THE
BALLOT,
THE
STREETS,
OR
BOTH?

First published in English under the titles
Lenin's Electoral Strategy from Marx and Engels through the Revolution of 1905:
The Ballot, the Streets—or Both, 1st edition
by August H. Nimtz published by Springer Nature America Inc.
and
Lenin's Electoral Strategy from 1907 to the October Revolution of 1917:
the Ballot, the Streets—or Both, 1st edition
by August H. Nimtz published by Springer Nature America Inc.

This edition published in 2019 by
Haymarket Books
P.O. Box 180165
Chicago, IL 60618
773-583-7884
www.haymarketbooks.org
info@haymarketbooks.org

ISBN: 978-1-60846-035-7

Distributed to the trade in the US through Consortium Book Sales and Distribution
(www.cbsd.com) and internationally through Ingram Publisher Services International
(www.ingramcontent.com).

This book was published with the generous support of Lannan Foundation and Wallace
Action Fund.

Special discounts are available for bulk purchases by organizations and institutions.
Please call 773-583-7884 or email info@haymarketbooks.org for more information.

Cover photograph of revolutionaries outside the State Duma in St. Petersburg during the
October Revolution courtesy of the Library of Congress. Cover design by Rachel Cohen.

Library of Congress Cataloging-in-Publication data is available.

Entered into digital printing November, 2020.

THE BALLOT, THE STREETS, OR BOTH?

From Marx and Engels to Lenin and the October Revolution

AUGUST NIMTZ

Haymarket Books
Chicago, Illinois

CONTENTS

PREFACE

Three years after the Bolshevik-led triumph in Russia in October 1917, Lenin declared that his party's "participation . . . in parliaments . . . was not only useful but indispensable" in its success. If true, this means that the Russian Revolution was the first and only revolution in history to employ the parliamentary arena for working-class ascent to state power. But what exactly did Lenin mean by "participation in parliaments"? This book aims to answer that very question and in the process to understand and sustain the validity of Lenin's claim. The Bolshevik example offers, therefore, potentially rich lessons for today's "protestors" in whatever corner of the globe. Yearning for something (however inchoate) more fundamental than what is often touted as "change" (not just new apps but a new operating system), many are torn between the "streets" and the "ballot box" for its realization. The solution Lenin fought for to this apparent dilemma was what he called "revolutionary parliamentarism"— the subject of this book.

The book makes four arguments. The first is that no one did more to utilize the electoral and parliamentary arenas for revolutionary ends than Vladimir Ilych Ulyanov—Lenin. The second argument is that Lenin's position on the "streets" versus the "ballot box"—no, it wasn't either/or—was squarely rooted in the politics of Karl Marx and Frederick Engels. Third, the historic split in international Marxism between communism and social democracy was long in place before the Guns of August 1914 exploded, owing in large part to two very different conceptions of how Marxists should comport themselves in the electoral/parliamentary arenas—with Lenin on one side and what would become twentieth and twenty-first century social democracy on the other side. The last claim is that the head-start program the founders of the modern communist movement gave Lenin on electoral politics goes a long way toward explaining why the Bolsheviks, rather than any other political current, were hegemonic in October 1917.

To make my case I do the following: For the first argument, I extract and summarize from the entire in print Lenin corpus all of his electoral activities, especially his leadership of the Bolshevik wing of the Russian Social Democratic Labor Party (RSDLP) in the four State Dumas from 1906 to the beginning of the First World War. This is no easy task since it's likely that on no other question apart from than that of the peasantry did Lenin spill so much ink. But it's doable because Lenin often reiterated the same claims for different venues. As for my argument that he was squarely rooted in Marx and Engels, I draw on my two earlier books on their politics. As many forests as have been felled for the Marxological industry, it is telling that this is the first synthesis of Marx and Engels's views on the electoral process. The Leninologists have also been derelict. Particularly striking about their enterprise is the almost complete absence of any sustained or, certainly, book-length discussion of Lenin's political kinship with Marx and Engels despite their frequent denial of such paternity. This book is, thus, a correction of two intellectual deficits. In the process, I show that no one of Lenin's generation understood Marx and Engels as well as he did. As for the argument about the roots of the historic split in international Marxism, I cull in chronological order from Lenin's writings and actions his awareness of the growing disagreements and divide between him and Western European Marxists. The record reveals—admittedly in hindsight—that the formal split that took place when the First World War erupted was the culmination of a decade-long process.

Finally, as for the "so what" question—what difference did it make that Lenin got Marx and Engels right?—this book argues that there is enough circumstantial evidence to show that his electoral/parliamentary strategy was decisive in the Bolshevik-led triumph in 1917, probably the only revolution to have been realized in such fashion. This is, therefore—and surprisingly, given all that's been written about it—the first study to trace the connection between the politics of the two founders of the modern communist movement and the Russian Revolution. Though not a definitive explanation for the Bolshevik success, a tentative case—given what's at stake in politics today—is infinitely superior to none at all. Just ask the protesters in Tahrir Square!

When I'd tell someone what I was working on while researching and writing this book, my words would often be greeted with a look of incredulity. "Lenin's electoral strategy"? That sounded oxymoronic. Such a reaction is not surprising. No figure in modern political history has been as misrepresented as Lenin. The reason is that not only his enemies but also many of his so-called friends are culpable. His enemies can easily justify their disdain simply on the basis of what has been done in Lenin's name for almost a century. The Stalinist counterrevolution that replaced the rule of the proletariat with that of the bureaucracy, and all the accompanying horrors, has indeed enabled his enemies' ever-present campaign to fault Lenin for what occurred after his death. But that reading of Lenin can only be sustained if there is indeed evidence of a causal link between his actions and Stalin's horrors; that the latter followed the former is no proof of Lenin's culpability. Lenin's more than decade-long work in electoral/parliamentary politics between 1905 and 1918 is inconvenient for his enemies and that is why—in almost Stalinist-like fashion—it has been deleted in Leninological accounts.

Lenin's smarter enemies know that *post hoc* explanation is unpersuasive—hence their never-ending quest to find the proverbial smoking gun, some evidence that he parented Stalin. And if that can't be found, it can be invented. Others have been less brazen and mainly impugn Lenin by innuendo. Rather than clutter the text with a discussion of that constant campaign, I confine it largely to the appendix, "A Critical Review of the Literature." One enemy's effort, though, is worth pointing out here: Richard Pipes's *The Unknown Lenin: From the Secret Archive* (1996). Because he was one of the first Western scholars granted permission to peruse formerly closed archives after the collapse of the Soviet Union and owing to his renown as a Leninologist, Pipes's book was highly anticipated. If anyone could find the smoking gun, surely he could. But Pipes fired a dud because the documents he reproduces from before the October Revolution contain no seed of the Stalinist counterrevolution. And one can be sure that if there was anything in that trove of documents that put Lenin, "a thoroughgoing misanthrope," in a positive light, it didn't find its way into the Pipes selection. For different reasons, Lenin's "friends," both real and fictitious—such as the hagiographers in Moscow and their cheerleaders elsewhere—are also complicit in veiling the rich record this book unearths. In the conclusions, I discuss what I call a conspiracy of silence by both foe and friend that helps make "Lenin's electoral strategy" sound so incongruous.

Though this book isn't about the Stalinist counterrevolution, it's a matter that can't be ignored. Along with mention of Lenin's unsuccessful fight from his sickbed to arrest the development, I devote a couple of pages at the end of chapter seven toward an explanation. Leon Trotsky's time-tested theory of Stalinism is what I employ. Lenin's second-in-command in the October Revolution, head of the Red Army in the civil war, a witness to the counterrevolution and eventually one of its many victims, Trotsky argued that political contingency best explains what happened. In other words, the Stalinist outcome was no more preordained than were the counterrevolutions that overthrew Radical Reconstruction after the US Civil War or the Paris Commune in 1871. There's no smoking gun to be found. I recognize that there's no convincing Lenin's *class* enemies, like Pipes, of the truth. But for those who are willing to suspend judgment until learning about this hitherto ignored side of Lenin, I offer this advice: The same kind of historical perspective needed to make judgments about the United States revolution, both phases—the war for national liberation and the social revolution that overthrew slavery (as viewers of Steven Spielberg's *Lincoln* might agree)—is also required for the Russian Revolution.

Lest it be construed that only reactionary forces have disdain for Lenin, let me mention another crowd. The reader will probably be struck by Lenin's unsparing criticism of Russian liberalism and the Cadet Party in particular—the "treachery of liberals," as he called it. At times he vented more anger at them than at the Czarist regime. Inveterate apologists for the latter, the liberals almost always vacillated at critical moments in Russia's democratic quest. Because they tried to inculcate workers and peasants with their anti-revolutionary politics, Lenin constantly hammered on the difference between democracy and liberalism and made special use of election campaigns to that end. His scathing denunciation of Russian liberals has earned him no friends in the liberal academy. The forces in Russia they are likely to identify with—despite pretenses of being "objective" in their accounts about the Russian Revolution—proved to be just what Lenin predicted: hand-wringing prevaricators. And that Lenin was so accurate in his predictions about them is even more galling. Lenin, informed by the lessons Marx and Engels drew on the Revolutions of 1848–49, read the politics of liberals better than any modern figure and they've never forgiven him for it.

I'm not sure I would have written this book had I not read many years ago *Lenin as Election Campaign Manager*, a twenty-three-page pamphlet that, fortunately—because it's still the best introduction to the topic and, thus, to this book—remains in print. Deep in my memory banks, it began to prick my consciousness a few years ago as I was reading a classic by a doyen of the academy that claimed that working-class participation in the electoral/parliamentary arena was inevitably compromising. According to political scientist Adam Przeworski, working-class parties, because they represented a minority of the population, had to enter into coalitions with parties representing other social layers and, thus, had to attenuate their demands and pursue a reformist political course a la Western European social democracy. But I vaguely remembered a different scenario: the Bolshevik experience. I revisited the pamphlet and found what I was trying to recall—Lenin's argument that the Russian movement also heard the siren call of opportunism but didn't succumb, at least in its revolutionary wing. In a 2010 article, I critiqued Przeworski—mainly for his dishonest treatment of Marx's and Engels's views on electoral/ parliamentary politics—and concluded that until the Russian case had been looked at closely, his hypothesis must remain no more than that. This book is that examination and it refutes Przeworski's claim of the inevitability of reformism. In my book *Marx and Engels: Their Contribution to the Democratic Breakthrough* (2000), I told readers that I'd address in a subsequent book what happened to their project after their deaths. This book also constitutes the first—belated largely because of the rich database I had to mine—down payment on that promise.

The chronological organization of this book is dictated by its four arguments. Chapter 1, "What Marx and Engels Bequeathed," provides the necessary evidence for the second argument, that Lenin's electoral/parliamentary strategy was squarely rooted in their politics. It distills and summarizes what the two founders of the modern communist movement said and did about electoral politics from the Revolutions of 1848–49 to the fight against reformism Engels was engaged in at the time of his death in 1895. It ends with their judgments about the revolutionary prospects for Russia—also necessary in making a determination about Lenin's continuity with their program. Chapter 2, "Revolutionary Continuity: Lenin's Politics Before 1905," seeks to understand how he responded when the first opportunity for electoral/parliamentary activity in Czarist Russia presented itself. What were his views from the time he entered politics in 1894 to the beginning of "Russia's Spring" in 1905, on democracy in general, parliamentary democracy, constitutional government etcetera and their relation to socialist revolution? And how did the democratic norm inform his views on the working class organizing itself into a party?

Chapters 3 to 6 constitute the empirical heart of the book, the very rich details about the leadership Lenin provided for the RSDLP for the elections to and participation in the four State Dumas from 1906 to 1914. Issues such as whether to boycott or participate in undemocratic elections, how to conduct election campaigns, whether to enter into electoral blocs and the related (and ever current) "lesser of two evils" dilemma, how to keep deputies accountable to the party, how to balance electoral politics with armed struggle, all had to be addressed. And most important, how could the electoral/parliamentary process be utilized to forge a revolutionary coalition of the majority, the worker-peasant alliance? Throughout the process, the often-contentious issue of internal party politics, specifically the growing split between the RSDLP's Bolshevik and Menshevik wings, looms large. That conflict, the evidence shows, mirrored the growing divide between revolutionary and reformist social democracy at the international level. This part of the narrative is framed by the Revolution of 1905, its defeat, the revival of revolutionary activity in 1912, and the outbreak of the First World War two years later.

Chapter 7, "'The Great War,' 1917, and Beyond," begins with the Bolshevik Duma deputies' response to the outbreak of the war, their arrest and trial, and the split in international social democracy. The February Revolution in 1917, the overthrow of Czarist rule, allowed Lenin to apply the lessons of a decade-long experience in the electoral arena—specifically, how "to count one's forces"—to determine when the Bolsheviks should lead an armed uprising of Russia's proletariat to take state power. There is sufficient evidence, as this chapter reveals, to make a more than credible case that the Bolshevik-led revolution in October, under Lenin's direction, was very much informed by the electoral/parliamentary strategy of modern communism's two founders—the first reading of the October Revolution to show its roots in Marx and Engels. Lenin's October Revolution balance sheets lend credence to this claim.

Last, in the conclusions, I begin with a summary of each chapter's contents and interrogate the book's four arguments to see if the evidence presented is convincing. I then offer an explanation for the silences in the literatures of foe and friend about Lenin's rich record in electoral/parliamentary politics. I end with a discussion of the potential relevance of Lenin's strategy of "revolutionary parliamentarism" for activists today in a variety of settings around the world.

Lenin's voice is prioritized and not, as is all too frequent in Leninological accounts, the author's. His voice is heard more than my own in chapters two to seven. Readers, I think, will be pleased with that decision as they learn what Lenin actually said as opposed to what is often attributed to him and understand why he is too often silenced. Lenin's detractors' accounts of him assume the reader has not and will not read him in his own words. Otherwise they would take far more precautions, make more hedges, or be less categorical than any of them have. Here Lenin is allowed to speak for himself. Virtually every word between quotation marks in the text is that of one of the protagonists of this story with the citation usually in reasonable proximity. If quotations come from the same writing, I provide the citation at the last one—to minimize the number of footnotes. To avoid confusion with quoted material, I have refrained as much as possible from the all-too-common practice of employing "scare quotes."

For Lenin's voice, I rely almost exclusively on the 1976 printing of V. I. Lenin, *Collected Works* in forty-five volumes, the English edition of the slightly more extensive Russian edition, which is now online at http://www.marxists.org/archive/lenin/works/cw/index.htm; for that reason I employ its spellings such as "Cadets" rather than "Kadets." I'm aware that not all that Lenin wrote is in print—and not just the unpublished documents Pipes's aforementioned selection drew on. Lenin's wife, Krupskaya, reported that much of their archives had to be burned before they fled Finland at the end of 1907, no doubt including many documents related to the second State Duma. And then there are the gargantuan Cracow archives that Lenin and Krupskaya had to abandon when the First World War broke out, reported to dwarf the *Collected Works* by at least a factor of ten. For some reason they have never found their way into print; they too are no doubt rich in relevant documents, especially about the third and fourth State Dumas. That I rely primarily on the *Collected Works* may for some readers raise a red flag. Shouldn't I employ other voices in a more "even-handed" way? First, the aim of this book is to present what Lenin actually said given the silences in other accounts. Relying on his *Collected Works* is the only feasible way to do that. Second, as for differing opinions on significant issues, the reader will see that Lenin, who was writing in real time, often copiously reproduced his opponents' views in his polemics in order to take them on. Unlike today, his audience had access to both sides of the debate and I assume with some confidence, therefore, Lenin had to be faithful in quoting opponents. What I can't determine, admittedly, is what Lenin didn't quote. Yet as the reader will see, he had to be convincing to be effective, which meant addressing his opponents' arguments in good faith.

Every so often in politics a moment occurs that suggests history in the making. Only Minerva's owl and, more encouragingly, students of history can make a definitive judgment. At the risk of sounding tempocentric, the eruption that began at the end of 2010—in Tunis, and then Cairo (where Natalie, my companion, was able to put in a brief appearance), Madison (where she spent a lot of time), New Delhi, Tel Aviv, New York, Oakland, Athens, Madrid, and then back to New Delhi, nearby Dhaka, and now, as this is being written, the improbable Nicosia—appears to be the long-expected (at least by some of us) breakthrough in the more than three-decade-long lull in the global class struggle. And this time the axis has finally shifted from the long-overburdened Third World to the long somnolent advanced capitalist world, especially its capital, the United States. Since it is in essence a response to one of those rare moments in the 250-year history of the capitalist mode of production, a global economic crisis—the last time the masses have gone in motion on a near-global scale—we can have more confidence that this upsurge, despite its inevitable ebbs and flows, has staying power. Years of resistance, with all of the learning opportunities that come with such challenges to business as usual, are on the agenda for the world's toilers. What is needed are those prepared to participate in and distill the lessons of those opportunities, like the thirty-five-year-old Lenin in Russia's "dress rehearsal" of 1905. This book, along with all the unseen, unacknowledged efforts in every corner of the world, is offered to aid and abet the future Lenins—to ensure that this moment will one day be the stuff of history.

ACKNOWLEDGMENTS

I want to recognize and thank the many people who helped to make this book possible, roughly in the order in which they provided assistance. First, to the volunteers who put and maintain online the Lenin *Collected Works*, to whom I'm truly indebted. Not only did their labor facilitate the production of the book, but it makes it easier for readers to verify my citations. For those I know personally: Sergio Valverde, a PhD student in my department of political science at the University of Minnesota, gave me the first opportunity to present the project in a public setting at the Minnesota Political Theory Colloquium he organized in the fall of 2011. The feedback I received was most valuable, especially from my colleague Elizabeth Beaumont. What I say about the outcome of the Russian Revolution in chapter seven and how to position Lenin in relation to it is in many ways a response to the thoughtful questions she raised. About a year later, Linda Hoover organized a group presentation for the Minnesota Marxist Book Club where I was able to share what I'd written—about half of the manuscript—with her, Michael Livingston, Dean Gunderson, and Amit Singh. That too was quite rewarding, not only on matters of content relevant to activists in that milieu but on stylistic issues I hadn't considered. In the meantime, Bob Braxton, a long-time acquaintance with editorial and revolutionary political experience, volunteered to give me feedback on the first three chapters. His advice and suggestions, for which I'm forever grateful, have informed the subsequent chapters in various ways. Joseph Towns IV also provided invaluable editorial input on the first four chapters and raised important questions about formulations in the manuscript that required clarification to make for a more readable narrative. And to Carl Voss, who read the preface and conclusions, the rumors about your superb editing skills were indeed true. No one was more helpful in pointing me toward the mainstream literature I interrogate in the appendix, "A Critical Review of the Relevant Literature," than Theo Stavrou, distinguished professor of Russian history at the University of Minnesota. Another colleague, Bud Duvall, took time from his very busy schedule as chair of the Department of Political Science to help me think through the logic of my fourth argument as I was writing the conclusions. Lastly, to my long-time comrade and companion, Natalie Johnsen Morrison, the best of the working class, whose constant injunction was to make this accessible to the working class, your forbearance and patience will forever be appreciated. Of course, I am ultimately responsible for what found its way into the book.

[Minneapolis, Summer, 2013]

ADDENDUM

This paperback edition, which combines the original two hardback volumes published by Palgrave Macmillan in 2014 under the titles *Lenin's Electoral Strategy From Marx and Engels Through the Revolution of 1905: The Ballot, the Streets—or Both*, and, *Lenin's Electoral Strategy From 1907 to the October Revolution of 1917: The Ballot, the Streets—or Both*, would not have been possible without the persistence of Anthony Arnove and the collaboration of his team at Haymarket Books, to whom I'm indebted. The cost of the hardback edition was a constant source of embarrassment for me. The many inquiries I got about when a paperback edition would be available can now be answered. I want to thank Michelle Chen, acquisitions editor at Palgrave Macmillan, for granting permission to Haymarket to do this—as well as for the paperback edition in Turkish by the Yordam Kitap collective in Istanbul, to whom I'm also appreciative. I take the opportunity also to thank Doug Jenness for his very positive feedback about the book. His Pathfinder Press pamphlet, *Lenin as Campaign Manager*, planted, unbeknownst to me at the time, again, the seed that generated this project.

When Natalie, my companion, who will be pleased with the new title, introduced me to the "Impeach Bush" movement in 2007, I was dubious and had to figure out how to respond constructively and in an unsectarian way. "If we don't," I said, "impeach the system that gave us Bush, we'll have someone in the White House who'll make us long for Bush." I repeat such a claim even about the current occupant in the executive mansion. No, he's far from the worst that capitalism has to offer—employing not a crystal ball but the lessons this book has sought to distill and present.

Minneapolis, Spring, 2019

Lenin's Electoral Strategy from Marx and Engels through the Revolution of 1905

CHAPTER 1

WHAT MARX AND
ENGELS BEQUEATHED

IN THE IMMEDIATE AFTERMATH OF THE BOLSHEVIK Revolution in 1917, Lenin engaged in a heated debate with what would be the intellectual forebears of today's social democrats. He accused them—especially Karl Kautsky, the one-time "Pope" of European socialism—of misrepresenting Marx and Engels's politics. Kautsky, he protested, "has turned Marx into a common liberal . . . [he] has beaten the world record in the liberal distortion of Marx."[1] Of particular concern was how, in Lenin's estimation, they portrayed Marx and Engels's views on parliamentary democracy and the related issue of involvement in the electoral arena. These were vital questions, he argued, that went to the very heart of the significance of what the October Revolution had just instituted, the process by which it was achieved, and the potential lessons for aspiring revolutionaries elsewhere.

This chapter provides a synopsis of Marx and Engels's views on both themes from their earliest to final pronouncements.[2] I also include a summary of what they thought about the prospects for revolution in Russia. Knowing what Marx and Engels had to say about parliamentary democracy and the electoral arena allows for a determination whether or not Lenin was justified in his accusations. A review of what they thought about the Russian movement also answers the oft-debated question concerning whether Lenin constituted continuity with the two founders of the modern communist movement—at least for these issues.

"THE EUROPEAN SPRING"

The revolutions of 1848–49 required that Marx and Engels address concretely and substantively for the first time parliamentary democracy and the electoral process. Like the participants in the "Arab Spring," they, along with other activists, had to grapple with all the questions that come with the overthrow of despotic regimes—how to do it, what to replace them with, and how to ensure that the previously disenfranchised are actually in power.

Prior to the midcentury upheavals, Marx and Engels had certainly thought and written about the institution of democratic rule. The daily reality of absolutist Prussia, even in its more liberal domains where the two lived, the Rhineland, almost demanded that they do so. Marx's first political writings addressed the irritant of state press censorship he faced as a cub reporter. His realization that the most influential mind for his generation, Georg Hegel, offered no real solutions to Germany's democratic deficit propelled him on the road to communist conclusions. Constitutional monarchy, Hegel's proposal, was far from "true democracy—the sovereignty of the people."[3] Rather than the world of philosophy, the study, he decided, of "actuality" or "the real movement of history" provided better results. And in the world as it existed when he set out to make his inquiries, history and "actuality" offered only two examples of political overturns that resulted in political democracy: France and the United States of America. The American case, I argue, generated the most valuable lessons for Marx.

What was so striking about the US experience for the young Marx was the combination of the most politically liberal society in the world with the grossest social inequalities, not the least of which was chattel slavery.[4] If that was the best that liberal or political democracy had to offer, then clearly something else was required for "true democracy," or "human emancipation." How do we explain this apparent contradiction? In seeking an answer Marx arrived at conclusions that made him a communist. As long as inequalities in wealth, especially property, were allowed and reproduced— political economy—then "real democracy" was impossible. The wealthy minority could and would use their resources to ensure political outcomes that privileged their interests. Then how could "real democracy"—a classless society—be realized, and what segment of society had the interest *and* capability to do so? Political developments in Europe provided the answer— the proletariat. Marx's new partner, Frederick Engels, reached similar conclusions by another route. The task for the two new communists was to link up with Europe's vanguard proletarian fighters. The price for doing so, after winning key German worker-leaders to their views, was to write a document that proclaimed their new world view.

The *Manifesto of the Communist Party* sharply distinguished itself from the programmatic stances of other socialist tendencies in its position that the prerequisite for the socialist revolution was the democratic revolution—the necessity "to win the battle for democracy." In related pronouncements clarifying their views, they wrote that, like the Chartists in England, the German proletariat "can and must accept the *bourgeois revolution* as a precondition for the *workers' revolution.* However, they cannot for a moment accept it as their *ultimate goal.*"[5] In no uncertain terms, the *Manifesto*, in four successive locations, made clear that it would take "force" to "overthrow the bourgeoisie" in order to reach the "ultimate goal." Nevertheless, they maintained to the end that the means to that goal was the conquest of the "bourgeois revolution." When a critic charged in 1892 that they ignored forms of democratic governance, Engels demurred, "Marx and I, for forty years, repeated ad nauseam that for us the democratic republic is the only political form in which the struggle between the working class and the capitalist class can first be universalized and then culminate in the decisive victory of the proletariat."[6]

COMMUNISTS FOR THE BOURGEOIS DEMOCRATIC REVOLUTION

The ink was hardly dry on the *Manifesto* when the "European Spring" erupted. On February 22, 1848, street fighting and the erection of barricades began in Paris. The monarch Louis Philippe abdicated after two days and a provisional government was installed, the commencement of the Second Republic. The outcome in Paris inspired protests and uprisings in almost fifty other cities in Europe. A new phase in the age of the bourgeois democratic revolutions had opened—the struggle to institute republican government and parliamentary democracy for the first time in most countries on the continent. In France, the fight was for its reinstitution. Armed with a party, the Communist League, the body that commissioned the writing of the *Manifesto*, Marx and Engels immediately went into action. From Brussels, where they had been in exile, they moved to revolutionary Paris, where they made plans for realizing their new world view in Germany. They had to move quickly for on March 18, after two days of street fighting in Berlin, Frederick IV conceded to the demands of the demonstrators and agreed to grant a constitution.

The *Manifesto*, they recognized, needed to be supplemented given the new reality. Except perhaps for France, socialist revolution—what the document spoke to—was not on the immediate agenda in most countries, certainly not their homeland. Thus they composed, with the approval of the Central Authority of the League, the much neglected *Demands of the Communist Party of Germany*, effectively the extreme left position of the bourgeois democratic revolution. As a one-page leaflet it was disseminated much more widely than the *Manifesto*. The first three and thirteenth of the seventeen demands are instructive:

1. The whole of Germany shall be declared a single and indivisible republic.
2. Every German, having reached the age of 21, shall have the right to vote and to be elected, provided he has not been convicted of a criminal offence.
3. Representatives of the people shall receive payment so that workers, too, shall be able to become members of the German parliament . . .
13. Complete separation of Church and State. The clergy of every denomination shall be paid only by the voluntary contributions of their congregations.[7]

As well as constituting what they considered to be the essentials of a democratic republic, these were Marx and Engels's first public pronouncements as communists on universal suffrage and representative democracy.

The *Demands* addressed another issue that the *Manifesto* didn't—the peasant question. As the document stated, demands six through nine "are to be adopted in order to reduce the communal and other burdens hitherto imposed upon the peasants and small tenant farmers without curtailing the means available for defraying state expenses and without imperiling production."[8] Other demands indicated that the document did indeed have a multiclass audience in mind: "It is to the interest of the German proletariat, the petty bourgeoisie and the small peasants to support these demands with all possible energy. Only by the realization of these demands will the millions in Germany, who have hitherto been exploited by a handful of persons and whom the exploiters would like to keep in further subjection, win the rights and attain to that power to which they are entitled as the producers of all wealth." In other words, an alliance of the proletariat, petit bourgeoisie, and small peasant—what Engels referred to in earlier writings as the alliance of "the people"—was the coalition Marx and Engels envisioned "to win the battle for democracy," the bourgeois democratic revolution.

Once back in Germany, the Rhineland in particular, Marx and Engels sought to implement their vision. The subhead of their new newspaper the *Neue Rheinische Zeitung* [*New Rhineland Newspaper*] or *NRZ*, the *Organ der Demokratie* [*Organ of Democracy*], said it all. But not all Communist League members and contacts were in agreement with the perspective of the *Demands*. Regarding, first, the demand for a unified republic, Andreas Gottschalk, the League's leader in Cologne, objected on the grounds that such a call would frighten the bourgeoisie. A constitutional monarchy was less threatening, he argued. He also complained about the elections to the All-German Frankfurt Parliament and the Prussian Constitutional

Assembly in Berlin because workers would be required to vote for electors and have, thus, only an indirect vote. The elections, he urged, should be boycotted. Marx and Engels and the rest of the League leadership disagreed and argued for active participation in the elections.

Another difference of opinion concerned the coalition of class forces for instituting the democratic revolution, an issue that had implications (to be seen shortly) for Marx and Engels's electoral strategy. Not only Gottschalk but another key figure in the workers' movement, Stephen Born, thought that priority should be given to issues that directly affected the working class and looked skeptically on an alliance with the petit bourgeoisie and peasantry. This stance, which Marx and Engels criticized, betrayed the tendency on the part of craft workers still saddled with a guild or *straubinger* mentality to dismiss the importance of the democratic revolution—a kind of working-class provincialism. To be sectarian toward these other social classes threatened the realization of that revolution, given that workers constituted a minority of society. Such a posture meant effectively conceding the franchise for that fight to the bourgeoisie, who, as Marx and Engels had already begun to point out, would increasingly vacillate on the issue of democracy.

The differences of opinion that surfaced in the League pose the related question of democratic decision making within the organizations that Marx led—an issue that can only be briefly treated here. Suffice it to say that in Gottschalk's case, owing to his disagreement with the League's leadership about its electoral strategy, he was asked to tender his resignation. One of its rules stipulated that "subordination to the decisions of the League" was one of the "conditions of membership." He told Marx that he disagreed with the rule and would indeed resign because "his personal freedom was in jeopardy." What transpired gives credence to the argument that the League's norms anticipated those that Lenin is most associated with: democratic centralism.[9] Many years later Engels told a supporter in Denmark that the "labor movement depends on mercilessly criticizing existing society . . . so how can it itself avoid being criticized or try and forbid discussion? Are we then asking that others concede us the right of free speech merely so that we may abolish it again within our own ranks?"[10] There is no evidence that he and Marx ever acted contrary to this stance, including in the case of Gottschalk. It was his actions—opposition to the League's electoral strategy—and not his right to voice disagreement that were curtailed.

It is not entirely clear from the extant historical record how the League participated (if it did so) in the initial elections to the Frankfurt and Berlin parliamentary/constituent assembly bodies in May 1848.[11] What is

known is that sometime in June, Marx, acting in his capacity as the organization's leader, decided to suspend activities in its name owing mainly
to perceived political realities—an issue to be revisited shortly. In its place,
the editorial board of the *NRZ*, with Marx in the lead, served as the effective body to carry out its perspective and organize its work. The axis of its
activities—at times quite successful—was the effort to realize the alliance
of "the people"—that is, the coalition of the proletariat, the peasantry,
and urban petit bourgeoisie—and the popularization of the *Demands*.

Virgin Steps into the Electoral Arena

Just as in the "Arab Spring," the course of the "European Spring" was
impacted by developments in the neighborhood, and no country was more
important in this regard than France—the Egypt of the revolutions of
1848–49. In hindsight, the bloody defeat of the working-class insurgents
in Paris in June 1848 was the beginning of the end of the continental-wide
upsurge—though, also in hindsight, it signaled the inauguration of the age
of socialist revolution. The routing of the democratic forces in Vienna in
October was the final nail in the coffin but, again, only in retrospect, since
it would be another half year before it was clear that the democratic revolutions had been stillborn. Basically, what happened, Marx and Engels argued,
is that the cowardly behavior of the bourgeoisie emboldened the reactionary
forces. Ignoring whatever progress the deputies to the Prussian body had
made in the constitution they were writing, Frederick IV decided to impose
his own on December 5. It provided for a constitutional monarchy—
granting him, thus, ultimate power. His coup d'état presented revolutionary
forces with a dilemma, because his imposed constitution authorized elections for the new Prussian Assembly. To participate or not to participate in
the elections, and if so, how?

For Marx, participation in the elections was obligatory. The only
question was whether to vote for liberal bourgeois democrats who would
oppose the constitution, or put forward candidates representing the
"people's alliance" of workers, peasants, and the urban petit bourgeoisie,
or abstain. He advocated for the first option. The "party of the people,"
in his opinion, was not strong enough to run its own candidates (a position that would undergo self-criticism the next year); it "exists in Germany as yet only in an elementary form."[12] The principled stance, as he
argued at a meeting of the proletarian component of the alliance, was
opposition to feudal absolutism—that is, the imposed constitution. "We
are certainly the last people to desire the rule of the bourgeoisie . . . But
we say to the workers and the petty bourgeoisie: it is better to suffer

in modern bourgeois society, which by its industry creates the material means for the foundation of a new society that will liberate you all." Thus it was necessary to "unite with another party [at least that wing of the bourgeoisie] also in opposition, so as not to allow our common enemy, the absolute monarchy, to win."[13]

Even though opponents of the constitution won overwhelmingly in the Rhineland, its proponents in the rest of Prussia, with the backing of the bourgeoisie, were successful. The fact that big capital supported a document objectively against its interests confirmed unambiguously for Marx that the German bourgeoisie was incapable of acting in a revolutionary way. The opposition Rhineland vote, however, which was mobilized by the joint efforts of the working class and urban petit bourgeoisie organizations of the province, convinced the *NRZ* party that the potential for building the "people's party" was better than ever. In the elections "the petty bourgeoisie, peasants and proletarians ['the specifically *red* class'] emancipated themselves from the big bourgeoisie, the upper nobility and the higher bureaucracy."[14]

About three weeks after the January elections, an opponent newspaper accused the *NRZ* tendency of having been duped by the liberal democrats, whom it supported on the expectation that they would oppose the constitution—a hope that was quickly dashed. Marx's reply is instructive because it provides perhaps the first glimpse of his and Engels' approach to electoral politics in a concrete setting. After explaining why "we put *our* own views into the background" during the elections, he declared, "Now, *after* the elections, we are again asserting our old ruthless point of view in relation not only to the Government, but also to the official opposition."[15] As for the charge of having been duped by the liberal democrats, "It could be foreseen that these gentlemen, in order to be re-elected, would now recognize the imposed Constitution. It is characteristic of the standpoint of these gentlemen that *after* the elections they are disavowing in the democratic clubs what *before* the elections they assented to at meetings of the electors. This petty, crafty liberal slyness was never the diplomacy of revolutionaries."[16]

Thus the "party of the people"—while obligated, owing to the particular setting of mid-nineteenth century Germany, to ally with the liberal democrats in the elections—should entertain no illusions about the latter and should take political distance from them as soon as the elections are concluded. A year later, to be seen shortly, Marx and Engels would distill and codify the revolutionary implications of this position by calling for complete working-class political independence from liberal democrats, specifically by running workers' candidates in future elections.

LESSONS OF STRUGGLE

With the "European Spring" in full retreat and thus diminished political space, Marx and Engels withdrew from the battlefield. In London, they, along with other League members, sought to regroup and to plan their next moves. History would reveal that their most important work were the balance sheets that they drew on the preceding two years—the lessons of struggle. Three documents/writings proved to have long shelf life.

The Address of March 1850
The first and most immediate task was to assess the performance of the League itself. As its reelected head, Marx, with the assistance of Engels, wrote on behalf of the other leaders what has come to be known as the "Address of the Central Authority to the League, March, 1850." A ten-page document (see Appendix A), it is a concise distillation of many of the conclusions they had already reached based on what they had witnessed. What makes the document so significant for present purposes is that "Lenin, who knew them [it and the "Address . . . June, 1850"] by heart," according to the Bolshevik archivist David Riazanov, "used to delight in quoting them."[17] Employing them and the other balance sheets in the heat of Russia's 1905 Revolution—a veritable laboratory of the class struggle—allowed Lenin to rightly see that "in the activities of Marx and Engels . . . the period of their participation in the mass revolutionary struggle of 1848–49 stands out as the central point. This was their point of departure when determining the future pattern of the workers' movement and democracy in different countries."[18]

The central theme of the "Address"—again, based on the experience of the two preceding years—is that the working class had to be organized independently in the expected revival of the German revolution; "independently" or some variant appears on nine of the ten pages, sometimes more than once. The suspension of the League—here Marx made an implicit self-criticism—led its members to dissolve themselves into the work of the broader democratic movement and thus conceded unnecessarily leadership in the democratic revolution to urban middle-class democrats. But the bourgeoisie's betrayal of the antifeudal cause (the *Manifesto* held open the possibility of a worker-bourgeois alliance) meant that in the revived revolution it was precisely those democrats that the working class would have to ally with—a class, however, whose track record in the two-year fight for democracy left much to be desired. Much of the document is about how to avoid another betrayal and what to do next following the successful overthrow of the feudal order, including preparation for armed struggle. The document stated repeatedly that a working-class alliance with the "petit bourgeois democracy" was just that—an alliance and not unity. Only the working class, independently organized, could provide the leadership needed to consummate the democratic revolution. And only then could the "revolution in permanence" be assured—that is, socialist revolution.

The "Address" proposed an electoral strategy—Marx and Engels's first detailed statement. In another implicit self-criticism—of the stance that Marx took regarding the aforementioned elections to the Prussian Constituent Assembly in January 1850—Marx and Engels laid out a perspective designed to avoid the kind of betrayal that the liberal bourgeoisie had committed in the electoral arena. In the next elections to the national assembly, workers had to pursue a course completely independent of not only the liberal bourgeoisie but the petit bourgeoisie as well. To be clear, what they outlined was a strategy for the postfeudal period where a degree of political democracy existed for the working class to contest elections. Most relevant are the instructions for the working-class party:

> [T]hat everywhere worker's candidates are put up alongside the bourgeois-democratic candidates, that they are as far as possible members of the League, and that their election is promoted by all means possible. *Even when there is no prospect whatever of their being elected, the workers must put up their own candidates in order to preserve their independence, to count their forces and to lay before the public their revolutionary attitude and party standpoint.* In this connection they must not allow themselves to be bribed by such arguments of the democrats as, for example, that by so doing they are splitting the democratic party and giving the reactionaries the possibility of victory. The ultimate purpose of all such phrases is to dupe the proletariat. *The advance which the proletariat party is bound to make by such independent action is infinitely more important than the disadvantage that might be incurred by the presence of a few reactionaries in the representative body.* If from the outset the democrats come out resolutely and terroristically against the reactionaries, the influence of the latter in the elections will be destroyed in advance.[19]

The first sentence I've italicized makes clear, in no uncertain terms, that for Marx and Engels electoral victories were subordinate to independent working-class political action. Rather than the number of seats won, the test of an election for the working-class party was how much it revealed its real strength—"their forces." Implicit here is an unarticulated way of how "to count" other than "being elected." Related and just as important is how well the party conducted itself in the election. Did it truly "lay before the public their revolutionary attitude and party standpoint"? Also significant are the subsequent sentences, because they address the conundrum that would bedevil many a progressive and working-class party in the next century and afterward—the "wasted vote" and "lesser of two evils" dilemmas in the electoral arena. Marx and Engels asserted, again unequivocally, that the potential gains from independent working-class political action outweighed the risks of "reactionaries" being elected. As for what they meant by "terroristically," one can only speculate, because nothing here or in subsequent pronouncements provides clarification.

Three Notable Balance Sheets

Marx and Engels produced three other assessments of the 1848–49 events that make points relevant to this discussion. One has to do with how they saw universal suffrage: what it could and could not do. In a series of articles written in 1850 that came to be called *Class Struggles in France*, Marx drew a balance sheet on the French revolution. He noted the "fundamental contradiction" of the political arrangements that came with the new provisional government and the constitution under which it governed:

> The fundamental contradiction of this constitution, however, consists in the following: The classes whose social slavery the constitution is to perpetuate—proletariat, peasantry, petty bourgeoisie—it puts in possession of political power through universal suffrage. And from the class whose old social power it sanctions, the bourgeoisie, it withdraws the political guarantees of this power. It forces the political rule of the bourgeoisie into democratic conditions, which at every moment help the hostile classes to victory and jeopardize the very foundations of bourgeois society. From the ones [first group] it demands that they should not go forward from political to social emancipation; from the others that they should not go back from social to political restoration.[20]

The granting of universal manhood suffrage created an inherently unstable situation for the bourgeoisie that could "jeopardize" its interests. The fundamental incompatibility between the interests of labor and capital was aggravated by the newly obtained political rights of the working classes. But even with universal suffrage, the bourgeois character of the constitution prevented the working class from going "forward from political to social emancipation."[21]

Implicit in Marx's argument is a crucially important distinction. The "possession of political power through universal suffrage" for the working class and its allies was not to be conflated with the actual exercising of that power for "social emancipation." The latter would require inroads on the "very foundations of bourgeois society"—that is, private property—exactly what the constitution prohibited. The "fundamental contradiction," Marx argued, was resolved in May 1850 when the National Assembly, representing the interests of the bourgeoisie, abolished universal suffrage. Alexis de Tocqueville, one of the body's leading lights, had characterized its rule, after the crushing of the Parisian proletariat in June 1848, as a "parliamentary dictatorship." For Marx, it was the "bourgeois dictatorship."[22]

Marx put the actions of the Assembly in perspective. "Universal suffrage had fulfilled its mission. The majority of the people had passed through the school of development, which is all that universal suffrage can serve for in a revolutionary period. It had to be set aside by a revolution or by the reaction."[23] For the revolutionary process, universal suffrage was means to an end, not an end in itself.

The end of universal suffrage emboldened, as Marx had anticipated, Louis Bonaparte to end the Second Republic with his coup d'état in December 1851. In his well-known analysis of the coup written in 1852, *The Eighteenth Brumaire of Louis Bonaparte*, Marx pointed out that any assessment of bourgeois democracy had to take context into account both in space and time, specifically continental Europe on the one hand and America on the other. In Europe in the middle of the nineteenth century, where capitalist relations of production were rapidly expanding along with the necessary class differentiation within feudal governmental forms, the republic was the governmental form that an insurgent bourgeoisie needed. In the United States, which lacked a feudal background and where class relations and thus the class struggle were still fluid and not fixed, the republic by the middle of the nineteenth century had come to embody the conservative form of bourgeois rule.

Engels drew a balance sheet on the German revolution also in a series of articles titled *Revolution and Counter-Revolution in Germany*. Although important gains, following mass working-class revolts in Berlin and Vienna in March 1848, were made in the convening (based on a limited franchise) of both a Prussian and all-German constituent assembly, respectively in Berlin and Frankfort, both proved incapable of leading a fight to advance and thus save the revolution. As was true with the National Assembly in Paris, the middle-class reformers in the two bodies (almost a fourth in Frankfort were professors on the state payroll) were more afraid of the masses in motion than the threat of the Prussian monarchy to end this brief democratic opening. Those in Frankfort honestly but tragically believed that the writing of a democratic constitution, more liberal than what was produced in Paris, would be sufficient for instituting liberal democracy in Germany for the first time. Engels is unsparing in his criticism of them:

> These poor, weak-minded men, during the course of their generally very obscure lives, had been so little accustomed to anything like success, that

they actually believed their paltry amendments, passed with two or three votes' majority, would change the face of Europe. They had, from the beginning of their legislative career, been more imbued than any other faction of the Assembly with that incurable malady, *parliamentary cretinism*, a disorder which penetrates its unfortunate victims with the solemn conviction that the whole world, its history and future, are governed and determined by a majority of votes in that particular representative body which has the honor to count them among its members, and that all and everything going on outside the walls of their house—wars, revolutions, railway-constructing, colonizing of whole new continents, California gold discoveries, Central American canals, Russian armies, and whatever else may have some little claim to influence upon the destinies of mankind—is nothing compared with the incommensurable events hinging upon the important question, whatever it may be, just at that moment occupying the attention of their honorable house.[24]

Engels's biting sarcasm gets to the heart of his and Marx's view of the legislative arena. While the parliamentary process was not to be ignored and could be of benefit for the revolutionary process, the developments that were decisive in understanding the course of history took place not within but rather outside its apparently hermetic walls—not the least important being revolutions. Marx's previously quoted comment about the fate of universal suffrage in the French upheaval—"It had to be set aside by a revolution or by the reaction"—is an instantiation of his claim. What's decisive, in other words, in the fate of the electoral process itself takes place outside its very parameters. No one, as we'll see, identified as much with this position as did Lenin. "Parliamentary cretinism" came to be his favorite label for those who failed to understand this basic political truth.

"A NEW ERA" IN THE CLASS STRUGGLE

The end of the "European Spring" in 1849 resulted in a more than decade-long lull in revolutionary politics in that part of the world. While Marx and Engels, in their new residence, closely watched British politics and made occasional comments about its electoral arena, it was only in 1863, when Marx declared that "the ERA OF REVOLUTION has now FAIRLY OPENED IN EUROPE once more," that they would not only engage in a sustained discussion about the electoral arena but actually act to shape it in the interest of the working class.[25] Presciently, Marx, speculating on the outcome of the German revolution, said at the end of 1848 that its fate was tied to the successful outcome of the worldwide revolutionary process that combined national liberation and antifeudal and anticapitalist struggles "waged in Canada as in Italy, in East Indies as in Prussia, in Africa as on the Danube."[26] Armed with a global perspective, he accurately recognized in 1860 the importance of two developments that foreshadowed a resurgence of the class struggle in Europe—the attack of the abolitionist John Brown on Harper's Ferry, Virginia, and the abolishment of servitude by the Russian Czar. Ending slavery and other precapitalist modes of exploitation was essential for the democratic revolution, a prerequisite for labor's struggle against capital.

THE INTERNATIONAL WORKING MEN'S ASSOCIATION

If there is one thing Europe's working classes learned once the US Civil War was under way, it was that *their* governments did not represent their interests, particularly when it came to foreign policy. This was especially true for British workers. London, beckoning to the call of the textile barons and their need for Southern cotton, took the side of the slave owners and threatened to intervene on their behalf. Despite the fact that textile workers in their thousands lost their jobs owing to the Northern blockade of ships taking Southern cotton across the Atlantic, they instinctively and consciously mobilized to support the antislavery cause and oppose London's threats. Workers increasingly recognized that they had to have their own foreign policy. This exigency was one of the factors that led to the founding in 1864 of the International Working Men's Association (IWMA), the First International.

From the beginning, Marx, who had already lobbied in the press on behalf of the Northern cause, played a key role in the new organization as the representative of the German workers and soon emerged as its effective leader. The central message of the founding document he wrote, *Inaugural Address*, was that while a reform such as the British Parliament's limiting (in law at least) the work day to ten hours was a victory for the working class, "the lords of land and the lords of capital will always use their political privileges for the defence and perpetuation of their economic monopolies . . . they will continue to lay every possible impediment in the way of the emancipation of labour . . . *To conquer political power has therefore become the duty of the working classes.*"[27] What this meant and how it would be implemented would take another seven years before it was concretized. In the meantime, the main task was to ensure the survival of the organization. Instrumental in doing so, it earned for Marx the moral authority needed for that moment.

In the second foundational document of the IWMA, also written by Marx, *Provisional Rules of the Association*, the other central message that

guided its work was stated at the very beginning: "[T]he emancipation
of the working classes must be conquered by the working classes themselves."[28] The key lesson of the 1848 revolutions weighed heavily on
Marx's brain when he wrote this. Unlike that of the *Inaugural Address*, this
message was given force and executed within weeks of the organization's
founding. After more than a month of working with some of the petit-
bourgeois figures on the General Council (GC), the executive committee
of the IWMA, Marx told Engels that "one has to be all the more careful
the moment men of letters, members of the bourgeoisie or semi-literary
people become involved in the organization."[29] To address that concern,
Marx initiated organizational norms that severely limited middle-class participation in the IWMA leadership. When a prominent lawyer who had
collaborated with it sought a seat on the GC, Marx convinced other members to reject his request. "I believe him an honest and sincere man; at the
same time, he is nothing and can be nothing save a Bourgeois politician."
Exactly because the lawyer aspired to a seat in Parliament, "he ought to be
excluded from entering our committee. We cannot become *le piedestal* for
small parliamentary ambitions . . . [Otherwise] others of his class will follow, and our efforts, till now successful at freeing the English working class
movement from all middle class or aristocratic patronage, will have been in
vain."[30] From its commencement, therefore, Marx opposed any attempts
to turn the International into an electoral conduit for, certainly, the petit
bourgeoisie and bourgeoisie itself. Whether and how to make it into such
a vehicle for the proletariat was a discussion and debate that eventually
would take place.

With its headquarters in London, the IWMA could not avoid the electoral arena. Six months after its founding, the GC, with Marx's support,
helped to found the Reform League, the working-class organization that
played a key role in pressuring Parliament to enact the 1867 Reform Act,
which extended the suffrage to the middle class and parts of the better-off
workers. At Marx's urging, the GC had agreed that it would only support the demand of universal manhood suffrage. A year later, however,
he reported that two of the GC's trade unionists "[W. R.] Cremer and
[George] Odger have both *betrayed* us in the Reform League, where they
came to a *compromise with the bourgeoisie* against our wishes."[31] The two
gave in to the liberal bourgeois elements in the League who would only
support household and not universal suffrage. Not only was the GC's
perspective compromised by Cremer and Odger, but the fledgling organization's own agenda suffered as a result of the time and energy that its
members devoted to League activities (one of the main reasons why the
IWMA did not hold a congress in its first year). At the beginning of 1871,

Marx wrote to a former Chartist leader who he still had relations with, "I regret saying, most of the workmen's representatives use their position in our council only as a means of furthering their own petty personal aims. To get into the House of Commons by hook or crook, is their *ultima Thule* ['most cherished goal'], and they like nothing better than rubbing elbows with the lords and M.P.'s by whom they are petted and demoralised."[32] What Marx witnessed (not for the first time in English politics) was the labor movement—or to be more precise, its leadership—subordinating the interests of the proletariat to those of the bourgeoisie. The International would have to institute explicit policies to prevent that from happening again.

A possible alternative to the class-collaborationist tendencies in the labor movement was what was being instituted in Germany. Beginning in 1862 the workers' movement, centered in Berlin and Leipzig, stirred anew after a decade of hibernation. Owing to his activist past in the 1848 events as well as his ties to Marx and Engels, Ferdinand Lassalle was asked by the workers to lead the fledgling body, the General Association of German Workers, founded in May 1863. However, his help came with a price—the insertion of ideas and a mode of functioning that were antithetical to the interests of independent working-class political action. While Marx and Engels waged a relentless campaign against his influence in the German worker's movement after his death in 1864—he was mortally wounded in a duel—they had to be careful in taking him on during his brief tenure as the movement's leader in order not to throw out the baby, the first truly German workers' association, with the bath water of Lassalleanism.

A year earlier, after a visit from Lassalle, Marx had concluded that there was no basis any longer of a "political PARTNERSHIP" with him, "since all we had in common politically were a few remote objectives."[33] Aside from the fact that he "gives himself all the airs of a future working men's dictator," Marx objected to his panaceas for the social emancipation of the German proletariat, among which was universal suffrage and Prussian state socialism. As Marx sarcastically noted to Engels, the "workers . . . are to agitate for *general suffrage,* after which they are to send people like himself into the Chamber of Deputies, armed 'with the naked sword of science.'"[34] Again, Marx was sober about universal suffrage. He also objected to Lassalle's proposal that "they organize workers' factories, for which the *state* advances the capital and, BY AND BY, these institutions spread throughout the country."[35] Despite its deformed birth, the General Association of German Workers was the best the German working class had to offer, and from afar Marx and Engels sought to shape its development and the larger German workers' movement. A successful breakthrough came in 1869 with the formation of an alternative that they helped to nurture: the Social Democratic Workers Party. It was able to win two seats—held by August Bebel and Wilhelm Liebknecht—in the Reichstag, the best example of independent working-class political action.

In addition to the class collaborationists, there was another tendency in and around the IWMA that Marx and Engels had to confront—the anarchists. Under the influence of Mikhail Bakunin, they basically disagreed with what was implicit in the central messages of the founding documents of the International that Marx had written—namely, that the working class should employ the political arena as a means for its emancipation. What was implicit, Marx increasingly realized, would have to be made explicit.

After the victory of the Union over the slavocracy in the United States, the most important political event in the history of the International occurred in Paris in the spring of 1871 when the working class rebelled and held power for almost three months—the Commune. Marx's most enduring contribution to the Communards was his *The Civil War in France*, published within a month of its demise on behalf of the IWMA. As well as a defense of the insurgents, it provides an analysis of what took place and distills the most important lesson of the Commune. After quoting from the manifesto that the Commune's Central Committee issued to justify its actions on March 18—"The Proletarians of Paris . . . have understood that it is their imperious duty and their absolute right to render themselves masters of their own destinies, by seizing upon the governmental powers"—Marx declared, "But the working class cannot simply lay hold of the ready-made State machinery, and wield it for its own purpose."[36] The insurgents quickly realized that in order to carry out fundamental social transformations to advance the interests of Paris's working masses, a radically new form of democratic governance, the Commune, had to be instituted. The liberal democratic state of the Third Republic was at best inadequate—not unlike the Second Republic that emerged in February 1848. So important was this conclusion that Marx and Engels repeated it in the Preface to the 1872 German edition of the *Manifesto*, the only correction they ever made to the founding document of the modern communist movement. The revolutionary program in the second part, they noted, had "in some details become antiquated. One thing especially was proved by the Commune, *viz, that* 'the working class cannot simply lay hold of the ready-made State machinery, and wield it for its own purposes.'"[37] The bourgeois republic, in other words, could not be a vehicle for socialist transformation—a lesson either ignored or unknown by twentieth-century social democracy, to its peril.

PLANTING THE SEED FOR WORKING-CLASS POLITICAL PARTIES

The long-simmering debate within the IWMA about working-class political action was finally put on its agenda at a meeting that convened in London in September 1871. The basic question was whether the abstentionist-anarchist perspective of Bakunin's followers or the class-collaborationist views of the English trade unionists were the only alternatives for workers. In his intervention, Engels distilled the essence of his and Marx's politics:

> [F]or us abstention is impossible. The workers' party already exist as a political party in most countries . . . The experience of real life and the political oppression imposed on them by existing governments . . . force the workers to concern themselves with politics, whether they wish or not. To preach abstention would be to push them into the arms of bourgeois politics. Especially in the aftermath of the Paris Commune which placed the political action of the proletariat on the agenda, abstention is quite impossible.
>
> We seek the abolition of Classes. What is the means of achieving it? The political domination of the proletariat . . . revolution is the supreme act of politics; whoever wants it must also want the means, political action, which prepares for it, which gives the workers the education for revolution and without which the workers will always be duped . . . But the politics which are needed are working class politics; the workers' party must be constituted not as the tail of some bourgeois party, but as an independent party with its own objective, its own politics.
>
> The political freedoms, the right of assembly and association and the freedom of the press, these are our weapons—should we fold our arms and abstain if they seek to take them away from us? It is said that every political act implies recognition of the status quo. But when this status quo gives us the means of protesting against it, then to make use of these means is not to recognize the status quo.[38]

Engels's speech was clearly directed at the anarchists. Their abstentionist line, however revolutionary it might sound, "would . . . push [the workers] into the arms of bourgeois politics" or make them be party, unwittingly perhaps, to the class-collaborationist line of the English trade unionists. Only if the workers had their own "independent party with its own politics" could they avoid the deadly trap of "bourgeois politics." Hence workers not only had an inherent interest in defending basic democratic rights but were obligated to do so since their existence gave them the space to further their own class interests. The alternative, therefore, to both the Bakuninist and class-collaborationist lines was independent working-class political action, the bottom line of both the Inaugural Address and the Preamble—and the heart and soul of the politics of Marx and Engels for at least a quarter of a century. The task now, seven years after both documents had been adopted and after the experience of the Commune, was to make this line a living reality.

In one of his speeches at the London conference under this point, Marx specifically addressed the matter of workers in parliaments, which "must not be thought that it is of minor importance." When governments prevent duly elected workers' representatives from exercising their parliamentary rights, "the effect of this severity and intolerance on the people is profound." He, too, as had Engels in a letter to Spaniard comrades, offered the German example for what was possible when more political space existed:

> Whereas if, like [August] Bebel and [Wilhelm] Liebknecht, they are able to speak from this platform, the entire world can hear them—in one way or the other it means considerable publicity for our principles . . . When during the [Franco-Prussian War] Bebel and Liebknecht embarked on the struggle against it, and to disclaim responsibility on behalf of the working class with regard to what was happening—the whole of Germany was shaken, and even Munich . . . was the scene of great demonstrations demanding an end to the war.
>
> The governments are hostile to us. We must answer them by using every possible means at our disposal, getting workers into parliament is so much gaining over them, but we must choose the right men and watch out for the Tolains.[39]

Worker participation in parliaments, therefore, was a means to an end—"a platform . . . for our principles." In another set of minutes, Marx is recorded as having said, "Since the July Revolution [1830] the bourgeoisie has always made every effort to unnoticeably create obstacles, in the workers' way. Our newspapers are not reaching the masses—the speakers' platform is the best means of publicity." Again, the importance of the parliamentary "platform" or rostrum is emphasized as a means to disseminate party ideas especially when other avenues were blocked; no one, as we'll see, again, took this advice more to heart than Lenin.

Marx repeated Engels's point about the logic of the abstentionists' "revolutionary" posture: "[B]y adjourning politics until after the violent struggle they are hurling the people into the formalist, bourgeois opposition—which it is our duty to combat, as well as the powers-that-be."

In concluding both his remarks and the debate, he addressed what other speakers had raised: governmental repression of the IWMA in the aftermath of the Commune. "We must tell [these governments] . . . we know that you are the armed force opposing the proletariat—we shall act against you peacefully wherever possible—and take up arms when that is necessary."[40] Thus if the peaceful road through the employment of basic democratic rights and the parliamentary option was closed to the workers' movement, then the International was prepared to pursue armed struggle.

Independent working-class political action—this was the essence of Marx and Engels's intervention. This, precisely, was the core of their *Address of March 1850*, including the need for workers to have their own candidates in elections—the main lesson they drew from the 1848–49 upheavals. They won the overwhelming majority of the conference attendees to this perspective and were authorized to later draw up the resolutions as well as a new set of rules agreed to at the conference. A month later they presented to the GC the now famous resolution "IX. Political Action of the Working Class," which incorporated the majority sentiment on this debate.[41] A year later at a more representative meeting, The Hague Congress—effectively the last for the International—the resolution was adopted by the delegates against the opposition of the Bakuninists. The resolution's historic significance is that it constitutes the first explicit call for what would eventually be Europe's mass working-class political parties. While much would need to be done to make it a reality, it nevertheless gave those who were predisposed to move in that direction the authority,—that is, the prestige of the International—to go forth boldly.

THE FIGHT FOR PROGRAMMATIC INTEGRITY

Between 1875, three years after The Hague Congress, and 1894 more than 11 working-class parties in Europe were founded—the largest block at any one time.[42] These were the parties that came together to later form the Socialist or Second International and to constitute European social democracy. Hobbled by poor health in his final years, Marx provided what assistance he could to these fledgling organizations, particularly the French party. With his death in 1883 it fell to Engels, who outlived him by 12 years, to continue that work. Even before then the two recognized that their assistance and counsel could not guarantee that these parties actually adhered to and would remain loyal to their program. Thus until his last days Engels waged a concerted campaign to try to ensure fealty to his and his partner's lifelong project.

German Social Democracy and the "Parliamentary Disease"

The German movement, as noted earlier, had been in the vanguard of independent working-class political action—a source of inspiration for others. Marx and Engels, aware of its problematic birth—Lassalle's panaceas—were more sober. Thus their optimism when the Social Democratic Workers Party, closer to their views, was founded in 1869 as an alternative to the Lassallean-influenced General Association of German Workers. In 1875, however, the two organizations fused to form the German Socialist Workers Party (SAPD). Within a couple of years Marx detected problems, as he explained to a longtime comrade: "In Germany a corrupt spirit is asserting itself in our party, not so much among the masses as among the leaders (upper class and 'workers'). The compromise with the Lassalleans has led to further compromise with other waverers . . . not to mention a whole swarm of immature undergraduates and over-wise graduates who want to give socialism a 'higher, idealistic' orientation, i.e. substitute for the materialist basis . . . a modern mythology with its goddesses of Justice, Liberty, Equality and *Fraternité*."[43] What Marx detected in 1877 were the pernicious effects of liberalism on the workers' movement and what would later morph into "reformism" and "opportunism." As for one of the transmission belts for these influences, "immature undergraduates and over-wise graduates," more will be explained about them shortly.

When both the Social Democratic Workers Party and the General Association of German Workers made significant gains in the 1874 Reichstag elections—from two to six seats for the former, and three seats for the first time for the latter—Engels warned, "it can hardly be doubted that measures to restrict the franchise will follow, though not for a year or two."[44] He was off by two years, because it was not until 1878 that Bismarck, fearful of the SAPD—again, the product of the fusion in 1875—had it banned. Neither Engels nor Marx was under any illusion that Bismarck or any bourgeois government would respect its own legal order when it came to the electoral arena.

While Bismarck's Anti-Socialist Law banned the SADP and its press in 1878, it provided for an important exemption; it allowed the party to run candidates in elections and hold seats in the provincial and national Reichstags. An immediate issue posed by the law was how, while in exile in Zurich, the editorial committee for the new party organ, the *Sozialdemodrat*, should function in relation to the rest of the party and its elected leadership. The broader political question was whether the party should accommodate itself to Bismarck's crackdown by adopting a more moderate posture or maintain its revolutionary stance.

THE CIRCULAR LETTER OF 1879

The proposed editorial committee in Zurich consisted of what Marx derisively called a "social-philanthropist" ("the first man to buy his way into the party") and two adherents of Eugen Dühring (the target of Engels's famous polemic *Anti-Dühring*), one of whom was the then 29-year-old Eduard Bernstein. When this committee published an article that confirmed their worst fears, Marx and Engels reacted with a stinging denunciation. Their letter to Bebel and the rest of the party leadership, which has come to be known as the *Circular Letter*, ranks, as Hal Draper rightly argues, in importance with the *Manifesto*, the *Address of March 1850*, the *Inaugural Address*, and the *Civil War in France*.[45]

Written by Engels with Marx's collaboration, the document has two key themes. One, it unequivocally affirmed the historic program of the communist party in opposition to Bernstein (one of the "over-wise graduates" Marx had in mind two years earlier) and the other authors of the article that Engels sardonically called the "Manifesto of the Zurich Trio." In their "Manifesto," Bernstein et al. had proposed that the SAPD abandon its proletarian orientation, make an appeal to both the petit bourgeoisie and the bourgeoisie, and adopt a less threatening posture toward Bismarck's regime. "If," Engels replied, "they [the 'trio'] think as they write, they ought to leave the party or at least resign from office [i.e., the editorial committee]. If they don't, it is tantamount to admitting that they intend to use their official position to combat the party's proletarian character. Hence, the party is betraying itself if it allows them to remain in office."[46] Engels threw down the gauntlet because the clear implication of their position, as he bitingly and sarcastically put it, was

> Therefore elect bourgeois!
>
> In short, the working class is incapable of emancipating itself by its own efforts. In order to do so it must place itself under the direction of 'educated and propertied' bourgeois who alone have 'the time and the opportunity' to become conversant with what is good for the workers. And, secondly, the bourgeois are not to be combatted—not on your life—but *won over* by vigorous propaganda.[47]

The goal of the "trio," in Engels's skillful dissection of their diluted politics, was "to relieve the bourgeois of the last trace of anxiety" by showing it "clearly and convincingly that the red spectre really is just a spectre and doesn't exist." But to shore up its left flank, the "Manifesto" made clear that the party's "programme is not to be *relinquished*, but merely *postponed*—for some unspecified period." More precisely, "They accept it [the 'programme']—not for themselves in their own lifetime but posthumously, as an heirloom for their children and their children's children. Meanwhile they devote their 'whole strength and energies' to all sorts of trifles, tinkering away at the capitalist social order so that at least something should appear to be done without at the same time alarming the bourgeoisie."[48] Engels's sarcasm resonates so well because its target is ever so present. Precisely because "we are still only too familiar with all these catch-phrases of 1848," could Engels and Marx be so insightful about the "trio." "These are the same people . . . whose fear of any kind of action in 1848 and '49 held back the movement at every step and finally brought about its downfall; the same people who never see reaction and then are dumbfounded to find themselves at last in a blind alley in which neither resistance nor flight is possible."[49] Engels then showed how the *Communist Manifesto* had foreseen this kind of development in the German movement and suggested what to do about it. Those who truly believe what "their Manifesto"—namely, that of the "trio"—put forward should form their own party, a "Social-Democratic petty-bourgeois party" separate and apart from a "Social-Democratic Workers' Party" with whom the latter "could negotiate with . . . and, according to circumstances, form an alliance with."[50] Under no circumstances should they be permitted to be in the leadership of the SAPD, and they should "remain aware that a break with them is only a matter of time."

The other major issue in Engels's *Circular* concerned the SAPD's Reichstag group or *Fraktion*. Here he addressed a problem that would bedevil many a twentieth-century workers' party wherever it had a parliamentary group—that is, how to make it accountable to the party as a whole. Engels, again in opposition to the Zurich "trio," came to the defense of a rank-and-file SAPD member who had publicly and sharply criticized a Fraktion member for voting for one of Bismarck's capitalism-from-above ventures—a whiff of the "stench" left behind by Lassalle's support to Bismarckian "state socialism." Engels agreed that the vote had "infringed party discipline" and that the deputy deserved to be handled "roughly" since the SAPD's program had specifically opposed both indirect taxation (the means by which the venture would be financed) and the "first and fundamental rule of our party tactics: not a farthing for this government" (from the slogan that Liebknecht made famous in 1871, *"diesem system keinen Mann und keinen Groschen!"*—"for this system, not one man and not one penny!").[51] In a didactic letter to Bebel two months later, Engels made the point—consistent with his and Marx's fundamental views—often forgotten by many a "social-democrat" in the subsequent century that warrants highlighting: "Social-Democratic deputies must always uphold the vital principle of consenting to nothing that increases the power of the government vis-à-vis the people."[52]

However despicable the vote of the deputy or the *Fraktion* as a whole for the Bismarckian project, the bigger problem was the uproar, as reflected by the "trio," of the party leadership to the rank-and-file criticism of the vote. "[H]as German Social-Democracy indeed been infected with the parliamentary disease, believing that, with the popular vote, the Holy Ghost is poured upon those elected, that meetings of the faction [*Fraktion*] are transformed into infallible councils and factional resolutions into sacrosanct dogma?"[53] To combat this "disease," what Engels labeled in 1850 "parliamentary cretinism," the party had to uphold the norm that the parliamentary representatives be subordinate to the will of the party as a whole.

Clearly, it was the issue of the composition of the editorial committee that most concerned Marx and Engels. In concluding the *Circular*, Engels warned that if the "trio" constituted the new committee, "then all we could do—much though we regret it—would be publicly to declare ourselves opposed to it and abandon the solidarity with which we have hitherto represented the German party abroad. But we hope it won't come to *that*."[54] In terms less diplomatic, Marx explained to a longtime comrade a day later what was at stake: "Engels has written a circular (letter) to Bebel, etc. (just for *private circulation* among the German leaders, of course), in which our point of view is plainly set forth. So the gentlemen are forewarned and, moreover, are well enough acquainted with us to know that this means bend or break! If they wish to compromise themselves, *tant pis*! In no circumstances shall we allow them to compromise *us*. . . they are already so far infected with parliamentary cretinism as to believe themselves *above criticism* and to denounce criticism as a *crime de lèse majesté*!"[55]

In effect, the *Circular* constitutes Marx and Engels's major programmatic statement against opportunism or what would later be called reformism or revisionism. That one of the targets of their polemic, Bernstein, would some two decades later come to be called the father of revisionism is probably no accident. No other joint document of Marx and Engels so clearly anticipated and critiqued the course of social democracy in the twentieth century. Politically, it stands in direct descent from the *Manifesto* and the *1850 March Address*. That the document only became public in its entirety for the first time in 1931, in a Stalinist publication, when it was then in Moscow's interest to expose the reformist character of social democracy, is also not fortuitous.

Marx and Engels's threat of "bend or break" to the leadership of the SAPD forced Bebel, accompanied by Bernstein, to travel to London to resolve their differences with the "old ones"—testimony to their influence and what was at stake. Though the matter was settled to the satisfaction of both parties, allowing Bernstein to become editor of the *Sozialdemokrat*, the subsequent history of the party and Bernstein himself revealed that the issue of reformism in the German party would continue to be a problem.[56]

Lest it be construed that the "old ones" were unduly harsh with the German leadership, Marx's comment to the aforementioned longtime comrade a few months later is instructive: "[W]e have eschewed any kind of *public* intervention. It does not befit those who are peacefully— *comparativement parlant*—ensconced abroad to contribute to the gratification of government and bourgeoisie by doing anything to aggravate the position of those who are operating in the homeland under the most difficult circumstances and at considerable personal sacrifice."[57] Neither did they view themselves acting authoritatively—in the worst sense of the term, by imposing their views. Two years later Engels described to Bernstein their modus operandi vis-à-vis national parties: "[A]ny attempt to influence people against their will would only do us harm, destroy the old trust that dates from the International."[58]

THE ELECTORAL ROAD TO SOCIALISM—"PEACEFUL" OR "FORCIBLE"?

Once working-class parties were able to participate in the electoral arena, Marx and Engels paid close attention. In the aftermath of the adoption of Resolution IX by The Hague Congress of the IWMA, this was even more the case. Engels's brief but very rich comments to one of the leaders of the Social Democratic Workers Party about its gains in the 1874 Reichstag elections are exemplary:

> Jacoby's conduct is irresponsible. If he did not wish to take up his seat he should have requested the Party Committee in advance just to put him forward as a mere "name" in completely hopeless constituencies. The workers have neither the money nor the time to squander on empty gestures of this sort. The most strenuous efforts will be needed to get Bracke in, and victory there is doubly important since it is in a *rural* constituency. Jacoby has disqualified himself for good with this. The man is just *too much of a sage*. And his reasons are so trivial and vulgar-democratic! He hurls abuse at *force* as something reprehensible in itself, even though we all know that when it comes down to it, nothing can be achieved without force. If [one of the liberal party candidates] had written such things, that would not be

so bad . . . but a candidate of our party! . . . And in fact it is all very fine and logical: on the one hand, he rejects *force*, on the other, parliamentary *legal* action—what is left then but pure Bakuninist abstention?[59]

Since it's not possible to do justice here to all that Engels raises, I note only the bare essentials. First, Johann Jacoby had been a left-wing liberal in the ill-fated Frankfurt and Prussian assemblies in the 1848–49 events, one of the "parliamentary cretins" that Engels ridiculed. Disillusioned by his parliamentary ambitions owing to Fredrick IV's imposition of the Imperial Constitution, he gravitated to more radical politics. He was a Social Democratic Workers Party candidate for the 1874 Reichstag elections and in the second round of voting actually won a seat representing a Leipzig constituency. However, to the party and Engels's consternation, he refused to take the seat in order to register his protest against the imposed constitution.

Engels's angry reaction is instructive. Working-class political parties had to take elections seriously—which meant collective decision making—despite how undemocratic they might be. Unlike Jacoby, he was under no illusion that the parliamentary arena was the venue for real change; it offered at best an opportunity to propagandize their ideas—as he and his partner had explained in the *Address of March 1850.* And when a real opportunity for winning presented itself, being serious was even more necessary. Protests about the democratic deficit were of more value from the parliamentary "platform" or rostrum than Jacoby's liberal gesture. What he protested against, that it was "force" that promulgated the constitution, revealed his own political naïveté. "We"—that is, communists and not "vulgar democrats"—"all know that when it comes down to it, nothing can be achieved without force." Last, if Jacoby was on principle opposed to the use of "force" and was unwilling to use available political space ("*legal* action"), then all that remained for him was an abstentionist posture—what Marx and Engels polemicized against at the London Conference of the IWMA.

Engels's comment about the double importance of winning "in a *rural* constituency" is most significant. It underscores one of the key lessons of the 1848–49 experience and points to the future: the importance of using the electoral arena to build the worker-peasant alliance. No alliance was more necessary in Marx and Engels's strategy for working-class ascendancy. Finally, as the results of the 1874 Reichstag elections were becoming available, Engels, three weeks earlier, applauded what he considered to be the correct conduct for working-class parties in elections that required runoffs: "[F]irst vote for our own man, and then, if it is clear that he won't get in on the second round, vote for the opponent of the government, whoever he happens to be."[60] There is no evidence that Engels ever abandoned this runoff strategy.

Commenting on the Reichstag debate leading up to Bismarck's crackdown in 1878, Marx made a more general observation about force and the parliamentary road to social transformation.

> An historical development can remain "peaceful" only for so long as its progress is not forcibly obstructed by those wielding social power at the time. If in England, for instance, or the United States, the working class were to gain a majority in PARLIAMENT or CONGRESS, they could, by lawful means, rid themselves of such laws and institutions as impeded their development . . . However, the "peaceful" movement might be transformed into a "forcible" one by resistance on the part of those interested in restoring the former state of affairs; if (as in the American Civil War and the French Revolution) they are put down by *force*, it is as rebels against "lawful" force.[61]

If, even in the United States and England, there was some likelihood that the peaceful road was ruled out—in a speech six years earlier after The Hague Congress Marx appeared to be more certain about such an option in both countries[62]—then clearly it was unlikely in Bismarck's Germany. Its impending crackdown against the SAPD "is the necessary prelude to forcible revolutions."[63] Until the end of his life Engels waged an uphill battle within the German party against the "disease" of parliamentary cretinism to drive home this point.

Bismarck's ban of the SAPD gave—perhaps intentionally—its parliamentary *Fraktion*, which tended to be to the right of the membership, far more influence in the party than before. While Engels had no objection to the *Fraktion* taking the lead given the constraints of the ban on open party activities, it functioned, he told Kautsky six months after the ban was lifted in 1890, as "a dictatorship that, was of course, essential and excellently managed."[64] He held, however, that "they can neither demand nor impose the implicit obedience [of the membership] that could be demanded by the former party leadership, *specifically* elected for the purpose. Least of all under present circumstances, without a press, without mass meetings."[65] In this, Engels was stating an essential principle later associated with democratic centralist organizing—that is, centralism in action required full democracy in decision making. Because he had more faith in the party's ranks than its leadership, he was especially concerned that they have sufficient freedom of action—an issue to be returned to shortly.

Engels also reiterated that elections were important, but under capitalism, at least, they not an end in themselves. In his newly published book, *Origin of the Family, Private Property and State*, which was reprinted as an excerpt in *Sozialdemokrat* in connection with the upcoming 1884 Reichstag elections, one of the key political conclusions he made was that "universal suffrage is the gauge of the maturity of the working class. It cannot and never will be anything more in the present-day state; but that," he continued, "is sufficient. On the day the thermometer of universal suffrage registers boiling point among the workers, both they and the capitalists will know where they stand."[66]

Cognizant of Bismarck's censors, Engels could not be as forthright with his metaphor as he was eight years later when he made this very same point to Paul Lafargue, following electoral gains for the party in France, about the value of elections for the revolutionary process.

> Do you realize now what a splendid weapon you in France have had in your hands for forty years in universal suffrage; if only people knew how to use it! It's slower and more boring than the call to revolution, but it's ten times more sure, and what is even better, it indicates with the most perfect accuracy the day when a call to armed revolution has to be made; it's even ten to one that universal suffrage, intelligently used by the workers, will drive the rulers to overthrow legality, that is, to put us in the most favorable position to make the revolution.[67]

Engels, therefore, left no doubt, contrary to later efforts to make him into a reformist, that elections under capitalism were only a means— a "gauge," the best in his opinion—to determine when to resort to armed struggle.[68] And this was a gauge to be employed not just in Bismarck's Germany.

This is the framework in which Engels's, as well as Marx's, pronouncements on elections and the use of force for socialist transformation must be understood. In 1880 he and Marx helped to draft the electoral program of what was in Marx's opinion the *"first real workers' movement* in France."[69] In the preamble, Marx made perhaps his most succinct and popular rationale for the participation of the workers' party in elections. He began with the premise, "That the emancipation of the producing class ['or proletariat'] is that of all human beings without distinction of sex or race." Also, only on the basis of "collective ownership" of the means of production would liberation be assured. Such an "appropriation" required the "revolutionary action of the producing class . . . organized into an independent political party." To this end, "all of the means at the disposal of the proletariat, including universal suffrage," should be utilized. Taking part in the elections, he emphasized, was a *"means of organization and struggle."*[70]

Regarding the successes of the SAPD in the 1884 elections, Engels told Bebel, "I am less concerned just now with the number of seats that will eventually be won . . . the main thing is the proof that the movement is marching ahead . . . [and] the way our workers have run the affair, the tenacity, determination and above all, humor with which they have captured position after position and set at naught all the dodges, threats and bullying on the part of the government and bourgeoisie."[71] In other words, the self-organization of the working class was the decisive gain. About the successes in the 1887 elections, he said, "But it's not the number of seats that matter, only the statistical demonstration of the party's irresistible growth."[72]

Finally, remarking on the 1893 elections, he reiterated, "[T]he number of seats is a very secondary consideration. The principal one is the increase of votes . . . [especially in the] rural districts . . . without which we cannot expect to be victorious."[73] Again, the rural vote was crucially important. Although the *Sozialdemokratische Partei Deutschlands* or SPD, the new name the party adopted after the ban was lifted in 1890, didn't do as well in the runoff elections in terms of seats, Engels said, "I am prouder of the defeats than of the successes . . . What we won we owe—for the first time—entirely to our own strength . . . [and not to] the help of the liberals and democrats."[74] All these assessments only make sense when seen from the perspective of elections as a gauge for the best moment when to employ revolutionary force.

Within this framework, Engels was sober about the German vote. As for the gains made in the 1884 elections, "In Germany it is easy to vote for a Social Democrat because we are the only real opposition party and because the Reichstag has no say in things, so that ultimately it doesn't matter whether one votes at all, or for which of the 'dogs that we are' one does vote."[75] Thus he recognized the reality of the protest vote in relation to the so-called wasted vote.

Engels like Marx was unequivocal on the necessity of force. To Bebel in 1884, when the prospects for lifting the ban against the SAPD seemed likely in return for its renunciation of violence, he counseled steadfastness on principles: "No party, unless it was lying, has ever denied the right to armed resistance *in certain circumstances.* None has ever been able to renounce that ultimate right." But "we shall not go into action as long as we have a military power against us. We can bide our time until the military power ceases *to be a power against us.*"[76] To a cothinker in Denmark in 1889, he wrote, "That the proletariat cannot seize political power, which alone will open the doors to a new society, without violent revolution is something upon which we are both agreed."[77] In his commentary on the

SPD's new program in 1891, the so-called Erfurt Program, Engels argued that the reality of Germany "proves how totally mistaken is the belief that a . . . communist society, can be established in a cosy, peaceful way."[78] To an Italian critic in 1892, Engels replied publicly, "I have never said the socialist party [the SPD] will become the majority and then proceed to take power. On the contrary, I have expressly said," echoing an aforementioned comment, "that the odds are ten to one that our rulers, well before that point arrives, will use violence against us, and this would shift us from the terrain of majority to the terrain of revolution."[79]

Finally, there was Engels's angry reaction to the most famous bowdlerization in the history of the socialist movement: Liebknecht's cut-and-paste job in the party newspaper *Vorwärts* on his 1895 "Introduction"—which summarized his and his partner's approach to universal suffrage and electoral politics—to Marx's *Class Struggles in France*. What Engels objected the most to about Liebknecht's self-serving editing, as he explained to Kautsky and Lafargue, was that it was done "in such a fashion that I appear as a peaceful worshiper of legality at any price" in order "to support the tactics of *peace at any price and of opposition to force and violence*."[80] Even the version that he approved for publication in the SPD's theoretical journal, *Die Neue Zeit*, edited by Kautsky, after watering it down because of the leadership's fears about government reprisals, had a key paragraph removed. The unexpurgated text made clear that "street fighting" was still on the revolutionary agenda in most places, if not everywhere, but that it would "have to be undertaken with greater forces."[81] This was his last word on the matter, since he died five months later. Had Engels known beforehand that it would be the expurgated version, which made him appear as an opponent of "street fighting," that subsequent generations of social democrats would be reared on, he no doubt would have resisted the entreaties to tone it down.

THE ELECTORAL ARENA IN MARX AND ENGELS'S POLITICS

Underlying Engels's position was a very fundamental principle that informed him and Marx even before they became conscious communists—that is, the need for the working class to take time to make adequate preparations to take power under the best circumstances. Elections were the best means to do so because they revealed what the party's strengths were and its level of support and organization. This was the point he was getting at in an article in *Sozialdemokrat* shortly after the government's ban on the party had expired in September 1890, though in language more couched and less provocative. "The attempt must be made to get along with legal methods of struggle for the time being"—the qualifier at the end being crucial. Should the party, he asked, "build barricades" if the regime banned it again? "It will certainly not do its opponents this favor. It will be saved from this by the knowledge of its own position of strength, given it by every general election to the Reichstag. Twenty per cent of the votes cast is a very respectable figure, but this also means that the opponents together still have eighty per cent of the vote." But given the rate of the gains that the party was making in each election, "it would be mad to attempt a putsch."[82]

While reformists have tried to use this statement to justify their politics, it's at best a very tortured reading of Engels that flies in the face of his overall strategy as argued here. His other public and private pronouncements at the time make clear that his call for revolutionary restraint in the *Sozialdemokrat* was exactly that. Precisely because of the gains the party had just made, doubling its vote to 1.5 million from the 1887 election, he expected that Bismarck would take preemptive action. "No doubt they will be the first ones to fire. One fine day the German bourgeois and their government, tired of standing with their arms folded, witnessing the ever increasing advances of socialism, will resort to illegality and violence."[83] However, the regime should remember, he warned in the party press that "at least one-half of the German socialists have passed through the army" and there are "amongst them too many who have learned to stand at order arms in a hail of bullets till the moment is ripe for attack."[84]

In letters to Paul and Laura Lafargue, Engels revealed the strategy behind his warning—playing for time. In spite of Bismarck's expected actions,

> it is our duty not to let ourselves be prematurely crushed. As yet only one soldier out of four or five is ours—on a war footing, maybe one in three. We are making headway in rural areas . . . In three or four years' time we shall have won over the farm laborers and hired hands, in other words the staunchest supporters of the status quo . . . That is why we must, for the time being, advocate lawful action, and not respond to the provocations they will lavish upon us.[85]

Elections, therefore, were the means by which the party could garner the effective forces to successfully wage the violent struggle. And until the most propitious moment, there would be revolutionary restraint. Of course, Engels recognized, consistent with his and Marx's earlier views, that while it would be a "great misfortune" if—because of, for example, a war with Russia—the party was brought "to power prematurely, we have to be prepared for that eventuality."[86] Being "armed" meant above all having a leadership in place that understood what had to be done in such a scenario.

If there is any doubt about how Engels viewed elections, read his comment to Bebel on the eve of the 1890 Reichstag elections in which the SPD was expected to make (and did make) significant gains: "[M]y only fear is that we shall obtain *too many* seats. Every other party in the Reichstag can have as many jackasses and allow them to perpetrate as many blunders as it can afford to pay for, and nobody gives a damn, whereas we, if we are not to be held cheap, must have nothing but heroes and men of genius."[87] Quality and not quantity was the goal—not the demand of a bourgeois politician.

It should be noted that nowhere does Engels say anything about winning a majority of the electorate through elections. The reason, as already suggested, is that he didn't expect the ruling class to allow the electoral process to go that far. Thus what was crucial for success was winning not just a simple majority in elections but rather effective supporters—that is, those who were willing to vote with their feet to resist the regime and especially those who knew how to use arms. Participating in the electoral process made it possible to determine when the requisite number of such forces had been accumulated. This is why the conduct of the party's proletarian ranks in the process was more important for him than just the number of votes obtained or seats won. Engels was also aware that the electoral process itself was flawed. Given the constraints on universal suffrage (e.g., neither women nor anyone under 25 could vote), or the gross inequities in the apportionment of electoral districts, the elections were far from an accurate measure of majority sentiment. Last, by taking preemptive action—that is, overthrowing the electoral process—the regime would forfeit its claims to legality and thus strengthen the workers' party politically in its use of force. The government then, to employ the previously cited point that Marx made, would be acting as "rebels against 'lawful' force"—that is, the majority.

One of the features of the "parliamentary disease," as Engels explained in his aforementioned critique of the so-called Erfurt Program of the SPD in 1891, was the tendency of "striving for the success of the moment" at the expense of the "future of the movement"—namely, "opportunism." In the electoral arena this translated into the disease of "vote-catching." It was exactly this secondary affliction, specifically the "striving" by reformist forces in both the German and French parties to win the peasant vote at the expense of communist principles, that convinced Engels to write in 1894, seven months before his death, *The Peasant Question in France and Germany*. This text came to constitute his and Marx's most comprehensive programmatic views on the peasant question. At the heart of it is the strategy not just for winning the peasant vote on a principled basis but for ensuring the worker-peasant alliance needed for working-class ascendancy.

Commenting on that wing of the SPD, led by Georg Vollmar, that wanted to "catch the peasant vote" at the expense of programmatic integrity, Engels told Paul Lafargue, "You will have seen in *Vorwärts* [the official organ of the SPD] Bebel's speech in the 2nd electoral constituency of Berlin. He complains with reason that the party is going bourgeois. That is the misfortune of all extreme parties when the time approaches for them to become 'possible.'"[88] Not surprisingly it was Bebel who complained about the reformist direction of the party, an assessment with which Engels agreed. Of all the SPD leaders, including Kautsky, as well as party leaders anywhere in the world, it was Bebel for whom Engels had the highest regard. To an old comrade he wrote in 1884, "There is no more lucid mind in the whole of the German party, besides which he is utterly dependable and firm of purpose."[89]

The reformist trend that Bebel called attention to was one that both Marx and Engels had earlier diagnosed—what Engels later called "opportunism." Engels's hope was that principled political differences would provoke the right wing into a split after the ban was lifted in 1890, hence the necessity of programmatic integrity. As for Bebel's prognosis about the SPD, Engels responded that "our Party cannot go beyond a certain limit in this respect without betraying itself."[90] Only would hindsight reveal that, contrary to what Engels thought, the "bourgeois" trend had indeed gone "beyond a certain limit." The parliamentary disease had metastasized into a cancer within the SPD. The campaign for catching the peasant vote signaled the beginning of revisionism in the German party. Vollmar was its political leader, and Bernstein, not long afterwards, became its theoretician. The consequences would be devastating results for all humanity.

BERNSTEIN AND KAUTSKY

This is the appropriate place, near the end of Engels's life, to say a few words about what he and Marx thought about two of the individuals in the German movement with whom they collaborated, specifically Bernstein and Kautsky (especially because they will reappear when attention turns to Lenin). As already discussed, Marx and Engels first encountered the young Bernstein in and about 1879 and severely chastised him and others—in the *Circular Letter of 1879*—who wanted to take the German party in a reformist direction. They thought (erroneously, as history later revealed) that they had won him over to revolutionary politics after the resolution of the kerfuffle. While Engels was more tolerant and patiently tried to bring him along politically—including efforts to "counteract his enthusiasm for Fabianism"[91]—it is worth noting that Marx continued to have doubts. Three months before his death in 1883, Engels told him, "You are right when you say that Bernstein doesn't always allow himself adequate time for reflection."[92] No doubt Marx's suspicions about the "educative elements," the "immature undergraduates and over-wise graduates," continued to influence his opinion of Bernstein.

That attitude about the "educative elements" was certainly on display in Marx's first encounter with Kautsky in 1881. To his daughter Jenny, he wrote, "He's a mediocrity, narrow in outlook, over-wise (only 26 years old), a know-all, hard-working after a fashion, much concerned with statistics out of which, however, he makes little sense, by nature a member of the philistine tribe . . . I unload him onto *amigo* Engels as much as I can."[93] Nothing in the two remaining years of Marx's life indicates that he changed his mind. Engels's comment on a series of articles Kautsky wrote in 1889 on the French Revolution is typical of his opinion of his writings. Engels, ever the dialectician, admonished him, "Altogether you generalize far too much and this often makes you absolute where the utmost relativity is called for . . . I would say a great deal less about the modern mode of production. In every case a yawning gap divides it from the *facts* you adduce and *thus* out of context, it appears as a *pure abstraction which* far from throwing light on the subject, renders it still more obscure."[94]

And then there was a comment Engels made about his political sense or lack thereof when it came to publishing. He accused Kautsky of having "lost touch with the living party movement. A few months ago he showed an inconceivable want of tact in proposing to sling a purely academic discussion of the general strike *in abstracto*, and of its pros and cons generally, into the midst of a movement engaged in a life and death struggle against slogans advocating such a strike."[95] Engels was criticizing him for having invited Bernstein to write an article on the general strike in *Die Neue Zeit* just as the Austrian party was engaged in a major fight with opponents about its use in the campaign for universal suffrage. Kautsky's penchant for abstraction at the expense of grounded context was in Marx and Engels's opinion characteristic of the "over-wise graduates" of Germany's universities.

Both criticisms are significant because Kautsky would come to exercise enormous influence through his writings. One in particular, *The Class Struggle (Erfurt Program)*, a popular presentation of the SPD's 1891 program, came to be widely seen after its publication in 1892 as the best one-volume introduction to the political program of Marx and Engels and, later, as the founding "text" of "orthodox" or "classical Marxism." It was intended, Kautsky said, to serve as a "catechism of Social Democracy."[96] His sobriquet, "the Pope of Marxism," was apropos given the popularity and influence of the book. As for what Engels thought about it, he told Kautsky, "I have only been able to read the first 16 pages. If I were you I should omit the better part of the introduction . . . [and] plunge straight into it . . . So overwhelmed am I by work."[97] His priority, as he explained, was the completion of Volume Three of *Capital*—a task only fulfilled about eight months before his death. While his suggestion about the introduction was taken, it's not clear if Engels ever read the published book. His relationship with Kautsky was clearly strained at the end due to three issues: Kautsky's foot dragging on completing Volume IV of *Capital* (*Theories of Surplus Value*); his shabby treatment of his estranged wife, Louise; and, last, his failure to inform Engels that he was writing and editing a multivolume history of socialism.

Speculation is all that is possible about what Engels thought of *The Class Struggle* in the absence of concrete evidence, but speculation can be informed. In one of the sections most relevant for this book, "9. The Political Struggle," Kautsky writes,

> Great capitalists can influence rulers and legislators directly, but the workers can do so *only* through parliamentary activity . . . By electing representatives to parliament, therefore, the working-class can exercise an influence over the governmental powers. The struggle of all classes which depend upon legislative action for political influence is directed, in the modern state, on the one hand toward an increase in the power of the parliament (or congress), and on the other toward an increase in their own influence within the parliament . . . [P]roletariat . . . parliamentary activity . . . is *the most powerful lever* that can be utilized to raise the proletariat out of its economic, social and moral degradation.[98]

If ever there was an example of "parliamentary cretinism," then this could surely be nominated for Exhibit A. Not only the tone but the language on display here is precisely what Marx and Engels polemicized against. Nothing in the Marx-Engels arsenal would support the claim that "only through parliamentary activity" can the working class influence the ruling class. Just the opposite! They argued that it was *outside* the parliamentary arena where the working class was more efficacious. Furthermore, to say that "parliamentary activity . . . is the most powerful lever" at the disposal of the working class for its advancement is to challenge the only addendum that Marx and Engels ever made to their *Manifesto*. I suspect that if Engels read what Kautsky alleged in 1892, he would not have been surprised. In 1894, as quoted before, he wrote that Bebel "complains with reason that the party is going bourgeois."

***

There is a respected body of literature that argues that twentieth-century social democracy traces its programmatic roots to Kautsky's "catechism."[99] It's beyond the scope of this book to interrogate that claim in any kind of detail. What can be argued with confidence is that the previously quoted sentences from the book—the reader can verify that they are not taken out of context—are diametrically opposed to the historic program of Marx and Engels based on the evidence presented here. To return to the question that opened this section and to conclude, Engels's approach to the electoral arena—with its roots in his and his partner's balance sheet on the "European Spring" of 1848–49, the *Address of March 1850*—was to view it as only as a means—the best in his opinion—to determine when to use revolutionary force. Electoral victories, specifically, were also a means to an end: access to the parliamentary "platform" or "rostrum," a most advantageous venue for propagating revolutionary ideas. These claims I make are most credible when coupled with the main lesson that Engels and Marx drew from the experience of the Paris Commune—that "the working class cannot simply lay hold of the ready-made State machinery, and wield it for its own purposes."

The question now is whether there was any continuity with Marx and Engels's program. Had they successfully recruited a committed cadre to their project? If Kautsky's "heresy" suggests that they were not to be found in the leadership of the German party—other than Bebel—were there forces anywhere prepared to pick up their mantle?

"AND ONCE THE FUN BEGINS IN RUSSIA, THEN HURRAH!"

When Marx and Engels determined in 1860 that a new revolutionary era had begun, they pointed to the peasant movement then under way in Polish Russia—evidence that in the new era "the lava will flow from East to West." However, it took Marx specifically about seven years to make direct contact with Russia's nascent revolutionary movement. In the meantime, and symptomatic of developments there, revolutionaries in Moscow took the initiative to have *Capital* published in Russian, its first translation into a language other than German.

While conducting his political economy research, Marx gained a better appreciation of Russia's importance, which spurred him in early 1870 to learn Russian. As his wife Jenny described it, "he has begun studying Russian as if it were a matter of life and death."[100] Marx wrote Engels that "the most important book published since your work on the *Condition of the Working Class*" was by the Russian Narodnik socialist N. Flerovsky, titled *The Condition of the Working Class in Russia*.[101] After reading Flerovsky, Marx felt "deeply convinced that a most terrible social revolution . . . is irrepressible in Russia and near at hand. This is good news. Russia and England are the two great pillars of the present European system. All the rest is of secondary importance, even *la belle France et la savante Allemagne*."[102] Five years later Engels accurately foresaw—clearly, it took longer than he expected—that the social revolution in Russia would "have inevitable repercussions on Germany."[103] From this point to the very end of their lives both Marx and Engels prioritized developments in Russia over any other country—a fact that virtually every Marxological account ignores.

MARX TAKES THE LEAD

Owing in part to the enormous impact that *Capital* had in Russia—the Russian edition sold better than any other—as well as his renown in connection with the IWMA, a group of Russian émigrés in Geneva asked Marx in March 1870 to represent them on the GC in the IWMA. This was the beginning of his formal links with the generation of Russian revolutionaries from whose ranks would emerge the leadership of the Russian Revolution. Given his and Engels's long-standing and well-known antipathy for Russia—the bulwark of European reaction—Marx found it ironic that he would "be functioning as the representative of *jeune Russie*! A man never knows what he may achieve, or what STRANGE FELLOWSHIP he may have to suffer."[104] One of these young émigrés, Elisaveta Tomanovskaya, worked closely with Marx and Engels during the Commune. That these Russian youth adamantly opposed Bakunin no doubt helped to deconstruct the essentialist views—largely negative—that Marx and Engels had long harbored about the "Russian race." Very soon Engels would say of these youth, "As far as talent and character are concerned, some of these are absolutely among the very best in our party." And in anticipation of a Lenin, "They have a stoicism, a strength of character and at the same time a grasp of theory which are truly admirable."[105]

It's instructive to note that the Geneva exiles wanted Marx to represent them because "the practical character of the movement was so similar in

Germany and Russia, [and] the writings of Marx were so generally known and appreciated by the Russian youth."[106] Although the standard Marxological charge is that Marx and Engels's perspective did not speak to peasant societies such as Russia, young Russian radicals in the 1870s begged to differ. They sought his views on the prospects and course of socialist revolution in their homeland. Specifically, they wondered if Russia would have to undergo a prolonged stage of capitalist development or if it could proceed directly to socialist transformation on the basis of communal property relations that prevailed in much of the countryside at that time.

Exactly because of the socioeconomic changes then underway in Russia, Marx was reluctant to make any categorical judgments. In a letter never mailed to the editorial board of the publication of a group of Russian populist Narodniks in 1877, he warned against turning his "historical sketch of the genesis of capitalism in Western Europe" in *Capital* "into a historical-philosophical theory of general development, imposed by fate on all peoples, whatever the historical circumstances in which they are placed."[107] What he was willing to say about Russia, based on intense study, was that if it "continues along the path it has followed since 1861, it will miss the finest chance that history has ever offered to a nation, only to undergo all the fatal vicissitudes of the capitalist system."[108]

When a related question was posed to him in 1881 by one of the founders of the Marxist party in Russia, Vera Zasulich, specifically about whether the Russian peasant commune could survive in the face of the ever-expanding capitalist mode of production, Marx was again cautious. In order for it to be saved and be the basis for socialist property relations, "it would first be necessary to eliminate the deleterious influences which are assailing it from all sides."[109] In other words, as one of the drafts of his letter put it, "To save the Russian commune, a Russian revolution is needed."[110] The drafts on which this reply was based went into far greater detail on the peasant question and revealed how extensively Marx had been following developments in Russia.

While Marx was cautious about the question, Engels seemed to be more certain that the commune would not survive capital's penetration into the countryside—at least in the context of a polemic with a Russian who, in Engels's opinion, romanticized the peasant. As it turned out, it fell on Engels's shoulders to bring more clarity to this question, because in outliving Marx by 12 years, he witnessed developments in Russia's countryside that Marx could only anticipate.

As for the politics and strategy of socialist revolution in Russia, Engels in the aforementioned polemic first predicted what would be involved. Rejecting the view that the Russian peasant was "instinctively revolutionary," he warned against "a premature attempt at insurrection," since "Russia undoubtedly is on the eve of a revolution." He provided a quite accurate sketch of what would occur, though not when he expected but three decades later: "[A] growing recognition among the enlightened strata of the nation concentrated in the capital that . . . a revolution is impending, and the illusion that it will be possible to guide this revolution among a smooth constitutional channel. Here all the conditions of a revolution are combined, of a revolution that, started by the upper classes of the capital, perhaps even by the government itself, must be rapidly carried further, beyond the first constitutional phase, by the peasants, of a revolution that will be of the greatest importance for the whole of Europe."[111] Marx saw a similar scenario, and when the Russo-Turkish War broke out in 1877, they both thought it would precipitate Russia's social revolution. They got the algebra if not the mathematics right, because it was indeed a war, the Russo-Japanese War in 1905, that helped catalyze the process culminating in 1917.

In the aforementioned polemic, Engels made clear that given Russia's reality a revolution that began with a conspiracy was certainly justifiable. Never "at any time in my political career [have I] declared that conspiracies were to be universally condemned in all circumstances."[112] Later, both he and Marx praised Russian revolutionaries—one of whom, Vera Zasulich, they would establish close ties with—who either carried out or attempted individual acts of terror against Russian rulers. "Against such wild animals one must defend oneself as one can, with powder and lead. Political assassination in Russia is the only means which men of intelligence, dignity and character possess to defend themselves against the agents of an unprecedented despotism."[113]

Both also held that the opening of the social revolution in Russia would spread westward, leading to "*radical change throughout Europe*."[114] In fact, the "overthrow of Tsarist Russia . . . is . . . one of the first conditions of the German proletariat's ultimate triumph."[115] In 1882 Engels counseled that the formation of the next international should only be done when conditions were ripe: "[S]uch events are already taking shape in Russia where the avant-garde of the revolution will be going into battle. You should—or so we think—wait for this and its inevitable repercussions on Germany, and then the moment will also have come for a big manifesto and the establishment of an *official*, formal International, which can, however, no longer be a propaganda association but simply an association for action."[116] This was most prophetic, since it was indeed the Russian Revolution in 1917 that lead to the formation in 1919 of the Third or Communist International, which proudly proclaimed its adherence to the Marx program.

Finally, in the Preface to the second Russian edition of the *Manifesto* in 1882, they wrote that "Russia forms the vanguard of revolutionary action in Europe." As for the future of the peasant commune in Russia, they provided their clearest answer yet: "If the Russian Revolution becomes the signal for a proletarian revolution in the West, so that the two complement each other, the present Russian common ownership of land may serve as the starting point for communist development."[117] To the end of his life, which was only 15 months away, Marx continued to devote his attention to the peasant question in Russia. Not coincidentally, this is the question that Lenin would begin his revolutionary studies with.

<h3 style="text-align:center">ENGELS IN CHARGE</h3>

With Marx gone, it fell to Engels to render assistance to the many national movements that sought his counsel. But none held his attention as did the Russian movement. He continued to believe, as Marx had, that it was in Russia where Europe's revolutionary "vanguard" existed. "And once the fun begins in Russia," he told his main contact in the United States in 1887, "then hurrah!"[118] The Russian "lava," in other words, "will flow . . . West."

The spate of political assassinations that began in 1877 had impressed him and Marx with Russia's volatility. Just as was true for Vera Zasulich's assassination attempt, they praised the assassins—members of *Narodnaya Volya* [*People's Will*]—of Czar Alexander II in 1881. To his daughter Jenny, Marx wrote that they were "sterling chaps through and through, without melodramatic posturing, simple, matter-of-fact, heroic . . . [T]hey . . . are at pains to teach Europe that their *modus operandi* is a specifically Russian and historically inevitable mode of action which no more lends itself to moralizing—for or against—than does the [recent] earthquake in Chios [Greece]."[119] For Engels, they were "our people," whose actions had helped to create a "revolutionary situation" in Russia.[120]

As Marx's comment to Jenny indicates, neither he nor Engels praised terrorism as a tactic suitable for all places at all times. Thus in the same article in which he condemned a terrorist bombing in London in January 1885—"Irish hands may have laid the dynamite, but it is more than probable that a Russian brain and Russian money were behind it"—he publicly defended *Narodnaya Volya*: "The means of struggle employed by the Russian revolutionaries are dictated to them by necessity, by the actions of their opponents themselves. They must answer to their people and to history for the means they employ. But the gentlemen who are needlessly parodying this struggle in Western Europe in schoolboy fashion . . . who do not even direct their weapons against real enemies but against the public in general, these gentlemen are in no way successors or allies of the Russian revolutionaries, but rather their worst enemies."[121] In the specific conditions of Russia, terror was justifiable, but it was not in Western Europe, at least at that moment.

Because Engels closely followed the debate within the Russian movement on the use of terror—"these Russian quarrels are not uninteresting," he told Laura Lafargue[122]—he could respond to Zasulich's request to comment on Georgi Plekhanov's polemic, *Our Differences*, against *Narodnaya Volya's* overall perspective and tactics. The Russian situation was so unstable, he pointed out, that it "is one of those special cases where it is possible for a handful of men to *effect* a revolution . . . Well, if ever Blanquism, the fantasy of subverting the whole of a society through action by a small group of conspirators, had any rational foundation, it would assuredly be in St. Petersburg." However—a most important qualifier— "Once the match has been applied to the powder, the men who have sprung the mine will be swept off their feet by an explosion a thousand times more powerful than they themselves."[123]

For Engels, then, the important thing was "that revolution should break out," and it was "of little concern to me" whether it be conspirators or not since the pent-up energy in Russia was such that "1789, once launched, will before long be followed by 1793"—that is, the "revolution in permanence." "Men who have boasted of having *effected* a revolution have always found on the morrow that they didn't know what they were doing; that once *effected*, the revolution bears no resemblance at all to what they had intended."[124] From its beginnings, the Marx-Engels project, based on the "real movement of history," lacked guarantees—a revolutionary project without guarantees.

At this time Engels began a regular correspondence and contact with Zasulich, Plekhanov, and other leaders of the recently formed Emancipation of Labor group, the first explicitly Russian Marxist organization.[125] As he and Marx had earlier commented, the seriousness with which the Russians took the study of their writings was singular among all their party contacts. They sought his views on the key theoretical issue that Marx had been asked to address—whether Russia could bypass capitalist development and proceed directly to socialism based on the common ownership of property of the traditional peasant commune. There were of course enormous political implications in the answer to this most vital question.

After almost a decade and a half had lapsed since his and Marx's last detailed comments, in 1894 Engels made his final and definitive judgment on Russia's trajectory. Its recent development, as he and Marx had suspected, was decidedly capitalist, and the "proletarianisation of a large proportion of the peasantry and the decay of the old communistic commune proceeds at an ever quickening pace." Whether enough of the traditional communes remained for a "point of departure for communistic development," Engels could not say.

> But this much is certain: if a remnant of this commune is to be preserved, the first condition is the fall of tsarist despotism—revolution in Russia. This will not only tear the great mass of the nation, the peasants away from the isolation of their villages . . . and lead them out onto the great stage . . . it will also give the labour movement of the West fresh impetus and create new, better conditions in which to carry on the struggle, thus hastening the victory of the modern industrial proletariat, without which present-day Russia can never achieve a socialist transformation, whether proceeding from the commune or from capitalism.[126]

In no uncertain terms, then, and contrary to all the future Stalinist distortions of Marx and Engels's views, Russia could "never achieve a socialist transformation" *without* the overthrow of the bourgeoisie in Western Europe by its own proletariat. Not only would Russia be the "impetus" for the socialist revolution in the West, as Marx and Engels had been saying for two decades, but its own revolution was inextricably linked to that outcome. This forecast would be profoundly and tragically confirmed by subsequent history.

Engels also noted in his final pronouncement that the Russian bourgeoisie, like its German counterpart, was content to allow a despot—the Czar—to rule in its place because the autocracy "offers it more guarantees than would changes even of a bourgeois-liberal nature." This was advantageous to the socialist revolution because the bourgeoisie's cowardly stance meant that Russia's small but growing proletariat, just as was true for Germany, would be forced to combine the fight for economic and social advancement with the struggle for political democracy; this would ensure, in other words, that the revolution would go beyond the boundaries of its bourgeois-democratic tasks to become "permanent." In Western Europe, it was the German proletariat that was expected to be the immediate recipient of Russia's "impetus." It was exactly this point, the vanguard role of the proletariat in Russia's as well as Germany's coming revolution, that Engels made to Zasulich at his last New Year's Eve celebration—a forecast she quickly relayed to her comrades in the Emancipation of Labour Group.[127] History would again confirm Engels's prescience.

***

If the prospects for a revolutionary leadership in Germany at the end of Engels's life looked dim, it didn't discourage him. He and his partner died with their eyes on Russia—a fact ignored in virtually every standard account of their lives. Part and parcel of Engels's fight for the political soul of the German party, to prevent it from "going bourgeois," was also an antiwar cause—to try to prevent what would be the First World War.[128] Russia was very much part of that strategy. In 1888 he wrote that "revolution in Russia at this moment would save Europe from the horrors of a general war and would usher in universal social revolution."[129] Three years later he was uncannily prophetic. While a general European war was not inevitable, "one thing is certain": "This war, in which fifteen to twenty million armed men would slaughter one another and devastate Europe as it has never been devastated before . . . would either lead to the immediate triumph of socialism, or it would lead to such an upheaval in the old order of things, it would leave behind it everywhere such a heap of ruins, that . . . the socialist revolution, set back by ten or fifteen years, would only be all the more radical and more rapidly implemented."[130] And a year later in 1892, he wrote, "If war breaks out, *those who are defeated* will have the opportunity and duty to bring about a revolution—and that's that."[131] Without a crystal ball, all that Engels—and Marx—could foresee was that a European conflagration was intimately linked with revolutionary prospects for Russia and the rest of Europe. The task now is to see if his and Marx's expectations were justified.

CHAPTER 2

REVOLUTIONARY CONTINUITY

LENIN'S POLITICS PRIOR TO 1905

"BLOODY SUNDAY," JANUARY 9, 1905, IN ST. Petersburg initiated the "Russian Spring"—the beginning of the end of the three-hundred-year-old Romanov dynasty. Like Frederick IV in Prussia, or the military regime that replaced the dethroned Hosni Mubarak, Nicholas II was forced in October after months of near nationwide mass protests to grant the semblance of representative democracy. While Marx and Engels had mistakenly thought that Russia's bourgeois revolution would come sooner, they were right that Europe's last remaining absolute monarchy was on life-support. They did all they could to influence its expected death in the interests of the toilers through their writings and collaboration with Russia's nascent Marxist movement.

To understand how Lenin responded to "Bloody Sunday" and its revolutionary aftermath, it is necessary to step back in time to see what his politics were prior to then. What was his understanding of the nature of the Russian Revolution? What was his conception of the role of democracy itself in organizing to make a revolution? Most important for this book, what was his attitude toward representative democracy and the electoral process—the concessions that Nicholas was forced to make? And for all these questions, last, how did Marx and Engels inform Lenin, or perhaps more correctly, how did he think they informed him, and was he right? I beg the reader's indulgence, because what follows is a detailed compilation of what Lenin actually said and did—necessary, I think, given the success of the Leninologists in having painted him with an antidemocratic brush. Perhaps the best way to challenge that all-too-familiar image is to let Lenin speak for himself.[1]

BUILDING ON THE LEGACY BEQUEATHED

When Engels in 1872 wrote to a longtime comrade in Germany and veteran of 1848–49 about the Russian youth he and Marx were now collaborating with, he compared them favorably to a prior generation of Russian revolutionaries. Unlike those "who came to Europe earlier on— noble, aristocratic Russians, among whom we must include Herzen and Bakunin and who are swindlers to the last man . . . those who are com- ing now, all of whom are of the *people*. As far as talent and character are concerned, some of these are absolutely among the very best in our party. They have a stoicism, a strength of character and at the same time a grasp of theory which are truly admirable."[2] Though only two years old when Engels penned these comments, Lenin would come to epitomize more than anyone what Engels was describing.

APPRENTICESHIP

If any one of the three qualities that Engels noted about the Russian youth came to distinguish Lenin, it was clearly his "grasp of theory." Critically important in understanding why were his extraordinary language skills.[3] At the encouragement of his mother, with roots in Germany, he and his siblings were fluent readers from a fairly early age of not only German but also French and English. His German skills made it possible for him to read *Das Kapital* at age 18, in 1888—an auspicious beginning for learning how to "grasp theory." Precisely because of what Marx and Engels bequeathed, the young Lenin was able to enter the political arena with a communist perspective about five years earlier than they had at a comparable age.

It was in Samara, in the Volga region and severely impacted by the 1891– 92 famine—a transformative event for Lenin according to Trotsky—where he moved to in 1889, that Lenin qualitatively deepened his understanding of Marx's politics and analysis. A year later, he translated the *Manifesto* into Russian for use by a study circle there that he had contact with.[4] During and immediately after the famine he immersed himself in the study of volumes one and two of *Capital* (Engels did not complete volume three until 1894[5]). The Samara period, owing to his intense study, specifically 1891–92, is when, Trotsky argues, Lenin became a conscious Marxist for the first time. As to when he became familiar with Russian social democracy, "Lenin told [Karl] Radek on a walk they took together that he had studied not only *Das Kapital* but also Engels' *Anti-Dühring* before he got hold of any publications of the Emancipation of Labor Group . . . [H]is acquaintance with the works of Plekanov, without which one could not have arrived at Social Democratic positions, must have taken place in 1891." In a party questionnaire in 1921, Lenin wrote that his revolutionary activities began in Samara in 1892–93.[6]

Lenin, in 1904, said that prior to Marx and Engels, it was Cherny- shevsky who "had a major, overpowering influence on me."[7] Marx, it

should be noted, thought very highly of Chernyshevsky's political economy writings, which, like *Capital*, owed a significant debt to Ludwig
Feuerbach and the young Hegelians. Marx might have agreed, therefore,
that reading Chernyshevsky would be a good place to begin for a young
Russian wanting to understand his analysis.[8]

Reading *Capital* is one thing—applying it is another. This is just what
Lenin began doing at the end of his Samara period (1889–93)—that is,
using Marx's analysis to understand Russia's reality, particularly the peasantry and the penetration of capitalist property relations in the countryside.
That this was exactly the question that occupied Marx at the end of his
life—probably unbeknownst to Lenin—indicates how well-tuned he was
to his mentors. Employing *Capital* in his first analytical writing, he reached
essentially the same conclusion that Engels, as noted in the previous chapter, would a few months later in 1894: "[T]he transformation of the country into a capitalist industrial nation . . . proceeds at an ever quickening
pace." To reach similar conclusions—independently—testifies to how well
Lenin had graduated from apprenticeship to mastery of Marx's method.

LENIN THE "SOCIAL-DEMOCRAT"

What the "Friends of the People" Are was Lenin's opening salvo. Written in
1894, this two-hundred-page polemic took on a then influential current
in radical circles: the populist Narodniks and their chief spokesperson,
Nikolai Mikhailovsky. It began with a defense of *Capital* for understanding Marx's methodology. Interestingly, it was Mikhailovsky who was the
target of Marx's criticism in 1877 (noted in Chapter 1) for having turned
his "historical sketch of the genesis of capitalism in Western Europe" in
Capital "into a historical-philosophical theory of general development,
imposed by fate on all peoples, whatever the historical circumstances in
which they are placed." Whether Lenin then knew of Marx's criticism
is uncertain. But for present purposes what is significant about Lenin's
employment of Marx is its defense of the political struggle, specifically
the fight for democracy.

Despite the illusions the Narodniks had about the small peasantry—
that the preservation of small landowners was somehow revolutionary—
Marxists, Lenin argued, were not neutral in the historic fight of this petit
bourgeois class against the large landowning class. The latter represented
the "survivals of the medieval epoch and of serfdom," and any struggle
against them was the "democratic side" to the peasant struggle.

> [A]lthough the Marxists completely repudiate petty-bourgeois theories,
> this does not prevent them from including democracy in their programme,

but on the contrary, calls for still stronger insistence on it . . . Social-Democrats unreservedly associate themselves with the demand for the complete restoration of the peasants' civil rights, the complete abolition of all privileges of the nobility, the abolition of bureaucratic tutelage over the peasants, and the peasants' right to manage their own affairs.

In general, the Russian communists, adherents of Marxism, should more than any others call themselves **SOCIAL-DEMOCRATS**, and in their activities should never forget the enormous importance of **DEMOCRACY** . . . it is the direct duty of the working class to fight side by side with the radical democracy against absolutism and the reactionary social estates and institutions—a duty which the Social-Democrats must impress upon the workers, while not for a moment ceasing also to impress upon them that the struggle against all these institutions is necessary only as a means of facilitating the struggle against the bourgeoisie, that the worker needs the achievement of the general democratic demands only to clear the road to victory over the working people's chief enemy, over an institution that is purely democratic by nature, *capital*, which here in Russia is particularly inclined to sacrifice its democracy and to enter into alliance with the reactionaries in order to suppress the workers, to still further impede the emergence of a working-class movement . . . political liberty will primarily serve the interests of the bourgeoisie and will not ease the position of the workers, but . . . will ease only the conditions for their struggle . . . *against this very bourgeoisie.*[9]

In his very next writing a few months later, *The Economic Content of Narodism and the Criticism of It in Mr. Struve's Book,* Lenin returned to what he calls the "progressive" side of the Narodnik program for the peasantry "relating to self-government, to the 'people's' free and broad access to knowledge, to the 'raising' of the 'people's' (that is to say, small) economy by means of cheap credits, technical improvements, better regulation of marketing, etc." These are what he called "general democratic measures."

The Narodniks in this respect understand and represent the interests of the small producers far more correctly [than Struve], and the Marxists, while rejecting all the reactionary features of their programme, must not only accept the general democratic points, but carry them through more exactly, deeply and further. The more resolute such reforms are in Russia, the higher they raise the living standard of the working masses—the more sharply and clearly will the most important and fundamental (already today) social antagonism in Russian life stand out. The Marxists, far from "breaking the democratic thread" or trend, as [an opponent] slanderously asserts they do, want to develop and strengthen this trend, they want to bring it closer to life.[10]

The comments from both writings are Lenin's first pronouncements—at the outset of his political career—on the bourgeois democratic revolution and its relation to the socialist revolution.[11] As will be seen, they constituted the basic stance he adhered to going into the 1905 Revolution and continued to inform his practice during the heady days of 1917. They were, I argue, thoroughly informed by Marx and Engels's politics beginning with the *Manifesto*, particularly the last section, and ending with Engels's retort in 1892 to a critic who claimed that he and his partner had ignored forms of governance: "Marx and I, for forty years, repeated ad nauseam that for us the democratic republic is the only political form in which the struggle between the working class and the capitalist class can first be universalized and then culminate in the decisive victory of the proletariat."[12] It should be recalled that while the *Manifesto* didn't include the peasantry as a potential ally for workers, the later *Demands* that Marx and Engels drew up did so. Given that it's unlikely that Lenin knew that when he wrote this, his inclusion of them testifies once again to how thoroughly he had grasped their theory and politics.

Also noteworthy about what Lenin wrote is his usage of "social-democracy" as a way to make more explicit the content of the communist program. Given what "social-democracy" would later come to mean—a not unimportant issue that Lenin would address after 1917—his semantic move here in 1894 is instructive and prescient, more evidence of his deep understanding of Marx and Engels's project. He also made clear that Marxists supported reforms if they indeed put the toilers in a better position to wage the decisive fight against capital. Contrary to what Struve alleged, the "fight for reforms" was always part of Marx's strategy: "[H]e said in the *Manifesto* that the movement towards the new system cannot be *separated* from the working class movement (and, hence from the struggle for reforms), and when he himself, in conclusion, proposed a number of practical measures."[13] Last, and most important in understanding his politics in 1905 and afterward, is his claim about Russian capitalists—that is, their group's inclination to "sacrifice its democracy and to enter into alliances with the reactionaries in order to suppress the workers." The centrality of this claim to his politics can't be overstated. It, too, originates in Marx and Engels—the central lesson they took from the "European Spring" of 1848–49.

In making his case, Lenin drew almost exclusively on Marx and Engels and not subsequent recruits to their program such as Kautsky and Georgi Plekhanov. He certainly respected the latter two and acknowledged, as already noted, a debt to them. But by being able to go straight to the source, he had the confidence, I argue, to break with them when he later thought their reading of Marx and Engels was faulty. To argue, also, as I do that the paternity from Marx and Engels to Lenin was direct and not through Kautsky and Plekhanov, as some claim, means that it is to the former and not the latter that attention must be directed in understanding Lenin's politics and perspective.[14] In an early self-reflective moment, Lenin wrote, "Let us not believe that orthodoxy means taking things on trust, that orthodoxy precludes critical application and further development, that it permits historical problems to be obscured by abstract schemes. If there are orthodox disciples who are guilty of these truly grievous sins, the blame must rest entirely with those disciples and not by any means with orthodoxy, which is distinguished by diametrically opposite qualities."[15]

Lenin's first trip to Europe in 1895—much of it spent in libraries— allowed him to quantitatively deepen his knowledge of the writings of Marx and Engels as well as related issues, not the least important being the Paris Commune. His article "Fredrick Engels," written shortly after his death, registered how productive the five-month trip had been. As always, he never missed the opportunity to extract the relevant political lessons:

> Marx and Engels, who both knew Russian and read Russian books, took a lively interest in the country, followed the Russian revolutionary movement with sympathy and maintained contact with Russian revolutionaries. They both became socialists after being *democrats*, and the democratic feeling of *hatred* for political despotism was exceedingly strong in them. This direct political feeling, combined with a profound theoretical understanding of the connection between political despotism and economic oppression, and also their rich experience of life, made Marx and Engels uncommonly responsive *politically*. That is why the heroic struggle of the handful of Russian revolutionaries against the mighty tsarist government evoked a most sympathetic echo in the hearts of these tried revolutionaries. On the other hand, the tendency, for the sake of illusory economic advantages, to turn away from the most immediate and important task of the Russian socialists, namely, the winning of political freedom, naturally appeared suspicious to them and was even regarded by them as a direct betrayal of the great cause of the social revolution. "The emancipation of the workers must be the act of the working class itself"—Marx and Engels constantly taught. But in order to fight for its economic emancipation, the proletariat must win itself certain *political* rights. Moreover, Marx and Engels clearly saw that a political revolution in Russia would be of tremendous significance to the West-European working-class movement as well. Autocratic Russia had always been a bulwark of European reaction in general . . . Only a free Russia, a Russia that had no need either to oppress the Poles, Finns, Germans, Armenians or any other small nations, or constantly to set France and Germany at loggerheads, would enable modern Europe, rid of the burden of war, to breathe freely, would weaken all the reactionary elements in Europe and strengthen the

European working class. That was why Engels ardently desired the establishment of political freedom in Russia for the sake of the progress of the
working-class movement in the West as well. In him the Russian revolutionaries have lost their best friend.[16]

Again, for Lenin the fate of Russia's socialist revolution depended on the
fight for "political freedom," for "political rights"—for democracy. In
hammering home the necessity for what the *Manifesto* called "the battle
for democracy," Lenin was criticizing another group of opponents, the
"economists"—that is, those who tended to prioritize economic struggles
while dismissing political democracy. And Russia's democratic quest, he
insisted, had implications beyond its borders, not just for the oppressed
nations within the Czar's domain but elsewhere. Here is Lenin's first
explicit statement—following Engels, and Marx as well—that Russia's
revolution was linked to Europe's proletarian revolution.

While in prison in 1895–97, following his first confrontations with the
regime as a communist, Lenin composed a "Draft and Explanation of a
Programme for the Social-Democratic Party." Like the *Manifesto*, it was not
a program for the organization he was a member of, the League of Struggle,
but rather the "social-democratic party" of Russia in a broad historical sense
just as Marx and Engels's document was written for the "communist party"
and not the League of Communists that actually commissioned the program. The "Draft" was basically an update of a program Plekhanov composed a decade earlier that called for, among other things, all the essentials
of bourgeois democracy.[17] The "Explanation" is all Lenin's voice. What he
had to say about the section in the "Draft" on the aims of the "Russian
Social-Democratic Party" vis-à-vis workers is particularly relevant:

> What is meant by these words: the struggle of the working class is a political
> struggle? They mean that the working class cannot fight for its emancipation
> without securing influence over affairs of state, over the administration of
> the state, over the issue of laws . . . Thus we see that the struggle of the work-
> ing class against the capitalist class must necessarily be a political struggle.
> Indeed, this struggle is already exerting influence on the state authority, is
> acquiring political significance. But the workers' utter lack of political rights,
> about which we have already spoken, and the absolute impossibility of the
> workers openly and directly influencing state authority become more clearly
> and sharply exposed and felt as the working-class movement develops. That
> is why the most urgent demand of the workers, the primary objective of the
> working-class influence on affairs of state must be *the achievement of politi-
> cal freedom*, i.e., the direct participation, guaranteed by law (by a constitu-
> tion), of all citizens in the government of the state, the guaranteed right of
> all citizens freely to assemble, discuss their affairs, influence affairs of state

through their associations and the press. The achievement of political freedom becomes the "*vital task of the workers*" because without it the workers do
not and cannot have any influence over affairs of state, and thus inevitably
remain a rightless, humiliated and inarticulate class.[18]

Here Lenin, for the first time, specified what "political freedom" means—
that is, all the characteristics of bourgeois democracy, including civil liberties. These were essential, once again, in aiding the working class in
its quest for political power, without which they would continue to be
subject to "the domination of the capitalist class."[19]

THE TASKS OF THE RUSSIAN SOCIAL DEMOCRATS

Out of jail and in exile in Siberia, Lenin had time to reflect on the most
tumultuous events of his political career so far: the St. Petersburg textile
workers' strikes in 1896—in many ways his baptism of fire. He drew some
preliminary lessons in commenting on the government's new legislation that
sought to assuage workers with some improvements in working conditions
such as the length of the working day. One of the lessons, he pointed out, is
that "the Russian Government is a far worse enemy of the Russian workers
than the Russian employers are, for the government not only protects the
interests of the employers, not only resorts, for this purpose, to brutal persecution of the workers, to arrests, deportations and the use of troops against
unarmed workers, but what is more, protects the interests of the *most stingy*
employers and resists any tendency of the better employers to yield to the
workers."[20] And from that fact another lesson was to be drawn about the
government's new policies: "[A]s long as the Russian workers, like the Russian people in general, stand disenfranchised in face of a police government,
as long as they have no political rights, no reforms can be effective."[21] Again,
the primacy of the struggle for political democracy.

As for the broader lessons of St. Petersburg and beyond, Lenin wrote a
widely distributed pamphlet at the end of 1897, *The Tasks of the Russian
Social-Democrats*, which provided greater precision about the democratic
content of social democracy and the strategy for its implementation. Of
Lenin's political writings prior to 1905, the pamphlet ranks in importance with *What Is to Be Done?*, published three years later. Russian social
democrats make clear from the beginning that their task in leading the
proletarian class struggle had two sides, "as the name they have adopted"
indicates: "socialist (the fight against the capitalist class aimed at destroying the class system and organising socialist society), and democratic
(the fight against absolutism aimed at winning political liberty in Russia
and democratising the political and social system of Russia)."[22] He then

detailed what the socialist task is with reference to the activities of the League of Struggle for the Emancipation of the Working Class in the recent St. Petersburg strikes. Essentially this involved a combination of winning urban industrial workers to a communist perspective and taking part in their fights with the capitalists. In prioritizing the industrial proletariat, Lenin assured his readers that this didn't mean ignoring other toilers. To the contrary, he argued, a class-conscious, fighting industrial proletariat was the best aid the other toilers had in their own struggles.

> We have pointed to the inseparably close connection between *socialist* and *democratic* propaganda and agitation, to the complete parallelism of revolutionary activity in both spheres. Nevertheless, there is a big difference between these two types of activity and struggle. The difference is that in the economic struggle the proletariat stands absolutely alone against both the landed nobility and the bourgeoisie, except, perhaps, for the help it receives (and by no means always) from those elements of the petty bourgeoisie which gravitate towards the proletariat. In the democratic, *political* struggle, however, the Russian working class does not stand alone; at its side are all the political opposition elements, strata and classes, since they are hostile to absolutism and are fighting it in one form or another. Here *side by side* with the proletariat stand the opposition elements of the bourgeoisie, or of the educated classes, or of the petty bourgeoisie, or of the nationalities, religions and sects, etc., etc., persecuted by the autocratic government.[23]

The question then was what kind of alliance should the working class have with these other forces in the democratic struggle?

> The attitude of the working class, as a fighter against the autocracy, towards all the other social classes and groups in the political opposition is very precisely determined by the basic principles of Social-Democracy expounded in the famous *Communist Manifesto*. The Social-Democrats support the progressive social classes against the reactionary classes, the bourgeoisie against the representatives of privileged landowning estate and the bureaucracy, the big bourgeoisie against the reactionary strivings of the petty bourgeoisie. This support does not presuppose, nor does it call for, any compromise with non-Social-Democratic programmes and principles—it is support given to an ally against a *particular* enemy. Moreover, the Social-Democrats render this support in order to expedite the fall of the common enemy, but expect nothing *for themselves* from these temporary allies, and concede nothing to them. The Social-Democrats support every revolutionary movement against the present social system, they support all oppressed nationalities, persecuted religions, downtrodden social estates, etc., in their fight for equal rights.[24]

Thus Marx and Engels provided the answer, specifically in Part IV of the *Manifesto*. As his mentors had taught, the alliance of the proletariat with other forces willing to fight for democracy and the support rendered was specific, "temporary and conditional" as he put it. Most important, it did not "presuppose" or mean a "compromise" of social democracy's eventual goal of socialist revolution.

Lenin then explained why what Marx and Engels fought for, "independent working class political action," was necessary in the democratic struggle. He recognized that this might be misread by potential allies. "We shall be told that 'such action will *weaken* all the fighters for political liberty at the present time.' We shall reply that such action will *strengthen* all the fighters for political liberty. Only those fighters are strong who rely on the *consciously recognised* real interests of certain classes, and any attempt to obscure these class interests, which already play a predominant role in contemporary society, will only weaken the fighters. That is the first point." In other words, the class position of the proletariat—so central to Marx and Engels's analysis—justified putting it into the proverbial driver's seat. But that was only the beginning of wisdom, Lenin recognized. Comparisons with the other social layers were necessary.

> The second point is that, in the fight against the autocracy, the working class must single itself out, for it is the *only* thoroughly consistent and unreserved enemy of the autocracy, *only* between the working class and the autocracy is no compromise possible, *only* in the working class can democracy find a champion who makes no reservations, is not irresolute and does not look back. The hostility of all other classes, groups and strata of the population towards the autocracy is *not unqualified*; their democracy always looks back. The bourgeoisie cannot but realise that industrial and social development is being retarded by the autocracy, but it fears the complete democratisation of the political and social system and can at any moment enter into alliance with the autocracy against the proletariat. The petty bourgeoisie is two-faced by its very nature, and while it gravitates, on the one hand, towards the proletariat and democracy, on the other, it gravitates towards the reactionary classes, tries to hold up the march of history, is apt to be seduced by the experiments and blandishments of the autocracy . . . is capable of concluding an alliance with the ruling classes against the proletariat *for the sake of* strengthening its own *small-proprietor* position.

Though virtually nowhere in the document does Lenin have anything to say explicitly about the small peasantry—the heroes for the Narodniks—it can be safely assumed, based on prior writings cited earlier, that they are included with the "small-proprietor."

But if the "hostility" of the bourgeoisie and petty bourgeoisie toward the autocracy is "not unqualified," unlike that of the proletariat, then might not there be other social layers that could be as solid in their opposition to the autocracy as that of the proletariat? If so, they were not, Lenin said, to be found in the ranks of at least one of two possible candidates:

> Educated people, and the "intelligentsia" generally, cannot but revolt against the savage police tyranny of the autocracy, which hunts down thought and knowledge; but the material interests of this intelligentsia bind it to the autocracy and to the bourgeoisie, compel it to be inconsistent, to compromise, to sell its oppositional and revolutionary ardour for an official salary, or a share of profits or dividends. As for the democratic elements among the oppressed nationalities and the persecuted religions, everybody knows and sees that the class antagonisms within these categories of the population are much deeper-going and stronger than the solidarity binding all classes within any one category against the autocracy and in favour of democratic institutions.

The intelligentsia, unlike oppressed nationalities, could not be expected to be as resolute as the proletariat in the democratic quest. Lenin's almost matter-of-fact but unsparing read of Russia's intelligentsia is reminiscent of Engels's comments about the parliamentary cretins in Germany in 1848–49, of which a large component were university professors on the state payroll.

The proletariat was unique. It "alone can be the *vanguard fighter* for political liberty and for democratic institutions. Firstly, this is because political tyranny bears most heavily upon the proletariat whose position gives it no opportunity to secure a modification of that tyranny—it has no access to the higher authorities, not even to the officials, and it has no influence on public opinion." And then Lenin gets to what I argue is the heart of his position—what any assessment of his views on democracy has to come to terms with: "Secondly, the proletariat alone is capable of bringing about the *complete* democratisation of the political and social system, since this would place the system in the hands of the workers." Nothing was more fundamental to his stance, as well to that of Marx and Engels. Only with the working class in power, in other words, is real democracy possible—exactly the conclusion that the young Marx and Engels reached a bit more than a half century earlier.

There were tactical and strategic consequences for such a conclusion, as alluded to earlier:

> That is why the *merging* of the democratic activities of the working class with the democratic aspirations of other classes and groups would *weaken*

the democratic movement, would *weaken* the political struggle, would make it less determined, less consistent, more likely to compromise On the other hand, if the working class *stands out* as the vanguard fighter for democratic institutions, this will *strengthen* the democratic movement, will *strengthen* the struggle for political liberty, because the working class will *spur on* all the other democratic and political opposition elements, will push the liberals towards the political radicals, will push the radicals towards an irrevocable rupture with the whole of the political and social structure of present society.

Though Lenin doesn't cite Marx and Engels's *Address of March 1850* for support, I think it likely that it was the inspiration for his stance. As pointed out in Chapter 1, the document stressed repeatedly that in the event of a new revolutionary upsurge the proletariat party had to avoid the mistake it previously made. Rather than "unity" with nonproletarian democratic forces, it should only enter into an alliance with them. Though Lenin employed—or at least his translators do—"merging," what he warned against here was exactly in the spirit of Marx and Engels's admonition. Although it's not clear when he did so, the Bolshevik's leading archivist, David Riazanov, said, again, Lenin committed the *Address* to memory.

There is one additional point from *The Tasks*—at least at this stage of the exposition—that merits mention. It refers to the state bureaucracy not only in Russia but in England as well. While it was unmistakable in Russia that the institution in all its myriad incarnations served the interests of the privileged,

> Even in England we see that powerful social groups support the privileged position of the bureaucracy and hinder the complete democratisation of that institution. Why? Because it is in the interests of the proletariat alone to democratise it *completely*; the most progressive strata of the bourgeoisie defend certain prerogatives of the bureaucracy and are opposed to the election of all officials, opposed to the complete abolition of electoral qualifications, opposed to making officials directly responsible to the people, etc., because these strata realise that the proletariat will take advantage of such complete democratisation in order to use it *against* the bourgeoisie. This is the case in Russia, too.[25]

Lenin made clear here that his indictment of the Russian ruling class did not exempt its counterparts elsewhere, including in settings where bourgeois democracy was in place. Particularly significant is his reference—for the first time, as far as I can determine—to the electoral process. This reveals that he had no illusions about bourgeois democracy if and when it finally came to Russia—crucial in understanding what his response would be.

TAKING INTO ACCOUNT RUSSIAN REALITIES

All the positions discussed so far that Lenin held on political freedom, civil liberties, democracy in general, bourgeois democracy, and its relation to the socialist revolution were repeated in one form or another in his subsequent writings, including the soon to be discussed *What Is to Be Done?* Nothing new of significance was added, though to be sure, there were some elaborations and occasional tweaks. For example, "[W]hile our allies in the bourgeois-democratic camp, in struggling for liberal reforms, will always glance back . . . the proletariat will march forward to the end . . . we will struggle for the democratic republic . . . The party of the proletariat must learn to catch every liberal just at the moment when he is prepared to move forward an inch, and make him move forward a yard. If he is obdurate, we will go forward without him and over him."[26] Or, to the list of "general democratic reforms" in the old party program, which already included "universal franchise" and "salaries for deputies" among other basic rights, "it would be well to add: 'complete equality or rights for men and women.'"[27] And last, the all-important democratic alliance of workers and peasants was flushed out in "A Draft Programme for Our Party" at the end of 1899; in *The Tasks* it was only implied. To that end the most popular presentation of the aforementioned positions was in Lenin's widely distributed pamphlet *To the Rural Poor*. For the first time, Russian peasants learned about social democracy and what it meant for them.

If Lenin's views should, as I contend, sit well with real liberal democrats, what about his "dictatorship of the proletariat"? In many ways the previously mentioned liberal who has to be gone "over" alludes, in fact, to the controversial concept. Lenin's first other-than-cursory usage of the "dictatorship of the proletariat" came, in fact, almost at the same time in 1902 and thus offers a hint for his meaning. Marx and Engels coined the phrase and employed it, according to the most exhaustive inquiry, 12 times.[28] Hal Draper argues that once it got into Russian hands its original meaning changed—an issue I'll revisit. Suffice here to note what Lenin wrote about it—an attempt to provide clarity to Plekhanov's usage in the 1885 Russian party program: "To effect this social revolution the proletariat must win political power, which will make it master of the situation and enable it to remove all obstacles along the road to its great goal. In this sense the dictatorship of the proletariat is an essential political condition of the social revolution."[29] Again, this was Lenin's first try at defining the term. He would employ it extensively during the 1905 Revolution, and I argue that only then will it become clear what he meant. Until that discussion I think it important to point out that though Marx and Engels didn't use the phrase in the *Manifesto*, which Lenin was intimately familiar with, they did say

in four successive locations in the document that "force" would be necessary for the proletariat to carry out socialist transformation.[30] A case can
be made, I think, that if not in the letter, Lenin's first try at a definition—
"remove all obstacles"—captures the spirit of their program.[31]

In defending his politics, including the need for the dictatorship of the
proletariat, Lenin often noted how Russia differed from Western Europe
and the social democratic parties in place there. At the level of methodology, Lenin argued that difference had to be taken into account: "We do not
regard Marx's theory as something completed and inviolable; on the contrary,
we are convinced that it has only laid the foundation stone of the science
which socialists *must* develop in all directions if they wish to keep pace with
life." And that task was even more incumbent on Russian socialists, since
Marx's theory "provides only general *guiding* principles, which in *particular*,
are applied in England differently than in France, in France differently than
in Germany, and in Germany differently than in Russia."[32]

In the old party program of Plekhanov, Zasulich, and others, rather
than parliamentary democracy, it called for "direct people's legislation."
Lenin thought that given "the specific features of Russia," it would be
better to demand parliamentary representative democracy. "The victory
of socialism must not be connected, in principle, with the *substitution* of
direct people's legislation for parliamentarism." Direct democracy, though
preferable, was—drawing on the research of Kautsky—more suitable for
societies at a higher level of sociopolitical development. While "we are not
in the least afraid to say that we want to imitate the Erfurt Program of the
German Social Democratic Party," Lenin felt its demands for "direct legislation of the people by means of the initiative and referendum" and an
electoral system with "proportional representation" and other very democratic features were inappropriate for the Russian reality.[33] "We, therefore,
believe that at present, when the autocracy is dominant in Russia, we
should limit ourselves to the demand for a 'democratic constitution.'"[34]
Lenin reiterated this position in *What Is to Be Done?* with the additional
point about representative democracy within the revolutionary party—an
issue to be discussed in the second part of this chapter.

Shortly afterward in a polemic against opponents who called themselves social democrats but subordinated the political to the economic
struggle—the "economists"—Lenin spelled out his earlier pronouncements. "What is meant by the overthrow of the autocracy?"

> It implies the tsar's renunciation of absolute power; the granting to the
> people of the right to elect their own representatives for legislation, for
> supervision over the actions of the government officials, for supervi-
> sion over the collection and disbursement of state revenues. This type of

government in which the people participate in legislation and administration is called the *constitutional* form of government (constitution = law on
the participation of people's representatives in legislation and the administration of the state). Thus, the overthrow of the autocracy means the
replacement of the autocratic form of government by the constitutional
form of government . . . It means the convening of a Zemsky Sobor ["A
central representative assembly"] of representatives of the people for the
elaboration of a constitution ["to win a democratic constitution"; people's
constitution, drawn up in the interests of the people], as it is put in the
draft programme of the Russian Social-Democrats published in 1885 by
the Emancipation of Labor Group.[35]

Here in very clear language for the first time Lenin stated what he meant
by "constitutional government." He then reiterated his previously stated
views about the necessity of such government, the democratic revolution,
for the socialist revolution.

Some pages later, Lenin addressed the ridicule of the opponents about
the fact that social democrats like him "'incessantly give first place to the
advantages of workers' activities in a parliament [nonexistent in Russia],
while completely ignoring . . . the importance of workers' participation' in
the employers' legislative assemblies, on factory boards, and in municipal
self-government." Lenin was only too happy to respond, pedagogically:

If the advantages of parliament are not brought into the forefront, how
will the workers learn about political rights and political liberty? If we
keep silent on these questions—as does Rabochaya Mysl [the opponent
newspaper]—does this not mean perpetuating the political ignorance of
the lower strata of the workers? As to workers' participation in municipal
self-government, no Social-Democrat has ever denied anywhere the advantages and the importance of the activities of socialist workers in municipal
self-government; but it is ridiculous to speak of this in Russia, where no
open manifestation of socialism is possible and where firing the workers with enthusiasm for municipal self-government (even were this possible) would actually mean distracting advanced workers from the socialist
working-class cause towards liberalism.[36]

Thus in unambiguous terms Lenin defended the participation of workers
in parliaments and other forms of representative government—a means
to "learn about political rights and political liberty." When that opportunity opened in Russia, Lenin, as we'll see, did all he could to make it a
reality. But in the absence of that opportunity—that is, political liberty—
advocating what the opponents wanted would actually divert the most

"advanced workers" from the democratic revolution—the fight that no
liberals were willing to pursue.

ON TERRORISM AND ARMED STRUGGLE

Crucial in understanding much of the opposition to Lenin's politics was
precisely the absence of political liberty. Russia was the world's largest
remaining absolutist state. It was effectively a police state. To many no-
doubt-sincere revolutionaries, to argue as he did that it was necessary to
think about how to utilize the parliamentary arena seemed naïve. But there
was nothing in Lenin's politics that ruled out armed struggle or even, perhaps, terror—just as for Marx and Engels, as noted in Chapter 1—as a
means for ending the monarchy and instituting parliamentary democracy.
What Lenin argued against, based on the historical record, was conspiratorial armed struggle or terror that was divorced from the mass movement. His first substantive comments on terror made at the end of 1899
in his "Draft Programme" began to make this point. The 1885 program
contained under the principles section a point on the "means of political
struggle" that he thought should be eliminated. "The programme should
leave the question of means open, allowing the choice of means ['even
terror'] to the militant organisations and to the Party congresses that determine the *tactics* of the Party." Thus terror was a tactic and not a principle,
and its use should be decided through collective discussion, which was
urgently needed.

It was needed, Lenin perceptibly noted, because "the growth of the
movement leads of its own accord, spontaneously, to more frequent cases
of the killing of spies and to greater, more impassioned indignation in
the ranks of the workers and socialists who see ever greater numbers of
their comrades being tortured to death in solitary confinement and at
places of exile." Unless, in other words, the rightful anger generated by
the terror of the police state was not handled in a conscious and strategic
way, the desire for revenge could get out of hand and be unproductive—
precisely why an organized discussion was necessary. Lenin's call for
collective discussion was, as we'll see shortly, a cardinal principle in his
political work.

Lenin then concluded, "In order to leave nothing unsaid, we will
make the reservation that, in our own personal opinion, terror is *not*
advisable as a means of struggle *at the present moment,* that the Party
(as a party) must renounce it (until there occurs a change of circumstances that might lead to a change of tactics) and concentrate *all of its
energy* on organization and the regular delivery of literature."[37] The task

now was to do the propaganda work to win the working class to social democracy.

Two years later in *What Is to Be Done?* Lenin noted what appeared to be a paradox—the agreement in opinion of "an Economist," one of the aforementioned opponents that Lenin had been polemicizing against, and a "non-Social-Democratic terrorist." But actually it wasn't, he asserted: "The Economists and terrorists merely bow to different poles of spontaneity . . . it is no accident that many Russian liberals—avowed liberals and liberals that wear the mask of Marxism—whole-heartedly sympathise with terror . . . [C]alls for terror and calls to lend the economic struggle itself a political character are merely two different forms of *evading* the most pressing duty now resting upon Russian revolutionaries, namely, the organisation of comprehensive political agitation."[38] Lenin's book, as we'll discuss, was part of his campaign for party organizing, and the problem with terrorism was that it hindered that objective. "Comprehensive" was exactly that—organizing designed to attract the largest numbers. And any organization that included "terror in its programme, calls for an organization of terrorists, and such an organisation would indeed prevent our troops from establishing closer contacts with the masses, which, unfortunately, are still not ours, and which, unfortunately, do not yet ask us, or rarely ask us, when and how to launch their military operations."[39] For Lenin the existence of a police state was not reason enough to call for terrorism. He opposed it, again, not on principle, but because it was an obstacle to building a mass movement. In that sense a principle was indeed at stake—that of the need for a movement that was the most inclusive. And only a mass movement could sanction the launching of "military operations."

In 1901 a new opponent organization was founded, the Socialist Revolutionary Party. In many ways this was a rebirth of the Narodniks with a socialist label. And as was the case with their predecessors, they, too, subscribed to the use of terror. Lenin's brother Alexander, it should be noted, was hanged in 1888 for trying to carry out a Narodnik assassination of the Czar. Lenin knew personally the futility of such schemes, a factor no doubt in his decision to take on its new advocates. "In their naïveté, the Socialist-Revolutionaries do not realize that their predilection for terrorism is causally most intimately linked with the fact that, from the very outset, they have always kept, and still keep, aloof from the working class movement . . . *without* the working people all bombs are powerless, patently powerless . . . Without in the least denying violence and terrorism in principle, we demanded work for the preparation of such forms of violence as were calculated to bring about the direct participation of the masses and which guaranteed that participation."[40]

And in their aloofness they committed the "principal mistake of terrorists" in not providing leadership for a proletariat in motion:

> At a time when the revolutionaries *are short of* the forces and means to lead the masses, who are already rising, an appeal to resort to such terrorist acts as the organisation of attempts on the lives of ministers by individuals and groups that are known to one another means, not only *thereby* breaking off work among the masses, but also introducing downright disorganization into that work . . . it even leads to apathy and passive waiting for the next *bout*. . . [A] revolutionary party is worthy of its name only when it guides *in deed* the movement of a revolutionary class . . . the working people are literally straining to go into action, and that their ardour runs to waste because of the scarcity of literature and leadership, the lack of forces and means in the revolutionary organisation . . . On the other hand, shots fired by the "elusive individuals" who are losing faith in the possibility of marching in formation and working hand in hand with the masses also end in smoke.[41]

These were certainly not Lenin's last words on terror, but it would be difficult to match the clarity in what he wrote here. It can't be stressed enough how central to his politics was the mobilization of the masses. The oft-made accusation thus—that he subscribed to putschism, overthrowing governments by a small group of revolutionaries—is simply not supported by the historical record, at least prior to 1905.[42]

As with terror, Lenin regarded armed struggle as a tactic and not a strategy. At a conference in 1902 that helped to prepare what would be the Second Congress of the Russian Social Democratic Labor Party (RSDLP) the following year, Lenin sketched a resolution on its "immediate political task." Not surprisingly, by now it was the "overthrow of the autocracy." As for the means to do that, he recommended "boycotts, manifestations at theatres etc., as well as organized mass demonstrations." And then he proposed that the conference "advises all Party committees and groups [the branches of the party in various cities] to devote due attention to the need for preparatory measures for a nation-wide armed uprising against the tsarist autocracy."[43] This was Lenin's first mention of armed struggle in a party document, but it provided no details. It wasn't a call to do so but to take "preparatory measures" toward that end. And he treated it as one of a number of means to be employed—a tactic in that sense. Last, note that he called it a "nation-wide armed uprising." To do that would obviously require a mass movement—exactly what he accused those who regarded terror as a strategy of not wanting to bring into existence.

Lenin played a key role in the Second Congress, including the drafting and editing of resolutions. The "Draft Resolution on Demonstrations" began with the point that they are "a highly important means of political education of the masses." It was therefore necessary that "the participation of the broad *masses* of the working class in the demonstrations" be secured. It also recommended that "preparations for armed demonstrations should be begun, strictly observing instructions of the Central Committee in this respect."[44] And to that end he repeated the point made at the earlier conference about the need for party locals to help in those preparations.

Lenin drafted another resolution titled "The Army," which for some reason wasn't submitted to the Congress—possibly, I suspect, for security reasons. "The Congress calls the attention of all Party organisations to the importance of Social-Democratic propaganda and agitation in the army, and recommends that all efforts should be made for the speediest strengthening and proper channelling of all the existing contacts among the officers and other ranks. The Congress considers it desirable to form special groups of Social-Democrats serving in the army, in order that these groups should occupy a definite position in the local committees (as branches of the committees), or in the central organisation (as institutions formed directly by the Central Committee and subordinated directly to it)."[45] Lenin was dead serious about winning the "broad masses"—including those within the army. This perspective of boring from within the military was completely consistent with his notion of the democratic alliance, particularly that between workers and peasants. The ranks of the military, as he would later say, were simply workers and peasants in uniform. The fruit of this work, over the course of about 14 years, would pay off for the Bolsheviks in October 1917, as we'll see. Finally, it should be noted that Lenin drafted a resolution on "Terrorism" in which he basically distilled in a short paragraph the points discussed earlier. The Congress voted in favor of the resolution, making it the official stance of the party.

Before turning to Lenin the party organizer, a few words about an issue that will get more attention later but that had its origins in the pre-1905 period: Because of its prestige in international social democracy, the course and actions of the German Social-Democratic Party (SPD) were followed closely by Lenin and cothinkers in other parties. As noted earlier, he wasn't afraid to admit that he wanted "to imitate the Erfurt Program" or at least "what is good" in it. The qualifier is significant, I think, when coupled with a later comment in *What Is to Be Done?*, almost in passing, about the SPD—its "weak points." Though it isn't clear what the latter refers to, Lenin was well acquainted with the reformist or "opportunist" wing of the German party led by Edouard Bernstein as soon as it appeared in 1898, and he carried out a fight against its echo within the Russian movement. Little did he know, however, that a cleavage was in the making that would sharply distinguish the Russian party from its fraternal organizations in most of Western Europe—imitating the Erfurt Program notwithstanding.

***

A final observation—for now: What pervades all Lenin's pronouncements and actions about Russia's yet-to-come democratic revolution is a profound sense of optimism. He truly believed that, other than the most privileged, no segment of Russian society—most important, the peasantry, the majority— was immune to the democratic virus. Nor was there any hint in his writings that an antidemocratic virus, as some would have it, lurked deep within the souls of the Russian people, making the democratic quest a nonstarter.[46] What was needed was for Russian social democracy to "raise the general-democratic banner, in order to group about itself all sections and all elements capable of fighting for political liberty or at least of supporting that fight in some way or another."[47] No better example of this deep faith was his proposal to the Second Congress in 1903 that the RSDLP make a special effort to reach out to "members of religious sects . . . so as to bring them under Social-Democratic influence." After all, "the sectarian movement . . . represents one of the democratic trends in Russia." The specific project was to be the publication of "a popular newspaper entitled *Among Sectarians*."[48] The first issue—with a different name, *Rassvet* [*Dawn*]—appeared in January 1904. After nine issues the monthly folded, owing to an insufficient number of writers, as Lenin was forced to admit. Despite its brief existence, the "experiment," which he had fought to keep on life-support, had been worth pursuing: "Something . . . has been accomplished: contacts among the sects are broadening, both in America and in Russia."[49]

BUILDING A PARTY

At about the same time that he and Engels were making the case in London in 1871 for the necessity of independent working-class political action, Marx offered similar advice to a supporter in the United States. In a most didactic letter, he distilled the essence of the political struggle: "The POLITICAL MOVEMENT of the working class naturally has as its final object the conquest of POLITICAL POWER for this class, and this requires, of course, a PREVIOUS ORGANISATION of the WORKING CLASS developed up to a certain point, which arises from the economic struggles themselves."[50] For the working class to seize political power, it must have, in other words, an organization already in place. Fast forward to 1901: Lenin's debates with the "Economists." Against their view that political agitation and building revolutionary organizations weren't essential in quiescent times, he countered, "[I]t is precisely in such periods and under such circumstances that work of this kind is particularly necessary, since it is too late to form the organization in times of explosion and outbursts; the party must be in a state of readiness to launch activity at a moment's notice."[51] Having a "previous organization" in place for the working class to take power was necessary because it would be "too late" to try to construct one in the heat of revolutionary turbulence.

Lenin's important addition to Marx's insight anticipated probably his most enduring contribution to his mentor's project. It registers how thoroughly he had grasped not only Marx's theory of political economy but his politics as well. In the remainder of this chapter the focus is on what kind of "previous organization" Lenin did seek to realize—again, prior to 1905—and how did democracy figure in as a means and end.

SOWING THE SEEDS

It was in Lenin's initial political declaration, *What the "Friends of the People" Are*, that he revealed his earliest thoughts on organizing a revolutionary party. But only toward the end of the two-hundred-page document did he address the issue. He rejected the claim of those who "foist upon Marx the most senseless fatalistic views . . . [T]hey assure us, the organization and socialization of the workers occurs spontaneously." The history of social democracy refutes such a claim, he argued. "Social-Democracy—as Kautsky very justly remarks—is a fusion of the working class movement and socialism," and that would not happen spontaneously; it required the "utmost energy" and "many, many persons." Socialists were therefore obligated to popularize Marxist theory and "help the worker to assimilate it and devise *the form of organization* most **SUITABLE** *under our conditions for disseminating Social-Democratic ideas and welding the workers into a political force.*"[52] By suitability "under our conditions" Lenin was referring to the absence of "political liberty" in Russia, which required the use of "secret circles"—as was true, he noted, for Marx and the Communist League in 1848. From the outset, then, Lenin considered his call to form an organization to be in the tradition of social democracy going back to Marx and Engels.

Lenin was already aware of the charge that in this scenario—socialists schooled in Marx's theory fusing with workers—the outcome would be an intellectual elite heading the organization. If the project, he said earlier in the document, was truly about "promoting the organization of the proletariat," then "the role of the 'intelligentsia' is to make special leaders from among the intelligentsia unnecessary."[53] Lenin recognized—as had

Marx and Engels—that the inequalities of class societies could impact the revolutionary party itself and therefore had to be addressed.[54] It's reasonable to assume that Lenin counted himself—at least at this stage of his political work—among the "intelligentsia." Thus he provided a reasonable criterion for the evaluation of his own practice. To what extent, in other words, did he act from then on to make those of his class background unnecessary for the working class's liberation?

Again, within months of the appearance of What the "Friends of the People" Are, Lenin experienced his political baptism of fire. In St. Petersburg in 1895, textile workers took the lead in staging Russia's first mass industrial strikes. Lenin and other social democrats were obligated to take part in whatever way they could. To coordinate their work, he helped found what would be the League of Struggle for the Emancipation of the Working Class.[55] Their activities led to his arrest and others' at the end of the year. He used his more than four-year-long imprisonment and Siberian exile to draw the lessons of the struggle, including its organizational tasks. To understand why, consider a comment he made in What Is to Be Done? To make his case that prior organizational work norms during the days of the strikes left much to be desired and that being more "professional" was needed now, he confessed,

> Let no active worker take offense at these frank remarks, for as far as insufficient training is concerned, I apply them first and foremost to myself. I used to work in a study circle that set itself very broad, all-embracing tasks; and all of us, members of that circle, suffered painfully and acutely from the realization that we were acting as amateurs at a moment of history when we might have been able to say, varying a well-known statement: "Give us an organization of revolutionaries, and we'll overturn Russia!" The more I recall the burning sense of shame I then experienced, the bitterer become my feelings towards those pseudo-Social-Democrats whose preachings "bring disgrace on the calling of a revolutionary," who fail to understand that our task is not to champion the degrading of the revolutionary to the level of an amateur, but to raise the amateurs to the level of revolutionaries.[56]

With real-life experiences under his belt, Lenin now sought to convince other social democrats to take organizing more seriously.

In his popular pamphlet written at the end of 1897, Tasks of the Russian Social-Democrats, Lenin wrote that the "creation of a durable revolutionary organization among the factory, urban workers is . . . the first and most urgent task confronting Social-Democracy."[57] He made clear what it would not be. He rejected the argument of a Narodnik opponent that such a party would effectively mean "organizing a political conspiracy . . .

The Social-Democrats . . . are not guilty of such a narrow outlook; they do not believe in conspiracies; they think that the period of conspiracies has long passed away, that to reduce political struggle to conspiracy means, on the one hand, immensely restricting its scope, and, on the other hand, choosing the most unsuitable methods of struggle." As for the same opponent's claim that "the Russian Social-Democrats take the activities of the West as an unfailing model," Lenin also begged to differ. "Russian Social-Democrats have never forgotten the political conditions here, they have never dreamed of being able to form a workers' party in Russia legally, they have never separated the task of fighting for socialism from that of fighting for political liberty. But they have always thought, and continue to think, that this fight must be waged not by conspirators, but by a revolutionary party based on the working-class movement."[58] The party that Lenin envisioned would have to operate, unlike fraternal social democratic parties in Western Europe, illegally given the absence of political liberty in Russia. And despite that glaring reality, its orientation would not be conspiratorial but rather toward the education and organization of the proletariat in its broadest numbers.

If there was a "model," Lenin wrote, it was that of the short-lived St. Petersburg League of Struggle and the work it conducted in Russia's first proletarian upsurge—the "embryo of a revolutionary party." Lenin's participation in the League was too brief, owing to his arrest, to draw any conclusions about his own organizational norms. In exile he wrote a leaflet that he appended to his pamphlet in support of the League as it came under increasing state oppression. Of significance was its call for a "strengthening and development of revolutionary discipline, organization and underground activity . . . And underground activity demands above all that groups and individuals specialize in different aspects of work and that the job of co-ordination be assigned to the central group of the League of Struggle, with as few members as possible."[59] This last recommendation would seem to contradict earlier pronouncements that suggested a more inclusive mode of functioning and opposition to conspiratorial organizing. What this confirms, rather, is that for Lenin organizational norms were flexible and to be adapted to the concrete situation; he had already said as much in distinguishing between the Russian and West European contexts for doing political work. The intent of the recommendation was to make it difficult to destroy the whole organization if individual members were arrested.[60] The leaflet, interestingly, was not appended to subsequent editions of the pamphlet.

In March 1898, a small group of social democrats who had been able to avoid the Czar's dragnet met secretly in Minsk to found the Russian Social-Democratic Labor Party. Though unable to attend because of his exile, Lenin applauded its work. The meeting was significant for another reason. It revealed a core characteristic of Russian social democracy often underappreciated and unacknowledged (certainly by Leninologists) from its official inception—its willingness to risk incarceration and sometimes life and limb to reach decisions through democratic discussion, debate, and vote and provide an account of its deliberations. No other political current, on either side of the spectrum, as far as I can determine, displayed such a similar trait. Russian social democracy, from the beginning, voted literally with democratic feet.

Events soon made clear that the party's founding was a stillbirth. Almost all the delegates who attended the Minsk meeting were arrested shortly afterward. Despite the setback, Lenin—again, in exile—labored arduously to write for what was to be the new party's central organ. A series of articles—though never published owing to the police state—formally initiated his party-building campaign. He set the tone for how to have a discussion in a preliminary piece criticizing an economist "credo" or manifesto: "We invite all groups of Social-Democrats and all workers' circles in Russia to discuss the above-quoted *Credo* and our resolution, and to express a definite opinion on the question raised, in order that all differences may be removed and the work of organizing and strengthening the [RSDLP] may be accelerated." Open discussion and debate to resolve differences to advance the party—that was the modus operandi Lenin advocated, and not for the last time.

His article *Our Immediate Task* was his first writing, as the title might suggest, devoted entirely to party building. It anticipated almost all the themes he would elaborate on in *What Is to Be Done? (WITBD)* two years later. The most important lines (certainly, for purposes here) had to do with what Lenin rightly saw as a potential tension in a mass revolutionary party "under conditions that are quite different from those of Western Europe." And precisely because of the latter fact, "there are no ready-made models to be found anywhere." He framed the issues with two questions: "1) How is the need for the complete liberty of local Social-Democratic activity to be combined with the need for establishing a single—and, consequently, a centralist—party?" Lenin recognized, in other words, at the outset the tension in a revolutionary party between the needs of centralization and democracy from below. The second question is even more instructive: "2) How can we combine the striving of Social-Democracy to become a revolutionary party that makes the struggle for political liberty its chief purpose with the determined refusal of Social-Democracy to organise political conspiracies, its emphatic refusal to 'call the workers to the barricades' . . . , or, in general, to impose on the workers this or that 'plan' for an attack on the government, which has been thought up by a company of revolutionaries?"[61] From a practical angle, he then said how these questions should not be answered. "This is not a solution that can be made by a single person or a single group; it can be provided only by the organized activity of Social-Democracy as a whole." Lenin's words are worth a reread because they challenge virtually every standard or Lenino-logical account that portrays his project as exactly the opposite—a small elite with him in the lead imposing its will on the working class. Little wonder that they have been treated with silence.[62]

The solution Lenin proposed to both questions was the *"founding of a Party organ that will appear regularly and be closely connected with all the local groups.* . . The organization and disciplining of the revolutionary forces and the development of revolutionary technique are impossible without the discussion of all these questions in a central organ, without the collective elaboration of certain *forms and rules for the conduct of affairs,* without the establishment—through the central organ—of every Party member's *responsibility* to the entire Party."[63] Note, again, Lenin's emphasis on collective discussion—exactly what a central organ could guarantee. Regarding his later proposals for a party program, "it is to be hoped that in the discussion of the draft programme all views and all shades of views will be afforded expression, that the discussion will be comprehensive." Though, again, these and the related articles were never published in Lenin's lifetime, they offer an invaluable window into his thinking leading up to *WITBD.*

THE "ISKRIST PARTY"

When conditions finally permitted in 1901 for having not only a party newspaper, *Iskra,* but a magazine as well, *Zarya,* Lenin—now abroad—registered two relevant opinions. First, he disagreed with the custom elsewhere in the world of social democracy (Germany in particular) where the newspaper was popularly pitched to a working-class audience while the magazine was for the more "educated":

> [W]e wish particularly to emphasise our opposition to the view that a workers' newspaper should devote its pages exclusively to matters that immediately and directly concern the spontaneous working-class movement, and leave everything pertaining to the theory of socialism, science, politics, questions of Party organisation, etc., to a periodical for the intelligentsia. On the contrary, it is necessary to combine all the concrete facts and manifestations of the working-class movement with the indicated questions; the light of theory must be cast upon every separate fact; propaganda on questions of politics and

Party organisation must be carried on among the broad masses of the working class; and these questions must be dealt with in the work of agitation.[64]

Nothing could be "more dangerous and more criminal than the demagogic speculation on the underdevelopment of the workers" and the assumption that they couldn't grasp theory.[65] Hence the only difference, he argued, between the two publications should be the length of their articles, not their content.

His second opinion had to do with, again, the apparent tension between centralism and democracy and how to ensure the latter:

[W]e desire our publications to become organs for the *discussion* of all questions by all Russian Social-Democrats of the most diverse shades of opinion. We do not reject polemics between comrades, but, on the contrary, are prepared to give them considerable space in our columns. Open polemics, conducted in full view of all Russian Social-Democrats and class-conscious workers, are necessary and desirable in order to clarify the depth of existing differences, in order to afford discussion of disputed questions from all angles, in order to combat the extremes into which representatives of various views, various localities, or various "specialities" of the revolutionary movement inevitably fall.[66]

Both opinions provide more evidence for Lenin's democratic credentials: specifically how to ensure (1) real working-class leadership in a party that purported to advance its interests and (2) democratic discussion and debate. His answers would find their way into *WITBD*.

The two publications were the product of a political fusion of the new generation of social democrats headed by Lenin with the older one in exile headed by Plekhanov. The six-person editorial board consisted of Lenin, Alexander Potresov, and Julius Martov representing the youth, and Plekhanov, Zasulich, and Pavel Axelrod representing the "old ones." The board, increasingly known as the "Iskrists" or "Iskrist Party," functioned as an ersatz party in waiting. In essence, this was Lenin's first opportunity, as editor-in-chief, to work in a body in which votes were taken to make decisions and for which there is some account. His letter to Plekhanov early in the newspaper's life, for example, is instructive. Negotiations on behalf of the committee with the aforementioned Struve on a joint publication proved to be politically unproductive, he reported: "I have made a copy of this letter, and am appending it to the Minutes of today's meeting as a statement of my protest and of my 'dissenting opinion,' and I invite you too to raise the banner of revolt . . . If the majority expresses itself in favour—I shall, of course, submit, but only after having washed my hands of it beforehand."[67] It's not clear if he had to "submit" to the will of the majority—because the negotiations eventually broke off—but he was "of course" willing to do so. Some months later a majority of the board did vote against his wording of an article, which he accepted with apparent magnanimity in a report to Plekhanov.[68] The available evidence reveals that in his two-and-a-half-year editorship he collaborated with the others—some with whom he had significant political disagreements—in a principled and aboveboard manner.[69]

WHAT IS TO BE DONE?

Very little of relevance in Lenin's most famous publication before 1905 had not been previewed in his prior writings discussed here. In the order of presentation in the book, let's begin with "the vanguard" question (implicit, I contend, in the prior writings).

In the aforementioned writing in which Lenin labeled "dangerous" and "criminal" any assumption about the political incapacities of the Russian proletariat, he was challenging the central argument of a recently formed committee of social democrats in Kiev in 1899. He offered, to the contrary, a litany of examples of how Russian workers had engaged in political struggle. If the response was that these were merely examples of just "spontaneous outbursts rather than political struggles," Lenin countered pedagogically, "Can one find in history a single case of a popular movement, of a class movement, that did not begin with spontaneous, unorganized outbursts, that would have assumed an organized form and created political parties without the conscious intervention of enlightened representatives of the given class?" The history of the class struggle, he argued, had demonstrated that within subjected classes some of its members are more "enlightened" than others—that is, they understand better the interests of the class and have the skills to organize the struggle to advance them. In other words, every class—dominant as well as subject ones—had a vanguard. What was missing in Russia, he went on to say, wasn't, contrary what the committee alleged, a lack of proletarian political struggles but rather a vanguard—those willing to organize and lead the numerous examples of local struggles to a successful conclusion: a political revolution. Lenin's argument rested on what he saw as the facts of history—Marx and Engels's "materialist conception of history"—and thus a counterargument would have to dispute him on that terrain.

Two years later Lenin was more explicit. It is in the 15-page section, "The Working Class as Vanguard Fighter for Democracy," of the third chapter that Lenin discussed the term for the first time. But it soon becomes clear that, rather than the label, it is a set of actions that concerned Lenin the most. The task for social democracy, he argued, is how to bring "class political consciousness" to the working class. Such consciousness required workers to think beyond their own immediate economic interests, and this is what social democrats were uniquely suited to assist in. As one of the more well-known lines of *WITBD* put it, "the Social-Democrat's ideal should not be the trade union secretary, but *the tribune of the people*, who is able to react to every manifestation of tyranny and oppression, no matter where it appears, no matter what stratum or class of the people it affects."[70] A couple of pages later Lenin elaborated on how this ideal could be realized; in the process he called attention—of importance for this book—to the role that parliamentary activity could play when available:

> The principal thing . . . is *propaganda* and *agitation* among all strata of the people. The work of the West European Social-Democrat is in this respect facilitated by the public meetings and rallies which *all* are free to attend, and by the fact that in parliament he addresses the representatives of *all* classes. We have neither a parliament nor freedom of assembly; nevertheless, we are able to arrange meetings of workers who desire to listen to *a Social-Democrat*. We must also find ways and means of calling meetings of representatives of all social classes that desire to listen to *a democrat*; for he is no Social-Democrat who forgets in practice that "the Communists support every revolutionary movement," that we are obliged for that reason to expound and emphasise *general democratic tasks before the whole people*, without for a moment concealing our socialist convictions. He is no Social-Democrat who forgets in practice his obligation to be *ahead of all* in raising, accentuating, and solving *every* general democratic question.[71]

Thus Lenin defined a vanguard as those who are "*ahead of all* in raising, accentuating, and solving every general democratic question." In the reality of Russia in 1902, that was what Lenin asserted a vanguard to be—no more, no less!

To be even clearer, he then ridiculed some self-proclaimed vanguard social democrats: "[I]t is not enough to call ourselves the 'vanguard,' the advanced contingent; we must act in such a way that all the other contingents recognize and are obliged to admit that we are marching in the vanguard. And we ask the reader: Are the representatives of the other 'contingents' such fools as to take our word for it when we say that we are the 'vanguard'?" A few months later Lenin reiterated this point about the problem with self-proclamation. In his second draft of a party program, Plekhanov wrote something about "advancing Social-Democracy *to the very first place* . . . In my opinion, we should not talk at all about the very first place: that is self-evident from the entire program. Let us leave it to history to say this about us, rather than say it ourselves."[72] Only history, in other words, would determine whether a party was in the vanguard or not.

Despite the contortions and discomforts the label has given to some sincere democrats, I contend that there is nothing in Lenin's understanding of a "vanguard" they should fear. If anything, he should be applauded. The actions of those who are "ahead of all" were intended to ensure the democratic revolution. Nor should there be concern about his claim that within classes there are those who step forward before others to provide leadership. There is nothing inherently undemocratic about that time-tested truth. If read in real time and not hindsight, Lenin's arguments were compatible with the democratic quest. The reader can, again, verify my claim by reading the entire section from which the quotes I've selected come.

As for the second issue, it may be remembered that Lenin in his very first programmatic statement wrote that the "role of the 'intelligentsia' is to make special leaders from among the intelligentsia unnecessary." This is exactly the issue addressed in "The Scope of Organizational Work" in the fourth chapter of *WITBD*. Lenin like other social democrats recognized that there were an insufficient number of cadre to carry out the necessary work, but he strongly disagreed with those who argued that the working conditions of the "average worker"—especially the 11.5-hour workday—meant that the most important tasks of revolutionary work, other than "agitation," "fall mainly upon the shoulders of an extremely small force of intellectuals." He especially disliked the notion that "pedagogics" was needed to bring workers up to speed to do more complex tasks. Such thinking "proves that our very first and most pressing duty is to help to train working-class revolutionaries who will be on the same level *in regard to Party activity* as the revolutionaries from amongst the intellectuals (we emphasize the words 'in regard to Party activity,' for, although necessary, it is neither so easy nor so pressingly necessary to bring the workers up to the level of intellectuals in other respects). Attention, therefore, must be devoted *principally to raising* the workers to the level of revolutionaries." And to achieve that goal required organizational adjustments.

Lenin then began to spell out what he meant by "to the level of revolutionaries" and what was required:

> To be fully prepared for his task, the worker-revolutionary must likewise become a professional revolutionary. Hence B-v [the opponent who provoked his dissent] is wrong in saying that since the worker spends eleven and a half hours in the factory, the brunt of all other revolutionary functions (apart from agitation) "*must necessarily* fall mainly upon the shoulders of an

extremely small force of intellectuals." But this condition does not obtain out of sheer "necessity." It obtains because we are backward, because we do not recognize our duty to assist every capable worker to become a *professional* agitator, organizer, propagandist, literature distributor, etc., etc.[73]

It wasn't workers, because of the conditions in which they labored, who were the problem but rather "we"—that is, those who claimed to be revolutionary social democrats. Lenin then detailed how the German SPD took steps to recruit "capable working class men" to become "professional" revolutionaries, August Bebel being Exhibit A. By "professional"—a label, like "vanguard," that often contorts many sincere democrats—Lenin meant no more than a worker who had the requisite skills to "wage a stubborn struggle against its excellently trained enemies."

With the German movement as a reference point, he specified what the Russian movement needed to do:

> A worker-agitator who is at all gifted and "promising" *must not be left* to work eleven hours a day in a factory. We must arrange that he be maintained by the Party; that he may go underground in good time; that he change the place of his activity, if he is to enlarge his experience, widen his outlook, and be able to hold out for at least a few years in the struggle against the gendarmes. As the spontaneous rise of their movement becomes broader and deeper, the working-class masses promote from their ranks not only an increasing number of talented agitators, but also talented organisers, propagandists, and "practical workers" in the best sense of the term (of whom there are so few among our intellectuals who, for the most part, in the Russian manner, are somewhat careless and sluggish in their habits). When we have forces of specially trained worker-revolutionaries who have gone through extensive preparation (and, of course, revolutionaries "of all arms of the service"), no political police in the world will then be able to contend with them, for these forces, boundlessly devoted to the revolution, will enjoy the boundless confidence of the widest masses of the workers. We are directly to *blame* for doing too little to "stimulate" the workers to take this path, common to them and to the "intellectuals," of professional revolutionary training, and for all too often dragging them back by our silly speeches about what is "accessible" to the masses of the workers, to the "average workers," etc.[74]

If there are any doubts about Lenin's sincerity in acting on his dictum to make those of his class background unnecessary for working class liberation, what he outlines here—particularly the concreteness of the proposals—must surely be reassuring. No one in the nascent Russian social democratic movement, as far as I can determine, was as conscientious as he in the recruitment of workers to its leadership. Subsequent events will reveal whether or not his efforts were rewarded.

The third and last issue of importance in *WITBD* concerns the previously discussed issue of direct versus representative democracy. Earlier, as noted, Lenin thought that given the reality of autocratic, underdeveloped Russia, the latter form of democracy—that is, parliamentary government—was preferable. But what about the party itself? Couldn't a case be made for direct democracy in the revolutionary party? Lenin demurred. The issue was part of a larger question—could the kind of revolutionary party he was proposing conform to the "broad democratic principle"—that is, "full publicity" and "election to all offices"? If that was the standard, then in the "frame of our autocracy" such norms could not be met. Under such conditions the "only serious organizational principle for the active workers of our movement should be the strictest secrecy, the strictest selection of members, and the training of professional revolutionaries." But—and this is important—it "would be a great mistake to believe that the impossibility of establishing real 'democratic' control renders the members of the revolutionary organization beyond control altogether."

What if direct democracy was possible in Russia? The history of the working-class movement itself, Lenin argued—citing the lessons of the English trade-union movement drawn by "Mr. [Sidney] and Mrs. [Beatrice] Webb's book" and "Kautsky's book on parliamentarism"—demonstrated after lots of trials and errors that even in settings where political liberty existed workers learned "the necessity for representative institutions, on the one hand, and for full-time officials, on the other."[75] To demand direct or "primitive democracy" by those who should have known these lessons, or the application of the "broad principle of democracy" in the reality of the Russian police state, was to engage in "playing at democracy," "democratism," or a mere "striving for effect."[76]

In criticizing those "striving for effect," there is not the slightest hint of Lenin making virtue out of necessity. A highly centralized and secretive mode of functioning with "professional" cadre not subject to the "broad democratic principle" was necessary in autocratic Russia, not desirable. This will be confirmed, as we'll see, when political space opened for the first time in the heady days of 1905–6.[77]

LETTER TO A COMRADE

When Lenin received a letter from a worker in St. Petersburg in the fall of 1902 that sought his opinion on revolutionary organizing, it allowed him to concretize two key themes in his recently published book—how to ensure that workers actually lead the revolutionary party and how to do effective revolutionary work under the constraints of a police state. His response, "A Letter to a Comrade on Our Organizational Tasks," in fact, should be read alongside *WITBD* to fully understand Lenin's arguments.[78] Written, as its title suggests, in a very comradely tone—in contrast to the polemical style of the book—Lenin addressed in order the points the worker wanted an opinion about. Relevant for purposes here was the second: a party central committee "should consist of both workers and intellectuals, for to divide them into two committees is harmful":

> This is absolutely and indubitably correct. There should be only one committee of the Russian Social-Democratic Labour Party, and it should consist of fully convinced Social-Democrats who devote themselves entirely to Social-Democratic activities. We should particularly see to it that as many workers as possible become fully class-conscious and professional revolutionaries and members of the committee. Once there is a *single* and not a dual committee, the matter of the committee members *personally* knowing many workers is of particular importance. In order to take the lead in whatever goes on in the workers' midst, it is necessary to be able to have access to all quarters, to know very many workers, to have all sorts of channels, etc., etc. The committee should, therefore, include, as far as possible, all the principal *leaders* of the working-class movement from among the workers themselves; it should direct *all* aspects of the local movement and take charge of *all* local institutions, forces and means of the Party.[79]

"As many workers as possible" on the central committee and "from among the workers themselves"—that was Lenin's ideal. In the accompanying footnote, he wrote, "We must try to get on the committee revolutionary workers who have the greatest contacts and the best 'reputation' among the mass of workers." Lenin's affirmative-action perspective, if implemented, would begin to reduce the weight of the "intellectuals" in the revolutionary workers' party. And having a unified central committee would aid this process, for if the intellectuals were to have their own space, they would likely exercise undue influence owing to the skill advantages that class society had bequeathed to them.

Though not in the order of presentation in the inquiry, there was a related point that Lenin took up—"the factory circles. These are particularly important to us: the main strength of the movement lies in the organisation of the workers at the *large* factories, for the large factories (and mills) contain not only the predominant part of the working class, as regards numbers, but even more as regards influence, development, and fighting capacity. Every factory must be our fortress." But this most vital work needed to be at the very center of revolutionary organizing and not ghettoized as was often the case where "the traditional type of purely labour or purely trade-union Social-Democratic organization" existed. To avoid this, the "factory group . . . should consist of a very small number of *revolutionaries*, who take their instructions and receive their authority to carry on all Social-Democratic work in the factory *directly from the [central] committee*. Every member of the factory committee should regard himself as an agent of the [central] committee, obliged to submit to all its orders and to observe all the 'laws and customs' of the 'army in the field' which he has joined and from which in time of war he has no right to absent himself without official leave."[80] Putting the factory groups at the center of the party would ensure that its leadership consisted overwhelmingly of industrial workers.

Almost every page of Lenin's letter refers to the overarching context— the Russian police state. That reality, more than any other, explained the party's necessary modus operandi, which Lenin distilled:

> The whole art of running a secret organisation should consist in making use of *everything possible*, in "giving everyone something to do," at the same time retaining *leadership* of the whole movement, not by virtue of having the power, of course, but by virtue of authority, energy, greater experience, greater versatility, and greater talent. This remark is made to meet the possible and usual objection that strict centralisation may all too easily ruin the movement if the centre *happens* to include an *incapable* person invested with tremendous power. This is, of course, possible, but it cannot be obviated by the elective principle and decentralisation, the application of which is absolutely impermissible to any wide degree and even altogether detrimental to revolutionary work carried on under an autocracy. Nor can any rules provide means against this; such means can be provided only by measures of "comradely influence," beginning with the resolutions of each and every subgroup, followed up by their appeals to the C[entral].O[rgan]. and the C[entral].C[ommittee]., and ending (if the worst comes to the worst) with the *removal* of the persons in authority who are absolutely incapable. The committee should endeavour to achieve the greatest possible division of labour, bearing in mind that the various aspects of revolutionary work require various abilities, and that sometimes a person who is absolutely useless as an organiser may be invaluable as an agitator, or that a person who is not good at strictly secret work may be an excellent propagandist, etc.[81]

Real elections for the selection of the party's leadership, as Lenin had pointed out before, required a set of conditions that simply didn't exist "under an autocracy."

If decentralization, like the "elective principle," could neither prevent an admitted potential danger with "strict centralization"—that is, the abuse of power—this didn't mean that Lenin dismissed it. To the contrary, his final main point was about the advantages of decentralization for a centralized party:

> [W]hile *the greatest possible centralisation* is necessary with regard to the ideological and practical *leadership* of the movement and the revolutionary struggle of the proletariat, *the greatest possible decentralisation* is necessary with regard to keeping the Party centre (and therefore the Party as a whole) *informed* about the movement, and with regard to *responsibility* to the Party. The leadership of the movement should be entrusted to the smallest possible number of the most homogeneous possible groups of professional revolutionaries with great practical experience. Participation in the movement should extend to the greatest possible number of the most diverse and heterogeneous groups of the most varied sections of the proletariat (and other classes of the people) . . . This decentralisation is an essential prerequisite of revolutionary centralisation and an *essential corrective to it.*[82]

Diversity in action at the local level and the information about it was exactly what a highly centralized organization needed to be an effective working-class revolutionary party. Under the conditions of the autocracy this was, as Lenin maintained, the only way to build what was needed to be "ahead of all" in the democratic revolution.

The richness of Lenin's 20-page document on organizational matters—which more workers read than *WITBD*—can only be glimpsed at here. Its details, for example, on how to deal with spies, agent provocateurs, and traitors—should they be killed or not?—or how to be prepared to respond to the arrests of leaders and cadre, are invaluable in understanding the daily repressive atmosphere in which revolutionaries had to function. Again, it can't be overstated how much that reality shaped Lenin's proposals. It should come as no surprise that almost all the surviving copies of the document came from police files.

THE SECOND CONGRESS AND AFTERWARD OR, *ONE STEP FORWARD, TWO STEPS BACK*

The Iskrists, with Lenin in the lead, were eventually successful in convening a congress of the RSDLP in July 1903. The undercover meeting took place in Brussels after two preliminary conferences inside Russia resulted in the arrests of most of their attendees. But even Brussels proved to be a dangerous venue, and after 13 sessions the congress was moved to London; it concluded there but again was forced to change venues. Lenin didn't exaggerate in writing later about "all of the tremendous effort, danger and expense" that went into holding it.[83] The danger was especially real for those delegates not already in exile but traveling from Russia. They had the challenge of not only getting out but also returning and then avoiding arrest for having been a participant. The approximately sixty attendees left a record of their proceedings not only for themselves but for posterity and recognized the risks involved—a potentially convenient tool for the police. Great care, then, had to be exercised by the minute takers, such as, for example, the use of gender-neutral pseudonyms given the number of women delegates. Such details underscore, again, the point made before about the often underappreciated extent to which Russian social democracy uniquely went to have democratic discussion, debate, and decision making.

Of the issues debated and resolved (or perhaps not) at the gathering, three are particularly relevant for this book. First, the delegates adopted the draft program that Plekhanov and Lenin had largely written that called for (among other points) the democratic republic with all the necessary trappings, like a "legislative assembly," "universal suffrage," and civil liberties as discussed earlier. Lenin's democratic agenda had now become the official program of Russian social democracy.

The second issue—and maybe the most contentious at the time—concerned the requirements for party membership. The proposal that Lenin offered stipulated, "A Party member is one who accepts the Party's programme and supports the Party both financially and by personal participation in one of its organizations." But what if someone, Pavel Axelrod objected, who supported the party couldn't be actively involved in a party organization—such as a university professor? What the ensuing debate exposed was the long-simmering differences of opinion about the role of intellectuals in a revolutionary workers party. Lenin, as already discussed, saw their role as that of making themselves expendable. To do as Axelrod wanted would allow them to have their cake and eat it too—to be fashionably revolutionary without having to pay the costs. But there were enough opponents of Lenin's proposal—for very different reasons—to have it modified.

After the congress Lenin revisited the issue, along with others, in his analysis of the overall outcome of the historic meeting, *One Step Forward, Two Steps Back* (*OSFTSB*). The differences on the question were not for him "a matter of life and death for the Party"; they could be resolved. Two years later, in fact, the opponents of his position, who had now crystallized into what came to be known as the Mensheviks, agreed with him. But their concern about intellectuals like university professors in the way Axelrod and kindred minds voiced it revealed for him something much more problematic. If Lenin was ever a member of the intelligentsia or the intellectual crowd, he burned whatever remaining bridges he had to them in *OSFTSB*. They—as well as sincere revolutionaries like Rosa Luxemburg and Leon Trotsky—took special umbrage to his characterization of them. A letter in the "new *Iskra*," now in Menshevik hands, provoked him. The writer, the anonymous "Practical Worker," "denounces me for visualizing the Party 'as an immense factory' headed by a director in the shape of the Central Committee." Lenin gladly took the bait:

> "Practical Worker" never guesses that this dreadful word of his immediately betrays the mentality of the bourgeois intellectual unfamiliar with either the practice or the theory of proletarian organisation. For the factory, which seems only a bogey to some, represents that highest form of capitalist co-operation which has united and disciplined the proletariat, taught it to organise, and placed it at the head of all the other sections of the toiling and exploited population. And Marxism, the ideology of the proletariat trained by capitalism, has been and is teaching unstable intellectuals to distinguish between the factory as a means of exploitation (discipline based on fear of starvation) and the factory as a means of organisation (discipline based on collective work united by the conditions of a technically highly developed form of production). The discipline and organisation which come so hard to the bourgeois intellectual are very easily acquired by the proletariat just because of this factory "schooling." Mortal fear of this school and utter failure to understand its importance as an organising factor are characteristic of the ways of thinking which reflect the petty-bourgeois mode of life and which give rise to the species of anarchism that the German Social-Democrats call *Edelanarchismus*, that is, the anarchism of the "noble" gentleman, or aristocratic anarchism, as I would call it.[84]

For "Practical Worker," and presumably an avowed Marxist, to treat the world of the factory in such an undifferentiated way was most telling about the "new Iskra."

This wasn't Lenin's first incision regarding intellectuals. An earlier one in the book complemented his rebuke of "Practical Worker":

> No one will venture to deny that *the intelligentsia, as a special stratum* of modern capitalist society, is characterized, by and large, *precisely by individualism* and incapacity for discipline and organization . . . This, incidentally, is a feature which unfavorably distinguishes this social stratum from the proletariat; it is one of the reasons for the flabbiness and instability of the intellectual, which the proletariat so often feels; and this trait of the intelligentsia is intimately bound up with its customary mode of life, its mode of earning a livelihood, which in a great many respects approximates

to the *petty-bourgeois mode of existence* (working in isolation or in very small groups, etc.).[85]

Lenin's unflattering portrait was completely consistent with his campaign to make, as he had said at the outset of his political career, the intelligentsia expendable for the working class. Not for naught, I suspect, the intellectual world in general has ever since looked askance on him—aside from his politics. As always, for Lenin, it wasn't personal but political.[86]

On a related note, Lenin restated what he had said at the congress about "professional revolutionaries" in response to what his critics alleged. "'It should not be imagined that Party organizations must consist solely of professional revolutionaries. We need the most diverse organizations of all types, ranks, and shades, beginning with extremely limited and secret and ending with very broad, free, *lose Organisationen.*' This is such an obvious and self-evident truth that I did not think it necessary to dwell on it."[87]

The third relevant issue of the congress was the fateful decision by the majority of delegates to select a central committee and new editorial board for *Iskra*, the now officially adopted organ of the party, whose respective compositions gave Lenin more influence. In the case of *Iskra* the delegates voted (in a most contentious session) to reduce its editorial board from six to three: Lenin, Martov, and Plekhanov. Thus two of the "old ones," Zasulich and Axelrod, and a "new one," Potresov, were no longer on the board. This vote, in hindsight, and not the dispute on membership, set into motion what would be the historic split in the RSDLP between the majority, the Bolsheviks, and the minority, the Mensheviks. Not content to be outvoted, the latter, with Martov leading the way—he refused to remain on the editorial board—rejected the decisions of the majority. What was at stake, Lenin argued in *OSFTSB*, was a basic democratic question—the "sovereignty of the congress." That was the principle, more than any other one, he defended in the two-hundred-page book. "If people really want to work together, they should also be willing to submit to the will of the majority, that is, of a congress."[88] In his retort to Luxemburg's criticism of his book, he asked, "[D]oes the comrade consider it normal for supposed party central institutions to be dominated by the minority of the Party Congress?—can she imagine such a thing?—has she ever seen it in any party?"[89] Lenin's opponents and enemies didn't see it that way, and thus began the story of "Lenin the ogre." Both Trotsky and Luxemburg were its initial authors.[90]

As it was becoming increasingly clear that a split in the RSDLP was underway in the aftermath of the Second Congress, Lenin responded very comradely to an article Plekhanov had written asking what could be done to avoid it:

> [F]irst of all: do not conceal from the Party the appearance and growth of potential causes of a split, do not conceal any of the circumstances and events that constitute such causes; and, what is more, do not conceal them not only from the Party, but, as far as possible, from the outside public either . . . To be a party of the masses not only in name, we must get ever wider masses to share in all Party affairs, steadily elevating them from polit- ical indifference to protest and struggle, from a general spirit of protest to the conscious adoption of Social-Democratic views, from the adoption of these views to support of the movement, from support to organized mem- bership in the Party. Can we achieve this result without giving the widest publicity to matters on whose decision the nature of our influence on the masses will depend?

Lenin then agreed with Plekhanov's point about making sure "suitable persons" were promoted to the party's "central bodies." "And for that very reason *the whole Party*" had to be involved in the process, and that meant having all the necessary information about possible candidates, their strengths and weaknesses, "their victories and 'defeats.'" Plekhanov, he noted, was particularly insightful, owing no doubt to his wealth of experiences—giving him his deserved props—about understanding the reasons for successes and failures:

> And just because these observations are so acute, it is necessary that the whole Party should benefit by them, that it should *always see* every "defeat," even if partial, of one or other of its "leaders." No political leader has a career that is without its defeats, and if we are serious when we talk about influencing the masses, about winning their "good will," we must strive with all our might not to let these defeats be hushed up in the musty atmosphere of circles and grouplets, but to have them submitted to the judgment of all . . . Only through a series of such open discussions can we get a really harmonious ensemble of leaders; only given this condition will it be *impossible* for the workers to cease to understand us; only then will our "general staff" really be backed by the *good* and *conscious* will of an army that follows and at the same time directs its general staff![91]

Lenin's civil, pedagogical, and measured reply to Plekhanov's article gives lie, again, to "Lenin the ogre."[92]

Some final words about *OSFTSB*—it was in the context of the pre- viously quoted comment about party organizational norms in Western Europe that Lenin gave his first sustained discussion of a feature of social democracy that was still in its infant stage. "It is highly interesting to note that these fundamental characteristics of opportunism in matters of organisation (autonomism, aristocratic or intellectualist anarchism . . . are, *mutatis mutandis* with appropriate modifications), to be observed in all the Social-Democratic parties in the world, wherever there is a division into a revolutionary and an opportunist wing (and where is there not?)"[93] He then devoted about five pages to describing the feature, first in the German party—"where opportunism is weaker than in France and Italy"—and then he noted the similarities with the fledgling Russian party. While he considered Kautsky to be "one of the spokesmen of the revolutionary trend" in the German party, he wrote in a footnote that "Comrade Kautsky has sided with Martov's formulation, and . . . is mistaken."[94] Lenin sent his reply to Luxemburg's criticism of his book to Kautsky for publication in *Neue Zeit*, where her article appeared, but Kautsky refused to publish it. Lenin's initial comments on opportunism in the German party would not be his last.

Lenin's comradely reply to Plekhanov's article about the need for openness recalls the advice that Engels in 1890 gave to the young Vera Zasulich, who was piqued about some of the Western social democratic press airing the debates within Russian émigré circles: "[I]t would surely be to the advantage of the Russian movement itself if it ran its course somewhat more openly before the wider public in the West, rather than covertly, in small isolated circles which, for that very reason, become hotbeds of intrigue and conspiracy. To inveigle his adversaries out into the open, into the light of day, and to attack them in full view of the public, was one of Marx's most powerful and most frequently used ploys when confronted by clandestine intrigue."[95] It was exactly the "isolated circles," the "autonomists," and, as he derisively labeled it, the "family" atmosphere they bred that Lenin wanted to get rid of through centralization. His book was just what Marx would have advised—an "attack . . . in full view of the public." Tragically, it seems, Zasulich never fully appreciated Engels's advice. She, along with Martov, and Trotsky in tow, helped lead the charge against Lenin's project. No Russian, I contend, understood better what Engels was talking about than Lenin.

***

What were the theoretical and programmatic premises that informed Lenin and the Bolsheviks when the political opening came in 1905—that is, when the monarchy was forced to grant a semblance of representative government? That is what this chapter has sought to understand. Again, the focus has been on issues related directly or peripherally to that opening, such as the relationship between the democratic and socialist revolutions, parliamentary democracy and the electoral process. Thus other matters that occupied his time have been ignored or, as in the case of the all-important one of the peasantry, treated only briefly. Lenin, like Marx and Engels, understood that the electoral arena was only one component—important, certainly—in the larger totality of the revolutionary process. And not least important in understanding that process, particularly what the Bolsheviks were able to accomplish later, was Lenin's profound grasp of the need for adequate preparation. Again, as he put it, if a revolutionary party was not in place when a revolution exploded, it would be "too late" to try to do so. That insight, more than anything else, explains his bull-dogged insistence in party-building in order to avoid such a scenario. Hence the details provided about Lenin's fight for a revolutionary party are especially valuable not just for the sake of determining Lenin's democratic credentials but for understanding democracy as a means in the revolutionary process. As 1904 was drawing to a close Lenin began to sense, rightly, that Russia's long-expected democratic revolution was drawing near. The task now is to see if and how the preparatory work he carried out paid off.

CHAPTER 3

"The Dress Rehearsal" and the First Duma

As the "Arab Spring" of 2011 began to unfold, especially when it reached Cairo, questions immediately began to be posed about its course. Did the movement have staying power? Was the world witnessing something historic, a regime thought to be impregnable on the verge of collapse? What about the countryside? Was there sufficient antiregime sentiment there or not, or could Cairo and Alexandria do it alone? Further, what if the regime, in an effort to stay in power, made concessions such as a new constitution, real elections, and representative government for the first time—should these be accepted or not? But was it really about reforming the regime or getting rid of it? And of course, there was the military: whose side would it take, and could it be won over to regime change? Last, and not least important, was there a leadership with a program prepared to rule in the name of the movement? Not for the first time were such questions posed, mutatis mutandis, when that far-too-infrequent moment occurred—the masses making history. Nor will it be the last.

THE REVOLUTION OF 1905

Russia's first experiment with representative governance, as had often been the case in history, was the product of its first democratic revolution—a fact that was indelibly stamped on its course. But unlike its predecessors, the Russian revolution had a protagonist more conscious and conversant with the lessons of such revolutions than any of the prior overturns. That too would forever shape its outcome. The events of 1905, how they set the stage for the convening of the First Duma in 1906, and the role Lenin and the Bolsheviks played in that process are the subjects of the first part of this chapter.

"BLOODY SUNDAY" AND THE AFTERMATH

In 1877, Marx, sixty years old and in failing health, wrote the following to a long-time comrade: "Russia . . . has long been on the verge of an upheaval; all the elements are to hand. The gallant Turks have advanced the explosion by many years through the blows they have dealt not only to the Russian army and Russian finances, but also personally to the *dynasty in command* of the army . . . The upheaval will begin, *secundum artem* ['by the rules of the game'], with some constitutional tomfoolery, *et puis il y aura un beau tapage* ['and then there'll be a fine how-do-you-do']. Unless Mother Nature is exceptionally unkind, we shall yet live to see the fun . . . This time the revolution will begin in the East, hitherto the impregnable bastion and reserve army of counter-revolution."[1] Marx's "gallant Turks" refers to the advances Turkish armies were making in the war then underway between Russia and Turkey.[2] As was sometimes the case with his and Engels's forecasts, the elegance of the algebra outshone that of the arithmetic. Indeed, it was the "blows" of war that set into motion the "constitutional tomfoolery" that led to the "upheaval" that eventually resulted in "revolution"—but 26 years later. Mother Nature could not be expected to be that kind.

Russia and Japan went to war in 1904 and, as was true in the Russo-Turkish War, the Romanov monarchy proved to be just as inept. The defeat that Russian armies suffered at the hands of the modernizing capitalist state of Japan exposed just what Marx and Engels accurately saw: not just a regime but a socioeconomic system on its deathbed. In a leaflet/article to celebrate May Day that year, Lenin wrote, "The war is making the preposterousness of the tsarist autocracy obvious to all and is showing everyone the death-agony of the old Russia . . . The old Russia is dying. A free Russia is coming to take its place . . . Comrade workers! Let us then prepare with redoubled energy for the decisive battle that is at hand!"[3] Lenin probably didn't realize—in that moment at least—the imminence of his prediction.

Thinking the regime was now vulnerable to pressures to loosen up a bit, to be at least willing to look like it would grant democratic reforms, liberal forces began to press for change. The Romanovs had been forced to do the same decades earlier. Another war and defeat, the Crimean, had bared the regime's increasingly sclerotic constitution. In an attempt to salvage itself, it granted in 1864 limited local self-government in the form of bodies called *zemstvos*. About those concessions, Lenin wrote, in his 1901 pamphlet *The Persecutors of the Zemstvo and the Hannibals of Liberalism*, that the "question of the relation of the Zemstvo to political freedom is a particular case of the general question of the relation of reforms to revolution." The oft-made claim of liberals "that the 'principle of progress is

that the better things are, the better' . . . is as untrue as its reverse that the
worst things are the better."

> Revolutionaries, of course, will never reject the struggle for reforms, the
> struggle to capture even minor and unimportant enemy positions, *if* these
> will serve to strengthen the attack and help to achieve full victory. But they
> will never forget that sometimes the enemy himself surrenders a certain
> position in order to disunite the attacking party and thus to defeat it more
> easily. They will never forget that only by constantly having the "ultimate
> aim" in view, only by appraising every step of the "movement" and every
> reform from the point of view of the general revolutionary struggle, is it
> possible to guard the movement against false steps and shameful mistakes.[4]

At the end of 1904 the challenge for democratic forces was "to guard . . .
against false steps," in this instance the wink and nod from the regime that
it might grant the long-held hope of its liberal supporters by convening a
national *zemstvo*, or *Zemsky Sobor*—what some erroneously thought would
be Russia's *États-Généraux*. "If there is a single, repetitive theme in the history
of Russia during the last twenty years of the old regime," argues Orlando
Figes, "it is that of the need for reform and the failure of successive governments to achieve it in the face of the Tsar's opposition."[5] The liberal-inclined
minister who had made the ill-fated proposal to Nicholas recognized immediately the consequences of its rejection: "'Everything has failed,' he said
despondently to one of his colleagues. 'Let us build jails.'"[6] Lenin was right:
"[T]he tsar intends to preserve and uphold the autocratic regime. The tsar
does not want to change the form of government and has no intention of
granting a constitution."[7] Marx's prescience about the "constitutional tomfoolery" would be tragically confirmed on a wintry day a few weeks later.

Hopes for liberal reforms, which Lenin said the "proletariat must support,"[8] combined with the increasingly harsh reality of daily existence for
Russia's plebian classes explain why on January 9, 1905, tens of thousands of them peacefully attempted to petition the Czar to improve their
deteriorating situation. Bullets and saber blades greeted their plea. While
hundreds were killed and wounded, more important is that the masses
believed thousands had been slaughtered as word quickly spread beyond
St. Petersburg. For the next ten months the masses would vent their anger
in cities, small towns, and villages, to which the regime responded with
horrendous brutality. Whatever remaining illusions they had about the
monarchy were now shattered. Thus began the beginning of the end of
the three-hundred-year-old Romanov dynasty.[9]

Because Lenin, at the end of 1904, thought that "a tremendous popular
movement" was imminent,[10] he quickly went into action once the upsurge

that came in the wake of January 9, "Bloody Sunday," commenced. Characteristically, he sought counsel in the lessons of the past. "In the present moment," he wrote in February from Geneva, "we all stand on the shoulders of the [Paris] Commune."[11] In addition to writing and giving lectures in exile, Lenin immediately moved to make the necessary organizational response to the revolution. The new situation required democratic discussion and decision making—that is, a party congress. What was to have been the third congress of the Russian Social Democratic Labor Party (RSDLP) in April—again, in London—proved in fact to be a Bolshevik congress; the Mensheviks held their own concurrent meeting in Geneva.

Despite the brutality visited on them, Russia's insurgent toilers refused to be cowered. And it's exactly for that reason that the regime had to play its soft-cop card, once again. It floated in February the idea of representative government. In anticipation of what would later be known as the Bulygin Duma proposal, Lenin gave his first public stance on how the Bolsheviks should respond. As he told the delegates at the congress, "[I]t is impossible to reply categorically whether it is advisable to participate in the Zemsky Sobor. Everything will depend on the political situation, on the electoral system, and on other specific factors which cannot be estimated in advance. Some say that the Zemsky Sobor is a fraud. That is true. *But there are times when we must take part in elections to expose a fraud* [my italics]." Yes, the regime was offering only "sham concessions," but the RSDLP, as he put it in the relevant resolutions, "should *take advantage of them* in order, on the one hand, to *consolidate* for the people every improvement in the economic conditions and every extension of liberties with a view to intensifying the struggle, and on the other, steadily to expose before the proletariat the reactionary aims of the government . . . [The Party has] to make use of each and every case of open political action on the part of the educated spheres and the people . . . all legal and semi-legal channels." And to be clear, "while maintaining and developing their underground machinery," party units should take the necessary steps to prepare for "open Social-Democratic activity, even to the point of clashes with the armed forces of the government."[12]

To participate or not in the electoral process could not, Lenin argued, be answered in the abstract. Participation depended on the political context and, most important, on whether it offered opportunities to advance the revolutionary process, including material improvements and the extension of liberties for the masses. Also evident is that Lenin did not make virtue out of underground work; it was necessary only when the opportunity for "open political action" was not available. Note also that "clashes with the armed forces of the government" constituted one of the forms of "open political activity"; events would soon reveal why he

allowed for this possibility. Though these were Lenin's initial pronouncements on the subject in concrete circumstances, history would show that
they forever informed his approach to electoral politics. Also on display
here was his deep understanding of political contingency—a necessary
skill to meet the challenges of political struggle for the rest of his life.

The Third Congress addressed another contingency. What stance
should the Bolsheviks take if the regime was overthrown and replaced by
a provisional government? Should they take posts in it or not? The delegates resolved that they could, "provided that the Party maintain strict
control over its representatives and firmly safeguard the independence of
the [RSDLP]."[13] In his major intervention in the discussion and debate,
Lenin, it should be noted, drew on the authority of Marx and Engels.
Their *Address of March 1850* figured significantly in his argument—his
first detailed discussion of it—and revealed that he had a more accurate
reading of the document than Plekhanov.[14] Though the revolution never
got as far as a provisional government (in 1917 it would), the resolution
would have implications for the Bolshevik stance toward a Duma if instituted. That is, if the RSDLP decided to put forward candidates who were
elected, should they take their seats? A year later, this is exactly what happened, and not surprisingly, it was the Bolsheviks who insisted on party
control and political independence as a condition for their participation.

Not taking anything for granted, Lenin, sometime in June and July,
drafted a "Sketch of a Provisional Revolutionary Government." Though
more relevant for developments in 1917, his three-page very rough outline
(see Appendix B) reiterated his point about the need for extending "liberties": "Object of the struggle = *Republic* (including *all* democratic liberties,
the **minimum programme** and far-reaching social reforms)."[15] A republic
for Lenin, in other words, would institute social and democratic measures,
including civil liberties, just as he had been defining "Social-Democracy"
since 1894.

While Lenin had already been thinking about the possibility of
"clashes with the armed forces of the government," the events in Odessa
in June made that real for the first time and brought home the gravity of
the situation. There, mutinous sailors of the battleship *Potemkin* tried to
unite with the city's rebellious masses, immortalized in Sergei Eisenstein's
film by that name. And for their deeds, Odessians suffered the greatest
concentrated repression by the regime during the revolution, with two
thousand killed and three thousand wounded.

> The tremendous significance of the recent events in Odessa lies precisely
> in the fact that, for the first time, an important unit of the armed force of
> tsarism—a battle ship—has openly gone over to the side of the revolution.

The government made frantic efforts and resorted to all possible tricks to conceal this event from the people, to stifle the mutiny of the sailors from the outset. But to no avail. The warships sent against the revolutionary armoured cruiser *"Potemkin" refused to fight* against their comrades . . . the armoured cruiser *Potemkin* remains an unconquered territory of the revolution, and whatever its fate may be, the undoubted fact and the point of highest significance is that here we have the attempt to form the *nucleus of a revolutionary army*.

But Lenin cautioned that the revolution may have reached a stage such that its military side, as registered by the *Potemkin* mutiny and similar rebellions in the armed forces, was outpacing its political organization. And to forge the latter would be very difficult:

But we must not allow what in the present circumstances would be still more dangerous—a lack of faith in the powers of the people. We must remember what a tremendous educational and organising power the revolution has, when mighty historical events force the man in the street out of his remote corner, garret, or basement and make a *citizen* out of him. Months of revolution sometimes educate citizens more quickly and fully than decades of political stagnation. The task of the class-conscious leaders of the revolutionary class is always to march ahead of it in the matter of education, to explain to it the meaning of the new tasks, and to urge it forward towards our great ultimate goal. The failures inevitably involved in our further attempts to form a revolutionary army and a provisional revolutionary government will only teach us to meet these tasks *in practice*; they will serve to draw the new and fresh forces of the people, now lying dormant, to the work of solving them . . .

As for forging a "revolutionary army," Lenin sought to make clear what that actually meant:

Social-Democracy never stooped to playing at military conspiracies; it never gave prominence to military questions until the actual conditions of civil war had arisen . . . Social-Democracy has never taken a sentimental view of war. It unreservedly condemns war as a bestial means of settling conflicts in human society. But Social-Democracy knows that so long as society is divided into classes, so long as there is exploitation of man by man, wars are inevitable. This exploitation cannot be destroyed without war, and war is always and everywhere begun by the exploiters themselves, by the ruling and oppressing classes. There are wars and wars. There are adventurist wars, fought to further dynastic interests, to satisfy the appetite of a band of freebooters, or to attain the objects of the knights of capitalist profit. And there is another kind of war—the only war that is *legitimate* in capitalist society—war against the people's oppressors and enslavers.

Lenin concluded with the "minimum programme" of the RSDLP—"of course, this is only a tentative list"—"*six* such fundamental points that must become the political banner and the immediate programme of any revolutionary government . . . (1) a Constituent Assembly of all the people, (2) arming of the people, (3) political freedom, (4) complete freedom for the oppressed and disfranchised nationalities, (5) the eight-hour day, and (6) peasant revolutionary committees." And consistent with everything he had said prior to the momentous events he was speaking to, "for the proletariat, the democratic revolution is only the first step on the road to the complete emancipation of labour from all exploitation, to the great socialist goal. All the more quickly, therefore, must we pass this first stage."[16] Shortly afterward, Lenin restated the Third Congress resolution about what was needed for a "democratic republic": "an assembly of people's representatives, which must be popular (i.e. elected, on the basis of universal and equal suffrage, direct elections, and secret ballot), and constituent assembly."[17] As for "arming of the people," this had very much to do with the fact that the regime unleashed fascist-like hordes that came to be known as the Black Hundreds; Jews were especially targeted for its bloodletting. Given the "atrocities perpetrated by the police, the Cossacks, and the Black Hundreds against unarmed citizens," such preparations were obligatory.[18]

If the Occupy Wall Street movement and its inspirers in Tahrir Square could be faulted for not having specific demands when they went into motion, that's the last that could be said of the Bolsheviks when Russia's spring erupted. The head-start program Marx and Engels provided and the very capable student who was recruited to it years before goes a long way in explaining why. Lenin was so confident about what he had learned that he felt he could correct one of his mentors. The laboratory of the class struggle offered that opportunity. As the Russian events unfolded, Lenin milked all he could out of what they had bequeathed. Most relevant were their writings about the Paris Commune, the only overturn in their lifetime when the working class held, though briefly, political power. Although he didn't mention Engels specifically, Lenin, informed by the reality of the Russian revolution, disagreed with his famous comment about the Commune: "That was the dictatorship of the proletariat."[19] That "the socialist proletariat," Lenin cautioned, had participated in "a revolutionary government with the petty bourgeoisie . . . shows us . . . that the real task the Commune had to perform was primarily the achievement of the democratic and not the socialist dictatorship, the implementation of 'our minimum programme' . . . It is not the word 'Commune' that we must adopt from the great fighters of

1871; we should not blindly repeat each of their slogans; what we must do is to single out those programmatic and practical slogans that bear upon the state of affairs in Russia and can be formulated in the words 'a revolutionary-democratic dictatorship of the proletariat and the peasantry.'"[20] The creative application of Marx and Engels's analysis to concrete situations is what it meant for Lenin to be a Marxist, as opposed to others who called themselves "Marxists."

The fact that the Bolsheviks and Mensheviks held separate party congresses in April registered the deep differences that continued to divide the two wings of the RSDLP after the Second Congress in 1903. The response of the flagship of international social democracy, the German Social Democratic Party, was revelatory for Lenin. His complaint to the Secretariat of the International Socialist Bureau—that is, the Second International—in July showed why: "I am compelled to state that nearly all German socialist papers, especially *Die Neue Zeit* and *Leipziger Volkszeitung*, are entirely on the side of the 'Minority,' and present our affairs in a very one-sided and inaccurate way. Kautsky, for instance, also calls himself impartial, and yet, in actual fact, he went so far as to refuse to publish in the *Neue Zeit* a refutation of an article by Rosa Luxemburg, in which she defended disruption in the Party. In *Leipziger Volkszeitang* Kautsky even urged that the German pamphlet with the translation of the resolutions of the Third Congress should not be circulated!! After this it is easy to understand why many comrades in Russia are inclined to regard the German Social-Democratic Party as partial and extremely prejudiced in the question of the split in the ranks of Russian Social-Democracy."[21]

With the benefit of hindsight, admittedly, this was the moment that first revealed the collision course the Bolsheviks and the German party leadership were on. Whether Lenin was aware of what was now in motion is difficult to say. But as the Russian party deepened its involvement in electoral politics in the next decade, it became increasingly clear to him that the differences he had with the Mensheviks were similar to those he had with the German leaders—over how revolutionary social democrats should comport themselves in that arena. Not for naught did Kautsky find it easier to publish Menshevik rather than Bolshevik documents.

THE REVOLUTION DEEPENS AND THEN RETREATS

The revolutionary genie refused to be rebottled. The regime therefore was forced to concretize the representative government proposal it floated in February. On August 6 it issued an Imperial Manifesto that set the conditions and timetable for its institution. Named after the minister who drew up the guidelines, the Bulygin parliament or Duma would be elected by indirect vote based on a very limited suffrage. The electors of the deputies were to be elected in the curiae or electoral colleges of various categories of the population: landowners (which included the clergy), urban prop- erty owners, peasants on communal land, and last, city residents. High property qualifications existed for all the categories.[22] Russia's small but increasingly vocal working class was not included. It didn't take Lenin long to condemn the proposal: "a consultative assembly of representatives of the landlords and the big bourgeoisie, elected under the supervision and with the assistance of the autocratic government's servants on the basis of an electoral system so indirect, so blatantly based on property and social-estate qualifications, that it is sheer mockery of the idea of popu- lar representation."[23] Especially reprehensible was that the "*entire urban working class, all the village poor, agricultural labourers, and peasants who are not householders, take no part whatever in any elections.*"[24]

The proposal was so patently antidemocratic that even many liberals denounced it, calling for a boycott of the Duma, which Lenin endorsed. But "we must exert every effort to make the boycott of real use in extend- ing and intensifying agitation, so that it shall not be reduced to mere passive abstention from voting. If we are not mistaken this idea is already fairly widespread among the comrades working in Russia, who express it in the words: an *active* boycott. As distinct from passive abstention, an active boycott should imply increasing agitation tenfold, organizing meet- ings everywhere, taking advantage of election meetings, even if we have to force our way into them, holding demonstrations, political strikes, and so on and so forth." Just how active was active? It meant "advocating an insurrection and calling for the immediate organization of combat squads and contingents of a revolutionary army for the overthrow of the autoc- racy and the establishment of a provisional revolutionary government; spreading and popularizing the fundamental and absolutely obligatory program of this provisional revolutionary government, a program which is to serve as the banner of the uprising and as a model for all future repe- titions of the Odessa events."[25] For the first time, Lenin publicly called for an insurrection to overthrow the regime and replace it with a provisional government. As he and other revolutionary veterans of that era would later remark, 1905 was the "dress rehearsal" for 1917.

Not every oppositional current was on board with the insurrectionary road. As bourgeois liberal forces began maneuvering for partaking in the Duma, Mensheviks saw an opening. Perhaps real change could come via the parlia- mentary route in an alliance with such forces. Lenin rebuked them and drew on Marx and Engels to support his argument. To entertain such a possibility means "playing at parliamentarism when no parliament whatever exists. It has been well said: we have no parliament as yet, but we have parliamentary cretinism galore."[26] Rather than cozying up to the liberals, Lenin—to let the reader know he had been thoroughly schooled by his mentors—wrote, "[W]e must expose the venal soul of a 'Frankfurt Parliament windbag' in every [Russian liberal] adherent who shuns this slogan of insurrection."[27] Not for the last time Lenin would invoke Marx and Engels's phrase to criticize those who viewed the parliamentary arena as the engine of real politics as opposed to what was actually taking place in Russia—the masses in the streets.

Lenin's strategy regarding the Duma was based on the assumption that insurrection was still on the agenda; as long as that was true, all energy should be devoted to its realization. "Only an uprising holds out the possibility that the Duma farce will not be the end of the Russian bourgeois revolution, but the beginning of a complete democratic upheaval, which will kindle the fire of proletarian revolutions all over the world." To begin maneuvering for the parliamentary road, as the Mensheviks were now doing, would undercut that effort. Yet he was sober about the situation. The proletariat could be "defeated," and if it was, "a new era will be inaugurated . . . European history will repeat itself, parliamentarism will for a time become the touchstone of all politics." But until that happens, "prepare for insurrection, preach it, and organize it."[28] As he explained to the Bolshevik leader Anatoli Lunacharsky in St. Petersburg in early October, "[T]here is no parliament as yet . . . We must fight in a revolutionary way *for* a parliament, but not in a parliamentary way for a revolution."[29] For a "*detailed* analysis of the relation of 'parliamentarism' to revolution," Lenin recommended that he read "Marx on the class struggles in France in 1848."

In criticizing the Mensheviks, Lenin made clear that he was not opposed in principle to making deals with liberals. It all depended on context, as he explained in an article toward the end of October. "Under a parliamentary system it is often necessary to support a more liberal party against a less liberal one." (In the previously cited letter to Lunacharsky, he was more specific: "For example, when balloting, etc. Such action there would not in the slightest degree violate the independence of the class party of Social-Democracy.") "But during a revolutionary struggle for a parliamentary system it is treachery to support liberal turncoats [the Cadets] who are "reconciling" Trepov [a Czarist official] with the revolution."[30] To be seen later, Lenin's contextual approach to politics indeed informed his approach to electoral politics once the revolutionary upsurge had exhausted itself and the Duma became a reality.

Lenin had every reason to believe that insurrection was still an option. From the late summer until October a strike wave swept through Russia that was unprecedented in the annals of the world's working class. Nothing gives a better sense of the moment than the letter that the very agitated Lenin wrote to his Bolshevik comrades in St. Petersburg on October 16:

What is needed is furious energy, and again energy. It horrifies me—I give you my word—it horrifies me to find that there has been talk about bombs for *over six months*, yet not one has been made! And it is the most learned of people who are doing the talking . . . Go to the youth, gentlemen! That is the only remedy! . . . Do not demand any formalities, and, for heaven's sake, forget all these schemes, and send all "functions, rights, and privileges" to the devil. Do not make membership in the R.S.D.L.P. an absolute condition—that would be an absurd demand for an armed uprising. Do not refuse to contact any group, even if it consists of only three persons . . . Let the groups join the R.S.D.L.P. or *associate* themselves with the R.S.D.L.P. if they want to; that would be splendid. But I would consider it quite wrong to *insist* on it . . . You must proceed to propaganda on a wide scale . . . organise combat groups immediately, arm yourselves as best you can, and work with all your might; we will help you in every way we can, but *do not wait for our help*; act for yourselves . . . The principal thing in a matter like this is the initiative of the mass of small groups. They will do everything. Without them your entire Combat Committee is nothing. I am prepared to gauge the efficiency of the Combat Committee's work by the number of such combat groups it is in contact with. If in a month or two the Combat Committee does not have a minimum of 200 or 300 groups in St. Petersburg, then it is a dead Combat Committee. It will have to be buried. If it cannot muster a hundred or two of groups in seething times like these, then it is indeed remote from real life . . . But the essential thing is to begin at once to learn from actual practice: have no fear of these trial attacks. They may, of course, degenerate into extremes, but that is an evil of the morrow, whereas the evil today is our inertness, our doctrinaire spirit, our learned immobility, and our senile fear of initiative. Let every group learn, if it is only by beating up policemen: a score or so victims will be more than compensated for by the fact that this will train hundreds of experienced fighters, who tomorrow will be leading hundreds of thousands.[31]

Written in probably the most intense moment of the revolution, this letter instructively distills the core of Lenin the revolutionary organizer; it's a plea to the Bolsheviks to broaden their ties to the mass movement— "do not refuse to contact any group"—and to take initiatives—"do not wait for our help." It's also worth noting Lenin's awareness that fighters should learn to judge when a revolutionary process might "degenerate into extremes."[32] That insight, as well as the rest of this most instructive letter, bears revisiting when 1917 arrives.

Undoubtedly, the political high-water mark of the revolution was the establishment, in St. Petersburg on October 13, of a new form of representative democracy unique to Russia—the soviet, an experiment repeated in Moscow and fifty or so other cities. Originally a body to coordinate the strike movement with elected representatives of various work places, the soviet quickly evolved into a combination legislative/executive body for the working class and its allies and potentially—not unlike the Paris Commune—an alternative government. Trotsky, who had managed to sneak his way back into Russia as early as February, became its effective head. Given the increasing breadth of the strike wave, especially when Moscow, "the very heart of Russia," revolted that month, clearly "ridiculous are the hopes of transforming the Duma into a revolutionary assembly."[33] Lenin could now point to a viable alternative.

Buffeted by a near nationwide revolt, the regime relented once again. On October 17 the Czar issued a new manifesto. In Lenin's words, it "promises a regular constitution; the Duma is invested with legislative powers; no law can come into force prior to approval by the people's representatives, ministerial responsibility has been granted; civil liberties have been granted—inviolability of the person, freedom of conscience, speech, assembly and association." Whereas the Bulygin Duma would have been only a consultative assembly, the new one being proposed would actually have "legislative powers." The earlier proposal was effectively rendered to the dustbin of history—vindication for Lenin of the policy of "active boycott." The newly granted "concessions" were for Lenin profound confirmation of Marx and Engels's basic political premise—unlike what "parliamentary cretins" believed—that what takes place in the streets is decisive in explaining the fate of the parliamentary process, a point he would forever make.

Lenin, of course, was under no illusion about Nicholas's manifesto. The regime was simply buying time. "The workers will never forget that it was only by force, by the force of their organization, their unanimity and their mass heroism, that they wrested from tsarism a recognition of liberty in a paper manifesto; and only in this way will they win real liberty for themselves." That could be realized, more specifically, "*only* by a victorious rising of the people, *only* by the complete domination of the armed proletariat and the peasantry over all representatives of tsarist power, who, under pressure by the people, have retreated a pace but are far from having yielded to the people, and far from having been overthrown by the people. Until *that* aim is achieved there *can be no* real liberty, no genuine popular representation, or a really *constituent* assembly with the power to set up a new order in Russia."[34] And crucial in that fight was the need to "pay special attention to the army . . . [W]e must attract the soldiers to workers' meetings, intensify our agitation in the barracks, extend our liaisons to officers, creating, alongside of the revolutionary army of workers, cadres of class conscious revolutionaries among the troops as well."[35] This was no abstract proposal. The regime struck back using the terrorism of the Black Hundreds, particularly targeting Jews. "There were 690 documented pogroms—with over 3,000 reported murders—during the two weeks following the declaration of the October Manifesto . . . The worst pogrom took place in Odessa, where 800 Jews were murdered, 5,000 wounded and more than 100,000 made homeless."[36] If ever there was a need to win the ranks of the army to the fight for "real liberty," the time was now.

Despite the state-sponsored terrorism, Lenin and other émigrés eventually returned to Russia, sensing that there was now sufficient space for them to work in the open since for the first time the working class was mobilized and civil liberties were at least on paper. His immediate task was to reorient the Bolsheviks and to urge them out of their semisectarian existence with regard to the mass movement, particularly the St. Petersburg soviet. The latter, in his view, "should be regarded as the embryo of a *provisional revolutionary government*"—what would only be realized in 1917. His willingness, unlike a number of other Bolshevik leaders, to work with Trotsky, the effective head of the St. Petersburg soviet but an opponent since the Second Congress in 1903, also anticipated 1917. In addition to broadening the party, Lenin said "the elective principle" could now be implemented (or, as he put it a few months later, "should be applied from top to bottom"[37]); that is, the party could now elect its leadership, more evidence that he never made virtue out of underground work. Parenthetically, he noted at the time that *What Is to Be Done?* was written in "entirely different, now outdated conditions."[38]

PREPARING FOR THE "BEGINNING OF A HUMDRUM LIFE"

Lenin had long been sober about the revolution. As a student of history through the lens of Marx and Engels, he knew that all upsurges, even the most radical, eventually ebb. Signs began to appear that, though not defeated, the St. Petersburg proletariat was "exhausted." When sailors at Kronstadt mutinied at the end of October, the St. Petersburg's soviet called for a general strike in solidarity. The response was not massive enough to prevent the regime from quelling the uprising. It sensed, correctly, that the momentum was now on its side.

December was the decisive month. Both the St. Petersburg and Moscow soviets called for general strikes in response to the government's counteroffensive. On the third of December the regime arrested most of the deputies of the St. Petersburg soviet, including Trotsky. The initiative now passed to Moscow, where for a couple of weeks the outcome of the revolution hung in the balance. To tip the scales to its advantage, the government's chief minister, Sergei Witte, issued on December 11 a decree that modified the August 6 Bulygin Duma proposal. Industrial workers, who had been excluded in the earlier decree, would now be able to elect Duma deputies, albeit quite indirectly. Witte, who no doubt hoped that this concession would possibly mollify the working class and lessen its revolutionary ardor, would forever have his name associated with the First Duma after it assembled in April 1906. How determinative his tactic was is uncertain, but by December 19 the opposition in Moscow called an end to its strike—the effective end to the 1905 revolution.

As the fighting in Moscow was underway, Bolshevik leaders and cadre met to discuss and chart a course forward from December 12 to 17 in the Finnish town of Tammerfors (Tampere), a relatively close and safe site (they ended earlier than planned so that delegates could return to take part in the revolt). Aside from agenda points on the agrarian question and plans for a unity congress with the Mensheviks, the most urgent item was how to respond to the Duma proposals Witte had just announced. Should the active boycott be maintained or not? In a telling moment, Lenin and one other delegate voted against the majority who wanted to keep it in place. It may be remembered that for Lenin context was all-important in answering question of political strategy and tactics. As he argued in response to the Bulygin Duma proposal, the key factor was whether insurgency was still a possibility. The majority of the delegates (including Josef Stalin, who he met for the first time) felt it was. Lenin no doubt differed with them on this critical point, but he was willing to change his vote. The majority had been on the ground in Russia longer than he had, with closer contacts to the rank-and-file cadre. Thus Lenin felt, apparently, that he had to concede to their opinion—also telling.[39] Years later, however, he would admit that the boycott had been a mistake.

As a disciplined member of the Bolshevik faction, Lenin publicly defended their boycott of the Witte Duma, but in a most nuanced way. In a series of writings after the Tammerfors decision, he discussed very civilly the differences between the Bolsheviks and the Mensheviks, emphasizing that the crux of the matter was whether—drawing on the experience of Germany in 1847–49—revolution was still on the agenda or in "final exhaustion . . . and the beginning of a humdrum life under a dock-tailed constitution?"[40] The latter meant the less-than-exciting prospects of work in the parliamentary arena. The answer would have to be resolved at the upcoming "unity congress" of the two factions of the RSDLP. If the congress decided "that insurrection isn't possible . . . we must regard the State Duma as a parliament, even if a bad one, and not only participate in the elections, but also go into the Duma."[41] While arguing that the revolution was still alive, he also, notably, insisted that the "majority of the members of the party" would decide the issue and that "the minority must submit to it in its political conduct while retaining the right to criticize and to advocate a settlement of the question at the next congress."[42] On the basis, then, of "democratic centralism," which the congress would make official RSDLP organizational policy for the first time, the Bolsheviks would be obligated to carry out the Menshevik line if it won majority support. One can only wonder, therefore, if Lenin's messages weren't really directed at the Bolsheviks who wanted to boycott the Witte Duma. Subsequent events would suggest so.

As Lenin pointedly reminded the Mensheviks a few months later, prior to the Duma elections the Bolsheviks and Mensheviks issued a joint statement saying that "both sides agreed with the idea of a boycott and disagreed only about the stage [in the various rounds of the elections] at which it should be carried out." Also, "not a single Menshevik in any Menshevik publication advocated going into the Duma" should a party member actually win an election in, presumably, the second stage.[43] That silence would soon confront the RSDLP with an awkward situation.

Before the Fourth Congress began in Stockholm, April 10–25, the first set of staggered elections for the Duma got under way. The returns, which Lenin closely analyzed in an eighty-page pamphlet (his penchant for statistics was on display once again), indicated that the left-liberal Cadet party would be the principal winner with the largest bloc of deputies. The data and the assessments of others explained why: "All agree that the election returns are not so much a vote *for* the Cadets as a vote *against the government*. The Cadets achieved their victory largely *because they were. . . the most extreme Left party in the field*. The genuinely Left parties were kept out of the field by violence, arrests, massacres, the election law, and so forth. By the very force of circumstances, by the logic of the election struggle, all the discontented, irritated, angry and vaguely revolutionary elements were compelled to rally around the Cadets."[44] Much of the vote for the Cadets was, in other words, a protest vote.

Most significantly, Lenin began to visualize in his pamphlet what it would be like when political reality dictated the "humdrum life" of parliamentary work for the RSDLP, functioning in such a Duma with its own deputies. "In those circumstances, it would be our bounden duty to support the Cadet Party in parliament against all parties to the right of it. Then, too, it would be wrong categorically to object to election agreements with this party in joint elections . . . (if the elections were indirect). More than that. It would be the duty of the Social-Democrats in parliament to support even the Shipovites [moderate liberals who advocated for a constitutional monarchy known as the Octobrists] against the real, brazen reactionaries [such as the Black Hundreds]."[45] For Lenin then, temporary electoral alliances with the lesser of the two evils, the liberals, would be permissible in order "to isolate reaction"—in the language of the *Address of 1850*, "alliances but not unity."

But to make clear that tactical maneuvers in the parliamentary arena did not mean restraining revolutionary politics, Lenin employed a metaphor of Engels: "Our task is not to support the Cadet Duma, but to use the conflicts within this Duma, or connected with it, for choosing the right moment to attack the enemy, the right moment for an insurrection against the autocracy. What we have to do is to take account of how the political crisis in the Duma and around it is growing. As a means of testing public opinion and defining as correctly and precisely as possible the moment when 'boiling point' is reached, this Duma campaign ought to be of enormous value to us, but only as a symptom, not as the real field of struggle . . . Our task is to be at our post when the Duma farce develops into a new great political crisis; and our aim then will be . . . the overthrow of the autocratic government and the transfer of power to the revolutionary people."[46] For Engels, as noted in Chapter 1, "universal suffrage is the gauge of the maturity of the working class. It cannot and never will be anything more in the present-day state; but that," he continued, "is sufficient. On the day the thermometer of universal suffrage registers boiling point among the workers, both they and the capitalists will know where they stand."[47] Lenin was faithful to Engels's metaphor.

The more Lenin, I argue, had to grapple with electoral politics, the more conscious he was about how "West-European Social-Democrats" comported themselves in that arena. His most explicit comments to date came in this text. Those parties considered, just as had Marx and Engels, "the parliamentary struggle as the main form of struggle . . . only when . . . insurrections" were no longer on the agenda. The "opportunists" in social democracy, such as the "Bernsteinians" in the German party, were the problem. They "accepted and accept Marxism *minus* its directly revolutionary aspect. They do not regard the parliamentary struggle as one of the weapons particularly suitable for definite historical periods, but as the main and almost the sole form of struggle making "force," "seizure," "dictatorship," unnecessary."[48] "Orthodox" Marxists in the Russian party had to guard against that distortion being "smuggled into Russia 'on the sly.'" In hindsight, this may signal the beginning of the fight that would culminate in 1914.

Lenin ended his pamphlet very prophetically: "We have no reason to be envious of the Cadets' successes. Petty-bourgeois illusions and faith in the Duma are still fairly strong among the people. They must be dispelled. The more complete the Cadets' triumph in the Duma, the sooner will this be done. We welcome the successes of the Girondists ['the bourgeois moderates'] of the great Russian revolution! They will be followed by the rise of broader masses of the people; more energetic and revolutionary sections will come to the fore; they will rally around the proletariat; they will carry our great bourgeois revolution to complete victory, and will usher in the era of socialist revolution in the West."[49] As was often the case with Marx and Engels, Lenin may not have gotten the arithmetic correct, but the algebra was nonetheless elegant. The Cadets' day in the sun, as events would soon reveal, lasted only about three months. But it would take the proletariat another decade or so to verify Lenin's prescience.

Prior to the agenda items on the Duma and the elections at the Fourth Congress, Lenin had to address the long-term prospects of a revolution in an overwhelmingly peasant society—of relevance, given his basic premise that electoral politics was only a means to an end. In what is arguably the most prophetic of all his forecasts so far, he said that "the Russian revolution can achieve victory by its own efforts, but it cannot possibly hold and consolidate its gains by its own strength. It cannot do this unless there is a socialist revolution in the West. Without this condition restoration is inevitable . . . Our democratic republic has no other reserve than the socialist proletariat in the West."[50] Engels, it may be recalled, said as much in his last major pronouncement on the Russian question.[51] What Lenin asserted here—and repeated, it should be noted—goes a long way in explaining the outcome of October 1917.

As Lenin anticipated—and no doubt hoped for, I contend—the Fourth Congress, with the Mensheviks in a majority, voted to participate in the Duma elections and to form a party group or fraction in it should RSDLP candidates be elected. The very practical problem was that most of the elections had already taken place in the long-drawn out process. The Bolsheviks noted this in their defeated resolution—written by Lenin, Lunacharsky, and Ivan Skvortsov-Stepanov—as well as in the accompanying report given by Lenin, which continued to defend the boycott. But Lenin pointed out that "when people [the Mensheviks] talk about our 'self-elimination' from the elections, they always forget that it was the political conditions and not our desire that kept our Party out; kept it out of the newspapers and meetings; prevented us from putting up prominent members of the Party as candidates."[52] They criticized the Mensheviks for having illusions in the Cadet victory and for having entered into electoral agreements with them in some of the elections.

The resolution correctly foresaw what would come of the Cadet victory, calling for a prohibition: "[I]n view of the possibility that the government will dissolve the State Duma and convene a new Duma, this Congress resolves that in the subsequent election campaign no blocs or agreements shall be permitted with the Cadet Party or any similar non-revolutionary elements; as for the question whether our Party should take part in a new election campaign, it will be decided by the Russian Social-Democrats in accordance with the concrete circumstances prevailing at the time."[53] If Lenin had been open to electoral blocs with the Cadets as his pamphlet on their victory indicated, this suggests that his two Bolshevik comrades forced him to retreat. Nevertheless, his points rejecting "self-elimination" from the elections and promoting a likely "new election campaign" clearly held open the possibility of Bolshevik participation in a future Duma. The clearest affirmation of this was Lenin's response to the request from the delegates from the Caucasus region. "We voted for the amendment moved by the comrades from the Caucasus (to participate in the elections where they have not yet taken place, but not to enter into any blocs with other parties)."[54] According to Robert Service, "we" meant a minority of Bolsheviks.[55] Lenin, who evidently broke discipline with his Bolshevik faction, still had his work cut out for him.

The Congress then turned to the somewhat awkward matter of what to do with Menshevik candidates, such as those in the Caucasus region—mainly rural areas—who might win in the few remaining elections. Should they take their seats and form a Duma fraction? Prior to the elections, as already noted, "not a single Menshevik . . . advocated going into the Duma." Their "semi-boycott" tactic—that is, of later rounds—meant only limited participation in the elections.[56] Their solution to this apparently unforeseen situation, to now permit the formation of a Duma fraction, was, in the Bolshevik view, deficient. To ensure the group's authority, Lenin argued, it would be necessary "to ask the workers whether they wish to be represented in the Duma by those they did not participate in electing"; "nine-tenths of the class-conscious workers," he noted later, "boycotted" the elections.[57] Elsewhere he wrote, "I pointed out that the great bulk of the class-conscious proletariat had not voted. Would it be advisable under these conditions to impose official representatives of the Party on this mass of workers?"[58] That Lenin would be concerned about the party appearing to "impose" itself on the working class must certainly sound strange to anyone who accepts as gospel the lie spun by his bourgeois critics and others that he was an authoritarian.

To try to make sure a RSDLP Duma fraction actually represented the working class, the Bolsheviks tried to amend the Menshevik resolution.

Drawing on "the experience of the socialist parties in Europe . . . particularly their Left wings," Lenin advocated for the same "*triple control*" they demanded that parities have "over their members of parliament: first, the general control that the party exercises over all its members; secondly, the special control of the local organizations who nominate the parliamentary candidates in their own name; and thirdly, the special control of the Central Committee, which, standing above local influences and local conditions, must see to it that only such parliamentary candidates are nominated as satisfy general party and general political requirements." Given Russia's reality, where "our Party organizations cannot exercise open and public control over their members . . . we unquestionably require far greater prudence than that prompted by the experience of the revolutionary Social-Democrats of Western Europe."[59] As early as 1879 Marx and Engels in their *Circular* to the leadership of the German party had noted (discussed in Chapter 1) the problem of Reichstag deputies becoming increasingly unaccountable to the party ranks. It was no accident that Lenin looked to the "Left wings" of European social democracy for solutions to this problem; he would learn later of the *Circular* and make use of it.

To appreciate the significance of what Lenin was addressing, fast forward to Europe circa 2008 until the present day. Since the official onset of the world capitalist crisis that year, European social democracy has been in the forefront of implementing the austerity drive to effectively lower the standard of living of Europe's working class—capitalism's plutocratic answer to the crisis. Emblematic of this social democratic attack on workers is the Pasok Party of Greece, whose now disgraced head, former prime minister George Papandreou, continues to be the president of the Socialist International, social democracy's transnational body, and successor to the Second International. Like Pasok, S-D parties in Spain, Portugal, and Iceland also led the offensive against workers and have paid a political price with the working classes in each country. Could these parties have pursued such policies if they had been accountable to their rank and files? Opinion polls suggest otherwise. Whether the "triple control" could have made them so is beyond the purview of this book, but the problem Lenin sought an answer to is as current as ever.

The Bolsheviks didn't garner enough votes for their resolution; the congress passed the Menshevik resolution, which "declared it desirable that a Social-Democratic parliamentary group in this Duma should be formed." Lenin was far from despondent and no doubt felt the Bolshevik objections had had an impact, as he explained in a postcongress report. Although "unfortunately" not included in the published proceedings of the meetings, "The Congress instructed the Central Committee to inform *all* Party organizations specifically: (1) whom, (2) when, and (3) on what conditions it has appointed as Party representatives in the parliamentary group, and also to submit periodical reports of the activities of these Party representatives. This resolution instructs the local workers' organizations to which the Social-Democratic deputies in the Duma belong to keep control over their 'delegates' in the Duma."[60] Lenin took delight in the howls of protests against this instruction from Cadets like the one-time "Marxist" Struve. For "bourgeois politicians" like him, the idea that parliamentary deputies should be under the control of party organizations was ridiculous. Unaccountability was the norm of bourgeois parliamentary politics, as Lenin saw it—exactly what the working class had to avoid.

For the record, especially for those Bolsheviks who may have been despondent, Lenin wrote, "We must and shall fight ideologically against those decisions of the Congress which we regard as erroneous. But at the same time we declare to the whole Party that we are opposed to a split of any kind. We stand for submission to the decisions of the Congress . . . We are profoundly convinced that the workers' Social-Democratic organizations must be united, but in these united organizations there must be wide and free discussion of Party questions, free comradely criticism and assessment of events in Party life."

As for "submission to the decisions of the Congress," Lenin was referring to the historic organizational decision of the RSDLP. "We"—that is, Bolsheviks and Mensheviks—"were all agreed on the principle of democratic centralism, on guarantees for the rights of all minorities and for all loyal opposition, on the autonomy of every Party organization, on recognizing that all Party functionaries must be elected, accountable to the Party and subject to recall."[61] Along with the second sentence in the previous paragraph, Lenin spells out here the essentials of democratic centralism, the basic organizational norm of the RSDLP—"freedom of discussion, unity of action." Its democratic content, not just on paper, was commendable and apparently without equal in comparison to other parties in Russia. Never should it be forgotten that democratic centralism began as a joint project of the Bolsheviks and Mensheviks.[62]

Having lost on the Duma fraction vote—as well as on the agrarian question—Lenin was, understandably, concerned about ensuring the "freedom of discussion" side of democratic centralism. The norm was crucial when it came to programmatic questions. In the case of electoral politics, however, "the situation is somewhat different. During elections there *must* be complete unity of action. The Congress has decided: we will *all* take part in elections, wherever they take place. During elections there must be no criticism of participation in elections. *Action* by the proletariat must be united. We shall all and always regard the Social-Democratic group in the Duma, whenever it is formed, as *our* Party group."[63] Armed with democratic centralism, Lenin now had license to lead the Bolsheviks, some of them kicking and screaming, into the "humdrum" parliamentary arena—what he clearly had wanted to do for some time.

"WHAT THOU DOEST, DO QUICKLY": A BRIEF BUT INSTRUCTIVE EXISTENCE

After the defeat of the Moscow uprising in December 1905, the regime no longer felt the need to play its soft-cop card. The concessions it had made regarding the Duma began to be compromised. In February it moved to have the Imperial Council, the long-existent autocratic advisory body to the Czar, become the upper chamber to the Duma with veto powers over its decisions. In April it revamped the Fundamental Laws, effectively the Czar's constitution. Article 87 gave the monarch the right to dissolve the Duma and to enact emergency measures when it was not sitting. Further, the regime increasingly played its hard-cop card with the use of state terror. "In all, it has been estimated that the tsarist regime executed 15,000 people, shot or wounded at least 20,000 and deported or exiled 45,000 between mid-October and the opening of the first State Duma in April 1906."[64] Whatever pretense therefore that the August and October Imperial Manifestos would institute substantive representative democracy was dispelled for most Russians when the Duma finally convened on April 27. That only a handful of Bolsheviks like Lenin saw any value in participating in the Duma's deliberations is understandable. "Indeed there is no more accurate reflection of the Duma's true position than the fact that whenever it met in the Tauride Palace [its official site] a group of plain clothes policemen could be seen on the pavement outside waiting for those deputies to emerge whom they had been assigned to follow and keep under surveillance."[65] Soon, however, it would become clear why Lenin did think it important to partake in what most of his Bolshevik comrades saw as a charade.

THE FIRST DUMA CONVENES

Once the Duma convened, it didn't take Lenin long to go on the offensive. But effective Duma work had to be linked to mass work. The day before, the Bolsheviks began publishing a legal daily in St. Petersburg titled *Volna* [*The Wave*], thus taking advantage of the remaining political space. About a week after the ceremonial opening session that Nicholas disdainfully addressed, Lenin's first article in the daily ridiculed the Cadets who "think that they are the hub of the universe . . . [and] dream about peaceful parliamentarism." Despite the Cadets having the largest bloc of deputies, about 180 out of 480, real history, he asserted, would be made by the "people," "the crowd." He then offered advice: "Let us hope that the minority in the Duma, the 'Trudovik Group' and the 'Workers' Group,' will take a stand different from that of the Cadets . . . [and] concentrate all their efforts and all their activities on helping in some way to promote the great work ahead."[66] Lenin would not leave the fulfillment of that goal, shortly to be concretized, to chance.

By the "minority in the Duma" he meant, first, the 90 or so peasant deputies that grouped themselves loosely in what came to be known as the Trudovik party and, second, the 15 deputies that had been belatedly elected and authorized by the Fourth Congress as its Duma fraction. That he appealed to both Duma groups was no accident. They were the potential representatives of "the democratic dictatorship of the proletariat and peasantry," the coalition for the Russian revolution that Lenin proposed in his *Two Tactics of Social-Democracy in the Democratic Revolution* pamphlet, written on the eve of the April 1905 Bolshevik congress. Because the regime assumed that the peasantry was loyal to the monarchy, it permitted them a surprisingly large number of deputies, who it expected to align in the Duma with representatives of the nobility/landlord class. Lenin's appeal to them and the "Workers' Group" was his opening shot at trying to prevent that from happening.

As for the "Workers' Group," Lenin soberly explained who the 15 were and how they got into the Duma in his first major article on the Duma a day later: "They were not nominated by workers' organizations. The Party did not authorize them to represent its interests in the Duma. Not a single local organization of the R.S.D.L.P. adopted a resolution (although it might have done) to nominate its members for the State Duma. The worker deputies got into the Duma through non-party channels. Nearly all, or even all, got in by direct or indirect, tacit or avowed, agreements with the Cadets. Many of them got into the Duma in such a way that it is difficult to tell whether they were elected as Constitutional-Democrats or as Social-Democrats. This is a fact, and . . . [t]o hush it up, as many Social-Democrats are doing today, is unpardonable and useless . . . because it means keeping in the dark the electorate generally, and the workers' party in particular. Useless, because the fact is bound to come out in the course of events."[67] To be dishonest about how these deputies got elected and who they might be accountable to, would, in

effect, miseducate the working class and therefore undermine the potential value of parliamentary work—not the way to begin.

Lenin also argued that the Fourth Congress of the party inadequately
addressed this problem when it voted to authorize the deputies to be the
RSDLP Duma fraction. But "in fairness," the congress did adopt the previously quoted "instructions" that the Bolsheviks insisted on to make the
fraction accountable to the party. And because the Menshevik majority
Central Committee failed to publish the "instructions"—"unfortunately,"
as he once put it—Lenin gladly filled in the "very serious gap in the Central Committee's publication" by reproducing the three provisions for his
readers.

More important, Lenin continued, was the present situation and what
to do. "On entering the Duma, Mikhailichenko, the leader of the group,
proclaimed himself a Social-Democrat. Through him the Workers' Group
clearly expressed its desire to dissociate itself from the Cadets and become
a genuine Social-Democratic group. Such a desire is worthy of all sympathy. At the Congress we were opposed to the formation of an official parliamentary group. Our motives are set out precisely and in detail in our
resolution published yesterday." This refers to the previously discussed
proposal for "triple control" over Duma deputies. Publicizing it was part
and parcel of Lenin's strategy for revolutionary parliamentary work; being
able to do so underscored the importance of having an organ, especially a
daily one like *Volna*. "But it goes without saying that the fact that we did
not think it opportune to form an official parliamentary group does not
in the least prevent us from encouraging *any* desire of *any* workers' representative to *shift* from the Constitutional-Democrats [Cadets] towards
the Social-Democrats." In other words, despite its birth defect, including its all-Menshevik composition, the fraction should be embraced if its
pro-social democratic declarations were sincere. This is the hand that the
political reality of Russia in 1906 has dealt us, Lenin might have said, and
it is our obligation to try to play it to our advantage.

Lenin cautioned his readers, his most important audience, about what
was ahead: "It is not enough to proclaim oneself a Social-Democrat. To be
a Social-Democrat, one must pursue a genuinely Social-Democratic workers' policy. Of course, we fully understand the difficulties of the position
of parliamentary novices. We are well aware of the need to be indulgent
towards the mistakes that may be made by those who are beginning to pass
from the Constitutional-Democrats to the Social-Democrats. But if they
are destined ever to complete this passage, it will only be through open
and straight forward criticism of these mistakes. To look at these mistakes
through one's fingers would be an unpardonable transgression against the

Social-Democratic Party and against the whole proletariat." Principled and constructive criticism along with magnanimity is what Lenin promised—what the "novices" got their first dose of in the next paragraph.

Deigning to give a brief address to the opening session of the Duma, Nicholas made clear that his autocracy was not about to relinquish its privileges and power. Having the gauntlet thrown down before its feet, the Cadets, the Duma's leading party, had to respond in a way that would placate and dupe most peasant masses without riling a monarchy that could, under Article 87, summarily end their parliamentary hopes. Trying to strike the golden mean with their Address to the Throne, the Cadets angered both the right and the left—a bad omen for their future prospects. The RSDLP fraction abstained. That, Lenin said, was a "mistake."

> Over the heads of the Cadets, it should have openly and plainly stated for all to hear: "You, gentlemen of the Cadet Party, are taking the wrong tone. Your address smacks of a deal. Drop that diplomacy. Speak out loudly and say that the peasants are demanding all the land, that the peasants must obtain all the land without compensation. Say that the people are demanding complete freedom, and that the people will take full power in order to ensure real freedom, and not merely freedom on paper. Do not trust written 'constitutions,' trust only the strength of the fighting people! We vote against your address."

This would only be the first time Lenin offered advice to RSDLP Duma fractions. It encapsulated his most basic ideas about revolutionary parliamentary work. At its core was an effort to utilize the parliamentary arena to mobilize "the crowd" to think outside the box of that arena and plant the seeds for the "democratic dictatorship of the proletariat and peasantry."

Finally, Lenin took on the Mensheviks, not the novice deputies but their daily organ *Nevskaya Gazeta*, which began publication in early May. Their commentary about the dilemma the Cadets found themselves in sounded, to Lenin's ears, sympathetic, specifically regarding the fear that the regime would invoke Article 87: "This is the wrong tone. It is unseemly for Social-Democrats to pose as people who can in any way be responsible for the Duma. If the Social-Democrats had a majority in the Duma, the Duma would not be a Duma, or else the Social-Democrats would not be Social-Democrats. Let the Cadets bear all the responsibility for the Duma. Let the people learn to cast off constitutional illusions at their expense, and not ours." He ended with a piece of advice that recalled Marx and Engels's critique of the "parliamentary cretinism" of the Frankfurt Assembly: "We must not appraise the revolutionary situation in the country from the standpoint of what goes on in the Duma. On the contrary, we must appraise questions and incidents that arise in the Duma from the standpoint of the revolutionary situation in the country."[68] This is the criteria he employed from here on in assessing the Duma, at least when it was in session. His point about the improbability of a social democratic Duma—that is, one composed of real social democrats—is also instructive. It suggests that like Marx and Engels, he too thought that a capitalist regime would never permit such an outcome. The fate of the First Duma, as we'll see, offers powerful evidence for his assumption.

While *Volna* was Lenin's principal venue for linking Duma work with the far more important struggle going on outside its walls, he had the rare opportunity on May 9 to address a mass audience of three thousand in St. Petersburg, the majority of whom were workers. It was a debate with a Menshevik and another left opponent on the discussion taking place in the Duma about the Cadets' response to Nicholas. Under the pseudonym "Comrade Karpov," he used the event to put pressure on the Duma fraction, some of whom were probably in attendance, to stand firm when dealing with the Cadets. According to the *Volna* account, no doubt written by Lenin, he argued, "Exposing the Cadet Party . . . was . . . the necessary and most advisable means of drawing the broad masses of the people away from the liberal bourgeoisie . . . to the revolutionary democratic bourgeoisie, which was preparing for a decisive struggle for power . . . Of course, the time when the conflict will set in does not depend on our will but on the behavior of the government, and on the degree of the political consciousness and the temper of the masses of the people."[69] The revolution, in other words, could not be willed. It depended on the readiness of the masses—exactly what his parliamentary strategy sought to ensure.

At the end of his intervention, Lenin, never one to waste such an opportunity, proposed that the meeting adopt a resolution that he drafted. After criticizing the Cadets for their vacillating behavior vis-à-vis the monarchy, it ended,

> This meeting calls upon the Peasant ("Trudovik") and Workers' Groups in the State Duma resolutely to state their respective demands, and the full demands of the people, absolutely independently of the Cadets. This meeting calls the attention of all those who value the cause of freedom to the fact that the behaviour of the autocratic government and its utter failure to satisfy the needs of the peasants, and of the people as a whole, is making inevitable a decisive fight outside the Duma, a fight for complete power for the people, which alone can ensure freedom for the people and meet their needs. This meeting expresses confidence that the proletariat will continue to be at the head of all the revolutionary elements of the people.[70]

What the resolution, "carried almost unanimously,"[71] did therefore was to rectify the "mistake" the Duma fraction had made in failing to criticize the Cadets' Address to the Throne. A mass meeting made up primarily of workers went "over the heads of the Cadets" and "plainly stated" what it supported—the essence of the revolutionary dictatorship of the proletariat and peasantry. What Lenin carried out with his intervention was a model of revolutionary parliamentary work—taking the parliamentary debate to "the crowd" outside and in real time. The regime would make sure, as long as it was in power, that he would never have such an opportunity again.[72]

Three more deputies joined the 15-member RSDLP fraction as a result of belated election returns from the Caucasus region. Unlike the others, they had been elected on the basis of the Fourth Congress decision that required approval of party organizations and no electoral agreements with the Cadets. Therefore, Lenin said, "all of us, as members of a united party, will do all we can to help them to fulfill their arduous duties." But he advised sobriety, once again:

> In times such as Russia is now passing through, the participation of Social-Democrats in the elections does not at all mean that the masses really become stronger in the course of the election campaign. Without unfettered newspapers, without public meetings and without wide agitation, the election of Social-Democrats often expresses, not a consolidation of the proletarian and fully Social-Democratic Party, but only a sharp protest of the people. In such circumstances, large sections of the petty-bourgeoisie sometimes vote for any anti-government candidate. Opinions on the value of the boycott tactics for the whole of Russia, if based on the returns of the Tiflis elections alone, would be much too rash and ill-considered.

He cautioned that the RSDLP could become the beneficiaries of the protest vote just as the Cadets had been, particularly in the absence of sufficient democratic space where competing political perspectives could be openly debated. Lenin's instrumental approach to democracy explains his invocation at the end to the new deputies: "Let us wish our comrades from the Caucasus, deputies to the Duma, for the first time to speak from this new platform in full voice, to speak the whole, bitter truth, to expose ruthlessly belief in words, promises and scraps of paper, to fill the gaps in our newspapers, which continue to be restricted and persecuted for speaking frankly, and to call upon the proletariat and the revolutionary peasantry to pose their problems clearly and distinctly and to settle the impending final contest for freedom outside the Duma."[73] Thus he revealed another reason a Duma fraction was so needed. In the face of diminishing political space, its immunity gave a relatively safe "platform" from which to make the call for the only guarantee of real democracy—the empowerment of the working class and peasantry "outside the Duma."

Without the "support" of the peasantry, "the proletariat cannot even think of achieving the complete victory of our revolution." "The land question," as Lenin explained to *Volna* readers, "is the one that is most of all worrying the masses of the peasants; and the peasants have now become the principal and almost the sole allies of the workers in the revolution. The land question will show better than anything else whether the Cadets, who call themselves the party of people's freedom, are loyally serving the cause of people's freedom." To make his case Lenin closely followed the Duma deliberations and sought to influence the actions of not only the RSDLP fraction but the Trudoviks as well.

The Cadets offered a solution to the land question, which they submitted to the government in response to Nicholas's curt and unyielding address: "The greater part of the population of the country, the toiling peasantry, awaits with impatience the satisfaction of its urgent need for land, and the First Russian State Duma would not be fulfilling its duty if it did not draw up a law for the satisfaction of that vital need by requisitioning to that end state, appanage, cabinet and monastery lands, and by the compulsory expropriation of privately owned lands."[74] Trying to preempt the radical left and assuming the regime still felt the heat of 1905, the Cadets no doubt thought they had taken a bold stance. Not so, said Lenin: "Instead of a demand, they drew up a timid request." The fact that they didn't protest the regime's refusal to receive a deputation, when they tried to present their address, only confirmed, Lenin opined, their lack of spine.

Nevertheless, the Cadets called for a debate on the land question in the Duma. For Lenin it was an opportunity to broadcast the revolutionary socialist position. Just as he had done on countless occasions, he defended peasant demands for land, explaining in the process why it was in the interests of the working class to do the same. But real land reform, he insisted, could not be achieved in the absence of a democratic republic. And this was one of the two major problems with the Cadets' own program of "requisitioning" and "compulsory expropriations." It relied on the very undemocratic institutions of the state for its implementation. The other problem was that the Cadets' plan called for compensation to the landlord class; a similar policy in 1861 resulted in "ruining the peasants, enriching the landlords and strengthening the old state power."[75] Whatever the case, the "bureaucratic government ['headed by some of the richest landlord-bureaucrats'], of course, refuses to consider even a Cadet agrarian reform."

The Trudovik fraction had yet to formulate its position. "Let us hope that at least on this occasion [it] . . . will come out quite independently of the Cadets." In the meantime, and most importantly, "the socialist workers . . . should enlarge their organization in general, and their contacts with the peasantry in particular. They should explain to the peasants—as widely, clearly, minutely and circumstantially as possible—the significance of the question of compensation and of whether they can put up with leaving the agrarian reform in the hands of the old authorities."[76] These were the most concrete recommendations Lenin provided so far for "the socialist workers," the Duma fraction. There was no greater priority than that of winning the peasantry, and he did all he could to advance that process.

As Lenin predicted, on May 13 the regime rejected the Cadets' "timid request." He reproduced for his *Volna* readers the main passages of the government's statement and distilled their essence: "Neither land nor freedom." The ball, Lenin wrote, was back now not in the Cadets' court but that of the real protagonists. "We shall see whether the deputies to the Duma learn anything from this declaration. The Cadets will certainly learn nothing from it. The Trudovik and Workers' Groups must now show whether they have become at all independent of the Cadets—whether they have realized that it is necessary to give up petitioning—whether they are able to talk straightforwardly and clearly to the people."[77]

Lenin, of course, was not disposed to wait to "see" if the deputies "learn anything" or to "see" if "they are able to talk straightforwardly and clearly to the people." Through the pages of *Volna* he campaigned to make that a reality. "This is not," contrary to what the Cadets claimed,

> a parliamentary conflict, and the Duma itself is far from being a parliament as yet . . . It is only an indicator and a very feeble reflector of the people's movement, which is growing outside or independently of the Duma. The Duma's conflict with the government is only an *indirect* indication of the conflict between all the fundamental and mature aspirations of the masses of the peasantry and the working class and the whole intact power of the old regime . . . The Trudovik and Workers' Groups in the Duma must know that only by dissociating themselves from the Cadets, only by rising above schoolroom lessons in constitutionalism, only by loudly proclaiming all the demands and needs of the people, only by speaking the whole bitter truth, can they make their greatest contribution to the struggle for real freedom.[78]

Marxist as opposed to liberal civic lessons—this is what Lenin provided through positive encouragement to the "novices" he wanted to influence.

Again, he took advantage of the remaining political space to forge the worker-peasant alliance.

When the Trudoviks tried to get a vote on a bill abolishing capital punishment but were thwarted by the Cadets, Lenin immediately came to their defense. He quoted two of the Trudovik deputies, one of whom was a priest, and applauded what they proposed. It was "perfectly clear: appeal to the people, make demands and not requests, ignore the bureaucratic regulations, don't drag out questions, and don't send them to committees." Employing, however, what the Cadet Chair of the Duma said were the "rules of parliamentary procedure," the Trudovik initiative came to naught. "The Cadets prevented the Duma from appealing to the people . . . Evidently the Trudovik Group again yielded to the opportunities and threats of the Cadets, and did not keep to the resolute position it at first took up. The people, who realize the meaning of the struggle for freedom, must protest the Cadets' behavior in the Duma and call upon the Trudovik Group resolutely and emphatically to declare that it will appeal to the people and to *do so*!"[79] While denouncing the Cadets, Lenin displayed patience with the Trudoviks. Sidetracking them was just the most recent example for him of Cadet appeasement of the regime, and he continued to try to make them pay a price. To that end he publicized in *Volna* that the progovernment press gloated over the fact that the Cadets had outmaneuvered the Trudoviks.[80]

As Lenin had predicted, "the Cadets will certainly learn nothing from" the regime's rejection of their address. He responded with ridicule to the outrage of Struve, the one-time "Marxist" and now Cadet leader, over the government's dismissal. "They Won't Even Bargain!," the title of his sarcastic commentary on Struve's article, highlighted what caught Lenin's eye and got his ire up. Struve admitted that the Cadets had tried unsuccessfully to negotiate with the government over the demands in their address, including those in both the "political" and "economic spheres." The former referred to civil liberties, universal suffrage, and amnesty, and the latter to the land requisitions and confiscations. Had the government, Struve complained, shown more "statesmanship," a deal could have been reached. "Mark that well, workers and peasants!" warned Lenin; "the Cadet gentlemen believed 'statesmanship' to consist in striking a bargain with [D.F.] Trepov [Governor of St. Petersburg] over a curtailment of the people's demands expressed in the Address." No deal was possible, he argued, because the "conflicting interests" of the "proletariat and peasantry" on one side and those of the "old regime" on the other could never be reconciled. "That is precisely why the gentlemen who are trading in the people's freedom, and who serve as brokers during the revolution and as diplomats in time of war, are doomed to be disappointed again and again."[81] The prescience of Lenin's words would soon become evident.

About three weeks after the Duma convened, the "Workers' Group" issued an appeal "To All Workers of Russia." *Volna* printed it and Lenin added commentary: "We warmly welcome the manifesto of the Workers' Group of Duma deputies, who stand closer to us in their convictions than any other group. This is the first appeal that Duma deputies have made, not to the government, but directly to the people. The example of the workers' deputies should, in our opinion, have been followed by the Trudovik, or Peasant, Group in the Duma." Though I can't prove it, the appeal was likely the first concrete fruit of Lenin's Duma work.[82] Ten days earlier, in his very first advice to the fraction, he hoped that it—and the Trudovik fraction as well—would "take a stand different from that of the Cadets." Their appeal was a step in that direction and he applauded them. But along with positive reinforcement came constructive criticism: "[T]o strive to make the Duma prepare for the convocation of a constituent assembly," as the statement put it, was problematic—one of its "flaws." Only the Trudoviks and not the rest of the Duma parties, specifically the Cadets, should be looked to for the realization of a constituent assembly. "[T]he Russian liberals are too unreliable. The workers would, therefore, do better to concentrate on supporting the *peasant deputies*, in order to stimulate them to speak out independently, and to act like real representatives of the revolutionary peasantry."

Then Lenin called attention to the all-important "outside." The working class was "mustering its forces to launch another determined struggle, but to launch it only together with the peasantry. The workers' deputies are therefore right in calling upon the proletariat not to allow itself to be provoked by anyone, and not to enter, unless really necessary, into isolated collisions with the enemy. Proletarian blood is too precious to shed needlessly and without certain hope of victory."[83] Crucial in understanding Lenin's politics in this moment, especially his attitude toward the Duma, is exactly this fact—the very real probability of a new upsurge in the revolution. But to avoid what happened in Moscow in December— a defeat—coordinated action of both the proletariat and peasantry was necessary this time; thus his admonition, "launch it only together with the peasantry." What isn't certain is whether this is what was actually being organized or whether this is what Lenin was hoping would be organized. Whatever the case, Lenin, in pointing to the "workers' deputies," clearly felt that they could play a key role in helping to forge a worker-peasant alliance for the next upsurge and thus guarantee its success.

The Workers' Group manifesto illustrated another advantage of Duma work. The debates within Tauride Palace—unlike, sometimes, those on the outside—required competing parties to clarify and articulate their views, a necessary step for Lenin in the political education of the masses. "The more frequent and sharp these collisions become, the more definitely the masses of the people see the differences between the liberal landlords, factory owners, lawyers and professors—and the peasants."[84] Thus he was pleased when on or about May 23 the Trudoviks finally formulated their positions on not just the agrarian question but the political one as well—exactly what he had urged in applauding the Workers' Group for issuing its appeal a few days earlier. In a most didactic article for *Volna* readers, he was able to compare and contrast Cadet, RSDLP, and Trudovik views and, hence, provide advice for the Workers' Group. Regarding their "political programme . . . The Trudovik Group accepts almost in its entirety the workers' minimum programme, including an eight-hour day, etc. Obviously . . . the workers' party must support the Trudoviks in opposition to the Cadets."

While the Trudoviks, on the land question, "*go further* than the Cadets in the struggle against landlordism, and against the private ownership of land in general," they err as do the Cadets in thinking that the "landlord state" can be utilized for real agrarian reform. Yet it would be a "gross error" for the workers' party to "not support [them] in opposition to the Cadets. The fact that both parties are mistaken should not serve as an excuse for refusing to support the genuinely revolutionary bourgeois democrats." The Trudoviks are also mistaken to believe that "equalization" of land is the solution for small peasants, since this would be "impossible so long as the rule of money, the rule of capital exists." Lenin then put the differences between them and the Cadets in long-term perspective: "The Cadet illusions are an obstacle to the victory of the bourgeois revolution. The Trudoviks' mistakes will be an obstacle to the immediate victory of socialism (but the workers are not uselessly dreaming about an immediate victory for socialism). Hence the vast difference between the Cadets and the Trudoviks; and the workers' party must take this difference strictly into account."[85] Note that his advice was meant not just for the Duma fraction but the party as a whole—essential to his electoral strategy. Lenin's qualifier "but" underscores, once again, that for him it was the bourgeois revolution that was on Russia's agenda and not, as is so often alleged, the overturn of capitalism.

A day or so after the Trudoviks revealed their program, 35 of their deputies signed on to a motion that called for "for the immediate establishment of land committees, local, freely elected committees for settling the land question." The Workers' Group, Lenin proudly reported, "to a

man took the side of the peasants against the bureaucrats and liberals."
Although the Cadets were eventually successful in convincing the 35 to
withdraw the motion, Lenin saw their "success" as a victory for the campaign for the worker-peasant alliance. "We compelled them to admit in
public that *they do not want to give the peasants complete freedom and all
the land, and that they seek to aid the bureaucrats against the peasants.*"[86]
Clarifying and sharpening the political differences was, again, what the
Duma arena could provide, thus increasing the political maturity of
the working class.

One of the advantages Lenin had in appealing to the Trudoviks is that
the Socialist Revolution Party boycotted the Duma. Founded in 1901, it
was, as noted in Chapter 2, essentially the Narodniks reinvented with a
socialist veneer. Their audience, in theory, was the peasantry and hence
why land equalization was one of their shibboleths. But by maintaining their boycott—terrorism was their preferred modus operandi—the
Socialist Revolutionaries allowed the Bolsheviks free reign in bringing
a social democratic agenda to the peasantry in the electoral arena.

THE FIGHT OVER THE DUMA MINISTRY

In the previously mentioned admission, Struve didn't say what the government put, if anything, on the table for negotiations with the Cadets
over their address. And though Lenin didn't have access to the particulars,
he was right to assume that they were doing exactly as he had charged—
"trading in the people's freedom." Documents unearthed years later
revealed that the regime pursued a two-prong bargaining strategy with the
Cadets, with neither of the two sets of parties aware what the other was
doing—why, in part, the negotiations collapsed.[87] The issue in contention
had to do with a key demand in the Cadet address—the call for a council
of ministers responsible to the Duma. While an executive branch of government responsible to the legislative branch was the norm in parliamentary government, the Duma, as Lenin never ceased to remind the working
class and peasantry, was only an illusory parliament; only a constituent
assembly, he had long argued, offered a chance for a real parliament. The
Cadets, Lenin charged, wanted to put the cart of the parliament before
the horse of the democratic republic. Nicholas, too, gave a reality check
in his terse remarks to its opening session: Russia was an "autocracy" that
he would defend "with unwavering firmness." Because the last thing the
Cadets wanted to do was mobilize the "crowd" on the "outside," Nicholas's
stance was the real reason for the unsuccessful negotiations and the eventual downfall of the Cadets. Lenin welcomed every bit of news, sometimes

prematurely, that confirmed the Cadets' deal-making efforts. "What thou doest, do quickly," he advised the "Cadet gentlemen." It would only accelerate the political education of the proletariat and peasantry.

The Cadets, nevertheless, tried to garner support from other parties for a Duma ministry that effectively would have become a Cadet-led ministry, since they were the largest party in the body. Their efforts struck a responsive chord with some of the Mensheviks. Lenin therefore had to wage a campaign against the Menshevik line both in and outside the Duma. This was no mean feat since the Mensheviks constituted a majority of the RSDLP Central Committee, which in theory guided the work of the Duma fraction. Fighting for the ear of the fraction meant using not only his writings but—it should be assumed, since Lenin was now based in St. Petersburg—face-to-face contacts with its members.

The debate with the Mensheviks was not about the character of the coming Russian Revolution. Both wings of the party agreed that it would be a bourgeois democratic one. The heart of the debate concerned who among the bourgeois forces the working class should look to ally with to bring it about. Lenin argued—his 1905 *Two Tactics* pamphlet being his most detailed elaboration—that only the peasantry, bourgeois to the core owing to their quest to become individual land owners, had the interest and capability of being loyal allies. With Plekhanov leading the way, the Mensheviks, on the other hand, looked to the liberal bourgeoisie and therefore the Cadets. For Plekhanov, Lenin's denunciation of the Cadets for their "treachery" in its negotiations with the regime was ill timed. It threatened to undermine the legitimacy of the Cadets and thus the Duma itself. As the regime increasingly sent signals that it might "disperse" the Duma, Plekhanov and other Mensheviks felt even more compelled to defend the Cadets and the Duma. Not for want did Lenin accuse them of becoming cheerleaders for the Cadets and "chasing the *shadow* of parliamentarism." In so doing Plekhanov was providing "bad advice" for both the working class and the Duma fraction. "Comrade Plekhanov has wholly and completely taken on the likeness of the average German Cadet in the Frankfurt Parliament. Oh, how many matchless speeches these windbags delivered on the political consciousness of the people! How many magnificent 'constructive' laws they drafted for this purpose!" Parliamentary cretinism had claimed another victim. And then strikingly prophetic, drawing on the fate, again, of the Frankfurt Assembly in 1850, Lenin wrote, "And how nobly they protested when they were dispersed *after* they had bored the people to death and had lost all revolutionary importance."[88] He probably didn't know, once again, how imminent his forecast was.

In a direct challenge to the Menshevik line of the Central Committee on the Cadets, the St. Petersburg Committee of the RSDLP, where the Bolsheviks had a majority, adopted a resolution drafted by Lenin that opposed the Cadets' call for a ministry responsible to the Duma. "For the Cadets use the demand . . . as a screen to hide their desire to strike a bargain with the autocratic government and to weaken the revolution, to hamper the convocation of a constituent assembly." Instead of a Duma ministry, the resolution resolved "that the proletariat supports the idea of forming an Executive Committee consisting of representatives of the revolutionary elements in the Duma, for the purpose of coordinating the activities of the local free organizations of the peoples."[89] The Duma then, for Lenin, could be a site for organizing the worker-peasant alliance—his first explicit suggestion.

The St. Petersburg Committee resolution, not surprisingly, provoked an internal party debate on procedural issues. Lenin argued, against the opinion of the Central Committee, that party local committees could "work out independently . . . their own directives" as long as they were consistent with the resolutions adopted at the Fourth Congress. At issue was not only the substantive question regarding the Cadets and the Duma but also the need to sustain internal party democracy. "The St. Petersburg worker Social-Democrats know that the whole Party organization is now built on a *democratic* basis. This means that *all* the Party members take part in the election of officials, committee members, and so forth, that *all* the Party members discuss and *decide* questions concerning the political campaigns of the proletariat, and that *all* the Party members *determine* the line of tactics of the Party organisations."[90] Democratic centralism, as this debate revealed, was clearly a work in progress.

Nothing for Lenin demonstrated more the need to shatter "constitutional illusions" about the Duma than the pogrom from June 1 to 3 in Belostok (Bialystok) in Polish Russia, in which more than eighty people were killed, almost all Jews. Lenin's June 3 article in *Vperyod* [*Forward*] (the Bolsheviks' new daily since *Volna* had been shut down by the regime), "The Reaction is Taking to Arms," put the slaughter in context. "The Social-Democratic press has long been pointing out that the vaunted 'constitutionalism' in Russia is baseless and ephemeral. So long as the old authority remains and controls the whole vast machinery of state administration, it is useless talking seriously about the importance of popular representation and about satisfying the urgent needs of the vast masses of the people. No sooner had the State Duma begun its sittings—and liberal-bourgeois oratory about peaceful, constitutional evolution burst forth in a particularly turbulent flood—than there began an increasing number of attacks on peaceful demonstrators, cases of setting fire to halls where public meetings were proceeding, and lastly, downright pogroms—all organised by government agents." The Belostok pogrom was the most horrendous attack so far.

After disparaging the usual way in which the "investigation" of pogroms had been carried out, Lenin struck a positive note: "The Duma did the right thing by immediately discussing the interpellation on the Belostok pogrom, and sending some of its members to Belostok to investigate on the spot. But"—Lenin's now-familiar "but"—"the government's take on what took place and the Duma's discussion of it were appallingly lacking given the history of such 'investigations.'"

> Judge for yourselves. The authors of the interpellation say: "The inhabitants *fear* that the local authorities and malicious agitators may try to make out the victims themselves to be responsible for the calamity that has befallen them." "False information on these lines is being circulated." Yes, the downtrodden and tormented Jewish population is indeed apprehensive of this, and has every reason to be. This is true. But it is *not the whole truth*, gentlemen, members of the Duma, and authors of the interpellation! You, the people's deputies, who have not yet been assaulted and tormented, know perfectly well that this is not the whole truth. You know that the downtrodden inhabitants will *not dare* to name those who are *really responsible* for the pogrom. *You must name them.* That is what you are people's deputies for. That is why you enjoy—even under Russian law—complete freedom of speech in the Duma. Then don't stand *between* the reaction and the people, at a time when the armed reaction is strangling, massacring, and mutilating unarmed people. Take your stand *openly and entirely* on the side of the people . . . *Indict the culprits in unequivocal terms—it* is your direct *duty* to the people. Don't ask the government whether measures are being taken to protect the Jews and to prevent pogroms . . . Indict the government openly and publicly; call upon the people to organize a militia and self-defense as the *only* means of protection against pogroms.
>
> This is not in keeping with "parliamentary practice," you will say . . . Don't you realize that the people will condemn you if, even at a time like this, you do not give up playing at parliaments and do not dare to say straightforwardly, openly and loudly what *you really know and think?*

The speeches of some of the Cadet deputies, Lenin insisted, justified his impatience. He applauded "Citizen Levin" for pointing out how "the whole system," including the police who distributed leaflets, was involved in organizing the pogroms. "Quite right, citizen Levin! But while in newspapers we can only speak of the 'system,' you in the Duma ought to speak out more plainly and sharply . . . [Y]ou should have said in your interpellation: does the government think that the Duma is not aware of the commonly-known fact that the gendarmes and police send out those leaflets?" Last, he pleaded with the "gentlemen of the Duma . . . *to associate the reactionary government with the progromists!*"[91]

Noteworthy, immediately, about Lenin's impassioned plea in defense of Russian Jewry is that it was directed at mainly the Cadets. Before, his Duma audience had always been the workers and/or peasant deputies. It may be recalled that in his pamphlet on the Cadet Duma victory he entertained the possibility of joint work with the Cadets in order "to isolate reaction." For the particular issue of effectively opposing pogroms, an alliance with the liberal bourgeoisie was a necessity. His efforts signaled, to be confirmed shortly, increasing recognition that the unique potential value of the Duma as a political space—freedom of the press, for example—was shrinking. But that possibility had to be fought for—exactly what he was doing here.

THE DUMA'S FINAL DAYS: A NEW ROLE FOR THE FRACTION

"The Social-Democratic Group in the State Duma is on the eve of taking action. Undoubtedly, this Group can now render the cause of the working-class movement and of the revolution a great service by its bold and consistent utterance, by proclaiming with unmistakable clarity the demands and slogans of *consistent* democracy and of the *proletarian* class struggle for socialism." With this Lenin informed *Vperyod* readers on June 10 that the Duma fraction would now play a more central role in RSDLP tactics. "And we think that our Caucasian comrades were quite right to sign the notorious 'solemn pledge' of the members of the State Duma and to state in the press in this connection that 'we are signing this in order to be able to fulfill the mission with which the people have entrusted us, and we emphasise that the only political obligations we recognise are obligations to the people.'" The "solemn pledge" was basically an oath of fealty to the Czar that all Duma deputies were required to make. But since the Duma didn't have real power, no principles were at stake. More important, the fraction, by signing on, could with its immunity be the effective voice for the party as political space was diminishing.

As rumors grew that the regime was about to pull the plug on the Duma, accompanied by a new upsurge in rebellion in the countryside and in the barracks, the fraction came under increasing pressure from the Cadets and thus the Mensheviks to come to its defense. Lenin therefore had to be especially vigilant about the Menshevik-dominated Central Committee's instructions to the fraction. Careful not to appear sectarian or to violate the norms of democratic centralism, his modus operandi vis-à-vis the fraction was a combination of positive reinforcement and constructive criticism: "We regard it as our duty to note their successes in the Duma and to criticize—in a business-like way—their mistakes." He agreed, for example, with the advice in *Kuryer* [*Courier*], the Menshevik daily (*Nevskaya Gazeta* had been shut down by the government), that the fraction should avoid getting sucked into the minutia of law making: "Such activities, customarily called 'constructive' are certainly *harmful*. They are harmful 'because instead of presenting striking contrasts that everyone can see, such Bills *hopelessly confuse* the mind of the public with a welter of clauses and paragraphs' . . . This is quite true . . . This project-mongering obscures, blunts and corrupts the mind of the public, for 'in any case, these laws will never be put into operation. Before that can be done, *power must be wrested* from the hands of those who now hold it [in order to] . . . put in the place of the Duma itself a *far more powerful and democratic institution*.'" Rather than the Cadets' "project-mongering" and their bills, social democracy could be more effective by means of "'decrees,' 'proclamations' and appeals to the people through the medium of the Social-Democratic Group in the Duma (and, under certain conditions, with Trudoviks acting in conjunction with it), and by issuing those 'calls to the people to form a popular militia, which alone will be capable of protecting their lives and honour.'"[92] Lenin advised the Mensheviks that taking such action would ensure not just party "unity" but the "unity of the political actions of the proletariat."

The next day Lenin offered more positive reinforcement—with a "but." For the first time he quoted extensively and approvingly the intervention of a fraction member, one of the Caucasus comrades, in the Duma deliberations. "Comrade Ramishivili" declared that the Duma was increasingly becoming irrelevant and that what was taking place on the "outside" would, prophetically, in "a month from now, perhaps" be decisive. The ineluctable tendency of the Cadets to seek "conciliation" with "the old regime," Lenin argued, explained what the comrade accurately noted. Any support therefore for their demand for a Duma ministry was to be complicit in their effort to cut a deal with the regime—a "peaceful solution" to the crisis—and, thus a betrayal of the "fighting people." Hence the "but." "Yesterday we pointed out that the comrades of *Kuryer* were right in stating that the Bills drafted by the Cadets were stupid and harmful. Today it is to be regretted that these same comrades are advocating support for a Duma Cabinet, that is to say, a Cabinet that will carry through these stupid and harmful Bills!"[93] It's not that Lenin was surprised at the support the "comrades" offered to the Cadets. He knew there was a fundamental political divide that separated him from the Mensheviks—two very different assessments of which component of the bourgeoisie to look to, the peasantry or the liberal bourgeoisie. And until most workers recognized that fact, he had to at least appear to be comradely. Their actions were merely "regretted"—at least for now.

A day or so after accusing the Cadets of trying to find "a peaceful solution" to the crisis, *Vperyod* was shut down by the regime. Readers of the new Bolshevik daily *Ekho* [*Echo*], which debuted on June 22, learned that Lenin tried unsuccessfully to have the RSDLP fraction employ a draft he wrote for its first major public declaration in the Duma. It emphasized, among other well-known Bolshevik views, the necessity of the worker-peasant alliance and the international character of the RSDLP. But the fraction rejected Lenin's document and instead read from one drafted by the Central Committee. He admitted that from a "formal point of view"—that is, the party rules on organization—and from a "factional point of view," the Menshevik-dominated Central Committee had every right to insist that its version be read. But from a "Party point of view," he argued that the Bolshevik document was more faithful to the resolutions adopted at the Fourth Congress. All party members were asked to weigh the not-too-subtle differences of the two, especially concerning what attitude to take toward the Duma: "an organ of the popular movement" in the Central Committee version versus "*an instrument of the revolution*" in the Bolshevik version.

In what Lenin had hoped the fraction would read, he made an important admission: "In spite of the autocracy's gerrymandering electoral law, its massacre, torture and imprisonment of the finest fighters for freedom, the State Duma, after all, turned out to be hostile to the autocracy."[94] About a week later Lenin offered an explanation for this unanticipated outcome. In a continued defense of the boycott, he contended that the tactic required the government to "fight *for* the convocation of the Duma," and with its attention directed against the boycotters it made it possible for the "liberal bourgeoisie and non-party revolutionaries . . . to [get] into the enemy's rear and stealthily [make] its way into the Duma, penetrating the enemy camp in disguise."[95] The autocracy also recognized what Lenin admitted to—thus its need, increasingly, to pull the plug.

The phenomenon that radicalized the young Lenin, famine, was afflicting Russian peasants once again and with deadly consequences, though not of the same magnitude as the famine of 1891. This time he was in a position to possibly shape its outcome through the Duma fraction. "First of all we will remind the reader that the question that originally arose in the State Duma was the following: Would it be right to grant money to the government of pogrom-mongers, or should the Duma itself take the whole business of famine relief into its own hands?" He, as well as the fraction, applauded the leading Trudovik deputy for wanting to do the latter. But unfortunately the Cadets, through parliamentary maneuvering, derailed that initiative. Lenin faulted the fraction deputies, "a mistake," for not coming to the aid of the Trudoviks in that moment. He charged the Cadets with wanting to trade off real famine relief for posts in the cabinet. "The Duma refused to become the instrument of the revolution in this matter."

Since the Cadets could not be expected to offer a real solution to the famine, the "Social-Democratic deputies," Lenin wrote, would have to take the lead in alliance with the Trudoviks, whose constituents were most affected by the crisis. He then outlined a set of proposals for the fraction on how to effectively discuss the question in the Duma—his most detailed and context-specific instructions to date for the fraction. They revealed how savvy he was about the legislative process, including his knowledge about the Duma committees. Lenin was under no illusion that the crisis could be resolved without a fundamental reordering of Russian society—just as he had concluded some 15 years earlier. But at least "[v]oices will then be heard from the rostrum of the Duma relentlessly exposing the double game the Cadets are playing, exposing all the 'secrets' of the Russian Budget of the police pogrom-mongers—a Budget which squanders tens and hundreds of millions on assistance for landlords and capitalists, on military adventures, on 'relief' for spies and gendarmes, on rewarding all the high-placed heroes of the Manchurian tragedy [the Russo-Japanese War], and on maintaining a horde of thieving officials who tyrannise over the people"—a necessary step in that reordering.[96]

A few days later Lenin applauded the fraction for its intervention and resolve in the debate on the famine. "They spoke on the lines we suggested the other day"—the first fruit of his efforts to employ the parliamentary rostrum for revolutionary ends. The fraction's vote against channeling famine funding through the government may be explained by the fact that about a week earlier the St. Petersburg Committee in which Lenin and the Bolsheviks were dominant "decided to establish a permanent liaison between [it] . . . and the Social-Democratic Group in the Duma."[97] Particularly gratifying was that "the Trudoviks voted with the Social-Democrats." The only problem for Lenin, ever the stickler for details, was that "a roll-call vote was not taken."[98] In trying to forge the worker-peasant alliance, he needed the names of individual deputies.

In countering the pro-Cadet sympathies of the Mensheviks, Lenin had to address the all-very-familiar "lesser of two evils" or "shouldn't we be grateful for a few crumbs" argument. Isn't a Cadet ministry a lesser evil than the autocracy's ministry? Aren't some reforms better than none at all? "This is how all the opportunists, all the reformists argue; unlike the revolutionaries . . . all over the world. To what conclusions does this argument inevitably lead? To the conclusion that we need no revolutionary program, no revolutionary party, and no revolutionary tactics. What we need are *reforms*, nothing more." Two very different assumptions, Lenin explained didactically, informed the reformist and revolutionary perspectives, and the logic of the latter called for independent working-class political action:

> Only by such tactics can real progress be achieved in the matter of impor-
> tant reforms. This may sound paradoxical, but its truth is confirmed by the
> whole history of the international Social-Democratic movement. Reformist
> tactics are the *least* likely to secure real reforms. The most effective way to
> secure real reforms is to pursue the tactics of the revolutionary class struggle.
> *Actually*, reforms are won as a result of the revolutionary class struggle, as a
> result of its independence, mass force and steadfastness. Reforms are *always*
> false, ambiguous . . . they are real only in proportion to the intensity of the
> class struggle. By merging our slogans with those of the reformist bourgeoi-
> sie we *weaken* the cause of revolution *and, consequently, the cause of reform as
> well*, because we thereby diminish the independence, fortitude and strength
> of the revolutionary classes.

These were the lessons that "many Menshevik comrades tend to forget" in their support to the Cadet ministry. "Only if we pursue such ['rev-olutionary'] tactics will history say about us what Bismarck said about the German Social-Democrats: 'If there were no Social-Democrats there would have been no social reform.' Had there not been a *revolutionary* proletariat there would have been no October 17" and hence no Duma.[99] If Lenin's argument strikes a contemporary chord, it's because it helps explain the reformist outcome, with the German party in the lead, of Western European social democracy, a phenomenon whose early signs he witnessed and whose consequences resonate today. Not for naught did he feel compelled to wage a fight against the "Russian Bernsteinians."

Outside the Duma things were heating up. The "peasant war on the manors had revived in the spring with a ferocity equal to the previous autumn's."[100] Sailors and soldiers were becoming restless, and workers met to plan their next assault. This was the context for the Social Revolution-aries' proposal to reinstitute the Soviets of Workers' Deputies, the bodies that led the uprisings in St. Petersburg and Moscow in the fall. George Khrustalev-Nosar, the Menshevik chair of the St. Petersburg Soviet, sup-ported the SR call; Trotsky, his deputy but real chair, was still in jail. The Bolshevik-led St. Petersburg Committee disagreed with the proposal and passed a resolution to that effect.

Nevertheless, *Ekho* opened its pages to Khrustalev-Nosar to make his case, and in the same issue Lenin explained what was wrong with reviving the Soviets. Basically, it was premature to do so. Soviets, he argued, were instruments designed to organize a proletariat in battle. The overriding task of the moment, he contended, was to organize the peasantry to do battle *together* with the proletariat. October and December 1905 taught that unless the proletariat is accompanied in struggle by the peasantry, the overwhelming majority of Russia's producing class, the proletariat could not be victorious. Revolutionary restraint was what was required of the proletariat in order to bring the peasantry on board, to make sure the "rear-guard" caught up with the "vanguard." And to that end Lenin pointed to the resolution the St. Petersburg Committee adopted on June 5, its alternative to the Cadet ministry: "to support the idea of forming an Executive Committee representing the Left groups in the Duma for the purpose of coordinating the activities of the free organizations of the people."[101] The Duma, in other words, or more correctly a portion of it, would be the site for organizing the next stage of the revolution. This strikingly registers how far Lenin had shifted his views about the utility of the Duma.

On June 20 the regime threw down the gauntlet again; as always, the land question loomed large. In its "appeal to the people," and not the Duma—a not-too-subtle hint about what it thought of the crowd in Tauride Palace—the autocracy made clear that it was not about to give an inch to satisfy the land needs of the peasants. In Lenin's assessment, "It is an actual declaration of war on the revolution. It is an actual manifesto of the reactionary autocracy saying to the people: We shall tolerate no nonsense! We shall crush you!" The Cadets, with the Trudoviks "unfortunately" in tow, a few weeks later read drafts of their "appeal to the people" to the Duma—that is, their responses. "What a miserable, truly pitiful impression these two drafts create! . . . For shame, gentlemen, representatives of the people!" Obviously, Lenin was not impressed. If not a gauntlet, he issued a challenge: "But there are the Social-Democrats in the Duma; will they not come to the rescue?" He then offered a social democratic "appeal to the people" in five paragraphs addressed to "Peasants!" It called on them to recognize "that the Duma is powerless to give you land and freedom . . . Utilize your deputies in the Duma . . . unite more closely and solidly all over Russia and prepare for a great struggle . . . Peasants! We are doing all we can for you in the Duma. But you must complete the job yourselves." Lenin ended with another challenge: "Let the Cadets' appeal, the Trudoviks' appeal and our appeal be read at any peasant meeting! We will hear what the peasants say in answer to the question: Who is right?"[102]

The debate in the Duma the next day, July 5, encouraged Lenin, because the "intrinsic nature of the different political parties was revealed with a clarity that left nothing to be desired." He felt his articles, especially the one the day before, contributed to that clarification. They provided "the whole Left wing of the Duma" with needed ammunition to "come to the rescue." "Lednitsky," a Polish deputy, "even employed one of the sharpest expressions that we employed yesterday, and said that the proposed appeal was '*pitiful*.'" A Trudovik deputy argued just as Lenin had done in the afore-mentioned article on reforms and revolution: "'Did the State Duma come into being as the result of peace and tranquility?' And, recalling the October struggle, the speaker, amidst the applause of the Left, exclaimed: 'It is due to these "disorders" that we are here today.'" The debate, Lenin contended, marked real progress for social democracy in the Duma. "In spite of all the efforts of the Right-wing Social-Democrats, up to now there has not resulted any support of the Cadets, but what has resulted fortunately, is an independent policy of the proletariat backed by a section of the peasant deputies." The only shortcoming of the fraction—Lenin, ever vigil—was not to have read its own "appeal to the people." In the next session he urged them to do just that: "A Social-Democratic draft of an appeal to the people, even if it remains only a draft read in the Duma, will have an extremely valuable effect in uniting and developing the revolutionary struggle, and will win over to the side of Social-Democracy the finest elements of the revolutionary peasantry."[103] They wouldn't get that opportunity.

On the following day the government issued a none-too-veiled threat through one of its dailies that not only would it pull the plug on the Duma if it persisted in an "appeal to the people," but it would also invite the armies of Austria and possibly Germany to enter Russia to finally put an end to the revolution. While the Cadets, not surprisingly, quickly retreated, Lenin advanced:

> [W]e too have our powerful international reserve: the socialist proletariat of Europe, organised in the three million-strong party in Germany, in the powerful parties of all the European countries. We welcome the appeal of our government to the international reserve of reaction: such an appeal will, in the first place, open the eyes of the most ignorant people in Russia and do us a valuable service by destroying faith in the monarchy, and, in the second place, such an appeal will better than anything else extend the basis and field of action of the Russian revolution by converting it into a world revolution. All right, Mr. Trepov & Co.! Open fire! Call on your Austrian and German regiments against the Russian peasants and workers! We are for an extension of the struggle, we are for an international revolution![104]

I suspect Lenin knew this would be the last issue of *Ekho*. Not unlike the famous last issue of Marx and Engels's *Neue Rheinische Zeitung* in the final days of the 1848–49 revolutions, he decided to go out with a bang. Whether he actually believed "our international reserve" was prepared to defend the

Russian revolution is impossible to know; I think not. But such a scenario accurately pointed out that proletarian internationalism was the way forward for the revolution's survival—not only then but in 1917, as I'll argue—and Lenin had nothing to lose and much to gain in making such a boast.

A day later *Ekho*, indeed, was shut down. A similar fate awaited the Duma. On July 8, the following day, the autocracy ended, unceremoniously, the brief but instructive life of Russia's first ersatz parliament. It cannot be said with certainty if Lenin's increasingly confrontational interventions explain the timing of the regime's dissolution of the Duma. But because it had for some time been looking for an excuse to do so, he may very well have provided them that opportunity.

Totally surprised by what happened, the Cadets retreated to Vyborg in Finland to lick their wounds. The best they could muster was a manifesto registering their indignation and a few false threats. Just as Lenin had so accurately predicted—"how nobly they protested when they were dispersed *after* they had bored the people to death and had lost all revolutionary importance"—their brief moment in the sun ended ignominiously. It recalls Engels's forecast about a similar party of liberals (that included Alexis de Tocqueville) who were also unceremoniously dismissed by an autocrat— Louis Bonaparte when he dissolved the French National Assembly in 1851. They would "hide themselves in the darkest corner of their houses, or be scattered like dead leaves before the popular thunderstorm."[105] Such insight served Lenin well in his first real test in the cauldron of revolution.

***

It took Lenin almost a month, owing to the crackdown, to get something into print that assessed what happened. In a twenty-page pamphlet, he began with the obvious: "The dissolution of the Duma has most strikingly and clearly confirmed the views of those who warned against being obsessed with the external 'constitutional' aspect of the Duma . . . the constitutional surface of Russian politics during the second quarter of 1906 . . . Note this interesting fact: the Duma has been dissolved *on strictly constitutional grounds*. It has not been 'dispersed.' There has been no infringement of the law. On the contrary, it has been done strictly in accordance with the law, as under any 'constitutional monarchy' . . . The logic of life is stronger than the logic of textbooks on constitutional law. Revolution teaches." Because the Cadets' Duma delegation counted so many professors among its ranks, Lenin, who never tired of doing so, got a dig in on those reared on "textbooks," not unlike Engels's cutting critique of the "professors" in the Frankfurt Assembly in 1849.

Yet despite having been proven right by "life," Lenin declined to gloat: "The Social-Democrats will neither exult (we made some use even of the Duma) nor lose heart. The people gained . . . by losing one of its illusions . . . All laws and all deputies are *naught* if they possess no power. That is what the Cadet Duma *has taught* the people. Let us then sing praises to the eternal memory of the deceased, and take full advantage of the lesson it has taught." Lenin held the deep conviction that the working masses had the capacity to learn, and that his task was to make sure that happened.[106]

Lenin's admission that "we made some use even of the Duma" speaks to a still more important lesson: "The Cadet Duma imagined that it was a constitutional organ, but it *was* in fact a revolutionary organ (the Cadets abused us for regarding the Duma as a stage or an instrument of the revolution, but experience has fully confirmed *our view*)." Thus the Duma did in fact—through Lenin's efforts—become a useful "instrument" in the revolutionary process, which is why it was dissolved. Unlike his response to the boycott of the First Duma, Lenin, to be seen in the next chapter, actively opposed fellow Bolsheviks who wanted to boycott the Second Duma exactly because of what the first experience had demonstrated: the potential utility of the Duma in the "revolutionary task of the struggle for *power*."[107]

Commenting some nine decades later on the Cadets' fall from grace, historian Orlando Figes—no friend of Lenin—confidently described their subsequent trajectory: "Never again would the Kadets place their trust in the support of 'the people.' Nor would they claim to represent them. From this point on, they would consciously become what in fact they had been all along: the natural party of the bourgeoisie. Liberalism and the people went their separate ways."[108] But that's the benefit of hindsight. In real time such wisdom wasn't so apparent. Not every RSDLP leader saw as Lenin did what the Cadets "had been all along." He was able to do so because he had so thoroughly grasped the lessons Marx and Engels bequeathed. This required knowing how to apply these lessons to concrete situations—that is, comprehending their methodology. And not the least important lesson, that of the 1848–49 European Spring, was that the liberal bourgeoisie could no longer be expected to carry out the bourgeois democratic revolution. The example of Plekhanov taught, tragically, that being familiar as he was with their teachings did not guarantee wisdom; they had to be mastered. In the end, the rich arsenal Marx and Engels left behind and the actual behavior of the Cadets are what gave Lenin the deserved confidence to say on more than one occasion about them, "Whatever thou doest, do quickly."

Though brief in existence, the First Duma allowed Lenin to cut his teeth on parliamentary work. That would serve him well for round two.

CHAPTER 4

FROM REVOLUTION
TO "COUP D'ÉTAT"

THE SECOND DUMA

IN HIS UKASE DISSOLVING THE DUMA ON July 8, 1906, Nicholas decreed that another would be convened the following year on February 20. This chapter begins by describing Lenin's response to that decree: he took the necessary steps to avoid the "awkward" situation the Russian Social Democratic Labor Party found itself in when the First Duma convened. He was determined that this time the Bolsheviks would contest the elections and be prepared to form a party fraction or group should they be successful. Indeed, the party as a whole made significant gains, and Lenin made every effort to use the Duma "rostrum" to advance what was left of the revolution in order to forge the worker-peasant alliance. Only in hindsight was it clear that not much of the revolution remained in place. The Czar's dissolution of the Second Duma after only three months in existence registered that fact—the end of the Revolution of 1905.

TOWARD THE SECOND DUMA

Within days of the Czar's decision to pull the plug on Russia's first experiment with parliamentary government, the half-year-long simmering from below boiled over. Sailors at Sveaborg near Helsingfors (Helsinki) and Kronstadt mutinied. Lenin and the St. Petersburg Committee did all they could to put a lid on it—"to secure a postponement of action"—or at least try to provide some leadership. For Lenin, the rebellion, along with the jacquerie in the countryside, meant that the revolution that began 18 months earlier on "Bloody Sunday," January 1905, had not been exhausted. But without revolutionary restraint such actions were doomed to fail until the "rearguard" caught up with the "vanguard." The election campaign for the Second Duma and the conduct of the party's Duma fraction offered a potentially valuable opportunity and means to ensure such an outcome. Though the Czar's government didn't set a date for the elections for the Second Duma, Lenin went into campaign mode almost immediately.

FROM BOYCOTT TO GUERRILLA WARFARE AND/OR ELECTIONS

After assessing the significance of the dissolution of the First Duma, Lenin, in his first pronouncement, addressed the "what next" question. Insurrection, in his opinion, was still on the agenda, especially given what the regime had just done. But how could it be organized? Success would depend not only on timing but on the assurance that local uprisings could be coordinated. "Influential members of the Duma among the Social-Democrats and Trudoviks could also help to make simultaneous action successful."[1] His suggestion about "influential members of the Duma" reveals how much the parliamentary arena had become part of his revolutionary strategy. It's easy to understand why. "The peasants," he wrote shortly afterward, "have learned more from the Duma than anyone . . . The Cadets were unmasked, the Trudoviks were consolidated—such were the most important gains of the Duma period." As evidence he noted that "revolutionary manifestos" that called for insurrection after the dissolution, "'To the Army and Navy,' 'To All the Peasants' . . . were signed by the 'bloc' of all revolutionary organizations, including the Trudovik Group."[2] A new Duma therefore offered the possibility of deepening those gains.

Not for naught was Lenin's next major writing titled, six weeks after the dissolution, "The Boycott." By now he had a new or, more correctly, a revived organ, *Proletary*, an illegal weekly published in Finland; like the rest of the Left opposition, the Bolsheviks had to play hide and seek with the government censors. Because *Proletary* was a weekly, Lenin's published responses to developments on the ground came less often than what a daily could have offered. The very first sentence of the "Boycott" article made clear its purpose: "The Left-wing Social-Democrats must reconsider the question of boycotting the State Duma." After reviewing how the Russian party as a whole had employed the boycott and arguing why it had been advantageous to do so, he admitted that the Duma experience provided unexpected "lessons" and that it would be "pedantic obstinacy" to not acknowledge that fact. "History has shown that when the Duma assembles opportunities arise for carrying on useful agitation both from within the Duma and around it . . . [H]istory has undoubtedly proved that that institution is of some, although modest, use to the revolution as a platform for agitation, for exposing the true 'inner nature' of the political parties, etc." Therefore, "[t]he time has now come when the revolutionary Social-Democrats must cease to be boycottists. We shall not refuse to go into the Second Duma when (or 'if') it is convened."

In making a case for participation, Lenin was under no illusion about what was involved. Although the regime said there would be a new Duma, that couldn't be taken for granted, especially since in setting a date for its convening, February 20, it "did not fix—*contrary to the law*—the date of the elections." The government was understandably keeping its options open, he argued, and the temperature of the class struggle would be determinative. If the masses were in an insurgent motion, as he expected, the regime might see elections as way to divert that energy. If not, then they might decide there was no need for a potentially bothersome Duma. Nor, he noted very presciently, would it be known "what the electoral laws will be like." Whatever the case, the party needed to prepare for such eventualities by having a new congress. And high on the agenda had to be a discussion and decision about electoral blocs, since the Stockholm or Fourth Congress ruled them out. Lenin, not surprisingly, already had a position: "[T]here we shall resolve that *in the event of elections taking place*, it will be necessary to enter into an electoral agreement, for a few weeks, with the Trudoviks . . . And then we shall utterly rout the Cadets."[3] A few weeks later he was more explicit—"my own personal opinion" and, presumably, not necessarily that of the other Bolsheviks: "I would advocate the following at the Fifth Congress: no blocs or agreements whatever between the Social-Democrats and any other parties to be tolerated at the lowest stage of the elections. We must appear before the masses at election *time* absolutely independently. At the highest stages agreements with the Trudoviks may be permitted exclusively for the proportional distribution of seats and on the condition that we 'make' the non-party Trudoviks party men, counterposing the opportunists among them and the semi-Cadets (Popular Socialists, 'Popular Socialist Party,' etc.) to the revolutionary bourgeois democrats."[4] The experience of the First Duma taught that a worker-peasant electoral bloc was a real possibility; it could even result in a Duma majority. But note the all-important qualifier "for a few weeks" in the earlier comment. In other words, and in the spirit of Marx and Engels's *Address of March 1850*, an "electoral agreement" with petit bourgeois forces was not only permissible but a necessity—as long as it didn't entail unity. Independent working-class political action, what the "lowest stage of the elections" made possible, had to be ensured.

In calling for an end to the boycott, Lenin continued to defend its usage against the Witte or First Duma. Because he initially opposed the tactic and conceded to the majority to support it, but then later, in 1920, said it had been a mistake, it is difficult to say with any certainty how sincere was his defense. I suspect that despite what he wrote, Lenin continued to harbor doubts about, if not outright opposition to, the boycott of the Witte Duma; that he moved so quickly to reject the tactic when the opportunity presented itself is suggestive. But being loyal to a decision he didn't agree with probably made him more effective in convincing those Bolsheviks who supported the boycott (the vast majority) to abandon it for the Second Duma. To have said at this moment that he disagreed with the boycott risked making him sound like an "I-told-you-so." He resisted that temptation and thus enhanced his argument.[5]

Lenin began to see signs that suggested the regime would play its hard-cop card in regard to the new Duma. Petr Stolypin, now head of the Council of Ministers and architect of the dissolution, had already stepped up the repression. Peasant revolts and opposition attacks, including a Socialist-Revolutionary attempt on his life, gave Stolypin the convenient pretext to do so. On August 19 he instituted the notorious and much-hated field-court trials, which basically allowed for summary executions. "[N]early 60,000 political detainees were executed, sentenced to penal servitude or exiled without trial during his first three years in office."[6] When the leader of the industrial capitalist Octobrist Party gave his stamp of approval to Stolypin's crackdown, Lenin, on September 30, issued a warning: "Workers! Be prepared for the promulgation by the government of a Black-Hundred electoral law by the time of the elections! Peasants! Beware, the government is planning to change the electoral system so that peasant deputies, Trudoviks, *cannot* be elected to the Duma!"[7] Lenin's forecast was accurate. Stolypin did indeed carry out what Lenin called a "coup d'état"—but nine months later when he dissolved the Second Duma and instituted, in violation of the law, new electoral rules that ensured a much more friendly Third Duma. Again, it was elegant algebra, but wanting arithmetic. Lenin, a revolutionary and not a mathematician, was obligated to prepare for the worst rather than wait to see if his calculations were correct.

In a context of increasing repression in which an insurgency still seemed on the agenda, Lenin turned his attention to guerrilla warfare. Nothing he wrote at this time was fundamentally different from his earlier and briefer comments on the topic as discussed in Chapter 2. Rather than a strategy, guerrilla warfare, like parliamentary work, was simply one of many tactics that social democrats employed, depending on the situation. Most important, it had to be seen as part of and coordinated with the mass movement: "Guerrilla warfare is an inevitable form of struggle at a time when the mass movement has actually reached the point of an uprising and when fairly large intervals occur between the 'big engage-ments' in the civil war . . . [G]uerrilla actions must conform to the temper of the broad masses and the conditions of the working class movement."[8] And to avoid it becoming an end in itself—the more than forty-year-old guerrilla wars in Colombia might be Exhibit A for what's wrong when that happens—party "control" was necessary.

To underscore the fact that for Lenin guerrilla warfare had to be part of a larger movement, the Russian Social Democratic Labor Party (RSDLP) actively sought to recruit soldiers and sailors—"peasants in uniform," as they sometimes called them. At the end of 1906 they had 33 newspapers in various localities—just for the military![9] To coordinate military recruit-ment, the party held a couple of conferences in November 1906 that mapped out plans for deepening its influence among the armed forces. These meetings were significant because Stolypin used them to justify the dissolution of the Second Duma.

If the regime was able to hedge and keep its options open regarding the new Duma, Lenin could be just as agile. Exactly at the moment when he was thinking through armed struggle, he was writing his first detailed election campaign strategy document—just as Marx and Engels had pro-vided both an electoral and an armed strategy in their *Address of March 1850*. Lenin's twenty-page pamphlet, *The Social-Democrats and Electoral Agreements*, brought together for the first time all his views on electoral work. Its central theme detailed his position about electoral "blocs" or agreements. In the first round of elections, again, he advised complete independence for social democracy, even from the Trudoviks, and only in later rounds could agreements with other parties be permitted. Lenin also advised social democrats on how they should comport themselves at both stages: "[S]peak simply and clearly, in a language comprehensible to the masses, absolutely discarding the heavy artillery of erudite terms, for-eign words and stock slogans, definitions and conclusion which are as yet unfamiliar and unintelligible to the masses. Without flamboyant phrases, without rhetoric, but with facts and figures, they must be able to *explain* the questions of socialism and of the present Russian revolution." Finally, "we must take advantage of the election campaign to *organize the revolu-tion*, i.e. to organize the proletariat and the *really* revolutionary elements of bourgeois democracy."

Given the uncertainty and difficulty involved in not only getting but keeping his ideas in print, Lenin understandably had no qualms about repeating what he had published elsewhere. The pamphlet, published in St. Petersburg, November 1906, served as a convenient handbook for social democratic electoral work. The regime evidently saw it that way, too. In 1912 it was banned and "the remaining copies were destroyed at the printing press of the city authorities."[10]

"SPLITTING THE VOTE" AND THE "BLACK HUNDRED DANGER": THE LESSER OF EVILS CONUNDRUM

In his pamphlet Lenin addressed for the first time an issue that has bedeviled many a working-class party in multiparty elections—the "danger of splitting the vote." Marx and Engels first raised the issue in their *Address*. In calling for the proletariat to put forward its own candidates in elections, even though "there is no prospect whatever of their being elected . . . they must not allow themselves to be bribed by such arguments of the democrats . . . that by so doing they are splitting the democratic party and giving the reactionaries the possibility of victory. The ultimate purpose of all such phrases is to dupe the proletariat. The advance which the proletarian party is bound to make by such independent action is infinitely more important than the advantage that might be incurred by the presence of a few reactionaries in the representative body." To these kernels of wisdom, Lenin added the necessary body.

The "few reactionaries" Lenin had to deal with were the fascist-like "pogrom mongers," the Black Hundreds. And for that reason the issue of vote splitting had to be taken "seriously": "It cannot be denied," he admitted, that in the absence of a "bloc of the Lefts," "Black-Hundred electors may be elected . . . And there is no doubt that the general public will take this [possibility] . . . into account; they will be afraid of splitting the vote, and because of that will be inclined to cast their votes for the most moderate of the opposition candidates."

The first thing that had to be taken into account, he said, was "the present electoral system in Russia." Elections were held in two to four rounds in four curia or electoral colleges, for landowners, urban dwellers, peasants, and workers. In the initial rounds the voting was for electors who eventually elected the deputies to the Duma. (The following figures make clear that due to the law of December 11, 1905, there was nothing representative about the elections: "one elector to every 2,000 voters in the landowner curia, one to each 7,000 in the urban curia, one to 30,000 in the peasant curia and one to 90,000 in the worker curia."[11]) In the first round, Lenin argued, when the mass of "primary voters go to the poll," the conundrum of vote splitting was most pronounced. In the subsequent rounds "when the elected representatives [or electors] vote, the general engagement is over; all that remains is to distribute the seats by partial agreements among the parties, which *know* the exact number of their candidates and their votes." The Black Hundreds were likely only to be elected from the cities, which contributed less than 10 percent of the seats to the Duma; in the countryside the electoral process was generally nonpartisan.

So should social democracy enter into electoral agreements in the first rounds—that is, have joint lists of candidates with other parties, especially Cadets, to block the election of the Black Hundreds? For Lenin that would be a mistake: "We would undermine the principles and the general revolutionary significance of our campaign for the sake of gaining a seat in the Duma for a liberal! We would be subordinating class policy to parliamentarism instead of subordinating parliamentarism to class policy. We would deprive ourselves of the opportunity to gain an estimate of *our* forces. We would lose what is lasting and durable in all elections—the development of the class-consciousness and solidarity of the socialist proletariat. We would gain what is transient, relative and untrue—superiority of the Cadet over the Octobrist."[12] Furthermore, the "arithmetic possibility of splitting the vote," he argued, based on an analysis of the returns for the First Duma, was minimal. But in later rounds, again, electoral agreements were not only permissible but necessary to block the Black Hundreds. That meant, more specifically, blocs with the Trudoviks to defeat the Cadets and blocs with the Cadets to defeat the Black Hundreds. This was Lenin's ranking of the evils, from lesser to greater.

Given the Mensheviks' orientation toward the Cadets—on full display in the First Duma—it is not surprising that they objected to Lenin's call for a prohibition on electoral agreements in the first rounds of voting. Such a policy, in their view, would be an obstacle to their pas de deux with the liberals. At a party conference in Tammerfors (Tampere), Finland, November 3–7, the Menshevik-dominated Central Committee had enough delegates to adopt a resolution that allowed for electoral agreements with the Cadets in the first rounds. Because it was a conference, the decisions, as Lenin pointed out later, were only "advisory." The Bolsheviks submitted, for discussion in local organizations, a "dissenting opinion" that reiterated their call for a ban on electoral agreements in the first rounds, but with a qualification: "Exceptions to this rule are permissible only in cases of extreme necessity and only in relation to parties that fully accept the main slogans of our immediate political struggle, i.e., those which recognize the necessity of an armed uprising and are fighting for a democratic republic. Such agreements, however, may only extend to the nomination of a joint list of candidates, without in any way restricting the independence of the political agitation carried on by the

Social-Democrats." But there was an exception to this exception: "*In the workers' curia the Social-Democratic Party must come out absolutely independently and refrain from entering into agreements with any other party.*"[13] If Lenin was willing to be a bit flexible on the general stricture on blocs in the first rounds of elections, that didn't apply to the arena devoted exclusively to the proletariat—the one place where social democracy had to be pure and unadulterated in order to accurately assess its support. More than anything to date, the differences at Tammerfors revealed the collision course the Bolsheviks and Mensheviks were on.

The "Black-Hundred danger," the Mensheviks insisted, justified first-round electoral agreements with the liberal Cadets—a claim that has a very familiar ring to it for anyone acquainted with Left politics in advanced capitalist countries since the Second World War. Lenin took this head-on in "Blocs with the Cadets," his first major writing after Tammerfors.

There were three basic "flaws" with the Menshevik argument. The first is that it assumed an alliance with the Cadets would actually lessen the Black Hundred danger. But there was nothing, he pointed out, in the track record of the Cadets that warranted such a claim. Look, he said, at their behavior in the First Duma. As a liberal-monarchist party, the Cadets were apologists for the Czar—"*the known leader of the Black Hundreds.* Therefore, by helping to elect Cadets to the Duma, the Mensheviks are not only failing to combat the Black-Hundred danger, but are hoodwinking the people, are obscuring the real significance of the Black-Hundred danger. Combating the Black-Hundred danger by helping to elect the Cadets to the Duma is like combating pogroms by means of the speech delivered by the lackey [Cadet] Rodichev: 'It is presumption to hold the monarch responsible for the pogrom.'"

"The second flaw . . . is that . . . the Social-Democrats tacitly surrender hegemony in the democratic struggle to the Cadets. In the event of a split vote that secures the victory of a Black Hundred, why should *we* be blamed for not having voted for the Cadet, and not the *Cadets* for not having voted for us?" Social democrats "must not allow themselves to be bribed"—as Marx and Engels counseled in their *Address*—by what had always happened whenever they embarked on independent working-class political action in the electoral arena, "the howling and barking of the liberals, *accusing the socialists of wanting to let the Black Hundreds in.*" Why should the Cadets be allowed to pose as democrats? To the contrary, they had to be fought: "Now or later, unless you cease to be socialists, you will have to fight independently, in spite of the Black-Hundred danger. And it is easier and more necessary to take the right step now than it will be later on . . . But the *real* Black-Hundred danger, we repeat, lies not in the Black Hundreds obtaining seats in the Duma, but in pogroms and [field] military courts; and you are making it more difficult for the people to fight this real danger by putting Cadet blinkers on their eyes." Ceding "hegemony in the democratic struggle to the Cadets" was to miseducate the masses and therefore disarm them in waging the "real" fight.

The "third flaw" was related to the second—"its inaccurate appraisal of the Duma and its role." Implicit in the Mensheviks' "tactics of partial agreement," as they called them, was the assumption that what transpired within the elegant walls of Tauride Palace was decisive in the class struggle. Trying to utilize the "Duma as a whole, i.e. the Duma majority"— again, in their own words—was the best way for "fighting the autocratic regime." It was just the opposite for Lenin and the Bolsheviks: "We think it is childish to imagine that the elimination of the Black Hundreds from the Duma means the elimination of the Black-Hundred danger." The Black Hundred danger, he argued, would be overcome in the only place it could—in the streets. The Mensheviks, Lenin charged, had succumbed to "parliamentary cretinism"—not the first and not the last well-intentioned revolutionaries to have met such a fate.

Although Lenin's answer to the vote-splitting/lesser-evil conundrum took into account the then existent electoral rules in Russia, there is nothing to suggest that it would have been qualitatively different for a different set of rules. At the heart of his position was a cost-benefit calculation informed by the assumption that what took place outside the parliamentary arena was decisive in politics. To the extent that participation in the electoral arena advanced independent working-class political action then it was worth taking part. If, however, such involvement interfered with that course, then the costs outweighed the benefits. Forming a bloc with the Cadets in the first round of elections incurred, in his view, an unjustifiable cost—the miseducation of the working class and its allies. It would be better to abstain—as the Bolsheviks did with the Bulygin Duma proposal—than to risk such an outcome. Even in the likelihood of the Black Hundreds obtaining a majority in the Duma, Lenin would have had the same answer; the Third and Fourth Dumas bear that out. However frightening that prospect might have been to some, Lenin knew that in the final analysis the "real" fight with the Black Hundreds had to take place outside Tauride Palace. "Everywhere we have a single policy: in the election fight, in the fight in the Duma, and in the fight in the streets—the policy of armed struggle. Everywhere our policy is: the Social-Democrats with the revolutionary bourgeoisie"—that is, the peasantry—"against the Cadet traitors."[14] Nothing distinguished the Bolsheviks more from the Mensheviks than that stance.

LENIN IN CAMPAIGN MODE

"Comrade workers, and all citizens of Russia! The Duma elections are approaching. The Social-Democratic Party, the party of the working class, calls upon you all to take part in the elections and so help to rally the forces that are really capable of fighting for freedom . . . Comrade workers, and all citizens of Russia! Vote for the candidates of the Russian Social-Democratic Labour Party!" Thus read the opening and closing paragraphs in Lenin's first explicit election campaign literature. Published on November 23, in *Proletary*, it came two weeks before the government set a date, February 6, 1907, for the Second Duma elections. Lenin couldn't wait to get out of the starting blocks.

A few days later he produced his first campaign poster, "Whom to Elect to the State Duma," included in the same issue of *Proletary*. Under the unwieldy subtitle, "Citizens See to It That the Whole People Clearly Understand What the Chief Parties are that are Fighting in the Elections in St. Petersburg and What Each of Them Strives for!" it explained, laid out in three and two columns, respectively the differences between the social democrats, the Cadets, and the Black-Hundreds on the one hand and between the social democrat and Trudovik parties on the other (see Appendix C). His not-too-subtle message drew strict lines between social democrats and Cadets while underscoring the vacillating character of the still inchoate peasant parties. The poster's text adhered strictly to his advice that "Social-Democrats must speak simply and clearly, in a language comprehensible to the masses."

The Stolypin administration sought to discourage enthusiasm for a campaign like Lenin's. No sooner had it announced the date for elections than it began to undermine them. "The other day [December 12]," Lenin reported, "an *order* was promulgated prohibiting the issue of election forms to unregistered parties." Effectively, this meant that only the Black-Hundred parties could get the forms. Also, "newspapers are being more and more summarily suppressed. Arrests are becoming more and more frequent. Premises are being raided and searched with the most transparent object of obtaining the names of electors and influential voters, in order to 'remove' them. In short, the election campaign is in full swing, as the witticism of Russian citizens puts it." This was why Lenin had no patience with those who "reduce the Black-Hundred danger to the danger of a Black-Hundred victory in elections"—elections "faked by the government!"[15] The government itself aided and abetted the Black Hundred danger. But Lenin would not be deterred. Three weeks before elections began he wrote that "there is still no doubt that the mood of the masses will decide the elections, and the decision will certainly not to be in favor of the government and its Black Hundreds."[16] In St. Petersburg in particular, the claim that a split in the Cadet and social democratic vote would lead to a Black Hundred victory was "an obvious absurdity . . . a *deception of the people* spread by the Cadets, the 'radicals' and the opportunists of every brand."[17]

Lenin threw himself into the electoral campaign because he anticipated, correctly, that in spite of the stepped-up repression, these would be the most democratic elections Czarist Russia would ever permit. Most important, social democracy was openly, for the first time, contesting the elections—hoping to both expose and win the masses to its program. A teaching moment unlike any in the history of Russia was being offered, and ground zero was St. Petersburg, to where "the eyes of all Russia are now turned . . . [and] the pulse of political life beats faster . . . than elsewhere." Two weeks into the month-long election process, Lenin wrote, "The election campaign in St. Petersburg has already provided an amazing abundance of political-educational material, and *day by day* continues providing more. This material must be assiduously studied. It must be systematically collected, and serve to bring out in the greatest possible relief the *class* basis of the various parties. And this live, direct knowledge, which interests and agitates everybody, must be carried to the broadest possible strata of workers and to the most remote rural areas."

What he called the "third stage" of the process was clearly what he enjoyed the most—the opportunity to assess and shape "the mood of the masses":

> The election campaign begins. Election meetings are being held. The Mensheviks, who very, very rarely speak at these meetings, blather timidly about agreements with the Cadets. The Bolsheviks, who speak at all meetings, call upon proletarians and semi-proletarians to join a united workers' party—the Social-Democratic Party; they call upon all revolutionary and democratic voters to form a united revolutionary bloc against the Black Hundreds and the Cadets. The Cadets are shouted down, while the Bolsheviks are applauded. The democrats in the city—the workers and the petty bourgeoisie—are swinging towards the Left and shaking off the Cadet yoke.[18]

Lenin, no doubt, attended—incognito, I suspect, for security purposes—and participated in these meetings. It helps explain why his assessment about gains for the Left at the expense of the Cadets proved to be accurate. He was able to experience what Plekhanov, the Menshevik leader, missed by remaining in Geneva.

Again, the elections were indirect. Duma deputies were elected by electors who in turn were elected in four different arenas or curia, for landowners, peasants, urban dwellers, and workers. And in each curia there were rounds or stages—two for landowners and urban dwellers, three for workers, and four for peasants—thus the possibility of electoral agreements or blocs. The meetings he was describing were those in St. Petersburg leading up to the first round elections for its curia. And very much on the agenda in those meetings was the vote-splitting/Black Hundred–danger/lesser-evil conundrum—what middle-class "democrats in the city" were especially sensitive to.

The debate between the Bolsheviks and Mensheviks regarding electoral agreements came to a head at a conference of the St. Petersburg RSDLP on January 7. The majority of the 71 delegates voted for the "dissenting opinion" submitted to the Tammerfors meeting by the Bolsheviks that prohibited blocs with the Cadets in the first rounds. The 31 Menshevik delegates "walked out" in disagreement. Effectively, this meant that there would be no uniform RSDLP policy on this question for the elections about to take place. Their deputies to the Second Duma would be elected in different ways, some completely independent and others in agreement with Cadets or Trudoviks and/or Social Revolutionaries. The latter, who had boycotted the First Duma, realized by now that they needed to take part this time; otherwise the social democrats would have unfiltered access to their constituents—the peasantry.

Lenin later revealed that the Bolsheviks themselves had differences on electoral agreements. While the "purists" didn't want agreements with any party, the "dissenters" like himself argued that "the socialist proletariat cannot refuse the non-socialist petty-bourgeois masses *to follow its leadership* in order that it may emancipate them from the influence of the Cadets." He was able to convince the "purists" to offer the Trudoviks and Social Revolutionaries, in return for their support to a joint "Left bloc" list in the first round, the following distribution of the six seats to the Duma allocated to St. Petersburg: "two places to the worker curia, two to the Social-Democrats, and two to the Trudoviks."[19] It was crucial, he argued, to defeat the Cadets in St. Petersburg, and having a social-democrat-Trudovik list separate and apart from a Cadet list—unlike what the Mensheviks wanted—would not enable victory for a Black Hundred list. Lenin thus waged war on a number of fronts, and the only power he had at his command was that of persuasion.

Though the details can't be gotten into here, Lenin's description of the democratic decision-making procedures the St. Petersburg Conference employed is instructive. His informative reports on the meeting constitute key documents in the history of democratic centralism.[20] It's worth noting his observation about RSDLP norms versus those of opponent organizations: "The bourgeois parties settle big political questions from case to case by a simple ruling of one or other party 'authority,' which secretly concocts various political nostrums for the people. Only the workers' Social-Democratic Party actually practices democracy in organization, in spite of the enormous difficulties—and even heavy, sacrifices—which this entails for an illegal party."[21] According to Lenin then, the democratic credentials of the RSDLP were more deserved than those of any other party, including the liberal Cadets.[22]

Bolshevik participation in campaign meetings was of utmost importance given that the regime placed severe limits on their ability to make their case in print. As an illegal weekly (and then later semimonthly), *Proletary* could not be easily circulated. They did manage to publish a legal weekly, *Ternii Truda* [*Thorns of Labor*] for two weeks before it was closed down by the government and then another, *Zreniye* [*Vision*].[23] Though the latter's existence was even briefer, Lenin wrote two key campaign literature articles for its two and only issues.

"How to Vote in the St. Petersburg Elections: Is There a Danger of the Black Hundreds Winning the St. Petersburg Elections" was the lead article in the first issue on January 25. A most didactic piece, it presented the Bolshevik arguments in very accessible language. As for the main Cadet/Menshevik claim that if the social democrats put forward their own list it would allow the Black Hundreds to win, "*This is not true*. We are going to prove to you that even in the *worst possible* case of a split vote, i.e., even if the votes are *evenly* divided between the Cadets and the Social-Democrats in *all* election wards of St. Petersburg—even in that case a Black-Hundred victory in St. Petersburg is *impossible*." For proof, Lenin examined the returns for the First Duma elections in St. Petersburg that were won by the Cadets at the expense of the Black Hundreds. What if the social democrats had been on the ballot and split the Cadet vote? Would that have allowed a Black Hundred victory? Lenin presented the data for each ward in the city and concluded, "These figures show clearly that even in the most unfavorable case of a split in the Cadet vote, the Black Hundreds would have been successful in the 1906 elections *in only three* wards out of the *twelve*. . . This means that the Black Hundreds *could not* have been elected to the Duma at the first elections even if the Cadet vote had been split equally between the Cadet and the Social-Democratic candidates in *all* wards . . . *Thus, those who are trying to scare the voters with the possibility of a Black-Hundred victory if the Cadets and Social-Democrats split the vote*, **are deceiving the people**." Lenin then offered what he said was the real reason for the scare tactic: "The Cadets are deliberately spreading false rumors of a 'Black-Hundred danger' so as to deter the voters from voting for the *socialists.*" He argued, looking at the ward data, that it "is *quite possible* for the Social-Democrats in St. Petersburg to gain a victory over the Black Hundreds and the Cadets."

Unlike his earlier-cited article about the Black Hundred danger, written mainly for a proletarian audience, "How to Vote" was directed at the urban petit bourgeois democrat. The detailed attention to election return data and probabilities of outcomes recognized that the latter was more susceptible to the vote-splitting/Black Hundred danger claim, and therefore a case had to be made to allay its fears. For the proletariat, Lenin appealed to their instinct for independent working-class political action. Therefore, as well as fighting for the proletariat, Lenin sought to win over the middle class—at least those who were capable of being won over. There was another reason they were susceptible to the Cadet argument: "Taking advantage of the government's ban on Social-Democratic newspapers, the Cadet newspapers are dinning into their readers' ears that a Social-Democratic victory at the elections is inconceivable without the aid of the Cadets."[24] Though limited, the Bolsheviks were at least able to challenge that din in St. Petersburg. In Moscow, they didn't even have a newspaper. But again, Lenin would not be discouraged.

ANALYZING THE ELECTION RESULTS: THE WORKERS' CURIA AND ST. PETERSBURG

"The elections of workers' delegates are an extremely important event in the political life of Russia and in the history of our labor movement, an event that has not yet been properly appreciated." Lenin was referring to the workers' curia elections. The Czar's feudal-like electoral system, he recognized, offered the Bolsheviks a unique opportunity—unlike any, probably, in the history of the communist movement. The proletariat, a nonexistent estate in feudal society, wasn't, it may be remembered, included in the regime's original electoral procedures. Eventually it was, because the regime felt the heat of working-class insurrection in December 1905.

The three-stage workers' curia elections involved, first, the selection of representatives by workers at the factory level who then chose electors that later voted for the Duma deputies. An enterprise with 50 to 1,000 workers could have one representative and additional ones for every thousand workers. At the last stage, the workers' curia electors met with those from other curia to elect the Duma deputies. Under the law, "workers ['male'] themselves were permitted to decide whether a plurality or a majority was required to elect a delegate, and whether voting would take place by ballot, a show of hands, or some other method."[25] The process, especially at the first stage, was indeed unique, as Lenin explained in his first assessment of the outcome of the first two stages of the elections in St. Petersburg: "For the first time *all* parties with any standing among the proletariat have come *before the masses* of the workers, not with general programs or slogans, but with a definite practical question: *to the candidates of which party* will the masses of the workers entrust the defense of their interests?"[26] Trade unions, as Victoria Bonnell describes in her classic work on the subject, played a key role in this regard: "The Petersburg Central Bureau of Trade Unions set the general tone when it urged that 'representatives of the socialist parties be given every assistance in explaining their program' . . . Election literature and lists of socialist party candidates were circulated through union channels."[27]

To appreciate the significance of the workers' curia elections, imagine what it would be like for a communist today to be able to debate every credible opponent before an audience composed exclusively of industrial workers, in their own workplaces. This is exactly what the Bolsheviks were able to do for two or more months throughout the Russian empire at the beginning of 1907. This probably has never happened before or since, anywhere. Engels would have been ecstatic; recall his chiding Paul Lafargue for not appreciating how elections could be used for revolutionary purposes.[28] Why would the regime allow such a process? Lenin, employing Marx and Engels's historical materialist method, would have had no difficulty in explaining as suggested in his discussion of the differences between the outcomes of the elections in "Russia proper and Poland"—the backwardness of the regime. In a more advanced capitalist country, the bourgeoisie would never have permitted communists to have such an opportunity. For Lenin, the elections were so significant that he issued the first of a frequent appeal to local Bolshevik leaders: "Unless our Party officials, and especially the advanced workers themselves, undertake the necessary and extremely important task of *studying* the course and the results of the elections in the worker curia, we can definitely say that we shall lose extremely valuable and necessary material for the future development of Party work and Party agitation."

As for the big picture, the elections confirmed Lenin's most basic political premise. "The general impression produced by the elections in the worker curia in Russia is unanimously summed up by all newspapers as follows: complete victory for the extreme Lefts, primarily the Social-Democrats, the Socialist-Revolutionaries coming second." The results "have fully borne out the fundamental thesis of Social-Democracy: as a class, the proletariat is revolutionary. The proletarian *masses* are Social-Democratic in their aspirations and sympathies. The proletariat is the most revolutionary class in Russia." But there was a disturbing fact about the outcome, one that caused "despondency" among some Bolsheviks. The Social Revolutionaries did far better than expected. "In Moscow the Social-Democrats gained a complete victory over the Socialist-Revolutionaries. According to some reports, not yet fully verified it is true, about 200 Social-Democratic delegates were elected, as against a mere 20 Socialist-Revolutionary delegates!" But the situation was different in St. Petersburg to where, again, "the eyes of all Russia are now turned." Estimates suggested that the Social Revolutionaries had won a third of the delegates, which if true was "*actually* a defeat for the Social-Democrat in the capital." It was a defeat because elsewhere, as in Moscow, the social democrats had trounced them. "This is a fact of tremendous importance. In St. Petersburg the extreme Left bourgeois democrats deprived the socialists of their *overwhelming* preponderance in the worker curia. It is our duty to give this fact the closest attention. *All* Social-Democrats must set to work to study this phenomenon carefully and find the correct explanation for it."

Preliminary reports allowed Lenin to conclude that "(1) it was at the *biggest* factories, the strongholds of the most class-conscious, the most revolutionary proletariat, that Socialist-Revolutionaries inflicted the most telling defeat on the Social-Democrats; (2) the Socialist-Revolutionaries defeated *mostly* and in the main the *Menshevik Social-Democrats*. Where a Socialist-Revolutionary candidate opposed a Bolshevik Social-Democratic candidate, the Social-Democrats were far more often, *in most cases in fact*, victorious." Social Revolutionaries' gains, thus, came at the expense of the Mensheviks and not the Bolsheviks. "The supreme significance of both these conclusions is obvious. We must therefore take good care that these are not mere impressions but *conclusions* drawn from exact and verified data that can leave no room for two interpretations."[29]

Details in an accompanying article about the elections in the Neva district, one of the major industrial suburbs in the capital, allowed Lenin to offer an explanation for the difference in the Bolshevik-Menshevik vote. The elections began a day after the Mensheviks walked out of the January 7 RSDLP conference; they wanted, as it was later learned, to resume their negotiations with the Cadets for an electoral agreement. This angered the most class-conscious workers, who hated the Cadets, and it was the Menshevik candidates who reaped that opprobrium. They penalized the Mensheviks by voting for other "socialists"—that is, Socialist Revolutionaries—not knowing, as Lenin pointed out, that they too, covertly, were engaged in negotiations with the Cadets. In the factories where the Bolsheviks were in the leadership, their candidates didn't suffer such a fate.

Before any definite conclusions could be drawn, details about other elections had to be gathered "so as not to gloss cravenly over our mistakes and short comings, but subject them to Party criticism and exert all our efforts to eliminate them. We *cannot* conduct consistent Social-Democratic work in St. Petersburg unless we pay close attention to the way in which the *masses of the workers* have voted for the candidates of the various parties. For the bourgeois parties it is important only to win so many seats. For us it is important for the masses themselves *to understand* the tenets and tactics of *Social-Democracy* as distinct from all petty-bourgeois parties, even though they may call themselves revolutionary, socialist parties. We must therefore strive to obtain exact and complete data on the voting at the elections in the St. Petersburg worker curia."[30] To that end Lenin drew up a questionnaire that was circulated to all local RSDLP units that asked for specific data about the elections, such as the number of workers who actually voted, the political identity of the candidates they voted for, and the actual number of votes for each candidate. The data confirmed by and large the preliminary conclusions he had drawn about the reason for the relative success of the Social Revolutionaries: "[T]he opportunist Social-Democrats"—that is, the Mensheviks—"are discrediting Social-Democracy in the eyes of the advanced proletariat."

In the meantime the workers' curia elections were entering their final stage. By mid-January all the factory elections had taken place. A total of 272 delegates had been elected with more than half (147) social democrats, more than a third (109) identified to one degree or another as Social Revolutionaries, and the remainder of various hues. The Bolsheviks then set out to win the delegates to their Left bloc that was formed on January 25, consisting of Bolsheviks, Trudoviks, and Social Revolutionaries. Except for a minority of them, the Mensheviks continued to "grovel at the feet" of the Cadets. At a meeting of 200 to 250 factory delegates on January 28, a resolution was passed overwhelmingly that supported the Left bloc—"fully endorsing *the tactics of the Bolsheviks*," as Lenin reported—and requested "that our Menshevik Social-Democratic comrades should enter into agreement with the Lefts and contribute to the success of the Left lists in the St. Petersburg elections." The request was spurned. A few days later the social democrat factory delegates met with the St. Petersburg RSDLP committee to select the 14 candidates for the Left bloc electors list, "published in all newspapers on the eve of the elections," that took place on February 1. The results were "a victory for the united Social-Democrats. *The St. Petersburg Committee's list was elected in toto.* All fourteen electors are Social-Democrats! . . . *eight* are Bolsheviks, four are Mensheviks [representing the minority who supported the Left bloc]," and the remaining two were unaligned social democrats.[31]

The outcome, in other words, was a clear victory for Lenin's strategy of independent working-class political action, a vindication of his "intransigence," as his opponents labeled it. This is no doubt the moment when the Bolsheviks assumed leadership of St. Petersburg's proletariat. Until then the Mensheviks had been more influential; their majority on the Central Committee registered that fact. Therefore the elections for the Second Duma, specifically those for the workers' curia, are when the Bolsheviks bested the Mensheviks, a defeat from which they never recovered. As Lenin was so fond of saying, "revolution teaches."

The St. Petersburg urban curia elections had yet to be completed. But three days before the results were in, Lenin wrote, "At the beginning of the election campaign in St. Petersburg the whole opposition, all the Lefts, were opposed to the Bolsheviks. Everything possible or conceivable was done against us. *Yet everything turned out as we said.*" He was relishing the fact that the arguments in his 1905 book, *Two Tactics,* regarding "the government's attitude towards the liberals and the attitude of the petty-bourgeois democrats towards the proletariat" had been confirmed by events leading up to the elections. The failure of the Cadets to put together an electoral bloc to oppose what the Bolsheviks sought to build was not unexpected. Stolypin was the main obstacle, and the other was the wavering of the petty bourgeoisie, the peasant parties, between the Cadet and Bolshevik alternatives. Confident in their politics, the Bolsheviks maintained a steady course. "And all who were *capable of fighting* followed us. The Left bloc became a fact. The hegemony of the revolutionary proletariat became a fact. *The proletariat* led *all* the Trudoviks and a large part of the Mensheviks, even intellectuals. The banner of *the proletariat* has been raised at the St. Petersburg elections. And whatever the outcome of the first serious elections in Russia in which all parties have participated—the banner of the independent proletariat, which is pursuing its own line, has already been raised. It will be held high in the parliamentary struggle and in *all other* forms of struggle that will lead to the victory of the revolution." The confidence Lenin and the Bolsheviks gained in this phase of the "dress rehearsal" of 1905–7 goes a long way in explaining, I argue, their success in 1917.

While the elections were underway in St. Petersburg on February 7, Lenin assessed the returns that had come in from elsewhere: "We have before us a Duma that is undoubtedly more Left than the previous one . . . and [thus] a new even more formidable and more unmistakable *revolutionary crisis*. . . A new clash is inexorably approaching—either the revolutionary people will be victorious, or the Second Duma will disappear as ingloriously as the First, followed by the repeal of the election law and a return to the Black-Hundred absolutism *san phrases*." The challenge now was how to temper revolutionary ardor. "We shall do all in *our* power to make this new struggle as little spontaneous and as conscious, consistent, and steadfast as possible . . . Therefore," as Engels would have advised, "no premature *calls* for an insurrection! No solemn manifestos to the people. No pronunciamentos, no 'proclamations.' The storm is bearing down on us of its own accord. There is no need of sabre-rattling."[32] The previous two years had amply demonstrated why behaving otherwise was now inadvisable. Two days before Lenin counseled revolutionary restraint, he wrote, "*In September 1870, six months before* the [Paris] Commune, Marx gave a direct warning to the French workers: insurrection would be an act of desperate folly . . . Marx knew how to warn the leaders against a premature rising." But his advice "was that of a practical advisor, of a participant in the struggle of the masses," and not that "of an intellectual philistine who moralizes: 'It is easy to foresee . . . they should not have taken up'" arms, as he charged Plekhanov with having done about the unsuccessful uprising in December 1905 in Moscow.[33]

Lenin summarized the St. Petersburg returns once they were all in: "The Cadets won the elections, but it must be stressed that the Left bloc polled 25 per cent of the total number of votes in St. Petersburg and that they were victorious in the Vyborg District. In many districts the Cadets won by a very small majority. In five districts it would have been enough to gain a further 1,600 votes to ensure a victory for the Left bloc . . . The Mensheviks, therefore, prevented a victory of the Left parties in St. Petersburg; nevertheless, the revolutionary Left is, in general, stronger in the Second Duma than it was in the First."[34] On one issue he felt especially vindicated—the Black Hundred danger: "The elections have proved that it was non-existent. Our repeated declarations and warnings, reiterated in all Bolshevik publications . . . have been fully confirmed. The Black Hundreds could not have won in St. Petersburg, no matter how the votes had split between the Cadets and the Lefts!"[35] As for the surprising number of votes for the Socialist Revolutionaries, "such results can only fortify our conviction that today, more than ever, our duty and the guarantee of our success lie in joint work, not with the liberal bourgeoisie, who want to put an end to the revolution, but with the democratic peasantry, against the baseness and treachery of the bourgeoisie."

Finally, the relatively close vote between the Cadets and the Left bloc in half of the districts was encouraging. For Lenin, the glass was half full: "If we work tirelessly . . . we *can* win, in every district, hundreds of shop-assistants, clerks, etc., from the party of the bourgeois liberals who are bargaining with Stolypin . . . The Cadets will not survive another election struggle against the Left bloc in St. Petersburg! They will be completely routed under the present electoral law." Winning social layers beyond the industrial proletariat and peasantry, in other words, was a necessity for success for the bourgeois democratic revolution. As for the "present electoral law," Stolypin no doubt read or knew what Lenin was thinking, reinforcing the conclusions about it that he had already drawn.

THE SECOND DUMA CONVENES

"The primary task of the Social-Democrats entering the Second Duma is to wrest away from the liberals those democratic elements that are still under their sway; to become the leader of those democrats; to teach them to seek support in the people and join ranks, with the masses down below; to unfurl *our own* banner before the whole of the working class and before the entire impoverished and famine-stricken peasant masses." In other words, "this Party must show it is the vanguard of the entire democratic movement."[36] Thus were Lenin's instructions to the just-elected social democratic fraction in the first issue of the new Bolshevik daily, *Novy Luch* [*New Ray*], launched on the day the Second Duma convened—just as they did when the First Duma commenced. This time, though, the regime tolerated their organ for only a week—an early sign of what was ahead.[37]

AGAINST THE "CRIMINAL MENSHEVIK POLICY"

The Second Duma that convened on February 20 was indeed, as Lenin predicted, much more to the left than the First. Of the 518 deputies, 65 were social democrats, 47 more than in the First. The almost 97 percent of all the workers' curia electors who either were or sympathized with the social democrats explains in part their success: "Despite the false assertions of the liberals who want to depict it as party of revolutionary intellectu-als, the Russian Social-Democratic Party is, therefore, a real *working-class* party."[38] Of the social democratic deputies, 36 were Mensheviks—who continued to do well among oppressed nationalities in the Caucasus and elsewhere—and 18 were Bolsheviks, with the remaining not formally attached to either wing of the party.[39] The largest peasant party, the Tru-doviks, increased its presence from 85 to 120 deputies, while the smaller

Social Revolutionaries who boycotted the First Duma now had 37, giving the peasant parties a total of 157 deputies, the largest group in the Second Duma. The gains of the Left bloc, especially those of the social democrats, came at the expense of the Cadets—"despite the tremendous power of the Cadet daily press, the legal status of the Cadet organization, the Cadet falsehood about the danger of a Black Hundred victory and despite the illegal status of the Lefts."[40] Cadet numbers declined by almost half, from 184 to 99. Also, it was clearly a more polarized Duma; the combined Black Hundred parties increased their presence from 45 to 64 deputies.

The first test for the social democrat fraction was the vote on the presidium, the chair and two vice-presidents of the Duma. As the party learned in the First Duma, these were not unimportant posts; their occupants decided who could speak in a Duma session. The Menshevik majority of the fraction, with some of the Bolsheviks reluctantly in tow, blocked with the Cadets to elect two of their deputies to the chair—F. A. Golovin—and one of the vice-president posts, and a Trudovik to the other one. The rationale they gave was the need to prevent a Black Hundred presidium.[41] Lenin disagreed and pointed to an article in the previous issue of *Novy Luch* that demonstrated that the Black Hundreds didn't have the votes to capture the presidium if the Left bloc voted against the Cadets. Their error was a learning opportunity for the inexperienced fraction. A crucially important principle, independent working-class political action, was at stake and needed to be defended if they were to successfully navigate their way through the new Duma and avoid the mistakes made by the previous fraction:

> What must the policy of the Social-Democrats be? Either abstain, and, as socialists, stand aside from the liberals, who betray liberty and exploit the people, or give the lead to the democratic petty bourgeoisie that is capable of struggle, both against the Black Hundreds and against the liberals. The former policy is obligatory for socialists when there is no longer any substantial difference between *any* of the bourgeois parties from the standpoint of the struggle for democracy. That is what happens in Europe. There is no revolution. All the bourgeois parties have lost the ability to struggle for democracy, and are struggling only for the petty, selfish interests of big *or small proprietors*. Under such circumstances, Social-Democracy *alone* defends the interests of democracy, and in so doing persistently unfolds its own socialist views to the masses. The latter policy is obligatory when the conditions of a bourgeois-democratic revolution obtain, when, in addition to the working class, there are certain bourgeois and petty-bourgeois strata capable of struggle for the democracy that is essential to the proletariat. In present-day Russia the second policy is obligatory. Without ever forgetting their socialist agitation and propaganda, and the organization of the

proletarians into a class, Social-Democrats must, *jointly* with the demo-cratic petty bourgeoisie, *crush* both the Black Hundreds and the *liberals*, as the situation may demand.

Lenin then showed how these general principles—one of his best concise explanations of the different tasks of social democracy vis-à-vis liberal democracy—would have been applied for the vote on the presidium:

> [T]he Social-Democrats should have said: we do not want our own pre-sidium. We support the *whole* list of Lefts or Trudoviks *against the Cadets*, that is, we support all three candidates for the presidium, against the Cadet candidates, and will abstain if the Trudoviks follow in the wake of the Cadets, despite our warnings. In any case it would be essential to put up a candidate from the Lefts even though there would be no chance of his being elected; at the first voting, the number of votes given for him would show what forces the Social-Democrats could rely on in the event of a struggle against the Cadets. And if it should turn out that he obtained more votes than the Cadet, even if it were less than the absolute majority required for election, the voting would show the people clearly that this is not a Cadet Duma, and that the Cadet *is not everything* in the Duma.[42]

His advice was designed to extract the maximum advantage for inde-pendent working-class political action in the parliamentary arena and a guide for future fraction work. The presidium vote therefore wasn't "mere bagatelle."

The Menshevik-dominated Central Committee, despite the disap-proval of the proletariat in St. Petersburg, persisted in courting the Cadets. It undermined, Lenin lamented, the work the Duma fraction should be doing: "This is just what is so *criminal* about the Menshevik policy in the Duma—they will not, or cannot, tell the people from the Duma platform the whole truth about the class nature of the various parties," particularly the reality of the Cadets and the deals they were willing to cut with the Stolypin government.[43] To help the readers of *Die Neue Zeit*, the German party journal, understand the division in opinion in the Russian party on the Cadets, Lenin provided one of his clearest explanations of the Bolshevik position:

> One wing (the Minority, or "Mensheviks") regard the Cadets and liberals as being the progressive urban bourgeoisie as compared with the backward rural petty bourgeoisie (Trudoviks). It follows from this that the bour-geoisie is recognized as the motive force of the revolution, and a policy of support for the Cadets is proclaimed. The other wing (the Majority, or "Bolsheviks") regards the liberals as representatives of big industry, who are

striving to put an end to the revolution as quickly as possible for fear of
the proletariat, and are entering into a compromise with the reactionaries.
This wing regards the Trudoviks as revolutionary petty-bourgeois democrats, and is of the opinion that they are inclined to adopt a radical position
on a land question of such importance to the peasantry, the question of
the confiscation of the landed estates. This accounts for the tactics of the
Bolsheviks. They reject support for the treacherous liberal bourgeoisie, i.e.,
the Cadets, and do their utmost to get the democratic petty bourgeoisie
away from the influence of the liberals; they want to draw the peasant and
the urban petty bourgeois away from the liberals and muster them behind
the proletariat, behind the vanguard, for the revolutionary struggle. In its
social-economic content, the Russian revolution is a bourgeois revolution;
its motive force, however, is not the liberal bourgeoisie but the proletariat
and the democratic peasantry. The victory of the revolution can only be
achieved by a revolutionary-democratic dictatorship of the proletariat and
the peasantry.[44]

The differences had immediate implications for Duma work as well as for
the eventual fate of Russian social democracy.

To counter the Mensheviks' unrequited wooing of the Cadets, Lenin
took the opportunity to reply to an article in the short-lived Trudovik
legal daily *Noviye Sily* [*New Forces*]—it lasted two issues longer than *Novy
Luch*—about his criticism of the presidium vote. The author objected
to "our 'hackneyed' division of the bourgeoisie into petty, revolutionary
and liberal" in assessing the Cadets; for Lenin, it was another teaching
moment. After patiently explaining the class roots of the Cadets, "the
liberal bourgeoisie" and "liberal landlords"—and later the "bourgeois
intelligentsia"—and why it was "inevitable" and not "fortuitous" that
they had turned increasingly rightward, Lenin discussed how class analysis informed Bolshevik tactics in relation to the Cadets and Duma politics. As for the presidium vote, the "Social-Democrats had to *wrest* the
Trudoviks *away* from the Cadets, either by voting for the Trudoviks or
by demonstratively abstaining from voting and giving a reason for the
abstention. *Noviye Sily* now admits that it was a *mistake* for the Left to
take part in a conference with the Cadets [where the agreement to block
with them was entered into]. This is a valuable admission. *Noviye Sily*,
however, is sadly mistaken in thinking that 'it was a mistake of practical
expediency and not of principle.' This opinion, as we have shown, arises
out of a misunderstanding of the fundamentals, principles and tactics of
the socialist proletariat in the bourgeois revolution."

Lenin ended with a comradely retort that allowed him to sketch out
social democratic tactics for the most familiar component of parliamentary work—tabling bills:

Legislative work "must inevitably be placed in the hands of the Constitutional-Democrats." Nothing of the sort. The Cadets, as leaders of the liberal "Centre" in the Duma, have a majority over the Black-Hundred group, without our support. We must therefore table our own Social-Democratic bills, not liberal and not petty-bourgeois, bills that are written in revolutionary language, not in official jargon, *and must put them to the vote*. Let the Black Hundreds and the Cadets turn them down. We shall then go over to a ruthless criticism of the Cadet bill and regularly submit amendments. When the amendments end we shall abstain from voting on the Cadet bill as a whole, leaving the Cadets to defeat the Black Hundreds, thereby taking no responsibility on ourselves before the people for the poverty and worthlessness of Cadet pseudo-democracy.

If Lenin could be patient and comradely with an unknown Trudovik writer, that wasn't true when dealing with a known Menshevik. His favorite polemical tactic, sarcasm, was on full display in response to the attempt of "Comrade D. Koltsov" to defend Menshevik support for the Cadets with the *Communist Manifesto*: "From the bottom of our heart we welcome this Menshevik turn to the study of the *fundamental* principles of our disagreement on tactics. It is high time." He then dared the "comrade" to put in writing as a resolution to be debated at the much anticipated Fifth Congress that the "Cadets are *the progressive urban bourgeoisie* and the Trudoviks *the backward rural bourgeoisie*." Because "the peasant struggle for land" is the key issue in the Russian revolution and "without the democratic reorganization of the state the peasants cannot overcome the feudal-minded landlords," the resolution would have to offer evidence that the Cadets and not the Trudoviks were capable of advancing such "reorganization." But nothing in the Cadet's recent history, such as their performance in the First Duma, even hinted at such a possibility. "We therefore welcome the frankness and directness of Comrade Koltsov, and repeat our challenge: let the Mensheviks try to formulate *these* ideas concerning the Cadets and the Trudoviks, and express them clearly and unequivocally."[45]

ON A COLLISION COURSE

Only a week after its convening, the "papers are full of news, rumors and surmises about the imminent dissolution of the Duma." Six months earlier Lenin had warned workers and peasants to be prepared for Stolypin doing exactly that. The task now for social democracy, especially the Duma fraction, was how to respond to the "rumors." "They should tell the people, simply and clearly, *from the rostrum of the Duma, the whole truth*, including the reason why the dissolution of the Duma, a coup d'état, and a return to pure absolutism are inevitable. The government *need* [sic] silence on this. The people *need* to know it. The representatives of the people—while they still are representatives of the people!—should say this from the rostrum of the Duma."[46]

The "rumors" began to subside when Stolypin addressed the Duma on March 6 to defend his government's iron hand after the dissolution of the First Duma and to present its legislative agenda, the most important moment in the short life of the Second Duma. The olive branch he held out to the body along with the unsheathed sword gave, as intended, the Cadets a ray of hope and new determination to not rock the boat. Leading up to the speech, they tried to orchestrate a nonconfrontational response—specifically, to not have a no-confidence vote on Stolypin's government. They proposed to the Left that his address be greeted with silence and a motion to pass immediately on to the regular order of business. The social democrats disagreed, saying Stolypin, with all the blood on his hands, had to be confronted, and they would do so, if necessary, alone: "Some Kadets with the approval of the Social-Revolutionaries suggested that all fractions leave the hall in protest against the Social-Democratic speech, but the Trudoviki and Popular-Socialists [the right wing of the Trudoviks] objected"—the first time in the session that the Trudoviks deserted the Cadets to support the social democrats.[47]

The social democrats differed on how they should respond to Stolypin's address. While the Bolsheviks wanted, like the Mensheviks, a statement that clearly indicted the regime for its crimes, they felt it should also include the social democratic program. The Menshevik majority, with the backing of the Central Committee, objected, contending that it would be repetitious, since the party had already laid out its program in the First Duma.[48] When the fateful day arrived, I. G. Tsereteli, the Menshevik faction leader from Georgia, along with two other Menshevik deputies, roundly denounced Stolypin's soft-cop/hard-cop message—much to the discomfort of the Cadets. G. A. Alexinsky, the Bolshevik faction leader and also from the Caucasus, added more fire. But Stolypin, who sat stoically through the denunciations, would not be intimidated: "These attacks count on paralyzing the will and thoughts of the government. They all come down to two words directed at authority: 'hands up.' To these two words, sirs, the government with complete calm, with a consciousness of its uprightness can reply in two words: 'you will not frighten us' (*ne zapugaete*)."[49] This scenario, more than any other, encapsulated the fate of the Second Duma—two irreconcilable parties on a collision course.

Lenin had drafted a statement for the fraction, "Apropos of Stolypin's Declaration," but it was rejected by the Menshevik majority. While it repeated some of the main points in Tsereteli's statement about all that was wrong with the regime, it challenged the prime minister in a way that the Mensheviks were not prepared to do. Lenin correctly knew what would be missing in Stolypin's feigned attempt at conciliation: "There is one thing this announcement does not say and which must be said to the people by those deputies they sent to the Duma and who remain faithful to the people's interests—the government does not say that its announcement signifies an irrevocable and inevitable decision to dissolve the Second Duma without even giving it an opportunity to express the will of the people, to express the needs of the peasants, workers and soldiers, of all working people, and to express anything the people included in the mandates they gave the deputies when they sent them to the Duma." And then, Lenin reminded the deputies why they were there in the first place, his most basic claim about parliaments: "Duma deputies and an entire Duma capable of helping the people are meaningless without the people. If Russia has obtained even tiny liberties for a short period, if Russia has been granted popular representation even if only for a brief period, this is only because it has been won by the struggle of the people, the selfless struggle for liberty by the working class, the peasantry, the soldiers and the sailors."[50]

That Mensheviks in the Duma like Tsereteli were willing, early in the life of the Second Duma, to make the Cadets uncomfortable (if not to the extent Lenin was) is noteworthy. Unlike the Menshevik-dominated Central Committee of the party, and Plekanov in particular, they had a more intimate and thus informed opinion of the Cadets owing to almost daily contact. The combination of Lenin's vigilance of the conduct of the fraction, I suspect, and the incessant tendency of the Cadets to bend to Stolypin at the expense of workers and peasants goes a long way in explaining why they increasingly found themselves closer to Lenin's politics than those of the Central Committee. It also explains Lenin's more comradely critique of the fraction than that of the Central Committee. He recognized that the fraction deputies, despite the Menshevik label for most of them, were teachable—just as those in the First Duma.

Three weeks after Lenin called attention to the "rumors" about the dissolution of the Duma, he wrote that the situation had changed: "The government will not dare dissolve the Duma without a budget and an agrarian law the latter has approved. The government is *afraid* to dissolve the Duma and, at the same time, is vociferating about dissolution and is putting into motion the entire Black-Hundred machinery . . . so as to scare the timid and incline the wavering to compliance. It wants to try and drag concessions out of the Duma by gagging it with the threat of dissolution."[51] Under the Fundamental Laws, the government's budget had to be approved by the Duma. Though a provision allowed the government to continue with the prior budget if approval wasn't obtained, having the Duma sign on facilitated the regime's ability to borrow from lenders outside Russia. "Whether the European financial magnates' faith in the durability and solvency of the firm of Stolypin & Co. will be strengthened or weakened, depends to a great extent on the Duma."[52]

THE DEBATE ON THE AGRARIAN QUESTION

But first, there was the land question, the most important agenda item for the Second Duma—just as for the First. This time there was greater urgency, because following the dissolution of the First Duma, Stolypin, acting under the emergency provisions of Fundamental Law 87, embarked on his own solution. Lenin characterized it as "the Prussian type" as opposed to "the American type"—that is, an agrarian revolution from above. Essentially, his "reforms" involved the dismantling of the peasant commune by creating a class of rich peasants or kulaks financed by the state. It effectively meant that Russia, like Prussia, would not experience a bourgeois democratic revolution with all the implications for the worker-peasant alliance and socialist revolution. But Stolypin needed the Duma to implement and legitimize his scheme. Lenin pointed to articles in the Cadet organ *Rech* that hinted Stolypin had reached a deal with them and issued a warning: "Trudoviks of all shades—do not allow yourselves to be tricked! Stand guard over the interests of the people! Prevent this filthy deal between the Cadets and the government! Social-Democrat comrades! We are certain you will understand the situation, that you will stand at the head of all revolutionary elements in the Duma, that you will open the eyes of the Trudoviks to the shameful treachery of the liberal-monarchist bourgeoisie. We are sure that from the rostrum of the Duma you will loudly and boldly expose this treachery to the whole people."[53]

To do exactly that, Lenin wrote a speech on the agrarian question for Alexinsky, the Bolshevik faction leader when the first sustained debates began on March 19. Owing to time constraints, he couldn't deliver every word of Lenin's thirty-page document, but the summary of the stenographic account reveals that he presented its essence.[54] Fully on display in Lenin's draft was his more than decade-long research on the question, but it was written in a most accessible and didactic manner. The peasant deputies were his primary audience, and with characteristic sarcasm and ridicule he enjoyed ripping into the Right/Black Hundred deputies who defended what amounted to "*serf* farming" despite the "emancipation" of 1861. "And those gentlemen on the Right benches talk about the

Jews exploiting the peasants, about Jewish usury! But thousands of Jewish merchants would not skin the Russian muzhik in the way the true Russian, Christian landlords do! The interest claimed by the worst usurer is not to be compared with that claimed by the true Russian land lord, who hires a muzhik in winter for summer work or who forces him to pay for a dessiatine [2.7 acres] of land in labour, money, eggs, chickens, and God alone knows what else!" The Right's defense revealed the essence of the debate—"whether or not to preserve landed proprietorship."

> And I must give special warning to the peasants and the peasant deputies—evasion of *the real substance* of the issue must not be allowed. You must trust in no promises no fine words, until the *most important* thing has been made clear—will the landed estates remain the property of the landlords or will they pass into the peasants' hands? *If they remain the property of the landlords, labour service and bondage will remain.* Constant hunger and want for millions of peasants will also remain. The torment of gradual extinction from starvation—that is what the retention of landed proprietor ship means for the peasants.[55]

But the main thrust of Lenin's attack was reserved for the Cadets. Given the Menshevik majority in the Central Committee and fraction and their reluctance to expose the Cadets, and the democratic centralist norm for doing Duma work, Lenin had been prevented from taking on the Cadets. But owing to a breach of the agreement the Mensheviks had with them to not attack the Trudoviks and social democrats but only the Right in the debates on the land question, Lenin now had license. One of the Cadet fraction members, apparently to the surprise of the rest of his comrades, did exactly what the agreement prohibited, charging that the Trudovik and social democrat proposals were, respectively, "impractical" and of "the greatest injustice." Lenin relished the opportunity to go after him because it allowed him to take on, indirectly, the Mensheviks who had been cozying up to the Cadets.

With a Marxist scalpel, Lenin methodically dissected "what Deputy Kutler, in his argument against my Party comrade [Tsereteli], called 'the greatest injustice.' 'It seems to me . . . that the abolition of private property in land [the key plank in the Social Democratic program on the agrarian question] would be the greatest injustice, as long as other forms of property, real and personal estate, still remain! . . .' And then farther: 'Since nobody proposes to abolish property in general, it is essential that the existence of property in land be in every way recognized.'" This was red meat for Lenin. "This is the first time I have been confronted by a liberal, and such a moderate, sober, bureaucratically-schooled liberal at that, who proclaims the principle of '*everything or nothing*'! For, indeed, Mr. Kutler's argument is based entirely on the principle of 'everything or nothing.'" Or, as Lenin put it more concisely in the first issue of the new Bolshevik legal daily, *Nashe Ekho* [*Our Echo*], a few days later, "Since we cannot take two steps forward *this very day*, then 'it is essential' to refuse to take a simple step forward! Such is the logic of the liberal. Such is the logic of landlord avarice."[56] Kutler's absolutist stance, what liberals like him often accused the Bolsheviks of adopting, invited tongue-in-cheek sarcasm: "I, as a revolutionary Social-Democrat, must positively declare against such a method of argument."

Very didactically—again, the peasantry and its Duma deputies were his real audience—Lenin offered an analogy to show what was wrong with Kutler's argument while making ever-so-clear social democracy's position on the agrarian question:

> Imagine, gentlemen, that I have to remove two heaps of rubbish from my yard. I have only one cart. And no more than one heap can be removed on one cart. What should I do? Should I refuse altogether to clean out my yard on the grounds that it would be the greatest injustice to remove one heap of rubbish because they cannot both be removed at the same time?
>
> I permit myself to believe that anyone who *really* wants to clean out his yard *completely*, who sincerely strives for cleanliness and not for dirt, for light and not for darkness, will have a different argument. If we really cannot remove both heaps at the same time, let us first remove the one that can be got at and loaded on to the cart immediately, and then empty the cart, return home and set to work on the other heap. That's all there is to it, Mr. Kutler! Just that and nothing more!
>
> To begin with, the Russian people have to carry away on their cart all that rubbish that is known as feudal, landed proprietorship, and then come back with the empty cart to a cleaner yard, and begin loading the second heap, begin clearing out the rubbish of capitalist exploitation!
>
> Do you agree to that, Mr. Kutler, if you are a real opponent of all sorts of rubbish? Let us write it into a resolution for the State Duma, using your own words: "recognizing, jointly with Deputy Kutler, that capitalist property is no more praiseworthy than feudal landlord property, the State Duma resolves to deliver Russia first from the latter in order later to tackle the former."

Lenin knew, of course, that Kutler's class position would never allow him to sign on to such a resolution. It was, rather, another way to expose the Cadets, "the so-called 'people's freedom' party." Kutler's attempted sleight of hand, to substitute "capitalist property" for "landed property," was glaringly instructive for the peasantry and those Mensheviks who were still capable of being instructed: "Nobody in the world will agree to call or consider democrats those people who, in an epoch of struggle for freedom, qualify as 'the greatest injustice' the abolition of that which is destroying freedom, which is oppressing and suppressing freedom"—that is, "feudal, landed proprietorship."

Lenin also defended the Trudovik deputies from Kutler's charge that their "land nationalization bill" was "impractical" given the prevailing "political conditions": "Mr. Kutler's arguments in their entirety boil down to this—since ours is not a democratic state there is no need for us to present democratic land bills! No matter how you twist and turn Mr. Kutler's arguments, you will not find a grain of *any other* idea, of *any other* content, in them. Since our state serves the interests of the landowners we must not (*representatives of the people must not!*) include anything displeasing to the landowners in our agrarian bills . . . no, Mr. Kutler, that is not democracy, that is not people's freedom—it is something very, very far removed from freedom and not very far removed from servility."[57]

More important for Lenin than responding to Kutler's attacks on the social democrats and Trudoviks was a convincing critique of the Cadets' own proposals on the land question. But that wasn't easy at this stage in the debate. Rather than lay out their program, the Cadets, with Kutler again in the lead, honed in on the imprecisions in the Trudovik figures and criteria for the amount of land they demanded to be taken from "the state, crown, church and privately-owned lands" to fulfill the needs of the peasants. Lenin, again, came to the defense of the peasant deputies. The questions Kutler raised "only serve to confuse the *basic issue*; should we take 72 million dessiatines of the landlords' land for the peasants or not? . . . he simply avoided giving an answer to the question of *whether he and his party agree to hand over all the landlords' land to the peasants.* Whoever *does not agree* to hand over literally *all* the landlords' land to the peasants (remember, I made the proviso that each landowner be left with 50 dessiatines so that nobody would be ruined!) *does not stand for the peasants and does not really want to help the peasants.*"

If the Cadets wouldn't say what they were for, their "silences," Lenin wrote, would have to be a stand-in. As well as avoiding the Trudovik demand for the 72 million dessiatines, their failure to say what they thought of the issues raised by "my comrade Tsereteli" was also telling. They boiled down to the following question "which Kutler evaded and confused": "will a democratic government" at both the national and local level "have to solve the agrarian problem, or should the present government?"

And don't try to tell me that the Duma is impotent, helpless and without the necessary powers. I know all that very well . . . The matter in hand is this—the Duma must clearly, definitely and, most important of all, correctly express the real interests of the people, must tell them the truth about the solution of the agrarian problem, and must open the eyes of the peasantry so that they recognize the snags lying in the way of a solution to the land problem.

The will of the Duma, of course, is still not law, that I am well aware of! But let anybody who likes do the job of limiting the Duma's will or gagging it—*except the Duma itself!*

To make clear what he was and was not expecting of the Duma, Lenin reiterated his core position about the role of the Duma in Russia's revolution: "In the final analysis, it is not the Duma, of course, that will *decide* the agrarian question, and the decisive act in the peasants' struggle for land will not be fought out in the Duma. If we really wish to be *representatives of the people*, and not liberal civil servants; if we really want to serve the interests of the people and the interests of liberty, we *can* and *must help* the people by explaining the question, by formulating it *clearly*, by telling them the *whole* truth with no equivocation and no beating about the bush."

Lenin reserved the last section of his draft for a comradely critique of the Trudoviks, specifically the intervention of a "Reverend Tikhvinsky . . . a peasant deputy who deserves all respect for his sincere loyalty to the interests of the peasants, the interests of the people, which he defends fearlessly and with determination." As well as respect, Lenin prefaced his comments with honesty: "The Social-Democrats do not share the views of the Christian religion . . . [W]e . . . have a negative attitude towards the doctrines of Christianity. But, having said that, I consider it my duty to add, frankly and openly, that the Social-Democrats are fighting for complete freedom of conscience, and have every respect for any sincere conviction in matters of faith, provided that conviction is not implemented by force or deception." Lenin knew that this was a unique opportunity he might not have again to forge the worker-peasant alliance, and being respectful and principled was critical for success.

The equal distribution of land was the core of the Trudovik land-reform program. Lenin quoted Reverend Tikhvinsky in its defense:

This is the way the peasants, the way the working people look at the land: the land is God's, and the labouring peasant has as much right to it as each one of us has the right to water and air. it would be strange if anyone were to start selling, buying or trading in water and air—and it seems just as strange to us that anyone should trade in, sell or buy land. The Peasant Union and the Trudovik Group wish to apply the principle—all the

land to the working people. With regard to compensation for the land—
how the above is to be effected, by means of compensation or by simple
alienation without compensation, is a question that does not interest the
laboring peasantry.

Lenin, without a hint of sarcasm or patronizing, responded that though
the deputy's position "springs from the most noble motives," the "error,
the profound error of the Trudoviks is their *not* being interested in the
question of compensation and the *ways of implementing* the land reform,
although whether or not the peasantry will achieve liberation from landlord oppression *actually* depends on this question." And behind it was a
more fundamental issue—the "still more burdensome, still more oppres-
sive power over working people of today, *the power of capital, the power
of money.*" Without any hint of condescension, Lenin sought to educate
the deputy on the basics of the capitalist mode of production. He urged
him to look beyond the countryside and recognize the pervasive power of
capital to transform not only land but human "labor-power" itself into a
commodity and think about the implications of that fact:

> [C]an you imagine equalitarian land tenure or prohibiting the sale and pur-
> chase of land as long as the power of money, the power of capital, continues
> to exist? Can the Russian people be delivered from oppression and exploi-
> tation if the right of every citizen to an equal-sized piece of land is recog-
> nized, when, at the same time, a handful of people own tens of thousands
> and millions of rubles each, and the mass of the people remain poor? No,
> gentlemen. As long as the power of capital lasts, no *equality* between land
> owners will be possible, and any sort of ban on the purchase and sale of land
> will be impossible, ridiculous and absurd. Everything, not merely the land,
> but human labor, the human being himself, conscience, love, science—
> everything must *inevitably be for sale* as long as *the power of capital* lasts.

In concluding, Lenin emphasized that the critique of the deputy was
in no way meant to impugn the justice of the peasant struggle or to "belit-
tle its significance":

> Worker Social-Democrats give their full support to the peasants against
> the landlords. But it is not petty owner ship, even if it is equalitarian, that
> can save mankind from the poverty of the masses, from exploitation and
> from the oppression of man by man. What is needed for that is a struggle
> for the destruction of capitalist society, and its replacement by large-scale
> socialist production. This struggle is now being conducted by millions of
> class-conscious Social-Democrat workers in all countries of the world. It
> is only by joining in this struggle that the peasantry can, having got rid of

their first enemy, the feudal landlord, conduct a successful struggle against the second and more terrible enemy, the power of capital![58]

Nothing that Lenin wrote for Alexinsky, his most extensive intervention to date in the Duma proceedings, had not been said in previous writings and speeches. New this time is the tone and the way in which he presented his ideas. It reveals a principled and agile politician who knew how to speak to different audiences in very accessible language in a venue very different from his usual theaters of operation. Only the Duma stenographic account would reveal how much of the draft found its way into Alexinsky's intervention. Its significance, however, is that it pointed the way forward for not only what but how to say what was necessary in forging the essential alliance for Russia's bourgeois democratic revolution.

Engels often pointed to the speeches of August Bebel as models of communist speech making in the legislative arena. Relevant to my claim that Lenin's parliamentary perspective stood on the shoulders of Marx and Engels, I argue that had he lived long enough to see what he and Marx accurately anticipated about the Russian theatre, he would have pointed to this speech as well.

"An Indispensable Weapon" from the Marx-Engels Arsenal

While the evidence is strong that Lenin's parliamentary perspective was indeed informed by Marx and Engels, it's not clear if he knew about their all-important *Circular Letter of 1879* that criticized the first reformist lurch of the German party. The answer to that question came on April 6, 1907, when he wrote the "Preface" to the Russian translation of *Letters by Johannes Becker, Joseph Dietzgen, Frederick Engels, Karl Marx, and Others to Friedrich Sorge and Others*: "Of particular interest to Russian socialists in the present revolutionary period are the lessons which the militant proletariat must draw from an acquaintance with the intimate aspects of the activities of Marx and Engels in the course of nearly thirty years (1867–95)"—which is exactly what the hitherto unpublished letters made possible.[59] "And running like a scarlet thread through all these opinions is . . . a warning against the 'Right wing' of the workers' party, a merciless (sometimes—as with Marx in 1877–79—a *furious*) war against *opportunism* in Social-Democracy."

Marx's "furious war" refers precisely to the events surrounding the *Circular Letter*, which Lenin discovered for the first time. He summarized in a couple of pages the relevant correspondence and chided the then most authoritative biographer of Marx and Engels, Franz Mehring, because he "attempts to tone down Marx's attacks—as well as Engels's later attacks—against the opportunists and, in our opinion, rather overdoes it." While one might quibble about this interpretation, more important, he said, is "Marx's assessment *in principle*, of definite *trends* in socialism in general." As for one of those trends, Lenin read the later correspondence to mean that this "forecast of Bernsteinism, made in 1882, was strikingly confirmed in 1898 and subsequent years. And after that, and particularly after Marx's death, Engels, it may be said without exaggeration, was untiring in his efforts to straighten out what was being distorted by the German opportunists."

Lenin flagged for readers a series of letters Engels wrote three years after Marx's death in which he criticized the Reichstag fraction for voting for a Bismarck steamship subsidy: "The 'philistinism' of the Social-Democratic deputies was *'colossal.'* 'A petty-bourgeois socialist parliamentary group is inevitable in a country like Germany,' said Engels . . . [I]n general, it was preferable that 'the Party should be better than its parliamentary heroes, than the other way round.'" He then summarized the significance of the correspondence:

> We thus see that for more than ten years Marx and Engels systematically and unswervingly fought opportunism in the German Social-Democratic Party, and attacked intellectualist philistinism and the petty-bourgeois outlook in socialism. This is an extremely important fact. The general public know [sic] that German Social-Democracy is regarded as a model of Marxist proletarian policy and tactics, but they do not know what constant warfare the founders of Marxism had to wage against the "Right wing" (Engels's expression) of that Party. And it is no accident that soon after Engels's death this concealed war became an open one. This was an inevitable result of the decades of historical development of German Social-Democracy.

By 1907, if not before, Lenin knew therefore that Marx and Engels had mounted a campaign against the reformist tendencies, including its parliamentary work, of international social democracy's flagship party—key evidence for one of the four arguments of this book. For Lenin, in battle against Menshevik "opportunism" vis-à-vis the Cadets, the publication of the letters was most timely. Not for naught did he say that they "should serve as an indispensable weapon for all Russian socialists."[60]

Shortly after writing the "Preface," Lenin pointed, with license now from Engels, to the "Right wing of the German Social-Democrats"—the "Bernsteinians." It came in a commentary on an article about the politics of the Second Duma in *Die Neue Zeit* written by Mehring, who "[r]eaders will, of course know . . . are ['the entire editorial board'] on the side of revolutionary Social-Democracy." Lenin read Mehring's article—which, interestingly, employed the lessons Marx and Engels drew about the events of 1848–49—as praise for the Bolsheviks. Their "positive work" in countering the "disgusting orgy" of the Cadets vis-à-vis the Stolypin regime was not unlike what Marx and Engels had done to challenge the liberals who betrayed Germany's bourgeois democratic revolution a half century or so earlier. An article in the leading Bernsteinian organ *Sozial-istische Monatshefte*, on the other hand, castigated the "Leninians" for the stance they took on the elections to the Second Duma in opposing a bloc with the Cadets. "The Mensheviks," Lenin noted, "*especially Plekhanov*," come in for praise as the "*realist wing* of Russian Social-Democracy." In addition, the article applauded the "saving the Duma" campaign of "the opposition taken as a whole" and recommended that "the socialists . . . not 'waste their forces in a completely useless struggle against the Cadets.'"

This was Lenin's clearest recognition so far that the split in the Russian party mirrored a similar one in its German counterpart and that the electoral arena figured significantly in the equation—crucial evidence for my claim that the later split in international social democracy was fore-shadowed many years earlier in that very arena.

THE FIFTH PARTY CONGRESS: THE "TREACHERY OF LIBERALISM"

Not long after Lenin pointedly noted that the "model of Marxist proletar-ian policy and tactic" had been criticized by Marx and Engels for more than a decade because of its "Right wing," he warned against blindly imitating "West-European Social-Democratic parties" and the German party in particular. The context was the opening of the Fifth Party Con-gress and the debate about its agenda. He disagreed with the Mensheviks who argued that "all questions of principle" should be removed from the agenda in order, supposedly, to avoid major conflict. The Russians, they contended, would be able to conduct a more "business-like" congress, like those of West European counterparts. Lenin demurred: "We must not take from the experience of other parties things that bring us down to the level of some period of everyday routine. We must take that which brings us up to the level of general questions, of the tasks of the entire revolutionary struggle of the entire proletariat. We must learn from the best examples, and not from the worst."[61]

The deep differences in the RSDLP about "questions of principle" required, as Lenin had long recognized, a congress where they could possibly be resolved. After numerous logistical challenges, often related to security—only by escaping from Siberia could Trotsky, for example,

attend—the most representative congress of the party to date took place
from April 30 to May 19 in London. Of the more than three hundred
delegates, each representing five hundred rank and file members, the Bolsheviks had a slight majority—a registration of what they had achieved
largely at the expense of the Mensheviks since the Fourth Congress in
Stockholm a year before. With the support of sympathetic delegates from
the Polish/Lithuanian and Latvian parties, like Rosa Luxemburg, they
were able to make sure "questions of principle" would be on the agenda—
the most important being the attitude of Russian social democracy toward
bourgeois or nonproletarian parties. Two-thirds of the three-week sessions
were devoted in one way or another to the Duma.

The order of the agenda required a discussion on the conduct of the
Duma fraction itself, which proved to be contentious, before the debate
on bourgeois parties. Tsereteli and Alexinsky—absent from the Duma for
three weeks—gave counter reports. Regarding the appraisal of the former that "'Even though we may have made blunders, we were not guilty
of political vacillation,'" Lenin, in agreement with Alexinsky, responded,
"I believe that it would be absolutely wrong to blame a young Duma
group, which is only just beginning to function, for its mistakes. But
the fact of the matter is that there was *vacillation* in the very policy of
the group. And we must frankly admit this vacillation, and make it our
business to get rid of it, not for the purpose of condemning individuals, but in order to educate the proletarian party as a whole." Because
Tsereteli justified Menshevik bending to the Cadets on the basis of his
reading of the events of 1848—the necessity of "some sort of alliance with
bourgeois democracy"—Lenin charged him with "revisionism": "[B]oth
the revolution of 1848 and subsequent historical experience have taught
international Social-Democracy the very opposite, namely, that bourgeois
democracy takes its stand more and more against the proletariat, that the
fight for freedom is waged consistently only where it is led by the proletariat. The year 1848 does not teach us to make alliances with bourgeois
democrats, but rather the need to free the least developed sections of the
masses from the influence of bourgeois democracy, which is incapable of
fighting even for democracy." In playing to the Cadets, Tsereteli had succumbed to "bourgeois parliamentarianism."

An example of vacillation, Lenin said, was the fraction's decision, against
the objections of its Bolshevik wing, to grant voting rights to an "expert"
liberal economist in its deliberations—an issue that challenged working-
class delegations in the parliamentary arena from the beginning—that
is, the need for information that only the educated had. "[Sergei] Prokopovich is a man of letters whose works are known to everyone. He is

the type of bourgeois intellectual who has penetrated into our Party with
definite, opportunist aims. His joining the Party in the Railway District
[of St. Petersburg] was sheer hypocrisy. It was a screen for work *in the
Duma milieu*. And our [Central Committee] is to blame for his having
used such a screen. Our Duma group is to blame for having made it easy
for liberal writers collaborating with *Tovarishch* [a left Cadet organ] who
do not work in the Party and who are hostile in principle to the Party, to
enter our Party by the back door, making use of the Duma."[62]

Four days later the congress finally took up the central question, the
"Attitude Towards Bourgeois Parties." This, Lenin began his report, "is
the nub of the differences in matters of principle that have long divided
Russian Social-Democracy into two camps."[63] There was nothing of substance in his report he hadn't said before, at least as for the Bolshevik position. New was a careful and concise dissection of the Menshevik position.
Lenin had to be at his persuasive best. The audience included not only
the most conscious of the rank and file of the RSDLP in the audience—
that is, the three-hundred-plus delegates—but also the leadership of the
Mensheviks like Plekhanov, Martov (the leader of the "Centre"), Trotsky,
and Rosa Luxemburg (as well as one undistinguished attendee with only
observer status: Stalin). If the "nub" was the "attitude to the bourgeois
parties," the essence of that difference could be distilled, he wrote later, to
two claims of the Bolshevks—the "treachery of liberalism ['the Cadets']
and the democratic capacity of the peasantry." The facts on the ground,
he argued, confirmed the Bolshevik stance on both scores while discrediting that of the Mensheviks. The facts included what had taken place in
the Duma. By the time he gave his report, May 12, Lenin had convincing
evidence from not only the First Duma but almost all the Second Duma;
less than three weeks later Stolypin pulled its plug. Employing Marx
and Engels's method—class analysis in all its concreteness and not just
genuflecting before it, as he charged the Mensheviks were prone to do—
is what allowed, he said, the Bolsheviks to accurately predict the course of
the Cadets and thus be persuasive.

Non-Bolsheviks, like Trotsky and Luxemburg, could agree with Lenin
about the "treachery of liberalism," thus guaranteeing enough support
for the Bolshevik line. They were less persuaded, it should be noted, by
the essential second half of Lenin's argument—the democratic potential
of the petit bourgeoisie, particularly the peasantry.[64] Lenin acknowledged
such skepticism, specifically about Trudovik delegates who still vacillated,
with a call to action at the end of his report:

> In all such cases we must be able to unmask the irresolute democrats openly,
> even from the Duma platform. "Peasants!" we must say in the Duma in

such circumstances, "peasants! You should know that your representatives are betraying you by following in the wake of the liberal landlords. Your Duma deputies are betraying the cause of the peasantry to the liberal windbags and advocates." Let the peasants know—we must demonstrate this to them by facts—that *only* the workers' party is the genuinely reliable and thoroughly faithful defender of the interests, not only of socialism but also of democracy, not only of all working and exploited people, but also of the entire peasant masses, who are fighting against feudal exploitation.[65]

Despite "such cases," the "totality of voting in the Second Duma speaks most clearly in favor of a 'Left bloc' policy, and against the policy of support for the Cadets."[66] On balance, the peasant deputies voted more often with the social democrat deputies than with the Cadets—crucial evidence for his claim that the peasants had better democratic credentials than the latter.

The penultimate agenda item was a resolution on the Duma and the party's fraction. Basically, it reaffirmed, with minor changes, the Stockholm decisions. The last business of the meeting was the election of a new Central Committee. This time, unlike at Stockholm, the Bolsheviks won more seats than the Mensheviks: five to four. Six other seats were divided between the Bund and the Polish and Latvian parties. In many ways, Cadet "treachery" assured Bolshevik ascendancy.

"SLAP AND THEY ARE GONE!": THE DISSOLUTION OF THE SECOND DUMA

Shortly after the congress, Lenin pointed to an interview Struve gave that indicated that the Cadet leader was willing to abandon his party and embrace the right-wing bourgeois Octobrist Party. The move, not unanticipated, "is to our advantage, for it brings clarity and definiteness into the situation. A new landlord Duma; a new election law that separates, splendidly and with all-desirable precision, the reliable landlords and bourgeois tycoons from the unreliable peasants, urban petty-bourgeoisie and workers."[67] Stolypin, in other words, now had political cover from a wing of the Cadets to do what he had long wanted to do—to create a Duma to his own liking. Events a few weeks later would confirm Lenin's foresight.

If the debate on the land question best revealed the collision course the regime and the Duma were on—just as was true for the First Duma—that on the budget question was next in importance. Despite having little formal power for approving the government's budget, the Duma did in fact exercise influence. As Lenin explained to *Nashe Ekho* readers, "without the Duma's direct or indirect consent," it would be difficult for Stolypin et al. to have access to West European creditors. Thus "the Duma's discussion of the budget and voting on it will have double political significance":

In the first place, the Duma must open the eyes of the people to all the methods employed in that organized robbery, that systematic, unconscionable plunder of national property by a handful of landlords, civil servants and all kinds of parasites, plunder which is called "the state economy" of Russia. To explain this from the Duma rostrum is to help the people in their struggle for "people's freedom" . . . Secondly, ruthless and *open* criticism of the budget and consistently democratic voting on it are of importance to Europe and European capital . . . Whether the European financial magnates' faith in the durability and solvency of the firm of Stolypin & Co. will be strengthened or weakened, depends to a great extent on the Duma . . . The *entire* European public will *immediately* learn of the discussion and *decisions* of the Duma, so that in this respect the voice of the Duma is of tremendous significance. Nobody else could do so much to deprive Stolypin & Co. of European financial support as the Duma can.

As for what to do, "*Only* the Social-Democrats have done their duty." He pointed to "Deputy Alexinsky's budget speech . . . [It] posed the question in a more principled manner than anybody else . . . There could be added to the declaration an exposition of the socialist view of the budget of a bourgeois class state."

Although the available archival record is opaque, it's most likely that Alexinsky's one-and-a-half-hour speech on March 22 was, like his intervention on the agrarian question, written by or received major input from Lenin. The reference, for example, to an article in the London *Economist* that indicated it closely followed the Duma's involvement in the budget deliberations smelled of Lenin's hand. That the article scandalized the Black Hundred crowd because it seemed to question the legitimacy of the Czar's dissolution of the First Duma could only have pleased him. And then there's this excerpt from a summary of the stenographic record: "The duma's task, Aleksinskii declared, was to criticize the entire budget and the financial policy of the government; to expose its true character to the West. The Kadets, he held, were as willing as ever to make an arrangement with the old order on conditions which were unfavorable to the population." If this wasn't Lenin in his own words, it was certainly his message. The only thing missing, "the socialist view of the budget of a bourgeois class state"—what Lenin meant by "there could be added"—was due to the Menshivik-headed fraction / Central Committee having enough votes to bar its inclusion.[68]

Unlike for the First Duma, where it was possible to see almost daily what Lenin was doing, the public record of Lenin's involvement in the fraction's activities in the Second Duma is less transparent. The reason is that by this time the regime understandably denied him space to maneuver. Related to this fact was Stolypin's very conscious effort to limit as much contact as possible between the Duma deputies and the workers and peasants. Lenin thus had to be more careful. The precariousness of a legal daily—*Nashe Ekho*, for example, survived for only two weeks—also contributes to a cloudy picture. Police reports, I suspect, would confirm what I assume was Lenin's intimate work with Alexinsky and other Bolsheviks in the fraction, as the budget speech suggests.[69]

Just as was true for his agrarian proposal, Stolypin was unable to get Duma agreement for his budget. The obstinacy on the part of the regime to share with the Duma its data on the fine details of its proposal and the resistance of the Left deputies, led by Alexinsky and the Bolsheviks, resulted in an impasse. For Stolypin it was increasingly clear that the Duma irritant had to be removed. Needed was a pretext. Nicholas, in fact, suggested as much not long after the Duma convened: "One must let them do something manifestly stupid or mean, and then—slap and they are gone!"[70]

If there was one component of society the regime tried its best to prevent the Left bloc in the Duma from having contact with, it was the military. It was no state secret that the RSDLP had since the beginning of the revolution in 1905 sought to win sailors and soldiers to its ranks. Stolypin, in fact, told the Duma in March that he was familiar with the party's Stockholm or Fourth Congress resolution on winning the army to the revolution. And as noted earlier, the party had 33 army newspapers by the end of 1906.[71] Stolypin had tried to get Duma support for a law to keep "politicals" from being drafted into the military and to criminalize underground political work in its ranks. His failure to do so explains why he finally decided on April 17 to make the Second Duma history. But needed, in addition to a pretext, was a new electoral law, to be announced when the dissolution actually took place, that would allow him to get a more pliable Duma.

Given the RSDLP's history, there was nothing unusual, from its point of view, that some soldiers in early May approached the St. Petersburg committee of the party to obtain the support of the Duma fraction to intervene on their behalf to improve their situation and have closer collaboration. But once the reports of informants about the meeting reached Stolypin's desk, the prime minister decided he had found his pretext. He would confront the Duma with the information, saying that the social democrat deputies had violated at least two laws—inappropriate contact with the military and dealings with an illegal organization, the RSDLP— and demand that they be stripped of their parliamentary immunity. Assuming that the Duma would balk, he would then be in a reasonably strong political position to get rid of the thorn in his side. Also, the timing was good, because he finally had in hand proposals for a new electoral law that would guarantee the kind of Duma he wanted.

When Stolypin did confront the Duma on May 30 to demand that it surrender for arrest virtually the entire social democrat fraction, thus Mensheviks and Bolsheviks, he offered as evidence not only the aforementioned transgressions but, interestingly, the resolutions of the Fourth Congress. His prosecutor was more specific. The accused were "plotting for the violent overthrow of the established form of government by means of a popular uprising, and the creation of a democratic republic in its stead." The Duma fraction constituted a "criminal society" because it "had subordinated itself to the central committee" of an illegal organization, the RSDLP, to carry out these goals. "It had directed the activities of local criminal organizations (local Social-Democratic groups) and had sent out circular letters with the intention of inciting the population against the government, military officials, nobles, and landowners . . . Then it had entered into relations with secret organizations which aimed to arouse a mutiny in the army . . . It has served as a center for the reception of revolutionary demands calling for the convocation of a constituent assembly."[72] As Stolypin had correctly anticipated, the Duma wouldn't go along. The charges were so blatantly political that not only did the peasant deputies defend the social democrats but many of the Cadets did as well. Only the Octobrist and Black Hundred deputies were elated with the charges.

With the Czar's approval, Stolypin informed the world on June 3 that the Duma had been dissolved and a new one would replace it on November 1. Elections would take place on September 1 under a new set of procedures detailed in the decree. In a final act of defiance, the social democrat fraction issued a declaration. It "exhorted the people to give no credence to the accusations . . . [and] charged the administration with faithlessness in violating the immunity of the Social-Democratic deputies by arresting them and cutting off all protest; with violating the October Manifesto and increasing its own arbitrary power; and with an attempt to prevent the duma from thoroughly examining the budget . . . [The government] feared the rejection of the budget and its foreign obligations and therefore dissolved the duma. The Kadet policy of cooperation with the government, even at the cost of yielding basic rights for a part in legislation had failed entirely. For the government grew more arrogant and sought to regain its absolute power when it observed that the revolution was on the ebb. The policy of 'guarding' the duma only lowered its dignity . . . and weakened its ties with the population."[73] That Menshevik and Bolshevik deputies wrote the declaration registered how far the former had moved toward Lenin's position. Having had a front row seat to "the treachery of the Cadets," they epitomized his dictum that "revolution teaches."

The absence of any kind of real protest against Stolypin's "coup d'état" of June 3 signaled the end of the Revolution of 1905. The all-important energy "outside" the walls of Tauride Palace had dissipated. Many of the fraction members, including Tsereteli and Alexinsky, were arrested and brought to trial six months later and sentenced for varying years to "hard labor" or exile.[74] Of interest in the trial is the point made by one of the members about the Stockholm resolutions—especially the one on armed struggle—that had figured so prominently in the regime's charges. He noted that at the London Congress armed struggle wasn't on the agenda. "For the party realized that the revolutionary wave was receding and that if it should attempt to organize an uprising artificially it would become liable to charges of plotting . . . the party would then be guilty of digression from the real Social-Democratic policy: the political education of the masses and their organization for struggle."[75] Again, if these were not Lenin's own words, it was certainly his message.

Lenin indeed anticipated the end of the revolution at the London Congress, as his comments at the end of his speech on the "Attitude Towards Bourgeois Parties" indicate:

> Even if the revolution suffers defeat, the proletariat will learn, first and foremost, to understand the economic class foundations of both the liberal and the democratic parties; then it will learn to hate the bourgeoisie's treacheries and to despise the petty bourgeoisie's infirmity of purpose and its vacillations.
>
> And it is only with such a fund of knowledge, with such habits of thinking, that the proletariat will be able to approach the new, the socialist revolution more unitedly and more boldly.[76]

I argue that the Second Duma experience contributed significantly to "such a fund of knowledge," enabling the Bolsheviks to be successful in "the new, the socialist revolution"—October 1917.

A few months later Lenin wrote a "Preface" for a collection of his major writings to date, one of which was *What Is to Be Done?* As for the critics who claimed that the "pamphlet" had "incorrect or exaggerated ideas on the subject of an organization of professional revolutionaries," Lenin begged to differ. In light of the previous two years, "these statements look ridiculous":

> Compare our Social-Democratic Party during this whole period with the other parties in respect of unity, organization, and continuity of policy. You will have to admit that *in this* respect our Party is *unquestionably* superior to *all* the others—the Cadets, the Socialist-Revolutionaries, etc. . . . Despite the split, the Social-Democratic Party earlier than any of the other

parties was able to take advantage of the temporary spell of freedom to build a legal organization with an ideal democratic structure, an electoral system, and representation at congresses according to the number of organized members. You will not find this, even today, either in the Socialist-Revolutionary or the Cadet parties . . . And take the elections to the Second Duma, in which all parties participated—did they not clearly show the superior organizational unity of our Party and Duma group?[77]

***

Reflecting on Stolypin's coup d'état of June 3, Alfred Levin wrote that there "was nothing in the political scene to make a serious digression from the [October] Manifesto inevitable. The changes wrought by the law of June 3, could not positively have been foreseen even though they might have been feared by the liberals and wishfully thought of by the revolutionaries."[78] In fact, the "changes" were foreseen. Nine months earlier, Lenin, in his article "A New Coup d'État in Preparation," argued that the logic of the situation required Stolypin to radically rewrite the electoral laws. Again, if Lenin, like his mentors Marx and Engels, didn't always get the arithmetic correct, it's because he employed their method and not a crystal ball. And neither did he "wishfully" hope that Stolypin would act as he did—the time-worn charge that for Lenin "the worst the better." To the contrary, he tried in that article to mount a campaign to prevent the regime from revamping the electoral laws exactly because it wasn't inevitable that they could get away with it. For Lenin it was always about how to forge the worker-peasant alliance, the masses in their majority, for the bourgeois democratic revolution—the necessary step for the socialist revolution—and having access to the Duma rostrum was critical in his strategy.

EXCERPT FROM "ADDRESS OF THE CENTRAL COMMITTEE TO THE COMMUNIST LEAGUE"

KARL MARX AND FREDERICK ENGELS

LONDON, MARCH 1850[1]

BROTHERS!

In the two revolutionary years of 1848–49 the League proved itself in two ways. First, its members everywhere involved themselves energetically in the movement and stood in the front ranks of the only decisively revolutionary class, the proletariat, in the press, on the barricades and on the battlefields. The League further proved itself in that its understanding of the movement, as expressed in the circulars issued by the Congresses and the Central Committee of 1847 and in the Manifesto of the Communist Party,[2] has been shown to be the only correct one, and the expectations expressed in these documents have been completely fulfilled. This previously only propagated by the League in secret, is now on everyone's lips and is preached openly in the market place. At the same time, however, the formerly strong organization of the League has been considerably weakened. A large number of members who were directly involved in the movement thought that the time for secret societies was over and that public action alone was sufficient. The individual districts and communes allowed their connections with the Central Committee to weaken and gradually become dormant. So, while the democratic party, the party of the petty bourgeoisie, has become more and more organized in Germany, the workers' party has lost its only firm foothold, remaining organized at best in individual localities for local purposes; within the general movement it has consequently come under the complete domination and leadership of the petty-bourgeois democrats. This situation cannot be allowed to continue; the independence of the workers must be restored . . .

2. To be able forcefully and threateningly to oppose this party, whose betrayal of the workers will begin with the very first hour of victory, the workers must be armed and organized. The whole proletariat must be armed at once with muskets, rifles, cannon and ammunition, and the revival of the old-style citizens' militia, directed against the workers, must be opposed. Where the formation of this militia cannot be prevented, the workers must try to organize themselves independently as a proletarian guard, with elected leaders and with their own elected general staff; they must try to place themselves not under the orders of the state authority but of the revolutionary local councils set up by the workers. Where the workers are employed by the state, they must arm and organize themselves into special corps with elected leaders, or as a part of the proletarian guard. Under no pretext should arms and ammunition be surrendered; any attempt to disarm the workers must be frustrated, by force if necessary. The destruction of the bourgeois democrats' influence over the workers, and the enforcement of conditions which will compromise the rule of bourgeois democracy, which is for the moment inevitable, and make it as difficult as possible—these are the main points which the proletariat and therefore the League must keep in mind during and after the approaching uprising.

3. As soon as the new governments have established themselves, their struggle against the workers will begin. If the workers are to be able to forcibly oppose the democratic petty bourgeois it is essential above all for them to be independently organized and centralized in clubs. At the soonest possible moment after the overthrow of the present governments, the Central Committee will come to Germany and will immediately convene a Congress, submitting to it the necessary proposals for the centralization of the workers' clubs under a directorate established at the movement's center of operations. The speedy organization of at least provincial connections between the workers' clubs is one of the prime requirements for the strengthening and development of the workers' party; the immediate result of the overthrow of the existing governments will be the election of a national representative body. Here the proletariat must take care:

1) that by sharp practices local authorities and government commissioners do not, under any pretext whatsoever, exclude any section of workers;

2) that workers' candidates are nominated everywhere in opposition
    to bourgeois-democratic candidates. As far as possible they should
    be League members and their election should be pursued by all
    possible means. Even where there is no prospect of achieving their
    election the workers must put up their own candidates to preserve
    their independence, to gauge their own strength and to bring their
    revolutionary position and party standpoint to public attention.
    They must not be led astray by the empty phrases of the democrats,
    who will maintain that the workers' candidates will split the demo-
    cratic party and offer the forces of reaction the chance of victory.
    All such talk means, in the final analysis, that the proletariat is to
    be swindled. The progress which the proletarian party will make
    by operating independently in this way is infinitely more impor-
    tant than the disadvantages resulting from the presence of a few
    reactionaries in the representative body. If the forces of democracy
    take decisive, terroristic action against the reaction from the very
    beginning, the reactionary influence in the election will already
    have been destroyed . . .

Although the German workers cannot come to power and achieve the
realization of their class interests without passing through a protracted
revolutionary development, this time they can at least be certain that the
first act of the approaching revolutionary drama will coincide with the
direct victory of their own class in France and will thereby be accelerated. But they themselves must contribute most to their final victory,
by informing themselves of their own class interests, by taking up their
independent political position as soon as possible, by not allowing themselves to be misled by the hypocritical phrases of the democratic petty
bourgeoisie into doubting for one minute the necessity of an independently organized party of the proletariat. Their battle-cry must be: *The
Permanent Revolution.*

APPENDIX B

"SKETCH OF A PROVISIONAL REVOLUTIONARY GOVERNMENT"

SETTING: TSARISM IN ST. PETERSBURG STRUCK DOWN, the autocratic government overthrown—struck down but not utterly destroyed, not killed, *not annihilated*, not extirpated.[1]

The provisional revolutionary government appeals to the people. Workers and peasants *take the initiative*. Complete freedom. The people organise their own lives. The *government programme* = *full* republican liberties, peasant committees for the *complete* reform of agrarian relations. The Programme of the Social-Democratic Party *is a thing standing by itself*. Social-Democrats in the provisional government = people delegated, *commissioned* by the Social-Democratic *Party*.

Next—the Constituent Assembly. *If* the people have risen, they . . .[2] *may* (even though not immediately) find themselves in the majority (peasants and workers). *Ergo*, the revolutionary *dictatorship* of the proletariat and the peasantry.

Frantic resistance of evil forces. Civil war *in full sweep*— *annihilation* of tsarism.

Organisation of the proletariat grows, propaganda and agitation of the Social-Democrats increases ten thousandfold—all the government printing-presses, etc., etc. *"Mit der Gründlichkeit der geschichtlichen Aktion wird auch der Umfang der Masse zunehmen, deren Aktion sie ist."*[3]

The peasantry takes *all* agrarian relations, *all* the land, into its own hands. *Then nationalisation* becomes a fact.

Tremendous growth of productive forces—the entire rural intelligentsia, all technical knowledge, is brought into action to increase agricultural production, to get rid of fettering influences (uplifters, Narodniks, etc., etc.) . . . Gigantic development of **capitalist** progress . . .

War: the *fort* keeps changing hands. Either the bourgeoisie overthrows the revolutionary dictatorship of the proletariat and the peasantry, or this dictatorship sets Europe aflame, and then . . . ?

If we are to consider the question of revolutionary dictatorship from the standpoint of Marxism, we shall have to reduce it to an analysis of the *struggle of the   c l a s s e s*.

Ergo, what major social forces should be taken into account? *Ordre de bataille*?

(α) The bureaucratic, military, and Court elements stand *for* absolutism *p l u s* the unenlightened elements among the people (a rapidly disintegrating conglomerate, yesterday all-powerful, tomorrow powerless). (Dynastic and other conflicts within inevitable.)

Degree of organisation very high—maximum

(β) The more or less big, moderately-liberal bourgeoisie.

((Here I include the liberal landlords, the top financiers, the merchants, manufacturers, etc., etc. This = σ lords and masters of a bourgeois country. "Can do anything."))

Degree of organisation very slight

Conflicts between the groupings inevitable; but all stand for a Constitution even now, and still more so tomorrow.

Ideological leaders—in abundance, from among the officials, landlords, and journalists.

(γ) The petty-bourgeois and peasant section. Tens of millions.

The "people" *par excellence*.

Degree of organisation—minimum

Greatest state of benightedness and disorganisation.

Their plight most desperate, they have most to gain *directly* from the revolution. The greatest instability (to day—for the revolution, tomorrow—for "law and order" after slight improvements).

D e m o c r a c y. Ideological leaders—a great number of democratic intellectuals. The Socialist-Revolutionary "type."

(δ) The proletariat.

Very high level of organisation, and discipline

Revolutionary-minded. Critical attitude towards the petty bourgeoisie. Has *fewer* ideological leaders than all the others—only the Social-Democratic intelligentsia and the educated Social-Democratic workers. Compared with the preceding groups numerically very much weaker, but *Kampffähigkeit*[4] very much stronger.

Object of the struggle = *Republic* (including *all* democratic liberties, the **m i n i m u m   p r o g r a m m e** and far-reaching social reforms).

α—absolutely against.

β—*for* a Constitution, *against* the Republic (½ and ½). ((Bargaining.))

γ—in a revolutionary moment (not firmly) for the Republic ((the unstable elements of the struggle)).

δ—wholly and entirely *for* the Republic.

June–July 1905

"Whom to Elect to the State Duma"

Citizens! See to it That the Whole People Clearly Understands What the Chief Parties Are that Are Fighting in the Elections in St. Petersburg and What Each of Them Strives For![1]

What Are the Three Chief Parties?		
The Black Hundreds	*The Cadets*	*The Social-Democrats*
They are—the Union of the Russian People, the monarchists, the Party of Law and Order, the Union of October Seventeenth, the Commercial and Industrial Party, the Party of Peaceful Renovation.	They are—the party of "people's" freedom or Constitutional-"Democratic" (in reality liberal-monarchist) Party, the Party of "Democratic" Reforms, the radicals, etc.	*The Russian Social-Democratic Labour Party.* It is the party of the class-conscious-workers of all the nationalities of Russia, of Russians, Letts, Poles, Jews, Ukrainians, Armenians, Georgians, Tatars, etc.
Whose Interests Do the Three Chief Parties Defend?		
The Black Hundreds defend the present tsarist government, they stand for the landlords, for the government officials, for the power of the police, for military courts, for pogroms.	*The Cadets* defend the interests of the liberal bourgeois, the liberal landlords, merchants and capitalists. The Cadets are a party of bourgeois lawyers, journalists, professors and such like.	*The Social-Democrats* are the party of the working class, defending the interests of all the working and exploited people.

What Do the Three Chief Parties Strive For?

The Black Hundreds strive for the preservation of the old autocracy, the lack of rights of the people, the unlimited rule over it of the landlords, officials and police.	*The Cadets* strive for the transfer of power into the hands of the liberal bourgeoisie. The monarchy; by preserving the police and military regime, is to safeguard the capitalists' right to rob the workers and peasants.	*The Social-Democrats* strive for the transfer of all power into the hands of the people, i.e., a democratic republic. The Social-Democrats need complete freedom in order to fight for socialism, for the emancipation of labour from the yoke of capital.

What Kind of Freedom do the Three Chief Parties Want to Give the People?

The Black Hundreds do not give the people any freedom, any power. All power is for the tsarist government. The rights of the people are: to pay taxes, to toil for the rich, to rot in gaol.	*The Cadets* want the kind of "people's freedom" which will be subordinated, firstly, to the Upper Chamber, i.e., to the landlords and capitalists; secondly, to the monarchy, i. e., the tsar with the irresponsible police and armed forces. One-third of the power to the people, one-third to the capitalists and one-third to the tsar.	*The Social-Democrats* want complete freedom and all power for the people, all officials to be elected, the soldiers to be freed from barrack servitude, and the organisation of a free, people's militia.

How Do the Three Chief Parties Regard the Peasants' Demand for Land?

The Black Hundreds defend the interests of the feudal landlords. No land for the peasants. Only the rich to be allowed to buy land from the landlords by voluntary agreement.	*The Cadets* want to preserve the landlord system of agriculture by means of concessions. They propose redemption payments by the peasants which already once before in 1861 ruined the peasants. The Cadets do not agree that the land question should be settled by local committees elected by universal, direct and equal suffrage by secret ballot.	*The Social-Democrats* want to abolish our landlord system of agriculture. All land must be transferred to the peasants absolutely, with out redemption payments. The land question must be settled by local committees elected by universal, direct and equal suffrage by secret ballot.

What Can the Three Chief Parties Achieve if Their Whole Struggle is Successful?

The Black Hundreds, using every possible means of struggle, can cause the people to be finally ruined and all Russia subjected to the savagery of military courts and pogroms.	*The Cadets*, using only "peaceful" means of struggle, can cause the pogrom-mongers' government to buy off the big bourgeoisie and the rich in the countryside at the cost of petty concessions, while it will chase out the liberal chatter-boxes for insufficiently servile speeches about the beloved, blameless, inviolable, constitutional monarch.	*The Social-Democrats*, using every possible means of struggle, including an uprising, can, with the aid of the politically conscious peasantry and urban poor, win complete freedom and all the land for the peasants. And with freedom, and with the help of the class-conscious workers of all Europe, the Russian Social-Democrats can advance with rapid strides to socialism.

Citizens! Vote at the Elections for Candidates of the Russian Social-Democratic Labour Party! Social-Democrats and the Trudovik Parties

Citizens! Anyone who wants to take an intelligent part in the elections to the State Duma must first of all clearly understand the difference between the three main parties. The *Black Hundreds* stand for pogroms and the violence of the tsarist government. The *Cadets* stand for the interests of the liberal landlords and capitalists. The *Social-Democrats* stand for the interests of the working class and all the working and exploited people.

Anyone who wants to uphold intelligently the interests of the working class and all working people must know which party is really able most consistently and resolutely to defend these interests.

Which Parties Claim to Defend the Interests of the Working Class and all Working People?

The party of the working class, the *Russian Social-Democratic Labour Party*, based on the standpoint of the class struggle of the proletariat.	*Trudovik parties*, i.e., parties based on the standpoint of the small proprietor: *The Socialist-Revolutionary Party*.	*The Trudovik* (Popular Socialist) Party and *the non-party Trudoviks*.

Whose Interests do these Parties Actually Defend?

The interests of the proletarians, whose conditions of life deprive them of all hope of becoming proprietors and cause them to strive for completely changing the whole basis of the capitalist social system.	The interests of the petty proprietors, who struggle against capitalist oppression, but who, owing to the very conditions of their life, strive to become proprietors, to strengthen their petty economy and to enrich themselves by means of trade and hiring labour.

How Steadfast are These Parties in the Great World-Wide Struggle of Labour Against Capital?

The Social-Democrats cannot allow of any reconciliation of labour and capital. They organise the wage-workers for a ruthless struggle against capital, for the abolition of private ownership of the means of production and for the building of socialist society.	*The toilers' parties* dream of abolishing the rule of capital but, owing to the conditions of life of the petty proprietor, they inevitably waver between fighting jointly with the wage-workers against capital and striving to reconcile workers and capitalists by the conversion of all the working people into petty proprietors, with equal division of land, or guaranteed credit, and so on.

What Can These Parties Achieve by Completely Fulfilling Their Ultimate Aims?

The conquest of political power by the proletariat and the conversion of capitalist into social, large-scale, socialist production.	The equal distribution of land among petty proprietors and small peasants, in which case there will inevitably be a struggle between them again, giving rise to a division into rich and poor, workers and capitalists.

What Kind of Freedom for the People are These Parties Trying to Achieve in the Present Revolution?

Complete freedom and full power for the people, i. e., a democratic republic, officials to be subject to election, the replacement of the standing army by universal arming of the people.	Complete freedom and full power for the people, i.e., a democratic republic, officials to be subject to election, the replacement of the standing army by universal arming of the people.	A combination of democracy, i.e., full power of the people, with the monarchy, i.e., with the power of the tsar, police and officials. This is just as senseless a desire and just as treacherous a policy as that of the liberal landlords, the Cadets.

What Is the Attitude of These Parties to the Peasants' Demand For Land?

The Social-Democrats demand the transfer of all the landlords' land to the peasants with out any redemption payments.	*The Socialist-Revolutionaries* demand the transfer of all the landlords' land to the peasants without any redemption payments.	*The Trudoviks* demand the transfer of all the landlords' land to the peasants, but they allow redemption payments, which will ruin the peasants, so that this is just as treacherous a policy as that of the liberal landlords, the Cadets.

Citizens! Vote at the Elections for Candidates of the Russian Social-Democratic Labour Party!

November 23, 1906

A CRITICAL REVIEW OF THE
RELEVANT LITERATURE

THIS BOOK, CONSCIOUSLY AND INTENTIONALLY, PRIVILEGES LENIN'S voice, and hopefully the reader who has read it appreciates that decision. For that reason I thought it best not to encumber the text, including the endnotes (for the most part) with other voices. Now is the time to bring the Leninologists into the conversation, given how extensive and influential their literature and voice is. But in no way does this interrogation pretend to be exhaustive. The focus here is solely on those who speak to Lenin's electoral and parliamentary strategy and differ in one way or another with what I present. Admittedly, attention is given mainly to those with most visibility, and I recognize that I may have missed voices that didn't get the attention they deserve. What I cover here could easily become a stand-alone article or even maybe a book—but not at this time. If it ends up being no more than an outline, sketch, or even an inspiration for either, then it has served its purpose. The organization of this review follows the order of the subject matter of the book and prioritizes the literature alluded to in the endnotes in reference to the text.

One body of literature neglected here, only for lack of language skills, is the Russian scholarship. What I can say is that I'm aware of its existence because it figures sometimes into the English-language scholarship, which is often about correcting the heavy hand of Stalinist orthodoxy. Thus in responding to the English-language literature, I indirectly address at least some of the Russian-language scholarship.

CHAPTER 1: WHAT MARX AND ENGELS BEQUEATHED

One thing, hopefully, this chapter has done is put to rest the long-standing myth as reiterated by David Lane in 1981: "Marx and Engels were principally concerned with the anatomy and dynamics of capitalism. While they both believed that inherent laws governing the system would lead to the victory of the proletariat, they said very little about the tactics of the struggle, they provided no interpretation of the ways that the proletariat had to be organized or the kind of alliances which had to be arranged for the working class to become a ruling class. Lenin, however, was particularly concerned with these questions and with the political organization of the proletariat in Russia."[1] Thirty years later Sheri Berman made a similar claim: "[O]rthodox Marxism could not furnish them ['Parties acting in Marx's name'] with a strategy for using their power to achieve any practical goals. Orthodox Marxism in general had little to say about the role of political organizations, since it considered economic forces rather than political activism to be the prime mover of history."[2]

My book *Marx and Engels* refutes this widely held but thoroughly disingenuous orthodoxy and, more pertinent here, its blinders to their electoral/parliamentary strategy and practice.[3] This chapter distills the relevant findings of the book. One of the striking things about most standard accounts of the history of European social democratic parties is the failure to acknowledge the critical role of Marx and Engels in their origins, as I document. A notable example is Stefano Bartolini's *The Political Mobilization of the European Left, 1860–1980*, which otherwise provides a thoughtful discussion about the ideological roots of those parties.[4] There is, however, an important exception to this myopia. Two heralded books of Adam Przeworski took seriously (or appeared to) the pronouncements of the two founders of communism about electoral politics.[5] He argued, in fact, that the reformist outcome of European social democracy can be traced to their electoral strategy. Encouraging, as they did, working-class parties to enter the electoral/parliamentary arenas inevitably resulted in their class-collaborationist character. As representatives of a minority layer of society, they were forced to attenuate their demands in order to win parliamentary seats.

Prezworski's argument, which continues to be accepted as wisdom in political science, is based, however, on an egregious misrepresentation of Marx and Engels and a selective reading of the social democratic experience. I document in a 2010 article the numerous ways in which he distorted their texts—in at least one case putting words into Marx's mouth.[6] If Przeworski is to be believed, Marx and Engels, and not the subsequent leaders of social democracy, were responsible for its reformist outcome. And to try to make his case, Przeworski, in *Paper Stones*, offers apparently convincing evidence based on the actual record of those parties that such an outcome was unavoidable. But his is a selective reading of the evidence, because there is at least one social democratic party missing in his account—the party that Lenin led. This book, which details the Bolshevik experience in the electoral/parliamentary arena is—as I could only suggest in my article—therefore a refutation of Przeworski's claims.

Przeworski isn't alone in distorting Marx and Engels's electoral strategy. Others have done the same, especially when it comes to Engels. The latter is alleged to be the real author of social democratic reformism. An example is Manfred Steger's attempt, like that of Przeworski, to justify Bernstein's subsequent revisionism; see his "Friedrich Engels and the Origins of German Revisionism: Another Look," in Steger and Terrell Carver, *Engels after Marx* (University Park: Pennsylvania State University Press, 1999). A more recent version of this tendency is Tristam Hunt's *Marx's General: The Revolutionary Life of Friedrich Engels* (New York: Metropolitan Books, 2009), 338–44. The evidence I provide in this chapter on Engels in his final years, especially his fight against opportunism, gives lie to all such efforts to defang him.

As for Marx and Engels's writings and activities in relation to the Russian movement, the last section of this chapter, the striking thing about the Marxological and Leninological literatures is the virtual absence of any mention of them. The reason, I suspect, has to do with the social democratic leanings of most of their authors, who have a vested interest in defending the alleged Chinese Wall between Marx and Engels on one side and Lenin on the other. Why until now the dots between the former and the latter, specifically the making of the Bolshevik Revolution, have never been connected is therefore understandable.

CHAPTER 2: REVOLUTIONARY CONTINUITY; LENIN'S POLITICS PRIOR TO 1905

Allowing Lenin to speak for himself as this book does stands in sharp contrast, as discussed in the Conclusion to *LES1917*, to that of a classic Leninologist account: Alfred G. Meyer's *Leninism* (New York: Frederick A. Praeger, 1962), particularly Chapter 3, "Democracy." While Meyer provides quotes from Lenin, easily three-fourths of the text is his voice—to prove that Lenin wasn't really a democrat despite what the quotes say. Meyer, I suspect, like so many of his kindred, is a victim of what I call in the Preface the *post hoc* fallacy—a tendency to read pre-October 1917 Lenin through the lens of what later occurred in the Soviet Union—that is, the Stalinist counterrevolution. Since he couldn't find the antidemocrat smoking gun in Lenin's words or actions prior to 1917, he had to invent it with his spin on the quotes he did provide.

Robert Service's trilogy three decades later, *Lenin: A Political Life*, is also, like Meyer's *Leninism*, a selective reading of Lenin, but because of its length, it is more elaborate and informed.[7] He included, for example, a few lines from *What the "Friends of the People" Are* but conveniently omitted any mention of Lenin's emboldened words "**Social-Democrats**" and

"**Democracy**."[8] Any evidence that Lenin took civil liberties seriously, as in his 1897 "Draft and Explanation of a Program for the Social Democratic Party," is also absent in Service's account.

More important than the Leninological misrepresentations is Hal Draper's claim that Lenin himself misrepresented Marx and Engels's "dictatorship of the proletariat," therefore "facilitating (though certainly not causing) the societal counterrevolution represented by Stalin."[9] If the Leninologist crowd hasn't found the smoking gun to make their case, then perhaps someone more capable and credible has. According to Draper, the dictatorship of the proletariat for Marx and Engels "meant nothing more and nothing less than 'rule of the proletariat'—the 'conquest of political power' by the working class, the establishment of a workers' state in the immediate postrevolutionary period."[10] But Marx and Engels were not, as Draper seems to imply, interested in the proletariat's "conquest of political power" as an end in itself but rather the use of that power to carry out socialist transformation. And the latter would require, as the *Manifesto of the Communist Party* makes all so clear, "despotic inroads" on capital and its property—that is, the use of force. In four successive locations the *Manifesto*, which, again, Lenin knew all so well, explicitly or indirectly sanctions the use of force.[11] To fault, as Draper does, Lenin for incorporating the use of force into his usage of the dictatorship of the proletariat—the misrepresentation charge—is to engage in what the latter sometimes called pettifogging or, perhaps more correctly, only a textual rather than a political analysis of what they meant by the term. Such a reading of Lenin, I argue, is what Draper is alluding to when he writes that Lenin's first take on the term is "about the Plekhanov-type *abrogation of democratic rights in specific situations* and nothing else."[12] But Draper never addresses the more important political question that Lenin in the later context of the Revolution of 1905–7 had to answer: whether "despotic inroads" includes the "abrogation of democratic rights" and therefore whether they are legitimate from a revolutionary point of view and one that Marx and Engels would have endorsed.

Less important (at least for purposes here) is Draper's other charge that Lenin's "two-class dictatorship," specifically his democratic dictatorship of the proletariat and peasantry, clashed with Marx and Engels's understanding of class politics. I disagree because, as I point out in my *Marx and Engels*, they promoted and defended the revolutionary "people's alliance" in the context of the 1848–49 upheavals, a coalition not unlike, I argue, Lenin's "two-class dictatorship."[13] To say that it "is not our present task, fortunately, to discuss the merits and demerits of this solution of Lenin's to the crucial problem of the Russian revolution"

(p. 85) sounds like a cop-out that permits textual at the expense of political analysis.[14] Draper's failure to even acknowledge—in what purports to be an exhaustive exposition of Lenin's views on the dictatorship of the proletariat, specifically the latter's most concrete defense of his formulation after its initial launching in 1905—his polemic with Martov in 1909[15] gives credence to such a characterization. It's worth noting in this context Lenin's disagreement—rightly, in my opinion—with Engels's labeling of the Paris Commune as the "dictatorship of the proletariat."[16] Exactly because Lenin had to function in the laboratory of the class struggle could he confidently do so—the only instance I know of in which he disagreed with either of the founders of the communist movement.

Lenin the putschist is another favorite hobbyhorse of Lenin bashers. This calumny derives from their time-worn misrepresentation of how the Bolsheviks led the working class to power in October in 1917. It is in turn employed to search for the smoking gun in Lenin's background, the roots of his supposed propensity for a conspiratorial-putschist minority-led revolution. But if the actual record prior to 1917 doesn't yield such evidence, as the quotes I provide on his views on terrorism and armed struggle would suggest, then its employers are compelled to invent it—exactly what Service and Figes do. While the former only hints at the culprit,[17] the latter spins a full-flung tale. The "Russian revolutionary tradition . . . of conspiratorial politics . . . [and] putschist tactics" via the Narodniks, especially Peter Tkachev (who was once the target of Engels's critique of such a modus operandi), is what really informed Lenin's politics, his Marxist protestations notwithstanding.[18] Lars Lih, who devotes six pages to the allegation, rightly concludes that the "idea that Lenin used Tkachev as a reliable guide to on-going political decisions in 1904–5 or any other time is totally absurd."[19]

When it comes to Lenin's party-building project, Leninology gets quite creative. About his first take on the subject, *The Tasks of the Russian Social-Democrats* (1897), Service writes, "He urged social-democrats to set about 'the education, disciplining and organization of the proletariat.' The imagery is trenchantly hierarchical; its bursts through all the qualifying language of the sentences around it. Discipline was always a key theme in his thought."[20] But rather than reproduce "the qualifying language of the sentences around" what Lenin actually wrote, as I do in presenting the text, Service offers his own "qualifying language." Here is the complete sentence that Lenin wrote: "[Russian social democrats] think that the fight against the autocracy must consist not in organizing conspiracies, but in educating, disciplining and organizing the proletariat, in political agitation among the workers which denounces every manifestation of absolutism, which pillories all the knights of the police government and compels this government to make concessions"[21]—not quite the "trenchantly hierarchical" tone that Service imputes.

But innuendo isn't sufficient for Service. When the counterfactuals are all too evident, he suffers a bout of myopia. Lenin, in his *Our Immediate Task* (1899), posed two key questions about how to reconcile rank-and-file control from below with the need for a centralized party in the context of near-absolutist Czarist Russia, both of which I reproduce in full. In this instance Service is especially duplicitous. Not only does he conveniently ignore the second question, but he baldly misrepresents what Lenin actually wrote: "But significantly, [Lenin] left his cumbersome phrased question unanswered."[22] As the reader can easily verify in Chapter 2, pp. 24–25, Lenin offered very concrete proposals on how to answer both questions, suggestions that, again, challenge the standard Leninological portrait of him as the domineering ogre who sought to impose his program on the working class.

"Lenin the ogre" and the related "Lenin the Jacobin" have their origin in the aftermath of the historic Second Congress of the RSDLP in 1903, which resulted in the Bolshevik-Menshevik split. Both Trotsky and Luxemburg were their original authors—Trotsky in particular, as his biographer Issac Deutscher convincingly documents.[23] Both polemicized against Lenin's book, *One Step Forward, Two Steps Back*, his assessment of the congress and defense of his position. Only in April 1917 did Trotsky put away his differences with Lenin—certainly on the organizational question—and join forces with him. As for what had been his position vis-à-vis that of Lenin, "its profound erroneousness," he wrote in 1941, "had been long ago demonstrated both in theory and practice."[24] There is no evidence that Luxemburg, unlike Trotsky, reconsidered her stance. In his response to her criticism of his book, Lenin argued that she misunderstood his approach to party organizing,[25] which lends credence to Lars Lih's argument that she actually never read the book.[26]

Perhaps the most egregious example of misrepresentation in the annals of Leninology was performed by Bertram Wolfe in his *Three Who Made a Revolution*.[27] After having begun for about a hundred pages somewhat objectively about Lenin, or at least pretending to, Wolfe had his supposed aha! moment—the proverbial smoking gun at last found. Buried in Lenin's polemic about the 1903 RSDLP conference, *One Step Forward, Two Steps Back*, was the incriminating evidence. In it, page unspecified, Wolfe alleges that

> centralism becomes a revolutionary virtue *per se* for all lands and all circumstances of struggle. One looks in vain in [*OSFTSB*] for what was in the

preceding works: some tribute to the desirability and corrective and educative force of democracy. On the contrary: "Burocratism versus democratism, i.e. precisely centralism versus autonomy, such is the organizational principle of revolutionary social democracy as against that of the opportunists. The latter principle strives to go from below upward, and therefore defends as far as possible and wherever possible autonomy and democracy . . . But the organizational principle of revolutionary social democracy strives to go from the top downward, and defends the enlargement of the rights and plenary powers of the central against the parts."

"This," Wolfe explains, "is the most naked expression of faith in hierarchy and distrust of democracy to be found in all of Lenin's writings. Only the isolation from the criticism of equals and the stubborn tendency to cherish most what was most under attack could have wrung from him such an extreme statement . . . [W]hen we seek to understand the Russian state after Lenin came to power, and when we watch the formation of the Communist International, we shall have to keep this one-sided utterance in mind, for it takes an authoritarian party to make an authoritarian state."[28] There, according to Wolfe, is the key to understanding the Stalinist counterrevolution that came in the wake of the Bolshevik triumph in 1917—this uncharacteristic "extreme statement" of Lenin in praise of "centralism" and "hierarchy" and of "distrust in democracy." I leave aside the pitfalls in Wolfe's reductionist argument about the reasons for the Stalinist counterrevolution, an issue I address in Chapter 3 in *Lenin's Electoral Strategy from 1907 to the Revolution of October 1917: The Ballot, the Streets—or Both*. The focus here is on the smoking gun that he claimed to have found.

Let's look now at what Lenin actually wrote—the full paragraph and this time with the page numbers. I embolden what Wolfe selected from the original, taking into account different translations.

Perhaps the only attempt to analyze the concept bureaucracy is the distinction drawn in the new *Iskra* (No. 53) between the "formal *democratic* principle" (author's italics) and the "formal *bureaucratic* principle." This distinction (which, unfortunately, was no more developed or explained than the reference to the non-*Iskra*-ists) contains a grain of truth. **Bureaucracy *versus* democracy** is in fact **centralism *versus* autonomism**; it is **the organizational principle of revolutionary Social-Democracy as opposed to the organizational principle of opportunist Social-Democracy. The latter strives to proceed from the bottom upward, and, therefore, wherever possible and as far as possible, upholds autonomism and "democracy,"** [Lenin's all-important scare quotes are dropped in Wolfe's rendering] carried (by the overzealous) to the point of anarchism. The former strives to proceed **from the top downward, and upholds an extension of the rights and powers of the center in relation to the parts.** In the period of disunity and separate circles, this **top** from which **revolutionary Social-Democracy strove to proceed organizationally** was inevitably one of the circles, the one enjoying most influence by virtue of its activity and its revolutionary consistency (in our case, the *Iskra* organisation). In the period of the restoration of actual Party unity and dissolution of the obsolete circles in this unity, this top is inevitably the *Party Congress*, as the supreme organ of the Party; the Congress as far as possible includes representatives of all the active organizations, and, by appointing the central institutions (often with a membership which satisfies the advanced elements of the Party more than the backward and is more to the taste of its revolutionary than its opportunist wing), makes them the top until the next Congress. Such, at any rate, is the case among the Social-Democratic Europeans, although little by little this custom, so abhorrent in principle to anarchists, is beginning to spread—not without difficulty and not without conflicts and squabbles—to the Social-Democratic Asiatics.[29]

Let's "cut to the chase." The "top" that Lenin was referring to and what Wolfe inexcusably omitted was "the Party Congress"—that is, the representative body ("as far as possible" under police state conditions) of the local organizations and committees and in power "until the next Congress." In countries that enjoyed greater political liberty, the congress was composed of democratically elected delegates from the local level. Thus the centralization that Lenin fought for was the kind of organizational structure that existed in virtually all social democratic parties. At the heart of the fight with the "autonomists" was their desire to maintain or reluctance to give up the local sovereignty that they had long been accustomed to exercising and not yield to the sovereignty of a higher body—that is, the party congress. Only an honest reading of Lenin's words—all of them—conveys what he actually meant.

As far as I can determine this is the first published exposure of Wolfe's legerdemain. Even Paul LeBlanc, in his sympathetic account about Lenin, *Lenin and the Revolutionary Party* (Atlantic Highlands, NJ: Humanities, 1990), and which makes a number of critical references about Wolfe's book, missed his machinations. It can't be overstated how influential the book was from its appearance in 1948—and it is still in print. It was greeted with accolades by luminaries such as Arthur Schlesinger Jr., Edmund Wilson, and Isaiah Berlin and was for decades required reading on many a university course syllabus. Again, because Wolfe was a former "insider," a functionary for Stalin, it gave his account credibility that none other had ever had. Note, also, what makes Wolfe's accusation effective—feigned surprise at what he supposedly discovered, in such contrast to "what was in [Lenin's] preceding works" that gave "tribute to the desirability and corrective and educative force of democracy." Wolfe's tenure as a staffer in Comintern makes it hard to resist recalling the title of Trotsky's instructive book about the organization's modus operandi, *The Stalinist School of Falsification*. If anyone could distort the real Lenin, Wolfe had the requisite credentials and skills. I suspect that the reason Wolfe hasn't been detected until now is that his claim sounds credible given the mainstream narrative—informed by a *post hoc* reading of the Russian revolution.

CHAPTER 3: "THE DRESS REHEARSAL" AND THE FIRST DUMA

J. L. Keep claims that Lenin "was exultant at the dissolution" of the First Duma, and to "many of his hearers the course which Lenin now recommended savored of 'Blanquism.'"[30] By the latter, Keep was referring to Lenin's call for the need to make preparations for a possible military confrontation with the regime. And consistent with Keep's Blanquist characterization of Lenin, the latter "advised the social-democratic deputies against trying to make contact with the electorate." Nothing could be further from the truth, as the evidence I provide, and what Keep is silent about, for Lenin's strategy for the RSDLP fraction shows. It was the regime that went to extraordinary lengths to prevent contact between the two. Keep betrays more confusion when he writes that Lenin "warned the workers with uncharacteristic caution not to strike until they were fully prepared, urging instead the formation of special committees to mobilize the peasants."[31] Only for those like Keep who didn't understand Lenin's politics was it "uncharacteristic" to advise revolutionary restraint.

It is possible to read, as Keep does, inconsistency into Lenin's tactics regarding the dissolution but only if one ignores that by end of the First Duma, as I think the evidence demonstrates and as Lenin admits, the institution had in fact—despite his initial skepticism—been of use. So the idea that he was "exultant" about its dissolution only makes sense if he hadn't changed his mind. Thus Keep is in a quandary in trying to explain why Lenin opposed boycott of the elections to the Second Duma. He, according to Keep, "seemed unsure of this position and took refuge in vague contradictory definitions of the new course. Perhaps the most plausible explanation of his change of tactics is that, although he was now aware of the improbability of an uprising in the near future, he dared not admit in public what he recognized in private"[32]—that is, "Lenin the devious." The contradictions reside only in Keep's reformist brain, which couldn't understand Lenin's revolutionary utilitarian or, better, Marxist approach to the electoral/parliamentary process.

Keep's real sympathies are revealed in his final comments about Lenin: "In so far as Lenin's deliberate policy of 'exposing' the Kadets helped to alienate popular support from the assembly and facilitate its dissolution, his tactics toward the first State Duma in 1906 may be said to have fore-shadowed his own forcible dissolution of the Constituent Assembly in 1918."[33] Not only did Lenin's actions in 1906 undermine Russia's first experiment with liberal democracy, we're told, but they explain the Stalin-ist counterrevolution that came in the wake of Lenin's death—two birds with one stone, and how convenient! Figes, forty years later, at least rec-ognizes that the Cadets were their own worst enemies and didn't need a Lenin to blame.

NOTES

PREFACE

1. V. I. Lenin, *"Left-Wing" Communism—An Infantile Disorder,* in *Collected Works,* vol. 31 (Moscow: Progress Publishers, 1978), p. 61. Hereafter, citations from his Collected Works will be designated as in this case: *31,* p. 61.

2. Like Marxologists (and unlike Marxists and Leninists), Leninologists pretend to be non-partisan in pursuit of "objective research." The reality in both cases is otherwise; for the duplicity of the Leninologists, see my Appendix: A Critical Review of the Literature. I owe the distinction to Hal Draper, *Karl Marx's Theory of Revolution,* vol.1 (New York: Monthly Review Press, 1977).

3. I recognize that Lenin's portrait by his enemies is complicated. Some of them actually praise what they see as his organizing skills while disdaining his politics. A classic example is Samuel Huntington's assessment in his *Political Order in Changing Societies* (New Haven, CT: Yale University Press, 1967). Huntington's portrait may in fact be the inspiration for such neoconservatives as William Kristol; "neoconservative foreign policy thinking has all along indulged a romance of the ruthless—an expectation that small numbers of people might be able to play a decisive role in world events, if only their ferocity could be unleashed" (Paul Berman, *New York Times Book Review,* March 26, 2006).

4. At the end of his influential career, Leninologist Leopold Haimson appears to have had a more balanced view of the Bolshevik leader. But he couldn't resist reading him through the lens of the Stalinist outcome of the Russian Revolution. See his "Lenin's Revolutionary Career Revisited: Some Observations on Recent Discussion," *Kritika* 5, no. 1 (2004): 79.

5. See the appendix, "A Critical Review of the Literature: chapter two," for what might be the most blatant example.

6. Richard Pipes, *The Unknown Lenin: From the Secret Archive* (New Haven, CT: Yale University Press, 1996).

7. I discuss in my *Marx, Tocqueville, and Race in America: The "Absolute Democracy" or "Defiled Republic"* (Lanham, MD: Lexington Books, 2003), pp. 161–71, how these two overturns were actually linked.

    Just as I was completing the manuscript, I discovered Roland Boer's *Lenin, Religion, and Theology* (New York: Palgrave Macmillan, 2013), a most informative treatment of a hitherto neglected dimension of the Bolshevik leader. I didn't have time to give it more than a cursory glance other than the references to Lenin vis-à-vis Duma politics—none of which appear to be problematic. However, I beg to differ with his claim about those who argue, like Trotsky and Krupskaya (Lenin's widow), that "Lenin was thoroughly consistent and faithful to Marx throughout his life, operating with a grand socialist narrative that moved . . . to the glorious construction of communism. The problem with this position," according to Boer, "is not only that it must end with a narrative of disappointment, for Lenin found after the revolution that events did not turn out as expected, but also that it must smooth over the many times Lenin took an unexpected direction" (p. 7). Readers of this book will be able to determine if one of "many times" applied to his electoral/parliamentary strategy. Relevant here, though, is the false assumption that neither Lenin nor his mentors, Marx and Engels, were prepared for defeats or counterrevolutions. Nothing could be further from the truth. The authors of the *Communist Manifesto* recognized this reality about the class struggle in the second paragraph in the first part of the document. Proletarian defeats, a few pages later, were more common than victories. And the living class struggle, from the coup d'état of Louis Bonaparte in 1851 to the defeat of the Communards of Paris in 1871—whose lessons Lenin had internalized—made theory real.

8. Doug Jenness, *Lenin as Election Campaign Manager* (New York: Pathfinder Press, 1971).
9. "Marx and Engels's Electoral Strategy: The Alleged versus the Real," *New Political Science* 32, no. 3 (September 2010): 367–87.
10. *Marx and Engels: Their Contribution to the Democratic Breakthrough* (Albany: State University of New York Press, 2000).
11. Nadezhda Krupskaya, *Memories of Lenin* (London: Panther Books, 1970), p. 145.
12. Robert Service, *Lenin: A Political Life*, vol. 2 (Bloomington: Indiana University Press, 1991), p. 353n32.

CHAPTER 1

1. V. I. Lenin, *Collected Works*, vol. 28 (Moscow: Progress Publishers, 1978), pp. 241–42. Hereafter, the designation will be as follows: *28*, pp. 241–42.
2. For another discussion of the topic, see my "Marx and Engels's Electoral Strategy: The Alleged versus the Real," *New Political Science* 32, no. 3 (September 2010): 367–87.
3. "Contribution to the Critique of Hegel's Philosophy of Law," in *Marx-Engels Collected Works*, vol. 3 (New York: International Publishers, 1975–2004), pp. 28–29. Hereafter, citations from the *MECW* are designated as follows: *MECW* 3, pp. 28–29. For details on Marx and Engels's political evolution, see my *Marx and Engels: Their Contribution to the Democratic Breakthrough* (Albany, NY: SUNY Press, 2000), ch. 1, and my *Marx, Tocqueville, and Race in America: The "Absolute Democracy" or "Defiled Republic"* (Lanham, MD: Lexington Books, 2003), ch. 1.
4. Chapter 1 in my *Marx, Tocqueville* distills Marx's path to communist conclusions based on his reading of the US case.
5. *MECW* 6, p. 333.
6. *MECW* 27, p. 271.
7. *MECW* 7, p. 3.

8. Engels reproduced a somewhat abridged version of the *Demands* in his article "On the History of the Communist League" in 1885, *MECW* 26, pp. 312–30, which did not include, for reasons not clear, the sixth demand and the accompanying clarification quoted here; it's possible that forty years later he didn't have a clean copy of the original. This might explain why Lenin, as far as I can tell, did not employ the *Demands* to support his arguments about the peasantry, specifically the alliance between workers and the small peasantry. Had he known what Marx and Engels had advocated I have no doubt that Lenin would have drawn on their authority to support his case.

9. For details, see my *Marx and Engels*, specifically the Index entries "democratic centralism," "party: internal democracy," "norms and obligations," "rules."

10. *MECW* 48, p. 425. See also Engels's more detailed comment on internal party democracy in *MECW* 49, p. 11.

11. In Cologne, at least, the League, owing to Gottschalk's opposition, boycotted the elections. Jonathan Sperber, *Karl Marx: A Nineteenth-Century Life* (New York: Liveright, 2013), p. 221.

12. *MECW* 8, p. 227–28. On the discussion within the worker's movement on this question, see Oscar Hammen, *The Red '48ers: Karl Marx and Frederick Engels* (New York: Charles Scribner's Sons, 1969), pp. 360–61. Contrary to Hammen, the context for this quote makes clear that the "party" is indeed the "people's alliance" of the *Demands* and not the communist party of the *Manifesto*.

13. *MECW* 8, p. 514.

14. Ibid., pp. 288–89.

15. Ibid., p. 390.

16. Ibid., p. 391.

17. David Riazanov, *Karl Marx and Friedrich Engels: An Introduction to Their Lives and Works* (New York: Monthly Review, 1973), p. 100.

18. *13*, p. 37.

19. *MECW* 10, p. 284, my italics.

20. Ibid.

21. In my "Marx and Engels's Electoral Strategy," I criticize Adam Przeworski for flagrantly misrepresenting Marx and Engels's view on this and subsequent points.

22. For a comparison of Marx and Engels's assessment of the 1848 revolution in France and that of Tocqueville, see Chapter 5 in my *Marx and Engels*.

23. *MECW* 10, p. 137.

24. *MECW* 11, p. 79. It might be noted that this is not a translation, because the original series was in English—published in the *New York Daily-Tribune* under Marx's name.

25. *MECW* 41, p. 453. Uppercase indicates that the original is in English.

26. *MECW* 8, p. 215.

27. *MECW* 20, p. 12, my italics.

28. Ibid., p. 14.

29. *MECW* 42, pp. 54–55.

30. Ibid., pp. 92–93. Marx, in a letter to Engels in May 1865, voiced similar suspicions about the one-time Chartist leader Ernest Jones: "[B]etween ourselves, *he* is *only* trying to use our Association for electoral agitation" (Ibid., p. 155). When Jones asked Marx in November 1868 to assist his parliamentary bid, he politely declined. The GC, he said, "does not get mixed up ELECTIONEERING" (*MECW* 43, p. 166). If the reader is wondering how Marx dealt with the fact of his own class origins in his role in the IWMA, see my *Marx and Engels*, pp. 185–88.
31. *MECW* 42, p. 314.
32. *MECW* 44, pp. 100–101.
33. *MECW* 41, p. 400.
34. Ibid., p. 467. Unbeknownst to Marx at the time, the summer of 1863, Lassalle met secretly with Bismarck to effect such a quid pro quo. In his letter to the chancellor, which included the statues of the GGWA, Lassalle gloated over "the constitution of *my* empire, which perhaps you'd have to envy me! But this miniature picture will plainly convince you how true it is that the working class feels instinctively inclined to dictatorship if it can first be rightfully convinced that such will be exercised in its interests." He then proposed to Bismarck that the Crown become, in partnership with him lording over the German working class, a "social dictatorship." Hal Draper, *Karl Marx's Theory of Revolution*, vol. 4 (New York: Monthly Review, 1990), p. 55. How perceptive Marx had been in suspecting Lassalle of aspiring to be "a future working men's dictator"!
35. *MECW* 41, p. 467.
36. *MECW* 22, p. 328.
37. *MECW* 23, p. 175. Almost 25 years later Engels reiterated this point; see *MECW* 50, p. 276.
38. *MECW* 22, pp. 417–18.
39. *MECW* 22, p. 617. Henri Tolain, a French member of the IWMA who had been elected to the National Assembly "as a representative of the Working classes" prior to the outbreak of the Commune, sided with Versailles against the insurgents. Because of his actions, the IWMA expelled him as a traitor; see ibid., p. 297.
40. Ibid., p. 618.
41. Ibid., p. 427.
42. Donald Sassoon, *One Hundred Years of Socialism: The West European Left in the Twentieth Century* (New York: New Press, 1996), p. 10. Though not on Sassoon's list, I'm including the French party of Jules Guesde that Marx collaborated with.
43. *MECW* 45, p. 283.
44. Ibid., pp. 6–7.
45. Draper, *Karl Marx's Theory of Revolution*, vol. 2, pp. 516 and 600.
46. *MECW* 45, p. 403.
47. Ibid.
48. Ibid., p. 405.
49. Ibid., pp. 406–7.

50. Ibid., p. 408.
51. Ibid., p. 399.
52. Ibid., pp. 423–24. As the reader probably realizes, *social democracy* had a different meaning in the Marxist movement at this stage from what it would acquire subsequently.
53. Ibid., p. 400.
54. Ibid., p. 408.
55. Ibid., pp. 413–14.
56. Contrary to what David McLellan, *Karl Marx: His Life and Thought* (New York: Harper and Row, 1973), p. 438, suggests, Marx did have an opinion of Bernstein and company, at least in September 1879, which was not very flattering: "They are poor *counter-revolutionary* windbags" (Ibid., p. 413).
57. *MECW* 46, p. 42.
58. Ibid, p. 150.
59. *MECW* 45, p. 9. For useful details about the elections, see my *Marx and Engels*, specifically the Index entries "democratic centralism," "party: internal democracy," "norms and obligations," "rules." Regarding Jacoby's biography, see Hal Draper, *The Marx-Engels Glossary* (New York: Schocken Books, 1986), p. 103.
60. *MECW* 45, p. 7.
61. *MECW* 24, p. 248.
62. *MECW* 23, p. 255.
63. *MECW* 24, p. 249.
64. *MECW* 49, p. 135.
65. *MECW* 46, p. 8.
66. *MECW* 26, p. 272.
67. *MECW* 50, p. 29. For Engels's first usage of the military analogy regarding elections, see *MECW* 48, pp. 39–40.
68. See "A Critical Review of the Relevant Literature: Chapter 1" for examples of literature that subscribe to the defanged Engels allegation.
69. *MECW* 46, p. 44.
70. *MECW* 24, p. 340.
71. *MECW* 47, p. 210
72. *MECW* 48, p. 30.
73. *MECW* 50, p. 155.
74. Ibid., pp. 159–60.
75. *MECW* 47, p. 342.
76. Ibid., p. 223.
77. *MECW* 48, p. 423.
78. *MECW* 27, p. 227.
79. Ibid., p. 271.
80. *MECW* 50, pp. 486 and 489.
81. *MECW* 27, p. 519.
82. Ibid., pp. 78–79.
83. Ibid., p. 241.
84. Ibid., pp. 6 and 10.

85. *MECW* 48, p. 456.
86. *MECW* 49, p. 267.
87. *MECW* 48, p. 452.
88. *MECW* 50, p. 369.
89. *MECW* 47, pp. 201–2
90. *MECW* 50, p. 369.
91. *MECW* 49, p. 502. As for Engels's opinion of the Fabians, "its chief object is to convert your *bourgeois* to socialism and so introduce the thing *peacefully* and *constitutionally*" (*MECW* 48, p. 449).
92. *MECW* 46, p. 413.
93. Ibid., p. 82.
94. *MECW* 48, pp. 267–68.
95. *MECW* 50, p. 261.
96. Karl Kautsky, *The Class Struggle (Erfurt Program)* (New York: W. W. Norton, 1971), p. 2.
97. *MECW* 49, pp. 367–68.
98. Kautsky, *The Class Struggle*, pp. 186–88, my italics. Note that the version I employ is a "somewhat condensed English translation" of the original (p. 2).
99. Przeworski's *Capitalism and Social Democracy*, the second chapter, is the most persuasive. See also Sheri Berman, "Social Democracy's Past and Potential Future," in *What's Left of the Left: Democrats and Social Democrats in Challenging Times*, ed. James Cronin, George Ross, and James Shoch (Chapel Hill, NC: Duke University Press, 2011).
100. Maximillien Rubel and Margaret Manale, *Marx without Myth: A Chronological Study of His Life and Work* (New York: Harper and Row, 1975), p. 251. This rendering compares favorably to that of *MECW* 43, p. 551.
101. *MECW* 43, p. 424.
102. Ibid., p. 450.
103. *MECW* 45, p. 103. "Longer than he expected" refers to the revolutionary upheavals in Germany that came in the wake of the Russian Revolution in October 1917.
104. *MECW* 43, p. 462.
105. *MECW* 44, p. 396.
106. Institute of Marxism-Leninism, *The General Council of the First International, 1868–1870: Minutes* (Moscow: Progress Publishers, 1974), p. 220.
107. *MECW* 24, p. 200.
108. Ibid., p. 199.
109. Ibid., p. 359.
110. Ibid., p. 371.
111. Ibid., p. 50.
112. Ibid., p. 37.
113. Ibid., p. 252. For Marx's praise of Russian terrorists like Zasulich, see *MECW* 46, pp. 45 and 83.
114. *MECW* 45, p. 296.
115. *MECW* 24, p. 103.

116. *MECW* 46, p. 198.
117. *MECW* 24, p. 426.
118. *MECW* 48, p. 46.
119. *MECW* 46, p. 83.
120. Ibid., p. 208.
121. *MECW* 26, p. 294.
122. *MECW* 47, p. 264.
123. Ibid., p. 280.
124. Ibid., p. 281.
125. On some details about Zasulich's close relationship with Engels, especially after she moved from Geneva to London in 1894, see Jay Bergman, *Vera Zasulich: A Biography* (Stanford: Stanford University Press, 1983), ch. 4.
126. *MECW* 27, p. 433.
127. Draper, *Karl Marx's Theory of Revolution*, vol. 2, p. 272.
128. For details, see Draper and E. Haberkern, *Karl Marx's Theory of Revolution, Vol. V: War & Revolution* (New York: Monthly Review, 2005), especially ch. 8.
129. *MECW* 48, p. 135.
130. *MECW* 27, p. 245.
131. *MECW* 50, p. 20.

CHAPTER 2

1. See "A Critical Review of the Relevant Literature: Chapter 2" in *Lenin's Electoral Strategy from 1907 to the October Revolution of 1917* (hereafter, *LES1917*) for details.
2. *Marx-Engels Collected Works*, vol. 44 (New York: International Publishers, 1975–2004), p. 396. Hereafter, citations from the *MECW* are designated as follows: *MECW* 44, p. 396.
3. Much ink has been spilt on Lenin's familial situation and its influence on his political trajectory, especially the execution of his brother Alexander, all of which is beyond the purview of this book. On his biography, Leon Trotsky's *The Young Lenin* (New York: Doubleday, 1972) is particularly useful.
4. V. I. Lenin, *Collected Works*, vol. 1 (Moscow: Progress Publishers, 1977), p. 540. Hereafter, citations from his *Collected Works* will be indicated as in this case: *1*, p. 540.
5. Lenin anxiously tried to get a copy as soon as it was available (*37*, p. 68). Interestingly, the Russian Narodnik Nikolar Danielson, living in St. Petersburg, appears to have been the first party contact to receive from Engels the publisher's galleys (*MECW* 50, p. 280)—another indication of the importance that he and Marx lent to the Russian movement.
6. Trotsky, *The Young Lenin*, p. 185.
7. Philip Pomper, *Lenin, Trotsky, and Stalin: The Intelligentsia and Power* (New York: Columbia University Press, 1990), pp. 32–33.
8. Lars Lih, *Lenin Rediscovered: What Is to Be Done in Context* (Leiden: Brill, 2006), pp. 377–84, correctly disputes the frequent charge that Lenin never

got over the Narodnik influence but misses an opportunity to show how Marx himself found Chernyshevsky attractive.

9. *1*, pp. 289–92, italics and bold in the original.

10. Ibid., p. 504.

11. Both documents are inconvenient for Leninologists. See "A Critical Review of the Relevant Literature: Chapter 2" in *LES1917*.

12. *MECW* 27, p. 271. In his "Appendix II," Lenin cites the relevant texts of Marx and Engels to make his case. Particularly noteworthy is the young Lenin's familiarity with the Marx-Ruge correspondence, 1842–43. These letters, underappreciated until today, reveal the process by which Marx broke with the young Hegelians, a necessary step on his road to communism. That Lenin could so early unearth them and see their significance speaks volumes about how well schooled he was in Marx's project.

13. Ibid., p. 439.

14. Lars Lih's claim that Lenin was essentially an offspring of the German Social Democratic Party, Kautsky specifically, was the target of my critique, "A Return to Lenin—But without Marx and Engels?" *Science and Society* 73, no. 4 (October 2009): 452–73.

15. *4*, pp. 92–93.

16. *2*, pp. 26–27.

17. Robert Service, *Lenin: A Political Life*, vol. 1 (Bloomington: Indiana University Press, 1991), pp. 61–62.

18. *2*, pp. 117–18. See "A Critical Review of the Relevant Literature: Chapter 2" in *LES1917* for Leninological myopia about Lenin's views on civil liberties.

19. Ibid., p. 107.

20. Ibid., p. 278.

21. Ibid., p. 285.

22. Ibid., p. 328.

23. Ibid., p. 333.

24. Ibid., pp. 333–34. Subsequent quotations can be found on pages 335–38.

25. Ibid., pp. 335–37.

26. *5*, p. 343.

27. *4*, p. 239.

28. Hal Draper, *Karl Marx's Theory of Revolution, Vol. 3: The "Dictatorship of the Proletariat"* (New York: Monthly Review, 1986).

29. *6*, pp. 26–27. Plekhanov's original states, "[I]n order to effect its revolution, the proletariat must have command of political power, which will make it master of the situation and enable it ruthlessly to smash all the obstacles it will come up against on the road to its great goal. In this sense the dictatorship of the proletariat is an essential political condition of the social revolution" (Ibid., pp. 21–22). Lenin's marginal notes are intriguing: "'Master of the situation,' 'ruthlessly to smash,' 'dictatorship'??? (The social revolution is enough for us.)" Do his question marks suggest that he was uncertain about Plekhanov's usage of the term or of the term itself? His proposed rewording appears to be his effort to clarify.

30. See my "Marx and Engels's Electoral Strategy: The Alleged versus the Real," *New Political Science* 32, no. 3 (September 2010): 375 for details.

31. Lenin's comments on the *Manifesto—4*, p. 49—about the "dictatorship of the proletariat" are evidence for Draper's claims. See "A Critical Review of the Relevant Literature: Chapter 2" in *LES1917* for a discussion of Draper's position.

32. *4*, pp. 211–12.

33. For the complete wording of the two demands in the Erfurt Program, see Gary Steenson, *After Marx, Before Lenin: Marxism and Socialist Working Class Parties in Europe, 1884–1914* (Pittsburgh: University of Pittsburgh Press, 1991), pp. 298–99. Regarding Lars Lih's position that Lenin was a "Russian Erfurtian," see his *Lenin Rediscovered*, pp. 111–58, and my critique in "A Return to Lenin—But Without Marx and Engels?"

34. *4*, pp. 238–39.

35. Ibid., p. 265.

36. Ibid., pp. 273–74. The program adopted by the Second Congress of the RSDLP in 1903 begins by calling for the "overthrow of the Tsarist autocracy and its replacement by a democratic republic, the constitution of which would ensure: 1. Sovereignty of the people—that is, concentration of supreme state power wholly in the hands of a legislative assembly consisting of representatives of the people and forming a single chamber. 2. Universal, equal and direct suffrage, in elections both to the legislative assembly and to all local organs of self-government." *1903: Second Ordinary Congress of the RSDLP, Complete Text of the Minutes* (London: New Park Publications, 1978), p. 6.

37. *4*, p. 238.

38. *5*, pp. 418–20.

39. Ibid., p. 512,

40. *6*, pp. 187–89, 193.

41. Ibid., pp. 190–94.

42. For a discussion of this frequently made charge, see "A Critical Review of the Relevant Literature: Chapter 2" in *LES1917*.

43. *6*, pp. 103–4.

44. Ibid., p. 467.

45. Ibid., p. 478.

46. In 2005 two Russian scholars, also convinced that their forbearers had democratic instincts, published a study on the elections to the first two state Dumas from the vantage of three provinces to make their case. Since the few things they say about Lenin are positive, it's unfortunate that they didn't know what he thought about elections and the details of his involvement in the RSDLP elections to the Second Duma—what I suspect they would have welcomed and another rationale for this book. See Natal'ia Borisovna Selunskaia and Rolf Torstendahl, *The Birth of Democratic Cultures in Late Imperial Russia: Reforms and Elections to the First Two National Legislatures, 1905–1907* (Stockholm: Altus History, 2012).

47. *4*, p. 237.

48. *6*, p. 473.

204 NOTESNOTES

49. *Z*, p. 442. Regarding "America," the extant record isn't enlightening.
50. *MECW* 44, p. 258. Again, uppercase indicates the original in English.
51. *5*, p. 18.
52. *1*, p. 320.
53. Ibid., p. 298.
54. See my *Marx and Engels: Their Contribution to the Democratic Breakthrough* (Albany, NY: SUNY Press, 2000), ch. 2, for details on how they addressed the issue.
55. On how it came about and how it was organized, see Richard Pipes, *Social Democracy and the St. Petersburg Labor Movement, 1885–1897* (Cambridge, MA: Harvard University Press, 1963), pp. 83–86. The editors of the *Collected Works* also provide details on its organization in *2*, pp. 546–47.
56. *5*, pp. 466–67.
57. *2*, p. 330.
58. Ibid., p. 340–41.
59. Ibid., p. 349.
60. This reading of Lenin's words is markedly different from a Leninological spin on them. See "A Critical Review of the Relevant Literature: Chapter 2" in *LES1917*.
61. *4*, pp. 217–18.
62. Service is particularly duplicitous in this regard. See "A Critical Review of the Relevant Literature: Chapter 2" in *LES1917*.
63. *4*, pp. 218–19.
64. Ibid., p. 326.
65. Ibid., p. 291.
66. Ibid., p. 328.
67. *34*, p. 57.
68. Ibid., p. 74.
69. Later correspondence with Plekhanov and Axelrod (Ibid., pp. 81–85) reveals an atmosphere of give and take when it came to editorial and substantive differences. Chapter 3 in Israel Getzler's *Martov: A Political Biography of a Russian Social Democrat* (Melbourne: Melbourne University Press, 1967) is also useful.
70. *5*, p. 423,
71. Ibid., p. 425.
72. *6*, p. 53.
73. *5*, p. 472.
74. Ibid., pp. 472–73.
75. Sidney and Beatrice Webb, *Industrial Democracy* (London: Longmans, Green, 1897); Lenin and his wife Krupskaya translated it in 1900. Karl Kautsky, *Der Parlamentarismus, die Volksgesetzgebung und die Sozialdemokratie* (Stuttgart: J. H. W. Dietz, 1893).
76. Ibid., pp. 477–82.
77. Lars Lih's *Lenin Rediscovered* is an invaluable source for a number of reasons but not the least for the context for *WITBD*. Chapter 8, "The Organisational Question: Lenin and the Underground," is especially useful.

78. Fifteen months after it was written and disseminated, Lenin recognized in January 1904 that the letter had the same standing as *WITBD* as a founding document for the organization norms he fought for.
79. *6*, p. 235.
80. Ibid., pp. 241–42.
81. Ibid., p. 240.
82. Ibid., pp. 246–47.
83. *Z*, p. 208. See also *34*, p. 149.
84. *Z*, p. 389.
85. Ibid., p. 267.
86. Lenin's characterization of intellectuals drew heavily on conclusions that Kautsky had reached, as can be seen on pp. 322–24 of *OSFTSB*.
87. Ibid., p. 261. See also, *1903: Second Ordinary Congress of the RSDLP*, p. 314.
88. *Z*, p. 178.
89. Ibid., p. 474.
90. For details and one of the most brazen misrepresentations of Lenin's views, see "A Critical Review of the Relevant Literature: Chapter Two" in *LES1917*.
91. *Z*, pp. 115–17.
92. Lenin had certainly been no saint at the congress, as he admitted in correspondence and publicly. To Potresov, he wrote, "I realize that I often behaved and acted in a state of frightful irritation, 'frenziedly'; I am quite willing to admit *this fault of mine to anyone*" (*34*, p. 164). And in *OSFTSB* he wrote, "I had admitted my personal harshness openly both in the letter to the *Iskra*-ist and at the League Congress" (*Z*, p. 370).
93. Ibid., p. 395.
94. Ibid., p. 479.
95. *MECW* 48, p. 484.

1. *Marx-Engels Collected Works*, vol. 45 (New York: International Publishers, 1975–2004), p. 278. Hereafter, citations from the *MECW* are designated as follows: *MECW* 45, p. 278.
2. Behind the scenes, as the rest of the letter reveals, Marx was doing all he could to weaken Russia's diplomatic position vis-à-vis England.
3. V. I. Lenin, *Collected Works*, vol. 7 (Moscow: Progress Publishers, 1977), pp. 199–200. Hereafter, citations from his *Collected Works* will be indicated as in this case: *Z*, pp. 199–200.
4. *5*, p. 74. So much, then, for the oft-alleged "Leninist approach of 'the worse the better'" as repeated in the *Financial Times*, Oct. 28, 2010.
5. Orlando Figes, *A People's Tragedy: A History of the Russian Revolution* (New York: Viking, 1996), p. 171.
6. Ibid., p. 173.
7. *8*, pp. 21–22.
8. Ibid., p. 26.

9. For a general overview of the 1905 Revolution, see Sidney Harcave, *First Blood: The Russian Revolution of 1905* (New York: MacMillan, 1964). Figes is useful for more recent research.

10. *8*, p. 28.

11. Ibid., p. 208.

12. Ibid., pp. 375–78.

13. Ibid., p. 380.

14. Ibid., pp. 385–89.

15. Ibid., pp. 534–36.

16. Ibid., pp. 560–68.

17. *2*, p. 25.

18. Ibid., p. 204.

19. *MECW* 27, p. 191.

20. *2*, p. 141. As far as I can tell, it was Mary-Alice Waters who first pointed out in print Lenin's disagreement with Engels in her "The Workers' and Farmers' Government: A Popular Revolutionary Dictatorship," *New International* 1, no. 3 (1984): 44–45, 54. In what purports to be a definitive treatment of Lenin's usage of the phrase, Hal Draper's *The "Dictatorship of the Proletariat" from Marx to Lenin* (New York: Monthly Review, 1987), no mention of his correction to Engels is made.

21. *2*, p. 145.

22. See Alfred Levin, *The Second Duma: A Study of the Social-Democratic Party and the Russian Constitutional Experiment* (New Haven: Yale University Press, 1940), pp. 7–10, for details.

23. *2*, p. 179.

24. Ibid., p. 193.

25. Ibid., pp. 182–84.

26. Ibid., p. 258.

27. Ibid., p. 273.

28. Ibid., pp. 258–61.

29. *34*, p. 353.

30. *2*, pp. 383–84.

31. Ibid., pp. 344–46.

32. In "Tasks of Revolutionary Army Contingents," written at the end of October, Lenin elaborates a bit on the problem of "extremes . . . that should not be forgotten" (Ibid., p. 422).

33. Ibid., p. 354.

34. Ibid., p. 461.

35. Ibid., p. 431–32.

36. Figes, p. 197.

37. *10*, p. 163. For corroborating evidence from a fellow Bolshevik about how broadly the "elective principle" was applied in the new setting, see Lars Lih's "Fortunes of a Formula: From 'DEMOCRATIC Centralism' to 'democratic CENTRALISM,'" *John Riddell, Marxist Essays and Commentary* (blog),

April 14, 2013, http://johnriddell.wordpress.com/2013/04/14/fortunes-of-a
-formula-from-democratic-centralism-to-democratic-centralism.
38. _10_, pp. 20–21.
39. For some details on the Tammerfors conference, see ibid., p. 527. The evidence
    about Lenin's change of heart comes from B. Gorev, the other Bolshevik who
    initially opposed the boycott; see Robert Service, _Lenin: A Political Life_, vol. 1
    (Bloomington: Indiana University Press, 1991), p. 149. For more sources for
    Lenin's about-face, see J. L. H. Keep, "Russian Social-Democracy and the First
    State Duma," _Slavonic & East European Review_ 34, no. 82 (December 1955):
    198n90.
40. _10_, p. 136.
41. Ibid., p. 143.
42. Ibid., p. 111.
43. _11_, p. 80.
44. _10_, p. 212.
45. Ibid., p. 235.
46. Ibid., pp. 237–38.
47. _MECW_ 26, p. 272.
48. _10_, p. 249.
49. Ibid., p. 276
50. Ibid., p. 280.
51. _MECW_ 27, p. 433.
52. _10_, p. 295.
53. Ibid., p. 293.
54. Ibid., p. 362.
55. Service, vol. 1, p. 155. Tony Cliff, _Building the Party: Lenin 1893–1914_ (Chi-
    cago: Haymarket Books, 2002), p. 218, says "we" was a minority of one: Lenin.
56. According to Alan Woods, _Bolshevism, the Road to Revolution: A History of
    the Bolshevik Party from the Early Beginnings to the October Revolution_ (Lon-
    don: Wellred Publications, 1999), p. 276, the Mensheviks "originally refused
    to participate in elections, but then changed their position to one of a 'semi-
    boycott.'" Woods is presumably referring to the aforementioned joint state-
    ment they issued with the Bolsheviks prior to the elections.
57. _10_, p. 313.
58. Ibid., p. 361.
59. Ibid., pp. 303–4.
60. Ibid., p. 362.
61. Ibid., p. 314.
62. Lenin revealed that hard bargaining with the Mensheviks took place in agreeing
    to the organization question—mainly about the percentage of party members
    needed to call a congress—but only briefly (ibid., p. 372). Though Service
    devotes five pages to the Fourth Congress, vol. 1, pp. 151–55, his total silence
    on the democratic centralism decision is deafening.
63. Ibid., p. 380.
64. Figes, p. 202.

65. Ibid., pp. 215–16.

66. *10*, pp. 398–99.

67. Ibid., p. 402. For photos of the RSDLP Duma deputies in the First and Second Dumas, see A. J. Sack, *The Birth of the Russian Democracy* (New York: Russian Information Bureau, 1918), pp. 147–48 and 153–55, respectively.

68. *10*, pp. 402–5.

69. Ibid., p. 408. *Nevskaya Gazeta* also provided an account of Lenin's speech, p. 407, and the differences with that of *Volna* are instructive.

70. Ibid., p. 409.

71. Ibid., p. 554.

72. Lenin noted a couple of weeks later that the government "has banned public meetings and has announced that it will take proceedings against those responsible for the meeting" in which he spoke (ibid., pp. 444–45).

73. Ibid., pp. 424–25.

74. Geoffrey A. Hosking, *The Russian Constitutional Experiment: Government and Duma, 1907–1914* (Cambridge: Cambridge University Press, 1973), p. 19.

75. *10*, p. 457.

76. Ibid., pp. 414–17.

77. Ibid., p. 422.

78. Ibid., pp. 428–29.

79. Ibid., p. 431.

80. Ibid., pp. 440–41.

81. Ibid., pp. 432–33.

82. Definitive proof would require an analysis of *Nevskaya Gazeta* and *Kuryer* [*The Courier*], the two Menshevik dailies, to see if anyone in its camp was as active as Lenin in trying to influence the Duma fraction. I suspect not, since he made no mention of anyone in that daily doing the same; it would have been out of character for him not to do so.

83. Ibid., pp. 434–35.

84. Ibid., p. 486.

85. Ibid., pp. 458–59, and 438.

86. Ibid., pp. 486–87.

87. Hosking, p. 20.

88. *10*, pp. 449, 471, 480.

89. Ibid., p. 515.

90. Ibid., p. 501.

91. Ibid., pp. 510–13.

92. *11*, pp. 20–23.

93. Ibid., pp. 24–26.

94. Ibid., pp. 32–37.

95. Ibid., p. 79.

96. Ibid., pp. 43–47.

97. Ibid., p. 482.

98. Ibid., pp. 61–62.

99. Ibid., pp. 69–72.

100. Figes, p. 219.
101. _11_, pp. 90–93.
102. Ibid., pp. 96–100.
103. Ibid., pp. 101–4.
104. Ibid., p. 107. Hosking, pp. 20–21n25, notes the same article that Lenin referred to in the progovernment daily about an Austrian-German intervention. Unfortunately, he doesn't consider the significance of Lenin's reading of this and his response.
105. _MECW_ 6, p. 382.
106. For an opinion that claims that Lenin did "gloat" and thus welcomed the Duma's dissolution, see "A Critical Review of the Relevant Literature: Chapter 3" in _Lenin's Electoral Strategy from 1907 to the Revolution of October 1917: The Ballot, the Streets—or Both_.
107. _11_, pp. 111–17.
108. Figes, p. 221.

CHAPTER 4

1. V. I. Lenin, _Collected Works_, vol. 11 (Moscow: Progress Publishers, 1977), pp. 130. Hereafter, citations from his _Collected Works_ will be indicated as in this case: _11_, p. 130.
2. Ibid., pp. 138, 148.
3. Ibid., pp. 141–48.
4. Ibid., pp. 259–60.
5. The history of the norm of democratic centralism—still very much a work in progress at this point—would reveal that carrying out a line of action one disagreed with gave one more authority to challenge it, if necessary, later.
6. Orlando Figes, _A People's Tragedy: A History of the Russian Revolution_ (New York: Viking, 1996), p. 224.
7. _11_, p. 212.
8. Ibid., pp. 219, 224.
9. See Alfred Levin, _The Second Duma: A Study of the Social-Democratic Party and the Russian Constitutional Experiment_ (New Haven: Yale University Press, 1940), p. 280, for more details, including bibliographic sources.
10. _11_, p. 501.
11. Ibid., p. 514.
12. Ibid., pp. 284–85.
13. Ibid., p. 300, italics in original.
14. Ibid., pp. 313–16.
15. Ibid., p. 459. For details on how "from the beginning of the electoral campaign the administration actively interfered in an attempt to influence the results," see Levin, pp. 60–64.
16. _11_, p. 415.
17. Ibid., p. 465.
18. Ibid., p. 59.

19. _12_, pp. 18–19.
20. Specifically, "The Workers' Party Election Campaign in St. Petersburg," "The Social-Democrats and the Duma Elections" (both in _11_), and "The Protests of the Thirty-One Mensheviks" (in _12_). For the Menshevik view of the meeting, see Levin, pp. 57–58.
21. _11_, p. 426.
22. Recently published documents of Cadet internal deliberations ought to allow for an assessment of Lenin's claim. See Alexandra Korros, "The Kadet Party and the Elusive Ideal of Internal Democracy," _Kritika_ 5, no. 1 (winter 2004): 117–36.
23. They even, apparently, had a daily, _Trud_ [_Labor_], but it must have been only momentarily, since no copies have ever been found (_12_, p. 523).
24. Ibid., pp. 46–53.
25. Victoria Bonnell, _Roots of Rebellion: Workers' Politics and Organizations in St. Petersburg and Moscow, 1900–1914_ (Los Angeles: University of California Press, 1983), p. 309. Bonnell provides some useful details on how the workers' curia elections were conducted for the First Duma (pp. 309–10).
26. _12_, p. 62.
27. Bonnell, p. 314.
28. See _MECW_ 50, p. 29.
29. _12_, pp. 62–65.
30. Ibid., p. 74.
31. Ibid., pp. 89–91.
32. Ibid., pp. 115–17.
33. Ibid., pp. 108–11.
34. Ibid., p. 149. Beyond St. Petersburg, "The Social-Democrats drew heavily from the suppressed minorities in the Caucasian towns, the mining population of Siberia and the Caucasus, and the great Caspian and Black Sea ports with their aggressive seamen and longshoremen" (Levin, p. 67).
35. _12_, p. 120.
36. Ibid., p. 155.
37. The Bolsheviks also began about this time an illegal organ, _Rabochy_ [_Worker_], within St. Petersburg that lasted until June 1907. It's interesting to compare the tone of the two publications. _Novy Luch_, during its brief existence, was much more circumspect in an eventually unsuccessful effort to get by regime censors.
38. _12_, p. 198. This is from Lenin's article "The Elections to the Duma and the Tactics of the Russian Social-Democrats" for _Die Neue Zeit_, his most detailed analysis of the election returns. Written for a German-speaking social democratic readership, it's also didactic and provides a clear explanation of the differences between the Bolsheviks and Mensheviks. That Kautsky, the editor of the organ, was willing to grant space to Lenin is noteworthy. He had denied, it may be remembered, Lenin such an opportunity in 1904 when the Bolshevik leader wanted to respond to Luxemburg and Trotsky's critique of the Bolsheviks coming out of the Second Congress of the RSDLP. The difference this time, I

suspect, is that Kautsky recognized that Lenin was writing about a real revolution in which he was an important protagonist.

39. For details on the fraction, its election, social composition, and organization, see Levin, ch. 3.
40. *12*, p. 154.
41. See Levin, pp. 92–94, for details.
42. *12*, pp. 162–63.
43. Ibid., p. 168.
44. Ibid, p. 203.
45. Ibid., pp. 189–92.
46. Ibid., p. 187.
47. Levin, p. 112n24.
48. Ibid., pp. 112–23. Though Levin makes no mention of Lenin's involvement in all of this, his draft response to Stolypin's address (see following) shows that he was indeed an actor in the drama. Why he ignores Lenin's draft in what appears to be an otherwise thorough examination of the published record is not clear. Police reports, if still extant, might fill in the gaps.
49. Levin, p. 122.
50. *12*, pp. 194–95.
51. Ibid., p. 244.
52. Ibid., p. 309.
53. Ibid., p. 248.
54. See Levin, pp. 176–85, for details about the context.
55. *12*, pp. 273–75.
56. Ibid., p. 304.
57. Ibid., pp. 282–86.
58. Ibid., pp. 296–99.
59. The German original was published in Stuttgart, 1906.
60. *12*, pp. 361–74.
61. Ibid., pp. 439–40.
62. Ibid., pp. 448–50. For more details on Prokopovich and the issue of the fraction employing "expert" opinion, see Levin, pp. 74–75. Lenin's critique of Prokopovich is reminiscent of Marx's warning about "le pedestal" for the bourgeoisie in 1865 in the First International.
63. On the report, why Lenin was able to give it, and the significance of the outcome of the vote, see his very informative article, "The Attitude towards Bourgeois Parties," *12*. pp. 489–509.
64. Lenin's most explicit statement of his differences with Trotsky on the peasant question came two years later in "The Aim of the Proletarian Struggle in Our Revolution": "Trotsky's major mistake is that he ignores the bourgeois character of the revolution and has no clear conception of the transition from this revolution to the socialist revolution." Lenin then analyzes the "mistakes" that derived from the "major" one (*15*, pp. 371–74). Part of the problem, I contend, is that Trotsky, because he was imprisoned, didn't get a chance to witness what Lenin

did—the politicization of the peasantry along the line that the latter expected beginning with the First Duma.

65. _12_, pp. 456–68.
66. Ibid., p. 506.
67. Ibid., p. 508.
68. See Levin, pp. 200–201, 210–11, for details, and _12_, p. 229, on what a "socialist view of the budget" would look like.
69. Alexinsky's speech on political terror on March 22—Levin, pp. 266–67—would be another example. The trial of the social democratic deputies, to be discussed later, revealed that the _Okhrana_, or state security, indeed had an extensive collection of documents about the fraction's activities obtained largely from informants.
70. Levin, p. 123.
71. A related issue is a set of conferences in which the party participated in November 1906 to discuss its military and armed strategy. See Lenin's "Apropos of the Minutes of the November Military and Combat Conference of the Russian Social-Democratic Labour Party," _12_, pp. 409–18, and Levin, pp. 282–83.
72. Levin, p. 324.
73. Levin, p. 343.
74. On their fate, see Chapter 1, _Lenin's Electoral Strategy from 1907 to the Revolution of October 1917: The Ballot, the Streets—or Both_, p. 42.
75. Ibid., p. 348.
76. _12_, p.
77. _13_, pp. 101–3.
78. Levin, p. 353.

APPENDIX A

1. Original text available at http://www.marxists.org/archive/marx/works/1847/communist-league/1850-ad1.htm.
2. Original text available at http://www.marxists.org/archive/marx/works/1848/communist-manifesto/index.htm.

APPENDIX B

1. Original text available at http://www.marxists.org/archive/lenin/works/1905/jul/00.htm.
2. [Footnote from source] One word illegible.—_Ed._
3. [Footnote from source] "As the thoroughness of the historic action increases, the magnitude of the mass whose cause it represents will also increase."—_Ed._ (See Marx and Engels, _The Holy Family, or Critique of Critical Critique_ [Moscow: Foreign Languages Pub. House, 1956], p. 410.)
4. [Footnote from source] Fighting capacity.—_Ed._

APPENDIX C

1. [Footnote from source] The leaflet "Whom to Elect to the State Duma" was written prior to the elections to the Second Duma. In the article "The Government's Falsification of the Duma and the Tasks of the Social Democrats," Lenin called this leaflet a poster "about the three *chief* parties" that took part in the Duma elections. The leaflet was printed in Vyborg by the editorial board of *Proletary* as a supplement to No. 5; it appeared in three editions (one in full and two abridged) in St. Petersburg in 1906. In the abridged form it was also published by the Ivanovo-Voznesensk, Kostroma, and Kharkov committees of the RSDLP; by the Ob group of the RSDLP; the Central Committee of the Social-Democrats of the Lettish Territory; and the Central Committee of the Latvian Social-Democrats. Original text available at http://www.marxists.org/archive/lenin/works/1906/nov/23f.htm.

A CRITICAL REVIEW OF THE RELEVANT LITERATURE

1. David Lane, *Leninism: A Sociological Interpretation* (Cambridge: Cambridge University Press, 1981), p. 43.
2. Sheri Berman, *The Primacy of Politics: Social Democracy and the Making of Europe's Twentieth Century* (Cambridge: Cambridge University Press, 2006), p. 13.
3. *Marx and Engels: Their Contribution to the Democratic Breakthrough* (Albany: State University of New York Press, 2000).
4. Stefano Bartolini, *The Political Mobilization of the European Left, 1860–1980: The Class Cleavage* (New York: Cambridge University Press, 2000).
5. Adam Przeworski, *Capitalism and Social Democracy* (London: Cambridge University Press, 1986), and *Paper Stones: A History of Electoral Socialism* (Chicago: University of Chicago Press, 1986), coauthored with John Sprague.
6. "Marx and Engels's Electoral Strategy: The Alleged versus the Real," *New Political Science* 32, no. 3 (September 2010): 367–87.
7. Robert Service, *Lenin: A Political Life* (Bloomington: Indiana University Press, 1985–95).
8. Ibid., vol. 1, p. 51.
9. Hal Draper, *The "Dictatorship of the Proletariat" from Marx to Lenin* (New York: Monthly Review, 1987), p. 105.
10. Ibid., p. 26.
11. See my "Marx and Engels's Electoral Strategy," p. 375, for details.
12. Draper, *"Dictatorship of the Proletariat,"* p. 83.
13. Nimtz, *Marx and Engels,* p. 345n101.
14. Draper, *"Dictatorship of the Proletariat,"* p. 85.
15. V. I. Lenin, *Collected Works*, vol. 15 (Moscow: Progress Publishers, 1977), pp. 371–74. Hereafter, citations from his *Collected Works* will be indicated as in this case: *15*, pp. 371–74.
16. *9*, p. 141.

17. Service, vo1. 1, p. 38.
18. Orlando Figes, *A People's Tragedy: A History of the Russian Revolution* (New York: Viking, 1996), pp. 145–46.
19. Lars Lih, *Lenin Rediscovered:* What Is to Be Done *in Context* (Leiden: Brill, 2006), pp. 377–83.
20. Service, vol. 1, p. 77.
21. *2*, p. 341.
22. Service, vol. 1, p. 76.
23. Issac Deutscher, *The Prophet Armed: Trotsky, 1879–1921*, vol. 1 (New York: Vintage Books, 1965), pp. 83–97.
24. Trotsky, *Stalin: An Appraisal of the Man and His Influence* (New York: The Universal Library, 1941), p. 112.
25. *Z*, pp. 472–83.
26. Lih, pp. 526–27.
27. Bertram D. Wolfe, *Three Who Made a Revolution: A Biographical History* (New York: Stein and Day Publishers, 1984).
28. Ibid., p. 259.
29. *Z*, pp. 394–95.
30. J. L. H. Keep, "Russian Social-Democracy and the First State Duma," *Slavonic & East European Review* 34, no. 82 (December 1955): 195.
31. Ibid.
32. Ibid., p. 198.
33. Ibid., p. 199.

BIBLIOGRAPHY

PRIMARY SOURCES

Institute of Marxism-Leninism. *The General Council of the First International, 1866–1872: Minutes*. Moscow: Progress Publishers, 1974.

Lenin, V. I. *Collected Works*. Vols. 1–45. Moscow: Progress Publishers, 1977. This English edition is a translation of the fourth, enlarged Russian edition prepared by the Institute of Marxism-Leninism, Central Committee of the Communist Party of the Soviet Union.

Marx, Karl, and Frederick Engels. *Collected Works*. Vols. 1–50. New York: International Publishers, 1775–2005.

1903: Second Ordinary Congress of the RSDLP. Complete Text of the Minutes. Translated and annotated by Brian Pearce. London: New Park Publications, 1978.

SECONDARY SOURCES

Bergman, Jay. *Vera Zasulich: A Biography*. Stanford, CA: Stanford University Press, 1983.

Berman, Sheri. "Social Democracy's Past and Potential Futures." In *What's Left of the Left: Democrats and Social Democrats in Challenging Times*, edited by James Cronin, George Ross, and James Shoch. Chapel Hill, NC: Duke University Press, 2011.

Boer, Roland. *Lenin, Religion, and Theology*. New York: Palgrave Macmillan, 2013.

Bonnell, Victoria. *Roots of Rebellion: Workers' Politics and Organizations in St. Petersburg and Moscow, 1900–1914*. Los Angeles: University of California Press, 1983.

Cliff, Tony. *All Power to the Soviets: Lenin 1914–1917*. Chicago: Haymarket Books, 2004.

———. *Building the Party: Lenin 1893–1914*. Chicago: Haymarket Books, 2002.

Draper, Hal. *The "Dictatorship of the Proletariat" from Marx to Lenin*. New York: Monthly Review, 1987.

———. *Karl Marx's Theory of Revolution*. Vols. 1–4. New York: Monthly Review, 1977–90.

———. *The Marx-Engels Glossary*. New York: Schocken Books, 1986.

Draper, Hal, and E. Haberkern. *Karl Marx's Theory of Revolution: Volume Five— War & Revolution*. New York: Monthly Review, 2005.

Figes, Orlando. *A People's Tragedy: A History of the Russian Revolution*. New York: Viking, 1996.

Getzler, Israel. *Martov: A Political Biography of a Russian Social Democrat*. Melbourne: Melbourne University Press, 1967.

Haimson, Leopold. "Lenin's Revolutionary Career Revisited: Some Observations on Recent Discussion," *Kritika: Explorations in Russian and Eurasian History* 5, no. 1 (winter 2004): 55–80.

Hammen, Oscar. *The Red '48ers: Karl Marx and Frederick Engels*. New York: Charles Scribner's Sons, 1969.

Harcave, Sidney. *First Blood: The Russian Revolution of 1905*. New York: MacMillan, 1964.

Hosking, Geoffrey A. *The Russian Constitutional Experiment: Government and Duma, 1907–1914*. Cambridge: Cambridge University Press, 1973.

Huntington, Samuel. *Political Order in Changing Societies*. New Haven, CT: Yale University Press, 1967.

Jenness, Doug. *Lenin as Election Campaign Manager*. New York: Pathfinder, 1971.

Kautsky, Karl. *The Class Struggle (Erfurt Program)*. New York: W. W. Norton, 1971.

———. *Der Parliamentarismus, die Volkgesetzgebung und die Sozialdemokratie*. Stuttgart: J. H. W. Dietz, 1893.

Keep, J. L. H. "Russian Social-Democracy and the First State Duma." *Slavonic & East European Review* 34, no. 82 (December 1955): 180–99.

Korros, Alexandra. "The Kadet Party and the Elusive Ideal of Internal Democracy," *Kritika: Explorations in Russian and Eurasian History* 5, no. 1 (winter 2004): 117–36.

Krupskaya, Nadezhda. *Memories of Lenin*. London: Panther Books, 1970.

LeBlanc, Paul. *Lenin and the Revolutionary Party*. Atlantic Highlands, NJ: Humanities, 1990.

Levin, Alfred. *The Second Duma: A Study of the Social-Democratic Party and the Russian Constitutional Experiment*. New Haven: Yale University Press, 1940.

Lih, Lars. *Lenin Rediscovered: What Is to Be Done in Context*. Leiden: Brill, 2006.

McLellan, David. *Karl Marx: His Life and Thought*. New York: Harper and Row, 1973.

Nimtz, August H. *Marx, Tocqueville, and Race in America: The "Absolute Democracy" or "Defiled Republic."* Lanham, MD: Lexington Books, 2003.

———. *Marx and Engels: Their Contribution to the Democratic Breakthrough*. Albany: State University of New York Press, 2000.

———. "Marx and Engels's Electoral Strategy: The Alleged versus the Real." *New Political Science* 32, no. 3 (September 2010): 367–87.

———. "A Return to Lenin—But without Marx and Engels?" *Science and Society* 73, no. 4 (October 2009): 452–73.

Pipes, Richard. *Social Democracy and the St. Petersburg Labor Movement, 1885–1897*. Cambridge, MA: Harvard University Press, 1963.

———. *The Unknown Lenin: From the Secret Archive*. New Haven, CT: Yale University Press, 1996.

Pomper, Philip. *Lenin, Trotsky, and Stalin: The Intelligentsia and Power*. New York: Columbia University Press, 1990.

Przeworski, Adam. *Capitalism and Social Democracy.* New York: Cambridge University Press, 1985.

Riazanov, David. *Karl Marx and Friedrich Engels: An Introduction to Their Lives and Works.* New York: Monthly Review, 1973.

Rubel, Maximillien, and Margaret Manale. *Marx without Myth: A Chronological Study of His Life and Work.* New York: Harper and Row, 1975.

Sack, A. J. *The Birth of the Russian Democracy.* New York: Russian Information Bureau, 1918.

Sassoon, Donald. *One Hundred Years of Socialism: The West European Left in the Twentieth Century.* New York: New Press, 1996.

Selunskaia, Natal'ia Borisovna, and Rolf Torstendahl. *The Birth of Democratic Cultures in Late Imperial Russia: Reforms and Elections to the First Two National Legislatures, 1905–1907.* Stockholm: Altus History, 2012.

Service, Robert. *Lenin: A Political Life.* Vols. 1–3. Bloomington: Indiana University Press, 1985–95.

Sperber, Jonathan. *Karl Marx: A Nineteenth-Century Life.* New York: Liveright, 2013.

Steenson, Gary. *After Marx, Before Lenin: Marxism and Socialist Working Class Parties in Europe, 1884–1914.* Pittsburgh: University of Pittsburgh Press, 1991.

Trotsky, Leon. *Stalin: An Appraisal of the Man and His Influence.* New York: The Universal Library, 1941.

———. *The Young Lenin.* New York: Doubleday, 1972.

Waters, Mary-Alice. "The Workers' and Farmers' Government: A Popular Revolutionary Dictatorship." *New International* 1, no. 3 (1984).

Webb, Sidney, and Beatrice Webb. *Industrial Democracy.* London: Longmans, Green, 1902.

Woods, Alan. *Bolshevism, the Road to Revolution: A History of the Bolshevik Party from the Early Beginnings to the October Revolution.* London: Wellred Publications, 1999.

Lenin's Electoral Strategy from 1907 to the October Revolution of 1917

CHAPTER 5

"LEGAL AND ILLEGAL WORK"

THE THIRD DUMA

UNLIKE ITS TWO PREDECESSORS, THE THIRD DUMA completed its full term, from its convening in November 1907 to its scheduled dissolution in June 1912. It proved to be prerevolutionary Russia's longest uninterrupted experience with parliamentary government and thus Russian social democracy's as well. Also, unlike its predecessors, it was the product of the revolution's defeat. That fact more than any other determined its origins and its course. Lenin had to mount an even more vigorous campaign to convince his Bolshevik comrades to participate in a body that offered even fewer possibilities for revolutionary work. Contrary to the claims of a vocal minority, the choice wasn't either/or—either parliamentary or illegal work. Both, Lenin argued, not only could be done but indeed had to be done in order to make effective the work in each sphere of activity. What Lenin had to do to win the skeptics to his position is the subject of this chapter.

PREPARING FOR THE THIRD DUMA

Prime Minister Pyotr Stolypin's new electoral law, just as Lenin had forecasted, was crafted to render a Duma more to his liking or, as its chief architect put it, to "tear the State Duma from the hands of the revolutionaries, to assimilate it to the historical institutions, to bring it into the state system . . . To try, on the basis of a new law, to distil from Russia's chaos those elements in which there lived a feeling for the Russian state system, and from them to create the Duma as an organ for the reeducation of society."[1] Once most Bolsheviks were won to taking part in the rigged elections for the Third Duma, the next task was to achieve clarity about what was expected of revolutionary social democracy in a decidedly more reactionary legislative arena.

AGAINST BOYCOTT

"In June 1907 they were the majority among the Bolsheviks. But *Proletary* campaigned continuously against the boycott."[2] That most Bolsheviks, especially those in Moscow, didn't want to take part in the Third Duma required that Lenin be at his persuasive best. His key weapon in the campaign was a 32-page pamphlet, *Against Boycott.* Central to his argument, presented in a very pedagogical and nonpolemical tone, was context and historical contingency. Simply put, the boycott was a tactic appropriate in some situations and not others. In the specific context of Russia's first revolution, the boycott of the regime's proposed Bulygin Duma was a necessity. As long as it was possible to "set up *representative institutions* of a purely revolutionary type—Soviets of Workers' Deputies, etc., in place of the representative institutions of the police-liberal type," everything, including the boycott of the latter, had to be employed to ensure the institution of the former.[3]

The more difficult task, Lenin recognized, was determining the rhythm of a revolution, its ascent and descent, and thus knowing what measures and slogans to employ in its different phases. Regarding the previous thirty months, once "the phase of upswing (1905)" had ended and "the phase of decline (1906–07)" had set in, the boycott, he argued, was no longer useful. One measure of the "upswing" was that "[r]epression expanded the movement instead of reducing it." An even more important indicator was "that the slogans of the revolutionaries not only evoked a response but actually *lagged* behind the march of events."[4] That was no longer the case, he pointed out. "Now we are at a period of a lull in the revolution when *a whole series of calls* systematically *met with no response among the masses.* That is what happened with the call to sweep away the Witte Duma (at the beginning of 1906), with the call for an uprising after the dissolution of the First Duma (in the summer of 1906), *with the call for struggle* in answer to the dissolution of the Second Duma and the coup d'état of June 3, 1907."[5] To call for a boycott—more specifically, an "active boycott"—in such a climate made no sense. While Lenin continued to defend the boycott of the Witte or First Duma, it's possible to read this—knowing that he reluctantly went along with it—as an implicit admission that it was inappropriate given that the down swing had begun. The failure to prevent its convening should have made that clear.

What about the contention of some boycotters that unlike the First and Second Dumas, the Third would be qualitatively worst and thus offer no opportunities for social democratic participation? Lenin objected, the first two Dumas proved in fact to be only steps to the Octobrist [Third] Duma, yet we utilized them for the simple and modest purpose (propaganda and agitation, criticism and explaining to the masses what is taking place) for which we shall always contrive to utilize even the worst representative institutions. A speech in the Duma will not cause any "revolution," and propaganda *in connection with the Duma* is not distinguished by any particular merits; but the advantage that Social-Democracy can derive from the one and the other is not less, and sometimes even greater, than that derived from a printed speech or a speech delivered at some other gathering . . . [R]eaction inevitably drove us and *will continue to drive* us constantly into worse and worse quasi-constitutional institutions. Always and everywhere we shall uphold our convictions and advocate our views, always insisting that no good can be expected as long as the old regime remains, as long as it is not wholly eradicated. We shall prepare the conditions for a new upswing, and until it takes place, and in order that it may take place, we shall work still harder and not launch slogans which have meaning only when the revolution is on the upswing.[6]

Lenin concluded by addressing "the strongest and only Marxist arguments in favor of a boycott." That they found support among "the comrades who stand closest to direct proletarian work" had to be taken seriously. Weren't there signs, they contended, of a revival of the revolution, and couldn't the boycott slogan be used to assist in that process? Again, Lenin disagreed. First, it was necessary to recognize that there was in fact a "protracted lull" in the revolution and for very good reason— "the proletariat has not recovered . . . Indeed, the brunt of the October-December struggle was borne by the proletariat *alone*. . . No wonder that in a country with the smallest percentage of proletarian population (by European standards), the proletariat should have found itself utterly exhausted by such a struggle." (This demographic reality, I argue, explains why Lenin fought so insistently for the revolutionary alliance of workers *and* peasants.)

Second, while there was certainly evidence of an upswing, particularly the strikes of textile workers in Moscow—the reason for strong boycott sentiment among Bolsheviks there—it was only a "partial" one and not enough of a justification to issue a call to boycott the Third Duma. Third, there was no evidence of the kind of sentiment that existed leading up to the First Duma: "[N]o one believes in the Third Duma, i.e., among the strata of population that are capable of sustaining the democratic movement there is not and cannot be any of that enthusiasm for the constitutional institution of the Third Duma that undoubtedly existed among the public at large for the *First* Duma, for the *first* attempts in Russia to set up any kind of institutions provided they were *constitutional*." A boycott slogan now, therefore, "sounds rather odd." Last, the main task now was to act to "convert the partial upswing into a general upswing."[7]

Against Boycott constitutes Lenin's first balance sheet on the tactics of the revolutionary process in which he was a participant and constitutes a key document in his arsenal. Given the substantive issue around which it was weaved, it is evidence for the central claim of this book—namely, that the electoral and parliamentary arenas were at the center of his politics. That he also drew on the lessons of Marx and Engels, particularly the revolutions of 1848–49—which can be only noted here—to make his case is evidence also for one of the four arguments of this book.

Two weeks after the publication of *Against Boycott*, a delegated meeting of the St. Petersburg branch of the Russian Social Democratic Labor Party (RSDLP) met in Terijoki (Zelenogorsk) Finland to take a position on whether to participate in the Third Duma. Lenin presented his two-page "theses" that distilled his argument while highlighting and elaborating on the "what is to be done" question. Again, the immediate task was to "convert" what was essentially a "trade-union upswing" in Moscow and its environs "into a revolutionary assault." "Only when the efforts of the Social-Democrats in this direction have been crowned with success, only on the basis of an aggressive revolutionary movement that has already come into existence, can the boycott slogan acquire serious importance in its inseparable connection with a direct appeal to the masses for an armed uprising, for the overthrow of the tsarist regime, and the replacement of the latter by a provisional revolutionary government, for the convocation of a constituent assembly on the basis of universal, direct, and equal suffrage by secret ballot."[8] The boycott as a tactic, therefore, was not to be abandoned but to be utilized at the right moment. The majority of the delegates rejected the boycottist theses submitted by Lev Kamenev and voted for Lenin's position to take part in the Third Duma—testimony to the power of his argument and persuasive skills.[9] Lenin's advice anticipated in many ways (to be seen later) decisions that would have to be taken about representative institutions in the heady days after February 1917.

A week later, in a more secure location in Finland, Kotka, a delegated conference of the entire party met to debate and decide how to relate to the Third Duma. Three resolutions were put to a vote: Lenin's theses; one presented by the Menshevik leader Fedor Dan, which also called for participation; and a third, that of another Bolshevik, Alexander Bogdanov, which called for a boycott. Lenin's resolution carried, once again. Only in hindsight would it be clear that the division within the Bolshevik ranks portended an eventual split.

Though there is no mention of it in the extant real-time debate about whether or not to boycott the Third Duma elections, there was probably another issue that figured into the mix. Referring to a problem with a member of the Fourth Duma fraction (see Chapter 2), Lenin, a decade later, made an admission: "Following the unfortunate experience with several deputies from the First and Second State Dumas, we were not surprised that the 'high title' of State Duma member turned people's heads and sometimes 'ruined' them."[10] Evidently, some of the RSDLP deputies took their posts in the First and Second Dumas far more seriously than warranted—at least from a revolutionary communist perspective—and compromised their politics. Thus Lenin, in trying to convince the Bolshevik doubters about the need to participate in the Duma, probably had another hurdle to overcome.

In Anticipation of the Guns of August

Engels, in 1882, cautioned the newly emerging working-class parties in Europe against forming a new international; they should wait for the appropriate "moment." "Such events are already taking shape in Russia where the avant-garde of the revolution will be going in battle."[11] The two-decade delay in that "battle" explains, in part, why his advice wasn't heeded. By the time of his death in 1895, just such an organization was coming into existence: the Socialist or Second International. The German party, with the largest membership and biggest successes in the electoral arena, was widely recognized by then as its flagship affiliate. The RSDLP joined the organization after its founding, and in August 1907 Lenin was one of its delegates to its seventh congress in Stuttgart. "On a whole," as he later told the readers of *Proletary*, "the Stuttgart Congress brought into sharp contrast the opportunist and revolutionary wings of the international Social-Democratic movement on a number of cardinal issues and decided these issues in the spirit of revolutionary Marxism."[12] In a more detailed article, and to a larger audience, he was more specific: "The remarkable and sad feature in this connection was that German Social-Democracy, which hitherto had always upheld the revolutionary standpoint in Marxism, proved to be unstable, or took an opportunist stand . . . [O]n most issues, the representatives of Germany were leaders of opportunism." He quoted a comment Engels made in 1886 about the German party to explain this development: "'In Germany everything becomes philistine in calm times.'"[13] The absence of a revolutionary situation in Germany, in other words, enabled opportunism—an insight worth revisiting.

The agenda item that immediately revealed the "sad feature" was the "colonial question." With Georg Vollmar—Exhibit A for Engels's critique of revisionism in the party[14]—and Edouard Bernstein in the lead, the German delegation tried to defend Imperial Germany's colonial project in the name of a "socialist colonial policy" (the "stench of Lassalleanism" as Marx and Engels might have charged). The entire Russian delegation, Lenin proudly reported—that is, Bolsheviks, Mensheviks, and Socialist Revolutionaries—rejected, along with the majority of other delegates, the idea that colonialism could have a "civilizing effect."

Women's suffrage, another agenda item, also revealed opportunistic tendencies, this time in the Austrian party. Party leaders, including Viktor Adler, tried to defend its demand for only universal male suffrage on the grounds that including women would jeopardize its chances for success. Clara Zetkin, a leader in the German party, had criticized this line prior to the congress. The "Austrians," in Lenin's summary of her comments, "had opportunistically sacrificed principle to expediency." Another German woman delegate who criticized the Austrians made a point that Lenin had often made about reforms: "'In principle we must demand all that we consider to be correct . . . and only when our strength is inadequate for more, do we accept what we are able to get. That has always been the tactics of Social-Democracy. The more modest our demands the more modest will the government be in its concessions.'" "This controversy"—Lenin in his own words—"between the Austrian and German women Social-Democrats will enable the reader to see how severely the best Marxists treat the slightest deviation from the principles of consistent revolutionary tactics."[15] The RSDLP had included women in its call for universal suffrage from the very beginning.

"The most important resolution of the Congress" was "that on anti-militarism." The discussion/debate centered on the appropriate response to a "notorious" figure in French politics, the one-time anarchist Gustave Hervé, who "tried to defend a very untenable position. He was unable to link up war with the capitalist regime in general, and anti-militarist agitation with the entire work of socialism." Though Hervé's knee-jerk response to any war with "strike action or an uprising" left much to be desired as far as the "stringency of orthodox . . . Marxist analysis" was concerned, there was a kernel of truth in it, and it served, inadvertently, a useful purpose. The counterresolution August Bebel offered was lacking—"a dogmatic statement of the general truths of socialism" that "failed to indicate the active tasks of the proletariat"—and gave an opportunistic opening to Vollmar:

With the extraordinary conceit of a man infatuated with stereotyped parliamentarism, he attacked Hervé without noticing that his own narrow-mindedness and thick-skinned opportunism *make* one admit the living spark in Hervéism, . . . it was this aspect of the question, the appeal not to prize only parliamentary methods of struggle, the appeal to act in accordance with the new conditions of a future war and future crises, that was stressed by the revolutionary Social-Democrats, especially by Rosa Luxemburg in her speech. Together with the Russian Social-Democratic delegates (Lenin and [J.] Martov—who here spoke in full harmony) Rosa Luxemburg proposed amendments to Bebel's resolution, and these amendments emphasized the need for agitation among the youth, the necessity of taking advantage of the crisis created by war for the purpose of hastening the downfall of the bourgeoisie, the necessity of bearing in mind the inevitable change of methods and means of struggle as the class struggle sharpens and the political situation alters.

The amendments, in other words, were revolutionary social democracy's alternative to the "parliamentary cretinism"—the language Engels and Marx employed to refer to the mistaken belief that the legislative arena was the alpha and omega of politics[16]—of Vollmar, the "dogmatism and passivity" of Bebel, and the "semi-anarchist" stance of Hervé on how to respond to war and militarism.[17] Lenin quoted favorably Zetkin's assessment of what transpired: "'[T]he revolutionary energy [*Tatkraft*] and courageous faith of the working class in its fighting capacity won in the end, winning, on the one hand, over the pessimistic gospel of impotence and the hidebound tendency to stick to old, exclusively parliamentary methods of struggle, and, on the other hand, over the banal anti-militarist sport of the French semi-anarchists of the Hervé type.'"[18]

The amended resolution carried overwhelmingly, by "nearly 900 delegates of all [25] countries." The near unanimity was deceptive, however. History would reveal that only the Russian party, with Lenin in the lead, took to heart what was adopted. The adopted resolution informed Bolshevik activities, both illegal and legal—for the latter, specifically, the "legal" work of its Duma fraction in both the Third and Fourth Dumas. Only in hindsight would it become clear that the weaknesses of the German delegation on not just the colonial but the war question foreshadowed how social democratic deputies in the Reichstag would respond when the Guns of August exploded seven years later.

POLITICAL SOBRIETY AND CLARITY

Unlike for the First and Second Dumas, Lenin uncharacteristically provided few details about the election campaign leading up to the convening of the Third Duma. The primary reason is that he had far fewer venues for publicizing his ideas. The qualitatively diminished political space registered the extent of Stolypin's "June coup d'état." Also, as his companion Nadezhda Krupskaya reported, on the eve of their flight from Finland into exile at the end of 1907 they had to destroy a lot of records, many that no doubt dealt with Lenin's involvement in the party's campaign activities.[19]

The elections, again, were conducted under circumstances most prejudicial to workers and peasants. First, the new electoral law made for a smaller Duma, from 518 to 442 deputies, and they would be elected by provincial assemblies. Peasants would be the biggest losers and the landed elite the biggest gainers, because representation of the former in the assemblies "fell from 43 to 22 percent" while that of the latter increased from "34 to 51 percent."[20] Worker representation would be reduced by half, and while they could still select electors in their curiae, the latter would no longer elect deputies to the Duma; that would be also be done by provincial assemblies in which the workers' electors participated with those of other curiae. "Since . . . the wealthy landowners and [urban] burghers were given a majority in these assemblies, they controlled the selection of peasant and worker representatives."[21] But "if all the electors of a worker curia nominated a Social-Democrat, the rest of the participants in the Gubernia [Provincial] Election Meeting were obligated to vote for him."[22] The number of cities represented in the Duma was reduced from 26 to 7. This also diminished worker influence, since they "had been a perceptible force in the urban assemblies."[23] Last, Great Russians were given more representation at the expense of national minorities. The more than 50 percent reduction in representation for the Caucasus, for example, where the RSDLP had been successful, would also diminish working-class influence.

Details on RSDLP preparations for the elections and campaign activity are thin in the English edition of the *Lenin Collected Works*. According to its only report on the party's campaign, from a conference of the St. Petersburg branch held in Terijoki, Finland, at the end of October, "the police used brutal violence against the working class voters during the elections to the Third Duma, prevented the Social-Democrats from conducting their election campaign, and so on."[24] Other sources indicate that the party, with Lenin intimately involved, formally launched its campaign at the beginning of July 1907, though the actual machinery wasn't in place until the end of the month or early August.[25] "They had to be watchful of government interference but this did not seem to inhibit the 'flying groups' of orators or prevent the calling of meetings in shops and factories."[26] Prior to then the Central Committee issued a platform state-ment, which essentially restated the basic party positions put forward in the First and Second Dumas, and eventually produced a campaign leaf-let. Various party branches had discussions about electoral blocs and in general reaffirmed the position adopted at the London or Fifth Congress advocated by the Bolsheviks, which permitted alliances only with revolu-tionary parties, "left blocs," in the first rounds and none with the Cadets. In the workers' curiae, again, no blocs were permitted in the first rounds. On their behalf, the Menshevik leader J. Martov sought, not unexpect-edly, more flexibility when it came to the Cadets, and it seems that he had some success depending on the specific locality. The St. Petersburg branch, in spite of the security risks, held a citywide meeting at the begin-ning of September to come up with a list of candidates for deputy to the Duma. Six Bolsheviks were selected to be the RSDLP electors.

Once the first round of elections got under way in September, it was possible to gauge levels of participation among different strata of the population and estimate their consequences. As for the peasantry, there was clearly less interest in the elections owing to how the process was constructed against the background of the failures of the First and Second Dumas to meet their principal demand—land. "The combina-tion of indifference, apathy, absenteeism, political circumspection, and some clerical and official pressure were apparently effective in reducing the oppositional element among the peasantry."[27] Another likely factor was the boycottist stance of the Social Revolutionaries, who claimed to represent the interests of the peasants. That position certainly affected a layer of workers who were attracted to them as the elections to the Second Duma had revealed. "Absenteeism was rife, as in all other strata, exacerbated by the Social Revolutionary insistence on the boycott of the elections. In some localities from one-third to almost one-half of the constituencies did not participate in the primary elections." In fac-tories where they had influence, including in some of the industrial districts in St. Petersburg, the abstention rate was overwhelming. "The Moscow workers, on the other hand, showed considerable interest in naming electors to the" provincial assemblies.[28] This suggests that Len-in's antiboycott campaign had born fruit in the place that had once been the center for Bolshevik opposition to participating in the elec-tions and thus the need to see worker participation in larger perspective. "[C]onsidering the apathetic and pessimistic mood of the greater part of the electorate, the workers made an impressive showing in naming all of their electors. The boycott movement took its toll but they were accessible to the Marxist propagandists, and they were accustomed to demonstrating their economic and political power."[29]

With virtually all the election results in, Lenin offered analysis and advice: "According to a fairly accurate estimate the members elected are 18 Social-Democrats, 13 others of the Left, 46 Cadets, 55 members of groups standing close to them, 92 Octobrists, 21 members of groups belonging to allied trends, 171 members of various Right-wing trends, including 32 members of the Union of the Russian People, and 16 non-party deputies. Thus, not counting an insignificant number of non-party deputies, all the others may be divided into four groups: the extreme Left, constituting a little over 7 per cent, the Left (Cadet) Centre 23 per cent, the Right (Octobrist) Centre 25.1 per cent, and the Right 40 per cent; the non-party deputies are a little less than 4 per cent." As Lenin had correctly forecast, the Third Duma would be a Black Hundred or right-wing Duma. But it didn't have a clear majority. A coalition between it and the Octobrists would constitute the most stable majority—65 percent of the deputies. But there was another possibility, an Octobrist-Cadet coalition, because it could pick up a few nonparty deputies and the few remaining elections were likely to be in favor of either party. Despite the differences between the two majorities, they were both "counterrevolutionary" given the rightward trajectory of the Cadets in the first two Dumas. And therein lay a key—and also prophetic—political conclusion: "[The Third Duma] is *incapable of accomplishing the objective tasks of the revolution even in the most distorted form*. It cannot even partly heal the gaping wounds inflicted upon Russia by the old regime—it can only cover up those wounds with wretched, sour, fictitious reforms. The election results only confirm our firm belief that *Russia cannot emerge from her present crisis in a peaceful way*."

The biggest danger for social democracy, Lenin contended in his first analysis of the elections in *Proletary*, would be to subscribe to the expected Menshevik position that the differences between the two majorities were meaningful as far as the interests of the toilers were concerned. The Octobrist-Cadet majority, they'd say, could be employed to advance the bourgeois democratic revolution and thus required support. Nothing could be further from the truth, he cautioned: "With the best will in the world, revolutionary Social-Democracy and, together with it, all the other revolutionary-minded elements of the Third Duma cannot use these conflicts in the interests of the revolution other than for purely propaganda purposes; there can be no question whatever of 'supporting' any of the conflicting sides, because such support, in itself, would be a counter-revolutionary act." As for differences within the Octobrist-Cadet

majority, they "could be" utilized, but they too were "superficial and transient." While "not refraining" from using them, *Social-Democracy must
wage a stubborn struggle for democratic and revolutionary aims not only
against the government, the Black Hundreds, and the Octobrists, but also
against the Cadets.*"

More important is what social democracy stood for. The resolutions of
the Fifth or London Congress, he argued, were still operative. And particularly important, given the way in which the Third Duma came into
existence, was the second part of the London resolution on "the immediate political aims of Social-Democracy in the Duma . . . to explain
to the people the impossibility of achieving political freedom by parliamentary means as long as real power remains in the hands of the tsarist
government, and to explain the inevitability of an open struggle of the
masses against the armed forces of absolutism, a struggle aimed at securing complete victory, namely, the assumption of power by the masses
and the convocation of a constituent assembly on the basis of universal,
equal, and direct suffrage by secret ballot." While the electoral process for
the First and Second Dumas left much to be desired, that for the Third
didn't even try to pretend to be democratic. The fraction "must expose
this crime, of course, not from the liberal stand point of a formal breach
of the constitution, but as a gross and brazen violation of the interests of
the broad masses of the people, as a shameless and outrageous falsification
of popular representation."

And of course, there was the even larger picture about Duma work as
stated in the London resolution:

> [T]he general character of the Duma struggle should be subordinated to
> the entire struggle of the proletariat outside the Duma, it being particularly
> important in this connection to make use of mass economic struggle and
> to serve the interests of that struggle . . . Peaceful legislative work by the
> Social-Democrats in the Third Duma under conditions which make mass
> movements highly probable would not only be inadvisable, would not
> only be absurd quixotry, but a downright betrayal of proletarian interests.
> It is bound to lead Social-Democracy to 'a whittling down of its slogans,
> which can only discredit it in the eyes of the masses and divorce it from the
> revolutionary struggle of the proletariat.' The spokesmen of the proletariat
> in the Duma could commit no greater crime than this.

Finally, Lenin addressed the specifics of Duma work for the fraction:
"The Social-Democrats in the Duma will carry out all these agitational,
propaganda, and organizational tasks not only by their speeches from the
Duma rostrum but also by introducing Bills and making interpellations

to the government . . . of course, Bills and questions of a consistently democratic character." The party had under its belt some experience in carrying out these tasks, but in the new Duma it would be more difficult. The rules required having 30 deputies to sign on to the introduction of a bill or an interpellation. In the new Duma there would only be 18 social democratic deputies. The fraction therefore would have to reach out to the much-reduced peasant Trudovik fraction and "other groups"—only those "to the left of the Cadets"—to get the necessary signatures. Lenin advised them to do so as long as principles weren't compromised: "It is not, of course, a question of any bloc, but only of those 'joint actions,' which, in the words of the London Congress resolution, 'must exclude any possibility of deviations from the Social-Democratic programme and tactics and serve only the purpose of a general onslaught both against reaction and the treacherous tactics of the liberal bourgeoisie.'"[30]

Lenin's proposals became the basis for resolutions voted on at two delegated party meetings held to orient itself to the soon to be convened new Duma. The first was that of the St. Petersburg branch, which met on October 27 in Terijoki, Finland. The only addendum was a concrete measure to facilitate "joint actions" with the democratic opposition: "To avoid a repetition of the mistakes made by the Social-Democrats in the Second Duma, the Social-Democratic group should immediately propose to the Left, and only to the Left, deputies of the Duma (i.e., those capable of fighting the Cadets) the formation of an Information Bureau which would not bind its participants but would enable the workers' deputies to exert systematic influence upon the democratic elements in the spirit of Social-Democratic policy." By a vote of 37 to 12 the meeting adopted Lenin's resolution and in the process rejected a Menshevik proposal "supporting the 'Left' Octobrists in the Third Duma and voting for a 'Left' Octobrist in the elections to the Duma presidium."[31]

A week later at an all-party conference, the Fourth, in Helsingfors (Helsinki), the delegates in their majority voted in favor of Lenin's resolution, this time in opposition not only to the Mensheviks but to the Jewish Bundist party faction as well. It included another addendum with three directives to the now christened "Social-Democratic group": "(1) to come forward with a special declaration; (2) to make an interpellation concerning the coup d'état of June 3; (3) to raise in the Duma, in the most advisable form, the question of the trial of the Social-Democratic group in the Second Duma."[32] The third point referred to the impending trial of the 55 social democratic deputies arrested in Stolypin's June 1907 coup d'état.

The Bolshevik-Menshevik differences on the eve of the convening of the Third Duma posed, once again, the norms of democratic decision making within the RSDLP. One issue concerned the fact that the Mensheviks had formed—apparently after the London Congress, where they lost their majority position on the Central Committee—a secret center that they utilized to promote support for a Cadet-Octobrist majority in various branches of the party—in opposition to the decision of the July or Third All-Party Conference not to do so. The Fourth Conference adopted a resolution to strengthen the Central Committee so that, hopefully, this wouldn't happen again.

The other issue concerned what Menshevik leader Georgi Plekhanov had done—specifically, his decision to voice his disagreement with the Third Conference's opposition to support for a Cadet-Octobrist majority in the pages of a left-bourgeois publication. He suggested that he did no more than what Lenin had done when Lenin published his pamphlet scandalizing the then Menshevik-dominated Central Committee at the beginning of 1907 for trying to cut a deal with the Cadets on the eve of the elections for the Second Duma and for which he was later brought up on charges for violating party discipline. Lenin countered that he had every right to make his exposure because he was challenging the Central Committee for not upholding the decisions regarding electoral alliances of the Stockholm or Fourth Congress, the highest decision-making body of the party. Also, Lenin said, he went public with his opposition in a pamphlet, whereas Plekhanov employed the pages of a bourgeois publication with a long record of hostility to the RSDLP. The majority of delegates at both meetings—looking to the German party for guidance on this issue—agreed with Lenin "that *political* participation in the bourgeois press, especially the supposedly non-party press, is absolutely inadmissible."[33] The debate on party norms revealed, once again, that democratic centralism was still a work in progress.

The very public Bolshevik-Menshevik disagreements provoked an inevitable schadenfreude response, "malicious chuckling," from opponents. "But Who Are the Judges?" Lenin sarcastically asked. "The liberals," he charged, "sneer at the struggle within Social-Democracy in order to cover up their systematic *deception* of the public in regard to the Cadet Party . . . There are no records of the proceedings of the Cadet congresses. The liberals issue no figures of their party membership either as a whole or by organizations. The tendency of the different committees is unknown. Nothing but darkness . . . Lawyers and professors, who make their career by parliamentarism, hypocritically condemn the underground struggle and praise open activity by parties while actually flouting the democratic

principle of publicity and concealing from the public the different political tendencies with in their party."

As for the Socialist Revolutionaries, they, too, he charged, were no
paragons of transparency. Founded in 1901, the "December Congress of
the Party . . . in 1905 was the first and only one to publish minutes of
the proceedings." But even then it failed to take advantage of the then
existing political space in the way the social democrats had: "[D]uring the
period of the greatest liberties, the period of most direct influence upon
the masses, they *concealed* from the public the existence of two different
tendencies within the party. The differences of opinion were as great as
those within the Social-Democratic ranks, but the Social-Democrats tried
to clarify them, whereas the Socialist-Revolutionaries tried diplomatically
to conceal them . . . 'Not to wash one's dirty linen in public' is a thing the
S.R.'s are adept at." The RSDLP, he contended, was willing to do exactly
that because "there can be no mass party, no party of a class, without full
clarity of essential shadings, without an open struggle between various
tendencies, without informing the *masses* as to which leaders and which
organizations of the Party are pursuing this or that line. Without this, a
party worthy of the name cannot be built, and we are *building* it. We have
succeeded in putting the views of our two currents truthfully, clearly, and
distinctly before everyone." The problem for the Socialist Revolutionaries, he concluded, "is that it is impossible for them to create a mass
party, impossible for them to become the party of a *class*." Their penchant
for terrorism registered this fact. "Your terrorism, gentlemen, is not the
outcome of your revolutionism. Your revolutionism is confined to terrorism."[34] Subsequent history would confirm Lenin's judgment.

THE THIRD DUMA CONVENES

The circumstances under which the RSDLP's Duma fraction was
elected—Stolypin's prejudicial electoral law of June 1907—presented
the party with new challenges. And not the least of them was the fact
that Lenin had to exercise direction from a considerable distance. For
the First and Second Dumas he did so, if not always from St. Petersburg,
then from nearby Finland. For the Third Duma it would have to be from
Geneva, Paris, Crackow, and elsewhere, with all the logistical and security
challenges that presented. Coupled with a very inexperienced fraction—
almost all the previous members were either in jail or in exile—Lenin had
his work cut out for him.

FIRST UNSTEADY STEPS

The first substantive issue that the social democratic group had to deal with was the budget, specifically a Cadet proposal for "extending the budgetary powers of the Duma." As was true for the Second Duma, the budget debate—one of the reasons for its dissolution—had the potential, Lenin repeated, to expose the reality of parliamentary government in Czarist Russia. Therefore he criticized—both comradely and pedagogically—the fraction in the first issue of the Central Committee's illegal organ *Sotsial-Demokrat* for signing on to what was apparently just a procedural matter about the proposal.

The main problem was that the Cadet proposal, not surprisingly, sidestepped the obvious: "The Russian Duma has no budgetary powers, for '*by the law*' the rejection of a budget does not prevent it from being put into execution"—what had actually occurred when the Second Duma couldn't agree on Stolypin's budget. "Thus, the *only* object of raising and debating this question in the Duma could be that of exposing the whole truth. Practical reform activity could *not*, at this time and in this situation, be the aim of a *democrat*, because, first, the impossibility of reforms on the basis of the existing Fundamental Laws of the Duma's budgetary powers is obvious, and secondly, it would be absurd, in a Duma composed of Black-Hundred die-hards and Moscow merchants, to propose that *its* powers, the powers of such a Duma, should be extended . . . A democrat should reveal to the people the *gulf* that lies between the powers of parliament and the prerogatives of the monarch, and not deaden the public mind, not distort *the political struggle* by reducing it *to an office-routine correction* of the laws."

Before his critique Lenin offered some positive reinforcement: "The speech by the representative of the Social-Democrats, Pokrovsky 2nd, we gladly acknowledge, reveals a quite *different* spirit, presenting the issue in a *fundamentally* different way. The Social-Democrat stated bluntly and clearly that he considered popular representation in the Third Duma *falsified* (we are quoting *Stolichnaya Pochta* [Metropolitan Post, a Left Cadet St. Petersburg paper] for January 18, since the verbatim reports of this session are not yet available). He stressed not minor points, not the official derivation of the law, but the ruined and oppressed state of the masses, of the vast millions of the people. He rightly declared that 'one cannot speak of the budgetary powers of the Duma without irony,' that we were demanding not only the right to recast the whole budget . . . but to 'remodel the whole financial system' and 'reject the government's budget.' He concluded with a no less correct and, for a member of the workers' party, obligatory demand for 'full power of the people.' On all these points Pokrovsky conscientiously and correctly upheld the Social-Democratic point of view."

But by voting with the entire Duma to have the Cadet proposal sent to committee without any instructions, the social democratic group undermined, Lenin argued, the force of Pokrovsky's intervention. Especially egregious, "judging by newspaper reports," was the fraction having directed Pokrovsky to declare, "'*We support the proposal . . . because it tends towards an extension of the budgetary powers of a popular representative assembly.*'" In fact, the proposal, apparently unbeknownst to the fraction, had been effectively rendered null and void through an agreement the Cadets reached with the Octobrists. There was a lesson in this that Lenin tried to impart to the young fraction: "For the hundredth and thousandth time 'support' given to the Cadets led to those who supported them being deceived. For the hundredth and thousandth time the *facts* have revealed how shoddy and impermissible are the tactics of supporting liberal, Cadet proposals."

He then gave an example of a proposal, even if offered by the Cadets, that the fraction could have supported and the advantages in doing so:

> If the Cadets, instead of joining with the Octobrists, had *put to the vote* a declaration stating clearly and precisely that the Duma was powerless in financial matters, that popular representation was falsified, that the country had been ruined by the autocracy and a financial débâcle was unavoidable, and that under such circumstances the democratic representatives would not give their support to any loans—that would have been an honest act on the part of the bourgeois democrats, an act of struggle and not an act of dull-witted flunkeyism. It would have been our duty to support such an act, while not forgetting to stipulate our own independent Social-Democratic objectives. Such an act would have contributed to the enlightenment of the people and the exposure of the autocracy. The defeat of such a declaration in the Duma and the violent opposition such a proposal would have raised among the Black Hundreds would have been a historical service rendered by the democrats and probably a new phase in the struggle for freedom. But now the Cadets have once again *proved bankrupt.* Social-Democratic comrades in the Duma, protect the honour of the socialist workers' party! Do not allow yourselves to suffer failure by giving support to such liberalism!

In offering constructive criticism, Lenin was careful about the facts—thus we see the qualifiers "judging by newspaper reports," "so says *Stolichnaya Pochta*," or even "we should like to believe that *Stolichnaya Pochta* did not tell the truth." Being much farther from the scene, Lenin had to rely on sources that were not always as reliable—another challenge for Third Duma work.

Lenin's article on the budget was reprinted in the illegal Bolshevik paper *Proletary* with a "Postscript": "Unfortunately, the first budgetary speeches of our Duma comrades are very lame and deeply mistaken. In the next issue of *Proletary* we shall deal in detail with these mistakes and indicate what we believe to be the necessary line of action for Social-Democrats in the budgetary debates and voting." The tone here was more critical, and it anticipated increasing Bolshevik discontent with the social democratic group.

Saber Rattling in the Balkans

On February 27, 1908, the Duma addressed the foreign policy of the regime. This was a first, since neither of the two previous Dumas had ever done so. The opportunity came with a discussion on appropriations for the ministry of foreign affairs. While the regime applauded the deliberations and vote that day to fund its request, couched in thinly veiled language that endorsed domestic and foreign aggression, for Lenin it was "A Police-Patriotic Demonstration Made to Order." Not only did the Octobrists, as expected, wrap themselves in the banner of patriotism in bowing to the government's wishes, but the Cadets did as well. "The *entire* Russian bourgeoisie, *Left* as well as Right, had to be made to formally express its confidence in the government, in its 'peaceful policy,' its stability, its intentions and ability to pacify and tranquillise. It was necessary as the blank endorsement of a bill." In so doing, in other words, the Cadets and the rest of the bourgeoisie enabled Nicholas to have access to West European creditors.

> In three years Russian liberalism has gone through an evolution which, in Germany, took over thirty years, and in France over a hundred—an evolution from adherents of freedom to spineless and contemptible henchmen of absolutism. The specific weapon of struggle which the bourgeoisie possesses—the possibility of putting pressure on the purse, of withholding funds, of upsetting the "delicate" approaches for new loans—this weapon could have been used by the Cadets many times during the Russian revolution. And on each occasion, in the spring of 1908 just as in the spring of 1906, they surrendered their weapon to the enemy, licking the hand of the pogrom-makers and swearing loyalty to them.

Lenin noted that prior to this patriotic display of the Cadets in the Duma, Pyotr Struve, one of their leaders, had written an article to provide theoretical justification for this "evolution in the ideology of Russian liberalism." He "already advocates the idea of a 'Great Russia,' the idea of bourgeois nationalism; he attacks 'the intelligentsia's hostility to the state,' for the thousandth time striking out at 'Russian revolutionism,' 'Marxism,' 'renegades,' the 'class struggle,' and 'banal radicalism.'" Successfully playing the patriotic card required, therefore, an attack on revolutionary social democracy. Not surprisingly, Lenin welcomed Struve's article: "Mr. Struve wants a frankly counter-revolutionary liberalism. We want it, too, because this 'frankness' of liberalism will best of all enlighten both the democratic peasantry and the socialist proletariat." In hindsight, the February 27 session of the Third Duma, the unleashing of patriotism, signaled the opening shot in Russia's contribution to the Guns of August six years later.[35]

There was, however, as Lenin ended, one notable dissent from the February 27 love fest—also in anticipation of 1914: "[I]t should be said that the only honest and proud word of a democrat came from a *Social-Democrat*. Deputy Chkheidze took the floor and declared that the Social-Democratic group would vote *against* the Bill. He started to give the reasons, but after his first words: 'Our diplomacy in the West has always been a bulwark of reaction and served the interests of . . .' the Chairman stopped the mouth of the workers' deputy." Despite having been silenced, the deputy set an example: "The workers' deputy stood isolated on this question. This is all the more to his credit. The proletariat should show, and it will show, that it is capable of defending the behests of the democratic revolution despite all the treacheries of liberalism and the waverings of the petty bourgeoisie."[36]

Lenin's praise was timely, because within half a year he would call on the social democratic group to emulate Chkheidze. The occasion was a new upsurge in the world revolutionary process and the predictably counterrevolutionary response of Europe's last absolutist state, especially since it shared borders with the two countries most affected. In his first sustained writing about international affairs, "Inflammable Material in World Politics," Lenin explained that the Young Turks revolt and that lead by Sattar Khan in Persia were delayed echoes of Russia's own revolution. Nicholas had every reason, therefore, to make sure they didn't succeed. As well he saw an opportunity to take advantage of the turmoil in Turkey to lay claim, in cahoots with European governments, to Ottoman Empire possessions in the Balkans—the consequences of which would only become clear six years later. Because of the regime's conscious misrepresentation of the facts about what was taking place in Turkey and Persia and the thinly veiled enabling of Nicholas by the Cadets, "our

Duma deputies and all our Party organizations must bear in mind that we cannot make a single serious step forward in Social-Democratic propaganda and agitation about the Balkan events without revealing—from *the Duma rostrum*, in leaflets and at meetings—the *connection* between the reactionary policy of the autocracy and the hypocritical opposition of the Cadets. We shall never be able to explain to the people how harmful and reactionary the policy of the tsarist government is, unless we explain that Cadet foreign policy is *essentially the same*. We cannot combat chauvinism and the Black-Hundred spirit in foreign policy, unless we combat the phrase-mongering, the posing, the mental reservations and dodges of the Cadets."

After detailing the machinations of the regime and their Cadet cheerleaders in both the Persian and Turkish theaters, Lenin spelled out what was at stake for both the Duma fraction and other units of the party:

> An extremely onerous, but at the same time extremely noble and momentous task falls now to the Russian Social Democratic deputies in the Duma, where a statement by [Foreign Minister] Izvolsky and a question by the Cadets and Octobrists are expected. The Social-Democratic deputies are members of a body that is a screen for the policy of the chief reactionary power, the chief plotter of counter-revolution, and they must find in themselves the courage and ability *to tell the whole truth*. At a time like this, the Social-Democratic deputies in the Black-Hundred Duma are people to whom much is given and of whom much is required. For apart from them there is *no one* in the Duma to voice the protest against tsarism from positions *other* than those of the *Cadets* and Octobrists. And a Cadet "protest," at such times and in the present circumstances, is worse than no protest at all since it can be made only *from amidst the selfsame* capitalist wolf-pack, and on behalf of the selfsame wolfish policy.

It was crucial that the fraction and the other party organizations collaborate intimately in this task, because "agitation among the masses is now a hundred times more important than in ordinary times." Lenin then honed in on three issues the antiwar campaign should focus on. First, "[o]ur job is to reveal the *fact* that there exists a reactionary conspiracy of the [European] powers, a conspiracy which the governments are doing everything they possibly can to conceal behind the farce of public negotiations . . . Secondly, we should reveal the real, as distinct from the asserted, results of this conspiracy, namely, the blow to the Turkish revolution, Russia's assistance in strangling the Persian revolution, interference in the affairs of other nations, and violation of that fundamental democratic principle, the right of nations to self-determination." Last, "[a]ll the bourgeois parties, including the most liberal and 'democratic' in name, our Cadets included, support capitalist foreign policy. That is the third thing which the Social-Democrats must with special vigor bring to the knowledge of the people." The Cadets only differ with the Black Hundreds on how to carry out such a policy; "these liberal reproaches leveled at the government for lagging behind other countries (in rapine and intervention!) have the most corrupting effect on the masses." Social democracy demands, "Down with all colonial policy, down with the whole policy of intervention and capitalist struggle for the conquest of foreign lands and foreign populations, for new privileges, new markets, control of the Straits [of Dardanelles], etc.!"

When the saber rattling began in the summer of 1908, Lenin said, "a European war seemed dangerously close . . . [but now in October] it is much more probable that the whole thing will end up in shouting and clamor and war will be avoided."[37] Though right in the short run, Lenin's optimism wasn't rewarded by subsequent history. His Duma-centered antiwar campaign, however, proved to be prescient—a dress rehearsal for Russia's social democrats when the storm clouds returned in 1914.

"THE REVOLUTIONARY-DEMOCRATIC DICTATORSHIP OF THE PROLETARIAT AND PEASANTRY"

While Stolypin's electoral law effectively reduced peasant and worker presence in the Third Duma, from 157 to 13 and 67 to 18 respectively out of 442 deputies, the worker-peasant alliance that Lenin sought and fought for through the Duma process came closer to realization. And this was despite the fact that, owing to the law, peasant deputies had been "sifted through a number of police sieves, even though elected by land-lords, even though intimidated by the Duma diehards." That process also eliminated, for the most part, deputies who could be identified as Trudoviks, the bane of the regime in the two previous Dumas. So particularly heartening were the initiatives of "a group of non-party peasants, some of them from the *Right* wing," that called "for compulsory alienation of the land and for the local land institutions elected *by the whole population!*" Even one Cadet deputy had to admit that "'on the agrarian question the stand of the 'Right' peasants in all three Dumas has been more Left than the Cadets.'"

With more details about the initiatives, Lenin seized on a Cadet lamentation about the "Trudovik spirit" of the new deputies. Two bills had been submitted, one by peasant deputies and the other by clergy deputies, that both called for land committees "elected on the basis of universal, direct and equal suffrage by secret ballot." They were quite similar to the

Trudovik bills submitted in the First and Second Dumas and lobbied against by the Cadets. What the latter called for instead were committees that would "consist of an equal number of representatives of the peasantry and of the landlords, with a *representative of the government*, as a third party. In other words, the Cadets were betraying the muzhik [peasant] to the landlord, by assuring that everywhere the latter would have the majority (the landlords plus a representative of the landlord autocracy are always in a majority against the peasants)."

Lenin relished the fact that "even the clergy—those ultra-reactionaries, those Black-Hundred obscurantists purposely maintained by the government—have gone further than the Cadets in their agrarian Bill." And why could that be? "The village priest will have to return from the most police-ridden Duma into his own village: and however greatly the village has been purged by Stolypin's punitive expeditions and chronic billeting of the soldiery, *there is no return to it* for those who have taken the side of the landlords. So it turns out that the most reactionary priest finds it more difficult than the enlightened lawyer and professor to betray the peasant to the landlord."[38] In saying "*there is no return to it*" and "finds it more difficult," Lenin pointed to a reality about the countryside that was of enormous importance for his argument about the "nature" of Russia's revolution. The peasantry not only had more democratic credentials than the liberals but was willing to use force and violence to defend its interests—a point to which he returned.

When the land question was debated again later in the session, Lenin was furnished "with exceptionally valuable material" to make his case. First, the speeches of the Octobrist and Black Hundred representatives were particularly useful because of their blatant defense for the first time of the landlord interests—"[t]hese gentlemen cannot even imagine any capitalism that is not based on the preservation of landlordism, i.e. feudalist landownership"—and conscious counterrevolutionary sensibility. "For agitation among the masses, the study of extracts [of those] . . . speeches . . . is absolutely necessary . . . very valuable material for the awakening of those sections of the people who are politically unconscious or indifferent . . . [T]he speeches of the Right [are] incomparably more valuable material, both for the scientific analysis of the present situation and for purposes of agitation, than the speeches of the half-hearted and cowardly liberals."

Despite the attempt of the Cadet speakers to "reconcile the irreconcilable, to straddle two stools," Lenin distilled for his *Proletary* readers the fundamentally prolandlord antidemocratic feature of their proposal presented by a "Mr. Berezovsky," specifically the aforementioned composition of the local land committees to decide on compulsory alienation: "The 'democrats' fall so low that they try to prove to the Black-Hundred die-hards how inoffensive their actions and programs are at a time of revolution!" The speeches of the peasant deputies, on the other hand, were starkly different:

> Take a typical Right-wing peasant, Storchak. He begins his speech by repeating in full the words of Nicholas II about "the sacred rights of property," the impermissibility of their "infringement," etc. He continues: "May God grant the Emperor health. He spoke well for the whole people" . . . And he finishes: "But if His Majesty said that there should be justice and order, then, of course, if I am sitting on 3 dessiatines of land, and next to me there are 30,000 dessiatines, that is not order and justice"! Compare this monarchist with the monarchist Berezovsky. One is an ignorant peasant, the other an educated almost-European. The first is as innocent as a babe unborn and amazingly ignorant politically. The link between the monarchy and "order," i.e., the disorder and injustice which protect the owners of 30,000 dessiatines, is not clear to him. The second is a skilled politician who knows all the ins and outs to Witte, Trepov, Stolypin and Co., and who has studied the niceties of European constitutions. The first is one of those millions who toil and moil all their life on 3 dessiatines, and whom economic realities *drive* into mass revolutionary struggle against the holders of 30,000 dessiatines. The second is one of the tens of thousands or at most one hundred thousand landlords who wants "peacefully" to keep his "cultured estate" by throwing a sop to the peasant. Is it not clear that the first *can* make a bourgeois revolution in Russia, *abolish* landlordism and set up a peasant republic (however much this word may frighten him now)? Is it not clear that the second *cannot but* hinder the struggle of the masses without which the victory of the revolution is impossible?
>
> Those people who still cannot for the life of them understand what "the revolutionary-democratic dictatorship of the proletariat and the peasantry" means, should give some thought to this!

For Lenin, the contrasts between the speeches of Storchak and Berezovsky and the proposals they presented—Storchak submitted the same one the peasant deputies did in the earlier session—could not have been more instructive. They gave lie to the Menshevik claim that an alliance with the Cadets was needed for Russia's bourgeois revolution: "[C]lass-conscious workers will only be strengthened in their conviction, after reading the debates in the Third Duma, that a victorious bourgeois revolution in Russia is impossible without a joint onset by the worker and peasant masses, in spite of the waverings and betrayals of the bourgeoisie." Lenin quoted other peasant deputies who made clear that they and their constituents were prepared to defend with force their interests—more evidence for his "democratic dictatorship" formula.

An important measure of the road the peasant deputies had traveled politically is that "all politically conscious peasants ['Trudoviks'] supported nationalization" of the land. One of the two social democrats who spoke, Belousov, provided data, in a speech drafted by Lenin—and based on a soon to be published book—in support of nationalization. As for the interventions of the two social democrat deputies, both "comrades . . . did their duty properly . . . Both speeches by the Social-Democratic spokesmen in the Third Duma should be kept for handy reference by every member of the Party who carries on the work of propaganda and agitation." There was only one glitch: the failure to mention nationalization "without compensation," a key party demand. But the oversight wasn't intentional, which "would have been an important breach of our program."

Lenin's purpose was clear: to use the pages of *Proletary*—or any other venue at his disposal—to convince workers that a revolutionary alliance with the peasantry was doable. His evidence was the speeches and proposals presented in the Duma by all parties—to be used for "propaganda and agitation." No wonder he would continue to defend the value of Duma work in the face of growing opposition among some Bolsheviks.

THE "FLIGHT OF THE INTELLECTUALS"

Six months after Stolypin's coup, Lenin drew a balance sheet on the state of the party. "On the Straight Road" contended that the "worst was over." The repression had clearly taken a toll on the party. Most symptomatic of that fact, as one local report put it, the "intellectuals, as is well known, have been deserting in masses in recent months." As long as the revolution was in the ascent and space existed to do legal political work, intellectuals flocked to the revolutionary cause. The crackdown, however, made the cause less appealing to that social layer. But, as a growing number of new reports began to reveal, there was an upside to the "mass desertion": "[T]he general conclusion reached is that 'in a number of places responsible work, owing to the flight of the intellectuals, is passing into the hands of the advanced workers' . . . The Party has already entered the straight road of leadership of the working masses by advanced 'intellectuals' drawn from the ranks of the workers themselves." This change was reflected in the advances the party was beginning to make in trade union work—both legal and illegal—and in the cooperatives.

Lenin then made a significant admission about another arena of party legal work, the Duma, specifically the election of social democrat deputies to the Third Duma:

> Strange though it may sound, it is a fact that we cannot all at once raise the work of our parliamentary representatives to a Party level—just as we did not all at once begin to work "in a Party way" in the co-operatives. Elected under a law which falsifies the will of the people, elected from the ranks of Social-Democrats who have preserved their legality, ranks which have thinned very greatly as a result of persecution during the first two Dumas, our Duma Social-Democrats *in effect* inevitably were at first non-party Social-Democrats rather than real members of the Party.
>
> This is deplorable, but it is a fact—and it could hardly be otherwise in a capitalist country entangled by thousands of bonds inherited from serfdom and with a legal workers' party that has been in existence for only two years. And it was not only non-party people who wanted on this fact to base their tactics of setting up a non-revolutionary Social-Democracy, but also those . . . Social-Democrat-like intellectuals who clustered around the Duma group like flies round a honey-pot.

The circumstances under which the deputies were elected, against the background of mass arrests of social democrats or their being forced into exile, made for a fraction that had a lot to learn.

Lenin was cautiously optimistic that progress was being made while being realistic:

> We will not undertake to prophesy, nor shall we close our eyes to what vast efforts are still required to organize more or less tolerable parliamentary Social-Democratic work in our conditions. But we may note that in the first issue of the Central Organ [*Sotsial-Demokrat*] there is Party criticism of the Duma group, and a *direct resolution* of the Central Committee about better direction for its work. We do not by any means consider that the criticism in the Central Organ covers all the defects . . . What is basic and most important is that the transformation of the Duma group into a really Party organization now features in all our work, and that consequently the Party will achieve it, however hard this may be, and however the road may be beset with trials, vacillations, partial crises, personal clashes, etc.

Ensuring that the Duma fraction was "a really Party organization" required a real party, and that, Lenin felt, was being realized after the collapse: "A strong illegal organization of the Party Centers, systematic illegal publications and—most important of all—local and particularly factory Party groups, led by advanced members from among the workers themselves, living in direct contact with the masses: such is the foundation on which we were building, and have built, a hard and solid core of a revolutionary and Social-Democratic working-class movement. And this illegal core will spread *its* feelers, *its* influence, incomparably wider than ever before, both through the Duma and the trade unions, both in the co-operative societies and in the cultural and educational organizations."[39]

Having boycotted the Third Duma, the Socialist Revolutionaries felt they had license to "sneer at the *mistakes*" of the inexperienced social democratic group. As for their speeches, "'Who knows anything about these statements, about these votings and abstentions'?" "Yes," Lenin fired back, "our Social-Democratic deputies in the Third Duma have made many mistakes. And this very example the S.R.s chose to quote demonstrates the difference in the attitude of *a workers' party* and *a group of intellectuals*":

> A workers' party understands that in a period of political lull and collapse the latter must inevitably show itself in the Duma group too, since in the Third Duma it was even less capable than in the Second of assembling large party forces. Therefore the workers' party criticizes and corrects the mistakes of its deputies. Every organization, by discussing each speech and arriving at the conclusion that such-and-such a statement or speech was a mistake, provides material for political action by the masses . . . And our criticism of their mistakes is done publicly, and openly, before the masses. Our deputies learn from this criticism, the classes learn, the Party learns—the Party which has seen hard times, and knows that it is not by ranting but only by the stubborn and steadfast work of *all* organizations is it possible to emerge with honor from a difficult situation. Even *Proletary*, which, as a newspaper published abroad, realized that it was under an obligation to give its advice from afar with care, openly proposed measures for improving the work of the group. Our open Party criticism, added to the work of the group, achieves the result that the masses know both the Duma statements and the *nature* of the Party's corrections to them. And failure to appreciate the Duma work at a time when Party organizations and the Party press are facing the effects of the deep collapse, is a sign of boundless intellectualist irresponsibility.

Such transparency, he concluded, was necessary in meeting the main challenge the party faced: how "to combine open speeches in the Duma with illegal Party activity." Solving this problem would "guarantee" that "the proletariat will be able, under the leadership of Social-Democracy, to fight more ably and more unitedly, and to gain more decisive victories" when the next revolutionary phase opened.[40] Events within a few years would test the accuracy of Lenin's forecast.

It was in the Moscow branch of the RSDLP, it may be remembered, where the greatest opposition to participating in the Third Duma existed. Though Lenin won over the vast majority against the boycottists, it is no coincidence that it was in Moscow where a new anti–Third Duma tendency emerged, known as the otzovists or recallists. Fueled largely by the "mistakes" of the social democratic group, they—led by, again, Bogdanov—argued that the party should recall the deputies and effectively dissolve the fraction. At a party conference in Moscow in June 1908, the recallists failed to get the majority of the branch to support their position, but that didn't end their campaign. *Proletary* opened its pages in its November issue to their argument, to which Lenin responded publicly for the first time in "Two Letters."

Lenin methodically dissected and exposed the shortcomings of the otzovists' argument. Quoting the comrade who wrote one of the letters on their behalf, he charged that he "exaggerates" the importance of Duma work—the obverse of Menshevik parliamentary cretinism:

> Nowhere under any conditions, even in the most "ideal" bourgeois-democratic republic, would revolutionary Social-Democracy agree to recognize its parliamentary group either as the "natural fulfillment" of the Party or as *its* "diplomatic representative." Such a view is deeply fallacious. We send deputies into bourgeois and bourgeois-Black-Hundred representative institutions not for diplomacy, but for a special type of subsidiary Party work, for agitation and propaganda from a particular rostrum. Even when there is an "ideal" democratic franchise, the parliamentary group of a workers' party will always bear certain traces of the influence of the general bourgeois circumstances in which the elections take place: for example, it will always be more "intellectual" than the Party as a whole, and therefore we shall never recognize the group to be the "fulfillment" of the Party. The parliamentary group is not a general staff (if I may be allowed to use a "military" simile side by side with the "diplomatic" one used by the writer), but rather a unit of trumpeters in one case, or a reconnaissance unit in another, or an organization of some other auxiliary "arm."
>
> The otzovist comrade has transformed the parliamentary group from a *subsidiary Party organization* into the "fulfillment" of the Party in order, by *exaggerating* the significance of the group, to attribute an entirely wrong character to the activity of the contingent which we have sent into the bourgeois-Black-Hundred Duma.

As for the comrade's second argument that since the masses are "indifferent to all that goes on within the walls of Tauride Palace" and therefore it's a waste of time for social democrats to be there, Lenin drew out its implications:

> "If the masses are indifferent, then the Social-Democrats should be indifferent too." But we are a party *leading* the masses to *socialism*, and not at all one which follows every change in mood or depression in the spirits of the masses. All Social-Democratic parties have had to cope at times with the apathy of the masses, or their infatuation with some error, some fashion (chauvinism, anti-Semitism, anarchism) . . . but never do consistently revolutionary Social-Democrats yield to every changing mood of the masses. One can and must criticize the bad policy of Social-Democrats in the Third Duma, when they carry on a bad policy there; but to say that the agitation is of no value *because* of the complete indifference of the masses, means to talk in a non-Social-Democratic way.

The fundamental problem with the comrade's argument, Lenin charged, is that he wanted to throw out the proverbial baby with the bath water. The task before the party, rather, was how to correct "the bad policy of Social Democrats in the Third Duma," not to dissolve the fraction and walk away from Duma work—and that was "only just beginning":

> We have not yet had a single Party conference telling the group firmly and clearly that it must correct its tactics in such-and-such definitely specified respects. We have not as yet a central organ appearing regularly, following every step of the group on behalf of the whole Party and giving it direction. Our local organizations have done still very, very little in that field of work—agitation among the masses on the subject of every speech of a Social-Democrat in the Duma, explaining every mistake in this or that speech. Yet we are being asked to give it all up, to declare the struggle hopeless, to renounce use of the Duma rostrum at times like the present of 1908.

One of the problems the party faced was the glomming on to the fraction of "bourgeois 'well-informed persons'"—that is, liberal intellectuals who ("like flies round a honey-pot," as he put it earlier) sought to be its "advisors." A similar problem arose with the Second Duma, but with the Bolshevik leadership far from the scene this time, intellectuals like S. N. Prokopovich had better access to the deputies. But as Lenin pointed out, even that problem was now being confronted.

Lenin was especially vigilant about liberal intellectuals vis-à-vis the working class, and nothing he wrote is as insightful as what he said about one of them:

There is no need to fear the landlords' influence on the people. They will never succeed in fooling any considerable number of workers or even peasants for any lengthy period. But the influence of the *intelligentsia*, who take no direct part in exploitation, who have been trained to use general phrases and concepts, who seize on every "good" idea and who sometimes from sincere stupidity elevate their inter-class position to a *principle* of non-class parties and non-class politics—the influence of this bourgeois intelligentsia on the people is dangerous. Here, and here alone, do we find a contamination of the masses that is capable of doing real harm and that calls for the utmost exertion of all the forces of socialism to counteract this poison.[41]

After listing the "serious mistakes" of the fraction and making some concrete proposals about the direction of its work by the Central Committee, Lenin concluded: "Needless to say one should criticize the group, it is dishonest to hush up its mistakes. But all of us have also to strengthen our organizations in the local areas, and develop the agitation to make use of every act by the Duma group. Only the combination of the two forms of work is activity really worthy of consistent revolutionary Social-Democrats, and only this combination will help us to overcome 'the moment of stagnation' and hasten the arrival of a new upsurge."[42]

Earlier in the year, on the twenty-fifth anniversary of Marx's death, Lenin made a contribution to a symposium. His "Marx and Revisionism" drew a balance sheet on Marxism and its critics. Of particular relevance here is the claim of "liberals . . . that bourgeois parliamentarism destroys classes and class divisions, since the right to vote and the right to participate in the government of the country are shared by all citizens without distinction."

The whole history of Europe in the second half of the nineteenth century, and the whole history of the Russian revolution in the early twentieth, clearly show how absurd such views are. Economic distinctions are not mitigated but aggravated and intensified under the freedom of "democratic" capitalism. Parliamentarism does not eliminate, but lays bare the innate character even of the most democratic bourgeois republics as organs of class oppression. By helping to enlighten and to organize immeasurably wider masses of the population than those which previously took an active part in political events, parliamentarism does not make for the elimination of crises and political revolutions, but for the maximum intensification of civil war during such revolutions.[43]

Nothing better explains why Lenin was so insistent in maintaining a Duma fraction. It's useful to recall, in grasping his point, his retort to the otzovist comrade in "Two Letters." The basic tasks of revolutionary social democratic parliamentary work, he emphasized, didn't distinguish between "ideal" bourgeois republics as in some Western European countries and the not-so-ideal as the "Black Hundred representative institution," the Third Duma. He held social democracy to the same standards no matter the setting. This is important in understanding how he increasingly viewed—one of the arguments of this book—the participation of social democratic parties in Western European parliaments leading up to the First World War.

To "Organize Social-Democratic Parliamentarism in Russia on a Different Basis"

"We have not yet had a single Party conference telling the [Social Democratic] group firmly and clearly that it must correct its tactics in such-and-such definitely specified respects." Lenin's complaint in his "Two Letters" would soon be rectified. Two leadership meetings in Paris at the end of 1908 and in June 1909 took the proverbial bull by the horns. Only in hindsight would it be clear that the party's parliamentary work was put on a firmer footing—a corner had been turned. At the end of the Third Duma in 1912, the party, despite the bumps along the way, was in a much stronger position to effectively use Duma work when the long-expected revival in the class struggle materialized.

The Paris Meetings and a By-Election

"The conference was the first authoritative meeting of delegates from the biggest Party organizations to discuss the work of the Duma Social-Democratic group during the whole session."[44] Such was the significance, in Lenin's opinion, of the Fifth (All-Russian) Conference of the RSDLP, held in Paris from December 21 to 27. In many ways it codified the arguments he had been making for some time in defense of Duma work and how to make it more effective. Most important, it recognized "that the blame for the group's deviations does not rest on the group alone, for it has to work in the extremely difficult conditions of a reactionary Duma, but is shared to some extent by all the organizations of the Party and its Central Committee, which have not by far yet done all that was necessary and possible to organize the Party's work in the Duma on proper lines." And to achieve that goal, "attention must be focused on building up and strengthening the illegal Party organization; and that only under the unfaltering influence of this organization can all work among the masses, all control of the Duma group, all the activity of the Party around the Duma group, all use of legal and semi-legal organizations, be properly arranged, without any debasing of the class aims of Social-Democracy." This resolution was explicitly directed at a newly emerged tendency in the party, "the liquidationist trend," that argued that given the repression it faced the party should "legalize [itself] . . . at all costs, even at the price of an open renunciation of the Party program, tactics and organization." The liquidationists, as they would be called, were influenced, Lenin charged, by the "flight of the intellectuals."[45]

In his report on the conference, Lenin pointed out that the difficulty the party faced in making sure the Duma fraction acted in accord with "the *political line* of the Party" was not unique to Russian social democracy:

> In the history of West-European socialist parties there have been a number of instances of abnormal relations between the parliamentary groups and the Party; to this day these relations are quite often abnormal in the Latin countries, where the groups do not display sufficient Party spirit. We must from the very outset organize Social-Democratic parliamentarism in Russia on a different basis; we must at once establish team-work in this field—so that every Social-Democratic deputy may really feel that he has the Party behind him, that the Party is deeply concerned over his mistakes and tries to straighten out his path—so that every Party worker may take part in the general Duma work of the Party, learning from the practical Marxist criticism of its steps, feeling it his duty to assist it, and striving to gear the special work of the group to the whole propaganda and agitation activity of the Party.[46]

This clearly reveals, possibly for the first time—and relevant to one of the arguments of this book—that the more involved Lenin became in Duma work the more conscious he became of the shortcomings of social democratic parliamentary work elsewhere, particularly in Western Europe, and he increasingly criticized its modus operandi.

Precisely to avoid "abnormal relations" between the parliamentary group and the party, the conference provided "practical instructions" to the fraction, a first for such a meeting, specifically on how to vote on budget items. In general, the fraction should refrain from voting for a budget proposed by a Black Hundred government. When uncertain they should consult the Central Committee or some other party organizations (see Appendix A, "Practical Instructions on Voting for the Budget by the Social-Democratic Group in the Duma"). On this and the other resolutions suggested there was common agreement by the end of the conference. Subsequent events would soon reveal, however, that the near unanimity at the meeting was deceptive.

Two recallists attended the Paris conference but "did not raise the question openly," Lenin noted. However, in Moscow and St. Petersburg, with Bogdanov leading the charge, the recallists became increasingly vocal. They were joined by another tendency, which argued that the Duma fraction should be given an opportunity to mend their ways, and if they didn't then they should be recalled; they became known as the "ultimatumists." Because both tendencies arose among Bolshevik ranks, it became increasingly clear that another meeting, a Bolshevik one this time, would have to be held to see if the differences could be resolved. So important was this issue to Lenin that he wrote he would "leave the [Bolshevik] faction immediately" if the recallist line prevailed.[47]

In the meantime, there were signs that Lenin's effort to patiently work with the fraction was beginning to bear fruit. When the Duma began its debates in the spring of 1909 on the budget proposals for the state-funded Russian Orthodox Church, it opened a wide-ranging discussion for the social democrats about religion. For Lenin, it was a great opportunity to implement the decisions of the Paris conference—that is, the need to coordinate the activities of the Duma fraction, legal work, with party building, illegal work—to show the skeptics that Duma work could in fact be valuable. Using the pages of *Proletary* and *Sotsial-Demokrat*, he explained to their readers the basics of the Marxist position on religion, how it differs from a liberal critique of religion, why "Social-Democracy's atheist propaganda must be *subordinated* to its basic task—the development of the class struggle of the exploited *masses* against the exploiters," and the practical implications for recruiting workers who are religious and even priests. The speech of one of the two comrades who intervened in the debates was indispensable for party work:

> The Social-Democrat Surkov, representing the workers' party and the working class, was the only person in the Duma to raise the debates to the truly high level of principle, and said without beating about the bush what the attitude of the proletariat is towards the Church and religion, and what should be the attitude in this matter of all consistent and vigorous democrats. "Religion is the opium of the people . . . Not a farthing of the people's money to these murderous enemies of the people who are drugging the people's minds"—this straightforward, bold and outspoken battle-cry of a socialist resounded like a challenge to the Black-Hundred Duma, and met with the response of millions of proletarians, who will spread it among the masses and who will know how to translate it into revolutionary action when the time comes.[48]

And then Lenin gave specific instructions to the illegal wing of the party to ensure that the "masses . . . will know" what Surkov said: "[His speech] should be circulated by all the organizations. In its discussion of this speech the Duma group demonstrated that it is fulfilling its Social-Democratic duty conscientiously. It remains to express the wish that reports on discussions within the Duma group should appear more often in the Party press so as to bring the group and the Party closer together, to acquaint the Party with the difficult work being done within the group, and to establish ideological unity in the work of the Party and the Duma group."[49]

In June, a meeting of four members of the editorial board of *Proletary*, the five Bolsheviks on the Central Committee, and three representatives from the St. Petersburg, Moscow, and Ural party branches in Russia took place in Paris. The main agenda item was the question of otzovism, or recallism, and ultimatumism. With improvements in the functioning of the Duma fraction and therefore the recallists garnering less support, Lenin focused most of his attention on the arguments of the ultimatumists. A distinction, he argued, had to be made between those who saw the "ultimatum" to the fraction to improve its work as only an incentive or form of "pressure" versus those for whom it hung over their heads as a "sword of Damocles" that effectively "rules out *constructive, creative* Party work on the Duma group." The former were tolerable, because they held open the possibility of improvement, whereas the latter were not because the logic of their line was otzovism and eventually "syndicalism and anarchism." The former resembled a kind of otzovism that prevailed among a layer of workers "largely [as] a result of being uninformed about the work of the Duma group." "The best way to combat *this kind* of otzovism is, first, wide publicity among the workers to keep them fully informed on the work of the Duma group and, secondly, to afford the workers opportunities to come into regular contact with the group and influence it. Otzovist sentiment in St. Petersburg, for instance, could be counteracted to a large extent by arranging a number of talks between our comrades in the Duma and the workers of St. Petersburg."

Lenin's arguments were formalized in resolutions, and they passed on a ten-to-two vote and a ten-to-one and one abstention vote. Bogdanov was the main dissenter and stated that he couldn't go along with the decisions of the majority. The "extended editorial board of *Proletary* henceforth disclaims any responsibility for the political actions of Comrade Maximov [Bogdanov]." Rather than a split, his actions constituted effectively a "breakaway" from the Bolsheviks.[50]

Finally, and especially important, Lenin gave a speech in which he drafted a resolution that was the most detailed to date on Duma work, "The Tasks of the Bolsheviks in Relation to Duma Activity"(see Appendix B). In addition to concrete suggestions on how the speeches of the Duma fraction could be publicized through leaflets—"Parliamentary speeches will always say less than anything. The i's will be dotted by the leaflets"[51]—Lenin raised the "delicate matter" of the mechanics of coordinating the work of the fraction with the party. It was "delicate" because it involved working with the Menshevik leaders of the party, who weren't necessary on the same political page with Lenin about how to conduct this work. A special committee, the "Paris promotion group" or the "Promotion Commission for the Duma Social-Democratic group," was proposed, and Lenin thought that it "should be set up under the C.O."—that is, the Central Organ, *Sotsial-Demokrat*, of the party rather than the Central Committee. Also, "nothing can be done in the Duma group without well-informed persons from the Bolsheviks. For this we should legalize two or three men. One suggestion is Vadim, and perhaps Kamenev."[52]

In his "Tasks" speech, Lenin made for the first time in the form of a party resolution the distinction between the "revolutionary Social-Democratic use of the Duma and the reformist (or more broadly, opportunist) use." He spelled out how this distinction played itself out in regard to both the "external relations" of the Duma group and the "internal content of the group's activity." When Lenin writes that the experiences of "West-European Social-Democrats" should be utilized but "special care" had to be taken "to avoid the opportunist distortion" of the group's "internal" activities, the significance of the distinction is clear—key evidence for, again, my argument about his growing awareness of reformism in the West European parliamentary arena as he deepened his involvement in and defense of this work. The document serves as a blueprint for Bolshevik parliamentary work henceforth and thus warrants reproduction in full; see Appendix B.

To appreciate how committed Lenin was to the bourgeois democratic revolution and utilizing whatever extant space to advance its cause, consider the effort he made to get the St. Petersburg branch of the party to participate in a by-election in September 1909. The opportunity came about after a Cadet deputy was expelled from the Duma, but it was fraught with challenges: "The election is taking place in a situation where the Social-Democratic Party and all working-class organizations whatsoever have been totally outlawed, where it is utterly impossible to hold meetings of workers, where the workers' press is totally banned, where the 'opposition' is (through police measures) entirely monopolized by the Cadet Party, which has prostituted itself by a series of unprecedented acts of flunkeyism in the Black Duma." All the more reason, Lenin argued, why social democracy should participate—an opportunity to expose the Cadets "before the mass of petit-bourgeois voters and remind them of the aims of real democracy which have been forgotten by the bourgeois democratic parties and groups." He urged the St. Petersburg comrades to put forward a candidate and offered advice on how to conduct the campaign—his first opportunity to apply the resolutions adopted at the extended editorial board meeting of *Proletary* a few months earlier:

> [E]veryone can and must take part in the Social-Democratic election campaign. Some can draw up and distribute the election manifestoes of the Social-Democrats; others can help to circulate the Duma speeches of the Social-Democrats; some can organize a canvass of the electors in order to propagate Social-Democratic ideas and explain the aims of the Social-Democrats in the election campaign; others will speak at meetings of voters or at private meetings; still others can cull a bouquet of extracts from Cadet literature and Cadet speeches that will cure all honest democrats of any desire to vote for the Cadets; . . . but it is not for us in a newspaper published abroad to point out ways and means of agitation, ways and means will be found locally, in St. Petersburg, a hundred times richer, livelier and more varied. The members of the Social-Democratic group in the Duma can, by virtue of their position, render particularly valuable services to the election campaign in St. Petersburg; here the Social-Democratic deputies have a particularly useful and particularly grateful part to play. No administrative prohibitions, no police traps, no confiscations of Social-Democratic literature, no arrests of Social-Democratic agitators can prevent the workers' party from doing its duty, namely, to make full use of the election campaign to spread among the masses the whole, undiluted program of the socialist proletariat, the vanguard in the Russian democratic, revolution.

Lenin was heartened to learn after writing these lines that the Trudoviks "unanimously decided to support the candidature of the Social-Democrat Sokolov"—concrete evidence that the worker-peasant alliance he fought to forge via the electoral and parliamentary arenas was operative.[53]

"The masses must come out of this election campaign more party-conscious, more clearly aware of the interests, aims, slogans, points of view and methods of action of the different classes—that is the permanent result which the political trend represented by N. D. Sokolov values above everything."[54] Since there are no extant balance sheets that Lenin drew on the election campaign, it's difficult to say how successful it was as measured by these criteria. It didn't help, as Lenin complained, that Bogdanov and other ultimatumists "did *in effect* put a spoke in the wheel of the election campaign that had just begun" by getting the executive committee of the St. Petersburg organization to pass a resolution that discouraged active participation.[55] Though it was later rejected by a more representative meeting, the resolution seems to have taken a toll. Despite the decisions of the Paris meetings, the recallist-ultimatumist tendency continued to get a hearing as long as the Duma fraction hadn't perfected its modus operandi—what Lenin continued to work on.

"STEADY PROGRESS"

A year after the first Paris meeting, Lenin wrote, "The work of the Social-Democrats in the Duma makes steady progress, becoming free from the mistakes that were inevitable at the outset, overcoming skepticism and indifference, forging the weapon of revolutionary propaganda and agitation of organized class struggle, so valued by all Social-Democrats."[56]

The progress the fraction was making had much to do with the careful attention not only to political perspective but to details that Lenin provided. No better example of that were the corrections and suggestions he made on behalf of a Central Committee "subcommittee"—no doubt the aforementioned "Promotion Commission"—to a draft bill drawn up by a Duma fraction member calling for the eight-hour work day (see Appendix C).[57] Written sometime after the St. Petersburg by-election, his response constitutes the most concrete evidence so far of the close collaboration established at least by then between the social democratic group and Lenin on behalf of the party. Before addressing the specifics of the proposal, he made clear that the "main aim of the Bills introduced by the Social-Democrats in the Third Duma must lie in *propaganda and agitation* for the Social-Democratic program and tactics. Any hopes of the 'reformism' of the Third Duma would not only be ludicrous, but would threaten completely to distort the character of Social-Democratic revolutionary tactics and convert it into the tactics of opportunist, liberal social-reformism." He then listed "five conditions" for realizing this aim.

With these "basic premises" he dissected the draft of the "author"—so termed, I suspect, for security reasons. He complimented him for having adapted model eight-hour work day bills drawn up by Western European social democratic parties to "Russian conditions" but stated that "our subcommittee" felt it needed "a number of corrections" because in "a few cases the author . . . tries to adapt his Bill to the requirement of 'practicality.'" He offered some suggestions—for example, about the scope of the bill—and then a concrete proposal about "the question of the *gradual* introduction of the eight-hour working day." Most interesting was his point about how to explain why the proposed bill called for such an introduction—certainly "not in order to 'adapt' the Bill to the measure of the capitalist government"—whereas the "revolutionary Soviets of Workers' Deputies of 1905 called for *immediate* realization of the eight-hour working day." The explanatory note accompanying the bill should say that in a real revolutionary situation "it is *essential* not to stop at anything—in short, in conditions resembling those of November 1905—the Social-Democrats regard the *immediate* introduction of the eight-hour working, day as not only legitimate but even *essential*."[58] It will be useful, I argue, to revisit Lenin's suggestion in assessing Bolshevik policies in the heady days of 1917.[59]

The Duma group's response to "Stolypin's notorious declaration of March 31," 1910, revealed that it indeed had come a long way. The background to this was the ongoing tug of war between the monarchy and those in the Duma like the Cadets and Octobrists who wanted a constitutional monarchy. The specific issue was how much input the Duma had in funding the military.[60] As Lenin unceasingly explained, the Duma was the product of the mass uprising that forced Nicholas to grant concessions including the Fundamental Laws, the closest thing to a constitution in Romanov Russia. The inconclusive outcome of the revolution was reflected in the ambiguities of the laws. Article 96, more to the point, apparently gave the Duma the right to approve military expenditures, but another provision, Article 14, suggested that the monarchy had the last word. Even though the counterrevolution was victorious with Stolypin's June 3 coup in 1907, three years later it still had nightmares about the revolution (the proximity of Turkey's Young Turks' revolution in 1908 also weighed on their brains). Anything, however faint, that suggested the revolution was alive, such as the idea that the military should be subject to the "collective will," sent a cold shudder up their monarchial spines.

When the issue returned in 1910, Stolypin, in his declaration, sided with Nicholas and effectively overruled Article 96—"reduced to nullity"—in favor of Article 14. That the Octobrists approved of his actions was no surprise, but that the Cadets sounded like apologists for Stolypin was "just one more example of how low" their party "has fallen." The challenge for the social democratic group was how to denounce his actions without giving an inch to the "constitutional illusions" of the Cadets and Octobrists:

> [T]he Social-Democrats unquestionably undertook a complicated task *requiring able handling*; they were undoubtedly wielding a double-edged

weapon which with the slightest mistake or even awkward usage might wound the bearer. To speak without metaphors, it might imperceptibly lead the Social-Democrats astray from the policy of class struggle to the policy of liberalism.

The Social-Democrats would have made such a mistake if they had spoken purely and simply of "defending" these fundamental laws, without explaining the *special* character of this "defense." They would have made an even greater mistake had they turned the defense of the fundamental laws or legality in general into some sort of slogan such as "fight for legality"—that would have been in the style of the Cadets.

Fortunately, our comrades in the Duma did neither the one nor the other.

Lenin then excerpted the interpellations of the two comrades. The first, Gegechkori, defended, Lenin proudly reported, the fraction against the thinly veiled threats of the Rights to have it ejected from the Duma for questioning the "prerogatives of the 'imperial leader.'" The deputy then made clear that the fraction's interventions were in no way to be interpreted as "'upholding the prestige of the Third Duma, if it has such a thing.'" Their purpose was "'only . . . for exposing once again the hypocrisy of the government.'" "Gegechkori voiced the consistently democratic, republican views of the socialists when he said: 'our laws will correspond to the interests and requirements of the mass of the population only when they are dictated by the *direct will of the people*,' and the '*clamour from the right*' noted in this part of the verbatim report emphasized that the shaft had gone home."

The second comrade, Pokrovsky, "spoke even more clearly and definitely in his speech," referring to the political significance of the interpellation: "'Let them (the Octobrists) do this directly and openly. Let them frankly accept the slogan of the Rights: "Down with the right of the popular representative assembly, long live the ministerial antechamber!" There is no doubt that the majority is working to bring about a time in Russia when constitutional illusions will completely vanish, leaving a black reality from which the Russian people will draw the appropriate conclusions.'"

The two comrades acted in "the only correct Social-Democratic way of presenting the interpellation." The rest of the party now had a task:

[T]his is the aspect that must be brought to the fore in our Party agitation, at labor meetings, in our study circles and groups, and, finally, in private conversations with workers who do not belong to any organization. We must explain the role of the workers' party, which is *exposing* a bourgeois Black-Hundred fraud inside the bourgeois Black-Hundred Duma itself. Inasmuch as it was not possible in *such* a Duma to treat the question with *complete* clarity or to state in full detail the revolutionary Social-Democratic point of view, it is our duty to amplify what our comrades said from the tribune of the Taurida Palace and popularize their speeches, so that the masses can understand and appreciate them.[61]

THE FINNISH QUESTION

Another issue that warranted in Lenin's view the attention of Russian social democracy and the Duma group in particular was Stolypin's moves beginning in 1908 to end the limited sovereignty the Finish people had enjoyed until then. From 1809 when Finland came under Romanov rule, its prospects for self-determination depended on the ups and downs of the democratic revolution in Russia. At its height, the end of October 1905 through the first two Dumas, the Finnish people enjoyed their greatest freedom. With Stolypin's coup in June 1907, however, the regime sought to reestablish Romanov supremacy. That Finland had served as a safe house for revolutionaries like Lenin during Russia's "spring" was not the least important reason for doing so. The Octobrists took the initiative in this revanchist project in 1908 with a proposal that the "Black Hundred Duma" should act as the monarchy's police to bring the Finnish people to heel—an attempt to convince Nicholas that the Duma could be a loyal servant and thus he had nothing to fear about their constitutional monarchy project.[62] Though the particulars are lacking, the social democratic group, according to Lenin, voiced their opposition.

When the issue returned in 1909, he provided more details. While the "bandits' venture has everything in its favor," given the continuing lull in Russia's democratic movement, the "proletariat of Finland knows that from the outset of its new struggle it will have on its side the socialist proletariat of all Russia, ready, however onerous the conditions of the contemporary moment, to do their duty, *their whole duty.*" The Duma fraction had a special duty because their counterpart in the Finnish Diet

> has sent a deputation to the Social-Democratic group in the Third Duma in order jointly to discuss a plan of action against the coercionists. From the lofty tribune of the Duma our deputies will raise their voice, as they did last year, to brand the tsarist government and unmask its hypocritical allies in the Duma. Let then all the Social-Democratic organizations and all workers exert every effort so that the voice of our deputies in the Taurida Palace is not a cry in the wilderness, so that the enemies of Russian and Finnish liberty see that the whole Russian proletariat is one with the Finnish people. The duty of the comrades in each locality is to use every opportunity that presents itself to make manifest the attitude of the

proletariat of Russia to the Finnish question. Beginning with appeals to the
Russian and Finnish Social-Democratic groups, and proceeding to more
active forms of protests, the Party will find ways enough to break the dis-
graceful conspiracy of silence in which the Russian counter-revolution is
rending the body of the Finnish people.[63]

Whether or not Finland's proletariat knew that their Russian comrades
would be "on its side" is uncertain; what is clear is Lenin's call, a joint
response of the Duma group and party organizations campaign, to make
that a reality—exactly what he called for when the Guns of August
exploded in 1914.

In 1910 Stolypin took the initiative by introducing a bill in the Duma
that would put Finland's "internal affairs," which the Finnish people
had hitherto managed themselves, "under the jurisdiction of the arch-
reactionary Octobrist Duma! *The utter destruction of Finland's freedom*—
that is what is being undertaken by the autocracy." This time Lenin sought
to bring clarity to the debates for both the fraction and the readers of *Sotsial-
Demokrat*, specifically the role of the bourgeoisie in "reinforcing . . . the old
nationalism . . . of the autocracy." The championing of such a policy by
the Octobrists registered the "growing class-consciousness and consciously
counter-revolutionary attitude of our Russian bourgeoisie. Chauvinism
has grown among them with their growing hatred of the proletariat as an
international force. Their chauvinism has grown stronger parallel with the
growth and intensification of the rivalry of international capital. Chauvinism appeared as a thirst for revenge engendered by the losing of the war
with Japan and the powerlessness of the bourgeoisie against the privileged
landlords. Chauvinism has found support in the appetites of the true Russian industrialists and merchants who are glad to 'conquer' Finland after
failing to grab a slice of the pie in the Balkans. Therefore, the representative
assembly of the land lords and big bourgeoisie gives tsarism true allies for
settling with free Finland."

As for the liberal bourgeoisie, the Cadets, while they, "of course, are
against the persecution of Finland" and "will certainly not vote with the
Octobrists," they in fact enabled the "old nationalism" of the autocracy. Referring to the earlier debates on the Balkans and Struve's influential article, Lenin continued, "Was it not the Cadets who did their
utmost to rouse nationalist feelings and sentiments throughout Russian educated 'society'? How right the Social-Democratic resolution (of
December 1908) [the Paris party conference] was in saying that the
Cadets by their nationalist agitation were *in fact* rendering a service to
tsarism and no one else! . . . So now, most 'humane' gentlemen of the
Cadet Party, reap what you have sown." Lenin concluded prophetically,

"[E]ach act of tsarist policy, each month of the existence of the Third Duma is more and more mercilessly destroying the liberal illusions, more and more exposing the impotence and rottenness of liberalism, scattering ever wider and more abundantly the seeds of a new revolution of the proletariat."[64]

There is no way Lenin could have known that his real-time insight would be tragically confirmed by events four years later—the role of both the Right and Left bourgeoisie in promoting the autocracy's war drive. He was able to be prescient precisely because of what the Third Duma, "the representative assembly of the landlords and big bourgeoisie," taught— again, why he was so insistent that it was in the interest of the proletariat to take its deliberations seriously and to use it, however limited the opportunities, for offering a working-class alternative.

A couple of months after the fraction's "able handling" of Stolypin's Declaration of March 31, Lenin gave an extensive response to the just-produced "platform" of the recallists in his sixty-page pamphlet, *Notes of a Publicist*. He stated his central argument at the outset:

> The autocracy has entered a *new* historical period. It is taking a step towards its transformation into a bourgeois monarchy. The Third Duma represents an alliance with definite classes. The Third Duma is not an accidental, but a necessary institution in the system of this new monarchy . . . We are confronted by a *specific* historical period with *specific* conditions for the birth of a new revolution. It will be impossible to master these specific conditions and prepare ourselves for this new revolution if we operate only in the old way, if we do not learn to utilize the Duma tribune itself, etc.

Stolypin's bill on Finland would no doubt have been for Lenin a good example of his use of the Third Duma to convert the "autocracy . . . into a bourgeois monarchy." This, he argued, is what the recallists failed to grasp about the interim period: the unique role of the Third Duma, unlike the two previous ones, in consolidating the counterrevolution while preparing at the same time the conditions for the inevitable rebirth of the revolution. Therefore "*there can be no question* of utilizing the transition period without utilizing the Duma tribune. The peculiar tactics of using the very tribune from which the counter-revolutionaries speak *for the purpose* of preparing the revolution thus becomes a *duty* dictated by the specific character of the *entire* historical situation." If, as Lenin suspected, the recallists, or many who were attracted to their cause, found functioning in such a way in such a setting far less exciting than when the revolution was still in full bloom, he readily conceded:

But the transitional period is transitional precisely because its specific task is to prepare and rally the *forces*, and not to bring them into immediate and decisive action. To know how to organize this work, which is devoid of outward glamour, to know how to utilize for this purpose all those semi-legal institutions which are peculiar to the period of the Black-Hundred-Octobrist Duma, to know how to uphold *even on this basis* all the traditions of revolutionary Social-Democracy, all the slogans of its recent heroic past, the entire spirit of its work, its irreconcilability with opportunism and reformism—such is the *task of the Party*, such is the task of the moment.[65]

In an earlier retort, he was less diplomatic but more concrete:

Get this into your heads . . . when the conditions of acute and increasing reaction are really present, when the mechanical force of this reaction really severs the connection with the masses, makes sufficiently broad work difficult and weakens the Party, it is then that the specific task of the Party becomes to master the parliamentary weapon of struggle; and that . . . is not because parliamentary struggle is higher than any other forms of struggle; no, it is just because it is *lower* than them, lower, for example, than a struggle which draws into the mass movement *even* the armed forces, which gives rise to mass strikes, uprisings, etc. Then why does mastery of the lowest form of struggle become the specific (i.e., distinguishing the present moment from other moments) task of the Party? Because the stronger the mechanical force of reaction and, the weaker the connection with the masses, the more immediate becomes the task of preparing the minds of the masses (and not the task of direct action), the more immediate becomes the task of *utilizing* the methods of propaganda and agitation *created by the old regime* (and not a direct onslaught of the masses against this old regime).[66]

The lull in the revolutionary movement that enabled the counterrevolutionary policies that Stolypin and the autocracy pursued made clear to Lenin—if not from the outset—that work in the Third Duma had a very different character than that in its two predecessors.

In an article on the Bolshevik-Menshevik split in *Neue Zeit* published sometime in 1910, Trotsky charged that neither wing of the party knew how to function in legal organizations: "'Even the most important legal organization, in which the Mensheviks predominate, works completely outside the control of the Menshevik faction.'" Lenin knew better: "[T]he facts are as follows. From the very beginning of the existence of the Social-Democratic group in the Third Duma, the Bolshevik faction, through its representatives authorized by the Central Committee of the Party, has all the time assisted, aided, advised, and supervised the work of the Social-Democrats in the Duma. The same is done by the editorial board of the Central Organ of the Party, which consists of representatives of the factions."[67] Thus at the end of 1910 Lenin confirmed in print what the public record only suggested until then—that is, he was effectively the party's electoral and parliamentary director. No one else had taken on such a responsibility; the experience would serve him well for the Fourth Duma. But Trotsky's uninformed criticism was revelatory—most of the Duma fraction members were Mensheviks! Never did Lenin hint so much in his published utterances. Taking into account the way in which they were elected, he treated them as if they were teachable. Labels such as "Mensheviks" were simply that for him—another indication of how important this work was for him.[68]

SOCIAL DEMOCRATIC PARLIAMENTARY WORK: LESSONS FROM ELSEWHERE

In the discussions/debates about whether to participate or not in the parliamentary arena, Lenin (and his opponents as well) often referenced the experience of German social democracy. The historic debate Marx and Engels had with the anarchists about involvement in both arenas only intensified as working-class parties inspired by their vision came into existence. Owing to its size and success the German party was the favorite target of the anarchists, and Lenin had to take on their charge—which got an echo from the recallists—that the German party practiced "parliamentarism at any price." "In point of fact the German Social-Democrats, far from standing for parliamentarism at any price, not only do not subordinate everything to parliamentarism, but, on the contrary, in the international army of the proletariat they best of all have developed such extra-parliamentary means of struggle as the socialist press, the trade unions, the systematic use of popular assemblies, the socialist education of youth, and so on and so forth."

The German party's usage of the parliamentary space, he also argued, was determined by the particular situation it faced, and not the least important was the period in which Bismarck's Anti-Socialist Law was in effect, 1878 to 1890, during which the party, except for its Reichstag Fraktion, was banned—a situation not unlike what the Russian party faced after Stolypin's coup and the convening of the Third Duma. "The point is that a combination of a number of historic conditions has made parliamentarism a *specific* weapon of struggle for Germany over a *given period*, not the chief one, not the highest, not of prime and essential importance in comparison with other forms, but merely specific, the most characteristic in comparison with other countries. Hence, the ability to use parliamentarism *has proved to be a symptom* (not a condition but a symptom) of exemplary organization of the *entire* socialist movement, in *all* its branches, which we have enumerated above."[69]

But wasn't there a basis for the anarchist charge given that the German party gave birth to opportunism and reformism—Bernstein et al.? Lenin, of course, was well aware of this development from the very beginning and had drawn attention to it—such as his critique of the Germans at the 1907 Stuttgart Congress of the Second International. The party's 1910 Magdeburg Congress provided the most recent evidence. "Two Worlds," the title of his article about the gathering, were revealed in the German party: "the point of view of the proletarian class struggle" versus "the point of view of the reformist." Unlike the anarchists, however, Lenin felt the first tendency, led by Bebel, was hegemonic in the party. The evidence was the overwhelming defeat for those who advocated the reformist line.

Most relevant for the Russian experience was the substance of Bebel's attack on the reformists at the congress. In Lenin's reading of his speech, Bebel was preparing the party for "the maturing revolution in Germany." And key to Bebel's strategy, according to Lenin, was the continued usage of legality in anticipation of an "era of tremendous revolutionary battles" while knowing the bourgeoisie would be forced for that very reason to "shatter his own legality."[70] Rather than what the anarchists claimed about the German party, the Magdeburg Congress demonstrated that social democracy could make usage of the parliamentary arena without succumbing to opportunism. Whether Lenin's optimism about the Germans was warranted will, of course, be revisited. Clearly, his reading of Bebel and the congress reflected his views and actions that parliamentary work could be put toward revolutionary ends.

At the end of 1910, Lenin reviewed in the first issue of the legal Bolshevik daily *Zvezda* [*The Star*], the successor to *Proletary*, "an interesting attempt at a scientific investigation" to explain the emergence of the "two big trends" in the working-class movements in Europe and America "departing from Marxism"—"revisionism (opportunism, reformism) and anarchism (anarcho-syndicalism, anarcho-socialism)." Dutch Marxist Anton Pannekoek's recently published book, *The Tactical Differences in the Labor Movement*, reached "conclusions, which, it must be recognized, are quite correct." Three factors, according to Pannekoek, explained their emergence: (1) the "very growth of the labor movement"; (2) its heterogeneous character and development; and (3) the different tactics ruling classes employed to discipline the labor movement. When the latter decided, for example, to play the hard cop, as in Germany with Bismarck's Anti-Socialist Law, they engendered "the growth of anarcho-syndicalism." When they employed "the method of 'liberalism,' of steps towards the development of political rights, towards reforms, concessions, and so forth," it bred "opportunism in the labor movement." While the "revisionists . . . regard reforms as a partial realization of socialism," the "anarcho-syndicalists reject 'petty work,' especially the utilization of the parliamentary platform." "Both anarcho-syndicalism and reformism must be regarded as a direct product of this ['one-sided'] bourgeois world outlook and its influence. They seize upon *one* aspect of the labor movement, elevate one-sidedness to a theory, and declare mutually exclusive those tendencies or features of this movement that are a specific peculiarity of a given period, of given conditions of working-class activity. But real life, real history, *includes* these different tendencies, just as life and development in nature include both slow evolution and rapid leaps, breaks in continuity." Although Pannekoek's argument made no reference "to Russia *at all*," it "seems that he is alluding to [it] . . . only because the basic tendencies which give rise to definite departures from Marxist tactics are to be observed in our country too, despite the vast differences between Russia and the West."[71] The Menshevik and recallist currents in Russian social democracy were without doubt the "definite departures" Lenin had in mind.

As well as Germany, Lenin paid special attention to the course of the workers' movement in Britain. The conferences in 1911of the two organizations that would eventually form the Labor Party were most instructive given the context: "It is well known that Britain and Germany have been arming very intensively during the past few years. Competition between these two countries in the world market is becoming increasingly acute. The danger of a military conflict is approaching more and more formidably." Even more important, the "socialists of Britain and Germany, and also of France (whom Britain would be particularly glad to drag into war in order to have a continental land army against Germany) are devoting much attention to the threatening war, fighting with might and main against bourgeois chauvinism and armaments, and doing all they can to explain to the most backward sections of the proletariat and of the petty bourgeoisie what misfortunes ensue from a war which serves exclusively the interests of the bourgeoisie."

The conference deliberations of the two organizations, the British Social-Democratic Party and the Independent Labor Party, revealed that while their leaders, respectively Henry Hyndman and Ramsey MacDonald, pursued "opportunist" policies—at one point "MacDonald said with virginal opportunist innocence that Parliament was hardly the place for 'propaganda speeches'"—it was "really gratifying" to learn that "from their ranks firm and determined voices were heard protesting against" opportunism. This was especially important at this moment since opportunism enabled in both cases, as he noted, "jingoism" and "chauvinism." In concluding, Lenin admitted that the "Liberals of all countries, Russia included, are rejoicing and laughing now at the sight of the predominance of opportunism in the British labor movement. But 'he laughs best who laughs last.'"[72] Again, history would decide whether his judgment was warranted. What he pointed to, however—the links between opportunism and the war drive and how revolutionary social democracy should respond—proved, as will be seen, to be prescient.

THE END OF THE THIRD DUMA AND "CONSTITUTIONAL ILLUSIONS"

Once the election results for the Third Duma were in, Lenin concluded that it would be "*incapable of accomplishing the objective tasks of the revolution even in the most distorted form. It cannot even partly heal the gaping wounds inflicted upon Russia by the old regime—it can only cover up those wounds with wretched, sour, fictitious reforms. The election results only confirm our firm belief that Russia cannot emerge from her present crisis in a peaceful way.*" If that wasn't clear before, the "constitutional crisis" in the spring of 1911 removed all doubts. Stolypin's habit of riding roughshod over the Duma eventually led the Octobrists and Cadets—at least their leaderships—to break with him in May. He needed both wings of the bourgeoisie to carry out his main project of converting the autocracy into a bourgeois monarchy, and the Third Duma was to be the vehicle for doing so. But as Lenin explained, "Tsarism consulted the bourgeoisie when the revolution still seemed to be a force; but it gradually applied its jackboot to kick out *all* the leaders of the bourgeoisie . . . as soon as the revolutionary pressure from below slackened." As the regime's leading landlord, Nicholas had no material interest in providing a real solution to the most "gaping" of the "wounds inflicted upon Russia"—land inequality. And as long as the Left and Right bourgeoisie continued to be afflicted with "parliamentary cretinism," it could never conceive of the crisis being solved in the only way it could—outside the parliamentary arena and in the streets. "Stolypin's policy," Lenin concluded, "ended in failure."[73] His assassination by a Socialist Revolutionary in September 1911 was indeed the final nail in the coffin.

The frustrations of the Octobrists and Cadets and their eventual break with Stolypin in May had been salutary, Lenin contended: "[T]hey express, once more, the collapse of constitutional illusions—which is a

useful by-product of the 'constitutional' crisis."[74] He then put Stolypin's
tenure and assassination in broad context:

> Stolypin disappeared from the scene at the very moment when the Black-
> Hundred monarchy had taken everything that could be of use to it from
> the counter-revolutionary sentiments of the whole Russian bourgeoisie.
> Now this bourgeoisie—repudiated, humiliated, and disgraced by its own
> renunciation of democracy, the struggle of the masses and revolution—
> stands perplexed and bewildered, seeing the symptoms of a gathering new
> revolution. Stolypin helped the Russian people to learn a useful lesson:
> either march to freedom by overthrowing the tsarist monarchy, under the
> leadership of the proletariat; or sink deeper into slavery and submit to the
> Purishkeviches, Markovs and Tolmachovs [Black Hundred leaders], under
> the ideological and political leadership of the Milyukovs and Guchkovs
> [respectively Cadet and Octobrist leaders].[75]

With Stolypin gone, the final year of the Third Duma was compara-
tively uneventful. The Black Hundreds predominated and thus increasingly played the nationalist and chauvinist cards. Lenin continued to pay
attention to and to work closely with the Duma fraction. When famine,
for example, returned, he made suggestions to the party on how the fraction should be utilized to help combat it. Also, he helped them draft an
alternative to the government's so-called Workers' State Insurance bill. In
the process he noticed a speech that a fraction member, Kuznetsov, had
given on the bill. While it "must be said, in fairness to him, that, in general, he spoke very well," he nevertheless made a mistake by echoing the
Cadet call for electoral reform. But real reform required the existence of a
republic and that demand, absent in the Cadet formulation, should have
been included in his speech. After sketching out what "Kuznetsov should
have said," Lenin offered some general advice:

> Wherever a Social-Democrat makes a political speech, it is his duty always
> to speak of a republic. But one must know how to speak of a republic. One
> cannot speak about it in the same terms when addressing a meeting in a
> factory and one in a Cossack village, when speaking at a meeting of stu-
> dents or in a peasant cottage, when it is dealt with from the rostrum of the
> Third Duma or in the columns of a publication issued abroad. The art of
> any propagandist and agitator consists in his ability to find the best means
> of influencing any given audience, by presenting a definite truth, in such a
> way as to make it most convincing, most easy to digest, most graphic, and
> most strongly impressive.[76]

Last, when evidence was revealed in Duma deliberations in October 1911 of how the 55 social democratic deputies in the Second Duma had been illegally framed up, he urged a step up in the international campaign to free them that involved the Third Duma fraction and other party organizations.

In the last months of the Third Duma, an incident occurred that for Lenin was a teachable moment. A fraction member, Terenty Belousov, abruptly withdrew from the group but wanted to keep his seat in the Duma. The fraction unanimously voted that he resign from the Duma "since he was elected by the votes of Social Democrats and had been a member of the Social Democratic group in the Duma for four and a half years." Lenin agreed and advised that there was a larger issue at stake—the accountability of those elected by the working class to the working class. By wanting to stay in the Duma, Belousov betrayed a tendency in the parliamentary process of those who "grab mandates for personal gain." "This has been the case in all bourgeois parliaments, and everywhere the workers who are aware of their historic role are fighting these practices and, *in the process of the struggle*, are training their own working-class members of parliament, men who are not out for mandates, not out to profit by parliamentary manipulations, but are the trusted envoys of the working class."[77] And this was advice given even before Lenin learned that a group of capitalists in Belousov's constituency came to his defense and urged that he remain in the Duma.

***

Six months before the Third Duma formally came to a close, June 9, 1912, a Bolshevik leadership meeting took place in Prague, in part to make plans for the elections to the Fourth Duma. Along the way it adopted a resolution written by Lenin on the conduct of the fraction in the Third Duma:

> This Conference recognizes that the Social-Democratic group in the Duma made use of the Duma platform in accordance with the line defined by the December (1908) Party Conference [Paris], which must remain the guide for the direction of Party work in the Duma.
> The Conference, in particular, regards as consistent with the tasks of the proletariat that aspect of the group's activities that it has energetically defended the interests of the workers and all measures for improving their lot (for instance, the labor bills) and in so doing has endeavored to show all the partial tasks in their relation to the general aims of the liberation movement led by the proletariat, and points to the mass movement as the only way to rid Russia of the sufferings and shame to which she has been brought by tsarism.[78]

CHAPTER 6

"To Prepare for a New Russian Revolution"

The Fourth Duma

By the beginning of 1911, Lenin concluded that the worst of the counterrevolution was over and that there were signs of a "revival." The main task was to rebuild the decimated party, especially since there were influential voices who contended that an illegal organization wasn't necessary—the "liquidators." And no better opportunity, he argued, existed for doing that than the upcoming elections to the new Duma. In addition to party building, the elections birthed a new social democratic Duma group. Though slightly smaller than the previous, it proved to be a politically stronger fraction. Almost half, all Bolsheviks, were elected by industrial workers—an advance for Russian social democracy. If the five-year-long Third Duma was about the Russian party finding its parliamentary feet, the briefer Fourth was about putting that prior training into practice. From its convening in November 1912 to the onset of the First World War in August 1914, the Bolshevik wing of the party, under Lenin's direction, accomplished more in the parliamentary arena in as short a time as any revolutionaries had ever done and, probably, ever since—and with more to come.

Lenin in Campaign Mode

More than a year before the elections for the new Duma took place, and while the Third was in its last session, Lenin began campaigning. That meant drawing up a program and strategy for the elections while opposing the liquidators and the remaining recallists. Clarity on the differences, as always for Lenin, was of utmost importance, and at issue was one that went to the very heart of Marxism as he understood it—the distinction between democracy and liberalism. To give his perspective authority required a party discussion, debate, and vote. The challenge then was to implement those decisions, which took on a new urgency when it became evident in the spring of 1912 that the Russian Revolution was reawakening. Lenin the strategist, organizer, and taskmaster were all on full display.

"THE IRRECONCILABLE DIFFERENCE":
A "LIBERAL LABOR" VERSUS A MARXIST LABOR POLICY

"The elections to the Fourth Duma are due to be held next year. The Social-Democratic Party must launch its election campaign at *once*."[1] Thus began Lenin's first detailed campaign literature written in October 1911. Two months later in a clear warning to the recallists, he wrote, "[A]ny wavering as to the advisability, from the point of view of Marxism, of our participation in the elections, is impermissible."[2]

Launching the campaign was a necessity given that "we are at the beginning of a new phase of the counterrevolution." The student protests the previous year, peasant discontent bred by the famine, and "last but not least, the strike wave" opened up space for "intensified propaganda, agitation, and organization . . . and the forthcoming elections provide a natural, inevitable, topical 'pretext' for such work." To do so required rebuilding the decimated party from the bottom up. "Therefore the first task of all Social-Democrats is to take the initiative in organizing nuclei (a word excellently expressing the idea that the objective conditions call for the formation of small, very flexible groups, circles, and organizations); it is the task of *all* Social-Democrats, even where there are only two or three of them, to gain some 'foothold,' establish connections of one kind or another, and start work that is systematic even if very modest."

A campaign, especially a social democratic one, needed a platform— what Lenin sketched out in the first of a series of strategic and tactical writings that became the basis for the Bolsheviks' plan of action. But as he pointedly observed, to "every party at all worthy of the name a platform is something that has existed long before the elections; it is not something specially devised 'for the elections,' but an inevitable result of the whole *work* of the party, of the way the work is organized, and of its whole trend in the given historical period." In other words, exactly because of what Lenin had been doing for more than a decade could he hit the ground running when new opportunities arose. That legacy, when combined with the reality of "the current political situation," determined the key planks in the platform: "Very often it may be useful, and sometimes even essential, to give the election platform of Social-Democracy a finishing touch by adding a brief general slogan, a watchword for the elections, stating the most cardinal issues of current political practice, and providing a most convenient and most immediate pretext, as well as subject matter, for comprehensive socialist propaganda. In our epoch only the following three points can make up this watchword, this general slogan: (1) a republic; (2) confiscation of all landed estates, and (3) the eight-hour day." After spelling out the rational for the three demands, especially "a republic," he distilled their significance: "[T]he substance and mainspring of the Social-Democratic election platform can be expressed in three words; *for the revolution!*" Regarding the possible charge that calling for "a republic," an illegality in Romanov Russia, might suggest "that recognition of the importance and necessity of legal work is not seriously intended," Lenin responded constructively and pedagogically:

> We cannot legally advocate a republic (except from the rostrum of the Duma, from which republican propaganda can and should be carried on *fully* within the bounds of legality); but we can write and speak in defense of democracy *in such a way* that we do not in the least condone ideas about the compatibility of democracy with the monarchy; *in such a way* as to refute and ridicule the liberal and Narodnik monarchists; *in such a way* as to make sure that the readers and the audiences form a clear idea of the connection between the monarchy, precisely as a monarchy, and the despotism and arbitrary rule reigning in Russia.[3]

As the events of 1917 would show, the practice of "adding a brief general slogan, a watchword" to a platform would prove to be most effective for the Bolsheviks.

Lenin's demand for a republic is exactly what Engels found wanting in the draft program of the German party in 1891, the so-called Erfurt Program. Not including it, he charged, smacked of "opportunism"—"this sacrifice of the future of the movement for its present . . . which is gaining ground in a large section of the Social-Democratic press"—and dangerously suggested that not only a "republic, but also communist society, can be established in a cozy, peaceful way." If the Wilhelmian state prohibited its inclusion, then wording should be found, as Lenin did, to at least express its substance.[4] Note also Engels's suggestion about how the program should be written: "the short, precise phrase, once understood, takes root in the memory, and becomes a slogan"—advice that no doubt informed Lenin's "finishing touch" to his draft platform.[5]

The Bolshevik leader wasn't the only social democrat who drafted an election platform. The liquidators and their Menshevik sympathizers were doing the same. After reading an early edition of their platform and despite Martov's efforts to put the best social democratic face on it, Lenin told *Sotsial-Demokrat* readers, "There should be no illusions—we have *two* election platforms, that is a fact . . . [That of Martov et al.] which *claims to be Social-Democratic* is actually *the platform of a liberal labor policy.* Anyone who fails to understand the difference, the irreconcilable difference, between these *two* platforms of working-class policy cannot conduct the election campaign *intelligently.* He is sure to be haunted at every step by disappointments, 'misunderstandings,' and comic or tragic mistakes."

To understand Lenin's critique requires a bit of history. For about three years the liquidators, mainly in response to the blows Stolypin inflicted on the Russian Social Democratic Labor Party (RSDLP) and other opponents of the regime, had been arguing that an underground party was not only impossible but not necessary. Rather, the effort should be made to carve out legal space for Russian social democracy. As Martov put it, Lenin quoting him, "'The workers' party should strive . . . to prevail upon the propertied classes to take one step or another toward the democratization of legislation and an extension of constitutional guarantees.'" But that was exactly the problem, Lenin countered: "Every liberal concedes that it is quite legitimate for the workers to strive 'to prevail upon *the propertied classes*' to take one step or another; all that the liberal stipulates is that the workers should not dare to prevail upon *the non-propertied* to take 'steps' which are *not* to the liberals' *liking.* The entire policy of the British liberals, who have so profoundly corrupted the British workers, is to allow the workers to try 'to prevail upon the propertied classes,' but *not to allow the workers* to win for themselves the leadership of a movement of the whole people." Not for the first or last time would Lenin read electoral/parliamentary developments in Russia through the lens of what was taking place in Western Europe—evidence, again, for one of the central arguments of this book.

Carving out only political space for the proletariat and its party became the core of the liquidators' election platform and the tactical measures thus implied; hence "the irreconcilable difference" with what Lenin was proposing. In a subsequent and more detailed response, Lenin quoted Martov again: "We must conduct the entire election campaign under the banner of the struggle of the proletariat for the freedom of its political self-determination, of the struggle for its right to have a class party of its own and to develop its activities freely, for the right to take part in political life as an independent organized force. This principle [mark this!] must govern both the content and tactics of the election campaign

and the methods to be used for organizational work." Lenin gladly reproduced Martov's "principle" because it "correctly" expressed "the crux of
the matter . . . a liberal labor policy"—what made it so different from a
"Marxist labor policy."

> The liberal bourgeois tells the workers: you are justified in fighting, indeed,
> you must fight, for the freedom of *your own* political self-determination,
> for the right to have a class party of *your own,* for the right freely to develop
> your activities, for *the right to take part* in political life as an independent
> organized force. It is these principles of the liberal, educated, radical, to use
> the English or French term, bourgeoisie that Martov is offering the work-
> ers in the guise of Marxism.
>
>   The Marxist tells the workers: in order really and successfully to fight
> for the freedom of your "own" political self-determination, you must fight
> for the free political self-determination of the entire people, you must show
> the people what the successive democratic forms of its political existence
> should be, and win the masses and the undeveloped sections of the work-
> ing people away from the influence of the liberals. If your party is really
> to attain a full understanding of the tasks of the class, and if its activity
> is actually to be of a class nature and not of a guild nature, it is necessary
> for it not only to take part in political life, but, in spite of all the vacilla-
> tions of the liberals, to direct the political life and initiative of the broad
> strata on to a greater arena than that indicated by the liberals, toward more
> substantial and more radical aims. He who confines the class to an "inde-
> pendent" corner of "activity" in an arena, the bounds, form, and shape of
> which are determined or permitted by the liberals, does not understand the
> tasks of the class. Only he understands the tasks of the class who directs its
> attention (and consciousness, and practical activity, etc.) to the need for so
> reconstructing this very arena, its entire form, its entire shape, as to extend
> it beyond the limits allowed by the liberals.

The differences were indeed "irreconcilable," because what Martov and
the liquidators were proposing, in Lenin's view, negated the very essence
of Marxist politics. Their line "*excludes* the idea of the 'hegemony' of the
working class, whereas the second deliberately defines this very idea."[6]
Therefore an election platform, a real one that bridged these differences,
was a virtual impossibility. Russian social democracy went into the elections, hence, with two opposed lines—in Lenin's terms, democracy versus
liberalism.

Once the Cadets mapped out their campaign strategy, Lenin could
be even more concrete: "It is one of our most important tasks in the
Third Duma [still in session] in general, after the period 1906–11
in particular, and especially on the eve of the elections to the Fourth
Duma, to explain the profound difference between genuine democracy

and the liberalism of the Cadets (the liberalism of 'society') who take the name of democracy in vain"—a thread that ran through almost all his interventions leading up to the elections.[7] This obligation applied not just to the Cadets, because "for Marxists, the main task in the election campaign is to *explain* to the people the *nature* of the various political parties, *what* views are advocated and *who* advocates them, what are the real and vital interests behind each party, which *classes* of society shelter behind each party label."[8]

As for the nuts and bolts of the campaign, of prime importance, understandably, would be the elections in the workers' curiae. If the elections to the Third Duma had been about getting as many workers' deputies as possible to be social democrats, this time it was making sure they would be supporters of a Marxist rather than a liberal labor policy. The guarantee for such an outcome depended, as had been the case before, on concerted propaganda work at the factory level where the electors were selected. As for the other curiae, specifically the second or the petit bourgeois urban curiae, the Left bloc tactic was still operative. With concrete examples from various locations, Lenin showed how social democrats could have won more seats to the Third Duma had more thought gone into the calculus of forming tactical blocs at the second stage of the elections with the Trudoviks to keep out the Cadets and with the Cadets to keep out the Rights. The Mensheviks, it may be remembered, opposed the Left bloc tactic for the Third Duma elections because it prevented them from blocking with the Cadets at the first stage of the elections. In league with the liquidators this time they'd do the same, because their liberal labor policy depended on support from the Cadets.

By now not only Lenin's familiar attention to detail was on display but also his facility with the "intricate mechanism" of the cumbersome and undemocratic election laws. To get a flavor, consider his advice about what the workers' and Trudovik electors should do at the provincial assemblies if they couldn't immediately form blocs with liberals to defeat the Rights:

> [T]he tactics of the democrats should be to unite first with the liberals to defeat the Rights, and then *with the Rights to defeat the liberals*, so that neither are able to secure the election of their candidates (provided that neither the Rights nor the liberals command an absolute majority by themselves, for if they do the democrats cannot hope to get into the Duma). In accordance with Article 119 of the Regulations governing the elections, the assembly adjourns. Then the democrats, guided by the exact figures of the votes cast, form a bloc with the liberals, demanding a proportionate share of the seats. *In such cases it is essential that the liberals elect the democrat first and not the other way round*, for history and the entire experience of

Europe show that the liberals have often cheated the democrats, whereas the democrats have never cheated the liberals.

Consistent with the importance he lent to the worker-peasant alliance, Lenin also provided detailed advice on how social democrats could assist the Trudoviks to win more seats:

> The duty of the working-class democrats with regard to the peasants in the elections is perfectly clear. They must carry their purely class propaganda to a peasantry that is becoming proletarianized. They must help the peasants to unite their forces in the elections to enable them, even on the basis of the June Third electoral law, to send to the Fourth Duma their *own* representatives in as large numbers as possible despite the obstacles put in their way both by the supporters of the old regime and by the liberals. They must strive to consolidate the leadership of working-class democrats and explain the great harm caused by the vacillation of the peasant democrats toward the liberals.[9]

The task now was to have a collective discussion and vote on Lenin's proposals in order to put them into force.

THE PRAGUE CONFERENCE

For the Third Duma elections, the RSDLP had been relatively united. The London or Fifth Party Congress in 1907 approved a set of resolutions to guide the party for conducting the elections and directing the Duma group. The Central Committee that was elected with a slight Bolshevik majority ceased, in fact, after a year or so to function. The unresolved Bolshevik/Menshevik divide was the main reason. To this schism was added the differences with the recallists and ultimatumists and then later and more significant, the liquidators. The Paris conference in December 1908 proved to be last authoritative party meeting before Lenin and the Bolsheviks took the initiative to hold a new one—this time in Prague in January 1912. As the resolution on the "Constitution of the Conference" explained, the "extremely urgent practical tasks of the working-class movement and of the revolutionary struggle against tsarism (leadership in the economic struggle, general political agitation, proletarian meetings, the campaign in connection with the elections to the Fourth Duma, etc.) make it imperative that prompt and most energetic measures be taken to re-establish a competent practical Party center, closely linked with the local organizations." The upcoming elections, in other words, in combination with the new upsurge, required such a meeting.

"Despite a number of arrests made by the police, all the Party organizations functioning in Russia, with very few exceptions, are represented at the present Conference," the resolution reported. They came from "St. Petersburg, Moscow, Saratov, Kazan, Samara, Nizhni-Novgorod, Sormovo, Rostov, Ekaterinoslav, Kiev, Nikolayev, Lugansk, Baku, the Tiflis group, the Wilno group, the Dvinsk group, Ekaterinburg, Ufa, Tyumen, a number of places in the Central Region, and others." As Krupskaya described it, the "Prague Conference was the first Party conference with workers from Russia that we succeeded in calling after 1908."[10] Two Duma fraction members also attended. The call came from the Bolshevik-led Russian Organizing Commission, "which several months ago notified all Social-Democrats of its convocation and invited to the Conference all, without a single exception, organizations of our Party; furthermore, all organizations were given an opportunity to take part in the Conference." Nevertheless it was mainly a Bolshevik affair with only two Mensheviks participating and no liquidators. While Mensheviks were more sympathetic to the line of the liquidators, there were important exceptions— such as Plekhanov and, especially, most of the Mensheviks in the Duma fraction—and they came to be known as pro-Party Mensheviks. The resolution noted that "Bolsheviks and pro-Party Mensheviks in Russia worked in harmony" on the Organizing Commission. Also, the meeting was mainly a Russian affair, since none of the national parties such as the Poles, Lithuanians, or the Bund attended, despite having been "invited three times" and that "every facility has been provided for them to send their delegates."[11]

Party tasks and the upcoming elections specifically were the key agenda items at the three week meeting. "The main tasks of our Party in the elections, and equally of the future Social-Democratic group in the Duma itself—a task to which all else must be subordinated—is socialist, class propaganda and the organization of the working class." The strategy and tactics Lenin detailed in prior writings were distilled into a four-page resolution, "Elections to the Fourth Duma" (see Appendix D), the campaign's blueprint, adopted unanimously by the conference. It reaffirmed the all-important tactic of no blocs with other parties, including the liquidators in the workers' curiae elections. Also, the Left-bloc tactic was permissible only in the second stage of elections in the peasant and second urban curiae, "to conclude agreements with bourgeois democrats against the liberals, and then with the liberals against all the government parties." But as agreed to at the London Congress, there was a crucial proviso: "There can be no electoral agreements providing for a common platform, and Social-Democratic candidates must not be bound by any kind of political commitment, nor must Social-Democrats be prevented from resolutely criticizing the counter-revolutionary nature of the liberals and the half-heartedness and inconsistency of the bourgeois democrats."[12]

Combined with the other resolutions—especially "The Social-Democratic Group in the Duma" and "The Character and Organizational Forms of Party Work"—there is no better set of documents to understand how the Bolsheviks went into and conducted themselves in the election campaign. The former, for example, emphasized how the Duma fraction could use its remaining time in the Third Duma to promote the three slogans of the campaign for the Fourth Duma. The "Party Work" resolution spelled out "the use of the Duma speeches of the S.D. members, the training of workers to become legal lecturers, the creation (in connection with the elections to the Fourth Duma) of workers' and other voters' committees for each district, each street, etc., and the organization of Social-Democratic campaigns in connection with the elections to municipal bodies, etc."[13] Missing in the official account of the Conference—probably for security reasons—was a decision or discussion, if not a resolution, to launch a legal daily, *Pravda* [*Truth*], as it would be called.[14] Its role was indispensable to the campaign, as will be seen. A hint was alluded to in the point in the "Elections" resolution about the need to "pay the necessary attention to the strengthening and broadening of the legally existing workers' press."

The conference declared itself to be the highest body for the party until the next congress and elected a new Central Committee, which included in addition to Lenin future Bolshevik leaders like Lev Kamenev and Grigory Zinoviev; Stalin was later co-opted to it. As for the liquidators' group, the "Conference declares that by its conduct . . . [it] *has definitely placed itself outside the Party.*"[15] Prague launched not only the Bolshevik election campaign for the Fourth Duma but in hindsight the Bolshevik party itself. There was a fly, however, in the ointment. Unbeknownst to Lenin and other Bolsheviks, one of the newly elected Central Committee members was an agent of Russian state security, or Okhrana—Roman Malinovsky—the implications of which would become apparent only later.

With the authority of Prague behind him, Lenin moved quickly to write the first official campaign literature for mass distribution: "The Election Platform of the RSDLP" (see Appendix E). Addressed to "Worker comrades, and all citizens of Russia . . . each and every one of you who enjoy electoral rights, as well as the great majority deprived of rights," it began with an indictment of the regime for its unprecedented counterrevolutionary terror both domestically and abroad: "[It] tries to suppress all movements for freedom in Turkey, Persia, and China." After a popular and pedagogical presentation of the campaign's three slogans and explanation of the differences between the "three main parties . . . contesting the elections: (1) the Black Hundreds, (2) the liberals, and (3) the Social-Democrats," Lenin made clear what the latter hoped to get out of the elections:

> Our Party goes into the Duma, not in order to play at "reforms," not in order to "defend the Constitution," "convince" the Octobrists or "to dislodge reaction" from the Duma, as the liberals who are deceiving the people say they will, but in order to call the masses to the struggle from the Duma rostrum, to explain the teachings of socialism, to expose every government and liberal deception, to expose the monarchist prejudices of the backward sections of the people, and the class roots of the bourgeois parties,—in other words in order to prepare an army of class-conscious fighters for a new Russian revolution.

Lenin later said that missing in the platform was "a very important paragraph about socialism."[16] That would be rectified in future campaign literature. The immediate task was to make sure the platform was widely distributed. According to the editors of the *Lenin Collected Works*, it was published "as a separate leaflet and distributed in 18 localities including the main working-class centers. Reprinted from the leaflet, it appeared as a supplement to No. 26 of *Sotsial-Demokrat*. It was also reprinted by many local Bolshevik organizations and by the Russian Bureau of the C.C. of the R.S.D.L.P. in Tiflis."[17]

Regarding Lenin's point about preparing "for a new Russian revolution," it is noteworthy what the platform said about the demand for a republic:

> Time was, and not so long ago, when the slogan "Down with the autocracy" seemed too advanced for Russia. Nevertheless, the R.S.D.L. Party issued this slogan, the advanced workers caught it up and spread it throughout the country; and in two or three years this slogan became a popular saying. To work then, worker comrades and all citizens of Russia, all those who do not want to see our country sink finally into stagnation, barbarity, lack of rights and the appalling poverty of tens of millions. The Russian Social-Democrats, the Russian workers will succeed in making "Down with the tsarist monarchy, long live the Russian Democratic Republic!" a nation-wide slogan.

This is significant. If Lenin was correct—and there is no reason to doubt the accuracy of his claim—then it was Russian social democracy, with him leading the way, that planted on a mass scale the idea of overthrowing the three-hundred-year-old Romanov dynasty and replacing it with a democratic republic. A credible case can then be made that the February Revolution in 1917 in which Nicholas was dethroned had its origins in the Bolshevik campaign for the Fourth Duma—key evidence for one of the claims of this book that Bolshevik success in the October Revolution can be traced to Lenin's electoral strategy.

The "Revolutionary Upswing" and Pravda

On April 4 about five hundred striking workers in the gold fields of Lena in Siberia were brutally killed or wounded by the regime's armed forces. When a social democrat deputy in the Duma demanded an explanation, the government's minister of the interior infamously replied, "So it was and so it will be!" Outrage and protests erupted throughout Russia and gave the already planned May Day demonstrations additional energy—the largest political protests since 1905. Both developments underscored, Lenin insisted, the importance of the elections to the Fourth Duma: "This thickening of the revolutionary atmosphere casts a vivid light on the tasks of the Party and its role in the election campaign . . . Russia has entered a period of revolutionary upswing."[18]

At the Prague Conference, as already noted, the decision was made to launch a legal RSDLP daily newspaper.[19] Shortly thereafter Lenin met with two members of the Duma fraction in Leipzig to map out plans. The original idea was to convert Zvezda [*The Star*], a weekly, into a daily. But that would not be easy, as Lenin's comment to Gorky suggested: "I am very, very glad that you are helping Zvezda. We are having a devilish hard job with it—internal and external and financial difficulties are immense."[20] Though sometimes described as a "Bolshevik" or "semi-Bolshevik" paper, Zvezda more accurately was a collaborative venture between Lenin, the St. Petersburg Central Committee, and members of the Duma fraction. Because of parliamentary immunity, deputies could serve as publishers of papers and not fear arrest as so often happened with opposition publications; a Bolshevik Duma member, Nikolai Poletayev, served as Zvezda's publisher. But the rest of the fraction—again, predominantly Menshevik—also had close ties to the paper. A comment Lenin made to a fellow Bolshevik about them in relation to the decision of the Prague Conference to break with the liquidators is telling: "The Duma Social-Democratic group is *directly* neither for us nor for them. But (1) there were *two* deputies at our Conference; (2) Zvezda has *nine* Social-Democratic deputies on its list of contributors, while the

liquidationist *Zhivoye Dyelo* [*Vital Cause*, a short-lived legal daily] has *four*."[21]
A few months later he remarked that the liquidationists "hate the [Duma]
group . . . Why? Because the majority of the group, in which pro-Party
Mensheviks have always predominated, have always fought with determi-
nation against the liquidators and helped to make them quite harmless in
St. Petersburg."[22]

The "neither for us nor for them" character of the Duma group
probably explains the friction between Lenin and the editorial board—
"internal . . . difficulties," as he told Gorky—especially in the aftermath
of Prague when new battle lines were drawn. The board members, all
Bolsheviks, were reluctant, I suspect, to do as Lenin wanted and give
unequivocal support to the antiliquidationist decisions taken at Prague—
for fear of alienating many of the pro-Party but "neither for us nor them"
Mensheviks in the fraction with whom they had collaborated on *Zvezda*.
Whatever the case, it wasn't the first or last time that Lenin, from "afar,"
and his comrades in St. Petersburg weren't all on the same political page.

The first clear indication of problems was his very pointed letter to the
board accompanying his just sent "Election Platform": "This platform
is being sent only for the *information of all*, particularly the *compilers* of
platforms. It is time to *cease writing* platforms when there already *exists*
one confirmed and published by the Central Committee . . . I would *very
strongly* advise the editors, known to you, *not* to approve *any* platform.
For the platform to be confirmed by anyone except the C.C. is a liquidationist trick. Besides, in essence, no good will be done by the editors
approving a platform. Let the editors agree with the existing platform
or remain silent." Revealed here was what Lenin correctly perceived six
months earlier—a struggle within Russian social democracy over which
election platform, a liberal labor or a Marxist labor policy, would be promoted. The specific issue on display was whether a party paper would
defend the platform approved by the Central Committee elected by the
Prague Conference (see Appendix E). Given the aforementioned nexus
between the Duma fraction and the editorial board, there were bound to
be disagreements—especially, again, in the aftermath of Prague. Added
to the mix was the police factor. One of the fraction members, Vasily
Shurkanov, who attended the Leipzig meeting where plans were made for
a legal daily, was later discovered to have been an Okhrana agent—as well
as the yet to be discussed Malinovsky, who was also there.[23]

The May Day demonstrations testified, in Lenin's opinion, to the
contest between the contending platforms and what was at stake. Lenin
was thoroughly heartened by the leaflet issued by the organizers in
St. Petersburg—"underground nuclei" that had to fill in and take initiatives

for the "shattered" St. Petersburg RSDLP Committee: "As a result of the arrests, there happens to be no hierarchic body able to decree the advancing of particular slogans. Hence the proletarian masses, the worker Social-Democrats and even some of the Socialist-Revolutionaries can be united *only* by slogans that are really indisputable for the masses, only by slogans that derive their strength not from a 'decree from above' (as demagogues and liquidators put it), but from the *conviction* of the revolutionary workers themselves. And," Lenin gleefully asked, "what do we find? . . . 'Let our slogans be,' the St. Petersburg workers wrote in their leaflet, 'a constituent assembly, an eight-hour working day, the confiscation of the landed estates.' And further on the leaflet launches the call: 'Down with the tsarist government! Down with the autocratic Constitution of June 3! Long live the democratic republic! Long live socialism!'" Not only was there an underground capable of organizing even in the absence of a "hierarchic body," but "*the slogans [it] adopted were those of the All-Russian Conference of the R.S.D.L.P. which was convened in January 1912*"—both outcomes diametrically opposed to the line of the liquidationists. The May Day protests, Lenin contended, showed that the slogans adopted by the Prague Conference were the real route to working-class unity, whereas the slogan Trotsky and the liquidators advocated, "freedom of association . . . a liberal labor policy," was "disregarded" by "the movement."

> The Social-Democratic proletariat of St. Petersburg has realized that a new revolutionary struggle must be started, not for the sake of one right, even though it should be the most essential, the most important for the working class, but for the sake of *the freedom of the whole people.*
>   The Social-Democratic proletariat of St. Petersburg has realized that it must generalize its demands, and not break them up into parts, that the republic includes freedom of association, and not vice versa, that it is necessary to strike at the center, to attack the source of evil, to destroy the whole system, the whole regime, of the Russia of the tsar and the Black Hundreds.[24]

May Day might have also offered lessons to the proponents of the liberal labor policy. If the Bolshevik slogans were more popular with Russia's proletariat, their candidates would likely gain more seats in the new Duma. This may explain comments Martov made in a liquidationist publication shortly afterward. "Martov," according to Lenin, "threatens in advance the future Social-Democratic group in the Fourth Duma that if it turns out to be anti-liquidationist like its crafty predecessor, then 'cases like the Belousov affair will not be exceptions, but the rule,' meaning, in plain language, that the liquidators will *split* the Duma group. Your bark, liquidator gentlemen, is worse than your bite. Had you had the strength to do so, you would long ago have formed your own liquidationist group in the Duma."[25] Belousov, as noted in Chapter 1, abruptly withdrew from the Duma fraction toward the end of the last Third Duma session and joined the liquidator's camp. If Lenin was right about what the liquidators were unable to do in the Third Duma, he would be wrong when it came to the Fourth.

With increasingly taut battle lines leading up to the elections, the need for a legal daily was all the more necessary—but a paper in which Lenin and the editors could be on the same political page. For that he would have to wage a struggle. Getting the *Zvezda* editors on board with the election campaign was the immediate task. To that end he worked with them to put out a *Voter's Handbook*, which included some of his earlier articles in *Zvezda* on electoral strategy and tactics, to aid in the campaign work. When they were slow in getting a copy back to him, he complained, "We received the *Voter's Handbook two and a half weeks after publication!* Yet to send it at once would have cost *5 kopeks.*"[26] Other party institutions also learned about Lenin the task master. To the Central Committee, about his platform along with a list of other complaints, he wrote, "No precise reply in writing about the platform either. Will it be published? When? Has it been approved completely? We have to print it in the Central Organ [*Sotsial-Demokrat*], but have no precise information."[27]

Lenin also began to be anxious about the status of the daily: "Let us know as soon as possible about the daily paper. What will be the size? What length of article can be sent?" Unbeknownst to Lenin—testimony to the shaky relations he had with the editorial board—the date of his inquiry, April 22, is when the first issue of *Pravda* [*Truth*] appeared. For complicated legal reasons, *Zvezda* had to cease operations on that date and the new paper became the legal daily envisioned at the Prague Conference.[28] The extant regular correspondence with the editorial board began a couple of weeks later when Lenin's first articles appeared. By July it was clear that Lenin saw the daily as an organizer for the upcoming elections:

> I would very much advise you to send a reporter to the City Council, find out *how many* applications [to register to vote] they are getting from tenants and set about publishing this *systematically* (encouraging successful districts and appealing to the unsuccessful). Very little time is left, and the paper should make itself responsible for the *whole* business.
>
> You should get from the City Council, through any statisticians among your acquaintances (or officially from the editors and the members of the State Duma), *all* the statistical material (if they don't exist, then buy *Rech*

[*Speech*, the Cadet daily] for those years and months, or some other paper) about the elections to the *First, Second* and Third State Duma + Petersburg statistics (housing, population, etc.). With such material in your hands, and with an intelligent reporter visiting the City Council daily or 2–3 times a week, you can run a *good* section in the paper about the course of the elections.[29]

The biggest challenge Lenin faced with the editorial board of *Pravda* was how they should deal with him and the liquidators—the "neither for us nor for them" problem. Lenin, of course, wanted to take them on in the pages of the new daily. The editors, again, due possibly to their ties with the pro-Party Mensheviks, were hesitant—the reason they didn't publish every article he submitted. "There is not," he contended, "and cannot be any middle course."[30]

By avoiding "painful questions," [*Nevskaya*] *Zvezda* and *Pravda make themselves* dry and monotonous, uninteresting, uncombative organs. A socialist paper *must* carry on polemics: our times are times of desperate confusion, and we can't do without polemics . . . You can't hide differences from the workers (as *Pravda* is doing): it's harmful, fatal, ridiculous . . . *Pravda* will *perish* if it is *only* a "popular," "positive" organ, that is certain . . .

It would certainly be victorious if it were not afraid of polemics, talked straight about the liquidators, became lively through argument . . . A paper must be a step *ahead of everyone*, and that goes for both *Nevskaya Zvezda* and for *Pravda*. Side by side with the two "positive" little articles, *Pravda* must provide *polemics* . . .—a feature article ridiculing the liquidators— and so forth. Monotony and lateness are incompatible with the newspaper business. And *Pravda* has in addition a special and exceptionally important duty: "whom is it going to *lead*"—this is what *everyone* is asking, what *everyone* is trying to read between the lines.[31]

Stalin, whom Lenin sent to collaborate directly with the editors in order to make his case, also, to Lenin's ire, succumbed to the Rodney King "Why can't we all get along?" syndrome.[32] Conciliationists, Lenin learned, came in all stripes, including those of Bolsheviks.

Toward the Elections

"[T]he elections are quite near at hand—a mere seven to nine weeks. We must take steps to redouble our effort with regard to all aspects of our pre-election work." Lenin's article, "The Significance of the St. Petersburg Elections," in the July 1 issue of *Nevskaya Zvezda* [*The Neva Star*] was a call to action to "worker democrats" in Russia's capital. St. Petersburg, he proposed, should be a "*model* of the election campaign which worker democrats have to undertake in the incredibly difficult conditions of Russian reality."

One thing that distinguished the capital is that "there is a tolerably well-organized working-class press, one which, for all the fierce persecution it is subjected to, for all the fines and the arrests of its editors, for all the instability of its position, and for all that it is kept down by the censorship, is able to reflect, to some little degree, the views of worker democrats . . . Nowhere else are the workers in a position to hold an election campaign *visible* to everyone." The latter qualification was significant because it testified, once again, to Lenin's larger vision—"free political self-determination of the entire people." Yes, the workers' curiae elections "are highly important, but there the workers cannot come up against the other classes of the population, and therefore cannot present on an *adequate* scale the *national* demands, and the views on the tasks involved in a *common policy*, which have been worked out by the progressive, proletarian democrats, so *that* they may serve all democrats in general as a guide."

What St. Petersburg offered, unlike any other setting, was a direct contest between "the liberals and the democrats," specifically in the elections in the urban second curiae. It was direct because the "electoral law now in force permits of a second ballot, so that no blocs are required, or permissible, at the first stage." That fact, coupled with the "absence of a Black Hundred danger," meant that "Russian Marxists" had a reasonable chance, given that the "elections to the Second Duma showed that Cadet 'domination' among the democratic urban voters is very far from being solid," in "freeing petty-bourgeois democrats from liberal influence." Hence the "election struggle in St. Petersburg is a struggle for hegemony between the liberals and the worker democrats within the whole of Russia's emancipation movement." Because of the nationwide significance of the elections, he urged that "[a]ll Russia should also help St. Petersburg."[33]

Having what no other city had—*Pravda*, with a daily press run of about 40,000, and, of lesser importance, *Nevskaya Zvezda*—was certainly a plus for the campaign, but there were limitations, aside from the conciliationist tendencies on the editorial board that Lenin had to struggle against. He suggested as much when referring to "censorship" and the "little degree" to which "the views of worker democrats" could be presented in the paper. More candid about the "legal *Marxist* press" in the illegal *Rabochaya Gazeta*, he wrote, "[I]t is fearfully handicapped, and does not dare utter a word about a republic, our Party, uprising, or the tsar's gang." At least, though, it is the worker's "*own* press and defends Marxism *theoretically.*"[34]

Lenin made a convincing case why *Pravda* indeed was the worker's "*own* press" in his longest contribution to date in the daily, "The Results of Six Months' Work." Published in mid-July in a series of articles, it analyzed monthly contributions to *Zvevda*, *Nevskaya Zveda*, and *Pravda* from 49 towns for six months. Five-hundred four groups made contributions. He then looked at comparable data for the two liquidator publications, *Zhivoye Dyelo* and *Nevsky Golos*, and reported, again with tables and figures (and glee), that "the group of liquidationist intellectuals succeeded in enlisting the support of *15 groups of workers in all* . . . . Could one imagine a more specific proof of the fact that we are in the presence of a group of liquidationist intellectuals who are capable of publishing a semi-liberal magazine and newspaper, but totally lack any serious support among the proletarian masses?"[35] The lesson, among others, was that factory workers could sustain and advance a working-class daily newspaper.

Sandwiched between the statistics was the import of the upcoming elections:

> [A] newspaper is required by the workers in general, and for carrying out elections to the Fourth Duma in particular. The workers know very well that they can expect no good either from the Third or from the Fourth Duma. But we must take part in the elections, firstly, to rally and politically enlighten the mass of the workers during the elections, when party struggles and the entire political life will be stimulated and when the *masses* will *learn politics* in one way or other; and, secondly, to get our worker deputies into the Duma. Even in the most reactionary Duma, in a purely landlord one, worker deputies *have done*, and can do, a great deal for the working-class cause, provided they are true worker democrats, provided they are connected with the masses and the masses learn to direct them and check on their activity.[36]

At the end of July, Lenin wrote in the illegal press, "Our Party has already made use of the elections, and very extensively too. No amount of 'interpretation' by the police, no amount of falsification of the Fourth Duma . . . can nullify *this* result. Propaganda, organized strictly on Party lines, has already been carried out everywhere and has *set the tone* for the entire election campaign of the Social-Democrats."[37]

If the legal press couldn't be overtly used to promote the election campaign, it could be a great venue for proletarian education—what Lenin meant when he said it "defends Marxism *theoretically.*" From July through the elections in October and November, Lenin supplied numerous articles to *Pravda* inspired, probably, by a resolution passed at the Prague Conference on the party's press. It asked "that more space be devoted to articles of a propagandist nature, and that the articles be written in a more popular style, so as to make them more intelligible to the workers."[38]

Usually no more than a page—making them convenient for campaign leaflets—the articles covered a rich range of topics, and while they couldn't explicitly call for a vote for the candidates of the outlawed RSDLP, campaign supporters could fill in between the lines in discussions and meetings. There were, for example, a group of articles employing basic Marxist analysis to examine and explain current wage rates, working hours, and capitalist profits in Russia. These were complimented by articles that discussed the economic reality of peasants. Also, as the campaign got under way, Lenin responded to Cadet and Octobrist condemnation of the regime's manipulation of the electoral rules to get more priests from the rural areas elected. His disagreement with their objections was consistent with his electoral strategy: "A democrat is absolutely hostile to the slightest *falsification* of suffrage and elections, but he is absolutely *in favor* of the widest masses of any priesthood being directly and openly drawn into politics. Non-participation of the priest hood in the political struggle is the most harmful hypocrisy. In reality the priesthood has *always* participated in politics covertly, and the people would only benefit if it were to pass to overt politics."[39]

Most instructive for purposes here was an article that took on the pro-monarchist Black Hundred daily, *Novoye Vremya* [*New Times*]. In an article about the 1912 US presidential elections, the paper self-righteously deplored "'the power of money' in America, relating with malicious joy the facts about the monstrous venality of Taft, Roosevelt, Wilson and, indeed, *all* Presidential candidates put up by the bourgeois parties. Here is a free, democratic republic for you, hissed the venal Russian newspaper." Lenin rejected the self-serving spin of an autocratic cheerleader and countered with the ABC's of Marxism: "The class-conscious workers will reply to that calmly and proudly: we have no illusions about the significance of broad democracy. No democracy in the world can eliminate the class struggle and the omnipotence of money. It is not this that makes democracy important and useful. The importance of democracy is that it makes the class struggle broad, open and conscious. And this is not a conjecture or a wish, but a fact."[40]

But it was the war question—specifically the First Balkan War, the interimperialist rivalry over the breakup of the Ottoman Empire that began in October 1912—that Lenin lent most attention to leading up to and during the elections: "Austria has torn off a chunk (Bosnia and

Herzegovina) and Italy has torn off another (Tripoli [Libya]); it is now our turn to enrich ourselves—such is the policy of *Novoye Vremya*." To explain to the readers of *Pravda* why this was happening, he resorted, again, to Marxist basics—and in the process anticipated his classic work of a few years later, *Imperialism: The Highest Stage of Capitalism*: "In a society of wage slavery, every merchant and every proprietor plays a game of chance, saying as it were: 'I shall either be ruined or make a profit and ruin others.' Every year hundreds of capitalists go bankrupt and millions of peasants, handicraftsmen and artisans are ruined. The capitalist countries play a similar game of chance with the blood of millions, whom they send into a carnage now here, now there with the aim of seizing foreign territory and plundering their weaker neighbors."[41] As for a working-class response,

> Democrats in general and workers in particular are opposed to all "protection" of the Slavs by foxes or wolves, and advocate the complete self-determination of nations, complete democracy, and the liberation of the Slavs from *all* protection by the "Great Powers."
>
> The liberals and nationalists are arguing about *different ways* of plundering and enslaving the Balkan peoples by the European bourgeoisie. Only the workers are pursuing a genuinely democratic policy, for freedom and democracy everywhere and completely, against all "protection," plunder and intervention![42]

As for the masses of the Balkans embroiled in the war and the liberals who profess to promote their "liberty,"

> Never and nowhere has "liberty" been won by the oppressed peoples through one people waging *war* against another. Wars between peoples merely increase the enslavement of peoples. Real *liberty* for the Slav peasant in the Balkans, as well as for the Turkish peasant, can be ensured *only* by complete liberty inside *every* country and by a federation of completely and thoroughly democratic states.
>
> The Slav and the Turkish peasants in the Balkans are brothers who are equally "oppressed" by their landlords and their governments.[43]

Though written a century ago, there is a remarkable currency to Lenin's counsel.

The Elections Begin

"Safarov and Inessa, close comrades, went from Paris to St. Petersburg to make preparations for the election campaign . . . Inessa stopped at

Cracow . . . and stayed with us for two days," reports Krupskaya.[44] In the summer of 1912, Lenin and his companion moved to Cracow in Poland—to be closer to the work they were directing. Knowing the challenges the campaign faced, the Central Committee, with Lenin's instructions, sent Inessa Armand, a Bolshevik leader, and G. I. Safarov, an Armenian comrade, to reestablish the St. Petersburg branch of the party— the repression of the regime following the May Day protests had taken a toll—to bring the editors of *Pravda* on board politically, and to begin preparations for the all-important workers' curiae elections.[45] After some frustrations on the first two fronts, Armand, working undercover, scored a success with the workers at the Putilov Works plant. After hearing her report on the Prague Conference, they decided to support the Bolshevik line and take part in the elections. She arranged a meeting on September 14 to select a slate of six Bolshevik candidates. Unfortunately, the police also knew of the meeting, and she and the others were arrested.[46]

Though jail would prevent Armand from seeing the results, the seeds she planted on September 14, the day of her arrest, bore not just any fruit but that of a protagonist who left a priceless eyewitness account of what happened afterward. Five weeks later, after much political drama— some of which foreshadowed the heady days of 1917—Alexei Badayev, a worker in the car repair shops of the Nikolaievsky Railway, was one of the four individuals elected at the St. Petersburg provincial council elections on October 20 to represent one of the capital's four class constituencies in the Fourth Duma. Badayev was also a Bolshevik.

The Bolsheviks in the Tsarist Duma, Badayev's recollections about his election to and experiences in the Fourth Duma, is indeed invaluable. After summarizing in the first chapter the Bolshevik (i.e., Lenin's) strategy for the Fourth Duma elections, he describes in the second in instructive detail the process that led to his election. The elections were a veritable obstacle course designed to discourage the participation of workers. Organization and planning ahead was a necessity because, as Badayev explains, the "precise date of the elections was not known beforehand. This was one of the tricks of the government, which, by fixing the election date suddenly, attempted to take the workers unawares and to decrease the number of voters."

Organizing the campaign required an office, and because of the newspaper's legal status, the "Bolshevik headquarters for the campaign were the editorial offices of *Pravda*." Having the space, however, was only one hurdle overcome. "Owing to the fact that incessant watch was kept by the police on every 'suspicious' worker, we had to resort to all sorts of subterfuges in order to gather together even in small groups. Usually, in order to avoid the attentions of the police, small meetings of not more than ten to twenty people were called. Summer helped us. Under the guise of picnic-parties, groups of workers went to the suburbs, mostly into the forest beyond the Okhta [River]. The forest was the best refuge from police spies, who would not venture beyond the outskirts, for it was easy to escape from there, and they were afraid of being attacked in some out-of-the-way spot."

Another and more serious problem concerned the selection of candidates. Because they "would certainly have been arrested . . . the names of the prospective candidates were kept secret, and the workers were only informed of them at the last moment before the elections." In some ways this actually aided the Bolsheviks, because in the debates with the Menshevik liquidators the latter wanted to make the campaign about "unity" and the personal characteristics of the candidates, whereas the former wanted the focus on the platform, particularly what Badayev calls "the three whales"—"the democratic republic," "an eight-hour day," and "the confiscation of all landlords' estates."

Not only did workers face obstacles. So too, to a lesser extent, did the petit bourgeois constituents for the second urban curiae elections—of major importance for Lenin. And for that reason "*Pravda*. . . conducted a great campaign against the absenteeism of the city democratic electors, calling upon them to safeguard their rights and to perform all the formalities required. Every issue of the paper reminded the electors to see to it that their names were not left out of the electoral lists and to make the requisite applications to the electoral commissions. *Pravda* called upon each of its readers to secure not less than three voters from among his comrades at the bench or his neighbors in the house where he lived." Convincing workers to participate in the elections was indeed a challenge, as Lenin told Gorky: "We are now 'up to the ears' in the elections. Absenteeism is damnably great. In the worker curia likewise."[47]

Badayev's election began in "the middle of the summer, [when he] learned that the Party organization had nominated me as a candidate." His standing among his coworkers was decisive in the choice, because the first stage in the workers' curiae elections was the selection of delegates at the factory level. On September 14 thousands of factory workers in their different work places met to select about eighty delegates for the next elections in the three-stage process. In Badayev's plant, after a heated debate between Bolsheviks, Menshevik-liquidators, and nonpartisan workers, he, along with another comrade, was elected to be a delegate from his plant to participate in the second stage. Because the regime wouldn't allow the eighty delegates to come together to discuss and debate who they wanted to be the six worker electors for the provincial assembly before the meeting scheduled to do so, October 5—the workers' curiae or second stage of the process—"the press campaigns," Badayev writes, "played an enormous part in the second stage of the elections." By this time, the Menshevik-liquidators, with financial support from the German party—a not unimportant fact to be discussed later—had their own daily, *Luch* [*The Ray*], to promote their line and candidates.

The workers' curiae met on October 5, but the regime, for reasons not clear, decided the day before to disqualify the elections in 21 work places, including the all-important Putilov Works. This led to massive citywide working-class protests, with the Putilov workers leading the way, and a turning point in the St. Petersburg elections. If just a few thousand workers took part in the election of delegates, tens of thousands—"more than 70,000 were involved in the movement"—now demanded in the streets that they had the right to do so. The actions forced the regime to grant new elections in the plants where they had been disqualified, and the result was a much more radical and politicized workers' curiae that convened anew on October 17. The day before the meeting, Lenin weighed in with an article in *Pravda*, "Deputy of the St. Petersburg Workers." After laying out what was at stake, he concluded,

> The workers need a deputy who will express the will of the majority and will know for certain *what* work he will carry out in and outside the Duma.
> The will of the majority has been stated, and the deputy for St. Petersburg should be a determined opponent of liquidationism and a supporter of consistent working-class democracy.[48]

On the day of the election, *Pravda*, as it had done for the October 5 meeting, "published lists of suitable candidates."[49]

Whereas the October 5 assembly was not allowed to have a debate, the reconvened curiae, with about twice as many delegates, met for four hours—registering what had been achieved in the streets: "The delegates decided to use this occasion to make a political demonstration and proposed a number of resolutions on current political conditions. Resolutions were passed, protesting against the Balkan war (which was then in progress); binding the future deputy to raise the question of retrying the case of the members of the Second Duma who had been exiled; and protesting against the sentences on the Black Sea sailors [accused of conspiring to mutiny]."

Most significant, writes Badayev, "at the end of the meeting, the St. Petersburg workers' instructions to their delegates, as proposed by the Bolsheviks, were unanimously adopted." Drafted apparently by Stalin, the one-page "instructions emphasized the importance of using the Duma tribunal for revolutionary propaganda and demanded that both the St. Petersburg deputy and the whole Social-Democratic fraction should fight for the 'unabridged' demands of the working class." Despite the unanimous vote for the Bolshevik "instructions," the outcome for the vote for the six electors was evenly divided between Bolsheviks and Mensheviks.[50] Unsuccessful discussions and negotiations took place between the two factions to try to reach an accord prior to the third stage of the process: the provincial assembly meeting that would select the four deputies to the Fourth Duma that would represent St. Petersburg.[51] The Bolsheviks argued that since the curiae voted unanimously for a Bolshevik platform, the six electors should unify around one of their three electors at the next stage. The Menshevik-liquidators, not surprisingly, didn't see it that way. The Bolsheviks even proposed that lots be drawn to settle the question, but that, too, was rejected.

The selection process at the St. Petersburg provincial assembly meeting on October 20, composed of 66 electors, began with the election of a deputy to represent the peasants. Of the five peasant electors, "four were Progressives ['a cross-breed of Octobrists and Cadets,' as Lenin described them] and one Right. We agreed to vote for the Progressive candidate on condition that, if elected, he would vote with the Social-Democratic fraction on bills concerning the workers. The candidate they nominated was elected. A Progressive was also successful for the houseowners [the second urban curiae], while an Octobrist was chosen to represent the landlords. Then the college proceeded with the election of a deputy to represent the workers. All the workers' electors, both Mensheviks and Bolsheviks, went to the ballot. When the votes were counted, I was declared elected, having received thirty-four votes against twenty-nine. The Liquidators received considerably less votes."[52] Needless to say, the Menshevik-liquidators were not pleased and "at once opened a slanderous campaign about the way the elections had been conducted"—foreshadowing the course of Bolshevik-Menshevik relations in the Fourth Duma.[53]

THE DUMA CONVENES

The Fourth Duma commenced on November 15, 1912, with a new RSDLP fraction. The election results, again the product of rules that severely prejudiced working-class representation, ensured the Czar an even more loyal Duma. Unlike for the Third Duma, the fraction this time, though slightly smaller, was almost evenly split between the two wings of Russian social democracy and more proletarian in composition. That fact and the two very different campaign lines, a liberal labor versus a Marxist labor policy, largely explain the intrafraction tensions that surfaced at the beginning. A Bolshevik leadership meeting was soon convened to make sure its wing of the fraction, along with the editors of *Pravda*, worked in accord. Progress was registered by the fact that by the time of the summer recess for the Duma, the differences between its deputies and those of the Menshevik-liquidators were clearer and increasingly unbridgeable. The situation required another leadership meeting.

"RESULTS OF THE ELECTIONS"

"An election campaign is of outstanding interest to any intelligent political leader because it furnishes *objective* data on the views and sentiments, and consequently interests, of the different *classes* of society. Elections to a representative body are comparable in this respect to a census of the population, for they provide political statistics." Analyzing them, Lenin cautioned, had to take into account the circumstances and rules of the elections—especially for the Fourth Duma given "their systematic rigging by the government." And only those afflicted with "parliamentary cretinism" would think them more important than "strike statistics." "Despite all these reservations, it is beyond question that elections supply *objective* data. Testing subjective wishes, sentiments and views by taking into account the vote of the *mass* of the population representing different classes should always be of value to a politician who is at all worthy of the name. The struggle of parties—in practice, before the electorate, and with the returns summed up—invariably furnishes data *serving to test* our conception of the balance of the social forces in the country and of the significance of particular 'slogans.'"[54]

Once all the returns were in, Lenin could indulge his penchant for number crunching—why he urged the editors of *Pravda* a week after the elections "not to break off the study of the election results."[55] The bare official results showed that social democrats won 14 seats and the Trudoviks 11 for a total of 25 for "Democracy" of the 442 seats in the new Duma. "Liberals," with the Cadets being the largest component, won 128 seats, while the "Rightists" won 283. "As a result, we have an even 'blacker' and even more Rightist Duma, but it is the Octobrists that today turn out to be the defeated party. The liberal opposition and revolutionary democracy (Social-Democratic workers and peasant bourgeois democrats) have almost managed to retain the status quo."[56]

Though the 14 seats the social democrats won were five less than in the elections to the Third Duma in 1907, of greater significance is that for the first time the Bolsheviks won all the six seats allocated to the workers' curiae. The Mensheviks won seven seats but in other curiae by block-ing with liberals and petit bourgeois democrats. The one other "Social Democrat," from Warsaw, was elected—due mainly to the maneuvers of the Bund—against the wishes of the Polish Social Democratic Party. After a heated debate between the Mensheviks and Bolsheviks about admit-ting him to the fraction, because he was seen by the former as an ally, a compromise was reached that granted him voice but not vote in internal fraction affairs. Thus the effective division in the fraction, from the begin-ning, was the "the seven" versus "the six." The Bolsheviks questioned the legitimacy of the Menshevik "majority," since one of its members was the choice of the provincial assembly in Siberia in which almost half of the electors from the worker's curia had been "disqualified" by the regime—what gave the Mensheviks, in Lenin's terms, an "accidental majority."

"Results of the Elections," a detailed examination of the returns, made a case for the correctness of the strategy agreed to at the Prague Confer-ence regarding the workers' curiae elections to campaign independently of the Menshevik-liquidators on the basis of the "three whales" or slogans of a Marxist labor policy. Winning all the six curiae in the most indus-trial regions of Russia meant that the latter was far more attractive to the working class than the "liberal labor policy"—"a test of slogans." As Lenin wrote later, "These figures speak for themselves!" Most instructive were the second-round elections to the second urban curiae. Not only had social democracy increased its vote over what it got in the elections for the Third Duma—"they are wresting more and more from the liberals"[57]—but the data showed that the most likely opponent of a social democratic nominee had been a Cadet. They were also more willing to enter into an alliance with a Right to prevent a social democrat from winning. The Cadets and Black Hundreds realized they had more in common with one another than they did with revolutionary democrats—the "'End' of The Illusions About the Cadet Party." The ever observant and honest analyst admitted that he had "continued to *overestimate*" the potential for a bloc with the liberals to prevent a Right from winning.[58] The returns steeled him even more in his conviction that any bending to liberals, as the Menshevik-liquidators were prone to do, must be vigorously opposed.

Based on the best data he had at his disposal about the actual member-ship of the RSDLP, Lenin argued that the Mensheviks were overrepre-sented in the new Duma—just as they had been in the Third—and that required an explanation:

> As a general rule, in all countries of the world the parliamentary represen-tatives of the workers' parties have a *more opportunist* composition than that of the workers' parties themselves. The reason is easy to see: firstly, all

the electoral systems of the bourgeois countries, even the most democratic, in practice *restrict* suffrage for the workers, either by making it conditional on age (in Russia it has to be 25 years), or on residence and permanence of work (six months in Russia), etc. And it is the young, more politically-conscious and resolute sections of the proletariat that these restrictions generally hit hardest of all.

Secondly, under *any* suffrage in bourgeois society, the non-proletarian elements of the workers' parties—officials of workers' unions, small proprietors, office employees, and particularly the "intelligentsia"—specialize more readily in the "parliamentary" profession (owing to their occupations, social standing, training, etc.).[59]

Lenin's insights about the electoral/parliamentary process—again, not limited to Russia—had real implications for fraction work in the Fourth Duma. All six Bolshevik deputies, like Badayev, were industrial workers, while three of the seven Mensheviks were from the intelligentsia. One of the latter, Nikolai Chkheidze, had headed the fraction in the Third Duma and thus was more knowledgeable than any of the 13 about the ways of the Duma; he was chosen, not surprisingly, to head the new fraction. The situation was complicated by the fact that one of the six Bolsheviks was Roman Malinovsky, the choice of Moscow's workers' curiae and also, as later discovered, the aforementioned "fly in the ointment"—a police agent. Aware of the political, class, and experiential unevenness of the fraction, Lenin tried unsuccessfully to bring them, at least the Bolsheviks, to Cracow before the Duma convened to plan their intervention. During the Duma's summer recess in 1913, he tried again, unsuccessfully—owing mainly to a lack of funds and arrests—to organize a school near Cracow where they could be instructed in the fundamentals of Marxism and other relevant topics to aid them in their Duma work. As he told Plekhanov in a letter of invitation "to deliver lectures . . . we . . . think it very useful that Party people, of various views should take part in an enterprise which seems to us extremely important for strengthening connections with the workers and reinforcing Party work."[60]

ORGANIZING AND WORKING WITH THE NEW FRACTION

The inexperience of the fraction was quickly revealed on the Duma's first day, November 15. Rank-and-file workers in the RSDLP and other organizations decided it would be a good opportunity to greet its opening with a protest. When the fraction got wind of their plans a few days earlier, they issued, with the Mensheviks leading the way, a "warning" to the organizers to cease and desist, because apparently the action hadn't been authorized by the leadership of the St. Petersburg branch. Lenin criticized their response. For him the protest was a "perfectly timed demonstration! Wonderful proletarian instinct, the ability to counter and contrast the opening of the Black-Hundred 'parliament' with red banners in the streets of the capital! . . . a truly popular, truly democratic, purely labor demonstration . . . a people's representative assembly." So "how could the Social-Democratic group 'warn'? How could it stoop to the level of Cadets—to a slavish level?"

If their concern was that the action was somehow intended to be a violent provocation engineered by the police, an excuse to victimize workers, then the objection was justifiable from "a *personal* point of view, but not *politically*." It is true that "one must not resort to violence when there is no question of it. One must warn against violence. But to warn against a peaceful strike at a time when the masses are *seething*? To warn against a *demonstration*?" The criticism then took a constructive tone—what "a real workers' deputy" would have done once plans for the protests were learned:

> The workers' deputy would have found his way to several influential workers. He would have realized that at *such* a time his place was alongside the prominent workers, that it was a hundred times more important to be there with the workers than at the meetings of the Duma group. He would have learned from the prominent workers, from two or three (or perhaps four or five) *influential* workers of the capital, *how matters stood*, what the workers *thought* about it, and *what the mood* of the masses was.
>
> The workers' deputy would have made inquiries about these things—he would have *known how* to make inquiries about them, and would have learnt that there was to be a strike (15 to 50 *thousand!!* according to the bourgeois press), that there was to be a demonstration, that the workers were not thinking of violence and disorders, and that, *consequently*, the rumor about a provocation was no more than a silly rumor.

Lenin's advice went to the very heart of his politics and parliamentary strategy—like that of Marx and Engels, the need to prioritize the world outside the parliamentary arena, specifically the masses in motion and its proletarian vanguard. As well as opposition to gratuitous violence, it captured the essence of what he would try to impart to the new deputies—an opportune teaching moment early in the life of the fraction. At the end he struck a sympathetic but principled chord: "It is a very, very sad mistake the Social-Democratic Duma group as a whole has made. And it would be gratifying to learn that this mistake was not made by all, and that many of those who did make it realize their mistake and will not repeat it."[61]

To assist the fraction in its first Duma intervention, the customary party declaration, Lenin sent a list of points that should be incorporated in the speech.[62] After intense negotiations between both wings of the fraction, Malinovsky, the vice chair of the fraction, was chosen, at the initiative of the Mensheviks, to deliver the declaration on December 7. The agreed on statement essentially combined their two lines. The only unexpected moment for the fraction in his presentation came, as Badayev related, when he "omitted a passage of considerable length criticizing the State Duma and demanding the sovereignty of the people."[63] Nevertheless, *Pravda* printed the full speech. Only in hindsight would it become clear why the omission was made.

Badayev and other fraction members forgave Malinovsky because they knew what it was like for a working-class revolutionary giving a maiden speech on clearly hostile terrain. Between the harangues and interruptions of the Black Hundred chair of the Duma and the hooting of the large Right presence in Tauride Palace, a fraction member could indeed be distracted, as Malinovsky claimed. A week later, Badayev made his first speech, an interpellation about the persecution of trade unions. Exactly because of the undemocratic obstacle course that governed Duma procedures, his intervention had to be carefully planned beforehand. His account of the experience is telling:

> The nervousness to which every workers' deputy was subject when making his first speech in the Duma was unique in his experience. When I mounted the rostrum I felt very keenly the responsibility which rested on a workers' representative. A speech in the Duma did not resemble in any way those speeches which I had to deliver at various illegal and legal meetings of workers . . . Each of us experienced great difficulty when making his first speech in this home of tsarist autocracy. It was a great strain to talk down the howling of the Black Hundreds, to fight against the continual interruptions of the chairman.[64]

If the atmosphere within Tauride Palace was hostile, except for the few workers who were allowed to attend, what was taking place outside helped to steel the nervous Badayev. The St. Petersburg party leadership called for and organized—unlike the actions that greeted the convening of the Duma on November 14—a one-day strike to coincide with his speech as an expression of support. As for the number of participants, there were "certainly not fewer than 60,000, i.e. the number employed in the largest works in St. Petersburg." The fraction was beginning to find its feet.

A year after the Prague Conference, the Bolshevik leadership met again, this time with four of "the six": Malinovsky, Badayev, Grigory

Petrovsky, and N. R. Shagov, the latter two elected respectively by the workers' curiae in Ekaterinoslav and Kostroma. The Duma's Christmas recess made that possible. The meeting, from December 26 to January 1, reaffirmed, in opposition to the Menshevik-liquidators, the necessity of underground work and made that the precondition for reconciliation with them. Another resolution applauded the "vigorous activity" of the fraction, "which found expression in a number of speeches in the Duma, the submission of interpellations and the reading of a declaration which in general correctly expressed the fundamental principles of Social-Democracy." The qualifier "in general" referred to one problem with the declaration. The compromise with the Mensheviks about its wording allowed for a slogan that violated an important provision in the party's 1902 program on the national question—an issue that would be revisited.

The resolution on the fraction also reaffirmed "our Party's established tradition . . . [that] the Duma Social-Democratic group is a body subordinate to the Party as a whole, in the shape of its central bodies . . . [C]areful attention should be paid to every step of the Social-Democratic group, and in this way Party control exercised over the group."[65] The London Congress in 1907, it may be remembered, formalized this "tradition." Three provisions in the resolution (unpublished for security reasons) gave concrete expression to this all-important norm. One called for a struggle with "the seven" to achieve equality in the fraction; another, that the four of "the six" who lent their names to be contributors to the liquidator's daily *Luch* when it came into existence should have them removed; and, third, that they "rally together for party work."[66] The latter probably referred to what Badayev most remembered about the meeting—the importance given "to the work outside the Duma . . . [for] 'the six' to whom the conference delegated many important tasks in connection with illegal party work." They were directed to use their parliamentary immunity and travel as often as possible to meet with their constituencies to do party-building work.

Before the Cracow conference, Lenin asked all the Bolshevik deputies to respond to a 19-point questionnaire about the process of their election. The encounter allowed him to have, except for Malinovsky, face-to-face contact with two-thirds of the fraction for the first time. Their responses to his 19 questions no doubt informed their discussions. "Lenin approached each deputy individually and succeeded in reinforcing in each of us," Badayev wrote, "the will to conduct an intense and sustained struggle."[67] Lenin sent his impressions to Gorky while they were together:

Malinovsky, Petrovsky and Badayev send you warm greetings and best wishes. They are good fellows, especially the first. Really, it is possible to build a workers' party with such people, though the difficulties are incredibly great. The base at Cracow has proved to be useful: our move to Cracow has fully "paid for itself" (from the point of view of the cause). The deputies confirm that a revolutionary mood is unquestionably growing among the mass of the workers. If we now create a good proletarian organization, without obstacles from the treacherous liquidators—the devil knows what victories we can then win when the movement from below develops.[68]

Having an organization in place "when the movement from below develops"—this is quintessential Lenin that goes back at least to *What Is to Be Done?*

A month and a half later, Lenin noted, again to Gorky, the first gains of the meeting: "Our six deputies in the Duma from the worker curia have now begun to work *outside the Duma* so energetically that it is a joy to see. This is where people will build up a real workers party! We were never able to bring this off in the Third Duma."[69] This was a real achievement, because the deputies were under intense police surveillance whenever they traveled, as Badayev detailed, and thus they had to resort to a lot of subterfuge.[70] Unbeknownst to them and Lenin, state security also knew—owing no doubt to reports from Malinovsky—about their party-building intentions. Last, Lenin asked Gorky, with undisguised pleasure, if he had seen the letter in *Luch* the four deputies had sent the daily requesting that their names be removed from its contributors list, as agreed to at the Cracow meeting. It registered another victory.

Badayev's account gives the impression that everyone was on the same page after Cracow. Lenin, certainly, gave more assistance to the Bolshevik wing of the fraction. For interventions in Duma debates, for example, he drafted a speech that Badayev gave on education reform—in which he pointed out that Russian peasants faired worst in comparison to the deplorable situation that confronted blacks in the United States—as well as providing suggestions on the always-important budget debate. But coordination between him and the Bolshevik deputies continued to be a challenge. Not the least of the "difficulties" was one of the "good fellows" he lauded. In the long run, however, and in hindsight, Cracow planted seeds that eventually bore fruit, and the party-building activities of the fraction were crucial in that development.

PRAVDA: A WORK IN PROGRESS

A month before Cracow, Lenin complained to the editor of *Pravda* that Badayev was not doing enough to help the daily: "A workers' paper in Petersburg without the cooperation of the workers' deputy for Petersburg (particularly as he is a *Pravda* supporter) is a stupid situation."[71] This was exactly one of the problems that the meeting sought to correct.

The 12-point resolution "On the Reorganization and Work of the *Pravda* Editorial Board" began by criticizing the board for its lack of "consistency of Party principle" and failure "to provide the necessary response to Party life among Social-Democratic workers in St. Petersburg." For that reason the "C.C. [Central Committee] is taking steps to reorganize" it. This was implicitly a criticism of Stalin, because until the conference he had been, for about half a year, the unofficial editor of the paper.[72] A new editor, Yakov Sverdlov, was designated. It was also resolved that the "Bolshevik section of the deputies must take part in the paper's broad editorial collegium [direction] and organize systematic and persistent participation in the literary and economic side of the business."[73] Badayev later explained, "On the recommendation of Comrade Lenin himself I was charged with the duty of publishing *Pravda*. Lenin told me that being the deputy for St. Petersburg, the representative of the St. Petersburg workers, I must take on that task. *Pravda* pursued not only educational and propagandist aims, but it was also the most important center for organization. He emphasized the point that my duty was to work there."[74]

For a few weeks afterward it looked to Lenin like the agreements reached at Cracow were being ignored. To *Pravda*'s new editor, he stressed why action had be taken immediately: "Unless we secure a reform and proper management in this field, we shall reach bankruptcy, both material and political. *Dyen* [the daily's code name] is the necessary means of organization for uniting and lifting up the movement . . . [T]he key to the whole situation is *Dyen*."[75] Ten days later he exhaled a sigh of relief: "Today we have learned of the beginning of reform in *Dyen*. A thousand greetings, congratulations and wishes for success. At long last you have managed to begin the reform."[76] Not only did *Pravda* have a new board, but the Bolshevik deputies were making "excellent" contributions in the form of articles and letters. Lenin even thought that one of the Menshevik deputies could be recruited to do the same.

Pravda's circulation testified to the progress that was being made for the four-page daily—"30–32 thousand on week-days and 40–42 thousand on holidays . . . The mass of workers are with us (40,000 *Pravda*, against 12,000 *Luch*)."[77] For the one-year anniversary of the paper, Lenin provided facts and figures. A comparison of "voluntary contributions" made by workers' groups to both dailies was, for him, most telling. From the first quarter of 1912 to the first ten days in April 1913, there had been 1,022 collections for *Pravda* and 256 for *Luch*. Also gratifying were the 177 contributions by workers' groups in Moscow for the paper launched there at the beginning of the year—one of the decisions made at Cracow.[78]

While things had improved, the paper faced objective problems. Four days after the editorial board changes, Sverdlov was arrested; a few days later the same happened to Stalin. Lenin couldn't understand why the Menshevik leader and editor of *Luch*, Dan, "lives quite freely" in St. Petersburg. "The liquidators have a mass of intellectuals, while all ours get arrested." And he didn't know that the solutions he proposed only aided and abetted the situation. "We have discussed with Malinovsky what measures to take." The lack of "intellectuals" was a related objective problem: "All the 'intelligentsia' are with the liquidators." Although *Pravda*'s working-class supporters "are producing their '*own*' intelligentsia," it was being done "slowly" and "with the greatest difficulty"—one of the reasons Lenin tried, again unsuccessfully, to organize a Marxist school during the summer recess of the Duma.[79] Given the shortage of skills required for the paper, Lenin stepped up his involvement, including especially the writing of more articles. He also offered advice on all kinds of matters, such as "Put in a telephone" or be more careful about "misprints" or know when to employ "large type." He acknowledged that the paper needed more variety and encouraged the editors to be more patient with a fledgling poet: "Don't find fault, friends, with human failings! Talent is rare. It should be systematically and carefully supported. It would be a sin on your conscience . . . against the democratic working-class movement, if you don't draw in this talented contributor and *don't help* him."[80]

Eventually, it became clear that relying on the working-class Duma deputies to put out the paper was not the solution. Party personnel with the requisite skills had to be in charge. But that, too, proved to be a problem. The new editor, Miron Chernomazov, and publisher, Vasily Shurkanov, were later discovered to be police agents.[81] Their presence probably explains an irritant that increasingly vexed Lenin—their willingness to give Bogdanov space in the paper to espouse what Lenin regarded as an idealist "god-making" philosophy. Only when he threatened to end relations with the paper did the situation improve. Keeping in mind that *Pravda* for Lenin was "the key to the *whole* situation"— that is, party building—it is understandable why he so insisted that it be a Marxist paper.

Another problem—no doubt related to the editor and publisher being double agents—was a tendency of the paper, increasingly by the fall of

1913, to run unnecessarily provocative pieces. To its editors Lenin wrote, "It seems to me that you are making a gigantic mistake in drifting unconsciously with the stream *and not changing* the tone of the paper. Everything suggests that both the tone *and the content* of the news section must he *changed*. It is essential to *achieve* legality, ability to pass the censor."[82] The overall situation only improved in February 1914 when Kamenev took over the editorship reins for the last six months of the paper. Daily circulation had risen back to 40,000 copies—"even reaching 130,000 on *Pravda*'s second anniversary" in April 1914—and was distributed in 944 cities.[83] Though it could never rival the capitalist/Czarist press in readership, it was clearly the favorite of Russia's working class.

Lenin's concerns about "legality" were justified, because beginning in July 1913 the daily was shut down on seven different occasions. Badayev provides fascinating detail on the steps that had to be taken to stay one step ahead of the regime's repressive apparatus to make sure the paper was published and distributed. As soon as it was suppressed, for example, it would resume publication in about a week with a new name, always some variant of *Pravda*. The cat-and-mouse game finally came to an end a year later.

"THE SEVEN" VERSUS "THE SIX"

The already-tense relationship in the Duma fraction rapidly deteriorated when the Bolshevik deputies asked that their names be removed from the list of contributors to the Menshevik-liquidator daily *Luch*. The seven Menshevik deputies charged that their action undermined fraction unity and retaliated with a series of measures that gave undue influence to the former in fraction matters.[84] They imposed, as Lenin charged, their "accidental majority" of one on the six deputies who had been elected by the workers' curiae. Thus the larger issue was which wing of the fraction actually represented Russia's working class, particularly when it came to the question of liquidationism.

When the editors of *Luch* prominently ran an article in one of its January issues, Lenin felt he had irrefutable evidence to make his case against the Menshevik-liquidators. So important he thought the article to be that he reproduced it in full with his commentary as a hectographed leaflet for wide distribution. The author found "deplorable" that "sympathy for the 'underground' is reviving and growing here and there among the workers"—"a resurgent respect for the underground" that was "reminiscent" of the popularity of "terrorism" in an earlier era of the movement. For Lenin, on the other hand, "he who considers" the revived interest and respect for underground work "deplorable is a liberal and not a Social-Democrat, a counter-revolutionary and not a democrat. Comparing the underground with terrorism is an unheard-of affront to revolutionary work among the masses. Only the underground poses and solves problems of the growing revolution, directing revolutionary Social-Democratic work and attracting the mass of the workers precisely by this work."[85]

There was, in Lenin's view, a more fundamental issue at stake. Through illegal as well as legal work a "working-class party is being built up. Workers' independence, the influence of the workers on *their own* parliamentary group, decisions by the workers themselves on questions of their own party—such is the great historical significance of what is going on." As was true for Marx and Engels, independent working-class political action was the bottom line of Lenin's politics. That meant party building, and to call "deplorable" the very necessary means of "the underground" for doing that flew in the very face of social democracy. "One cannot," he reminded the editors of *Pravda*, "unite the Party with the destroyers of the Party."[86]

The all-important issue of "the influence of the workers on *their own* parliamentary group"—what Marx and Engels called attention to in an early criticism of the German party—was also at stake. Only with a party would workers be able to direct their deputies:

> In the present struggle *the very* question at issue is that of defending the *basic* principles of party life. The question of *what* policy *it* wants conducted in the Duma, what attitude *it* has to an open party or an underground one, and whether it considers the Duma group to be *above* the party or vice versa, is confronting every workers' study circle starkly, in a form that demands an immediate and direct answer . . . The liquidators are out *to prevent* the workers from building up their own working-class party—that is the meaning and significance of the struggle between "the six and the seven."[87]

Lenin framed the debate in an instructive way reminiscent of the memorable point Engels made in 1847 that "communism is not a doctrine but a movement": "Socialism is not a ready-made system that will be mankind's benefactor. Socialism is the class struggle of the present-day proletariat as it advances from one objective today to another objective tomorrow *for the sake* of its basic objective, to which it is *coming nearer* every day. In this country called Russia, socialism is today passing through the stage in which the politically conscious workers are themselves completing the organization of a working-class party despite the attempts of the liberal intelligentsia and the 'Duma Social-Democratic intelligentsia' *to prevent* that work of organization."

Behind the conflict lay, of course, the long-existent one going back to the First Duma about the character of the Russian revolution: "[W]e are divided," Lenin told the German party in March 1913, "from the liquidators by profound differences of principle—above all on the question of another revolution in Russia."[88] For Mensheviks, the majority of whom had allied by now with the liquidators, Russia's bourgeois democratic revolution was one in which liberals, the Cadets, would take the lead. Subjecting their Duma deputies to the discipline of a workers' party, exercised through the norms of democratic centralism, was rejected as a constraint on their maneuvering in their still unfulfilled quest to convince the Cadets of their supposed destiny. For the Bolshevik deputies, on the other hand, the constant refrain of Lenin about the treachery of the liberals and the proclivity of the latter to verify his thesis increasingly convinced them that independent working-class political action and thus party building was the priority. Later, and famously, he wrote, "without an organization the working class is *nothing*."[89] That the proletarian masses were voting with their feet, drawn to the underground, was even more persuasive.

A split in the fraction was clearly looming. It may be remembered that Martov threatened as much early in the election campaign to the Fourth Duma; the two incompatible lines in the campaign were now embodied in the fraction. For Lenin, the only question now was how to carry out a split in a way that advanced the revolutionary process. That would require a party meeting.

While the Marxist summer school Lenin envisioned couldn't convene, a delegated Bolshevik meeting did take place in the same location not far from Cracow at the end of September 1913 during the summer recess of the Duma. All the Bolshevik deputies, except for one who was sick, participated in the second or Cracow II meeting. Duma strategy and tactics, as always, depended on the larger political context. The resolution on "The Present Situation," the first of nine, affirmed that the "situation in the country is becoming increasingly acute" and reaffirmed the currency of the "revolutionary slogans": the democratic republic, the confiscation of landed estates, and the eight-hour day. In the discussion and resolution on "Activities in the Duma," refinements were made on the tactics of bill writing and voting:

If bills, motions, etc., concern immediate and direct improvements in conditions for workers, minor salaried employees and working people generally (for example, reduction of hours, increase of wages, the removal of even minor evils in the lives of the workers and of broad sections of the population in general, etc.), the clauses that provide for such improvements should be voted for.

In cases when the conditions the Fourth Duma attaches to these improvements make them dubious, the group should abstain from voting, but must *unfailingly* formulate its motives for so doing, after having first discussed the question with representatives of workers' organizations.

This Conference affirms that:

on all questions, important bills, etc., the Socialist-Democratic group in the Duma must independently formulate its own motion to pass on to next business.

In cases of the group's vote against the government, after the Social-Democratic motion has been rejected, coinciding with the vote of other parties, the group must endeavor to formulate its own motives for voting for another party's motion, or part of a motion.[90]

On what was clearly the most pressing agenda item—the situation in the Duma group—the meeting, after describing how "the seven deputies encroach on the elementary rights of the six workers' deputies who represent the overwhelming majority of the workers of Russia," proposed a solution:

This Conference is therefore of the opinion that united action on the part of the Social-Democratic group in the Duma is possible only if the two sections of the group enjoy equal rights, and if the seven deputies abandon their steam roller tactics.

Notwithstanding irreconcilable disagreements in spheres of activity outside as well as inside the Duma, this Conference demands that the group should maintain unity on the basis of the aforesaid equality of rights of its two sections.

This Conference invites class-conscious workers to express their opinion on this important question and to exert all efforts to help preserve the unity of the group on the only possible basis, that of equal rights for the six workers' deputies.[91]

The "irreconcilable disagreements" meant that Lenin, certainly, had no hope that "the seven" would agree to equality in the fraction. Yet he clearly knew that for most workers the dispute was confusing and all they wanted was unity. So the proposal was phrased defensively, to put the burden of unity on "the seven."

PRELUDE TO THE "GREAT WAR"

With both the Duma fraction and Central Committee in agreement after a collective discussion about how to deal with "the seven," "the six" returned to St. Petersburg and threw down the gauntlet. The chief task was to prove that their politics were more popular with Russia's most class-conscious proletariat than those of the Menshevik-liquidators. They did so by employing a variety of measures in a society that didn't allow for open and free decision making. Outside of Russia, however, at least in the leadership circles of Western European social democracy, their opponents were more popular. Opportunism and reformism had taken their toll. But in the crisis-ridden circumstances of a three-hundred-year-old autocracy on life support, those who were willing to do all that was necessary to finally pull the plug only enhanced their credibility, notwithstanding the obstacles they faced. Whether planned or not, the regime managed to delay a showdown by firing the first shot in what came to be called the "Great War."

"Declaration" and Split

Shortly after the Fourth Duma reconvened, the Bolshevik deputies submitted to "the seven" the equality proposal and published it the next day as a "Declaration" in *Za Pravdu* [*For Truth*], the latest edition of *Pravda*. As expected it was rejected, and at the end of October 1913 "the six" designated themselves a separate fraction, the Russian Social Democratic Labor Group, as distinct from the Social Democratic Group in the Duma. The task now was to win the majority of workers to support the new fraction and *Pravda*, or whatever name the organ would have.

Given the understandable confusion the split created among many workers—which the Cracow discussion anticipated—making known the facts was crucial. In addition to what "the six" wrote and said, Lenin put together a package of data for a special issue of *Pravda*.[92] The focus was on two claims: first, that "the six," unlike "the seven," represented the majority of Russia's workers and, second, that the latter had unfairly used their "accidental majority" of one to thwart the equal participation of the former in the fraction. As for the first, Lenin elaborated on the significance of the workers' curiae elections and added data on other elections, specifically those to the governing boards of trade unions—especially the very powerful metal workers union—and the workers' sick insurance boards. In every case the Bolsheviks outdistanced the Menshevik-liquidators. Lenin added data on the circulation of the *Pravda* and *Luch*, which showed that the former was three to four times more popular.

Regarding the second claim, Lenin, with the input of the Bolshevik deputies, elaborated on the "steam roller tactics" of "the seven," specifically their over representation on Duma committees because of the one vote majority advantage they enjoyed in the fraction:

> Of the 26 committees on which the Social-Democrats are represented:
> the six deputies are represented on *seven*; the other seven deputies are represented on *thirteen*—nearly *twice as many*.
> Of the 20 committees on which there is one Social-Democratic representative:
> the six deputies are represented on *seven*; the other seven are represented on *thirteen*—nearly *twice as many*.
> Of the committees on which there are two Social-Democratic representatives:
> the six deputies are represented on *three*; the other seven are represented on *six*—*twice as many*.
> On each of three of these committees the seven had two representatives.
> Not one of the six deputies sits on more than two committees. Of the seven, *Chkhenkeli sits on six committees; Skobelev sits on six, and Mankov sits on four.*[93]

Both *Za Pravdu* and *Novaya Rabochaya Gazeta* (successor to *Luch*) mounted campaigns respectively for "the six" and "the seven." Workers were asked to send signed—with the risks that entailed—statements and/ or resolutions of support for either fraction. At the end of the year about ten thousand had been received. Almost seven thousand were in favor of the Bolshevik deputies as opposed to about three thousand for "the seven." Lenin ridiculed Martov's claim that "the six" had garnered just "slightly more than half" of the total. But there was a larger significance:

> No other political party in Russia can show, for the whole period of the counter-revolution in general and for 1913 in particular, a similar *open and mass opinion poll of all its members* on a most important issue of Party life. None of the legalized parties in Russia, none of the wealthy liberal and democratic parties, which have a host of intellectualist forces and all sorts of publications at their command, has done as much as the party of the working class, the party of propertyless proletarians, who have been driven underground and maintain their newspaper with the kopeks [pennies] they collect.[94]

Even more telling in Lenin's opinion were the collections that workers sent to the two Duma fractions "for the relief of comrades in prison or exile, for aid to strikers in different factories and industries, and for various other needs of the working-class movement." Owing to their parliamentary immunity, Duma deputies could (in theory at least) engage in such assistance.[95] From the end of October 1913 to June 1914, almost 1,300 workers' groups sent collections to "the six" as opposed to about 200 to "the seven." And in terms of the actual amounts, about half of what "the seven" got came from "non-workers," whereas the equivalent for "the six" was less than 10 percent—crucial evidence that, again, "the six" were the real representatives of Russia's working class.

The success of the support campaign for "the six" had broader and long-term significance. It took, as Lenin had always envisioned, Duma work to "the outside," beyond the walls of Tauride Palace, where it should be. Until then, the de facto split between the Bolsheviks and Mensheviks was mainly an internal party affair. Because of the campaign, as Badayev explained in convincing detail, "the Bolsheviks had carried new positions and considerably widened and deepened their influence among the workers . . . The campaign . . . resulted in an influx of workers into the ranks of the Party, and the whole of our Party work was infused with new vigor."[96] The success of the campaign for "the six" did more than anything to make the Bolsheviks known among the Russian working class. It explains why they had a head start in 1917. Another campaign involving "the six"—to be discussed shortly—was also influential.

As for "the seven," the admission in January 1914 of one of their leaders about the state of the group foretold the fate of the Mensheviks: "'[I]t has lost all influence, deserted the political life of the country, broken its connections with the workers and finally forced the most active members to leave the fraction and consequently brought the work of the fraction to a standstill.'"[97] The campaign for "the six" affirmed a principle dear to Lenin that has utmost importance for this book—the norm that a workers' parliamentary fraction should be subordinate to their will. The erosion of that principle in Western European social democracy would be tragically exposed a few months later—and reverberates until today.

The Cadets, not surprisingly, closely followed the fight within Russian social democracy and wrote, in Lenin's opinion, a very perceptive and telling article about it. "The seven," in the author's eyes, and for whom he was rooting, were, according to Lenin's quotes, "the parliamentary elements of Social-Democracy" around which "the entire intelligentsia" of the party grouped. "The six," on the other hand, constituted "the irreconcilables," the "non-parliamentary workers' majority." Russian social democracy could evolve in the direction of its Western Europe counterpart if it could function in an open legal way. But the "longer the transition to this normal existence is delayed . . . the more the reason will there be to anticipate that the parliamentary majority of the Social-Democratic intellectuals [i.e., 'the seven'] will be compelled to yield to the non-parliamentary workers' majority and to its present mood." In other words, the delay in instituting bourgeois democracy in Russia increased the likelihood of a revolutionary outcome. History would indeed confirm the author's insight.

But what the Cadet author couldn't see or admit to is how the "treachery" of his party aided and abetted the intransigence of the regime. The Cadets viscerally disagreed with Lenin's perspective about reforms, encapsulated best in what he wrote at the height of the 1905 upheaval: "[W]e must fight in a revolutionary way for a parliament but not in a parliamentary way for a revolution." Lenin knew—from the lessons of the "European Spring"—what every liberal feared, as Marx and Engels put it in their *Address of March 1850*: "the revolution in permanence." A revolutionary fight for a parliament might end, to their horror, just that way. Russian liberals would rather enable autocracy than risk democracy. The debates within Russian social democracy over a revolutionary versus a reformist electoral/parliamentary strategy, therefore, made not only Lenin increasingly aware of the parallels with Western Europe but the Cadets as well—most relevant, again, for one of the arguments of this book.

OPPORTUNISM AND REFORMISM IN WESTERN EUROPE

Parliamentary politics in Britain continued to attract Lenin's attention exactly because of the potential lessons for Russia's working class. "It is well known," he wrote as elections for the Fourth Duma were under way, "that in Britain there are two workers' parties: the British Socialist Party (BSP), as the Social-Democrats now call themselves, and the so-called Independent Labor Party . . . The Independent Labor Party (ILP) is a party of liberal labor policy. It is justly said that this Party is 'independent' only of socialism, but very dependent on liberalism." Its annual conference in 1912 was instructive. A debate and vote arose about whether its MP's should support their counterparts in the Liberal Party. Although the "opportunists carried the day," he was heartened by the size of the "opposition in the ranks of this very Party. The opponents of opportunism acted far more correctly than their like-minded colleagues in Germany frequently do when they defend rotten compromises with the opportunists."[98]

As for the British Labor Party, "which must be distinguished from the *two* socialist parties," it was the "workers' organization that is most opportunist and soaked in the spirit of liberal-labor policy." The vote of their parliamentary group on budget allocations for the British navy early in 1913 was also instructive. Only 15 of their 40 MP's supported the ILP motion to reduce spending. "There you have a striking example of how opportunism leads to the *betrayal* of socialism, the *betrayal* of the workers' cause . . . From the example of other people's mistakes, the Russian workers, too, should learn to understand how fatal are opportunism and liberal-labor policy."[99]

A highly visible by-election later in the year instantiated his characterization of the ILP, "for whom our liquidators express such tender feelings." The resignation, for personal reasons, of the head of the ILP, Ramsey MacDonald, made the election possible. Working-class rank-and-file members of the ILP in the constituency moved to back as a replacement a candidate of the British Socialist Party. "The I.L.P. Parliamentary group intervened and published a *protest* in the *Liberal* press (which, like [that of our Cadets] . . . helps the opportunists)" against the BSP candidate. Their action ensured the election of a Liberal. Lenin doffed his reporter's hat: "Class-conscious workers in various countries quite often adopt a 'tolerant' attitude toward the British I.L.P. This is a great mistake. The *betrayal* of the workers' cause in Leicester [the constituency] by the I.L.P. is no accident, but the result of the *entire* opportunist policy of the Independent Labor Party. The sympathies of all *real* Social-Democrats should be with those British Social-Democrats who are determinedly combating the Liberal corruption of the workers by the 'Independent' Labor Party in Britain."[100] This was Lenin's most explicit call to date for the need to oppose opportunism in a Western European working-class movement.

His allusion to the failings of the German party presaged the coming divorce. What's striking was Lenin's forbearance until then. In early 1913 he complained to its leadership, still his "comrades," about its very nonneutral stance vis-à-vis the split in its sister party: "Either for lack of information or for some other reason, the Vorstand [executive] has not displayed impartiality in respect of the liquidators and us." For example, the "Central Organ of the fraternal German Party (*Vorwärts*) sets aside whole columns for gross attacks by the liquidators on our" Prague conference. "During," also, "the election campaign, the Vorstand, despite our protests, gave cash assistance to the liquidators, but denied it to the Central Committee . . . And the liquidators used the German workers money to start their publication of a Konkurrenzorgan [rival organ] *Luch* . . . whose first issue appeared *on the very day of the election* [to the Fourth Duma] and helped to aggravate the split."[101]

And then there was Kautsky. As early as 1904, *Neue Zeit*, the party's theoretical organ that he edited, found pro-Menshevik views more palatable than those of Lenin. Nevertheless, the Bolshevik leader was willing, apparently, to ignore that history as long as Kautsky spoke like a revolutionary. But "Kautsky's Unpardonable Error," the title of Lenin's article in a December 1913 issue of *Pravda*, signaled the end of his patience. By saying at a meeting of the Socialist International on the split in the Russian movement that the RSDLP "had disappeared," Kautsky affirmed, in effect, the position of the liquidators. His "monstrous blunder," Lenin charged, "not only betrayed ignorance of the facts about the Russian working-class movement, but also revealed what sort of influence the liquidator whisperers abroad exercise upon our foreign comrades."[102]

A leading figure in the German party's Reichstag fraction (the SPD) published an account of his recent trip to the United States, where he was invited to address Congress. Lenin concurred with his praise "that in America the government provides every congressman not only with a private office fitted all modern conveniences, but also with a paid secretary to help him cope with a congressman's manifold duties"—amenities unavailable to deputies in the Reichstag and the Duma. But he severely chastised the SPD leader's proud defense of his speech for not having said anything "against capitalism and in favor of a mass strike." On display, Lenin argued, was just the most recent example of the degree to which opportunism had infected "the officers' corps" of the German working class. He recalled that at the 1907 Stuttgart Congress of the Socialist International, "half of the German delegation turned out to be sham socialists of this type, who voted for the ultra-opportunist resolution on the colonial question" (see Chapter 4 in the first volume, *LES1905*). The more that liberals and liquidators try to import such practices "*to our soil*, the more determinedly must they be resisted . . . the merits of German Social-Democracy are merits, not because of shameful speeches like those delivered by [the deputy] . . . but *despite* them. We must not try to play down the *disease* which the German party is undoubtedly suffering from, and which reveals itself in phenomena of this kind; nor must we play it down with 'officially optimistic' phrases. We must lay it bare to the Russian workers, so that we may learn from the experience of the older movement, learn what should not be copied from it."[103] Five months after he wrote these lines, "the disease" would reveal itself in a way that even Lenin could not have imagined.

Another publication in 1913 was the correspondence of Marx and Engels—the most complete to date. Although under the joint editorship of Eduard Bernstein and August Bebel, the hand of the former predominated. Given his "extreme opportunist views . . . Bernstein," Lenin opined, "should never have undertaken" the task.[104] His "prefaces are in part meaningless and in part simply false . . . Unfortunately, the eclectic attitude to Marx's ideological struggle against many of his opponents is becoming increasingly widespread among present-day German Social-Democrats." Despite the failings of Bernstein, the four-volume publication was sorely needed: "The more we have occasion in our day to observe how the working class movement in various countries suffers from opportunism . . . the more valuable becomes the wealth of material contained in the correspondence."[105]

One of the reasons why Bernstein exercised such influence on the publication is that Bebel was in declining health. When he died shortly after the four volumes appeared, Lenin used the moment to acquaint Russian workers with the history of the German movement. Bebel—unlike Kautsky, Lenin emphasized—was a worker, and though only 27 when he was elected as a social democrat to the new German parliament when it was established in 1869, his conduct provided enduring lessons: "The fundamentals of parliamentary tactics for German (and international) Social-Democracy, tactics that never yield an inch to the enemy, never miss the slightest opportunity to achieve even small improvements for the workers and are at the same time implacable on questions of principle and always directed to the accomplishment of the final aim—the fundamentals of these tactics were elaborated by Bebel himself or under his direct leadership and with his participation." Along with Wilhelm Liebknecht—and supported with the moral authority of Marx and Engels—he led the charge against the first signs of the "parliamentary disease" in the party: "Under the leadership of Bebel and Liebknecht the party learned to combine illegal and legal work. When the majority of the legally-existing Social-Democratic group in parliament adopted an opportunist position on the famous question of voting *for* the shipping subsidy, the illegal *Sozialdemokrat* [party organ] *opposed* the group and, after a battle four weeks long, proved victorious."[106] The parallels with the then current debates between "the six" and "the seven" were not lost on readers of *Pravda*.

If Lenin no longer had faith in the "officers' corps" of the SPD, that wasn't true when it came to the ranks of the party. Fifteen months before the Guns of August exploded, he reported with obvious pleasure on how a general meeting of the party in a constituency in Stuttgart demanded that the parliamentary fraction be unyielding in opposing armaments spending. If necessary, "mass strikes" should be employed to steel their determination. "There is slow but steady growth of awareness among German Social-Democrats that more resolute, active, mass struggle by the workers is necessary. If the opportunists, of whom there are many in the parliamentary group and among the officials of the labor movement, are opposed to such a struggle, the masses of workers accept it with greater and greater sympathy."[107]

Belgium was also on Lenin's radar screen. The general strike in 1913 that ended with only "a partial victory" offered lessons. Why had the strike, he asked *Pravda* readers, garnered "such *little* success" in a country where "political liberty" allowed workers to "have a broad and open road before them"?—a not unimportant question for a newspaper that put the fight for a democratic republic at the center of its program. There were two reasons: "The first is the domination of opportunism and reformism in a section of the Belgian Socialists, especially those in parliament. Being accustomed to move in alliance with the Liberals, these members of parliament feel themselves dependent on the Liberals in all their activity. As a result, there was hesitation in calling the strike, and hesitation could not but limit the success, strength and scope of the whole proletarian struggle." The second, basically, is that Belgian workers lacked "a strong, highly principled and strictly party organization which is true to socialism"—what the liquidators who also followed Belgian politics "have done wrong to ignore."[108]

Lenin's increasingly critical stance toward Western European social democracy, especially their parliamentary fractions, was justified given the actions of the leadership of the Socialist International, which met in July 1914 to discuss the split in the Russian movement. The meeting was, ostensibly, to be just an airing of differences before the International's "officers' corps" to help them understand what was at issue. Lenin provided a very detailed report, drawing on data he published before, to show that "the six" actually represented the mass of Russia's workers and proposed conditions for resolving the dispute. However, he decided not to attend and explained to Inessa Armand, who was out of jail and back in exile in Western Europe, why she should go and give the report instead of him. And it wasn't just a matter that her French—the meeting would be in Paris—was better than his: "We shall calmly (I am no good for that) . . . propose our conditions in the most polite (I am no good for that either) French."[109]

Lenin upped the ante for reconciliation. As well as equality in the fraction, he demanded that "the seven" recognize the authority of the Central Committee that came out of the Prague Conference because it was more representative of the Russian working class than any group the Menshevik-liquidators had in place. Not only did the executive committee reject his proposals, as Lenin no doubt expected, but they voted, effectively—and contrary to the stated purpose of the meeting to be simply an airing of differences—that the Bolshevik Central Committee suspend itself and thus "the six" also. It appeared that Lenin suffered a defeat. But developments far more important than the meeting in Paris soon revealed that the Socialist International itself was the loser. It would forfeit the moral authority needed to implement their decisions.

1905 Redux?

Back in St. Petersburg, "the six" were as busy as ever—outside the walls of Tauride Palace. The class struggle that revived in 1912 intensified in the opening months of 1914. From political protests commemorating the Lena goldfields massacre and celebrating May Day to struggles against economic exploitation in some of the city's largest factories, the proletariat of the capital increasingly looked like their counterparts in the heady days of 1905. This time they had representatives in the Duma who they looked to for assistance. The aforementioned contributions that workers' groups collected and sent to the deputies for strike and other aid were especially important. Fraction members were expected to help in other ways and did so. Because the biggest and most notable strike actions took place in St. Petersburg, Badayev was probably more active than any of his comrades in the fraction. At a certain moment he was confronted by the assistant to the minister of the interior with the facts his police had been gathering on him: "You are a deputy of the State Duma, your business is to legislate—that is why you were elected—but instead you spend your time at the workshops, hatching plots, issuing leaflets and publishing a newspaper which incites its readers to criminal acts." Badayev replied, "You cannot prevent me going to the factories. A deputy elected by the workers will never confine himself to speeches in the Duma while the workers are being beaten up in your police stations."[110] Parliamentary immunity allowed Badayev such freedom— exactly why the regime would have to do what it did with the social democratic group in the Second Duma.

Within the Duma, the fraction maintained its revolutionary posture. This is why, along with "the seven" and the Trudovik deputies, it was not invited to a "secret meeting" in March of all the other fractions to discuss how to increase armaments spending—four months before the Czar declared war on Germany. "When we denounced this fresh expenditure of the people's money on armaments," writes Badayev, "we were supported by a strike of 30,000 workers."[111] To protest the infringement on their speaking rights by the Duma president when trying to defend striking workers, the three fractions decided to obstruct the debate on the government's budget—reminiscent of what they did in the First and Second Dumas. The Octobrist president responded by suspending the members of all three fractions for 15 sessions. Most significant, tens of thousands of workers took to the streets in not only St. Petersburg but Moscow as well to protest the suspensions. Their actions coincided with those already planned for May Day a few days later—the largest since 1905–7. In anticipation of the fate of both fractions and *Pravda*, a leading Black Hundred publication blamed the upsurge on the "agitation carried on by the workers' press and in the activity of the Social-Democratic deputies."[112]

Badayev and his comrades were not opposed to doing what the government official demanded that they should only do—"to legislate." A month before their suspension they sought to do just that. The issue was one that the second Cracow meeting recognized to be an increasingly obvious fact: "The orgy of Black-Hundred nationalism, the growth of nationalist tendencies among the liberal bourgeoisie and the growth of nationalist tendencies among the upper classes of the oppressed nationalities, give prominence at the present time to the national question." The context was the Balkan Wars and the coming "Great War." To counter "the orgy," Lenin and the Bolsheviks mounted a campaign that took varied forms. His most detailed writings to date on the national question informed a bill that the fraction tried to introduce in the Duma: "A Bill for the Abolition of All Disabilities of the Jews and of All Restrictions on the Grounds of Origin or Nationality" (see Appendix F). While "the seven" were invited to sign on, it's not clear if they did. Even with Trudovik support they would not have had the required 33 signatures to introduce the bill for debate. Nevertheless, as they had done before, the fraction utilized *Pravda* to inform its readers of its contents. As Lenin explained in his introduction, "[W]e do not look to the nationalist [Black Hundred] Fourth Duma to abolish the restrictions against the Jews and other non-Russians. But it is the duty of the working class to make its voice heard. And the voice of the *Russian* workers must be particularly loud in protest against national oppression." About the work the fraction did on the inside, Badayev made a crucial point: "Had there been no workers' Bolshevik paper, our speeches would not have been known outside the wall of the Tauride Palace"—what the regime also knew.

A week after the May Day protests, "the six" became "the five." On May 8, Roman Malinovsky submitted his resignation to the president of the Duma. He said nothing to his comrades and disappeared. Bolshevik opponents, "the seven" especially, had a field day with Malinovsky's unexplained departure. There had long been rumors and suspicions about him but never hard evidence—at least to convince Lenin. After the October Revolution, when the Bolsheviks had access to the Czar's police files, it was learned that he had indeed been on their payroll. "He betrayed,"

Lenin revealed, "scores and scores of the best and most loyal comrades, caused them to be sentenced to penal servitude, and hastened the death of many of them."[113] And no doubt he helped stoke the factional side of the debate between the Bolsheviks and Mensheviks between at least the Prague Conference and his departure. A trial in 1918 resulted in his execution at the hands of a firing squad.

Reflecting later on Malinovsky, Lenin suggested that it was not coincidental when he went missing in action. It was when the class struggle in the spring of 1914 was beginning to look like a replay of the fall of 1905. Though he had been a valuable asset for the police, it was becoming increasingly clear that the movement was getting more out of him than the regime: "I should not at all be surprised if the secret police used the following argument for Malinovsky's removal from the Duma: that Malinovsky had turned out to be too closely involved with the Duma fraction and *Pravda*, which were carrying on their *revolutionary* work among the masses much too energetically to be tolerated by the police."[114] He was objectively aiding and abetting, contrary to what he no doubt preferred, the revolutionary process. The modus operandi of the Bolsheviks made that possible: collective discussion and debate, a democratic vote, and the expectation that everyone was obligated to carry out the will of the majority—in other words, democratic centralism. Lenin, in his later reflection about Malinovsky, said that "we had a rule whereby we did not allow those to the left of us to make speeches; if a speech was somewhat to the right, it was still possible to correct it, but more leftish statements could cause great harm. Apparently Malinovsky did not always like this line of conduct; he preferred bolder illegal work"—exactly what an agent provocateur sought, a pretext for the regime to crack down on the Bolsheviks.[115] Democratic centralism also served the party well in the case of Chernomazov, the problematic editor of *Pravda* and also a police agent. Precisely because he violated discipline—one of the resolutions adopted at the second Cracow meeting—it facilitated the Central Committee's replacement of him with the more effective Kamenev.

The revolutionary upsurge that began in early 1914 continued to deepen, and both "the five" and *Pravda* were intimately involved—the reason the government decided to pull, finally, the plug on the daily. On July 8 the police raided its offices, ransacked the premises, and arrested everyone on the site. Badayev's parliamentary immunity no longer protected the paper. The closing of *Pravda* was just the first of the opposition press to meet a similar fate. "In spite of this there were no signs of slackening and the movement continued to grow during the following days until July 12. The number of strikers increased to 150,000, and on July

9 barricades were seen in the streets of St. Petersburg. Tramcars, barrels, poles, etc., served as material for the construction of barricades which were built mainly in the Vyborg district. All traffic was interrupted and in many areas workers had complete control of the streets."[116]

Whether the July protests would have resulted in another October 1905 will never be known. On July 19, Nicholas II declared war on Germany. The patriotic fervor the announcement engendered effectively brought an end to the revolutionary upsurge—at least for a while. The Bolsheviks and their Duma fraction were now faced with new and unprecedented challenges in the history of social democracy.

***

Shutting down *Pravda* was probably—in hindsight, admittedly—the prelude to Nicholas's declaration, part of a well-orchestrated plan to stifle any organized opposition to his war drive. The paper had for more than two years spoken out, unlike any other, against the imperial ambitions of the autocracy. When the Balkan Wars began as the elections for the Fourth Duma were under way, Lenin, in language to get pass the government's censors, warned *Pravda* readers to beware of the "foxes or wolves," those who claimed to be "protecting the Slavs"—exactly how the autocracy sought to cloak its intrigues for initiating the "Great War." The Bolsheviks also worked to counter the regime's domestic chauvinist offensive, a necessary ingredient in its war drive. "A Bill for the Abolition of All Disabilities of the Jews and of All Restrictions on the Grounds of Origin or Nationality," which Lenin drafted and *Pravda* publicized, was just one component in that effort. They were the lone consistent voice among party organizations to confront the march to war. Their fraction's denunciation of new spending on arms in March 1914 and the strike of 30,000 workers in support of their stance made them a more dangerous opponent. The regime also probably knew, therefore, that it would not be enough to silence the organ of the Bolshevik fraction. The fraction itself would have to be shut down.

CHAPTER 7

THE "GREAT WAR,"
1917, AND BEYOND

ARGUABLY THE MOST CONSEQUENTIAL WORK OF ANY of the four Russian Social Democratic Labor Party Duma fractions came with the onset of the First World War. The antiwar actions of the five Bolshevik deputies in the Fourth Duma were for Lenin a model for what he would begin to call communist parliamentary work. But after they were arrested and exiled to Siberia, that work ceased to occupy his attention to the degree it once had. The reason is that with the overthrow of the Romanov dynasty in February 1917, Lenin would have to spend much of his time before and after the October Revolution defending soviet governance, for him a superior form of representative democracy. By no means did this signify a change of heart about the parliamentary arena. To the contrary, he maintained to the end that in the absence of soviets communists should make use of parliaments but based on the lessons drawn and codified by the new Communist or Third International. Subsequent history revealed, however, that only a few who claimed to do politics in his name were faithful to the legacy he bequeathed.

THE DUMA FRACTION AND ANTIWAR WORK

When Nicholas II declared war on Germany on July 19, 1914 (or August 2 in the new calendar)—in response to the German Kaiser's declaration a day earlier—the only question for the Duma was what would be the response of the social democratic deputies.[1] Would they get on board the war train as had every other fraction, including the Cadets? They had long opposed the Czar's imperial ambitions and the chauvinist campaigns that enabled them, and as an affiliate of the Socialist International, the RSDLP had signed on to the much publicized Basle Manifesto of 1912 when the Balkan Wars commenced. That proclamation, standing on the shoulders of the antiwar resolution of the 1907 Stuttgart Congress, called on its signers to oppose militarism. If war began, their parliamentary fractions should vote against any funding and call on the proletariat in their respective countries to turn it into a civil war against their own bourgeoisies.

THE HISTORIC "BETRAYAL" AND THE BOLSHEVIK RESPONSE

To the disbelief of every Russian social democrat, regardless of faction, the Reichstag fraction of the German party voted on August 4 to fund the war. The fateful action of the flagship party of international social democracy gave license to every other social democratic parliamentary group in Western Europe to follow suit. The Menshevik (and soon to be Bolshevik) Alexandra Kollontai was present when the vote was taken: "'I could not believe it,' she wrote in her diary that evening: 'I was convinced that either they had all gone mad, or else I had lost my mind.'"[2] Lenin, too, was apparently taken aback, despite having recently written about the creeping "disease" within the German movement. His reaction to the vote, "a feeling of the most bitter disappointment," suggests as much: "The responsibility for thus disgracing socialism falls primarily on the German Social-Democrats."[3] This wholesale "betrayal," as he and many other social democrats called it, of the basic principles of Marxism was soon recognized as a watershed in the history of the movement. For Lenin it was a teaching moment, as he explained to Kollantai at the end of the year: "The European war has brought this great benefit to international socialism, that it has exposed for all to see the utter rottenness, baseness and meanness of opportunism, thereby giving a splendid impetus to the cleansing of the working-class movement from the dung accumulated during decades of peace."[4]

How the Russian parliamentary group, both wings, would respond to the war drums now took on added significance in the aftermath of the vote of the German and other Western European parties. With the other Bolshevik fraction members out of town during the Duma's summer recess, it fell to Badayev to answer the deluge of questions from reporters working for St. Petersburg's bourgeois and monarchist press. "But what I said was altogether unsuitable for publication in their newspapers. I declared":

> The working class will oppose the war with all its force. The war is against the interests of workers. On the contrary, its edge is turned against the working class all over the world. The Basle Congress . . . in the name of the world proletariat, passed a resolution declaring that, in case of the

declaration of war, our duty was to wage a determined struggle against it. We, the real representatives of the working class, will fight for the slogan "War against War." Every member of our fraction will fight against the war with all the means at his disposal.[5]

If the prowar press ignored Badayev's message, the regime's police certainly did not. The two last sentences meant that from then on he and his other comrades would be under even closer surveillance.

In preparation for the reconvening of the Duma to vote on funding for the war, the Bolshevik, Menshevik-liquidator, and Trudovik deputies held discussions to see if they could come up with a joint declaration. After a number of meetings a statement was agreed on by only the Bolsheviks and Mensheviks. Though read at the session on July 26, Badayev reports that the Octobrist Duma president "censored it before it was printed in the stenographic report."[6] Regarding its contents, "Although our declaration did not contain a clear and precise characterization of the war or of the position of the working class and did not give a well-defined revolutionary lead, yet, when set off against the jingo background, it sounded a clear call of protest against the war madness." Badayev suggests that a joint statement with the Mensheviks required a watering down of the Bolsheviks' antiwar stance due in part to the patriotic fervor of the moment.[7] Nevertheless, the declaration and what the social democrats then did stood in sharp contrast to the rest of the Duma deliberations: "After its patriotic orgy, the State Duma proceeded to vote for the war budget. In accordance with decisions taken at all congresses of the International, our fraction refused to take part in the voting and left the hall. Our declaration and our refusal to vote war credits raised a storm of protest from the Duma majority. Deputies from all other parties, including the left Cadets and Progressives, lost their temper and attacked us in the lobbies." The walk out of all social democrats (Trudoviks as well according to other reports) was an instant cause célèbre and "soon became widely known among the workers." It initiated the Bolshevik's antiwar work, "which, under war conditions, rendered every member who was caught liable to trial by court-martial and almost certain death." Their Duma group would have to lead this campaign, because in the wake of the wholesale crackdown by the regime on the underground when the war began, it was the only Bolshevik unit that had some room to maneuver.

In consultation with what was left of the Central Committee based now in Finland, the Bolshevik fraction issued a number of antiwar proclamations: "[One] dealt with the necessity of conducting propaganda among the troops, with preparing for an armed struggle, and with the approaching revolution. Thus, the slogan of 'War against war' was evolving into a practical program of utilizing the war for the revolutionary struggle." The collaboration between the Bolshevik centers in St. Petersburg and Finland entailed a new and increasingly dangerous game of cat and mouse in court-martial-ruled Russia. The police assumed, rightly, that for the Bolsheviks to be able to produce and distribute their antiwar propaganda meant that the Duma deputies had to be intimately involved and that Badayev was probably the chief culprit. As one of their reports explained, "[T]hough 'the St. Petersburg Committee has ceased its activity . . . the restless youthful members of the illegal organizations are not content with their enforced inactivity and, under the influence of the Social-Democratic deputy, Badayev, have begun to issue a series of leaflets dealing with current events with the set purpose of discrediting the government's conduct of the war . . . All measures will be taken to obtain from persons arrested confessions which will prove that the deputy Badayev is engaged in revolutionary propaganda.'"[8] Again, the parliamentary immunity the deputies enjoyed—increasingly tenuous—allowed them to travel widely to do antiwar work and in the process rebuild the shattered party.

In contrast to the Bolsheviks, Western European social democrats embraced the war in the name of defending the homeland. The head of the Socialist International, Emile Vandervelde—the same individual who had only a month earlier at the Paris meeting directed the Bolsheviks to dissolve their faction, now a newly minted and proud cabinet member in Belgium's prowar government—sent a letter to the two Russian Duma fractions urging them to support the war and in effect end their antiwar stance. Not surprisingly, his appeal had no credibility with the Bolshevik deputies. It was a different story for the six Mensheviks. In his letter, Vandervelde asked the Russians to "share the common standpoint of socialist democracy in Europe." His appeal gave political cover to those Mensheviks who were looking for an opportunity to reject the position they took on July 26. After a heated debate they all did just that.[9] The five Bolsheviks were now the sole antiwar Duma fraction.

While social democratic deputies were making their stance in the Duma on July 26, Lenin, who was living in Austrian-controlled Poland—now a belligerent of Russia—was arrested and imprisoned for two weeks. Only after he and Krupskaya relocated in Switzerland was he able to reconnect with the fraction after an almost two-month hiatus. In the meantime, as well as drafting positions the Bolsheviks should take on the war, he gave public talks. In one instance a newspaper reported on his intervention at a talk that Plekhanov gave on the war in Lausanne: "Comrade Lenin . . . analyzed the duty of socialists in wartime. *Social-Democrats did their duty only when they fought chauvinist passions at home.* And the

Serbian Social-Democrats offered the best example of such fulfilment of duty." The Serbian social democrats were the first to have opposed the war and voted against war credits.

That the Serbians offered "the best example" of a response is significant. The joint statement Badayev and the other four Bolshevik deputies entered into with the Mensheviks on July 26 came with a political price that Lenin no doubt disagreed with, especially the provision that was greeted with broad applause when read in the nearly unanimous prowar Duma: "The proletariat, which is the constant defender of the freedom and interests of the people, will at all times defend the cultural wealth of the nation against any attack from whatever quarter."[10] For Lenin, this smacked of Western European social democracy's "defending the homeland" excuse for supporting the war. Thus his proposal on October 17 to the Central Committee member, based in Stockholm, who was in direct contact with the fraction: "[O]ur group should make a statement independent of the bloc, and should set forth a *consistent* point of view."[11] The declaration of "the bloc," as Badayev later admitted, "did not contain a clear and precise characterization of the war or of the position of the working class and did not give a well-defined revolutionary lead." In contrast to the July 26 declaration, the Bolshevik deputies' rejection of Vandervelde's entreaties to get on board the war train, a response that was published in *Sotsial-Demokrat*, appears to have had input from Lenin.[12]

LENIN'S THESES ON THE WAR

About a month after the war began, Lenin formulated a set of theses, positions the Bolsheviks should take, and submitted them for discussion and debate. A major factor in the "betrayal of socialism" by the Western European social democratic parties was due to their "making a fetish of the necessary utilization of bourgeois parliamentarism and bourgeois legality, and forgetting that illegal forms of organization and agitation are imperative at times of crises."[13] Nothing in the remaining theses was really new, and they were consistent with what Badayev told the press in the now renamed Petrograd ("St. Petersburg" sounded too German for the regime's chauvinist campaign) except for the sentence in the sixth thesis: "From the viewpoint of the working class and the toiling masses of all the peoples of Russia, the defeat of the tsarist monarchy and its army, which oppress Poland, the Ukraine, and many other peoples of Russia, and foment hatred among the peoples so as to increase Great-Russian oppression of the other nationalities, and consolidate the reactionary and barbarous government of the tsar's monarchy, would be the lesser evil by far."[14] That the Bolsheviks should welcome a defeat of the Czar's armies was a position that many of Lenin's comrades, especially those in Russia, found difficult to embrace. It was not the easiest stance, "revolutionary defeatism," as it came to be known—in contrast to the "defensist" position of most social democrats—to take in the midst of the patriotic fervor sweeping the country in the early days of the war.[15] Both the regime and opponents like the Cadets seized on the sentence to try to discredit the Bolsheviks and isolate them politically.

A close reading of Lenin's controversial thesis suggests that it was informed by his understanding of the national question and proletarian internationalism—the dialectic between the two. It was consistent, he argued, with "the fundamental truth of socialism, long ago set forth in the *Communist Manifesto*, that the workingmen have no country." The working class of the oppressor nation had to bend over backward to prove its proletarian internationalism, especially in time of war. Lenin assumed that the oppressed nations in the Romanov's oft-called "prison house of nations" would have the least problem with "revolutionary defeatism." A victory for the monarchy would only strengthen its ability to suppress them. And winning the oppressed nations was crucial in the formation of a revolutionary majority. This interpretation of Lenin's position is given added credence by the way in which he formulated in the seventh thesis his now familiar three slogans for Russia's bourgeois democratic revolution: "a struggle against the tsarist monarchy and Great-Russian, Pan-Slavist chauvinism, and advocacy of a revolution in Russia, as well as of the liberation of and self-determination for nationalities oppressed by Russia, coupled with the immediate slogans of a democratic republic, the confiscation of the landed estates, and an eight-hour working day."

With the Central Committee in exile in agreement, Lenin then submitted his theses to the Bolshevik Duma deputies in order that they organize—since they were the only party unit in a position to do so—a more representative meeting to debate and discuss them in order that they become official party policy. The long-existent Bolshevik practice of making collective decisions even under the very arduous conditions of court-martial-ruled Russia made such a meeting possible. In their updated version, "The War and Russian Social-Democracy," he praised the fraction for its stance on July 26—his reservations about the joint statement with the Mensheviks notwithstanding:

> Our Party, the Russian Social-Democratic Labor Party, has made, and will continue to make great sacrifices in connection with the war. The whole of our working-class legal press has been suppressed. Most working-class associations have been disbanded, and a large number of our comrades

have been arrested and exiled. Yet our parliamentary representatives—the Russian Social-Democratic Labor group in the Duma—considered it their imperative socialist duty not to vote for the war credits, and even to walk out of the Duma, so as to express their protest the more energetically; they considered it their duty to brand the European governments' policy as imperialist. Though the tsar's government has increased its tyranny tenfold, the Social-Democratic workers of Russia are already publishing their first illegal manifestos against the war, thus doing their duty to democracy and to the International.[16]

After taking as many precautions as possible, the five Bolshevik deputies held a secret meeting on the outskirts of Petrograd in early November with seven party delegates from various locales—elected in meetings that the deputies helped organize—who had successfully eluded very tight police surveillance. Kamenev, who represented the Central Committee, joined them from Finland. The main agenda item, Lenin's theses, was taken up on the second day of the conference, and according to Badayev, "no objections were raised to the principles outlined, although certain formal amendments were suggested . . . But before the conference could complete its work, the police broke into the room and arrested everyone present."[17] "This is terrible," Lenin said upon hearing the news. "We must be ready for the very worst: falsification of documents, forgeries, planting of 'evidence,' false witnesses, trial behind closed doors, etc., etc. . . . At all events, the work of our Party has now become 100 times more difficult. And still we shall carry it on! *Pravda* has trained up thousands of class-conscious workers out of whom, in spite of all difficulties, a new collective of leaders—the Russian C.C. of the Party—will be formed . . . Times are difficult, but . . . we shall get through!"[18]

"A MODEL OF REVOLUTIONARY PARLIAMENTARISM": THE TRIAL OF THE BOLSHEVIK DEPUTIES

Lenin's fears about the fallout from the arrests of the deputies, Kamenev, and the others were warranted. The government's second public announcement about the arrest of the five Bolshevik deputies said they were attending a conference that "was engaged in discussing a resolution which stated that 'the least evil is the defeat of the tsarist autocracy and its army' and in which the slogan was advanced 'to carry on as widely as possible among the troops propaganda for a socialist revolution' and 'the organization of illegal cells in the army.'"[19] As well as Lenin's theses, the police confiscated other incriminating evidence, the most damaging being the records of Martei Muranov, the deputy who represented the workers in Kharkov province. They detailed how he used his Duma post to do illegal work. The regime now had the smoking gun it had been looking for to deprive the Bolsheviks of their parliamentary immunity and put them on trial for violating martial law. The Petrograd party committee issued a leaflet denouncing the arrests of the five deputies and called on workers to stage protest meetings and one-day strikes. Despite massive steps the government took to prevent that from happening, a few actions did take place. But it was clear the patriotic offensive had sapped the revolutionary energy in place only a few months earlier. As the leaflet put it, "The war and the state of martial law has enabled the government to carry out their attack on the workers' deputies, who were so valiantly defending the interests of the proletariat."

To the surprise of the five arrestees, they learned that they would not be tried by court martial, which would have meant the death penalty, but in an ordinary court. Nicholas, himself, made the decision. He did so, the fraction felt, because by the time the trial was to take place, early 1915, the patriotic wave was beginning to ebb as setbacks on the battlefields began to mount and the workers' movement was beginning to recover. "The government could no longer count on the news of the punishment of the workers' deputies being received with patriotic shouts of joy." At the same time, the Black Hundred progovernment press, as the trial date approached, sought to paint the Bolshevik deputies in the worst possible light from a chauvinist/patriotic perspective. A frequent complaint was their failure to follow the example of their Western European counterparts when the Great War began:

> These unworthy bearers of a high title . . . played into the hands of Germany so obviously that there can be no question of any innocent error on their part while acting in conformity with the pernicious teaching of Socialism. Socialists exist in other countries too, but everywhere, in England, France and Belgium, the moment the war was declared, they renounced their internal struggles and joined the national ranks against the formidable enemy, German militarism.
>
> Even German Socialists renounced their Utopias for the duration of the war and are behaving like their bourgeois friends. It is only to Russian workers that the honorable Duma Socialists give their advice to act on theories of non-resistance to evil, peace at any price, etc., and it is only Russian Socialists who attempt to stir up internal disorders in war time.

As the trial drew nearer, Bolshevik organizations, against enormous odds, issued leaflets and organized workplace meetings to counter the slander campaign. The leaflet on the eve of the trial declared, "Comrades!

It is the working class which is in the dock, represented by deputies who were elected by the workers and who have acted in complete agreement with the workers . . . Strike on February 10, arrange meetings and demonstrations, protest against the tsarist mockery of the working class." While the stranglehold the regime still held on Russia prevented any large-scale protests, millions of workers now knew about the Bolshevik deputies and their politics, particularly their antiwar stances, owing to the pro and counter campaigns.

The trial itself was, as Lenin predicted, orchestrated and offered no surprises. The chief prosecutor repeated, for example, the complaint that the Bolshevik deputies hadn't acted like their namesakes in Western Europe by having "'voted for war credits and proved to be friends of the government.'" The regime also "took steps to suppress any speeches and evidence which might be used for agitational purpose. The military censorship ruthlessly cut out whole passages from the reports of the trial."[20] However, in order to make its case, the government inadvertently exposed, as Lenin put it, "a model of . . . *revolutionary* Social Democracy making use of parliamentarism." Exhibit A was the testimony of Muranov, who, rather than disowning his notes that the police had seized, took the proverbial bull by the horns: "'Realizing that the people did not return me to the Duma just to warm my seat there, I travelled about the country to ascertain the mood of the working class.' He admitted that he had undertaken the functions of a secret agitator of our Party, that in the Urals he organized workers' committees at the Verkhneisetsky Works, and elsewhere."[21] The trial "'uncovered' only a fraction of the activities our comrades were conducting in this field." Other fraction members "travelled, for propaganda purposes, throughout almost the whole of Russia and . . . Muranov, Petrovsky, Badayev and others arranged numerous workers' meetings, at which anti-war resolutions were passed, and so on."

Lenin admitted that some fraction members, in an effort to escape the possibility of capital punishment, had not acquitted themselves as principled as had Muranov—"who at the trial behaved better than the rest"[22]—and that opponents were trying to use that fact to impugn the integrity of Bolshevik politics. They were trying to obscure the real issue at stake: how to make use of the parliamentary arena. As opposed to the

European (i.e. servile) "socialist" parliamentarism . . . there are different kinds of parliamentarism . . . Some utilize the parliamentary arena in order to win the favor of their governments, or, at best, to wash their hands of everything, like the Chkheidze [Menshevik] group. Others utilize parliamentarism in order to remain revolutionary to the end, to perform their duty as Socialists and internationalists even under the most difficult circumstances. The parliamentary activities of some bring them into min-isterial seats; the parliamentary activities of others bring them—to prison, to exile, to penal servitude. Some serve the bourgeoisie, others—the pro-letariat. Some are social-imperialists. Others are revolutionary Marxists.[23]

There was an even more significant dimension about the proceedings, Lenin argued: "Thanks to the trial, the words cited in the indictment: 'The guns should be directed, not against our brothers, the wage slaves of other countries, but against the reactionary and bourgeois governments and parties of all countries'—these words will spread—and have already done so—all over Russia as a call for proletarian internationalism, for the proletarian revolution. Thanks to the trial, the class slogan of the van-guard of the workers of Russia has reached the masses of the workers."[24] The trial and its coverage in the press did more to publicize the antiwar stance of the Bolsheviks than anything prior to then. A few months after-ward, Lenin, most prophetically, wrote, "We cannot tell whether a pow-erful revolutionary movement will develop immediately after this war, or during it, etc., but at all events, it is only work in this direction that deserves the name of socialist work. The slogan of a civil war is the one that summarizes and directs this work, and helps unite and consolidate those who wish to aid the revolutionary struggle of the proletariat against its own government and its own bourgeoisie."[25] Not surprisingly, the five Bolsheviks were found guilty and sentenced to hard labor in Siberia. But unlike that of their comrades in the Second Duma, their stay in the Czar's prisons would be of shorter duration—exactly because the Great War began to develop into a civil war.

Without a Duma fraction, Lenin sought out any remaining legal space. Just such an opportunity arose when the government agreed to allow workers in the war industries to elect in the fall of 1915 representatives to committees established by the capitalist owners. Precisely because this was a thinly veiled attempt to get workers on board the war train that was increasingly unpopular by pretending that they would have some say so in the actual management of the industries, it opened a debate among the opposition about whether to participate. This was not unlike the debates about the elections for the First and Second Dumas—to boycott or not. The monarchy, in fact, had just prorogued the Fourth Duma because of increasing criticism of its conduct of the war by the Octobrists and other parties. Given the growing revival of the revolutionary process, the regime needed to improve its public image.

Based on "advice from comrades in Russia," Lenin made the following proposal: "We are opposed to participation in the war industries commit-tees, which help prosecute the imperialist and reactionary war. We are in

favor of utilizing the election campaign; for instance, we are for participation in the first stage of the elections for the *sole* purpose of agitation
and organization." And to be clear about what was and was not being
proposed, he added, "There can be no talk of boycotting the Duma.
Participation in the second ballot is *essential*. While we have no Duma
deputies from our Party, we must utilize everything that happens in the
Duma so as to advance the aims of revolutionary Social-Democracy."[26]
Even Nicholas's suspension of the Fourth Duma could not dissuade Lenin
from utilizing it whenever it resumed.

True to their word, the Bolsheviks used the elections to the war industries committees to campaign against the war. After the first round of
the elections, their resolution that called for a boycott of the committees
and a revolutionary solution to the war garnered more delegate support
than that of the Menshevik-liquidators. Since they chose not to participate in the second round of the process—demanded by the bosses, who
didn't like the outcome of the first round—the Menshevik position to
participate in the committees prevailed. But the overall balance sheet fell
far short of what the bourgeoisie wanted: "As a result of Bolshevik propaganda, elections to the 'workers' groups' [for the committees] were held
in only 70 areas out of a total of 239, and workers representatives were
actually elected only in 36 areas."[27]

Along with the proposal to participate in the elections to the war
industries committees, Lenin addressed in "Several Theses" two related
issues that had been raised in the discussion inside Russia—both of which
would soon be at the center of his politics. One concerned the demand
for a constituent assembly:

> The slogan of a "constituent assembly" is wrong as an independent slogan,
> because the question now is: who will convene it? The liberals accepted
> that slogan in 1905 because it could have been interpreted as meaning
> that a "constituent assembly" would be convened by the tsar and would
> be in agreement with him. The most correct slogans are the "three pillars"
> (a democratic republic, confiscation of the landed estates and an eight-
> hour working day), with the addition (cf. No. 9) of a call for the workers'
> international solidarity in the struggle for socialism and the revolutionary
> overthrow of the belligerent governments, and against the war.

As had always been the case for Lenin, the demand for a constituent
assembly depended on the context—the objective tasks and pace of the
movement.

The other issue, the all-important question of 1917, was posed
because some Bolsheviks thought that the elections to the war industries

committees opened up the possibility for such a demand. Lenin demurred: "Soviets of Workers' Deputies and similar institutions must be regarded as organs of insurrection, of revolutionary rule. It is only in connection with the development of a mass political strike and with an insurrection, and in the measure of the latter's preparedness, development and success that such institutions can be of lasting value."[28]

A constituent assembly or soviet government? No debate would dominate the political discourse in 1917 (when insurrectionary conditions did unfold) and afterward as much as this question. Lenin's theses of 1915, informed by all that he had said before, anticipated the stances he would take in that debate.

Lenin's ninth thesis, the one he drew attention to, is also worth noting, because it made clear that his revolutionary defeatist stance was applicable not just to a Czarist government: "If the revolutionary chauvinists won in Russia, we would be opposed to a defense of *their* 'fatherland' in the present war. Our slogan is: against the chauvinists, even if they are revolutionary and republican *against* them, and for an alliance of the international proletariat *for* the socialist revolution." Even if the Romanov dynasty were overthrown, the Bolsheviks would continue to call for a defeat of Russia's armies if the new regime pursued an imperialist course without the titular leadership of Nicholas. They proved to be true to their word.

To appreciate what the Bolsheviks lost with the arrests of their five comrades, consider Lenin's anxious letter in October 1916 to his primary contact, based in Sweden, with the Russian movement, A. G. Shlyapnikov: "The most pressing question now is the weakness of contacts between us and leading workers in Russia!! No correspondence!! . . . We can't go on like that. We *cannot* organize either the publication of leaflets or transport, either agreement about manifestos or sending over their drafts, etc., etc., without *regular* secret correspondence. That is the key question! . . . Two-thirds of the contacts, as a minimum, in each city, should be with leading *workers*, i.e., they should *write* themselves, *themselves* master secret correspondence (artists are made, not born), should themselves each train up 1–2 'heirs' in case of arrest. This should not be entrusted to the intelligentsia alone. Certainly not. It can and must be done by the leading workers. Without this it is *impossible* to establish continuity and purpose in our work—and that is the main thing."[29] A year later, exactly, the situation would be far different—owing in large part to what the Duma fraction had been able to accomplish before being exiled to Siberia.

"REVOLUTIONARY PARLIAMENTARISM" FOR A NEW INTERNATIONAL

Lenin's aforementioned points about "different kinds of parliamentarism" came in a document, *Socialism and War*—Zinoviev was coauthor—for what would be the founding meeting of the Communist or Third International, the famous Zimmerwald Conference of 1915. For the minority of European social democrats who saw the vote for war credits by the majority of Second International parties as a betrayal of the historic Marxist program, only one conclusion could be drawn—a new international had to be constructed. The pressing agenda item for the 38 delegates from 11 European countries who gathered in the small Swiss town that September was how to respond, in contrast to most social democrats, to the war in a revolutionary way. In the process they addressed other programmatic issues, and for Lenin none was as important as clarity on the Marxist approach to doing electoral and parliamentary work. After all, he contended—already noted in his first pronouncement on the war—a major factor in the "betrayal of socialism" by Western European social democracy was due to their "making a fetish of the necessary utilization of bourgeois parliamentarism and bourgeois legality, and forgetting that illegal forms of organization and agitation are imperative at times of crises."

Shortly before writing *Socialism and War*, Lenin, in preparing for the Zimmerwald meeting, offered a more detailed examination of the "betrayal" in his *The Collapse of the Second International*. Legality at any price, he argued, exemplified by the German party, doomed most social democratic parties. Once the war began, the "initiation of revolutionary activities would obviously have led to the dissolution of these legal organizations by the police, and the old party—from Legien [the German party leader whose trip to the United States earned, as noted in Chapter 2, Lenin's ire] to Kautsky inclusively—sacrificed the revolutionary aims of the proletariat for the sake of preserving the present legal organizations. No matter how much this may be denied, it is a fact. The proletariat's right to revolution was sold for a mess of pottage—organizations permitted by the present police law." Employing the tactics of warfare as an analogy, Lenin proposed, beginning hypothetically, an alternative, revolutionary course for the electoral and parliamentary arenas:

> Today there is no revolutionary situation, the conditions that cause unrest among the masses or heighten their activities do not exist; today you are given a ballot paper—take it, learn to organize so as to use it as a weapon against your enemies, not as a means of getting cushy legislative jobs for men who cling to their parliamentary seats for fear of having to go to prison. Tomorrow your ballot paper is taken from you and you are given a rifle or a splendid and most up-to-date quick-firing gun—take this weapon

of death and destruction, pay no heed to the mawkish snivelers who are afraid of war; too much still remains in the world that *must* be destroyed with fire and sword for the emancipation of the working class; if anger and desperation grow among the masses, if a revolutionary situation arises, prepare to create new organizations and *use* these useful weapons of death and destruction *against* your *own* government and your *own* bourgeoisie . . . This form of the class struggle stands in the same relation to participation in elections as an assault against a fortress stands in relation to maneuvering, marches, or lying in the trenches. It *is not so often* that history places this form of struggle on the order of the day, but then its significance is felt for decades to come. *Days* on which *such* method of struggle can and must be employed are equal to *scores of years* of other historical epochs.

While Lenin's perspective about the necessity of illegal work was clearly informed by the Russian experience, he didn't limit it to such settings where political space was severely circumscribed: "Not only in wartime but positively in any acute political situation, to say nothing of periods of revolutionary mass action of any kind, the governments of even the *freest* bourgeois countries will threaten to dissolve the legal organizations, seize their funds, arrest their leaders, and threaten other 'practical consequences' of the same kind. What are we to do then? Justify the opportunists on these grounds, as Kautsky does? But this would mean sanctifying the transformation of the social democratic parties into national liberal-labour parties." The government of one of the "freest bourgeois countries" proved Lenin right three years later when it jailed Socialist Party of America leader Eugene V. Debs for his antiwar stance. Twenty six years later, followers of Lenin in Minneapolis, Minnesota, witnessed the "arrest of their leaders" because of their opposition to the Roosevelt administration's war drive—a half year before Pearl Harbor![30]

The war, Lenin contended, had demonstrated that "pure legalism, the legalism-and-nothing-but-legalism of the 'European' parties, is now obsolete and, as a result of the development of capitalism in the pre-imperialist stage, has become the foundation for a bourgeois labor policy. It must be augmented by the creation of an illegal basis, an illegal organization, illegal Social-Democratic work, without, however, surrendering a single legal position." And there was no better example, he argued, of how to combine the two than what the five Bolshevik deputies had done: "Muranov, the workers' deputy in the Duma, who at the trial behaved better than the rest and was exiled to Siberia, clearly demonstrated that—besides '*ministeriable*' parliamentarism . . . there can be *illegal and revolutionary* parliamentarism. Let the Kosovskys and Potresovs [Mensheviks] admire the 'European' parliamentarism of the lackeys or accept it—we shall not tire of telling the workers that such legalism, *such* Social-Democracy of the Legien, Kautsky . . . brand, deserves nothing but contempt."[31]

For the follow-up meeting to the Zimmerwald conference, eight months later in 1916, Lenin submitted, in the name of the Central Committee of the Russian Social Democratic Labor Party, eight proposals for discussion. Most relevant is, first, an excerpt from the third: "Socialists do not refuse to fight for reform. Even now, for example, they must vote in parliament for improvements, however slight, in the condition of the masses, for increased relief to the inhabitants of the devastated areas, for the lessening of national oppression, etc. But it is sheer bourgeois *deception* to preach reforms as a solution for problems for which history and the actual political situation demand revolutionary solutions." Again, there's nothing here that Lenin had not already stated in one form or another for at least two decades. Its significance is that it was put forward as part of a campaign to win other forces, this time outside of Russia, to it and the other proposals as part of building a new international movement.

That was also the case with the seventh proposal, which in many ways was a reiteration of what he raised at the earlier meeting but with added political content:

> On the question of socialist parliamentary action, it must be born in mind that the Zimmerwald resolution not only expresses sympathy for the five Social-Democratic deputies in the State Duma, who belong to our Party, and who have been *sentenced* to exile to Siberia, but also expresses its solidarity with their tactics. It is impossible to recognize the revolutionary struggle of the masses while resting content with exclusively legal socialist activity in parliament. This can only arouse legitimate dissatisfaction among the workers, cause them to desert Social-Democracy for anti-parliamentary anarchism or syndicalism. It must be stated clearly and publicly that Social-Democratic members of parliament must use their *position* not only to make speeches in parliament, but also to render all possible aid outside parliament to the underground organization and the revolutionary struggle of the workers, and that *the* masses themselves, through their illegal organization, must supervise these activities of their leaders.[32]

Lenin's point, made not for the first time, that social democratic opportunism in the electoral arena and the reformism it bred—again, for Lenin fighting for reforms was not to be confused with reformism—gave "anti-parliamentary anarchism or syndicalism" a hearing has as much currency today as it did then. Witness the various global examples of the recent "occupation" movement in which anarcho-syndicalists were influential if not always hegemonic. Exactly because of the "betrayal" of modern-day social democracy could they appear as a credible working-class alternative.

Finally, there are Lenin's (seldom appreciated) pronouncements based on his direct involvement in working-class politics in one of, as he put it, "the *freest* bourgeois" countries in the world—Switzerland. Forced exile, for two and a half years, allowed him to generalize his electoral/parliamentary political strategy and tactics beyond absolutist Russia.[33] His "Tasks of the Left Zimmerwaldists in the Swiss Social-Democratic Party," written in October–November 1916, is most instructive. As the title suggests, Lenin was a leader of the most revolutionary current within the party and sought to win the majority to its course with the document. Among the many proposals that addressed not only the war but domestic matters as well were those under the heading, "Pressing Democratic Reforms and Utilization of the Political Struggle and Parliamentarism":

16. Utilization of the Parliamentary tribune and the right of initiative and referendum, not in a reformist manner, in order to advocate reforms "acceptable" to the bourgeoisie, and therefore powerless to remove the principal and fundamental evils suffered by the masses . . .

17. Abolition of *all* restrictions without exception on the political rights of women compared with those of men . . .

18. Compulsory naturalization . . . of all foreigners, free of charge . . . The disfranchisement and alienation of foreign workers serve to increase political reaction, which is already mounting, and weaken international proletarian solidarity . . .

19. Immediate propaganda for Social Democratic candidates in the 1917 Nationalrat [National Council] elections to be nominated only on the basis of a political platform that has been previously widely discussed by the electors.[34]

Further on in the document he specified what he meant by utilizing the parliamentary space in a nonreformist manner. Regarding the proposal for political equality for women, whether it was Lenin who first raised this demand in the Swiss party is uncertain, but it was not until 1971 that women gained the right to vote in Switzerland. In Russia, on the other hand, suffrage for women was one of the first acts of the new Bolshevik-led government. Last, he included a proposal on greater accountability and democratic functioning in the Swiss party.

In hindsight, all these documents, especially the platform for the Swiss party, constitute Lenin's initial drafting of what would eventually become the norms of communist electoral and parliamentary work wherever branches of the new international existed.

FROM FEBRUARY TO OCTOBER

Though Lenin declared, in a public lecture in Switzerland on January 9, 1917 (the twelfth anniversary of the beginning of the 1905 revolution), that "Europe is pregnant with revolution," he did not realize how soon the baby would arrive.[35] Long before, however, he correctly anticipated the way it would: "[I]t is quite possible, and historically much more probable," he wrote in 1901, "that the autocracy will collapse under the impact of one of the spontaneous outbursts or unforeseen political complications which constantly threaten it from all sides. But no political party that wishes to avoid adventurous gambles can base its activities on the anticipation of such outbursts and complications. We must go our own way, and we must steadfastly carry on our regular work, and the less our reliance on the unexpected, the less the chance of our being caught unawares by any 'historic turns.'" The fact is that he was "caught unawares" when the February Revolution began, but precisely because of having gone their "own way" and done "regular work" could he and the Bolsheviks quickly rebound, get their revolutionary feet, and eventually be victorious. The focus here cannot for obvious reasons be the richness of the transition from the February to the October Revolution but how, in a distilled presentation, the decadelong Duma experience informed Lenin's strategy and tactics for the Bolshevik ascent to power.

"Soviets of Workers' Deputies Must Be Organized"

With the abdication of Nicholas II on March 2, a provisional government composed of various opposition forces in the Fourth Duma was instituted. Lenin, who was still in exile, reacted critically to one of its first proclamations:

> In its manifesto, the new government promises every kind of freedom, but has failed in its direct and unconditional duty immediately to implement such freedoms as election of officers, etc., by the soldiers, elections to the St. Petersburg, Moscow and other City Councils on a basis of genuinely universal, and not merely male, suffrage, make all government and public buildings available for public meetings, appoint elections to all local institutions and Zemstvos, likewise on the basis of genuinely universal suffrage, repeal all restrictions on the rights of local government bodies, dismiss all officials appointed to supervise local government bodies, introduce not only freedom of religion, but also freedom from religion, immediately separate the school from the church and free it of control by government officials, etc. . . . Soviets of Workers' Deputies must be organized, the workers must be armed. Proletarian organizations must be extended to the army

(which the new government has likewise promised political rights) and to the rural areas. In particular there must be a separate class organization for farm laborers.[36]

Lenin's proposals were consistent with the historical program of the RSDLP and all that he'd been advocating about the electoral process and representative democracy for at least a decade. With necessary adjustments, they came to constitute the core of what he would struggle for in the next eight months.

Shortly afterward, Lenin addressed another issue that figured significantly in Russia's political debates for the next ten months. To one of the first group of Bolsheviks returning to Russia after the February Revolution, he responded to a request about the tactics they should pursue: "[N]o trust in and no support of the new government; Kerensky is especially suspect; arming of the proletariat is the only guarantee; immediate elections to the Petrograd City Council; no rapprochement with other parties." Because press reports contributed some confusion about his telegrammed advice, he clarified with a letter. First, what he sent was written "in the name of the Central Committee members *living abroad*, not in the name of the Central Committee itself." Second, and more important, "[r]eference is not to the Constituent Assembly, but to elections to *municipal* bodies. Elections to the Constituent Assembly are, so far, merely an empty promise. Elections to the Petrograd City Council could and should be held *immediately*, if the government is really capable of introducing its promised freedoms. These elections could help the proletariat organize and strengthen its revolutionary positions."[37] If Lenin had reservations about the constituent assembly—which he voiced, as already noted, in 1915—he harbored no qualms about plunging back into the electoral arena. For him it was mostly about picking up from where the Bolsheviks had left off before the arrest of their deputies in November 1914 and for the same reasons—to advance the revolution.

Prior to his return to Petrograd, Lenin penned his now famous "Letters from Afar," in which he outlined his vision for the next stage in Russia's revolution. Especially relevant were his comments on the Soviet of Workers' Deputies formed in Petrograd—a reflection, he said, of the lessons of 1905 and the Paris Commune. That it was "drawing in *soldiers'* deputies, and, undoubtedly deputies from rural *wage*-workers, and then (in one form or another) from the entire peasant poor" was most encouraging. The inclusion of the soldiers' deputies gave license to say that the Soviet comprised "*over 1,500* deputies of workers and peasants dressed in soldiers' uniform." "The prime and most important task, and one that brooks no delay, is to set up organizations of this kind in all parts of

Russia without exception, for all trades and strata of the proletarian and semi-proletarian population without exception . . . I shall mention that for the entire mass of the peasantry our Party . . . should especially recommend Soviets of wage-workers and Soviets of small tillers who do not sell grain, to be formed *separately* from the well-to-do peasants." Just as Lenin strove to use the Dumas to construct the worker-peasant alliance, he was now advocating that the soviets be the vehicle for doing that—a far more democratic representative body, akin to the Paris Commune.

Of crucial importance for the effectiveness of the soviets, he emphasized, was the organization of a "genuine *people's* militia, i.e., one that, first, consists of the *entire* population, of all adult citizens of *both* sexes; and, second, one that combines the functions of a people's army with police functions, with the functions of the chief and fundamental organ of public order and public administration." He underscored the necessity of including women in the militias: "If women are not drawn into public service, into the militia, into political life, if women are not torn out of their stupefying house and kitchen environment, it will be *impossible* to guarantee real freedom, it will be *impossible* to build even democracy let alone socialism." Organizing the soviets and their militias on this basis pointed the way forward to the replacement of the old state apparatus with a new one needed for the "transition from that first stage of the revolution to the second."[38] Again, the lessons of the Commune figured significantly in his vision, and thus, as he explained elsewhere, the soviets were "the harbinger of the 'withering away' of the state *in every form*."[39]

"NOT A PARLIAMENTARY REPUBLIC"

Lenin's task, once he returned to Russia, was to win the rest of the Bolshevik leadership to his perspective. Except for Kollantai, most of them, as once before, displayed conciliationist tendencies, this time toward the provisional government. Within hours of his arrival in Petrograd on April 3, he delivered what has come to be called his "April Theses" and had them published in the now resurrected *Pravda*. After addressing in the first of the ten theses the war question, he turned to, in the next four, the "basic question of every revolution," as he later put it: "state power."

> 2) The specific feature of the present situation in Russia is that the country is *passing* from the first stage of the revolution—which, owing to the insufficient class-consciousness and organization of the proletariat, placed power in the hands of the bourgeoisie—to its *second stage*, which must place power in the hands of the proletariat and the poorest sections of the peasants.
>
> 3) No support for the Provisional Government . . .

4) Recognition of the fact that in most of the Soviets of Workers' Deputies our Party is in a minority . . . As long as we are in the minority we carry on the work of criticizing and exposing errors and at the same time we preach the necessity of transferring the entire state power to the Soviets of Workers' Deputies, so that the people may overcome their mistakes by experience.

5) Not a parliamentary republic—to return to a parliamentary republic from the Soviets of Workers' Deputies would be a retrograde step—but a republic of Soviets of Workers', Agricultural Laborers' and Peasants' Deputies throughout the country, from top to bottom.

As for the future, "It is not our *immediate* task to 'introduce' socialism, but only to bring social production and the distribution of products at once under the *control* of the Soviets of Workers' Deputies." Last, "I argued that *without* the Soviets of Workers' and Soldiers' Deputies the convocation of the Constituent Assembly is not guaranteed and its success is impossible."[40]

Lenin's objection to "a parliamentary republic" did not in the least signify a retreat from his long-standing advocacy for representative democracy. To the contrary, he reaffirmed that stance by arguing that soviets, an increasing reality as a result of the February events, were a superior form of such democracy because of the way in which they were created and their modus operandi. His other well-known article of that period, "The Dual Power," distilled what he considered to be their model:

This power is of *the same type* as the Paris Commune[41] of 1871. The fundamental characteristics of this type are: (1) the source of power is not a law previously discussed and enacted by parliament, but the direct initiative of the people from below, in their local areas—direct "seizure," to use a current expression; (2) the replacement of the police and the army, which are institutions divorced from the people and set against the people, by the direct arming of the whole people; order in the state under such a power is maintained by the armed workers and peasants *themselves*, by the armed people *themselves*; (3) officialdom, the bureaucracy, are either similarly replaced by the direct rule of the people themselves or at least placed under special control; they not only become elected officials, but are also *subject to recall* at the people's first demand; they are reduced to the position of simple agents; from a privileged group holding "*jobs*" remunerated on a high, bourgeois scale, they become workers of a special "arm of the service," whose remuneration *does not exceed* the ordinary pay of a competent worker.[42]

No better concise description of the Commune exists in the annals of Marxism—the product of two decades of research, writing, and lecturing

on the topic. In the subsequent debate with Kamenev and other Bolsheviks in defense of his theses, Lenin was even clearer: "The parliamentary
bourgeois republic hampers and stifles the independent political life of
the masses, their direct participation in the democratic organization of
the life of the state from the bottom up. The opposite is the case with
the Soviets."[43] The oft-made claim, then, that Lenin lacked a democratic
vision—and thus the Stalinist outcome of the Bolshevik revolution—is
groundless.

In calling for the transference of power from the provisional government to the soviets, Lenin, Kamenev charged, was abandoning the more
than decade-long Bolshevik demand for the revolutionary democratic
dictatorship of the proletariat and peasantry—its virtue being a strategy
for winning the majority to Russia's bourgeois democratic revolution.
Lenin disagreed and pedagogically explained why: "The revolutionary-
democratic dictatorship of the proletariat and the peasantry has already
been realized, but in a highly original manner, and with a number of
extremely important modifications." It had been realized, Lenin contended, in the form of the soviets. But rather than take power, they,
specifically the soviet in Petrograd, ceded it to the bourgeois provisional
government. The tasks for "communists"—the label Lenin increasingly
employed in place of the now soiled "social democracy"—was to convince the soviets to take power for themselves. "As long as we are in the
minority," as the fourth thesis put it, "'patient' explaining" was necessary
to win "the majority of the deputies in all (or in most) Soviets" to the
view that the provisional government did not serve the interest of Russia's
producers.[44]

The Central Committee made clear in a resolution adopted on April 22
that the Bolsheviks were not demanding immediate transference of power
to the soviets despite such calls at a protest two days earlier against the
provisional government:

> The slogan "Down with the Provisional Government!" is an incorrect one
> at the present moment because, in the absence of a solid (i.e., a class-
> conscious and organized) majority of the people on the side of the revolu-
> tionary proletariat, such a slogan is either an empty phrase, or, objectively,
> amounts to attempts of an adventurist character.
>   We shall favor the transfer of power to the proletarians and semi-
> proletarians only when the Soviets of Workers' and Soldiers' Deputies
> adopt our policy and are willing to take the power into their own hands.[45]

Again, "patient explanation" to win the majority of the soviets to transference was the immediate task—exactly the tactic Lenin advised for the

RSDLP fractions in the four Dumas from 1906 to 1914 to convince the Trudovik peasant deputies to break with the Cadet liberals in order to forge the worker-peasant alliance. That experience—unappreciated until now—plus the force of argument, the betrayals of the provisional government, and the greater democratic space that existed after February ensured that Lenin's strategy would prove successful this time.

Soviet rule didn't mean opposition to republican government. But it meant something quite different from a "'parliamentary' republic":

> The people need a republic in order to educate the masses in the methods of democracy. We need *not only* representation along democratic lines, but the building of the entire state administration from the bottom up by the masses themselves, their effective participation in all of life's steps, their active role in the administration. *Replacement* of the old organs of oppression, the police, the bureaucracy, the standing army, by a universal arming of the people, by a really universal militia, is the only way to guarantee the country a maximum of security against the restoration of the monarchy and to *enable* it to go forward firmly, systematically and resolutely towards socialism, not by "introducing" it from above, but by raising the vast mass of proletarians and semi-proletarians to the art of state administration, to the use of the *whole* state power.[46]

A month after Lenin's return, Trotsky arrived in Petrograd, also from a more than decadelong exile. "I arranged with Comrade Kamenev"—his brother-in-law, by the way—"for a visit to the editorial office of *Pravda* on one of the first days after my arrival. The first meeting must have taken place on the 5th or 6th of May. I told Lenin that nothing separated me from his April theses and from the whole course that the party had taken since his arrival."[47] Three weeks later Lenin referred to him as "Comrade Trotsky."[48] The two had been bitter opponents since 1903 when Trotsky accused Lenin of being a Jacobinist—the debut of that timeworn charge—or, more condescendingly, "a *caricature* of Robespierre."[49] Three months before their meeting Lenin called him a "swine" for not aligning with the Left Zimmerwaldists.[50] It speaks volumes about the two of them and their politics that all that was now water under the bridge—arguably the most consequential reconciliation in the annals of politics.[51] From either "the 5th or 6th of May" 1917, both, until the ends of their lives, saw themselves as comrades in struggle.

"ALL POWER TO THE SOVIETS"

To bring the entire Bolshevik party on board to Lenin's theses required a delegated party meeting. The weeklong Seventh All-Russia Conference in April was the first legal Bolshevik gathering in Russia, with 133 voting delegates representing 80,000 members and 18 with voice—the most representative to date. The "freest of all the belligerent countries in the world," as Lenin called post-February Russia, made that possible. Also attending the conference were the five Fourth Duma deputies and the surviving ones from the Second Duma, freed from Nicholas's Siberian prisons.

The conference discussion around the soviets is of special relevance. Lenin ended the opening report on the current situation with the "what is to be done" question: "The Soviets must take power not for the purpose of building an ordinary bourgeois republic, nor for the purpose of making a direct transition to socialism. This cannot be. What, then, is the purpose? The Soviets must take power in order to make the first concrete steps towards this transition, steps that can and should be made . . . We cannot be for 'introducing' socialism—this would be the height of absurdity. We must preach socialism. The majority of the population in Russia are peasants, small farmers who can have no idea of socialism."[52] Despite what was achieved in February, Lenin was as sober as he had always been about what was and was not on the political agenda in Russia.

In the resolution on the soviets themselves, Lenin could be more specific:

This growth of the revolution in the provinces in depth and scope is, on the one hand, the growth of a movement for transferring all power to the Soviets and putting the workers and peasants themselves in control of production. On the other hand, it serves as a guarantee for the build-up of forces, on a national scale, for the second stage of the revolution, which must transfer all state power to the Soviets or to other organs directly expressing the will of the majority of the nation (organs of local self-government, the Constituent Assembly, etc.) . . .

It is, therefore, the task of the proletarian party, on the one hand, to support in every possible way the indicated development of the revolution locally, and, on the other to conduct a systematic struggle within the Soviets (by means of propaganda and new elections) for the triumph of the proletarian line.

The Conference repeats that it is necessary to carry out many-sided activity within the Soviets of Workers' and Soldiers' Deputies, to increase the number of Soviets, to consolidate their power, and to weld together our Party's proletarian internationalist groups within the Soviets.[53]

The resolution on the current situation, after five days of discussion and debate, composed by Lenin, concluded that the soviets could carry out practical work to deal with the real needs of the masses, "only when an overwhelming majority of the people has clearly and firmly realized the practical need for them; on the other hand their character guarantees that the reforms will not be sponsored by the police and officials, but will be carried out by way of voluntary participation of the organized and armed masses of the proletariat and peasantry in the management of their own affairs . . . Great care and discretion should be exercised in carrying out the above measures; a solid majority of the population must be won over and this majority must be clearly convinced of the country's practical preparedness for any particular measure."[54] For Lenin, again for the umpteenth time, "only when an overwhelming majority of the people" came on board could the revolutionary project go forward, this time via the soviets. In the May 15 issue of *Pravda*, Lenin raised publicly for the first time the slogan, *"All power to the Soviets of Workers' and Soldiers' Deputies! No confidence in the government of the capitalist!"*[55] The context makes clear that he did so for purposes of propaganda and not agitation—that is, to persuade rather than, at this time, to incite.

To underscore that the peasantry was still crucial in his equation for winning the majority to soviet governance, ten days later Lenin addressed a letter to the First All-Russia Congress of Peasants' Deputies representing their recently created soviets throughout the country. While it was indisputable that "Russia must become a democratic republic," the Bolshevik party, "the party of class-conscious workers and poor peasants, is . . . working for a democratic republic of another kind"—different from what the "majority of landowners and capitalists" wanted:

> We want a republic where there is no police that browbeats the people; where all officials, from the bottom up, are elective and displaceable whenever the people demand it, and are paid salaries not higher than the wages of a competent worker; where all army officers are similarly elective and where the standing army separated from the people and subordinated to classes alien to the people is replaced by the universally armed people, by a people's militia.
>
> We want a republic where all state power, from the bottom up, belongs wholly and exclusively to the Soviets of Workers', Soldiers', Peasants', and other Deputies.
>
> The workers and peasants are the majority of the population. The power must belong to them, not to the landowners or the capitalists.
>
> The workers and peasants are the majority of the population. The power and the functions of administration must belong to *their Soviets*, not to the bureaucracy.[56]

A week later at the First All-Russia Congress of Soviets of Workers' and Soldiers' Deputies, attended by more than a thousand delegates of whom the Bolsheviks and their allies comprised about 20 percent, Lenin reiterated his case for the need to transfer power to the soviets, despite the fact that there were now "near-socialist Ministers" such as Alexander Kerensky, a Socialist Revolutionary, in the provisional government. But this time he made what would be his constant refrain until October on why it was so necessary to do so. Only if the soviets took power, he implored the delegates, would the most pressing question confronting not just the producing classes in Russia but those elsewhere affected by the Guns of August be resolved—the war. As long as the soviets, the real power in Russia, conceded to the government of capitalists and landlords, the beneficiaries of the conflagration, the slaughter would continue. "Peace without annexations and indemnities"—that was the Bolshevik solution and what a government dominated by capitalists and landlords could never deliver. Because the latter had "a majority in the government the war will remain an imperialist war no matter what you write, no matter how eloquent you are, no matter how many near-socialist Ministers you have." But unlike anywhere else in the world, Russia, owing to the events of February, produced an institution, the soviets, that had the ability to implement a real working-class peace policy: "The Soviets are an institution which does not exist in any ordinary bourgeois-parliamentary state and cannot exist side by side with a bourgeois government. They are the new, more democratic type of state which we in our Party resolutions call a peasant-proletarian democratic republic."

> Only one country in the world can at the moment take steps to stop the imperialist war on a class scale, in the face of the capitalists and without a bloody revolution. Only one country can do it, and that country is Russia. And she will remain the only one as long as the Soviet of Workers' and Soldiers' Deputies exists . . . If you were to take power into your hands, if power were to pass to the revolutionary organizations to be used for combating the Russian capitalists, then the working people of some countries would believe you and you could propose peace.[57]

When a provisional government minister declared at the congress that the soviets couldn't take power because there was no party in them that was prepared to rule, Lenin famously replied—to both applause and laughter—"Yes, there is. No party can refuse this, and our Party certainly doesn't. It is ready to take over full power at any moment."

In a demonstration on June 18 that the Menshevik-Socialist Revolutionary leadership of the Petrograd soviet called to rally support for itself, "most of the 400,000 marchers who came out did so under" the Bolshevik banner of "All Power to the Soviets," much to the embarrassment of the former.[58] Three weeks later on July 4, a half million did the same in an action the Bolsheviks called to protest the provisional government's latest and unsuccessful battlefield offensive. In defending the demonstration and slogan, Lenin summarized what had transpired since the toppling of the Romanov dynasty:

> During the several months that have passed since February 27 the will of the majority of the workers and peasants, of the overwhelming majority of the country's population, has become clear in more than a general sense. Their will has found expression in mass organizations—the Soviets of Workers', Soldiers' and Peasants' Deputies.
>
> How, then, can anyone oppose the transfer of all power in the state to the Soviets? Such opposition means nothing but renouncing democracy! It means no more no less than imposing on the people a government which *admittedly* can neither come into being nor hold its ground *democratically*, i.e., as a result of truly free, truly popular elections.[59]

Lenin defended the slogan "All Power to the Soviets!" through to and after October, except for a moment beginning in mid-July. The context was the "July Days" when in response to the July 4 actions the provisional government went on a counterrevolutionary offensive.[60] Not only was *Pravda* shut down, but Bolshevik leaders like Trotsky were arrested while others like Lenin had to go into hiding. The authorities were aided and abetted in this by the Socialist Revolutionary-Menshevik leadership of the soviets. On the run, Lenin wrote, "The slogan 'All Power to the Soviets!' was a slogan for peaceful development of the revolution which was possible in April, May, June, and up to July 5–9, i.e., up to the time when actual power passed into the hands of the military dictatorship. This slogan is no longer correct, for it does not take into account that power has changed hands and that the revolution has in fact been completely betrayed by the S.R.s and Mensheviks."[61] As long as the soviets advanced the democratic process—that is, the revolution—they were to be supported. But once they had become an obstacle, that support, he now argued, should be denied—the same reasoning that informed his opposition to the Bulygin Duma in the Revolution of 1905. Also, Lenin never made an organizational fetish about soviets—one of his earlier differences with Trotsky.[62] Their appropriateness depended on the context of the class struggle. After debate and discussion, an overwhelming majority of the delegates to the party's semiclandestine Sixth Congress at the end of July, which Lenin didn't attend because he was in hiding, agreed with his argument.

By the beginning of September, however, when the revolution was on the offensive again, the Bolsheviks reembraced the slogan. Lenin made a "compromise" proposal to the Menshevik and Socialist Revolutionary leadership: "The compromise on our part is our return to the pre-July demand of all power to the Soviets and a government of S.R.s and Mensheviks responsible to the Soviets." The Bolsheviks "would refrain from demanding the immediate transfer of power to the proletariat and the poor peasants and from employing revolutionary methods of fighting for this demand." In exchange they would have "complete freedom of propaganda and the convocation of the Constituent Assembly without further delays or even at an earlier date." Freedom to conduct propaganda, which also meant the unbanning of *Pravda*, went hand in hand with, parenthetically, "new elections" for the soviets: "The Bolsheviks would gain the opportunity of quite freely advocating their views and of trying to win influence in the Soviets under a really complete democracy . . . Under a Soviet government, such freedom would be *possible* . . . *We* have nothing to fear from real democracy, for reality is on our side, and even the course of development of trends within the S.R. and Menshevik parties, which are hostile to us, proves us right."[63] Lenin's calculus proved accurate. The "new elections" to the soviets confirmed his prediction. As Trotsky put it about the new situation, seven weeks before the October Revolution, "the cry raised at the very beginning of the revolution by our party—'All Power to the Soviets!'—has become the voice of the whole revolutionary country."[64]

ELECTIONS AND ELECTORAL NORMS

Except for a one-page party resolution, there are no sustained discussions in Lenin's published corpus between February and October on elections, the tactics and strategy of campaigning, and related matters similar to what he produced in the run ups to the four Dumas.[65] What does exist, however, makes certain that all he had done in the electoral arena before was as valid for him, if not more, in the heady days of 1917. New this time in post-February Russia, with implications for his electoral strategy, was ample political space.

The Fourth or State Duma was reconvened after the dethronement of Nicholas, but the fact that it figures only in passing in Lenin's narrative testifies to its importance or lack thereof after February. His position had always been, going back to 1905, that soviets should be prioritized because they offered the greater possibility for genuine democratic governance—exactly what opened up with February. The aforementioned "truly free, truly popular elections" were indeed those to the soviets.

The election campaigns for the four State Dumas were always for Lenin an invaluable opportunity to educate workers on the differences between political parties—an experience that served him well for 1917. If there was one thing that characterized post-Nicholas Russia, it was the ubiquity of elections—this time not only to soviets but to local dumas as well. Immediately upon his return to Petrograd, he composed a piece of literature for mass distribution that resembled the leaflet he produced for the elections to the Second Duma in 1906 in which he laid out in three columns the differences between the Black Hundreds, the Cadets, and the social democrats (see Appendix C in the first volume, *LES1905*). The new piece appeared as articles intended for a leaflet but became a pamphlet for the July 4 demonstration. It retained the question/answer format but this time with answers for four categories of parties: "Parties and groups to the right of the Constitutional Democrats," the "Constitutional Democrats and kindred groups," the "Social-Democrats, the Socialist Revolutionaries and kindred groups," and, last, "Bolsheviks, the party which properly should be called the *Communist Party*."

Of significance here are the Bolshevik answers to three questions. As for what form of government they wanted, "A republic of Soviets of Workers', Soldiers', Peasants', and other Deputies. Abolition of the standing army and the police, who are to be replaced by the arming of the whole people; officials to be not only elective, but also displaceable; their pay not to exceed that of a competent worker." If the elective principle applied to government officials, shouldn't soldiers be able to elect their officers? "Not only must they be elected, but every step of every officer and general must be supervised by persons specially elected for the purpose by the soldiers." And if civilians could displace government officials, shouldn't soldiers enjoy the same right? "It is desirable and essential in every way. The soldiers will obey and *respect* only elected authorities."[66] Whether Lenin's pamphlet impacted soldiers is uncertain. It may have helped to generalize practices that were already in place as mounting losses on the battlefield sparked increasing rank-and-file resistance to the commands of officers. What is known is that Bolshevik success in October was due in large part to the support they enjoyed among soldiers and sailors, and the promise of democracy and the elective principle—what no other party put in writing—no doubt made them attractive.

In many ways the pamphlet was a stand-in for a new party program. The old one, based on a unified Russian Social Democratic Labor Party and a pre-February 1917 political reality, needed revisions. Some months later, authorized by delegated party meetings, Lenin began to put together a draft. A number of innovations are of import. He expanded on the elective principle in his pamphlet by first making clear that soviet governance was now the goal of the party: "[P]arliamentary representative institutions will be gradually replaced by Soviets of people's representatives (from various classes and professions, or from various localities), functioning as both legislative and executive bodies." Under soviet democracy, and to be enshrined in a future constitution,

> supreme power in the state must be vested entirely in the people's representatives, who shall be elected by the people and be subject to recall at any time, and who shall constitute a single popular assembly, a single chamber . . . proportional representation at all elections; all delegates and elected officials, without exception, to be subject to recall at any time upon the decision of a majority of their electors . . . Judges and other officials, both civil and military, to be elected by the people with the right to recall any of them at any time by decision of a majority of their electors . . . Public education to be administered by democratically elected organs of local self-government . . . teachers to be elected directly by the population with the right of the latter to remove undesirable teachers.[67]

There is no mention in the draft party program, unlike in his pamphlet, of the elective principle for soldiers, no doubt because the "police and standing army," as stated, were "to be replaced by the universally armed people."

At the end of May the 12 districts of Petrograd held elections for their respective dumas. The appearance of Lenin's soon-to-be pamphlet was most timely. At the party's delegated City Conference in the third week in April, a debate took place on how the Bolsheviks should conduct themselves in the elections. A key issue concerned the character of the parties in contention and the related one of electoral blocs. The struggle, he argued, was between three party groupings, Cadets and parties to their right, the Socialist-Revolutionaries and the Mensheviks who defended the war, and the Bolsheviks. Unlike the elections for the four State Dumas, proportional representation would be employed for those to the municipal dumas. There was, therefore, he proposed, "no need for a bloc"— that is, electoral blocs that the RSDLP sometimes entered into under the prior electoral rules; now "the minority is protected." Nevertheless, "I am decidedly in favor of placing on our tickets the names of the Menshevik candidates who are breaking with chauvinism. This is no bloc." His resolution that embodied these positions along with the basic stance that "under no circumstances can the municipal platform, particularly at the present revolutionary time, be reduced only to communal questions" was adopted—Lenin's only published writing explicitly devoted to electoral policy between February and October (see Appendix G).

As the Petrograd elections were about to take place, Lenin pointed to "two shortcomings in our Party organization and Party work." They concerned the Bolsheviks' list of candidates for one of the wealthiest districts in the city:

> Our list for Liteiny District has only 33 candidates as against the 63 of the Cadets and the Menshevik bloc . . . Apparently, our Party workers have not been able to find more than 33 candidates of the proletarian party in this wealthy district. But this is an obvious shortcoming in our work, an obvious indication that we have not gone down far enough into the midst of the working and exploited people. We must break with established custom. In the wealthy districts we must "go among the people" more energetically than ever, and waken more and more strata of the working and exploited people to political consciousness. We should get the non-party proletarian elements—especially the *domestic servants* for instance—to take an active part in the elections and not hesitate to put the most reliable of them into our proletarian list. Why should we fear a minority of non-party *proletarian* elements, when the majority are class-conscious internationalist proletarians?[68]

This admonition is most revealing because it suggests that while the published account of Lenin's activities during 1917 is relatively sparse regarding his input into Bolshevik electoral activities for that year, he was still as much the hands-on campaign organizer, strategist, and taskmaster as he'd been for the elections for the four State Dumas. And the call to recruit "domestic servants" is even more telling but entirely consistent with everything he'd advocated and done before. "Comrade workers!" he urged in a *Pravda* article on the eve of the elections, "Let us all get down to work, canvassing all the poorest homes, awakening and enlightening the domestic servants, the most backward workers, etc., etc."[69]

A few months later, elections to the Petrograd City Duma took place. William Rosenberg provides the most detailed account in English.[70] Of significance are the gains the Bolsheviks made over the prior elections, a 14 percent improvement, which foreshadowed their future fortunes. Given all that was at stake in the aftermath of the "July Days," the party went into full campaign mode, not only in Petrograd but in Moscow— where they increased their vote by 40 percent—and other locations where local duma elections were to take place. Keep in mind that this was the moment when the Bolsheviks were having second thoughts about the soviets as the best vehicle for democracy from below. If the soviets were in doubt, then local dumas (or, more specifically, the elections to them) would allow the party to measure what Engels had once said made elections so valuable for the revolutionary process and that Lenin knew all too well: the mood of the masses for the employment of armed struggle. In fact, and crucial evidence for one of the arguments of this book, subsequent memoirs say they regarded their gains "not only as a means of 'taking the revolutionary temperature of the masses,' but also as a potential aid in seizing power."[71] To recall Engels's formulation in *The Origin of the Family, Private Property and State*: "On the day the thermometer of universal suffrage registers boiling point among the workers, both they and the capitalists will know where they stand." A month after the counterrevolutionary offensive and two months before the October Revolution, such readings of public sentiment were more than ever needed.

Of tremendous assistance to the Bolshevik campaigns was the start-up of two party newspapers, *Proletary* and *Soldat*, in place of the banned *Pravda*. The Bolsheviks, as they could do for the State Duma elections, were now able to disseminate their program on a mass scale. Very reminiscent of the campaign literature Lenin had once written was the appeal to voters in three issues of *Proletary*: "Every worker, peasant, and soldier must vote for our list because only our party is struggling staunchly and bravely against the raging counterrevolutionary dictatorship of the bourgeoisie and large landowners. [Only our party] is fighting the reimposition of capital punishment, the destruction of worker and soldier organizations, and the suppression of all the freedoms won with the blood and sweat of the people. You must vote for our party because it alone is struggling bravely with the peasantry against large landowners, with workers against factory owners, with the oppressed everywhere against the oppressors."[72] This appeal and all the details of the campaign—the importance of Rosenberg's account—make it hard to believe that Lenin (who, again, was on the run, probably why the extant paper trail is so incomplete) was not the orchestrator and largely responsible for what was achieved. After all, no Bolshevik knew more about how to conduct an effective and successful election campaign.

The best circumstantial evidence is provided by Krupskaya. After returning to Petrograd, "my work at the secretariat bored me more and more," she wrote.

> I wanted to get into real mass work. I also wanted to see Ilyich [Lenin] more often . . . The district Duma elections took place in June. I went to Vasilevsky Island to see what progress was being made in the election

campaign . . . The elections to the district Dumas were over. I was elected to the Vyborg district council. The only candidates to be elected to this council were Bolsheviks and a few Menshevik-Internationalists . . . I learned a great deal from the work in the Vyborg district. It was a good school for Party and Soviet work. During the many years that I had lived abroad as a political exile, I never dared to make a speech even at a small meeting, and until that time I had never written a single line in *Pravda*. I needed such a school very much.[73]

Krupskaya's education speaks volumes about what was opened for the Bolsheviks with the new opportunity for "mass work" through the local duma elections. Again, it's highly unlikely that Lenin wasn't intimately involved with her new and more fulfilling political life.

More decisive than the elections to the local dumas, however, as history would show, were those to the soviets. From the time of his return to Petrograd, Lenin recognized their importance. When the aforementioned crisis in April revealed that the leadership of the Soviet of Workers' and Soldiers' Deputies was becoming an obstacle to the revolution, he called "upon all the workers and soldiers . . . to send as delegates to the [soviet] only such comrades who express the will of the majority. In all cases where a delegate does not express the opinion of the majority, new elections should be held in the factories and the barracks."[74] Unlike for the local dumas, elections to the soviets were more frequent and included the right of recall, the details of which, however, are not captured in the extant published Lenin corpus. A decisive turning point in the revolution came in July when the Bolsheviks—who, in Trotsky's words, "occupied a wholly insignificant sector" of the workers' section of the Soviet in April—now constituted "two thirds of its members" as a result of by-elections in the factories. "That meant that among the masses their influence had become decisive."[75]

Yet Lenin objected to the rules of representation in the Petrograd Soviet as new elections to it approached at the end of August. That "the soldiers have one representative to every 500 people, while the workers have 1:1000" was, he charged, a violation of democracy. "'One representative, everywhere, to an *equal* number of electors' is the ABC of democracy. Anything else is a *fraud*." He urged the party to pass

a resolution demanding *equal* suffrage (both in the Soviets and at trade union congresses), branding the *slightest* departure from equality as a *fraud*—using exactly this word—as *a Nicholas II method*. This resolution of the plenary meeting of the Central Committee must be written in a language everybody can understand and spread in leaflet form among the mass of the workers.

> We cannot tolerate a *fraud* of democracy if we call ourselves "democrats." We are not democrats but unprincipled people if we tolerate this!![76]

That the soviet failed to change its rules, owing mainly to Socialist Revolutionary opposition to Lenin's proposal, doesn't negate his democratic vision for how it should function. Despite this setback the Bolsheviks achieved a major victory in the Petrograd and Moscow Soviets on August 31 and September 5, respectively, when an overwhelming majority of delegates in both bodies passed their motions calling for a rejection of any compromises with the bourgeoisie and the transfer of "All Power to the Soviets!"—testimony to the deepening of the revolutionary process. About this moment, Trotsky writes, "The city dumas, which had made an effort to compete with the soviets, died down in the days of danger and vanished. The Petrograd duma humbly sent its delegation to the Soviet 'for an explanation of the general situation and the establishment of contact.'"[77]

The elective principle, last, applied to the party itself. Telling evidence that it was in full force after the February Revolution came in a comment Lenin made about the April 20 protest against the provisional government. Called for and organized by the Bolsheviks, the action went "a trifle more to the left" than planned, "a serious crime"—a problem of "disorganization" that had to be corrected. "Had we deliberately allowed such an act, we would not have remained in the Central Committee for one moment."[78] Lenin and other Central Committee members, in other words, would have been immediately recalled. Years of having to operate without elections did not dull Bolshevik sensibility for their need when the opportunity presented itself.

ON THE EVE OF OCTOBER

For more than a year, Lenin had been thinking about and working on what would be his last major writing before assuming the responsibilities that came with the October Revolution. *State and Revolution: The Marxist Theory of the State and the Tasks of the Proletariat in the Revolution*, as the subtitle suggests, brought together in one text what he had been saying on the topic for some time, of urgent necessity given the likely course of events in Russia at the end of the summer of 1917—a document that could theoretically inform the process even if he couldn't live to see its outcome.

The six-page section, "Abolition of Parliamentarism," which immediately follows a detailed discussion on the Paris Commune, is relevant here. There is nothing fundamentally new in his critique of parliamentarism that Lenin hadn't said before. Different this time was the way he framed the issue. The betrayal by the "practical socialists" of the basic lesson Marx and Engels had drawn about the Commune, that the working class cannot use parliamentary governance for socialist transformation, came with a political price—aside from the slaughter their fateful votes on August 4, 1914, enabled. By defanging Marx and Engels, they "have left all criticism of parliamentarism to the anarchists, and, on this wonderfully reasonable ground, they [the 'practical socialists'] denounce all criticism of parliamentarism as 'anarchism'!! It is not surprising that the proletariat of the 'advanced' parliamentary countries, disgusted with such 'socialists' . . . has been with increasing frequency giving its sympathies to anarcho-syndicalism, in spite of the fact that the latter is merely the twin brother of opportunism." If this sounds descriptive of politics since the onset of the world capitalist crisis in 2008 where social democracy, the "practical socialists," has been hegemonic, then it is.

But Marx, Lenin contended, did what the "present-day traitor to socialism" could not. He "knew how to break with anarchism ruthlessly for its inability to make use even of the 'pigsty' of bourgeois parliamentarism, especially when the situation was obviously not revolutionary; but at the same time he knew how to subject parliamentarism to genuinely revolutionary proletarian criticism." And it was the Commune, the living class struggle—what the producers had discovered on their own without, as Lenin was fond of saying, "the aid of any books"—that offered an alternative. Because of the actuality of socialist revolution in Russia in August 1917, he began to consider the implications of the Commune experience, his first concretization of what a socialist society would look like.

Important here is Lenin's continued defense of representative democracy, despite the betrayals of "the present-day 'Social-Democrat'":

> The way out of parliamentarism is not, of course, the abolition of representative institutions and the elective principle, but the conversion of the representative institutions from talking shops into "working" bodies. "The Commune was to be a working, not a parliamentary, body, executive and legislative at the same time." . . . We cannot imagine democracy, even proletarian democracy, without representative institutions, but we can and must imagine democracy without parliamentarism, if criticism of bourgeois society is not mere words for us, if the desire to overthrow the rule of the bourgeoisie is our earnest and sincere desire, and not a mere "election" cry for catching workers' votes.[79]

All this, once again, was consistent with what he had been saying for at least two decades. His views were informed not only by the reality of the

Russian revolution from 1905 but, again, by the opportunity to live and do political work in what was widely regarded as a paragon of parliamentary democracy—Switzerland. About the two experiences, Krupskaya writes, "It seems to me that had Ilyich not lived through the 1905 revolution and the second period in exile, he would not have been able to write his book, *State and Revolution*."[80]

What is apparently odd about this part of the text, especially since Lenin says in the preface that he'd address the lessons of 1905 to 1917, is the absence of any positive mention of the soviets, organs that he'd once lauded for their Commune-like characteristics. But there's no mystery. As he explained three months later about what was missing, "I had no time to write a single line of the chapter; I was 'interrupted' by a political crisis—the eve of the October revolution of 1917. Such an 'interruption' can only be welcomed . . . It is more pleasant and useful to go through the 'experience of revolution' than to write about it."[81]

Certainly, from the "July Days" until early September, Lenin and the Bolsheviks had doubts about the soviets as institutions of representative democracy to advance the interests of the proletariat—exactly when he was completing his book. But that skepticism soon evaporated. Again, in the first week of September, Lenin's enthusiasm for the soviets, having performed heroically in beating back the counterrevolution, was rekindled. But the demand "Power to the Soviets," as he warned at the end of September, had to be acted on: "Either all power goes to the Soviets and the army is made fully democratic, or another Kornilov affair occurs"— that is, another attempt at a counterrevolution.[82]

The debate among Bolsheviks in the lead-up to the October Revolution was whether they enjoyed sufficient support for leading an armed overthrow of the provisional government—an insurrection. Lenin, in the minority (Trotsky was the Central Committee member closest to his views on this) insisted that there was: "The Bolsheviks, having obtained a majority in the Soviets of Workers' and Soldiers' Deputies in both capitals, can and *must* take state power into their own hands . . . The majority gained in the Soviets of the metropolitan cities *resulted* from the people coming over *to our side*. . . Compare the elections to the city councils of Petrograd and Moscow with the elections to the Soviets. Compare the elections in Moscow with the Moscow strike of August 12. Those are objective facts regarding that majority of revolutionary elements that are leading the people."[83] For Lenin, again, elections were an invaluable tool for calculating the probability of success for the most important election, the masses voting with their feet—their willingness and ability to not only take power but defend it. Note the qualifier, the "majority of revolutionary elements that are leading the people"—those he regarded to be the most effective voters with their feet.

It's useful to recall his point made in 1913 about the elections to the Fourth Duma, because they, too, supplied "*objective data*. . . The struggle of parties—in practice, before the electorate, and with the returns summed up—invariably furnishes data *serving to test* our conception of the balance of the social forces in the country and of the significance of particular 'slogans.'" He reiterated this point about the value of elections five months after the October Revolution in the context of a debate about the prospects for a Bolshevik-like revolution in Germany: "As matters stood in October, we had made a precise calculation of the mass forces. We not only thought, we *knew* with certainty, from the experience of the mass elections to the Soviets, that the overwhelming majority of the workers and soldiers had already come over to our side in September and in early October. We knew . . . that the coalition [government] had also lost the support of the peasantry—and that meant that our cause had already won."[84]

The Socialist Revolutionary-Menshevik leadership of the executive of the soviet convened in mid-September the "Democratic Conference," which was basically an attempt to divert the energy boiling from below and increasingly led by the Bolsheviks into the parliamentary arena. Lenin urged the party's leadership not to be enticed: "It would be a big mistake, sheer parliamentary cretinism on our part, if we were to regard the Democratic Conference as a parliament; for even if it were to proclaim itself a permanent and sovereign parliament of the revolution, it would nevertheless *decide nothing*. The power of decision lies *outside* it in the working-class quarters of Petrograd and Moscow."[85] Consistent with all the lessons Marx and Engels had drawn about 1848 and the experiences of Russia's own revolution, Lenin explained in anticipation of Russia's future "civil war" and its outcome why what was "outside" the electoral and parliamentary arenas was more important: "A comparison of the data on the 'parliamentary' [local duma] elections and the data on the . . . mass movements [since April 20] fully corroborates, in respect of Russia, an observation often made in the West, namely, that the revolutionary proletariat is incomparably *stronger* in the *extra-parliamentary* than in the parliamentary struggle, as far as influencing the *masses* and drawing them into the struggle is concerned."[86] When Lenin decided that the Bolsheviks should boycott the conference, he drew on "the elements that went into shaping the correct tactics of boycotting the Bulygin Duma" in 1905 and the "incorrect" ones of "boycotting the Third Duma" in 1907.[87]

After delays and postponements, the provisional government finally set a date for elections to the Constituent Assembly: November 12. Having insisted for months that they be held, the Bolsheviks immediately made preparations to take part. Ever vigilant about a proletarian approach to the electoral process, however, Lenin criticized the composition of the list the Central Committee put together. There were two problems. First, more workers, "four or five times more," needed to be included, because in what would be an overwhelmingly "peasant Constituent Assembly . . . they alone are capable of establishing close and intimate ties with the peasant deputies." The second and related problem had to do with the political histories of many on the list: "It is absolutely inadmissible also to have an excessive number of candidates from among people who have but recently joined our Party and have not yet been tested . . . In filling the list with such candidates who should first have worked in the Party for months and months, the C.C. has thrown wide open the door for careerists who scramble for seats in the Constituent Assembly."

Lenin immediately made clear his intentions: "It goes without saying that from among the mezhraiontsi [members of the Inter-District Organization, the party that Trotsky had belonged to from 1913] who have been hardly tested in proletarian work in our Party's *spirit*, no one would contest the candidature of, say, Trotsky, for, first, upon his arrival, Trotsky at once took up an internationalist stand; second, he worked among the mezhraiontsi for a merger; third, in the difficult July days he proved himself equal to the task and a loyal supporter of the party of the revolutionary proletariat. Clearly, as much cannot be said about many of the new Party members entered on the list." About one of the latter, he said it would have been fine to include him if, like Trotsky, he had displayed "a desire to reform" his previous views. "But to get him into the Constituent Assembly within a week or so of his entry into the Party is *in fact* to transform the Party into the same kind of dirty stall for careerists as most of the European parties are."

Going into the Constituent Assembly required conscious party direction: "The serious work in the Constituent Assembly will consist in establishing close, intimate *ties* with the peasants. Only workers who are in touch with peasant life are fit for this. To pack the Constituent Assembly with orators and writers is to take the beaten track of opportunism and chauvinism."[88] Just as he had devoted innumerable hours to providing direction to the RSDLP deputies in the four State Dumas for forging the worker-peasant alliance as well as other tasks, Lenin envisioned Bolshevik participation in the Constituent Assembly for doing the same. No other party member had thought as long and hard about realizing this goal via the parliamentary arena nor had the experience for doing so.

That Trotsky was already on the list and that Lenin endorsed him in the way he did is especially instructive about the internal norms of the Bolsheviks. It was at the aforementioned semiclandestine Sixth Congress of the party at the end of July that Trotsky was not only formally admitted to the Bolshevik party but voted onto its Central Committee, while he was in jail and Lenin in hiding. The vote tally itself is revealing. The top four vote getters in descending order were Lenin, 133 of 134; Zinoviev, 132; Kamenev, 131; and Trotsky, 131. Despite a more than decade-long bitter dispute between him and Lenin and other Bolsheviks, all that, again, was now water under the bridge. Indicative of what happened to the Bolshevik party after Lenin was dead is that Trotsky's name continued to be omitted in the *Lenin Collected Works* in the list of those elected to the Central Committee. And only in the fifth Russian edition did Lenin's endorsement of him appear for the first time.[89]

The relative ease with which the revolution was carried out on October 25, marked by the absence of any real defense of the provisional government and thus minimum bloodshed, especially in Petrograd, offers convincing evidence that Lenin was indeed right that the effective majority of the population—those willing to vote with their feet—would support the insurrection. And nothing was as important in his calculus as the results of the various elections that preceded it.

Five years before October, Lenin came across letters Marx wrote, in the heat of the Paris Commune uprising, to a one-time acquaintance who charged that the insurgents were mistaken to have gone into revolt. To appreciate Marx's response, know that six months prior to the insurgency he counseled the Paris working class against doing just that; they lacked a leadership and sufficient allies to be victorious. But did Marx, Lenin asked, rain on the revolt once it began? "No. On April 12, 1871, Marx writes an *enthusiastic* letter to [Ludwig] Kugelmann—a letter which we would like to see hung in the home of every Russian Social-Democrat and of every literate Russian worker . . . when he saw the mass movement of the people, he watched it with the keen attention of a participant in great events marking a step forward in the historic revolutionary movement . . . The *historical initiative* of the masses was what Marx prized above everything else . . . Marx knew how to warn the *leaders* against a premature rising. But his attitude towards the heaven-storming *proletariat* was that of a practical adviser, of a participant in the *struggle* of the masses, who were raising the *whole* movement to *a higher level* in spite of the false theories and mistakes of [Louis] Blanqui and [Joseph] Proudhon."

Lenin then turned to Marx's critique of Kuglemann's "doubts" about the Communards, "referring to the hopelessness of the struggle and to realism as opposed to romanticism": "Marx immediately (April 17, 1871) severely lectured Kugelmann. '*World history*,' he wrote, '*would indeed be very easy to make, if the struggle were taken up only on condition of infallibly favorable chances* [Lenin's italics].' He realized that to attempt in advance to calculate the chances *with complete accuracy* would be quackery or hopeless pedantry. What he valued *above everything else* was that the working class heroically and self-sacrificingly took the initiative in *making* world history. Marx regarded world history from the standpoint of those who *make* it without being in a position to calculate the chances *infallibly* beforehand, and not from the standpoint of an intellectual philistine who moralizes: 'It was easy to foresee . . . they should not have taken up' . . . Marx was also able to appreciate that there are moments in history when a desperate struggle of the *masses*, even for a hopeless cause, is *essential* for the further schooling of these masses and their training for the *next* struggle."[90] Nothing presaged Lenin's course in fall 1917 as did these lines.

AFTER OCTOBER

Among Lenin's many tasks as leader of the new Russian state was the distillation of the lessons of the revolution. The newly founded Communist International, Comintern, or Third International, was just the venue for their discussion and dissemination. Not the least important of those lessons was how the Bolsheviks utilized the electoral and parliamentary arenas to take power. Two documents proved to be his definitive and final pronouncements on the topic. What happened to those lessons was inextricably linked to the fate of the revolution that unfolded within a few years of his death.

IN DEFENSE OF REVOLUTIONARY PARLIAMENTARISM

The central debate in 1917 about which form of representative democracy would prevail, soviet or parliamentary democracy—a proxy for the more fundamental issue, which class would rule Russia—was settled in January 1918. The day after the Bolshevik-led insurrection, the Second Congress of Soviets of Workers' and Soldiers' Deputies, where the Bolsheviks had a majority, took ownership of what had been done in its name. The era of soviet governance, commencing with a coalition of the Bolsheviks and Left Socialist Revolutionaries, had begun. As Lenin had always said, only with the workers and peasants in power would the convening of the Constituent Assembly be ensured. Elections for it finally began on November

12.[91] The Socialist Revolutionaries garnered the largest number of votes in the country as a whole while in Petrograd and environs the Bolsheviks were the clear winner. Lenin argued that because the Socialist Revolutionary lists were drawn up before the party split into a right and left wing the votes they got did not reflect actual popular will. The situation could only be rectified if voters had the right to recall elected deputies whose politics they disagreed with. The Central Executive Committee of the Soviets issued such a decree, setting the stage for the inevitable clash over which was the supreme political authority in Russia, the soviets or the Constituent Assembly. When the latter convened on January 5, the committee demanded that it recognize the hegemony of the soviets. Its failure to do so prompted Lenin the next day to call for its dissolution, which is exactly what the committee voted to do and what in fact occurred.

When Kerensky and Kornilov threatened to end soviet power in July and August of 1917, workers and peasants came to its defense, the prelude, in hindsight, to the October Revolution. But when soviet power threatened the just-born Constituent Assembly, no comparable class force voted with its feet to be its savior. Its brief moment in the sun ended unceremoniously on January 6. The difference speaks volumes about which of the two institutions of representative democracy enjoyed effective majority support. A similar point can be made about the outcome of the civil war that got under way soon afterward. Lenin, as noted already, anticipated such a conflagration and correctly predicted, based on the election data, the eventual defeat of the counterrevolution. Once soviet power was in place after October, he could be even more confident about his forecast. Because one of its first acts was to fulfill the Bolshevik pledge to grant land to poor peasants, it ensured support for soviet governance from Russia's largest constituency. Exactly because it was soviet power and not the long-delayed Constituent Assembly that made the decree is why the peasantry came to its defense in the most critical moment in the young revolution's existence and ensured its victory in the civil war.[92]

The dissolution of the Constituent Assembly required Lenin to defend soviet governance against critics such as Kautsky. His speech to the Central Executive Committee of the Soviets on January 6 that called for its demise went to the heart of his argument: "The Soviets, created solely by the initiative of the people, are a form of democracy without parallel in any other country of the world . . . At one time, we considered the Constituent Assembly to be better than tsarism and the republic of Kerensky with their famous organs of power; but as the Soviets emerged, they, being revolutionary organizations of the whole people, naturally became incomparably superior to any parliament in the world, a fact that

I emphasized," referring to his April Theses, "as far back as last April."[93] And later, in one of the best succinct distillations of the Marxist view of the alternative to the soviets, bourgeois democracy, he said, "No bourgeois republic, however democratic, ever was or could have been anything but a machine for the suppression of the working people by capital, an instrument of the dictatorship of the bourgeoisie, the political rule of capital. The democratic bourgeois republic promised and proclaimed majority rule, but it could never put this into effect as long as private ownership of the land and other means of production existed."[94] He provided his Exhibit A: "One of the most democratic republics in the world is the United States of America, yet nowhere (and those who have been there since 1905 probably know it) is the power of capital, the power of a handful of multimillionaires over the whole of society, so crude and so openly corrupt as in America. Once capital exists, it dominates the whole of society, and no democratic republic, no franchise can change its nature."[95]

A related issue that had to be addressed concerned the decision of the new soviet government to disenfranchise the bourgeoisie, which for Lenin was "not a necessary and indispensable feature of the dictatorship of the proletariat."[96] It had to do with the "*specific conditions* of the Russian revolution and the *specific path* of its development."[97] Doing so "does not mean . . . that a definite category of citizens are disfranchised for life. It applies, only to the exploiters, to those who, in violation of the fundamental laws of the socialist Soviet Republic, persist in their efforts to cling to their exploiters' status and to preserve capitalist relations . . . [I]n the very near future, the cessation of foreign invasion and the completion of the expropriation of the expropriators may, under certain circumstances, create a situation where the proletarian state will choose other methods of suppressing the resistance of the exploiters and will introduce unrestricted universal suffrage."[98] "We do not propose," for that reason, "our Constitution as a model for other countries."[99] The civil war, along with the other Russian realities, required such measures—not unlike those that Lincoln employed in the American Civil War.

While defending disenfranchisement of Russia's bourgeoisie—"barely two or three percent of the population"[100]—Lenin urged greater participation of women in the political process: "It is essential that women workers take a greater part in the elections. The Soviet government was the first and only government in the world to abolish completely all the old, bourgeois, infamous laws which placed women in an inferior position compared with men and which granted privileges to men . . . Therefore, elect more women workers, both Communist and non-Party, to the Soviet. If she is only an honest woman worker who is capable of managing work sensibly and conscientiously, it makes no difference if she is not a member of the Party—elect her to the Moscow Soviet."[101]

Last, the rationale for soviet governance needed to be spelled out for the first time in the party's program. The first two of the seven reasons he proposed embody their essence:

> The more direct influence of the working masses on state structure and administration—i.e., a higher form of democracy—is also effected under the Soviet type of state, first, by the electoral procedure and the possibility of holding elections more frequently, and also by conditions for re-election and for the recall of deputies which are simpler and more comprehensible to the urban and rural workers than is the case under the best forms of bourgeois democracy . . . secondly, by making the economic, industrial unit (factory) and not a territorial division the primary electoral unit and the nucleus of the state structure under Soviet power.[102]

When detailed figures for the elections to the Constituent Assembly became available a year later, Lenin's penchant for number crunching kicked into high gear. The data, he argued, explained not only why the Bolsheviks were able to take power in October but why they were winning the civil war at the end of 1919. Even Lenin's opponents grudgingly admit to the objectivity and validity of his analysis.[103] The essence of his claim in "The Constituent Assembly Elections and the Dictatorship of the Proletariat" was that by September 1917 his party had won to its side the majority of Russia's most efficacious voters—those willing to vote with their feet. The Bolsheviks then used that state power to win over the majority of Russia's peasants by decreeing land to them. And therein was a lesson applicable as well to advanced capitalist countries:

> [T]he proletariat cannot achieve victory if it does not win the majority of the population to its side. But to limit that winning to polling a majority of votes in an election *under the rule of the bourgeoisie*, or to make it the condition for it, is crass stupidity, or else sheer deception of the workers. In order to win the majority of the population to its side the proletariat must, in the first place, overthrow the bourgeoisie and seize state power; secondly, it must introduce Soviet power and completely smash the old state apparatus, whereby it immediately undermines the rule, prestige and influence of the bourgeoisie and petty-bourgeois compromisers over the non-proletarian working people. Thirdly, it must *entirely destroy* the influence of the bourgeoisie and petty-bourgeois compromisers over the *majority* of the non-proletarian masses by satisfying *their* economic needs *in a revolutionary way at the expense of the exploiters*.[104]

The fallacy of Kautsky et al., Lenin argued, was to "imagine that extremely important political problems can be solved by voting. Such problems are actually solved by *civil war* if they are acute and aggravated by struggle." To appreciate his point, think about the American Civil War. Neither the country's constitution nor presidential election of 1860 could resolve its "extremely important political problem"—its equivalent to Russia's long festering sore. Only a conflagration of biblical proportions was able to put an end to chattel slavery. In the midst of the carnage of the First World War and in language reminiscent of the most memorable sentence in Lincoln's Second Inaugural Address, Lenin wrote that "too much still remains in the world that *must* be destroyed with fire and sword for the emancipation of the working class."[105]

The last section of the article lists in thesis-like fashion ten points that summarized his argument (see Appendix H). "The Constituent Assembly Elections and the Dictatorship of the Proletariat" proved to be Lenin's penultimate declaration on the revolutionary employment of the electoral and parliamentary arenas, a summary and generalization of the Russian experience.

In defending soviet power, Lenin made absolutely clear what he didn't intend, as he told delegates to the party's Seventh party congress in 1918: "[W]e ought not in any way to give the impression that we attach absolutely no value to parliamentary institutions. They are a huge advance on what preceded them."[106] The third of his ten "theses" in the "Constituent Assembly Elections" article, in fact, underscored his point. In his better-known pamphlet, written four months later in 1920, *Left-Wing Communism: An Infantile Disorder*, Lenin made his most forceful case for participating in the parliamentary arena. The context was the growing attractiveness of the Bolshevik Revolution for aspiring revolutionaries elsewhere in the world, particularly those affiliated with the new Communist or Third International. Clarity on why and how the Bolsheviks took power was essential for any who wanted to emulate their Russian comrades. An emerging problem was the tendency to see the October insurrection as the magic bullet. His pamphlet—along with correspondence to revolutionaries such as Sylvia Pankhurst in Great Britain—and the Bolshevik intervention in the Second Congress of the International in 1920 sought to correct such a narrow reading of the Russian Revolution.[107]

Lenin began with his all-important and too neglected qualification of the historical place of the Russian Revolution. Now it was on center stage, but "soon after the victory of the proletarian revolution in at least one of the advanced countries, a sharp change will probably come about: Russia will cease to be the model and will once again become a backward country (in the 'Soviet' and the socialist sense)."[108] Then came his main point based on the actual Bolshevik experience: "The alternation of parliamentary and non-parliamentary forms of struggle, of the tactics of boycotting parliament and that of participating in parliament, of legal and illegal forms of struggle, and likewise their interrelations and connections—all this was marked by an extraordinary wealth of content."[109] After a brief description of the party's decadelong Duma experience, he distilled its significance:

> Today, when we look back at this fully completed historical period, whose connection with subsequent periods has now become quite clear, it becomes most obvious that in 1908–14 the Bolsheviks *could not have* preserved (let alone strengthened and developed) the core of the revolutionary party of the proletariat, had they not upheld, in a most strenuous struggle, the viewpoint that it was *obligatory* to combine legal and illegal forms of struggle, and that it was *obligatory* to participate even in a most reactionary parliament and in a number of other institutions hemmed in by reactionary laws (sick benefit societies, etc.).[110]

The "strenuous struggle" referred to the recurring debate on whether to boycott or participate in the Dumas. If the boycott of the Bulygin Duma in 1905 was correct, that "of the Duma in 1906 was a mistake although a minor and easily remediable one"—his first admission in print of the error and what the circumstantial evidence at the time suggested.

The Russian experience challenged those voices in the Third International who justified nonparticipation in parliaments, especially when they became centers for organizing the counterrevolution: "We Bolsheviks participated in the most counterrevolutionary parliaments, and experience has shown that this participation was not only useful but indispensable to the party of the revolutionary proletariat, after the first bourgeois revolution in Russia (1905), so as to pave the way for the second bourgeois revolution (February 1917), and then for the socialist revolution (October 1917)."[111] The word "indispensable" is itself indispensable for one of the arguments of this book—namely, that Lenin's electoral/parliamentary strategy goes a long way in explaining Bolshevik success in 1917.

As for the claim of some would-be revolutionaries that parliaments had now become "obsolete," Lenin responded, yes and no. The Paris Commune and the Russian experience did indeed show that a new era of representative democracy had opened. But both were only at the beginning of a historical development that could only be "counted in decades." In the meantime, and as long as the dictatorship of capital was in place, the "Lefts" would have to participate in them. It was true, he admitted, that it "is far more difficult to create a really revolutionary parliamentary group in a European parliament than it was in Russia. That stands to reason. But it is only a particular expression of the general truth that it was easy for Russia, in the specific and historically unique situation of 1917, to *start* the socialist revolution, but it will be more difficult for Russia than for the European countries to *continue* the revolution and bring it to its consummation."[112] Yes, he could "assure foreign communists" that doing parliamentary work in Russia was "quite unlike the usual West European parliamentary campaigns. From this the conclusion is often drawn: 'Well, that was in Russia, in our country parliamentarianism is different.' This is a false conclusion. Communists, adherents of the Third International in all countries, exist for the purpose of *changing*—all along the line, in all spheres of life—the old socialist, trade unionist, syndicalist, and parliamentary type of work into a *new* type of work, the communist."[113] In the debate at the Second Congress of the International, Lenin reminded delegates that though it was brief, Russia, too, after the February Revolution, experienced bourgeois democracy that the Bolsheviks had to figure out how to negotiate.[114]

Finally, there was another advantage in doing parliamentary work. Because, as the Russian experience showed, "in conditions in which it is often necessary to hide 'leaders' underground, the *evolution* of good 'leaders,' reliable, tested and authoritative, is a very difficult matter; these difficulties *cannot* be successfully overcome without combining legal and illegal work, and *without testing the 'leaders,' among other ways*, in parliaments." The problem with "bad leaders," such as in Germany, wasn't the parliamentary arena itself but "those leaders who are unable—and still more against those who are *unwilling*—to utilize parliamentary elections and the parliamentary rostrum in a revolutionary and communist manner."[115] It could be easier, in other words, being a communist doing "illegal work" but harder in the "legal" or parliamentary arena imbued with its daily temptations to compromise revolutionary politics. Combining the two areas of work would therefore be the best laboratory for communist training.

Left-Wing Communism unambiguously confirms that Lenin intended his electoral/parliamentary strategy for any country where the working class had political weight. Written two and a half years before he succumbed to his last and incapacitating stroke—its 82 pages being far longer than anything he wrote afterward—it constitutes, along with "The Constituent Assembly Elections," Lenin's final and definitive treatment of the topic. At the Second Congress of the Third International in 1920, "Theses on the Communist Parties and Parliamentarism," drafted by

Trotsky, Nikolai Bukharin, and Zinoviev, were adopted (see Appendix I). They were essentially an elaboration of Lenin's "The Constituent Assembly Elections" article and arguments in *Left-Wing Communism*. Among the 21 conditions for membership in Comintern that delegates to the Second Congress adopted, a debate and discussion in which he actively participated, was number 11. With the betrayals of the Second International in mind when the Guns of August exploded in 1914, it required affiliates to remove from "their parliamentary fractions . . . unreliable elements" and ensure that fraction members were subordinate to party executive committees "not just in words but in deeds" and demand that each "subordinate all of his activity in the interests of truly revolutionary propaganda and agitation."[116]

LENINISM AFTER LENIN

Aspiring revolutionaries affiliated with the Third International took Lenin's counsel to heart. Years later the Hungarian Marxist Georg Lukács remembered his youthful communism, a kind of "messianic sectarianism . . . My polemical essay attacking the idea of participation in bourgeois parliaments is a good example of this tendency. Its fate—criticism at the hands of Lenin—enabled me to take my first step away from sectarianism. Lenin pointed to the vital distinction, indeed to the paradox, that an institution may be obsolete from the standpoint of world history—as, e.g. the soviets had rendered parliaments obsolete—but that this need not preclude participation in it for tactical reasons; on the contrary."[117] But with Lenin gone—and later mummified—such advice would no longer be readily available.

The failure of revolutionaries elsewhere to do what the Bolsheviks had done, despite Lenin's best efforts, to lead their working classes to political power goes a long way in explaining the outcome of the Russian Revolution and, hence, Lenin's legacy. Marx and Engels at the end of their lives and Lenin as early as 1905 made clear that the consummation of a socialist revolution in Russia depended on it spreading to one of the advanced capitalist countries in Europe. For a moment it appeared that the Germans might duplicate what the Bolsheviks did. But the mistakes of the new communist party and the counterrevolutionary actions of social democracy made that impossible. The increasing isolation of the Russian Revolution, combined with the devastating toll of the civil war, became a breeding ground for the bureaucratic counterrevolution Stalin would soon lead. In his final months, Lenin realized what was happening— "a workers' state with bureaucratic distortions" is how he described the Soviet Union—and waged from his sick bed an eventually unsuccessful fight to halt that development.[118] Political and historical contingency, in other words, rather than some notion of a democratic deficit in Lenin, best explain the Stalinist counterrevolution.[119] Nothing in Lenin's program and practice prior to those contingencies could have predicted such an outcome. This book has by now, hopefully, amply and convincingly documented Lenin's profoundly democratic credentials. Certainly no one in Russia could rival him in this regard. Like Marx and Engels, he deeply understood that to be a democrat one had to be a revolutionary.

For this book there is no better evidence of the Stalinist counterrevolution that had taken place than the policy that Moscow imposed on the affiliates of the Third International at its Seventh Congress in 1935. In the name of fighting fascism, "Communists . . . *must strive to secure joint action with the Social-Democratic Parties, reformist trade unions and other organizations of the toilers against the class enemies of the proletariat, on the basis of short or long-term agreements.*" For the electoral arena it meant that "the Communists must seek to establish a united front with the Social-Democratic Parties and the trade unions . . . and exert every effort to prevent the election of reactionary and fascist candidates. In face of fascist danger, the Communist may . . . participate in election campaigns on *a common platform and with a common ticket of the anti-fascist front* [all italics in original]."[120]

If this sounds familiar to readers of this book, it should be. This was essentially the line that Lenin combatted in more than one Duma election. Mensheviks incessantly advocated support to the Cadets as the "lesser evil" in order, according to them, to prevent the election of the Black Hundreds—the fascist equivalent. Lenin vehemently disagreed and always fought, like Marx and Engels, for independent working-class political action despite the "Black Hundred scare." That the Seventh was the last Third International Congress is no coincidence. To convince bourgeois heads of state like Franklin Delano Roosevelt that the communists in his country were no longer a threat because of the new Popular Front policy, Stalin unilaterally pulled the plug on what had already been by then a comatose organization. For would-be revolutionaries who looked to Moscow for guidance, the vast majority in that era, Lenin's real electoral/parliamentary strategy would never be made available for them. Only the relatively small number of those who looked to Trotsky for leadership learned differently.

***

It fell to Trotsky to defend and fight for Lenin's real program. No one had better credentials. Once a bitter opponent of Lenin, the person who launched the Lenin-as-Jacobin charge, Trotsky embraced him in 1917 to ensure Bolshevik success and later died at the hands of one of Stalin's assassins in 1940 for leading the struggle against the counterrevolution. No better perspective exists on what the Soviet experiment sought to achieve than the final comments in his *History of the Russian Revolution*, written two decades after the Bolshevik triumph in October 1917:

> The historic ascent of humanity, taken as a whole, may be summarized as a succession of victories of consciousness over blind forces—in nature, in society, in man himself. Critical and creative thought can boast of its greatest victories up to now in the struggle with nature. The physico-chemical sciences have already reached a point where man is clearly about to become master of matter. But social relations are still forming in the manner of the coral islands. Parliamentarism illumined only the surface of society, and even that with a rather artificial light. In comparison with monarchy and other heirlooms from the cannibals and cave-dwellers, democracy is of course a great conquest, but it leaves the blind play of forces in the social relations of men untouched. It was against this deeper-sphere of the unconscious that the October revolution was the first to raise its hand. The Soviet system wishes to bring aim and plan into the very basis of society, where up to now only accumulated consequences have reigned.[121]

Unless it's assumed that the present examples of representative democracy—including the US Congress—constitute humanity's last word on the subject, then the Bolsheviks should be applauded for at least having tried to do better.[122] Lenin deserves the last word, because his insight about the reality of bourgeois democracy, made in 1908, is so nakedly instantiated today by the ways in which the ruling classes, employing the legislative process, seek to resolve the present capitalist crisis—on the backs of working people. "Parliamentarism does not eliminate, but lays bare the innate character even of the most democratic bourgeois republics as organs of class oppression."

Conclusion

THE NEWS FROM CAIRO AS THESE LINES are being written—late summer 2013—is that supporters of deposed Egyptian President Mohamed Morsi of the Muslim Brotherhood are bracing for a violent confrontation with the military. Morsi's government, the product of the mass protests that brought down the three-decade-old rule of Hosni Mubarak in January 2011, Egypt's edition of the "Arab Spring," was itself victim to "the streets." Increasingly, the latter felt that what they had achieved with Mubarak's overthrow was being undermined by the Islamist regime. But if the democratic movement knew what it was against, it couldn't agree on what it was for. Into that breach stepped the one institution in Egypt that at least had a leadership—the military. Four chapters and almost a year ago, I stated that Egypt's democratic revolution was still up for grabs and asked, "Is there a leadership with a program prepared to rule in the name of the movement?" The evidence so far suggests not.

In many ways this book—again, this and the companion volume, *Lenin's Electoral Strategy from Marx and Engels through the Revolution of 1905 (LES1905)*—is about whether history offers any lessons on how to forge a revolutionary leadership. The focus is Lenin and the Bolshevik Revolution and, more specifically, how he employed the electoral and parliamentary arenas to do just that. The task now is, first, to see if sufficient and convincing evidence has been presented in support of the four arguments around which the narrative is woven. Second, if a credible case has been made, then what explains the silences in the literature—by friends and foes alike—about this very rich and heretofore untold story? Last, does the Bolshevik experience offer any lessons to those not just in Tahrir Square but anywhere who seek for the world's toilers a working-class solution to a still-unfolding capitalist crisis of unprecedented scope?

AN OVERVIEW OF THE EVIDENCE AND FOUR ARGUMENTS

A summary of Lenin's electoral and parliamentary strategy and how it played out is in order before I interrogate the book's claims. His two basic premises, the subject of Chapter 1 in *LES1905*, were bequeathed by Marx and Engels. The first, based on the balance sheets the two founders of the modern communist movement drew on the "European Spring" of 1848–49, is that what takes place outside the parliamentary arena is decisive in politics. To believe otherwise is to be afflicted with parliamentary cretinism. It's what the masses do or do not do in the streets and on the barricades that determines which class rules. The unsuccessful upheavals of those two years also revealed that the liberal bourgeoisie no longer had a class interest in leading revolutions. No subsequent "outside the parliamentary arena" moment was as instructive as the Paris Commune of 1871, which provided the second and complimentary premise for Marx and Engels's perspective. The insurgent Communards, only two and a half months in power, quickly learned that they could not use the bourgeois state and its parliamentary apparatus to meet the social needs of the plebian orders. A new kind of state had to be constructed for socialist transformation, one that fused the legislative and executive functions of governance. For Marx and Engels, there was no parliamentary road to working-class conquest of state power and socialist transformation.

Though the electoral/parliamentary arena could not be a vehicle for working-class ascent to power, it offered, Marx and Engels contended, unique and invaluable assistance in that quest. But the working class had to have its own candidates in elections, "even when there is no prospect whatever of their being elected," to be able "to count their forces and to lay before the public their revolutionary attitude and party standpoint." Nor should the working class be deterred in this effort by the charge of liberals, who betrayed the 1848–49 revolutions, that "by doing so they are splitting the democratic party and giving the reactionaries the possibility of victory."[1] Independent working-class political action was the core message of one of Marx and Engels's balance sheets on the European Spring, the *Address of March 1850*—the founding document for their strategy and one Lenin not only knew by heart but "used to delight in quoting."[2] Two paragraphs before the previous citations in the *Address* is a detailed discussion of why "the workers must be armed and organized," making clear that Marx and Engels were prepared to employ armed struggle if necessary and were under no illusions that elections in and of themselves ensured working-class empowerment. Elections were merely one sphere of revolutionary work, albeit an important one. Their later books, articles, and letters on working-class involvement in electoral and parliamentary arenas are essentially, as detailed in Chapter 1 of *LES1905*, an elaboration of the themes of the *Address*, supplemented with advice based on the experiences of the first mass working-class parties, especially the German party.

Already well-versed in Marx and Engels's ideas, Lenin enthusiastically deployed them when the opportunity arose in 1906 with the convening of the First Duma, a concession the Russian monarchy was forced to grant owing to the masses' revolt of 1905. That is the subject of Chapter 2 in *LES1905*. Though the 15 Russian Social Democratic Labor Party (RSDLP) deputies who were elected were all Mensheviks—the Bolsheviks boycotted the elections—Lenin immediately embraced them. His main task, as Chapter 3 in *LES1905* explains, was to convince them of the need for an alliance with the deputies who represented the peasantry in order to undermine the efforts of the liberal Cadet party that wanted the peasant representatives' backing. A worker-peasant alliance rather than a liberal-peasant alliance was critical to Lenin's vision of Russia's bourgeois democratic revolution, the necessary vehicle for its socialist revolution. While the real and effective alliance of these two classes that he fought to forge lay outside the Duma walls, Lenin recognized that the legislative deliberations and the actions of the RSDLP Duma group or fraction, publicized by the Bolshevik press, could be invaluable toward that end. Success required a thoroughgoing critique of not only the Cadets but the Menshevik leadership who courted them on the assumption that Russia's liberal bourgeoisie, whom the Cadets represented, was the necessary class for a bourgeois democratic revolution. Lenin agreed that the coming Russian revolution was a bourgeois democratic one, but he looked not to the liberals but rather to the peasantry, who in its vast majority wanted to be property owners. And the peasant-elected deputies in the Duma were the closest thing the peasantry had to political representation. That was why Lenin followed the debates on the land question closely as well as intervening in them through his articles and drafts for the fraction members' speeches. As the dominant party in the First Duma, the Cadets, Lenin argued, would reveal their true counterrevolutionary colors. Informed by the lessons Marx and Engels drew from the European Spring, specifically the betrayal of the liberals, Lenin's forecast about the Cadets proved accurate.

By calcified Romanov standards, however, even a Cadet-led Duma proved too liberal, and it was sent packing after having sat for only three months. In the meantime the Bolsheviks and Mensheviks had a unity congress in Stockholm at which they agreed to important norms of how to do Duma work. The most significant was that the party had to exercise control over the Duma fraction. In anticipation of the Duma being prorogued and new elections being called, the congress also decided against electoral blocs with the Cadets. In response to Czar Nicholas's dismissal of the Duma, Lenin called on the RSDLP and peasant deputies to use their parliamentary immunity to organize armed resistance, a testament to how important Duma work—not just a venue to agitate and propagandize—had become for him.

With the First Duma experience under his belt, Lenin hit the ground running in preparation for the Second Duma—how Chapter 4 in *LES1905* begins. This time he made sure the Bolsheviks would not boycott the elections, and after an intense internal party debate and vote he won the majority to his position. It wasn't easy to make the case given the increasingly repressive policies of the regime. This was the moment when Lenin wrote the most he ever did on the organization of armed struggle. He then made preparations for the election campaign and composed the first of his key writings on the topic. The heart of the article was the ever-current issue of vote splitting and the lesser-evil conundrum that has always confronted progressive forces in the electoral arena. Wouldn't failure to form a bloc with the Cadets allow the fascist-like Black Hundreds to be victorious? Lenin, informed by Marx and Engels's *Address*, disagreed on both political and evidential grounds; for the latter, with his penchant for number crunching, he made a detailed analysis of election returns for the First Duma. It and related articles explained how to construct electoral blocs and conduct the election campaign in conformity with independent working-class political action. Once the Second Duma convened in February 1907 with a much larger representation of peasant and RSDLP deputies, respectively 157 and 67 out of 524 in total, Lenin immediately took up where he had left off with the First Duma, working closely with the fraction, most of whom were Mensheviks, to forge the worker-peasant alliance. The land question was again the central issue. The speeches Lenin drafted for the fraction were designed to convince the peasant deputies—and the larger public who read them in the Bolshevik press—why the working class and not the liberal Cadets were their real allies. The peasant deputies' votes and speeches gave Lenin reason to believe his strategy was working. Another and more inclusive party congress, in London this time, gave him more authority to lead that effort. It was success in that work that helped put the new Duma once again on a collision course with the government.

In June 1907 the regime pulled the plug on the Second Duma, arrested most of the RSDLP deputies, and decreed new elections, but this time under rules that would guarantee a Duma more to its liking. Chapter 1 in this volume commences with an account of how Lenin once again had to convince his Bolshevik comrades to take part despite the blatantly undemocratic new rules. In doing so, he offered his most succinct analysis of 1905's events and of how revolutionaries should partake in undemocratic elections. The debate eventually resulted in a split in Bolshevik ranks, with the departure of a minority who wanted either to boycott the elections or, later, to recall those RSDLP deputies they claimed comported themselves poorly in the Duma. While the paper trail for Lenin's role in the Third Duma election campaign is sparser than the Second Duma's, it's clear that he was just as active, even from afar. The new electoral rules achieved their purpose: both the RSDLP and peasant representation were significantly reduced in the new Duma, from 67 to 18 and 157 to 13, respectively, out of 442 deputies. Because the Third Duma's tenure from 1907 to 1912 coincided with the downturn in the class struggle—the counterrevolution was in full swing—it offered fewer opportunities to coordinate Duma work with mass work. Nevertheless, Lenin was able to deepen collaboration between the RSDLP and peasant deputies. In hindsight it also proved a useful training ground for what Lenin would call revolutionary parliamentary work, the combination of legal and illegal work. But that required a party leadership committed to such a method. That only occurred when the de facto Bolshevik-Menshevik split in the RSDLP became "official" in 1912, giving Lenin a clearer hand in leading the work.

The convening of the Fourth Duma at the end of 1912 coincided with a new upsurge in the class struggle, making it possible to use the parliamentary arena to "prepare for . . . a new Russian revolution"—the focus of Chapter 2. The axis of the Bolshevik election campaign was the clarification of the difference between liberalism and democracy, which in turn determined its approach to electoral agreements. The election results served as a "test" of these two very different perspectives before the electorate. Though the RSDLP fraction was reduced to 13, its 6 Bolshevik deputies, unlike the 7 Mensheviks, were firmly rooted in the industrial working class unlike ever before, owing in part to a unique electoral process that gave the working class its own electoral college. The 11-member peasant representation continued to work with the RSDLP deputies, especially the Bolsheviks. Armed with a daily, *Pravda*, that entailed a constant game of hide and seek with the government and its censors, Lenin, still from afar, was in a much better position to coordinate the legal and illegal work. Most important for posterity, one of the Bolshevik deputies left an invaluable eyewitness account. The insurmountable differences between the Menshevik and Bolshevik deputies resulted in a very public split in fall 1913, followed by a very awkward situation for the Bolsheviks: a fraction head on the payroll of the Czar's secret police.

All this came to a head with the near-revolutionary situation in July 1914 and then the Guns of August of the First World War. Only the

Bolshevik deputies, now down to five, stood up to the regime's chauvinist campaign and, using their parliamentary immunity status, actively campaigned against the war. Their counterparts in the German party and elsewhere in Western Europe, fearful of losing their legal status, failed overwhelmingly to do the same. For their efforts the Bolshevik deputies were arrested, put on trial, and sentenced to hard labor at the beginning of 1915. Their antiwar work and the comportment of one of the deputies at the trial became for Lenin a "model of revolutionary parliamentarism."

The overthrow of the three-hundred-year-old Romanov dynasty in February 1917, a consequence of the war, made it possible for Lenin and the Bolsheviks to use the revived parliamentary arena once again, but this time accompanied by a new kind of governing institution. Soviets, unlike the dumas, combined legislative and executive functions. The decadelong experience with the four state Dumas served the Bolsheviks well in carrying out this kind of work, as Chapter 3 shows. Elections to municipal dumas and the soviets permitted the Bolsheviks to do exactly what Marx and Engels had counseled about the advantages of universal suffrage for the working-class party: to "count their forces," to "gauge the maturity of the working class," to measure the "boiling point among the workers," and to indicate "with the most perfect accuracy the day when a call to armed revolution has to be made." This advice, crucial to Lenin's calculus, when combined with the Duma experience, explains not only when and why the Bolsheviks were able to lead the working class to state power in October 1917 but why that conquest was successfully defended. One of his many tasks afterward was to distill and generalize those lessons for aspiring revolutionaries elsewhere in the world.

The four claims this book makes, to repeat, are that, first, no one did more to use the electoral and parliamentary arenas for revolutionary ends than Lenin. Second, the framework he used and conclusions he reached were squarely rooted in the politics of Karl Marx and Frederick Engels. Third, the historic split in international Marxism between communism and social democracy was a de facto reality before the Guns of August of 1914 exploded, owing in large part to two very different conceptions of how Marxists should comport themselves in the two arenas—with Lenin on one side and what would become twentieth-century social democracy on the other side. Last, the head-start program the founders of the modern communist movement left to Lenin on electoral/parliamentary politics goes a long way toward explaining why the Bolsheviks were hegemonic in October 1917.

(1) It's possible that someone else did more than Lenin to use the electoral and parliamentary arenas for revolutionary ends—but there is

no written record of such a person. What does the record reveal about Lenin himself and about Lenin in relation to such a possible other? The reader, I suspect, has been surprised, as I was, to learn how much Lenin had to say about the electoral/parliamentary process. What's presented in these two volumes is at best 5 percent of what exists in the *Lenin Collected Works* (*LCW*), the most complete publication of his writings in English, exceeded only by the slightly longer Russian edition. The bulk of his writings on the topic are from between the 1905 Revolution and the 1915 trial of the five Bolshevik deputies, from volume 8 to 21 of the 45-volume collection and distilled in Chapters 3 and 4 in *LES1905*, and Chapters 1 and 2 in this volume. I estimate that in those 14 volumes only the peasant question received more attention—which was not separate from the electoral/parliamentary question, as his efforts to forge the worker-peasant alliance through Duma work show. For the entire collection, there are approximately as many entries in the subject index volume for the electoral/parliamentary topics as for topics related to his better known party-building project. The norm of democratic centralism, for example, was—unappreciated until now—intimately linked to electoral/parliamentary work. More concretely, should delegated party-meeting decisions be binding on the Duma fraction or not? In addition, it can be rightly assumed that the *LCW* doesn't include all that he ever wrote on the topics. Krupskaya, as noted, said that many records had to be destroyed before she and Lenin escaped Finland at the end of 1907, much of which, no doubt, had to do with the elections and activities of the party fraction to the Second Duma. Also known is that they abandoned troves of records when they were forced to flee Cracow when the war began. According to one estimate, it amounted to the equivalent of 640 volumes, or 14 times the size of the 45-volume *LCW*![3] It doesn't appear, from a close reading of the *LCW*, that any of that—much of which certainly dealt with the Fourth Duma—found its way into the 45 volumes.

It is patently clear, therefore, that electoral/parliamentary politics was as central to Lenin's project as anything else—unacknowledged in any of the standard Leninological accounts. More important is that the axis around which this work revolved, what this book details, was fidelity to revolutionary politics. Because the Bolsheviks had a significant core of skeptics within their ranks who doubted it could be done, Lenin was forced to make a case for participation and provide evidence that he was right. In addition to those Bolshevik were the abstentionist anarchist-minded forces, best represented by the Socialist Revolutionaries. The near-absolutist character of Czarist Russia understandably bred skepticism about participation in either arena.

On the other hand, there were the Mensheviks who were always inclined to do just what the skeptics feared—compromise revolutionary politics. A recurring theme in Lenin's polemics to them was the refutation of their lesser-evil/Black Hundred scare tactic, employed to justify support for the Cadets. The combination of the two tendencies required vigilance and agility on his part. The mistakes of the Third Duma fraction and the criticisms they engendered from the boycottists forced Lenin to not just defend participation in the Duma but produce positive results. Midway into the tenure of the Third Duma, Lenin took charge to make sure that would happen. In anticipation of the elections to the Fourth Duma and the need to prepare for them and avoid the weaknesses of the Third Duma fraction, Lenin took the fateful steps, the Prague Conference in 1912, that effectively put to bed the old RSDLP and birthed the new Bolshevik party—again, the nexus between electoral/parliamentary work and party building.

What about Lenin vis-à-vis a possible other? Was there anyone else who came close to producing such a corpus of writings either before or during his lifetime? It's unlikely, because had they existed Lenin would have made reference to them. When he began in 1905 to write in a sustained manner on the topic, he cited everything he could find that Marx and Engels had to say. Even before then, he cited Kautsky's 1893 book *Parliamentarism*, from which Lenin probably took the term. He looked closely at anything the German party (the SPD) did and said, since it was indeed the flagship institution of international social democracy. Rather than any particular writings, he more often pointed to the actions of the SPD and the examples of Bebel and Liebknecht as models for comportment in both arenas. There is no body of SPD literature as extensive, certainly, that details electoral/parliamentary work in the way that Lenin's output does. Buried, perhaps, in party archives is a treasure trove of documents waiting to be discovered. But until then, I stand by this claim. Nor for any other West European social democratic party is there anything comparable to what Lenin produced. Dutch Marxist Anton Pannekoek's *The Tactical Differences in the Labor Movement*, published in 1910, which Lenin praised, is the exception to the rule.

Neither did the Mensheviks nor any of their leaders like Martov produce anything as rich as did Lenin. Without having thoroughly plowed Menshevik sources, it's safe to make that claim, because here, too, Lenin's own record is instructive. Owing to their intense and public debates, he was unlikely to ignore any significant Menshevik interventions. There's more to be learned, for example, about Martov's views on the electoral/parliamentary work by reading Lenin than what his well-known and otherwise authoritative biography supplies.[4] The fact is that none of the Mensheviks were willing to put in the time and energy to be as vigilant as was Lenin in making sure that work hewed to revolutionary standards. Whereas the Mensheviks had an interest in minimizing differences with the Cadets—in constant quest for an alliance with them—Lenin seized every opportunity around Duma elections and Duma deliberations to educate workers on the differences between revolutionary social democracy and liberalism, arguably the most repeated theme in his interventions. That required far more ink. That the German movement didn't, apparently, produce anything comparable to what the Russians did probably had to do with the fact that by the time the latter came onto the parliamentary scene, the SPD had settled down into a kind of routinism without controversy. The consequences of a lack of debate about that modus operandi only became clear when the Guns of August exploded.

As for what happened after Lenin, nothing came close to equaling what he produced. Two reasons, I think, account for this. The proponents of Moscow's Popular Front policy, the vast majority of those who claimed to do politics in his name, had, as I suggested in Chapter 3, no interest in promoting and therefore expanding on what he'd done. For those, on the other hand, who wanted to emulate his example and had the good fortune to actually know what it was—most likely those allied with and/or descended from Trotsky's Left Opposition—their task, as they saw it, wasn't the reinvention of the wheel. Rather it was to put the wheel in motion. The lessons Lenin drew, codified in the Theses of the Second Congress of Comintern in 1920, had said all that was essential.

(2) What about the second claim, that Lenin's electoral/parliamentary strategy was squarely rooted in Marx and Engels's program? Lenin, as the record makes clear, certainly thought so. The question, though, is whether he was correct. Chapter 1 in *LES1905*, "What Marx and Engels Bequeathed," makes possible an informed answer. There were basically two debates in which he was engaged: one with the abstentionists, such as the boycottists, anarchists, and Socialist Revolutionaries, about whether to partake in electoral politics; the other, with the Mensheviks, Plekhanov, and Kautsky, about how revolutionary social democrats should conduct themselves in political spheres. Let's begin with the former, the easier of the two to address.

There is no instance in the Marx-Engels record of either ever advocating nonparticipation in the electoral arena. To the contrary, they enthusiastically embraced it. As soon as the 1848 revolt made it possible for workers to vote for a constituent assembly and parliament, Marx and Engels organized, even under prejudicial rules and in opposition to some in the workers' movement, a campaign in the name of the Communist League. When the workers' movement in Germany revived in the 1860s, they applauded its independent working-class political action. They pointed to the electoral gains of what would eventually be the SPD as a model for affiliates to the International Working Men's Association (IWA). At the London Conference in 1871, they opposed the abstentionist stance of the anarchists and succeeded in getting the IWA to make independent working-class political action including electoral participation official policy—the go-ahead for launching mass working-class political parties. In critiquing the Bolshevik boycotters and abstentionism of the Socialist Revolutionaries, Lenin therefore was indisputably carrying out the line of Marx and Engels.

What about his differences with the Mensheviks et al. about how the proletariat should comport itself in the electoral/parliamentary arena? Who was more faithful to Marx and Engels's program? This requires a closer reading of their texts. Plekhanov, certainly, and some of the Mensheviks, rested their case (wooing the liberal Cadet Party) on their reading of the *Communist Manifesto*, written before the 1848–1849 Revolutions began. Specifically, the sentence in Part IV of the document that states that communists must "fight with the bourgeoisie whenever it acts in a revolutionary way, against the absolute monarchy, the feudal squirearchy, and the petty bourgeoisie"[5] is what they pointed to in justifying their unending quest for an alliance with the Cadets. Lenin, who is said to have committed it to memory, countered with the *Address of March 1850* and other balance sheets Marx and Engels drew on the 1848–49 upheavals. The fact is that the liberal bourgeoisie in both Germany and France caved in to the authoritarian forces and could no longer be expected to lead the bourgeois democratic revolution—the basic lesson of the European Spring.[6] In Germany, the liberal bourgeoisie had succumbed to "parliamentary cretinism"—a label Lenin enjoyed tacking on to their homologues in Russia—and failed to recognize that the real fight for democracy lay outside the walls of the parliamentary arena. The French revolution and counterrevolution taught that universal suffrage was a means to an end, not an end in itself: "It had to be set aside by a revolution or by the reaction."

As the *Address* insisted, only independent working-class political action in the electoral arena could ensure victory for the democratic struggle— exactly what Lenin advocated and fought for. That required the workers' party to run its own candidates "alongside the bourgeois-democratic candidates . . . Even where there is no prospect whatever of their being elected." Doing so allowed it "to count their forces and to lay before the public their revolutionary attitude and party standpoint." The workers' party should not be misled by the claims of the democrats that in so doing "they are splitting the democratic party and giving the reactionaries the possibility of victory . . . The advance which the proletarian party is bound to make by such independent action is infinitely more important than the disadvantage that might be incurred by the presence of a few reactionaries in the representative body."[7] Lenin therefore had every reason to believe that in rejecting the Menshevik policy of courting the Cadets or forming electoral blocs with them he was acting in complete accordance with the historic program of Marx and Engels.

The next most important conclusion in the Marx-Engels arsenal, in chronological order, was the key lesson of the Paris Commune—namely, that the working class could not use the bourgeois republic to carry out socialist transformation; the Communards had to construct a new state form. That lesson—the only addendum Marx and Engels ever made to the *Manifesto*—informed, more than any other, Lenin's defense contra Kautsky et al. of the soviet state as a democratic form superior to the parliamentary republic. The similarity of soviet governance to the Commune, the way in which it performed before and after October 1917, and the fact that it was more popular with workers and peasants than parliamentary governance—neither voted with their feet in favor of the latter when push came to shove—also gave Lenin just reason to claim that his politics were more faithful than his opponents' to Marx and Engels's program.

Marx and Engels's *Circular Letter of 1879* was their principal statement about how working-class parties should conduct themselves in the parliamentary arena. One of its themes, that the parliamentary group must be subordinate to the party and its decisions, is precisely what Lenin insisted on about the Duma fractions and what increasingly put him at odds with the Mensheviks. They wanted more flexibility for the fraction in order that it be able to bend to the whims of the Cadets. The differences between the two on this and related matters resulted in the fraction being formally split in the Fourth Duma into two wings: one Bolshevik and the other Menshevik-liquidator. Again, as with other Marx-Engels foundational documents, the *Circular Letter* sounded more Lenin-like than Menshevik-like.

In other writings of the era when the German party was increasing its share of vote totals, Marx and Engels reiterated their utilitarian approach to universal suffrage and elections. The most notable comment came in Engels's *Origin of the Family, Private Property and the State*, written in connection with the approaching 1884 Reichstag elections: "Universal suffrage is the gauge of the maturity of the working class. It cannot and never will be anything more in the present-day state; but that is sufficient. On the day the thermometer of universal suffrage registers boiling-point among the workers, both they and the capitalists will know where they stand." He wrote more explicitly in a private communication: "[U]niversal suffrage . . . indicates with the most perfect accuracy the day when a call to armed revolution has to be made." No advice, as the events of 1917 reveal—detailed in Chapter 3—was as influential and consequential as this in Lenin's calculus for the timing of the Bolshevik-led insurrection.

With his partner in his grave, it fell to Engels to counsel the German party as well as others. On more than one occasion, he cautioned against thinking that the number of seats won in an election was decisive. To assume so was to indulge illusions of a peaceful route to the working class taking power. In his final years, Engels fought to dispel such a reading of his own views, particularly in the case of Germany: "I have never said the socialist party will become the majority and then proceed to take power. On the contrary, I have expressly said that the odds are ten to one that our rulers, well before that point arrives, will use violence against us, and this would shift us from the terrain of majority to the terrain of revolution."[8] In broad strokes, this comes awfully close to what actually happened in Russia in 1917 and why Lenin, against the objections of Kautsky—the issue of the majority—felt rightly that the Bolshevik-led insurrection was very much in the mold of Marx and Engels.

In sum, then, the totality of Marx and Engels's positions as detailed in Chapter 1 in *LES1905* offer convincing evidence that Lenin's electoral/parliamentary strategy was indeed more faithful to their politics than that of his opponents like Plekhanov, the Mensheviks, and Kautsky.

A final observation—both Marx and Engels, as pointed out in Chapter 1, expressed on occasion leeriness about Kautsky, his grasp of politics and theory, and his character. In contrast is the comment Engels made about the Russians that he and Marx were beginning to work with in 1872, worth repeating: "As far as talent and character are concerned, some of [them] . . . are absolutely among the very best in our party. They have a stoicism, a strength of character and at the same time a grasp of theory which are truly admirable." Though he was barely two years old when it was written, no Russian, I contend, better fitted that description than Lenin. Trotsky, a one-time opponent whose own Marxist theoretical credentials were second only to Lenin's—his theory of Stalinism being his most original contribution—was more qualified than anyone to write of Lenin, "Marx has never had a better reader, one more penetrating or more grateful, nor a more attentive, congenial, or capable student."[9]

(3) What about the argument that the historic split in international Marxism between communism and social democracy was effectively in place—irreconcilable differences—before the Guns of August of 1914 exploded due in large part to two very different conceptions of how Marxists should comport themselves in the electoral/parliamentary arenas, with Lenin on one side and what would become twentieth-century social democracy on the other side? In the immediate aftermath of the fateful vote for war credits, Lenin offered an explanation. The German party, the chief culprit, had made "a fetish of the necessary utilization of bourgeois parliamentarism and bourgeois legality." Afraid they'd lose their parliamentary immunity, their deputies failed to act as the five Bolsheviks did—to engage in revolutionary antiwar work. But even prior to this "betrayal of socialism," the leadership of the Second International "had long been preparing to wreck" the organization by succumbing to opportunism and bourgeois reformism, "the danger of which have long been indicated by the finest representatives of the revolutionary proletariat of all countries."[10] The question then is what evidence is there prior to August 1914 that supports Lenin's claims?

It was the debate on the colonial and antiwar questions at the 1907 Congress of the Second International (see Chapter 1) that first revealed for Lenin the tendency of the German party to bend to opportunism, the "sacrifice of the future of the movement for its present" as Engels defined it in his criticism of the party's draft program in 1891. The debate on militarism was especially instructive. Georg Vollmar, the leader of the SPD's right wing—and once the target of Engels's critique of that wing—exemplified "parliamentary cretinism." Instead of limiting antiwar work to "parliamentary methods" as he advocated, revolutionary social democracy, Lenin argued, should "utilize the crisis created by the war to hasten the overthrow of the bourgeoisie"—exactly what the Bolsheviks would do seven years later. Along with the fact that the Cadets and other liberals were now beginning to hold up the SPD as a model that the Bolsheviks should emulate, the conduct of the Germans at the congress no doubt prompted Lenin to look more closely at the party that had indeed once been his inspiration.[11] Clearly a portion of it, if not the whole, had succumbed to the "parliamentary disease."[12]

In the debates with the boycotters and recallists (see Chapter 1), Lenin came to the defense of the German party against accusations that it practiced "parliamentarism at any price." This might suggest that he backtracked on his increasing sobriety about the party in the aftermath of the 1907 Congress. The evidence reveals, rather, that he increasingly differentiated between the opportunist and revolutionary wings of the SPD.

He did the same with regard to the British movement (Chapter 2), and in both cases, especially for Germany, he expected that the revolutionaries, more prevalent in the ranks than in the leaderships, would be triumphant. Whether his optimism was warranted is debatable. The subsequent trajectories of both parties would suggest that it was misplaced. But that's the benefit of hindsight the historian enjoys. Lenin was first and foremost a politician who sought to influence outcomes as he did when in 1913 he called on the ranks in the British movement to challenge the opportunist electoral and parliamentary practices of their reformist leaders.

The growing split in the RSDLP Duma fraction in the Fourth Duma anticipated more than anything the eventual split in international social democracy. Kautsky exposed his heretofore pro-Menshevik sympathies by effectively siding with them when the split actually took place—his "unpardonable error" as Lenin called it in December 1913. His assumption that only parliamentary or legal work counted in determining the well-being of a workers' party was telling—why the German party was unwilling to jeopardize its legality and do what the Bolshevik five did when the Great War began. "We must not play down the *disease which* the German party is undoubtedly suffering from," Lenin wrote five months before August 4.

Finally, there was the conference in Brussels on the eve of the war that the leadership of the International called to discuss the split in the Russian party. Lenin had no illusions about its outcome. He assumed correctly that the "officers' corps" of Western European social democracy was more sympathetic to the Mensheviks than the Bolsheviks. When they ruled that the latter should liquidate themselves, it only confirmed what he had concluded by then—an irreconcilable split existed in international social democracy between a reformist wing and a revolutionary wing.

Not only were the differences between the two wings in place and increasingly acknowledged by Lenin, but they go a long way in explaining the two very different responses to the outbreak of the First World War: that of the five Bolshevik deputies on one side (along with the Serbian party) versus on the other not only the majority of the SPD Reichstag Fraktion but the seven Menshevik deputies as well. Unlike the Bolsheviks, the SPD and Mensheviks were unwilling to use their parliamentary status for antiwar work. The similar response or lack thereof of the latter two to the war suggests that the different response of the Bolsheviks can't be attributed to their operating in a different national environment. That the Menshevik parliamentary strategy was similar to that of the SPD—legality at any price (they were called liquidators because they wanted to end the kind of illegal work the Bolsheviks practiced)—is strong evidence that it was indeed political and not national differences that determined how parties responded to the war. Whether Lenin fully appreciated the significance of the difference is admittedly uncertain, since it appears that he, too, was surprised by the fateful vote of the SPD Fraktion. Nevertheless, the evidence is quite strong that before the outbreak of the Great War two irreconcilable groupings existed in international social democracy that centered on fundamental disagreements about how to carry out electoral and parliamentary work and that largely explain their differential responses to the war.

(4) The last argument, that the head-start program the founders of the modern communist movement left to Lenin on electoral/parliamentary politics was key in why the Bolsheviks were hegemonic in October 1917, is the most important, because it addresses the "So what?" question. That is, what difference did it make that electoral/parliamentary work was central to Lenin's politics and that it was squarely rooted in the project of Marx and Engels? Chapter 3 makes the case for the fourth argument. There are, first, the events in 1917 leading up to the Bolshevik-led triumph and, second, Lenin's post-October reflections.

Once Lenin returned to Russia after the February Revolution, he consciously and actively used the new and unprecedented political space to win the effective majority to socialist revolution—those willing to vote with their feet. Participation in the elections to the soviets and local dumas and their deliberations figured significantly in his strategy. Thus the rich experience of the Bolsheviks leading up to and in the four state Dumas, distilled in Chapter 3 in *LES1905* and Chapters 1 and 2 in this volume, could serve them well in carrying out this strategy. Compared, however, to the published record about those pre-1914 activities, what's available for what Lenin did after he returned in April is much sparser. The main reason, I suspect, is that once back in Petrograd he could have more face-to-face meetings, thus leaving a thinner paper trail. However, there is enough published evidence, I argue, to make the case.

For Lenin, after the July Days and the Kerensky-Kornilov putsch attempt, it was no longer a question of whether to take power but when. Decisive in his calculations were the elections to the soviets and local dumas. The advice of Marx and Engels, some of which he knew by heart, had currency for him like never before. From their *Address of March 1850* to Engels's *Origin of the Family, Private Property and the State* to a letter to Paul Lafargue decades later, elections, respectively, allowed workers "to count their forces," or were "the thermometer that registers the boiling point among workers," or, even more explicitly, indicated "with the most perfect accuracy the day when a call to armed revolution has to be made." No wonder, then, why Lenin went into full campaign mode for the municipal duma elections in July and August. The details of that campaign from other sources, including the memoirs of Bolshevik leaders who described the elections as a means of "taking the revolutionary temperature of the masses," Krupskaya's account about her own involvement in the election campaign, the tone and language of the campaign literature in the party press, all suggest that Lenin was indeed the orchestrator. His fingerprints, based on what he had done before not only in the elections to the four state Duma elections but in those to the municipal dumas in May 1917, were all over the campaign. The burden of proof is on those who argue otherwise.

Certainly, he pored over the vote totals. No other Bolshevik gave as much attention to election returns as Lenin. "The data on the parliamentary elections," as he explained to other Bolshevik leaders at the beginning of October in an effort to convince them of the need to take power, "are the objective facts regarding the majority of the revolutionary elements that are leading the people." Most of the Central Committee was won over. Not only, then, did Marx and Engels's advice inform the timing of Lenin's actions, but it proved to be efficacious, accounting for the relative ease with which the Provisional Government was overthrown.

After October, Lenin drew balance sheets on what the Bolsheviks had done and why they were successful. His analysis of the election returns for the Constituent Assembly was especially instructive. It revealed, he argued, why the Bolsheviks not only were victorious in October but would be in the civil war that was drawing to a close. And in his longest writing after the triumph, he attributed success in October to the decadelong experience of combining legal work, specifically participation in parliamentary work, and illegal work. That experience, he claimed, was "indispensable" in the Bolshevik victory—a lesson that would-be revolutionaries should absorb.

In showing that Lenin's electoral strategy was squarely rooted in Marx and Engels's project (this book's second argument), it becomes possible therefore to connect the dots between the politics of the two founders of the modern communist movement and the Bolshevik-led triumph in 1917. This is the first study—surprisingly, given all the forests felled for writing about the Russian Revolution—to do so. Demonstrating the historical links does not, certainly, make for a causal explanation. But for any credible explanation of a revolution, let alone a causal one—with all the difficulty that entails for social phenomena—connecting the political dots is a necessary step. Though the evidence is incontrovertible that Lenin attributed Bolshevik success to its electoral/parliamentary experience and saw it as thoroughly informed by Marx and Engels's politics, one could, of course, claim that he was simply wrong. For those who think so, I leave it to them to make that case. So far they have not.[13]

Many years ago I read an article Trotsky wrote toward the end of his life about the role of the individual in history.[14] The focus was Lenin— his indispensability to the outcome in October. Only now, after plowing through what was necessary to write this book, can I fully appreciate his claim. In the grand scheme of things, as Trotsky the historical materialist argued, socioeconomic-political conditions are indeed decisive in explaining history but only, as this investigation makes all so clear, if there is someone willing, in the best sense of the phrase, to take advantage of them. It is indisputable, as the particulars of the Russian Revolution clearly demonstrate, that Lenin was unique in doing so, and no one was better qualified than Trotsky to appreciate that fact. In other words, the subjective factor—leadership and program—is as critical to the outcome of the revolutionary process as are the objective factors.[15]

TOWARD AN EXPLANATION OF THE SILENCES

Lenin's political career began in 1893 and ended three decades later in 1923. The period when he was most active in electoral/parliamentary work was from 1905 to 1915—that is, a third of his political life. This fact is registered by his literary output if measured by the number of volumes in the 45-volume English edition of his collected works that covers that decade: volumes 8 to 21, almost a third. A close reading of those 14 volumes reveals that his electoral activities informed the bulk of what he wrote—evidence of how central that work was to his politics. But if it was so "indispensable" to the Bolshevik-led victory in October 1917, as the evidence demonstrates, then what explains the near silences in the literature of both friend and foe about such a copious and easily available (now online) record? As noted in the Preface in *LES1905*, the only writing I know that describes Lenin's electoral strategy (other than what he wrote) is *Lenin as Election Campaign Manager*, published originally in 1971 by Pathfinder Press. Still in print, the 23-page pamphlet is the best and, unfortunately, only introduction to the topic. That Pathfinder is the publisher is no accident. It is the publishing arm of the US Socialist Workers Party (SWP) that has its origins in the Left Opposition that Trotsky led against Stalin's counterrevolution. Trotsky, a leader of the Third International, coauthored, along with Bukharin and Zinoviev, "Theses on Communist Parties and Parliamentarism," which was adopted by delegates to the Second Congress in 1920. The document distilled and codified the lessons Lenin drew on not only the Russian but the Western European experience as well. The pamphlet acknowledges its roots in the "Theses" as well as the counsel that Trotsky, until his assassination in 1940, provided to fledgling parties such as the SWP that were inspired by the Bolshevik-led revolution. Therein lay in these facts a possible explanation of the silences, at least for Lenin's "friends."

Unlike what Trotsky sought to achieve, parties that took their lead from Moscow after the Popular Front strategy became de rigueur after 1935 placed proletarian revolution on the back burner. The priority now was making alliances with the "progressive" or "national" bourgeoisies of various countries, in the name of fighting fascism. Lenin's critique of such forces and his alternative—independent working-class electoral and parliamentary action—were now politically inconvenient. This had major implications for his writings in the hands of the growing Stalinist bureaucracy in worldwide pursuit of Popular Fronts. The vast majority of humanity would be introduced to him in his own words through what Moscow packaged—the various editions of his "selected" works. The daunting 45-volume complete works made such briefer editions popular. A close reading of them reveals that only one of Lenin's numerous writings on electoral politics, *Left-Wing Communism*, ever found its way into such collections, probably because it was too significant to be ignored and could be misread through a Popular Front lens. Also telling is that while Moscow put together numerous editions of selected writings of his on all kinds of topics, it never saw the need to do one on his electoral strategy.

Even with the collapse of the Soviet Union and its Eastern European allies, most of its one-time global affiliates still subscribe to the Popular Front strategy, the US Communist Party's continuing embrace of the Democratic Party being the prime example. Beijing, a Stalinist rival to Moscow after 1960, had its own version of the Popular Front strategy, the "bloc of four classes," and it too had no interest in promoting the real Lenin. Just as social democracy had no interest in publicizing the real Marx and Engels through such works as the *Address of March 1850* or the *Circular Letter of 1879*, Stalinism, in both incarnations, did the same for Lenin and for the same reason. Revolutionary electoral and parliamentary work a la Marx and Engels and later Lenin was incompatible with the opportunism of the former and the class-collaborationist orientation of the latter.

Only with the advent of the Cuban Revolution in 1959 did a major challenge to the Popular Front policy come into being. Unlike the movement that Mao Zedong led, Fidel Castro's July 26 Movement did not have roots in the Stalinist counterrevolution. In fact, it declared itself to the world an opponent of the class-collaborationist politics of Moscow and its affiliates in Latin America. The Second Declaration of Havana, issued at the beginning of 1962, in a not-too-subtle criticism of the modus operandi of the "communist" parties in Latin America, proclaimed that "in many countries of Latin America revolution is inevitable. The duty of every revolutionary is to make the revolution . . . it is not for revolutionaries to sit in the doorways of their houses waiting for the corpse of imperialism to pass by. The role of Job doesn't suit a revolutionary." This and other pronouncements of the young revolution, along with its actions, gave, perhaps unintentionally, the impression that what the Cubans had done, armed insurrection, was the only way forward.[16] Rather than a tactic as in Lenin's hands, it now became a strategy to the exclusion of parliamentary and other legal work.[17] Given the track record of the communist and social democratic parties in Latin America, such an outcome is not surprising. Leaders of Moscow's affiliate in Cuba, for example, served in the government of Fulgencio Batista, the dictator that Castro's July 26 Movement overthrew. If Batista is what legal work led to, then only, as many an aspiring revolutionary understandably inferred, illegal work such as armed struggle should be engaged in. Being unaware of Lenin's alternative—revolutionary parliamentarism—facilitated such conclusions. Only the small number of followers of Trotsky's Left Opposition would likely have known about it, but they didn't have the political weight to make a difference.

There is also a near silence on Lenin's electoral strategy in apparently sympathetic book-length accounts on the Bolsheviks and their leader; the reasons vary.[18] In the first volume, for example, of Tony Cliff's well-known biography, published originally in 1975, *Building the Party: Lenin 1893–1914*, encompassing the years he gave the most attention to that work, there are at best 15 pages on anything having to with the subject in the 200 pages of the 350-page volume covering the period from 1905 to 1915. While 5 pages are devoted to the debate about whether to boycott the Second Duma, and 8 to its deliberations about elections to and Bolshevik participation in the Fourth Duma, the reader would never know that it was Lenin who spent innumerable hours directing the Bolsheviks in winning seats to and participation in the four Dumas. On the other hand, an entire chapter of 10 pages is devoted to "Lenin on Armed Struggle," and there is another of 16 pages with the subtitle "Lenin Learns from Clausewitz."

The electoral lacuna in Cliff's account is not accidental, nor is the emphasis on armed struggle. He was a leader of the British Socialist Workers Party that for most of its history has rejected participation in electoral politics and counterposes to it direct action such as strikes and demonstrations. This was not unlike the stance of the Socialist Revolutionaries who disagreed with Lenin's electoral strategy. Anarcho-syndicalists, Lenin later pointed out, held similar views. Thus Cliff's own politics led him to distort the portrait, certainly for this period of Lenin's life, by understating one dimension of Lenin's practice and overstating the other—contributing to the miseducation of a generation or two of radicalizing youth who were looking for an alternative to the portraitures coming from Moscow.

In Neil Harding's two-volume narrative, *Lenin's Political Thought* (1977–78), the reader learns that early in his political life Lenin "imbibed his life-long regard for proper statistical preparation—an enduring trait in his writings."[19] But Harding provides not one iota of detail to illustrate the point when it came to his electoral/parliamentary work. Neither is there any mention of how Lenin employed that work to realize Harding's also correct claim about the centrality of the worker-peasant alliance to Lenin's politics. Of the 300 pages in the first and relevant volume of his book, at best 15 of them address Duma politics, and within that too-brief treatment Lenin's activities hardly amount to a couple of sentences. His "thought" and action in the electoral arena are evidently of minor interest to Harding.

Alan Woods's *Bolshevism: The Road to Power* (1999) is only a slight improvement over the previous accounts.[20] In the almost 300 pages covering 1905 to 1915, out of 600 pages, 37 are devoted to the Bolsheviks in the four state dumas, mainly the First, the Second, and the Fourth. The reader is able to get a glimpse of Lenin's role as director of the Bolshevik fraction in the Fourth Duma. However, there is nothing about him as election campaign manager in any of the duma elections or his work with the RSDLP fraction in the Third Duma, the longest sitting of all four. As is the case with Cliff, Woods's own politics might explain the inadequate attention to this crucial dimension of Lenin's practice. His organization, the International Marxist Tendency, as far as I can tell, like that of Cliff's, appears not to encourage election campaigns for its affiliates. Its self-description as a "Trotskyist" organization implies that having organic links to Trotsky's Left Opposition does not guarantee fealty to his politics, specifically those for the electoral arena.

More recently, Christopher Read's *Lenin: A Revolutionary Life* (2005), a work that doesn't appear to be connected with any political tendency as far as I can determine, replicates even more so the silencing done by the previous apparently sympathetic accounts.[21] In the relevant section of the three-hundred-page book, about eighty pages, Read manages to generate at best a page about Lenin's interest in Duma activities. And as the others do, he's treated as only an observer and never as a participant. Perhaps this had to do with Read being, as he describes himself, first and foremost an academic, a group that in general has little experience in actual political work. His greater attention to ideas in Lenin's biography suggests as much.

This might explain the character of an even more recent biography whose author, Lars Lih, is also an academic. His *Lenin* (2011) is filled with many fascinating and until now unknown facts about the Bolshevik leader.[22] But in the forty pages that cover the period from 1905 to 1915 of its two hundred pages, there are only three and a half pages about the party's parliamentary work—two and a half of which are quite riveting in illustrating Lenin's deep commitment to Duma work. For a biography whose purpose is to make the case for Lenin's emotional connect to his political project, this is an odd omission.[23] Nothing instantiates that tie better than all the time and energy he devoted to electoral and parliamentary work—testimony to his deep conviction in the revolutionary potential of the masses.

The silences of Lenin's "friends" enabled those of his enemies, those who explicitly oppose his perspective and politics—a conspiracy of silence. A survey of some of the most influential texts of that milieu is instructive.[24] Bertram Wolfe's highly acclaimed cold war text, *Three Who Made a Revolution* (1948) is a good place to begin.[25] The 25 pages or so devoted to Lenin's parliamentary work, out of 200 (Trotsky and Stalin are the other two figures around which the 600-page narrative is weaved), is, in general, an accurate distillation of the facts. But along the way Wolfe, as if surprised at what he found, saw the need to add gratuitous remarks that unfortunately soiled what was positive in his brief exposition.[26] His volume had a lot of cachet because it came from a one-time insider—Wolfe had once been a functionary for Moscow—and it introduced the first generation of post–Second World War readers to Lenin and the Bolsheviks.

Following Wolfe, an academic take on Lenin, with all the abstractions that often come with such an enterprise, achieved acclaim. Alfred Meyer's *Leninism* (1957) introduced an entire generation of aspiring academics to the Bolshevik leader.[27] It's a prime example of how not to read Lenin, what Lih calls a "textbook" rendering of him, and what this book consciously rejects. Meyer begins with a set of abstract categories related to Lenin's party activities and for which he claims to distill Lenin's views by drawing on various statements—no more than 5 percent of Lenin's text, if that—uttered at different moments of his political life but without the context. In effect the reader is given a set of conclusions about Lenin that Meyer has drawn to serve as premises for reading two historic moments in Lenin's life: the Revolution of 1905 and that of October 1917. Of relevance for purposes here is his assertion that by about 1914 Lenin had rethought his earlier supposed approval of "constitutional democracy" as a means for socialist revolution. This permits Meyer to contend that by then Lenin no longer entertained the possibility of "using both constitutional and unconstitutional means" for waging revolutionary struggles. With such a dubious conclusion—contradicted specifically by Lenin's work in relation to the Third Duma—Meyer could apparently convince himself why his duma work was nonexistent.[28] I count at best two sentences in the 160 pages that cover the relevant period that even hint—both having to do with his opposition to the boycottists and recallists—that Lenin engaged in parliamentary work. The silences are deafening.

A decade later, a storyteller, a journalist this time, took center stage because his biography, with endorsements from the illuminati, won a National Book Award in 1965—Louis Fischer's *The Life of Lenin*. Fischer, apparently a one-time fellow traveler, presented, in contrast to what preceded, a more balanced account for those who were suspicious of the heavy handedness of Lenin's enemies and sought something different. But this made Fischer's rendering all the more insidious. In the fifty relevant pages of his seven-hundred-page work, only five sentences came close to acknowledging that Lenin had been involved in duma work, his opposition to the boycotttists and recallists. Had that been all, Fischer could be accused of merely being a myopic sympathizer. But his specious charge that Lenin's call to dismiss the Constituent Assembly violated majority opinion, which, as discussed earlier, flies in the face of the facts on the ground, revealed only a velvet-gloved foe.[29]

Robert Service's three-volume opus, *Lenin: A Political Life*, published between 1985 and 1995, also came with rave reviews.[30] But he, too, like his predecessors in this category of writers, seems to have suffered from writer's block when it came to Lenin's electoral and parliamentary activities. Loquacious when it came to other issues, especially anything that might have cast a pall of suspicion over Lenin's democratic credentials, Service could only manage to write the equivalent of 13 pages on the subject in the 160 pages dealing with the period, out of a 1,000-page work. What is presented—never, as is true with the other foes, in Lenin's own words—is often tendentious and only occasionally accurate.[31] It's clear from the text and footnotes that Service was thoroughly familiar with Lenin's activities and knew far more than he let on and therefore consciously misrepresented the record.

Finally, there is Orlando Figes's *A People's Tragedy: A History of the Russian Revolution*, published in 1996 and also an award winner. Unlike the prior writings, it's a synthetic account of the revolution that drew on what was considered the best of the extant original research, making it authoritative in academic circles. In many ways it is quite informative—as some of my references to it demonstrate—as well as being very readable. But if he had his druthers, Figes would have airbrushed Lenin out of the story. Obviously, he couldn't, and when introduced as a protagonist in the nine-hundred-page narrative, Lenin is a "domineering personality," with a "cruel and angry streak," a "putschist" with "dictatorial tendencies" and "a profound mistrust of the revolutionary potential of the masses," and hence a "mistrust of democracy." With such an intro, it's easy to understand now the silences in this genre of the literature—why, as should be clear to any reader of this book, Figes, like Lenin's other enemies, had to conceal Lenin's electoral/parliamentary work. There is not even a hint of it in the relevant section of the narrative; only once, in passing, does his name even appear. Lenin the ogre, the portrait that the Leninological industry had worked long and hard to manufacture, is utterly incompatible with that work. Why would someone who had "a profound mistrust of the revolutionary potential of the masses" spend so much time in the elections to and fraction work in every Duma—certainly after the First—trying to forge a worker-peasant alliance—that is, winning the overwhelming majority to a revolutionary perspective? As long as the facts were concealed—the conspiracy of silence—his literary foes didn't have to explain the disconnect with their portraiture. I also suspect that Lenin's enemies, mainly liberal in composition, hated that he successfully used what they regarded as sacred space, the parliamentary arena, to build a mass revolutionary movement.

With the collapse of the Soviet Union, some state archives became accessible to scholars for the first time. One of the latter, the well-known Leninologist Richard Pipes, was able to sift through thousands of the documents and publish (113 in total) those that confirmed his long-standing antipathy for Lenin the "misanthrope" (he didn't reveal what else he had found). Pipes titled his book *The Unknown Lenin: From the Secret Archive.*[32] With a touch of sarcasm, I could have used the same title for this book (and with more cause) but with a slightly different subtitle: *From the Not So Secret Archive.*

SO WHAT? OR, TODAY'S REALITY

The question now is whether any of this largely unacknowledged history of Lenin's practice, though interesting and at times fascinating, has any relevance for today's activists—certainly the question Lenin would have asked. On occasion, as the close reader has noted, I've suggested that it indeed does. The challenges posed for activists in the "Arab Spring," for example, are not unlike what those who partook in the 1905 Revolution faced. When—one of the critical questions for revolutionary forces in both upheavals—should elections be boycotted or not? And then there is the ever-present "lesser of two evils" conundrum that progressive-minded forces confront in the electoral arena and that Lenin first addressed in the elections to the Second Duma. Do today's Black Hundreds—for example, in the US case, the Republican Tea Partiers—make the today's Cadets—the Democrats—the lesser of two evils? If so, does that mean Lenin would have objected to a bloc with the Democrats and their standard bearer Barack Obama in the recent presidential election just as he did with the Cadets? The present task is to be explicit. What follows can at best be only an introduction to how Lenin's course can inform progressive politics today. A recently published collection of essays conveniently provides an opportunity to do just that.

The Question of Strategy—Socialist Register 2013 is the latest *Socialist Register* annual that in 2010 began to address the then still-unfolding global capitalist crisis. Whereas the previous two volumes sought to explain the crisis, the current one "examines the choices faced by the left today, the models of strategy available to it, and the innovations that are being made by groups as they organize in diverse settings."[33] A premise of the collection is that while a "break from capitalism . . . an insurrectionary rupture might someday be possible, it hardly seems in the realm of possibility anytime in the near future . . . What, then, should an anti-capitalist strategy look like, when capitalism is likely to shape the landscape of social and political struggle, at least for the middle run?"[34] Within that framework, the essays begin with an analysis of the current state of the crisis and then concretize the response of activists in different settings— for example, trade unions and the various occupation movements in the United States, Left parties in Europe, specifically Italy and Greece, and then elsewhere in South Africa and Latin America. Feminist politics is given special attention. It concludes with a return to the "American Left" in historical perspective, Badiou's "idea of communism," and the "state and future of socialism." Scattered throughout the essays are more than passing mention of the Arab Spring, "los indignados" in Spain, and others in struggle. Most useful for purposes here is the editors' intention that the collection be an assessment of "the emergence of new socialist parties in light of the legacy of Leninist and social democratic traditions." Rather than a review, this is an interrogation of the essays through the lens of the findings of this book. Particular attention is given to those essays that explicitly raise the question of whether electoral/parliamentary work can be employed for the working class to take state power and embark on socialist transformation.

LENIN VERSUS LENINISM

Let's begin with the explicit references to Lenin, the Bolsheviks, the Russian Revolution or some variant, because whether his perspective has currency depends in part on how he is understood in progressive circles today. There are first, as anticipated in the collection's Preface, those that suggest, sometimes in passing, that there was Lenin the historical figure, on one hand, and what came to be known as "Leninism," on the other, and that never perhaps the twain shall meet. Such suspicions, if real, are salutary. In Chapter 3, I also employ "Leninism" to denote his reincarnation in the hands of his embalmer, Stalin. Only in Charles Post's essay, "What Is Left of Leninism? New European Parties in Historical Perspective," is there an attempt, in a few paragraphs, to make that distinction clear.[35] The novice reader to this literature, therefore, who might have missed what Post says could, unfortunately, come away thinking that anything that smacks of the Bolshevik leader's name or anything associated with him such as the Third or Communist International (Comintern) is to be avoided.

As Post explains, "'Leninism' as a distinct organizational theory and practice was invented during the 'Bolshevization' campaign of 1924–25 . . . After 1923, the Comintern leadership imposed what the twentieth-century left has come to know as 'Leninist norms of organization' . . . In the wake of these organizational changes, rank-and-file worker communists lost whatever control they may have exercised over the policies, action and leadership of their organizations." While this is essentially correct, it's important to add that while alive Lenin advised, as already noted in Chapter 3, that once an advanced capitalist country experienced a socialist revolution, "Russia will cease to be a model and will once again become a backward country (in the 'Soviet' and the socialist sense)." Extraordinary measures taken to defend the revolution, he also pointed out, were specific to Russian conditions: "We do not propose," again, "our Constitution as a model for other countries."

While "the 'Bolshevization' campaign" was largely an affair of Stalin, it had its roots in the Third Congress of Comintern in 1921, specifically the Theses on the Organizational Structure of the Communist Parties that it adopted. They detailed how party affiliates should organize themselves.

"The resolution is an excellent one," Lenin told delegates at the Fourth Congress the next year, "but it is almost entirely Russian . . . too Russian, it reflects Russian experience. That is why it is quite unintelligible to foreigners, and they cannot be content with hanging it in a corner like an icon and praying to it."[36] A few months before it was adopted, the Russian party voted at its Tenth Congress to suspend the long-standing Bolshevik party norm of the right to form factions—groupings in the party that disagreed with a party line and wanted a change of leadership. The context was the recently concluded civil war and a number of internal party debates that threatened a split. Given the reality of state power in 1921 and the hostile international environment, a permanently split or destroyed Bolshevik party would probably have resulted in the overthrow of the revolution. Although seen as a temporary measure, it became a permanent norm—a key weapon in Stalin's rise to power.

Writing 14 years later, Trotsky, who continued to defend the measure, was realistic: "But one thing is absolutely clear: the banning of factions brought the heroic history of Bolshevism to an end and made way for its bureaucratic degeneration."[37] Notably, the ban on factions did not suspend debate and democratic discussion; that came with the triumph and consolidation of the Stalin clique. But the suspension of factions found its way into the Theses and this is no doubt what Lenin meant when he said, "[W]e made a big mistake with this resolution." Trotsky later recognized the consequences of extending the Bolshevik party norm to "the young sections of the Comintern, thus dooming them to degeneration before they had time to grow and develop."[38] His *The Revolution Betrayed* (1937) remains the best explanation of what unfolded both in and outside the Soviet Union. A degenerated Comintern allowed Stalin to impose the class-collaborationist Popular Front policy, which had, as Post notes, "a *lasting* political and *social* impact on the communist parties of Europe." They basically became social democrats in communist garb, thus explaining their political nullity today in the face of the capitalist crisis. As this book contends, there was nothing in Lenin's politics and practice prior to the October Revolution—Chapter 2 in *LES1905* is especially useful in this regard—that could have predicted the Stalinist outcome. Historical contingency, rather than some "character defect" or other "smoking gun" or "skeleton" hiding in his background—as his detractors are prone to look for—explains better the counterrevolution.

If Post is essentially correct about the Stalinist corruption of Lenin's program, his own claims about the real Lenin and the Bolsheviks are problematic. First, his description of Leninist organizational norms as being "the construction of an organization of revolutionary worker

activists *independently* of the labor and parliamentary officialdom capable
of contesting the latter's leadership of the workers' movement" is a reading through the lens of the West European social democratic experience
and its reformist outcome. For Lenin, as the details of the Third and
Fourth Duma experience make quite clear, the emphasis was on how to
ensure *subordination* of the parliamentary work to the will of the party
and thus its rank-and-file members. The reason for this misreading of the
Bolshevik experience is revealed two pages earlier in the essay, the second
problem. With Lars Lih as a reference point, Post offers an explanation
for why the Russian movement didn't succumb to opportunism like its
fraternal organizations in Western Europe. The reason was "the absence of
parliamentary institutions and legal trade unions in Russia."[39] The Russians, it seems, had fewer opportunities to be politically compromised.

Only unawareness of Lenin's practice between 1905 and most of 1917
could inform such a claim. Not only were "parliamentary institutions" in
place in Russia, with all their limitations, but the opportunist response
that characterized the Western European parties found an echo there—
the Mensheviks. This, in fact, is exactly the point that Lenin made in his
Left-Wing Communism—An Infantile Disorder. Disputing would-be revolutionaries in countries where bourgeois democracy was more advanced
than what had existed in Russia and who thought, therefore, that the
Russian experience was inapplicable to their countries, Lenin begged to
differ. Most of them, like Post evidently, didn't know about the decade-
long electoral/parliamentary work the Bolsheviks had engaged in—true,
he acknowledged, under very different circumstances than those in the
Western Europe. But after February, certainly, Russia became the "freest country in the world," where bourgeois parliamentarism with all its
opportunist pitfalls flourished. The bourgeois democratic Provisional
Government, local dumas, and the soviets all confronted the Bolsheviks
with the same challenges West European revolutionaries faced. The decisive difference was the presence of a Lenin—what the pamphlet could
only imply. Lih's work, as discussed in the previous section, though admirable because of its rich textual analysis, is bereft of any details about
Lenin's electoral/parliamentary work—one of the consequences of relying, as Post does, on the writings of Lenin's "friends," in this case one that
covers a limited period in his political life.

Of the 21 contributions in the *Socialist Register* collection, only 2
explicitly embrace Lenin or at least claim to, implying that apparently
informed voices of the "anti-capitalist left" find it hard to disentangle
Stalinism from the real Lenin. With the attention-getting title, "Occupy
Lenin," Mimmo Porcaro boldly declares that the crisis "rings in, once

again, *the hour of Lenin*. . . if its eruption brings us back to Marx, its momentary 'solution' brings us to Lenin. That is, it brings us to the need to put classes, their struggle and the state at the centre of analysis and to imagine a social alternative that can no longer be just a corrective for the deeply ingrained responsibility of proposing a new and coherent mode of production." Porcaro is described by the editors as "a grassroots union activist in Turin and a member of Rifondazione Comunista," or the Italian Party of Communist Refoundation (PRC). As its name suggests, the PRC, founded in 1991 as the Soviet Union was disintegrating, was the product of the regrouping of those parties that once took their lead from Moscow. While many former Stalinist organizations quickly discarded the "communist" label, those who organized the PRC did not, thus why it or at least some of its members can still embrace Lenin—or more correctly, Lenin as they understand him.

Owing to the hardball tactics of capital's response to the crisis (which Pocaro rightly says renders increasingly null and void the once in-vogue claims of Michael Hardt and Antonio Negri)[40]—namely, capital's willingness to employ the "*heavy weapons* of *economic blackmail* and of *political force*"—"it is the general headquarters of capital and the state that must be seized." That makes the current situation a "Lenin moment," but not because of the "answers" that Lenin provided as embodied in "this or that thesis" on "imperialism," the "dictatorship of the proletariat," "the party," and "communism." Rather, it was how he responded to crises such as 1905 and 1917, his "style . . . that can be summed up as *continuous and constant change* in relation to the *given situation*. Lenin is the continuous redefinition of the given situation on the basis of the dynamic of the class struggle and of the spaces which open up from time to time, or which become closed, to the activism of the popular movement . . . Lenin, therefore, is a continuous *movement of rupture* in the face of convictions, of political lines and of organizational forms, which, having matured in a preceding situation, tend by inertia to repeat their problems and solutions and therefore to remain prisoners of the old class relations."

Porcaro's claim about Lenin's "style," one of "continuous rupture," is a reading of the Bolshevik leader at the level of appearances, not essences. Yes, it's true, as documented in this book, that he was often at logger heads with his comrades, many times in the minority, on one occasion even brought up on charges of indiscipline, and constantly challenging routinism. But his "ruptures" were informed by a steel core that went back to Marx and Engels, as this book hopefully makes clear—independent working-class political action. If Porcaro doesn't think there was such a core or, perhaps, disagrees with it and thinks it's no longer relevant in today's world, he should say so.

Because Porcaro says "this is no place" to argue about the supposedly out-of-date character of the "answers" Lenin provided, what he calls "this or that thesis," it is difficult to know what he means. If he is referring to the theses codified by Comintern before its Stalinization, then that requires a discussion. For example, there is the much-maligned—owing to "friend" and foe—dictatorship of the proletariat, a valid claim based on the actual history of the revolutionary process that the working class on the road to power and in power will have to impose its will by any means necessary. Unless Porcaro, who acknowledges the "hard power" capital is willing to employ today—in fact, its dictatorship—thinks capital will behave differently from its forbearers whenever they are defeated (i.e., by resorting to any means necessary to try to regain power), again, he should say so and try to make a persuasive case. Otherwise he inadvertently and unnecessarily disarms in advance the victorious proletariat from defending its conquest. No more tragic example in modern history exists of what happens when such a line is advanced—that the working class can take power disarmed, let alone to defend it—as Allende's Chile.[41]

But it is the party question that is most problematic in my opinion in Porcaro's "'Lenin moment' but without Lenin's 'answers.'" While he is rightly suspicious of those who, in reaction to "the party" that "has all too often given a poor account of itself," offer in place "diverse and autonomous 'movement institutions,'" what he proposes is unconvincing. Can he really be serious about "*Jacobin* . . . sects, germs perhaps of oligarchic or semi-authoritarian regression . . . political-intellectual groups" as an alternative given the track record of what's been done in the name of "Leninist vanguardism"? Perhaps a real and honest discussion about the modus operandi of the Italian Communist Party from which the PRC came took place, but what Porcaro proposes suggests that it did not. It never came to terms with its Stalinist past, a recognition that its "Leninist" norms had nothing to do with the real party that Lenin led, making the PRC understandably vulnerable to the criticisms of those who were right to be suspicious of "Leninism." The purpose of Chapter 2 in *LES1905* was exactly that, to recover the real Lenin from the beginning regarding his democratic credentials in both electoral/parliamentary matters and the revolutionary party. Again, there is nothing in that record that would have anticipated the Stalinist counterrevolution in his name— why a historical contingency argument is more convincing. From 1905 until the October Revolution 12 years later (the bulk of this narrative), what is striking is how the Bolsheviks were willing to risk life, limb, and imprisonment to have democratic debate, discussion, and a vote under the most difficult circumstances, unlike any other party in Russia, the liberal Cadets included.

Toward the end of his essay, Porcaro, almost in passing, recognizes the horrors of Stalinism, or more accurately, recognizes that others do so but says "we are not dealing with them here." This is in fact the political problem of a contribution that purports to make a case for embracing Lenin. Unless the crimes of Stalin are addressed and dealt with, even if only in an abbreviated fashion, such an effort will be for naught. Generations that have no idea what the real Marx, Engels, and Lenin stood for, but who've been reared on ruling-class narratives about the Stalinist counterrevolution—and that's exactly what it was—require a real and honest discussion about all the horrors that have been done in their names. It can't be swept under the rug. If this is the *Socialist Register*'s case for the Leninist alternative, then it's at best inadequate. Socialism and much that has been done in its name faces a similar challenge. The radicalization of Ayman Al-Zawahiri, Al Qaida's intellectual author, is as much a reaction to the homegrown Arab Socialism of Gamal Abdul Nasser and his successor Anwar al-Sadat as it was to the colonial/Western imperialism legacy. Because the ruling parties in Mubarak's Egypt and Ben Ali's Tunisia draped themselves in a socialist mantle, a real socialist alternative will also have to come to terms with both histories if they are to be persuasive.

Lenin's advice to the international delegates at the Fourth Congress of Comintern in 1922 bears repeating—that is, the need for them to carefully study the Russian Revolution. The history of Bolshevik organizational norms, as this book recounts, was very much a work in progress. The Organizational Theses of 1921 were an attempt to codify those practices for aspiring revolutionaries elsewhere. If Porcaro's point is that those norms were not set in stone, he's right. But is he talking about tweaking them to reflect new conditions or getting rid of them all together and starting over again? I disagree if the latter. If he is right about the "hard power" capital is prepared to use against the working class, which I think he is, then Lenin's trenchant point made in 1913 against those who thought that it wasn't necessary to have an illegal party, the liquidators, is as relevant now as then: "[W]ithout an organization the working class is nothing." Porcaro is right that at some moment there will be a need to seize "the general headquarters of capital." But does he really believe that can be done without a party, a disciplined one? Is the norm of democratic centralism, the real and not Stalinist-distorted one, obsolete?

Pocaro is rightly impressed with what Lenin did in 1917. Does he not recognize that was due precisely to Bolshevik prior organizational experience? No insight of Lenin's is as important today as his claim in 1902—what informed his *What Is to Be Done?*—that unless a revolutionary leadership already exists before the proverbial "shit hits the fan," it would be too late to try to form one in the heat of the battle. The two martyrs of Germany's failed revolution in 1918, Rosa Luxemburg, who disagreed in 1904 with Lenin's organizational perspective, and Karl Liebknecht, tragically confirm his insight. Just ask the progressive forces in Egypt and Tunisia today about what happens when you don't have an organization in place to compete with forces such as the Muslim Brotherhood and the Salafists who had been organizing beforehand—for decades in the case of the former. The best to be hoped for in both settings is that the space that was opened with the Arab Spring will last long enough—which requires fighting for it—for the working class and its allies to get its act together. The Russian example demonstrates that the revolutionary process often comes in different chapters that can spread over a number of years, enough time to organize for the next chapter—if you're lucky.

Of all the contributions in the *Socialist Register* collection, Atilio Borom's "Strategy and Tactics for Popular Movements in Latin America" speaks most directly to the rationale for this book. Borom, currently Director of the Latin American Program of Distance Education in Buenos Aires, is a highly respected and keen observer of progressive and revolutionary politics in the region. He begins by underscoring the political toll that Hardt and Negri's *Empire* took on progressive forces in the first decade of the millennium, leading many to incorrectly believe that strategy, tactics, and the need to take state power were all unimportant. Instead, it was all about social movements in their creative spontaneity, the "multitude." The current capitalist crisis that began at the end of 2007 has exposed the vacuity of that apolitical perspective, again as some of us predicted.[42] Borom notes that the collapse of the Soviet Union, the entrenchment of state capitalism in China and Vietnam, and the concessions to capitalism the Cubans were forced to make in the wake of the Soviet demise to maintain the basic foundations of their revolution all help to explain why the social-movement model became appealing. He acknowledges a positive for the model: "To some extent it could be said that social movements were able to break out of the straitjacket of electoral politics, something that could also be labeled the 'electoral cretinism' of political parties on the left . . . [I]f the leftist parties want to change the world and not only denounce its evils, much more than an adequate electoral strategy is in order."[43]

Borom then makes the case for the necessity of strategy, because the "heroism and militancy" often associated with the social movements is "not enough," and he employs Lenin for support. He disputes the "postmodernist left" and "traditional social democratic" view of Lenin as a Blanquist or putschist. Unlike what Blanqui stood for, "small conscious minorities at the head of the mass lacking consciousness," quoting Engels's criticism, "Lenin's theory is exactly the contrary; the party, and the leadership, must first gain the confidence of the crowds and only then launch the revolutionary attack." And the other lesson from Lenin, his "classic dictum: 'without revolutionary theory there can be no revolutionary movement,'" will be crucial in finding "the route to arrive at the haven of the good post-capitalist society."

In concluding, Borom calls for an end to the unproductive dichotomy between the two perspectives currently in vogue: "[I]f parties narrow their political range of choices when only engaged in the electoral arena, then social movements suffer the same consequences when they refuse to develop an institutional strategy to come to power while at the same time refusing to address a mass insurrectionary strategy to conquer state power. This is the worst of all possible outcomes: neither an institutional road nor an insurrectionary road. The result: the perpetuation of bourgeois rule."[44] The solution to the either/or dilemma that he has correctly diagnosed is exactly what this book has detailed—Lenin's strategy of revolutionary parliamentarism. It's obvious that Borom has some familiarity with Marx and Engels's views on the topic around the 1848–49 upheavals. "Electoral cretinism," for example, is, of course, their "parliamentary cretinism." But it's also obvious that he isn't familiar with Lenin's record; otherwise he would have employed it as he has done with Lenin's other insights. Through electoral and parliamentary work, in both the dumas and soviets, the Bolsheviks were able to realize precisely what he calls "Lenin's theory": to "gain the confidence of the crowds" in order to successfully "launch the revolutionary attack" in October.

In calling for an "insurrectionary strategy," Borom stands out among the *Socialist Register* contributors and hence provides an opportunity to broach a topic that others may have been wary of—armed struggle. As detailed in Chapters 2 and 3 in *LES1905*, armed struggle for Lenin was a tactic and not a strategy, only one of various means for working-class ascent, and it had to complement mass work; otherwise it could become counterproductive. The Revolutionary Armed Forces of Colombia (FARC)—the more than four-decade-old guerrilla movement in Colombia—is Exhibit A for what's wrong when armed struggle becomes a strategy. As with everything, Lenin approached armed struggle from a class perspective. Soldiers and sailors—but not the police—were for him workers and peasants in uniform. Therefore the revolutionary working-class party had the obligation to see them as potential recruits, and every effort had to be made to do just that. The thirty-some-odd newspapers that both the Bolsheviks and Mensheviks founded for the armed forces in 1905–6 inaugurated more than a decade of such work, and it was the former who were most consistent in doing so and who thus reaped the benefits in October 1917. One of the lessons of October is that successful recruitment of the rank and file of the military to the revolutionary cause helps minimize the amount of bloodshed in taking state power.

There is no reason to assume that Lenin's perspective is any less relevant today. Egypt's edition of the Arab Spring illustrates what happens—taking into account the particularities of civil-military relations in the country—when most of the rank and file in the military sympathizes with the masses in the streets. What's required there now, as elsewhere, is a conscious campaign along the lines of Lenin's perspective to ensure that the unplanned becomes planned and not be left to chance as was the case when the events in Tahrir Square erupted. Syria illustrates tragically what happens when there is no plan. For the United States, such planning will have to take into account that there are far more arms in civilian hands than in those of military personnel. And at a certain moment in the insurrectionary process, the most elemental and consequential task will be to make sure that the vast majority of those 290 million arms are pointed in the right direction.

The editors of the *Socialist Register* collection may be right that an "insurrectionary rupture . . . hardly seems in the realm of possibility anytime in the near future" in any of the advanced capitalist countries affected by the crisis (though Lenin, it must be remembered, thought in January 1917 that he wouldn't live to see a successful revolution), but Syria and other sad lessons from history show what happens when no forethought is given to it. The Bolshevik experience, on the other hand, demonstrates that it is the prior work, before things come to a head, that will determine the outcome, and an orientation toward winning over the ranks of the military will be decisive. It's no accident that near the top of the requirements for membership in the pre-Stalinist Comintern—the famous, or infamous, depending on one's politics, "twenty-one conditions"—was the fourth: "The duty to disseminate communist ideas carries with it a special obligation to conduct vigorous and systematic propaganda in the army." In the United States, certainly, where thousands join the military to find employment due to the crisis, many of them tragically and increasingly take their own lives—the shattered hopes of isolated workers. "Vigorous and systematic propaganda in the army" can therefore be salutary—basic proletarian solidarity.

The armed-struggle question, by the way, exposes a key problem with the 1 percent versus 99 percent distinction of the occupy movement in the United States. The American ruling class is actually less than 1 percent of the population, but it stays in power owing to the support of various layers of society that number far more than 1 percent (what I like to call "Stephen's people" after the unforgettable head slave on the Candie Land Plantation in Quentin Tarantino's *Django Unchained*). Not the least important of these layers, aside from the ideological defenders—many of whom are employed by the most prestigious institutions of higher learning—is the military apparatus; again, what makes having a working-class military strategy in place all so important.

APPLYING LENIN'S PERSPECTIVE

The *Socialist Register* collection includes five essays about settings in which independent working-class political action in the electoral/parliamentary arenas is not just a theoretical possibility but is being posed today to one degree or another: Greece, Italy, Germany, South Africa, and Bolivia. The task now is to see if any of what this book details speaks to the realities those essays reveal about the current situation in each nation.

In no country has the crisis so exposed the bankruptcy of social democracy as in Greece. Pasok was the ruling party that obediently carried out the orders of European bankers to implement drastic austerity measures against the Greek working class beginning in 2010. Most emblematic is the fact that the then prime minister, George Papandreou, was also the president of the Socialist International, the rump that was left of the Second International after the First World War. (It's worth noting that the ruling parties of both Mubarak in Egypt and Ben Ali in Tunisia were, before being dethroned, affiliates of the same body.) Pasok was not alone in the social democratic offensive against workers in Europe. In Iceland, Portugal, and Spain, the same was happening. So much, then, for the so-called parliamentary road to socialism thesis—a fraud exposed by Marx, Engels, and Lenin long ago. The two important political lessons of the twentieth century, taught respectively by social democracy and Stalinism, are that the capitalist state cannot be used to construct socialism and that socialism can't be constructed on the backs of the proletariat.

With the political collapse of Pasok in 2012, owing to the electorate's rejection of its proausterity policies, and the continuing nullity of the traditional Stalinist party, the possibility of a real working-class alternative was seriously posed for the first time in Greece. For many anticapitalist activists, that option appeared to be embodied in the coalition of left parties known as Syriza, which understandably garners the most attention in the collection—two articles exclusively and one partially. Syriza came within 2.8 percent of becoming the ruling coalition (though officially a "party" for the sake of the elections) in the general election in June 2012, winning 27 percent of the vote; with 71 of the 300 seats in the Greek parliament, it is the major opposition coalition to the ruling bloc headed by New Democracy in alliance with another capitalist party and the spent Pasok as a junior partner. The two contributions in the *Socialist Register* collection that deal just with Syriza come from two leading intellectuals intimately involved in the day-to-day activities of the coalition, one as an essay and the other an interview, by Michalis Spourdalakis and Aristides Baltas, respectively. Both provide useful background about the coalition, its evolution, the situation it faced in the spring of 2012 and the way forward. The interview with Baltas has a bit of the feel of high drama in that it took place on the eve of the June general election when it was very possible that Syriza would win and become the new governing party/ coalition.

From the vantage point of this book, the most promising thing about the two presentations is that both Spourdalakis and Baltas agree that there is a history that Syriza needs to come to grips with if it is to be true to its professed goals. For Spourdalakis, "Socialism needs once again to be put on the political agenda. But strategizing for socialism in the twenty first century requires a critical evaluation of all the previous efforts as they were historically articulated by all traditions—from the Fabians to the Leninists." And for Baltas, "[W]hat we consider extremely important for Greece and perhaps for the whole of Europe is the need to have a big discussion of the fate of socialism in the twentieth century, why it failed in China and why it failed in Eastern Europe . . . the feeling runs quite deep here that the left should reply as to the why of such failures . . . This involves going as far back as it takes through Lenin and Trotsky and Stalin so if even we perhaps make new mistakes, we surely do not [sic] to repeat the old ones."[45]

Such openness to a real discussion about this history is potentially salutary because, to paraphrase Trotsky's insight about the parties that joined the Third International or Comintern after Moscow imposed its line, Syriza was born with a birth defect; it carries the two genes of Stalinism and social democracy. That's clear in not only the two accounts about Syriza's origins between 2002 and 2004 but what the authors themselves have to say about that heritage. While acknowledging its parentage,

Syriza, according to Spourdalakis, is "leaving behind both the reformism of a bankrupt social democracy and the vanguardism of revolutionaries still dreaming of the storming of the winter palace. It hopes in this way to bridge the gap between reform and revolution and to define the radical transformation of capitalist society as a process of structural reforms directly connected to everyday struggles." To the question posed by Leo Panitch, one of the editors of the collection, about how Syriza would avoid the pitfalls of European social democracy given Syriza's "electoral path," Baltas responds that "our party members are incapable of wanting a social democratic party of the European variety. They are too aware of what Pasok did: despite its ideological agenda and its rhetoric, once it entered the state within a short period it instituted clientelism at a level not approached before and immersed itself in corruption of the worst kind . . . The social structure of Greece precludes social democratization of the Northern European type" because of the lack, for the most part, of a second-generation Greek working class. Also, unlike Northern Europe, "intellectuals here are integrated into the left." They would be able to provide the "expertise for running a new kind of state . . . we might even say that if we take the government, then the revolution will start" through the grassroots networks. "So if we reform the government and if we keep, let's say, the left flank [the working class] of our coalition ['the traditional and new petty bourgeoisie' being the other half] absolutely fixed, firm, then things will develop from below in a socialist sense."

The bottom line for both views is that Syriza—according at least to these two intellectuals/participants—believes it can use the capitalist state to carry out socialist transformation—exactly what the best that social democracy had to offer thought it could do and which nowhere, as Marx, Engels, and Lenin confidently predicted, has ever been successful, including southern Europe. That futile quest is what defines social democracy, and the degree of a society's proletarianization doesn't explain why it can become hegemonic. It has to be confronted politically, and that requires clarity about what it actually is. If there is one thing the numerous 24- and 48-hour general strikes in Greece since 2011 (the largest organized by the Pasok-affiliated trade unions) have proven, it's not enough for the masses to come into the streets and demonstrate their anger with the austerity measures of the bourgeois state. At a certain moment, they will have to take power into their own hands to stop the austerity drive and, like the Communards, begin to construct a new kind of state. It may not be a "storming of the winter palace," but it will have to be something comparable. The reader of this book knows that Lenin—again, the real Lenin and not the "Leninist" Lenin—said a

lot about reforms and revolution, and nothing better captures his position than his point made in the waning months of the revolutionary
upheavals of 1905–7: "[W]e must fight in a revolutionary way for a
parliament"—that is, reforms—"but not in a parliamentary way for a
revolution." What Spourdalakis and Baltas advocate comes close to what
he counseled against: the parliamentary road to socialism.

Spourdalakis at least recognizes that to even carry out the "structural
reforms" project he envisions requires the "building of a political party,"
the next and necessary stage in Syriza's coalitional existence. Success in
that arena would require, however, a thoroughgoing interrogation of what
has passed in Greece for "Leninism" both politically and organizationally.
To not do so threatens to reproduce the grotesqueness of the USSR and
its Eastern European clones even in the hands of well-intentioned "left"
intellectuals. Lenin, like Marx and Engels, fought for a perspective based
not on whether they'd actually live to see its execution but one that made
the preparations for what could be employed when the necessary conditions existed for its success. That's the difference between "dreaming of
the storming of the winter palace" and laying out a course to be ready to
do so when the time arises.

Hillary Wainwright's "Transformative Power: Political Organization in
Transition" also examines what Syriza has so far achieved but through the
experience of two prior left forays into the electoral/parliamentary arenas—
the Labour Party's Greater London Council campaign in the 1980s and
the Brazilian Workers' Party involvement in the Porto Alegre municipal
council between 1989 and 2004. Also an academic, at the University
of Bradford in the United Kingdom, hers is an effort about "rethinking
political organization beyond both Leninism and parliamentarism"—that
is, as I read it, neither Stalinism nor social democracy. The research question she poses, in fact, is similar to what this book asks: "whether the
vote is still a resource for social transformation or a perpetual source of
disillusion and alienation. In other words, can representation in the existing institutions of parliamentary democracy, along with efforts to change
these institutions, strengthen the wider struggle to bring somehow an end
to capitalist power—the power of the financial markets, private banks
and corporations, all intertwined with and guaranteed by state institutions?"[46] Of all the contributions in the *Socialist Register* collection, Wainwright's essay, therefore, speaks most directly to the specifics of this book.

The answer to her question, she says, is a conditional yes based "on an
understanding of citizenship as social and situated. In today's societies,
ridden as they are with inequalities, this implies an engagement with electoral politics while at the same time strongly challenging what has become

of the universal franchise: an abstract, formal political equality in a society that is fundamental unequal." The experiences of the forays of the Labour Party and Workers' Party, which resulted in some redistribution of resources at the local level, "illustrate a transition from socialist change as centered around the state to an understanding of transformative power organized in society." But in many ways, that's exactly the all-important point Marx and Engels made—and Lenin constantly employed—with their notion of "parliamentary cretinism": the mistaken assumption that the alpha and omega of politics is the legislative arena. Rather, they all understood that decisive in politics is what takes place outside that arena, what social democracy denies to its peril.

Wainwright is right to call for a "rethinking of the franchise," and Marx, Engels, and Lenin can be of assistance. The necessary complement today to "parliamentary cretinism," coined originally by Engels in 1849, might be called "voting fetishism"—that is, the modern but erroneous tendency to equate the right to register a preference for either a candidate or a policy in a public election with the actual exercise of political power. Stating a preference should never be mistaken for taking power; the consequences can be life threatening, because it can be literally disarming. There are two characteristics of voting that, if thought about, should disabuse anyone of such confusion. An electoral vote, in the ordinary sense of the term, is an action that is, first, usually private and, second, doesn't take much time—nothing that could be more remote from the exigencies of taking political power. Neither is a political demonstration—as the Greek masses frustratingly learn—the same as taking power; it's just that, a demonstration of preferences, though certainly more advanced than voting because it's public.[47] Exactly because Marx and Engels didn't confuse registering preferences with taking power could they put forward a strategy—elaborated on to effective usage by Lenin—that didn't subscribe to the either/or dilemma that Wainwright seeks an exit from—that is, take part in the electoral process and risk being compromised a la social democracy or boycott it and risk irrelevancy a la anarchism. Not only could elections be useful for propaganda purposes, to disseminate revolutionary ideas, but they offered revolutionaries an excellent opportunity to count preferences in order to determine the most propitious moment for actually taking power—"for storming the winter palace."

The Paris Commune allowed Marx and Engels to supplement their electoral strategy with the only addendum they ever made to the *Communist Manifesto*, an insight that anticipated what Wainwright came to recognize based on the London and Porto Alegre experiences. "We noted how actually existing parliamentary democracy effectively tends to occlude and reinforce inequalities of wealth and power unless directly challenged . . . entrenched institutions which take as given and as beyond their responsibility the inequalities and problems against which these struggles and the electoral mandate are directed." That's precisely the reality the insurgent Communards encountered, which is why they had to—a lesson that Lenin absorbed to the very core of his political being—not just challenge the status quo but construct a new state institution, what Russian workers discovered on their own in 1905 and repeated later in 1917: soviets. Unlike the French National Assembly and the Czarist State Duma, the Commune and the Soviet of Workers', Peasants', and Soldiers' Deputies fused the legislative and executive functions of governance. Owing to his participation in Swiss politics during his many years in exile there—one of the surprises of the research for this book—Lenin learned that even the most transparent bourgeois parliamentary institution would "occlude and reinforce inequalities of wealth and power," especially as long as those two functions were separated. Wealth could exercise its influence in the walled-off executive branch / state bureaucracy that had a life of its own independent of the parties that happened to be ruling parliament and thus the government.

Like Spourdalakis, Wainwright thinks that Syriza will have to transform itself into a "political party" if it is to be effective at all. Not only, she says, would such a party have to be actively engaged with "extra-parliamentary" work, but it would "require specific organizational forms to counter the pressures drawing representatives into the flytrap of parliamentary politics, with all of its tendencies towards a separate political class." What Wainwright is raising is related to the problem Marx and Engels detected as early as 1879 in German social democracy: the tendency for the parliamentary group to want to be less accountable to the rank-and-file members of its parent party. One of the important tests for Syriza as it goes forward and becomes, perhaps, a party is whether the parliamentary group, now headed by the charismatic Alexis Tsipras, will be willing to subordinate itself to the decisions, arrived at by Leninist and not Stalinist methods, of the party. Based on everything that the three contributions say about Syriza, I'm skeptical that will happen. Whatever the case, Lenin gave a lot of thought to this potential problem with parliamentary work and proposed a number of solutions to arrest its development. Once again, Wainwright's otherwise thoughtful analysis could have benefited tremendously from what Marx, Engels, and Lenin bequeathed.

It's commendable that Wainwright wants to draw on the lessons of history to estimate Syriza's chances for a real socialist transformation. But the fact is that the only example of a revolutionary movement employing the electoral/parliamentary arena to lead the working class to state power—which she readily admits never happened with social democracy a la the Labour Party or Workers' Party despite some success with the local "experiments"—is what the Bolsheviks under Lenin's leadership accomplished in 1917. Lenin's revolutionary parliamentarism offers another valuable lesson that all three contributions apparently assign low priority to—proletarian internationalism. As Wainwright points out, "the full development of both experiments was curtailed by the impact on parties of labour of the global momentum of neoliberalism." That's no surprise and exactly why Marx, Engels, and Lenin rejected the notion of socialism in one country and saw the need for an international body of workers that could provide solidarity to one another in their struggles against capital. If that was a necessity in the nineteenth and early twentieth century, it's even truer today. The ability of capital to impose its will on workers in Greece and elsewhere is aided and abetted by the absence of such solidarity. Perhaps in their desire to distance themselves from the "Leninist" Comintern, the three contributors have avoided this all-important issue. But that comes with a price. The lack of international working-class solidarity and a perspective on how to achieve it also aids and abets the nationalist response to the crisis, which in Greece has already taken a significant fascist turn—namely, Golden Dawn.

A final observation about the Greek case—both Spourdalakis and Baltas mention the anarchists but without any sustained discussion. An observation Lenin made about anarcho-syndicalism in 1912 is still relevant. The anarchists, he argued, were given a new lease on life at the beginning of the twentieth century precisely because of the increasingly opportunist character of social democratic parties in European parliaments. Revolutionary parliamentarism, he contended, would obviate the need for them. In this regard, Baltas's comment that despite their rejection of the state and traditional parties "almost all of the anarchists are actually voting . . . for Syriza" is instructive.[48] It would take us too far afield to fully dissect that fact—assuming its correct—but suffice it to say that as long as Syriza appears as a real and viable socialist alternative then the anarchist response is not surprising. Once in office, however, the story is likely to be very different given its problematic parentage.[49] Lenin's constant egging of the liberal Cadet party in the first and second state Dumas, "what thou doest, do quickly"—that is, take power and reveal yourselves so that the masses might learn—might apply, therefore, to Syriza.

Two other European countries have parties that share a similar history with Syriza: Die Linke [The Left] in Germany and the already mentioned Party of Communist Refoundation (PRC) in Italy. The former came into being in 2005, composed mainly of the reinvented Stalinist party of East Germany and left dissidents from the Social Democratic Party. The PRC was a similar reincarnation in 1991 but just of the Communist Party of Italy. Like Syriza, both were deformed at birth owing to their origins and thus suffer from the same problems it does. Stephen Hellman's "Whatever Happened to Italian Communism? Lucio Magri's *The Tailor of Ulm*" unintentionally shows why for the PRC an honest discussion about its Stalinist history never took place. The assessment in the aforementioned contribution of Charles Post is useful: "Despite their claims to be 'post-social democratic' and 'post-Leninist' . . . and [d]espite the purported programmatic differences—the PRC's 'anti-capitalism' and *Die Linke*'s anti-neoliberalism—both parties proved unable to consistently resist the lure of participation in government coalitions with the social liberals with the resulting embrace of austerity at home and imperialist wars abroad. Neither party has transcended the pre-1914 social democratic 'twin pillars' organizational norm where the party focused on electoral politics, while the union officialdom directed the day-to-day class struggle in the workplace and beyond."[50] The revolutionary parliamentarism gene was never a possibility for either.

Two essays in the *Socialist Register* collection focus on particular countries beyond Europe: Susan Spronk's "Twenty-First Century Socialism in Bolivia: The Gender Agenda" and John Saul's "On Taming a Revolution: The South African Case." Both share a commonality—parties in power that claim either a socialist or redistributive agenda or are widely perceived to do so. And in neither case has that been substantively realized.

Spronk, an academic at the University of Ottawa, describes how the ruling party of President Evo Morales, Movimiento de Socialismo (MAS), since being elected in 2005 has taken important steps toward the recognition of both women and indigenous rights in the still most underdeveloped country in South America. And while some material aid has been directed toward the most impoverished women in Bolivia, it is still inconsequential: "[U]ltimately, cash transfer programmes come nowhere close to providing the kinds of high quality, decommodified public services enjoyed by citizens in revolutionary contexts such as Cuba."[51] That admission is revealing and instructive. It explains in part why she argues "agrarian reform and food sovereignty—the existing demands of Bolivia's most radical [peasant] women's movements—should be seen as part of the agenda for gender justice." A "socialist-feminist agenda," in other words, "must center on a fundamental transformation of the social relations of production." MAS, then, has yet to do what the Bolsheviks and, later, the Cubans did (in both cases within two years of taking power):

complete the bourgeois democratic revolution with a real land reform—in a country that "has amongst the most unequal distribution of land in the region"—and embark on the road to socialist transformation. It's not clear if MAS ever inherited a social democratic gene, but it acts as if it did so. Like Marx and Engels, Lenin believed that the test of any society and revolution is the progress women have made. In Evo Morales's Bolivia, it's been so far more about appearances than substance, and the contrast with Cuba is telling. The danger as always with the equivocations of those who speak in the name of socialism is that it may convince—as discussed earlier about the lessons that revolutionaries in Latin America mistakenly drew about the Cuban Revolution—a new generation of would-be revolutionaries that there is nothing to be gained in utilizing electoral/parliamentary spaces.

John Saul, a longtime and highly respected commentator on and participant in the Southern African liberation movement and now professor emeritus of York University, seeks to explain why South Africa's ruling African National Congress, in power since 1994, has also apparently equivocated, presiding over a "disappointing path to the present." To answer that question, he expertly distills the history of the antiapartheid struggle to understand what he sees as the key moments and actors that account for the "taming of the revolution" and "jettisoning the more elaborate dreams of a socialist future." For some of us, however, who had long supported the liberation struggle in South Africa, we began in the mid-1980s to reassess the character of its revolution based on a closer reading of Lenin and concluded that what was on the agenda was not—as many of us assumed and/or hoped—a socialist revolution but rather a bourgeois democratic one and that the African National Congress (ANC) was capable and committed to leading that course. And unlike most of the grassroots activists of that era, Saul's real heroes and heroines, the ANC had a nose for state power, the necessary ingredient for uprooting the state-sponsored and enforced system of apartheid—and hence an important lesson for today's activists who dismiss the importance of state power. Its main programmatic statement, the Freedom Charter of 1955, was about a radical democratic revolution, and not—as some of us were prone to read it—a program for socialist revolution (just as Nelson Mandela explained a few months after it was adopted). A thoroughgoing bourgeois revolution as Lenin argued, just as Marx and Engels did, was the necessary condition—without a predetermined timetable—for a socialist revolution and thus was to be applauded and supported. With that reassessment, we recommitted to the South African struggle but with more clarity and sobriety.

From the perspective of that reevaluation, the most recent events in South Africa began to fulfill what we had expected and hoped for. We couldn't predict when it would occur, but we knew that the overthrow of apartheid would put the class question on the agenda, in a similar way that the overthrow of Jim Crow in the United States has done for its class struggle. The unprecedented strikes that began in the summer of 2012 of not only the miners but other workers, especially the rural proletariat farm workers—for the first time in their history—is the most important development since the overthrow of apartheid, without which they could not have occurred as they have.[52] And the fact that the upsurge begins to coincide with protests elsewhere due to the global capitalist crisis—which, too, affects South Africa—makes their timing even more potentially significant. Like in Bolivia, the land question looms large in South Africa—that is, the need for agrarian reform. A worker-peasant alliance is therefore required in both countries, and as Lenin demonstrated in practice, the parliamentary arena can be advantageous for its organization, the kind of space that didn't exist under apartheid. But to do so requires the kind of leadership Lenin and the Bolsheviks provided, and therein is a curious lacuna in Saul's account, the proverbial elephant in the room—the South African Communist Party. Its acronym, the SACP, is employed throughout the essay, but the reader who is new to the South African reality is never informed what it actually stands for.

The SACP, unlike the Bolsheviks, is a product of the Stalinized Comintern, and its more than half-century alliance with the ANC has essentially the character of a Popular Front in the so-called Triple Alliance—the two organizations plus the umbrella labor coalition, the Congress of South African Trade Unions (COSATU). The SACP continues to exercise inordinate weight within it, and it's impossible to understand, for example, the ANC's "modus operandi" or its politics without pointing to the Stalinist influence. The "popular front," the ANC in exile as "a small, elite led, top-down hierarchical party [with] strict democratic centralism . . . characteristic of the Soviet model," and other such scattered references throughout Saul's essay are very much the stuff of Stalinism. History has shown that the most principled of the ANC leaders—Mandela being the best example—were likely to have been imprisoned for many years at Robben Island and therefore were relatively immune from the cynical and corrupting influence that characterized ANC/SACP exile politics.[53] Of the Triple Alliance members, the SACP is the most conscious and ardent defender of its popular front character—what it calls the "national democratic revolution"—and it is therefore the biggest political obstacle to independent working-class politics in South Africa today.

An honest discussion about Stalinism and the price it cost the antiracist struggle in South Africa has never taken place, despite the pretense that it had.[54] The new upsurge has the potential to dislodge the hegemony of the Triple Alliance and bring into existence a new working-class leadership. Stalinism, especially in a setting like South Africa where unsophisticated anticommunism marked much of the history of its ruling class, could always pose as a viable working-class option as long as it didn't have state power. The more than 15 years that the Triple Alliance has been in power with the finger prints of the SACP all over it threatens to shatter whatever remaining illusions exist about it as a real option—Lenin's constant refrain about the Cadets, "what thou doest, do quickly," comes to mind. That possibility, rather than "disappointment," is what to look forward to and to be optimistic about. The missing elephant in his narrative notwithstanding, Saul is right to see—written before the recent upsurge—"the dawning of the 'next liberation struggle.'"[55]

THE US CASE

I conclude with the setting that understandably receives the most attention in the *Socialist Register* collection: the United States. Two articles are devoted to the Occupy movement in New York City and Oakland, one to the labor movement, one to the historical significance of the left, and one to socialist feminism in the United States and elsewhere since the crisis. But through the lens of this book, there is relatively less to be said about the US case, at least quantitatively. That's because in the other countries independent working-class political action is currently posed, while in the United States it remains an abstraction. This is still the only advanced capitalist country whose working class lacks its own political party. Engels offered an explanation in 1893: the winner-takes-all electoral system, US economic expansion and the resulting gains for workers (the "American dream"), and the divisions within the working class, especially the black/white and native/immigrant cleavages.[56] In 2003, I argued that owing to the fight to overthrow Jim Crow (i.e., racial segregation), the American working class is more integrated than ever not only racially but also by gender and nationality. That historic conquest, in combination with the crisis of late capitalism—"It's not a question whether . . . recession and depression . . . will come to the shores of the United States but only when"—opened up the possibility for a real working-class alternative for the first time.[57] I stressed that there were only favorable conditions for such an outcome; it wasn't inevitable. And indeed, it has yet to happen.

What's so telling about Sam Gindin's otherwise informative contribution on the US labor movement, "Rethinking Unions, Registering Socialism," is nary a single word about independent working-class political action. Though there is mention of "the cynical electoral tactics of the Republican Party," there isn't a peep about the cynical prostitution of the labor movement, in collusion with its leaders, by the Democratic Party. The head of a state trade union federation (AFL-CIO) told me in 2011 how, after he expressed dissatisfaction to Vice President Joseph Biden with the Obama administration's lackluster performance on labor, Biden shot back, "What are you complaining about? You know you have nowhere else to go!" The bitter truth is that Biden was right. As long as labor's officials refuse even to consider breaking with the Democrats, it will be exploited to its increasing peril. The most recent defeats at the ballot box, the failure to recall Governor Scott Walker in Wisconsin, and the failure to defeat the right-to-work legislation in Michigan demonstrate the utter bankruptcy of labor's class-collaborationist strategy in the electoral/legislative arenas.[58]

The political nullity of the US labor movement has been long in the making. Eli Zaretsky, a historian at the New School in New York City, argues correctly in his essay "Reconsidering the American Left" that only when there has been what he calls "a powerful, independent radical left" have democratic gains been made. The abolitionist movement constitutes for him the first example—though in fact it was armed white farmers and former slaves who overthrew the slavocracy. But that's a tolerable error. He is profoundly incorrect, however, in claiming that "the Popular Front leftists put social equality" on the political agenda during the Great Depression. Rather, it was the independent mobilizations of the working class between 1933 and 1936, before the US Communist Party began campaigning for Moscow's line, which forced the concessions from the Roosevelt administration known as the New Deal. What the Popular Front actually did was to help housebreak the labor movement by taking it into the debilitating embrace of the Democratic Party, where it has been submissively residing ever since. And not the least treacherous of its consequences was labor officialdom's support for the Roosevelt administration's war drive—in the name of fighting fascism—which obligated it to sign on to no-strike pledges during the Second World War; only the United Mine Workers of America refused to comply, and the Communist Party USA has to this day paid a price in the coal fields for its unsuccessful strike-breaking stance. Precisely because Zaretsky ignores this history can he with a straight face confess that Obama's election in 2008 was an "investment of the American left in a historic Presidency—the first African-American to win the office" and with further naïveté admit that the returns on that investment have proved "profoundly disheartening." For Zaretsky, in other words, "an independent radical left" today means cohabitation with a bourgeois party—exactly what Lenin would have soundly denounced and why the Popular Front's champions have no interest in promoting his real program. It's no wonder Zaretsky speculates on the reasons "for the marginalization of the left that began in the 1970s." The dear political price "the left" has paid for being cheerleaders for the Democratic Party doesn't figure into the "complex" explanation he offers.

The labor movement isn't the only casualty of this fatal embrace of the Democratic Party. Though there is no contribution in the collection that explicitly addresses it, the black rights movement—as I also argued in 2003—has suffered a similar fate. And the same goes for the organized movement for women's rights. Joan Sangster and Meg Luxton, in "Feminism, Co-optation and the Problems of Amnesia: A Response to Nancy Fraser," are right to call the renowned feminist theorist on the carpet for believing that Obama's election "could 'signal the decisive repudiation, even in the belly of the beast, of neoliberalism as a political project.'"[59] This is why the Occupy movements in Oakland and elsewhere were right to be suspicious of electoral politics and the Democratic Party leading up to Obama's reelection.[60] But without a revolutionary parliamentarism perspective, that healthy sentiment and energy was bound to be sucked into the black hole of the Democratic Party just as the anarchists in Greece have gravitated toward Syriza.

The biggest political obstacle today to independent working-class political action—not just in the United States—is lesser-evil thinking. Every working-class vote for the lesser-evil bourgeois politician is another step away from building a real working-class alternative. And every vote for a bourgeois politician helps reproduce bourgeois politics. Many a sincere revolutionary in the United States and elsewhere thought that support for Barack Obama over Mitt Romney was in the interest of the international working class. Aside from what the cold facts about the new Obama administration have already revealed—"what thou doest, do quickly"—what such support in fact did, as always with such strategies, was to drain precious time and energy away from what needs to be done. It's impossible to calculate, but much of the energy of the Occupy movements in the United States, with all their strengths and limitations, was siphoned off into the reelection of Barack Obama—a pattern seen with earlier mass movements in the run-ups to presidential elections, such as the Vietnam antiwar movement. The justification is always that failing to support the lesser evil allows the "greater evil," the reactionaries, to win. A major problem with this argument is its lack of clarity about what reaction actually is and how it advances. One thing is certain: the logic of capital dictates that unless there is a real working-class alternative, bourgeois politics will keep moving to the right—especially in the context of the still-unfolding crisis. Every delay in the pursuit of independent working-class political action only emboldens reaction.

Confusion about reaction, in US politics in particular, is closely related to confusion about fascism. In the 1906 elections to the Second Duma, Lenin first challenged the lesser-evil "Black Hundred scare"— that is, the claim of the Cadets and their Menshevik cheerleaders that a vote for a RSDLP candidate who had no chance of winning would take votes away from them and enable victory for the most reactionary party in Russia, the Black Hundreds. Fascism as a mass movement was then nonexistent. Present-day lesser-evil advocates might therefore argue that Lenin's objections are no longer relevant in today's world, where such movements are extant, Greece being the prime example. It is hence instructive to note Lenin's point, made in 1922 shortly before his last incapacitating stroke, that "the fascists in Italy" revealed that the Italians were "not yet ensured against the Black Hundreds."[61] It suggests that he saw similarities between both reactionary movements, and for good reason given the infamous pogrom-mongering actions of the latter. Despite the very real danger the Black Hundreds posed—far greater than any Republican Tea Partier who "clings to guns or religion"— Lenin refused to be swayed by the liberals' and fainthearted Mensheviks' "scare" campaign and went on to construct a working-class alternative that took state power in 1917.

Lenin built on the kernel of wisdom Marx and Engels planted in 1850: that the working class should not be deterred by liberals from independent political action just because it might allow "a few reactionaries" to be elected. Beginning in 1906, he wrote a series of articles based on the particulars of the Russian situation that fleshed out the logic of their argument in order to demonstrate its validity. Those writings are largely unknown to the working class, mainly because of the still hegemonic Popular Front policy. Lenin's stance, as the discussion in Chapter 4 in *LES1905* reveals, was not an absolutist one. Under extraordinary circumstances he was indeed willing to bloc with the Cadets to prevent the Black Hundreds from winning Duma seats, but only after the working class had made the most concerted campaign for independent political action. And in the final analysis, Lenin knew that the question of the Black Hundreds, and all such reactionary forces, would be settled only where it effectively could be—in mass militant mobilizations in the streets. Marx and Engels had hinted as much.[62]

Turning to the real Lenin does not mean there is nothing to add to that rich legacy. But to do so in the most remunerative way requires full knowledge of what he left us—not only his electoral/parliamentary strategy but also the record of his final fight, against the growing cancer that would become Stalinism. Lenin didn't live long enough to see fascism fully developed, but Trotsky did, and no body of writings on the subject is as valuable as his—the kind of analysis that not only failed to take place at the last Comintern congress in 1935 but could not have. An honest discussion would have exposed Stalin's criminal and disastrous line on Germany: "first the fascists, then us." Imposing the Popular Front necessitated the obfuscation of fascism—a problem that remains in most progressive-minded understandings of the phenomenon, its essence, how it came to be hegemonic, and how to fight it.

The noted Marxist scholar Alex Callinicos, in his contribution in the *Socialist Register* collection on the philosopher Alain Badiou, unfortunately repeats the timeworn fable that Marx "tended to assume that the overthrow of capitalism is inevitable."[63] Nothing could be further from the truth. A single sentence from a letter Marx wrote in 1852, no matter how important, cannot make that case. Marx and Engels claimed that class struggle is inevitable once class society appears—a central theme from the outset of part one of their *Communist Manifesto*. But *what's not inevitable is the class struggle's outcome*.[64] Otherwise there would have been no need to compose the manifesto, which is a call to action from beginning to end. Not only did they issue such a call—at the request of the revolutionary party of which they were members—but for the next four decades, until the end of their lives, they waged a concerted campaign to realize its message, so that the working class could have a better than even chance of being victorious. And no one understood their project better or did more to realize it than Lenin. His electoral strategy concretized what they bequeathed. I contend that not only Callinicos but all the contributors to the *Socialist Register* collection would benefit in one way or another from this understanding of Lenin's legacy.

For most of the twentieth century, the center of the world revolutionary process was in the so-called Third World. The unprecedented and still unfolding crisis of global capitalism has shifted the axis of politics to the advanced capitalist world, where there are far more opportunities in the electoral and parliamentary arenas—making Lenin's strategy of revolutionary parliamentarism more relevant than ever. But to realize its potential, it has to be used. This is a contribution toward that end for those who are truly anticapitalist and who not only seek but are willing to fight for a working-class alternative.

THE FIFTH (ALL-RUSSIAN) CONFERENCE OF THE RSDLP[1]

DECEMBER 21–27, 1908; JANUARY 3–9, 1909

PRACTICAL INSTRUCTIONS ON VOTING FOR THE BUDGET BY THE SOCIAL-DEMOCRATIC GROUP IN THE DUMA

FIRST VARIANT

VOTING FOR THE BUDGET AS A WHOLE is declared wrong in principle. The Conference is of the opinion that, as regards voting for particular items in the Budget, the Duma group should be guided by the principle of our program that Social-Democrats firmly reject reforms involving tutelage of the police and the bureaucracy over the working classes. Therefore the general rule should be to vote against particular items of the Budget, for they nearly always bring in their train not only such tutelage but also downright coercion by the Black-Hundred reactionaries. In cases where some improvement of the conditions of the working people seems likely in spite of these circumstances, it is recommended that the deputies should abstain from voting, but should without fail make a statement setting forth the socialist position. Lastly, in those exceptional cases when the group deems it necessary to vote for a particular item, it is recommended that they should not do so without consulting representatives of the Central Committee and, if possible, the Party organizations in the capital cities.

On the question of the Budget the Conference considers that on principle it is wrong to vote for the Budget as a whole.

It is also wrong to vote for items of the Budget of the class state which sanction expenditure on instruments for the oppression of the masses (the armed forces, etc.).

In voting for reforms or for items of expenditure for cultural purposes, point of departure should be the principle of our programme that Social-Democrats reject reforms involving tutelage of the police and the bureaucracy over the working classes.

Therefore the general rule should be to vote against the so-called reforms and items of expenditure for so-called cultural purposes introduced in the Third Duma.

In special cases where, in spite of the general conditions, some improvement of the conditions of the working people is no more than probable, it is recommended that the deputies should abstain from voting and state their reasons for doing so.

Lastly, in exceptional cases, where there is no doubt that the workers will benefit, it is permissible to vote for a particular item, but it is recommended that the deputies should consult representatives of the Central Committee and Party and trade union bodies.

December 25–26, 1908 (January 7–8, 1909)

CONFERENCE OF THE EXTENDED EDITORIAL BOARD OF *PROLETARY*[1]

JUNE 8–17 (21–30), 1909

SPEECH AND DRAFT RESOLUTION ON THE TASKS OF THE BOLSHEVIKS IN RELATION TO DUMA ACTIVITY

WE ARE COMING TO THE END OF the debate, and I don't think there is any need to fix it in a special resolution, because we need to be careful with that. The thing was after all to thrash the matter out among ourselves. In reply to Vlasov[2] on the use of legal opportunities, I will read a draft resolution:

"The Bolshevik Centre resolves: in order *in practice* to achieve—and to achieve in a *revolutionary* Social-Democratic spirit and direction—the objects now recognized by all Bolsheviks of making use of all 'legal opportunities,' all legal and semi-legal organizations of the working class in general and the Duma rostrum in particular, the Bolshevik section must definitely and clearly put before itself the aim of securing at any cost the training up of a body of experienced Bolsheviks, specialized in their job and firmly established in their particular *legal* post (trade unions; clubs; Duma committees, etc., etc.)."

Vlasov stated that this refers to the leaders. This is not the case. The trouble is that in our Bolshevik section the view prevails that such specialists are not required. Our forces are few: they must be utilized and allotted to the legal functions, and made responsible for carrying out these functions in the name of the section. If we speak of setting up Party cells, we must know how to do it. I have drafted a resolution on agitation by leaflets:

"Having discussed the question of the Bolsheviks' tasks in relation to Duma activity, the Bolshevik Centre resolves to draw the attention of all local organisations to the importance of agitation by leaflets (in addition to the local and regional press) which spread among the masses information about the Duma work of the Social-Democrats and give direction to this work. Subjects for such leaflets might be indications of questions to be highlighted from the Duma rostrum, the summing up of the Social-Democrats' activity in the Duma and the grouping of the different parties, outlines of propagandist speeches on these questions, analysis of the political significance of particularly important Social-Democratic speeches in the Duma, pointing out omissions or inaccuracies in Social-Democratic Duma speeches, and extracts from these speeches giving practical conclusions important for propaganda and agitation, etc., etc."

And I have also roughed-out in the form of a resolution the points on the question of our attitude to Duma activity which were discussed at the private meeting:[3]

"II. The difference between the revolutionary Social-Democratic use of the Duma and the reformist (or more broadly, opportunist) use can be described by the following indications, which do not pretend to be complete.

"From the standpoint of the external relations, so to speak, of the Duma Social-Democratic group, the difference between the revolutionary Social-Democratic use of the Duma and opportunist use consists in the following: the necessity to combat the tendency on the part of deputies and very often of the bourgeois intellectuals surrounding them—a tendency natural in all bourgeois society (and in Russia during a period of reaction especially)—to make parliamentary activity the basic, most important thing of all, an end in itself. In particular it is essential to make every effort that the group should carry on its work as one of the functions subordinated to the interests of the working-class movement as a whole, and also that the group should be in constant contact with the Party, not drawing apart from it but implementing Party views, the directives of Party congresses and the central institutions of the Party.

"From the standpoint of the internal content of the group's activity, it is essential to bear the following in mind. The aim of the activity of the parliamentary Social-Democratic group differs in principle from that of *all* other political parties. The aim of the proletarian party is not to do deals or haggle with the powers that be, not to engage in the hopeless patching-up of the regime of the feudalist-bourgeois dictatorship of counter-revolution, but to develop in every way the class-consciousness, the socialist clarity of thought, the revolutionary determination and all-round organization of the mass of the workers. Every step in the activity of the Duma group must serve this fundamental aim. Therefore more attention must be paid to promoting the aims of socialist revolution from the Duma rostrum. Efforts must be made to ensure that speeches should more often be heard from the Duma rostrum propagandizing the fundamental conceptions and aims of socialism, namely, of scientific socialism. Then, in the conditions of continuing bourgeois-democratic revolution, it is extremely important that the Duma group should systematically combat the torrent of counter-revolutionary attacks on the 'liberation movement,' and the prevalent tendency (both on the part of the outright reactionaries and of the liberals, especially the Cadets) to condemn the revolution and discredit it, its aims, its methods, etc. The Social-Democratic group in the Duma must bear high the banner of the revolution, the banner of the advanced class, leader of the bourgeois-democratic revolution in Russia.

"Furthermore it is essential to point out a task of the Duma Social-Democratic group, which is exceptionally important at the present time, namely, that of participating energetically in all discussions of labor legislation. The group must utilize the rich parliamentary experience of the West-European Social-Democrats, taking special care to avoid the opportunist distortion of this aspect of its activity. The group must not whittle down its slogans and the demands of our Party's minimum program, but draft and introduce its Social-Democratic Bills (and also amendments to Bills of the government and the other parties), in order to unmask to the masses the hypocrisy and falseness of social-reformism, in order to draw the masses into independent economic and political mass struggle, which alone can bring real gains to the workers or transform half-hearted and hypocritical 'reforms' under the existing system into strong-points for an advancing working-class movement towards the complete emancipation of the proletariat.

"The Duma Social-Democratic group and the whole Social-Democratic Party should take the same stand towards reformism within Social-Democracy, which is the latest product of opportunist vacillation.

"Finally, revolutionary Social-Democratic use of the Duma should differ from opportunist use in that the Social-Democratic group and the Party are bound to explain to the masses in every possible way the class character of all bourgeois political parties, not confining themselves to attacks on the government and outright reactionaries, but exposing both the counter-revolutionary nature of liberalism and the waverings of petty-bourgeois peasant democracy."

EXPLANATORY NOTE ON THE DRAFT OF THE MAIN GROUNDS OF THE BILL ON THE EIGHT-HOUR WORKING DAY[1]

II[2]

IN THE PRESENT, SECOND PART OF THE explanatory note we intend to dwell on the question of the *type* of the Social-Democratic Bill on the Eight-Hour Working Day for the Third Duma and on the *grounds* explaining the *basic features* of the Bill.

The original draft in the possession of the Duma Social-Democratic group and given to our subcommittee could be taken as a basis, but it has required a number of alterations.

The main aim of the Bills introduced by the Social-Democrats in the Third Duma must lie in *propaganda and agitation* for the Social-Democratic program and tactics. Any hopes of the "reformism" of the Third Duma would not only be ludicrous, but would threaten completely to distort the character of Social-Democratic revolutionary tactics and convert it into the tactics of opportunist, liberal social-reformism. Needless to say, such a distortion of Social-Democratic Duma tactics would directly and emphatically contradict the universally binding decisions of our Party, viz.: the resolutions of the London Congress of the R.S.D.L.P. and the resolutions, confirmed by the Central Committee, of the All-Russian Party Conferences of November 1907 and December 1908.

For Bills introduced by the Social-Democratic group in the Duma to fulfil their purpose, the following conditions are necessary.

(1) Bills must set out in the clearest and most definite form the individual demands of the Social-Democrats included in the minimum program of our Party or necessarily following from this program;

(2) Bills must never be burdened with an abundance of legal subtleties; they must give the *main grounds* for the proposed laws, but not elaborately worded texts of laws with all details;

(3) Bills should not excessively isolate various spheres of social reform and democratic changes, as might appear essential from a narrowly legal, administrative or "purely parliamentary" standpoint. On the contrary, pursuing the aim of Social-Democratic propaganda and agitation, Bills should give the working class the most definite idea possible of the *necessary connection* between factory (and social in general) reforms and the *democratic* political changes without which all "reforms" of the Stolypin autocracy are inevitably destined to undergo a "Zubatovist"[3] distortion and be reduced to a dead letter. As a matter of course this indication of the connection between economic reforms and politics must be achieved not by including in all Bills the demands of consistent democracy in their entirety, but by bringing to the fore the democratic and specially proletarian-democratic institutions corresponding to each individual reform, and the impossibility of realising such institutions without radical political changes must be emphasised in the explanatory note to the Bill;

(4) in view of the extreme difficulty under present conditions of legal Social-Democratic propaganda and agitation among the masses, Bills must be so composed that the Bill taken separately and the explanatory note to it taken separately *can achieve their aim* on reaching the masses (whether by being reprinted in non-Social-Democratic newspapers, or by the distribution of separate leaflets with the text of the Bill, etc.), i.e., can be read by rank-and-file unenlightened workers to the advantage of the development of their class-consciousness. With this end in view the Bills in their *entire* structure must be imbued with a spirit of proletarian distrust of the employers and of the state as an organ serving the employers: in other words, the spirit of the class struggle must permeate the whole structure of the Bill and ensue from the sum of its separate propositions;

finally (5) under conditions in Russia today, i.e., in the absence of a Social-Democratic press and Social-Democratic meetings, Bills must give a sufficiently *concrete* idea of the changes demanded by the Social-Democrats and not limit themselves to a mere *proclamation* of principle. The ordinary unenlightened worker should find his interest aroused by the Social-Democratic Bill, he should be inspired by its concrete picture of change so that later he passes from this individual picture to the Social-Democratic world outlook as a whole.

Proceeding from these basic premises, it has to be admitted that the type of Bill chosen by the author of the original draft of the Bill on the Eight-Hour Working Day is *more in accordance* with Russian conditions than, for example, those Bills on a shorter working day which were introduced by the French and German Social-Democrats in their parliaments. For example, the Bill on the Eight-Hour Working Day moved by Jules Guesde in the French Chamber of Deputies on May 22, 1894, contains two articles: the first forbids working longer than eight hours per day and six days per week, the second permits work in several shifts provided that the number of working hours per week does not exceed 48.[4] The German Social-Democratic Bill of 1890 contains 14 lines, proposing a 10-hour working day immediately, a nine-hour working day from January 1, 1894, and an eight-hour day from January 1, 1898. In the session of 1900–02 the German Social-Democrats put forward a still shorter proposal for limiting the working day immediately to ten hours, and subsequently to eight hours, at a time to be decided separately.[5]

In any case, of course, such Bills are ten times more rational from the Social-Democratic point of view than attempts to "adapt" oneself to what is *practicable* for reactionary or bourgeois governments. But whereas in France and Germany, where there is freedom of press and assembly, it suffices to draft a Bill with only a *proclamation of principle*, in our case in Russia at the present time it is necessary to add *concrete propaganda* material in the Bill *itself.*

Hence we regard as more expedient the *type* adopted by the author of the original draft, but a number of corrections need to be made in this draft, for in some cases the author commits what is in our opinion an extremely important and extremely dangerous mistake, viz., he lowers the demands of our minimum program without any need for it (e.g., by fixing the weekly rest period at 36 hours instead of 42, or by saying nothing about the need to have the consent of the workers' organizations for permitting night work). In a few cases the author, as it were, tries to adapt his Bill to the requirement of "practicability" by proposing, for example, that the *minister* should decide requests for exceptions (with the matter being raised in the legislative body) and by making no mention of the role of the workers' trade union organizations in implementing the law on the eight-hour day.

The Bill proposed by our subcommittee introduces into the original draft a number of corrections in the above-mentioned direction. In particular, we shall dwell on the grounds for the following alterations of the original draft.

On the question of what enterprises should come under the Bill, the sphere of its application should be extended to include all branches of industry, trade and transport, and all kinds of institutions (including those of the state: the post office, etc.) as well as home work. In the explanatory note put forward in the Duma the Social-Democrats must especially emphasize the need for such an extension and for putting an end to all boundaries and divisions (in this matter) between the factory, trading, office, transport and other sections of the proletariat.

The question may arise of agriculture, in view of the demand in our minimum program for an eight-hour working day "for all wage-workers." We think, however, that it is hardly expedient at *the present time* for the Russian Social-Democrats to take the initiative in proposing an eight-hour working day in agriculture. It would be better to make the proviso in the explanatory note that the Party reserves the right to introduce a further Bill in regard to both agriculture and domestic service, etc.

Further, in all cases where the Bill deals with the permissibility of exceptions to the law, we have inserted a demand for the consent of the workers' trade union to each exception. This is essential in order to show the workers clearly that it is impossible to achieve an actual reduction of the working day without independent action on the part of the workers' organizations.

Next, we must deal with the question of the *gradual* introduction of the eight-hour working day. The author of the original draft does not say a word about this, limiting himself to the simple demand for the eight-hour day as in Jules Guesde's Bill. Our draft, on the other hand, follows the model of Parvus[6] and the draft of the German Social-Democratic group in the Reichstag, establishing a *gradual* introduction of the eight-hour working day (immediately, i.e., within three months of the law coming into force, a ten-hour day, and a reduction by one hour annually). Of course, the difference between the two drafts is not such an essential one. But in view of the very great technical backwardness of Russian industry, the extremely weak organization of the Russian proletariat and the huge mass of the working class population (handicraftsmen, etc.) that has not yet participated in any big campaign for a reduction of the working day—in view of all these conditions it will be more expedient *here and now*, in the Bill *itself*, to answer the inevitable objection that a sharp change is impossible, that with such a change the workers' wages will be reduced, etc.[7] Laying down a gradual introduction of the eight-hour working day (the Germans protracted its introduction to eight years; Parvus to four years; we are proposing two years) provides an immediate reply to this objection: work in excess of ten hours per day is certainly irrational economically and impermissible on health and cultural grounds. The annual term, however, for reducing the working day by one hour fully suffices for the technically backward enterprises to come into line and introduce changes, and for the workers to go over to the new system without an appreciable difference in labor productivity.

The introduction of the eight-hour working day should be made gradual not in order to "adapt" the Bill to the measure of the capitalists or government (there can be no question of this, and if such ideas were to arise we should, of course, prefer to exclude any mention of gradualness), but in order to show everyone quite clearly the technical, cultural and economic practicability of the Social-Democratic program in even one of the most backward countries.

A serious objection to making the introduction of the eight-hour working day a gradual one in the *Russian* Social-Democratic Bill would be that this would disavow, even if indirectly, the revolutionary Soviets of Workers' Deputies of 1905, which called for *immediate* realization of the eight-hour working day. We regard this as a serious objection, for the slightest disavowal of the Soviets of Workers' Deputies *in this respect* would be direct renegacy, or at any rate support of the renegades and counter-revolutionary liberals, who have made themselves notorious by such a disavowal.

We think therefore that *in any case*, whether gradualness will be incorporated in the Bill of the Social-Democratic Duma group or not, *in any case* it is altogether essential that *both* the explanatory note submitted to the Duma *and* the Duma speech of the Social-Democratic representative, should quite definitely express a view which absolutely excludes the slightest disavowal of the actions of the Soviets of Workers' Deputies and absolutely *includes* our recognition of them as correct in principle, wholly legitimate and necessary.

"The Social-Democrats," so, approximately, the statement of the Social-Democratic representatives or their explanatory note should read, "do not in any case renounce the *immediate* introduction of the eight-hour working day; on the contrary, in *certain* historical conditions, when the struggle becomes acute, when the energy and initiative of the mass movement are at a high level, when the clash between the old society and the new assumes sharp forms, when for the success of the working class struggle against medievalism, for instance, it is *essential* not to stop at anything—in short, in conditions resembling those of November 1905—the Social-Democrats regard the *immediate* introduction of the eight-hour working day as not only legitimate but even *essential*. By inserting in its Bill at the present time a gradual introduction of the eight-hour working

day, the Social-Democrats merely desire to show thereby the entire possibility of putting into effect the demands of the programme of the
R.S.D.L.P. even under the worst historical conditions, even during the
slowest tempo of economic, social and cultural development."

Let us repeat: we consider *such* a declaration on the part of the Social-
Democrats in the Duma and in their explanatory note to the Bill on the
eight-hour working day as *absolutely* and under all circumstances essential, whereas the question of introducing a gradual establishment of the
eight-hour working day in the Bill itself is relatively less important.

The remaining changes made by us in the original draft of the Bill
concern particular details and do not require special comment.

THE SIXTH (PRAGUE) ALL-RUSSIA CONFERENCE OF THE RSDLP[1]

JANUARY 5–17 (18–30), 1912

ELECTIONS TO THE FOURTH DUMA

I

THIS CONFERENCE RECOGNIZES THE UNDOUBTED NECESSITY FOR participation by the R.S.D.L. Party in the forthcoming election campaign to the Fourth State Duma, the nomination of independent candidates of our Party and the formation in the Fourth Duma of a Social-Democratic group, which as a section of the Party is subordinated to the Party as a whole.

The main tasks of our Party in the elections, and equally of the future Social-Democratic group in the Duma itself—a task to which all else must be subordinated—is socialist, class propaganda and the organization of the working class.

The main election slogans of our Party in the forthcoming elections must be:

(1) *A democratic republic.*
(2) *The eight-hour working day.*
(3) *Confiscation of all landed estates.*

In all our election agitation it is essential to give the clearest possible explanation of these demands, based on the experience of the Third

Duma and all the activities of the government in the sphere of central as well as local administration.

All propaganda on the remaining demands of the Social-Democratic minimum programme, namely: universal franchise, freedom of association, election of judges and officials by the people, state insurance for workers, replacement of the standing army by the arming of the people, and so on, must be inseparably linked with the above-mentioned three demands.

II

The general tactical line of the R.S.D.L.P. in the elections should be the following: the Party must conduct a merciless struggle against the tsarist monarchy and the parties of landowners and capitalists supporting it, at the same time steadfastly exposing the counter-revolutionary views of the bourgeois liberals (headed by the Cadet Party) and their sham democracy.

Particular attention in the election campaign must be paid to dissociating the position of the proletarian party from that of *all* non-proletarian parties and explaining the petty-bourgeois essence of the sham socialism of the democratic (chiefly Trudovik, Narodnik and Socialist-Revolutionary) groups, as well as the harm done to democracy by their waverings on the question of consistent and mass revolutionary struggle.

As far as electoral agreements are concerned, the Party, adhering to the decisions of the London Congress, must:

(1) Put forward its candidates in all worker curias and forbid *any* agreement *whatsoever* with other parties or groups (liquidators);

(2) In view of the great agitational significance of the mere fact of nomination of independent Social-Democratic candidates, it is necessary to ensure that in the second assemblies of urban voters, and as far as possible in the peasant curias, the Party puts forward its own candidates;

(3) In cases of a second ballot (Article 106 of the Election Regulations) in the election of electors at the second assemblies of urban voters it is permissible to conclude agreements with bourgeois democrats against the liberals, and then with the liberals against all the government parties. One form of agreement can be the compilation of a general list of electors for one or several towns in proportion to the number of votes registered at the first elections;

(4) In those five cities (St. Petersburg, Moscow, Riga, Odessa, Kiev) where there are direct elections with a second ballot, it is essential in the first elections to put forward independent Social-Democratic candidates for the second urban curia voters. In the event of a second ballot here,

and since there is obviously no danger from the Black Hundreds, it is permissible to come to an agreement only with the democratic groups against the liberals;

(5) There can be no electoral agreements providing for a common platform, and Social-Democratic candidates must not be bound by any kind of political commitment, nor must Social-Democrats be prevented from resolutely criticising the counter-revolutionary nature of the liberals and the half-heartedness and inconsistency of the bourgeois democrats;

(6) At the second stage of the elections (in the uyezd assemblies of delegates, in the gubernia assemblies of voters, etc.), wherever it proves essential to ensure the defeat of an Octobrist-Black Hundred or a government list in general, an agreement must be concluded to share the seats, primarily with bourgeois democrats (Trudoviks, Popular Socialists, etc.), and then with the liberals (Cadets), independents, Progressists, etc.

III

All Social-Democrats must *immediately* commence preparation for the election campaign, and should pay special attention to the following:

(1) It is urgently necessary everywhere to form illegal Social-Democratic nuclei in order that they may without delay prepare for the Social-Democratic election campaign;

(2) To pay the necessary attention to the strengthening and broadening of the legally existing workers' press;

(3) The entire election campaign must be carried out in close alliance with workers' trades unions and all other associations of workers, and the form in which these societies participate must be chosen with due consideration paid to their legal status;

(4) Special attention must be paid to the organizational and agitation preparation of the elections in the worker curias of those six gubernias in which the election of deputies to the Duma from the worker curias is guaranteed (St. Petersburg, Moscow, Vladimir, Kostroma, Kharkov and Ekaterinoslav). Every single worker elector—here and in the other gubernias—must be a Social-Democratic Party member;

(5) Assemblies of workers' delegates, guided by the decision of the illegal Party organizations, must decide *who precisely* is to be elected to the Duma from the workers, and bind all electors, under threat of boycott and being branded as traitors, to withdraw their candidature in favor of the Party candidate;

(6) In view of persecution by the government, the arrest of Social-Democrat candidates, etc., it is necessary to carry out particularly

restrained, systematic and careful work, using every means to react quickly to all police tactics and nullify all the tricks and coercion of the tsarist government, and to elect Social-Democrats to the Fourth State Duma, and then in general to strengthen the group of democratic deputies in the Duma;

(7) The candidates of the Social-Democratic Party are endorsed, and instructions concerning the elections are given by the local illegal organizations and groups of the Party, under the general supervision and guidance of the Central Committee of the Party;

(8) If, despite all efforts, it proves impossible to convene a Party congress or a new conference before the elections to the Fourth Duma, the Conference empowers the Central Committee, or an institution appointed for the purpose by the latter, to issue concrete instructions on questions concerning the conduct of the election campaign in the various localities, or to meet special circumstances arising, etc.

THE ELECTION PLATFORM
OF THE RSDLP[1]

WORKER COMRADES, AND ALL CITIZENS OF RUSSIA!

The elections to the Fourth Duma are to be held in the very near future. Various political parties and the government itself are already energetically preparing for the elections. The Russian Social-Democratic Labor Party, the party of the class-conscious proletariat, that by its glorious struggle in 1905 dealt the first serious blow to tsarism and forced it to concede representative institutions, calls on each and every one of you who enjoy electoral rights, as well as the great majority deprived of rights, to play a most energetic part in the elections. All those who strive for the liberation of the working class from wage slavery, all those who hold the cause of Russia's freedom dear, must start work at once so that at the elections to the Fourth Duma, the landowners' Duma, they may unite and strengthen the fighters for freedom, and advance the class-consciousness and organization of Russian democrats.

It is five years since the government coup of June 3, 1907, when Nicholas the Bloody, the Khodynka Tsar,[2] "the victor and destroyer" of the First and Second Dumas, threw aside his pledges, promises, and manifestos, so that, together with the Black-Hundred landowners and the Octobrist merchants, he could take vengeance on the working class and all the revolutionary elements in Russia, in other words, on the vast majority of the people, for 1905.

Vengeance for the revolution is the hallmark of the entire period of the Third Duma. Never before has Russia known such raging persecution on the part of tsarism. The gallows erected during these five years beat all records of three centuries of Russian history. The places of exile, penal establishments and prisons overflow with political prisoners in unheard-of numbers, and never before has there been such torture and torment of the vanquished as under Nicholas II. Never before has there been such a wave of embezzlement, such tyranny and violence on the part of officials, who are forgiven everything because of their zeal in the struggle against "sedition"; never before have the ordinary people, and the peasants in particular, been so humiliated by any representative of authority. Never before has there been such avid, ferocious, reckless persecution of the Jews, and after them of other peoples, not belonging to the dominant nation.

Anti-Semitism and the most crude nationalism became the only political platform of the government parties, and Purishkevich became the one complete, undiluted, and perfect personification of all the methods of rule by the present tsarist monarchy.

And, what have these frenzied acts of the counter-revolutionaries led to?

The consciousness that it is impossible to continue living in this way is penetrating into the minds of even the "higher," exploiting, classes of society. The Octobrists themselves, the dominant party in the Third Duma, the party of landowners and merchants, terrified of the revolution and cringing before authority, are more and more expressing the conviction in their own press that the tsar and the nobility, which they have served so faithfully and truly, have led Russia into an impasse.

There was a time when the tsarist monarchy was the gendarme of Europe, protecting reaction in Russia and assisting in forcibly suppressing all movements for freedom in Europe. Nicholas II has brought things to such a pass, that he is now not only a European, but an Asiatic gendarme who, with the help of intrigues, money and the most brutal violence, tries to suppress all movements for freedom in Turkey, Persia, and China.

But no tsarist atrocities can halt Russia's progress. No matter how these feudal survivals, the Purishkeviches, Romanovs and Markovs, disfigure and cripple Russia, she is still advancing. With each step of Russia's development the demand for political freedom is becoming ever more insistent. In the twentieth century Russia cannot live without political freedom any more than any other country can. Is it possible to expect political reforms from the tsarist monarchy, when the tsar himself dissolved the first two Dumas and rode roughshod over his own Manifesto of October 17, 1905? Is it possible to conceive of political reforms in modern Russia, when the gang of officials mocks at all laws, knowing that in doing so, they have the protection of the tsar and his associates? Do we not see how, taking advantage of the tsar's protection, or that of his relatives, Illiodor yesterday, Rasputin today, Tolmachov yesterday, Khvostov today, Stolypin yesterday, Makarov today, trample under foot all and every law? Do we not see that even the tiny, ludicrously pathetic "reforms" of the landowners' Duma, reforms directed towards refurbishing and strengthening tsarist rule, are repudiated and distorted by the Council of State or the personal decrees of Nicholas the Bloody? Do we not know that the Black-Hundred gang of murderers who shoot at the backs of the deputies whom the rulers want out of the way, who sent to penal servitude the Social-Democratic deputies to the Second Duma, who are always organising pogroms, who insolently rob the treasury on all sides—do we not know that that gang enjoys the special blessings of the tsar and receives his poorly-disguised aid, direction and guidance? Look at the fate, under Nicholas Romanov, of the main political demands of the Russian people for the sake of which the best representatives of the people have been waging a heroic struggle for more than three-quarters of a century, for the sake of which millions rose up in 1905. Is universal, equal and direct suffrage compatible with the Romanov monarchy, when even the non-universal, unequal and indirect suffrage of the elections to the First and Second Dumas was trampled underfoot by tsarism? Is freedom of unions, associations, strikes, compatible with the tsarist monarchy, when even the reactionary, ugly law of March 4, 1906[3] has been brought to nought by the governors and the ministers? Do not the words of the Manifesto of October 17, 1905 about the "immutable principle of freedom of citizens," about the "real inviolability of the individual," about "freedom of conscience, speech, assembly, and unions," sound like mockery? Every subject of the tsar witnesses this mockery daily.

Enough of liberal lies! As if a union between freedom and the old rule were possible, as if political reforms were conceivable under a tsarist monarchy. The Russian people have paid for their childish illusions with the hard lessons of the counter-revolution. Anyone seriously and sincerely desiring political freedom, will raise the banner of a *republic* proudly and bravely, and *all* the live forces of Russian democracy will certainly be drawn to that banner by the politics of the tsarist-landowner gang.

Time was, and not so long ago, when the slogan "Down with the autocracy" seemed too advanced for Russia. Nevertheless, the R.S.D.L. Party issued this slogan, the advanced workers caught it up and spread it throughout the country; and in two or three years this slogan became a popular saying. To work then, worker comrades and all citizens of Russia, all those who do not want to see our country sink finally into stagnation, barbarity, lack of rights and the appalling poverty of tens of millions. The Russian Social-Democrats, the Russian workers will succeed in making "Down with the tsarist monarchy, long live the Russian Democratic Republic!" a nation-wide slogan.

Workers, remember 1905. Millions of toilers then were given new life, raised to class-consciousness, to freedom, through the strike movement. Tens of years of tsarist reforms did not and could not give you a tenth part of those improvements in your lives which you then achieved by mass struggle. The fate of the Bill on workers' insurance, made unrecognizable by the landowners' Duma with the aid of the Cadets, has once again shown what you can expect "from above."

The counter-revolution has taken away almost all our gains, but it has not taken and cannot take away the strength, courage and belief in their cause of the young workers, nor of the all-Russian proletariat that is growing and becoming stronger.

Long live the new struggle to improve the lot of workers who do not wish to remain slaves doomed to toil in workshops and factories! *Long live the 8-hour working day*! He who desires freedom in Russia must help the class which dug a grave for the tsarist monarchy in 1905, and which will throw the mortal enemy of all the peoples of Russia into that grave during the forthcoming Russian revolution.

Peasants! You sent your deputies, the Trudoviks, to the First and Second Dumas, believing in the tsar, hoping by peaceful means to win his agreement to the transfer of landed estates to the people. You have now been able to convince yourselves that the tsar, the biggest landowner in Russia, will stop at nothing in defense of the landowners and officials; at neither perjury nor lawlessness, oppression or bloodshed. Are you going to tolerate the yoke of the former serf-Owners, silently bear the affronts and insults of the officials, and die in hundreds of thousands, nay millions, from the agonies of starvation, from disease caused by hunger and extreme poverty, or will you die in the fight against the tsarist monarchy and tsarist-landowner Duma, in order to win for our children a more or less decent life, fit for a human being.

This is the question which the Russian peasants will have to decide. The working-class Social-Democratic Party calls on the peasants to struggle for complete freedom, for the transfer of all land from the landowners to the peasantry, without any compensation whatsoever. Sops thrown to the peasants cannot remedy their poverty or relieve their hunger. The peasants are not asking for charity, but for the land which has been drenched in their blood and sweat for centuries. The peasants do not need the tutelage of the authorities and the tsar, but freedom from officials and the tsar, freedom to arrange their own affairs.

Let the elections to the Fourth Duma sharpen the political consciousness of the masses and draw them again into decisive battles. Three main parties are contesting at the elections: (1) the Black Hundreds, (2) the liberals, and (3) the Social-Democrats.

The Rights, Nationalists, and Octobrists belong to the Black Hundreds. They all support the government; this means that any differences which may exist between them are of no serious significance whatsoever.

Merciless struggle against all these Black-Hundred parties—this must be our slogan!

The liberals are the Cadet Party (the "Constitutional Democrats" or "people's freedom" party). This is the party of the liberal bourgeoisie, which seeks to share power with the tsar and the feudal landowners in such a way, that their power is not basically destroyed, and does not pass to the people. While the liberals detest the government which prevents them from taking power, while they help to expose it, and introduce vacillation and disintegration into its ranks, their hatred of the revolution and fear of mass struggles is even greater than their hatred of the government, and their attitude towards the popular liberation movement is even more wavering and irresolute, so that in decisive moments they treacherously go over to the side of the monarchy. During the counter-revolution, the liberals, echoing the "Slavonic dreams" of tsarism, posing as a "responsible opposition," grovelling before the tsar as "His Majesty's Opposition," and pouring dirt on the revolutionaries and the revolutionary struggle of the masses, have turned away more and more from the struggle for freedom.

The Russian Social-Democratic Labor Party was able to raise the revolutionary banner even in the reactionary Third Duma, it has succeeded even there in helping the organization and revolutionary enlightenment of the masses, and the peasants' struggle against the landowners. The party of the proletariat is the only party of the advanced class, the class capable of winning freedom for Russia. Today, our Party goes into the Duma, not in order to play at "reforms," not in order to "defend the Constitution," "convince" the Octobrists or "to dislodge reaction" from the Duma, as the liberals who are deceiving the people say they will, but in order to call the masses to the struggle from the Duma rostrum, to explain the teachings of socialism, to expose every government and liberal deception, to expose the monarchist prejudices of the backward sections of the people, and the class roots of the bourgeois parties,—in other words in order to prepare an army of class-conscious fighters for a new Russian revolution.

The tsarist government and the Black-Hundred landowners have recognized to the full the tremendous revolutionary force represented by the Social-Democratic group in the Duma. Hence, all the efforts of the police and Ministry of the Interior are directed towards preventing the social democrats from entering the Fourth Duma. Unite then, workers and citizens! Rally around the R.S.D.L.P. which at its recent conference, recovering from the breakdown during the evil years, again gathered its forces and raised aloft its banner. Let each and every one take part in the elections and the election campaign, and the efforts of the government will be defeated, the red banner of revolutionary Social-Democracy will be hoisted from the rostrum of the Duma in police-ridden, oppressed, blood-drenched, down-trodden and starving Russia!

Long live the Russian Democratic Republic!

Long live the 8-hour day!

Long live the confiscation of all landed estates!

Workers and citizens! Support the election campaign of the R.S.D.L.P.! Elect the candidates of the R.S.D.L.P.!

Central Committee of the Russian Social-Democratic Labour Party

THE NATIONAL EQUALITY BILL[1]

COMRADES:

The Russian Social-Democratic Labor group in the Duma has decided to introduce in the Fourth Duma a Bill to abolish the disabilities of the Jews and other non-Russians. The text of this Bill you will find below.

The Bill aims at abolishing all national restrictions against all nations: Jews, Poles, and so forth. But it deals in particular detail with the restrictions against the Jews. The reason is obvious: no nationality in Russia is so oppressed and persecuted as the Jewish. Anti-Semitism is striking ever deeper root among the propertied classes. The Jewish workers are suffering under a double yoke, both as workers and as Jews. During the past few years, the persecution of the Jews has assumed incredible dimensions. It is sufficient to recall the anti-Jewish pogroms and the Beilis case.

In view of these circumstances, organized Marxists must devote proper attention to the Jewish question.

It goes without saying that the Jewish question can effectively be solved only together with the fundamental issues confronting Russia today. Obviously, we do not look to the nationalist-Purishkevich Fourth Duma to abolish the restrictions against the Jews and other non-Russians. But it is the duty of the working class to make its voice heard. And the voice of the *Russian* workers must be particularly loud in protest against national oppression.

In publishing the text of our Bill, we hope that the Jewish workers, the Polish workers, and the workers of the other oppressed nationalities will express their opinion of it and propose amendments, should they deem it necessary.

At the same time we hope that the Russian workers will give particularly strong support to our Bill by their declarations, etc.

In conformity with Article 4 we shall append to the Bill a special list of regulations and laws to be rescinded. This appendix will cover about a hundred such laws affecting the Jews alone.

A BILL FOR THE ABOLITION OF ALL DISABILITIES OF THE JEWS AND OF ALL RESTRICTIONS ON THE GROUNDS OF ORIGIN OR NATIONALITY

1. Citizens of all nationalities inhabiting Russia are equal before the law.
2. No citizen of Russia, regardless of sex and religion, may be restricted in political or in any other rights on the grounds of origin or nationality.
3. All and any laws, provisional regulations, riders to laws, and so forth, which impose restrictions upon Jews in any sphere of social and political life, are herewith abolished. Article 767, Vol. IX, which states that "Jews are subject to the general laws in all cases *where no special regulations affecting them, have been issued*" is herewith repealed. All and any restrictions of the rights of Jews as regards residence and travel, the right to education, the right to state and public employment, electoral rights, military service, the right to purchase and rent real estate in towns, villages. etc., are herewith abolished, and all restrictions of the rights of Jews to engage in the liberal professions, etc., are herewith abolished.
4. To the present law is appended a list of the laws, orders, provisional regulations, etc., that limit the tights of the Jews, and which are subject to repeal.

THE PETROGRAD CITY CONFERENCE OF THE RSDLP (BOLSHEVIKS)[1]

APRIL 14–22 (APRIL 27–MAY 5), 1917

RESOLUTION ON THE MUNICIPAL QUESTION

UNDER NO CIRCUMSTANCES CAN THE MUNICIPAL PLATFORM, particularly at the present revolutionary time, be reduced only to communal questions.

It must also contain a definite answer to all present-day key issues, especially those concerning the war and the tasks of the proletariat in regard to the central power.

Even in municipal questions, such as that of the militia, food supply, housing, and taxes, we cannot expect the petty-bourgeois parties to agree to revolutionary measures necessary to combat war and its consequences.

For all these reasons we must go to the elections without blocs, upon a straight issue of principles announced in the programme of the proletarian party, and explain to the people the fundamental differences between the three main party divisions, namely,(1) the Cadets and those to the right of them; (2) the parties of the petty bourgeoisie (Narodniks) and a section of workers who have fallen under the influence of the bourgeoisie (the Menshevik defencists); (3) the party of the revolutionary proletariat (the Bolsheviks).

The technical arrangements for the elections based on the system of proportional representation make blocs technically unnecessary.

It is advisable in every way to encourage closer relations and mutual exchange of opinions, on the basis of practical work, with those Mensheviks who are really breaking with revolutionary defencism and with support of the Provisional Government. With such comrades it is permissible to run a joint ticket, on condition that there be sufficient agreement on fundamentals. A concrete municipal programme should be worked out, particularly on the question of a proletarian militia to be paid for by the capitalists.

Pravda No. 46, May 15 (2), 1917

Excerpt from "The Constituent Assembly Elections and the Dictatorship of the Proletariat"[1]

THE COMPARISON OF THE CONSTITUENT ASSEMBLY ELECTIONS in November 1917 with the development of the proletarian revolution in Russia from October 1917 to December 1919 enables us to draw conclusions concerning bourgeois parliamentarism and the proletarian revolution in every capitalist country. Let me try briefly to formulate, or at least to outline, the principal conclusions.

1. Universal suffrage is an index of the level reached by the various classes in their understanding of their problems. It shows how the various classes are *inclined* to solve their problems. The actual *solution* of those problems is not provided by voting, but by the class struggle in all its forms including civil war.

2. The socialists and Social-Democrats of the Second International take the stand of vulgar petty-bourgeois democrats and share the prejudice that the fundamental problems of the class struggle can be solved by voting.

3. The party of the revolutionary proletariat must take part in bourgeois parliaments in order to enlighten the masses; this can be done during elections and in the struggle between parties in parliament. But limiting the class struggle to the parliamentary struggle, or regarding the latter as the highest and decisive form, to which all the other forms of struggle are subordinate, is actually desertion to the side of the bourgeoisie against the proletariat.

4. All the representatives and supporters of the Second International, and all the leaders of the German, so-called "independent,"

Social-Democratic Party, actually go over to the bourgeoisie in this way when they recognize the dictatorship of the proletariat in words, but in deeds, by their propaganda, imbue the proletariat with the idea that it must first obtain a formal expression of the will of the majority of the population under capitalism (i.e., a majority of votes in the bourgeois parliament) to transfer political power to the proletariat, which transfer is to take place later.

All the cries, based on this premise, of the German "independent" Social-Democrats and similar leaders of decayed socialism against the "dictatorship of a minority," and so forth, merely indicate that those leaders fail to understand the dictatorship of the bourgeoisie, which actually reigns even in the most democratic republics, and that they fail to understand the conditions for its destruction by the class struggle of the proletariat.

5. This failure to understand consists, in particular, in the following: they forget that, to a very large degree, the bourgeois parties are able to rule because they deceive the masses of the people, because of the yoke of capital, and to this is added self-deception concerning the nature of capitalism, a self-deception which is characteristic mostly of the petty-bourgeois parties, which usually want to substitute more or less disguised forms of class conciliation for the class struggle.

"First let the majority of the population, while private property still exists, i.e., while the rule and yoke of capital still exist, express themselves in favor of the party of the proletariat and only then can and should the party take power"—so say the petty-bourgeois democrats who call themselves socialists but who are in reality the servitors of the bourgeoisie.

"Let the revolutionary proletariat first overthrow the bourgeoisie, break the yoke of capital, and smash the bourgeois state apparatus, then the victorious proletariat will be able rapidly to gain the sympathy and support of the majority of the non-proletarian working people by satisfying their needs at the expense of the exploiters"—say we. The opposite will be rare exception in history (and even in such an exception the bourgeoisie can resort to civil war, as the example of Finland showed).

6. Or in other words:

"First we shall pledge ourselves to recognize the principle of equality, or consistent democracy, while preserving private property and the yoke of capital (i.e., actual inequality under formal equality), and try to obtain the decision of the majority on this basis"—say the bourgeoisie and their yes-men, the petty-bourgeois democrats who call themselves socialists and Social-Democrats.

"First the proletarian class struggle, winning state power, will destroy the pillars and foundations of actual inequality, and then the proletariat, which has defeated the exploiters, will lead all working people to the *abolition of classes*, i.e., to socialist *equality*, the only kind that is not a deception"—say we.

7. In all capitalist countries, besides the proletariat, or that part of the proletariat which is conscious of its revolutionary aims and is capable of fighting to achieve them, there are numerous politically immature proletarian, semi-proletarian, semi-petty-bourgeois strata which follow the bourgeoisie and bourgeois democracy (including the "socialists" of the Second International) because they have been deceived, have no confidence in their own strength, or in the strength of the proletariat, are unaware of the possibility of having their urgent needs satisfied by means of the expropriation of the exploiters.

These strata of the working and exploited people provide the vanguard of the proletariat with allies and give it a stable majority of the population; but the proletariat can win these allies only with the aid of an instrument like state power, that is to say, only after it has overthrown the bourgeoisie and has destroyed the bourgeois state apparatus.

8. The strength of the proletariat in any capitalist country is far greater than the proportion it represents of the total population. That is because the proletariat economically dominates the center and nerve of the entire economic system of capitalism, and also because the proletariat expresses economically and politically the real interests of the overwhelming majority of the working people under capitalism.

Therefore, the proletariat, even when it constitutes a minority of the population (or when the class-conscious and really revolutionary vanguard of the proletariat constitutes a minority of the population), is capable of overthrowing the bourgeoisie and, after that, of winning to its side numerous allies from a mass of semi-proletarians and petty bourgeoisie who never declare in advance in favor of the rule of the proletariat, who do not understand the conditions and aims of that rule, and only by their subsequent experience become convinced that the proletarian dictatorship is inevitable, proper and legitimate.

9. Finally, in every capitalist country there are always very broad strata of the petty bourgeoisie which inevitably vacillate between capital and labor. To achieve victory, the proletariat must, first, choose the right moment for its decisive assault on the bourgeoisie, taking into account, among other things, the disunity between the bourgeoisie and its petty-bourgeois allies, or the instability of their alliance, and so forth. Secondly, the proletariat must, after its victory, utilize this vacillation of the petty

bourgeoisie in such a way as to neutralize them, prevent their siding with the exploiters; it must be able to hold on for some time *in spite of this vacillation*, and so on, and so forth.

10. One of the necessary conditions for preparing the proletariat for its victory is a long, stubborn and ruthless struggle against opportunism, reformism, social-chauvinism, and similar bourgeois influences and trends, which are inevitable, since the proletariat is operating in a capitalist environment. If there is no such struggle, if opportunism in the working-class movement is not utterly defeated beforehand, there can be no dictatorship of the proletariat. Bolshevism would not have defeated the bourgeoisie in 1917–19 if before that, in 1903–17, it had not learned to defeat the Mensheviks, i.e., the opportunists, reformists, social-chauvinists, and ruthlessly expel them from the party of the proletarian vanguard.

At the present time, the verbal recognition of the dictatorship of the proletariat by the leaders of the German "Independents," or by the French Longuetists, and the like, who are *actually* continuing the old, habitual policy of big and small concessions to and conciliation with opportunism, subservience to the prejudices of bourgeois democracy ("consistent democracy" or "pure democracy" as they call it) and bourgeois parliamentarism, and so forth, is the most dangerous self-deception—and sometimes sheer fooling of the workers.

December 16, 1919

SECOND CONGRESS OF THE COMMUNIST INTERNATIONAL, 1920

THESES ON THE COMMUNIST PARTIES AND PARLIAMENTARISM[1]

1. THE NEW EPOCH AND THE NEW PARLIAMENTARISM.

THE ATTITUDE OF THE SOCIALIST PARTIES TOWARDS parliamentarism was in the beginning, in the period of the First International, that of using bourgeois parliaments for the purpose of agitation. Participation in parliament was considered from the point of view of the development of class consciousness, i.e. of awakening the class hostility of the proletariat to the ruling class. This relationship was transformed, not through the influence of theory, but through the influence of political development. Through the uninterrupted increase of the productive forces and the extension of the area of capitalist exploitation, capitalism, and with it the parliamentary state, gained continually increasing stability.

Hence there arose: The adaptation of the parliamentary tactics of the socialist parties to the "organic" legislative work of the bourgeois parliament and the ever greater importance of the struggle for reforms in the framework of capitalism, the domination of the so-called minimum program of social democracy, the transformation of the maximum program into a debating formula for an exceedingly distant "final goal." On this basis then developed the phenomena of parliamentary careerism, of corruption and of the open or concealed betrayal of the most elementary interests of the working class.

The attitude of the Communist International towards parliamentarism is determined, not by a new doctrine, but by the change in the role of parliament itself. In the previous epoch parliament performed to a certain degree a historically progressive task as a tool of developing capitalism. Under the present conditions of unbridled imperialism, however, parliament has been transformed into a tool for lies, deception, violence and enervating chatter. In the face of imperialist devastation, plundering, rape, banditry and destruction, parliamentary reforms, robbed of any system, permanence and method, lose any practical significance for the toiling masses.

Like the whole of bourgeois society, parliamentarism too is losing its stability. The sudden transition from the organic epoch to the critical creates the basis for a new tactic of the proletariat in the field of parliamentarism. Thus the Russian Labour Party (the Bolsheviks) had already worked out the nature of revolutionary parliamentarism in the previous period because since 1905 Russia had been shaken from its political and social equilibrium and had entered the period of storms and shocks.

To the extent that some socialists, who tend towards communism, point out that the moment for the revolution has not yet come in their countries, and refuse to split from parliamentary opportunists, they proceed, in the essence of the matter, from the conscious assessment of the coming epoch as an epoch of the relative stability of imperialist society, and assume that on this basis a coalition with the Turatis and the Longuets can bring practical results in the struggle for reforms. Theoretically clear communism, on the other hand, will correctly estimate the character of the present epoch: highest stage of capitalism; imperialist self-negation and self-destruction; uninterrupted growth of civil war, etc. The forms of political relations and groupings can be different in different countries. The essence however remains everywhere one and the same; what is at stake for us is the immediate political and technical preparations for the insurrection of the proletariat, the destruction of bourgeois power and the establishment of the new proletarian power.

At present, parliament, for communists, can in no way become the arena for the struggle for reforms, for the amelioration of the position of the working class, as was the case at certain times in the previous period. The center of gravity of political life has at present been removed finally and completely beyond the bounds of parliament.

On the other hand the bourgeoisie is forced, not only by reason of its relations to the toiling masses, but also by reason of the complex mutual relations within the bourgeois class, to carry out part of its measures one way or another in parliament, where the various cliques haggle for power, reveal their strong sides, betray their weak sides, expose themselves, etc.

Therefore it is the historical task of the working class to wrest this apparatus from the hands of the ruling class, to smash it, to destroy it, and replace it with new proletarian organs of power. At the same time, however, the revolutionary general staff of the class has a strong interest in having its scouts in the parliamentary institutions of the bourgeoisie in order to make this task of destruction easier. Thus is demonstrated quite clearly the basic difference between the tactic of the communist, who enters parliament with revolutionary aims, and the tactics of the socialist parliamentarian. The latter proceeds from the assumption of the relative stability and the indeterminate duration of the existing rule. He makes it his task to achieve reform by every means, and he is interested in seeing to it that every achievement is suitably assessed by the masses as a merit of parliamentary socialism. (Turati, Longuet and Co.).

In the place of the old adaptation to parliamentarism the new parliamentarism emerges as a tool for the annihilation of parliamentarism in general. The disgusting traditions of the old parliamentary tactics have, however, repelled a few revolutionary elements into the camp of the opponents of parliamentarism on principle (IWW) and of the revolutionary syndicalists (KAPD). The Second Congress therefore adopts the following Theses.

2. Communism, the Struggle for the Dictatorship of the Proletariat, and the Utilization of Bourgeois Parliaments

I

1. Parliamentarism as a state system has become a "democratic" form *of* the rule *of* the bourgeoisie, which at a certain stage *of* development requires the fiction *of* popular representation which outwardly appears to be an organization *of* a "popular will" that stands outside the classes, but in essence is a machine for oppression and subjugation in the hands *of* ruling capital.

2. Parliament is a definite form *of state* order; therefore it cannot at all be the form *of* communist society, which knows neither classes nor class struggle nor any state power.

3. Nor can parliamentarism be a form of proletarian state administration in the period of transition from the dictatorship of the bourgeoisie to the dictatorship of the proletariat. In the moment of sharpened class struggle, in the civil war, the proletariat must inevitably build up its state organization as *a fighting organization*, into which the representatives of the previous ruling classes are not permitted. In this stage any fiction of the "popular will" is directly harmful to the working class. The proletariat

does not need any parliamentary sharing of power, it is harmful to it. The form of the proletarian dictatorship is the soviet republic.

4. The bourgeois parliaments, one of the most important apparatuses of the bourgeois state machine, cannot as such in the long run be taken over, just as the proletariat cannot at all take over the proletarian state. The task of the proletariat consists in breaking up the bourgeois state machine, destroying it, and with it the parliamentary institutions, be they republican or a constitutional monarchy.

5. It is no different with the local government institutions of the bourgeoisie, which it is theoretically incorrect to counterpose to the state organs. In reality they are similar apparatuses of the state machine of the bourgeoisie, which must be destroyed by the revolutionary proletariat and replaced by local soviets of workers' deputies.

6. Consequently communism denies parliamentarism as a form of the society of the future. It denies it as a form of the class dictatorship of the proletariat. It denies the possibility of taking over parliament in the long run; it sets itself the aim of destroying parliamentarism. Therefore there can only be a question of utilizing the bourgeois state institutions for the purpose of their destruction. The question can be posed in this, and only in this, way.

II

7. Every class struggle is a political struggle, for in the final analysis it is a struggle for power. Any strike at all that spreads over the whole country becomes a threat to the bourgeois state and thus takes on a political character. Every attempt to overthrow the bourgeoisie and to destroy its state means carrying out a political fight. Creating a proletarian state apparatus for administration and for the oppression of the resisting bourgeoisie, of whatever type that apparatus will be, means conquering political power.

8. Consequently the question of political power is not at all identical with the question of the attitude towards parliamentarism. The former is a general question of the proletarian class struggle, which is characterized by the intensification of small and partial struggles to the general struggle for the overthrow of the capitalist order as a whole.

9. The most important method of struggle of the proletariat against the bourgeoisie, i.e. against its state power, is above all mass action. Mass actions are organized and led by the revolutionary mass organizations (trades unions, parties, soviets) of the proletariat under the general leadership of a unified, disciplined, centralized Communist Party. Civil war

is war. In this war the proletariat must have its bold officer corps and its strong general staff, who direct all operations in all theatres of the struggle.

10. The mass struggle is a whole system of developing actions sharpening in their form and logically leading to the insurrection against the capitalist state. In this mass struggle, which develops into civil war, the leading party of the proletariat must as a rule consolidate all its legal positions by making them into auxiliary bases of its revolutionary activity and subordinating these positions to the plan of the main campaign, the campaign of the mass struggle.

11. The rostrum of the bourgeois parliament is such an auxiliary base. The argument that parliament is a bourgeois state institution cannot at all be used against participation in the parliamentary struggle. The Communist Party does not enter these institutions in order to carry out organic work there, but in order to help the masses from inside parliament to break up the state machine and parliament itself through action (for example the activity of Liebknecht in Germany, of the Bolsheviks in the Tsarist Duma, in the "Democratic Conference," in Kerensky's "Pre-Parliament," in the "Constituent Assembly" and in the town Dumas, and finally the activity of the Bulgarian Communists).

12. This activity in parliament, which consists mainly in revolutionary agitation from the parliamentary rostrum, in unmasking opponents, in the ideological unification of the masses who still, particularly in backward areas, are captivated by democratic ideas, look towards the parliamentary rostrum, etc., should be totally and completely subordinated to the aims and tasks of the mass struggle outside parliament.

Participation in election campaigns and revolutionary propaganda from the parliamentary rostrum is of particular importance for winning over those layers of the workers who previously, like, say, the rural toiling masses, stood far away from political life.

13. Should the communists have the majority in local government institutions, they should a) carry out revolutionary opposition to the bourgeois central power; b) do everything to be of service to the poorer population (economic measures, introduction or attempted introduction of an armed workers' militia, etc.); c) at every opportunity show the limitations placed on really big changes by the bourgeois state power; d) on this basis develop the sharpest revolutionary propaganda without fearing the conflict with the power of the state; e) under certain circumstances replace the local administration by local workers' councils. The whole activity of the Communists in the local administration must therefore be part of the general work of disrupting the capitalist system.

14. Election campaigns should not be carried out in the spirit of the hunt for the maximum number of parliamentary seats, but in the spirit of the revolutionary mobilization of the masses for the slogans of the proletarian revolution. Election campaigns should be carried out by the whole mass of the Party members and not only by an elite of the Party. It is necessary to utilize all mass actions (strikes, demonstrations, ferment among the soldiers and sailors, etc.) that are taking place at the time, and to come into close touch with them. It is necessary to draw all the proletarian mass organizations into active work.

15. In observing all these conditions, as well as those in a special instruction, parliamentary activity is the direct opposite of that petty politicking done by the social democratic parties of every country, who go into parliament in order to support this "democratic" institution or at best to "take it over." The Communist Party can only be exclusively in favour of the revolutionary utilization of parliament in the spirit of Karl Liebknecht and of the Bolsheviks.

III

16. "Anti-parliamentarism" on principle, in the sense of absolute and categorical rejection of participation in elections and revolutionary parliamentary activity, is therefore a naive, childish doctrine below any criticism, a doctrine which occasionally has a basis in healthy nausea at politicking parliamentarians, but which does not see at the same time the possibility of a revolutionary parliamentarism. Moreover, this doctrine is often linked with a completely incorrect conception of the role of the party, which sees in the Communist Party not the centralized shock troops of the workers, but a decentralized system of loosely allied groups.

17. On the other hand an absolute recognition of the necessity of actual elections and of actual participation in parliamentary sessions *under all circumstances* by no means flows from the recognition in principle of parliamentary activity. That is dependent upon a whole series of specific conditions. Withdrawal from parliament can be necessary given a specific combination of these conditions. This is what the Bolsheviks did when they withdrew from the Pre-parliament in order to break it up, to rob it of any strength and boldly to counterpose to it the St. Petersburg Soviet on the eve of the insurrection. They did the same in the Constituent Assembly on the day of its dissolution, raising the Third Congress of Soviets to the high point of political events. According to circumstances, a boycott of the elections and the immediate violent removal of not only the whole bourgeois state apparatus but also the bourgeois parliamentary

clique, or on the other hand participation in the elections while parliament itself is boycotted, etc., can be necessary.

18. In this way the Communist Party, which recognizes the necessity of participating in the elections not only to the central parliament, but also to the organs of local self-government and work in these institutions as a general role, must resolve this problem concretely, starting from the specific peculiarities of any given moment. A boycott of elections or of parliament and withdrawal from the latter is mainly permissible when the preconditions for the immediate transition to the armed struggle and the seizure of power are already present.

19. In the process, one should always bear in mind the relative unimportance of this question. Since the center of gravity lies in the struggle for state power carried out outside parliament, it goes without saying that the question of the proletarian dictatorship and the mass struggle for it cannot be placed on the same level as the particular question of the utilization of parliament.

20. The Communist International therefore emphasizes decisively that it holds every split or attempted split within the Communist Parties in this direction and only for this reason to be a serious error. The Congress calls on all elements who base themselves on the recognition of the mass struggle for the proletarian dictatorship under the leadership of the centralized party of the revolutionary proletariat exerting its influence on all the mass organizations of the workers, to strive for the complete unity of the communist elements despite possible differences of opinion over the question of the utilization of bourgeois parliaments.

3. Revolutionary Parliamentarism

In order to secure the actual carrying out of revolutionary parliamentary tactics it is necessary that:

1. The Communist Party as a whole and its Central Committee, already in the preparatory stage, that is to say before the parliamentary election, must take care of the high quality of the personal composition of the parliamentary faction. The Central Committee of the Communist Party must be responsible for the whole work of the parliamentary faction. The Central Committee of the Communist Party must have the undeniable right to raise objections to any candidate whatever of any organization whatever, if there is no guarantee that if he gets into parliament, he will pursue really communist policies.

The Communist Party must break the old social democratic habit of putting up exclusively so-called "experienced" parliamentarians, predominantly lawyers and similar people, as members of parliament. As a rule it is necessary to put up workers as candidates, without baulking at the fact that these are mainly simple party members without any great parliamentary experience. The Communist Party must ruthlessly stigmatize those careerist elements that come around the Communist Parties in order to get into parliament. The Central Committees of the Communist Parties must only ratify the candidatures of those comrades who have shown their unconditional devotion to the working class by long years of work.

2. When the elections are over, the organization of the parliamentary faction must be completely in the hands of the Central Committee of the Communist Parties, irrespective of whether the whole Party is legal or illegal at the time in question. The chairman and the committee of the communist parliamentary faction must be ratified by the Central Committee of the Party. The Central Committee of the Party must have a permanent representative in the parliamentary faction with a right of veto, and on all important political questions the parliamentary faction shall ask the Central Committee of the Party in advance for instructions concerning its behavior. Before any big forthcoming action by the communists in parliament the—Central Committee has the right and the duty to appoint or to reject the speaker for the faction, and to demand of him that he previously submit the main points of his speech or the speech itself for approval by the Central Committee. A written undertaking must be officially obtained from every candidate on the proposed communist list that, as soon as he is called upon to do so by the Party, he is prepared to resign his seat, so that in a given situation the action of withdrawing from parliament can be carried out in a united way.

3. In those countries where reformist, semi-reformist or merely careerist elements have managed to penetrate into the communist parliamentary faction (as has already happened in some countries) the Central Committees of the Communist Parties have the obligation of carrying out a thorough purge of the personal composition of the faction proceeding on the principle that it is much more useful for the cause of the working class to have a small, but truly communist faction, than a large faction without consistent communist policies.

4. On the decision of the Central Committee, the communist member of parliament has the obligation to combine legal with illegal work. In those countries where the communist members of parliament enjoy immunity from bourgeois law, this immunity must be utilized to support the Party in its illegal work of organization and propaganda.

5. Communist members of parliament must subordinate all parliamentary action to the activity of their Party outside parliament. The regular introduction of demonstrative draft laws, which are not intended to be accepted by the bourgeois majority, but for the purposes of propaganda,

agitation and organization, must take place on the instructions of the Party and its Central Committee.

6. In the event of demonstrations by workers in the streets and other revolutionary actions, the communist members of parliament have the duty to place themselves in the most conspicuous leading place at the head of the masses of workers.

7. Communist members of parliament must use every means at their disposal (under the supervision of the Party) to create written and any other kind of links with the revolutionary workers, peasants and other toilers. Under no circumstances can they act like social democratic members of parliament, who pursue business connections with their voters. They must be constantly at the disposal of the Party for any propaganda work in the country.

8. Every communist member of parliament must bear in mind that he is not a legislator seeking an understanding with other legislators, but a Party agitator who has been sent into the enemy camp in order to carry out Party decisions there. The communist member of parliament is responsible, not to the scattered mass of voters, but to his Party, be it legal or illegal.

9. Communist members of parliament must speak a language that can be understood by every simple worker, every peasant, every washerwoman and every shepherd, so that the Party is able to publish the speeches as leaflets and distribute them to the most distant corners of the country.

10. Simple communist workers must appear in the bourgeois parliament without leaving precedence to so-called experienced parliamentarians—even in cases where the workers are only newcomers to the parliamentary arena. If need be the members of parliament from the ranks of the working class can read their speeches from notes, so that the speeches can be printed in the press and as leaflets.

11. Communist members of parliament must use the parliamentary rostrum for the unmasking not only of the bourgeoisie and its hacks, but also of the social-patriots, and the reformists, of the vacillations of the politicians of the "center" and of other opponents of communism, and for broad propaganda for the ideas of the Communist International.

12. Even in cases where there are only a few of them in the whole parliament, communist members of parliament have to show a challenging attitude towards capitalism in their whole behavior. They must never forget that only he is worthy of the name of a communist who is an arch enemy of bourgeois society and its social democratic hacks not only in words but also in deeds.

August 2, 1920

A CRITICAL REVIEW OF THE RELEVANT LITERATURE

THIS BOOK, CONSCIOUSLY AND INTENTIONALLY, PRIVILEGES LENIN'S voice, and hopefully the reader who has read it appreciates that decision. For that reason I thought it best not to encumber the text, including the footnotes (for the most part), with other voices. Now is the time to bring the Leninologists into the conversation given how extensive and influential their literature and voice is. But in no way does this interrogation of what they have to say pretend to be exhaustive. The focus here is solely on those who speak to Lenin's electoral and parliamentary strategy and differ in one way or another with what I present. Admittedly, attention is given mainly to those with most visibility, and I recognize that I may have missed voices that didn't get the attention they deserve. What I do here could easily become a stand-alone article or even maybe a book—but not at this time. If it ends up being no more than an outline, sketch, or even an inspiration for either, then it has served its purpose. The organization of this review follows the order of the subject matter of the book and prioritizes the literature alluded to in the footnotes in reference to the text.

One body of literature neglected here, only for lack of language skills—which I readily acknowledge—is the Russian scholarship. What I can say is that I'm aware of its existence because it figures sometimes into the English-language scholarship, which is often about correcting the heavy hand of Stalinist orthodoxy.[1] Thus in responding to the English-language literature, I indirectly address at least some of the Russian-language scholarship.

CHAPTER 1: "LEGAL AND ILLEGAL WORK": THE THIRD DUMA

If the Leninological literature is prone to ignore Lenin's contributions to the Marxist tradition of participating in the electoral process, there is one related issue that has never escaped their otherwise myopic eyes. The departure of Bogdanov has always given Lenin-bashers an opportunity to find what they are always in search of—"Lenin the ogre," by way of innuendo or being tendentious. After a somewhat convoluted description of what the editorial board of *Proletary* decided, Robert Service declares that "Bogdanov was to be driven out of the Bolshevik faction"[2]—in other words, a fait accompli before the actual vote. And if Orlando Figes is to be believed, it was because "Lenin always liked a fight," such as in "the campaign for the boycott of the Duma" (actually, it was against the boycott) and in "the campaign against Bogdanov."[3] The actual record of the meeting, as I've summarized, challenges such distortions. Krupskaya's distillation is enlightening: "[T]he enlarged meeting of the editorial board of *Proletarii* passed a resolution condemning the organization of this new fraction. Bogdanov declared that he would not submit to the decision of the meeting and was expelled from the fraction."[4] Though it's not clear if he included Bogdanov, Lenin later wrote in 1920 that "among" those expelled "were many splendid revolutionaries who subsequently were (and still are) commendable members of the Communist Party."[5]

Lenin's positive assessment of the work of the Russian Social Democratic Labor Party (RSDLP) fraction in the Third Duma at the end of this chapter would appear to be incompatible with Robert McKean's claim that "Lenin's most cherished goal was to break the unity of the Social Democratic parliamentary group, which in the Third State Duma had remained impervious to his efforts at control."[6] Of all Lenin's latter-day academic opponents, McKean is the only one to take seriously his electoral/parliamentary work, though very selectively and tendentiously. His overriding thesis is that none of the exile revolutionary leaders, including Lenin and the Bolsheviks, exercised any real influence on developments inside Russia, specifically St. Petersburg, from the counterrevolution in 1907 to the February Revolution in 1917. The actual target of his very detailed account, upon close reading, is official Soviet scholarship. Lenin, in his own words, never hid the fact, unlike his hagiographers in Moscow, that he was often at loggerheads with the internals—what McKean admits occasionally. The details provided in Chapter 1 confirm that fact as far as the Third Duma fraction is concerned. The main problem with McKean is that despite his rich excavation of the data, on everything else he is prone—as is the case here about Lenin's "most cherished goal"—to simply make such assertions without the supporting evidence. More important is that he either disagrees with Lenin's politics (which is the likely case) or doesn't understand them. That becomes clearer when examining his assertions about Lenin and the RSDLP fraction in the Fourth Duma.

CHAPTER 2: "TO PREPARE FOR A NEW
RUSSIAN REVOLUTION": THE FOURTH DUMA

Except for Lenin's opposition to the boycott of the Duma elections, Robert Service virtually ignores his electoral/parliamentary strategy. That changes with the Fourth Duma elections, the only time Service addresses any of his substantive writings on the topic. In this instance he disputes Lenin's analysis of the outcome that resulted in a significant drop in the number of liberals elected, particularly the Octobrists: "The newly ultra-right political complexion of the parliamentary chamber, according to Lenin, was the product of the calculations and manipulations of the authorities." Service disagrees: "A more cogent explanation is that opinion among most members of the property-owning classes, especially the gentry in the countryside, had spontaneously moved rightward . . . The Russian empire . . . was not a regime of total control."[7] But Lenin wasn't alone in charging "manipulation" of the elections by the regime: "This has been," Lenin wrote, "commented on quite sufficiently by the *entire* liberal and democratic press, and the Cadets' detailed interpellation in the Fourth Duma speaks of the same thing."[8] Subsequent scholarship sustains Lenin's point. About the biggest loser, the Octobrists, Geoffrey Hosking writes, "The indifference and disorganization of their followers combined with active administrative pressure by the government against their well-known left-wingers to ensure this. In some of the provinces, governors and police chiefs closed down Octobrist electoral meetings and disqualified their candidates." And there was another factor that Lenin also called attention to and commented on: "The Holy Synod mobilized the clergy in support of the Rights and Nationalists and warned against voting for the Octobrists."[9]

The real purpose of Service's bogus correction—which requires him to sound like an apologist for the regime—is that it pretends to yield a brilliant insight: "Lenin's conspiracy theory of the Fourth Duma elections divulged much about his own instincts about elections and majorities."[10] Aha, finally, the pre-1917 smoking gun. Lenin, in other words, was projecting his own supposed cynicism about elections onto the regime. This conveniently informs Service's introduction to the Prague Conference, where Lenin, he asserts, resorted to "manipulations [that] were blatantly factional" in order to pull off a "charade. His objective, we're told, was the confection of a 'Party Conference' which would be not merely a predominantly Bolshevik assembly but an assembly consisting mainly of Bolsheviks who supported Lenin's strategy . . . Democratic procedures were disregarded." Yet Service is forced to admit, since the record is all so transparent, that despite these largely unsubstantiated charges "this did not mean that it was a Conference made in Lenin's image."[11] And at the end of the gathering, the "seven elected members of the Central Committee . . . were not as solidly pro-Lenin as is usually thought."[12] This charge about Lenin's "instincts about elections and majorities" and the innuendos implied is probably de rigueur for the Leninological industry and one that requires a revisit.

McKean makes similar charges about the Prague meeting: "The transparency of the Bolshevik leader's motives—his desire to equate the Bolshevik faction with the party—the blatantly manipulative character of the 'election' of the two delegates from the capital, and the dubious legality of the entire proceedings deepened divisions within Social Democracy."[13] And like Service, he asserts more than he proves. In both cases, the security and logistical challenges that Russian revolutionaries faced in trying to hold a delegated meeting in exile—from the organizing of meetings in Russia where delegates could be elected to their travel abroad and back—are short shrifted or ignored.

What Service and McKean are incapable or unwilling to understand is what Trotsky later explained was wrong with trying to reconcile with the Liquidationists and the Conciliationists like himself and why Lenin, as history proved, was right. The Service and McKean crowd never address the political question that was at the heart of the debate, as did Trotsky some decades later:

> Certain critics of Bolshevism to this day regard my old conciliationism as the voice of wisdom. Yet its profound erroneousness had been long ago demonstrated both in theory and practice. A simple conciliation of factions is possible only along some sort of "middle" line. But where is the guaranty that this artificially drawn diagonal line will coincide with the needs of objective development? The task of scientific politics is to deduce a program and a tactic from an analysis of the struggle of classes, not from the [ever-shifting] parallelogram of such secondary and transitory forces as political factions. True, the position of the reaction was such that it cramped the political activity of the entire Party within extremely narrow limits. At the same time, it might have seemed that the differences of opinion were unimportant and artificially inflated by the émigré leaders. Yet it was precisely during the period of reaction that the revolutionary party was unable to train its cadres without a major perspective. The preparation of tomorrow was a most important element in the policy of today. The policy of conciliation thrived on the hope that the course of events itself would prompt the necessary tactic. But that fatalistic optimism meant in practice not only repudiation of factional struggle but the very idea of a party, because, if "the course of events" it capable of directly dictating to the masses the correct policy, what is the use of any special unification of

the proletarian vanguard, the working out of a program, the choice of leaders, the training in a spirit of discipline?[14]

No one has more credibility than Trotsky on this question, who functioned in real time as Lenin's most capable opponent—unlike those carp-
ing from the comfortable side lines of hindsight and what they find so
inconvenient about his verdict.

Because McKean's sympathies are with the seven Menshivik-
liquidators in the RSDLP fraction, he rejects the reasons the Bolsheviks
gave for the split in the fall of 1913: "On the flimsiest of pretexts, formulated by Lenin, which were mostly demonstrably false, the six Bolsheviks
broke away in the last week of October 1913 to form an independent
Russian Social Democratic Workers' Fraction."[15] In the accompanying footnote, he writes, "The pretexts included the unfounded charges
that the Menshevik seven deprived the Bolshevik six of opportunities
to address the House and of their due share of seats on parliamentary
commissions."[16] He cites the Bolshevik press for these charges but, once
again, provides no proof for his claim that they were "unfounded." As
the reader can see in Chapter 2, the charges are quite specific, and if
McKean knows better he is obligated to provide details for his claim that
they were "demonstrably false."

Regarding the "fly in the ointment," Roman Malinovsky, there has
been much speculation about why it took Lenin so long to be convinced
of his duplicity when so many others, including Bolsheviks, had doubts.
Even after Malinovsky mysteriously abandoned the fraction, Lenin
maintained civil and comradely relations with him until unimpeachable
damning evidence surfaced in 1917. R. C. Elwood's *Roman Malinovsky:
A Life without a Cause* (1977) remains the best source in English on the
actual details. Lenin-bashers like Service use such facts to accuse the
"party boss" of "naïveté," of allowing himself to not only be "flattered"
but be "fooled" by the provocateur.[17] Louis Fischer, in a kinder, gentler
form of Lenin-bashing, speculates that Malinovsky was able to convince
Lenin that in spite of how things might look Malinovsky had actually
been won to the cause—"so persuaded" was Lenin "of the all-conquering
force of revolution."[18]

At an inquiry of the Provisional Government in June 1917 about the
Malinovsky affair, Lenin offered in his deposition an explanation for his reluctance to rush to judgment: "After Malinovsky's resignation, we appointed a
commission to investigate the suspicions . . . We interrogated quite a few
witnesses, arranged personal confrontations with Malinovsky, wrote up hundreds of pages of transcripts of these testimonies . . . Definitely, not one
member of the commission was able to find any proof . . . the general

conviction of all three members of the commission was that Malinovsky was not a provocateur, and we stated so in the press."[19] Years later Trotsky came to Lenin's defense despite the harm Malinovsky had done: "[I]n those days suspicions, complicated at times by factional hostility, poisoned the atmosphere of the underground. No one presented any direct evidence against Malinovsky. After all, it was impossible to condemn a member of the Party to political—and perhaps even physical—death on the basis of vague suspicion . . . Lenin deemed it his duty to defend Malinovsky with the energy which always distinguished him."[20]

At the risk of overkill, let me offer an additional explanation that complements, I think, what Lenin and Trotsky said about the affair. Malinovsky, I suspect, was Lenin's "Eccarius problem." By this, I'm referring to the initially comradely, then awkward and eventually severed relationship that Marx had with Johan Georg Eccarius—one that revealed Marx's capacity for patience, for almost three decades. Eccarius was unique in the Marx circle because he was an actual worker, a tailor, and Marx did all he could—at times overlooking and apologizing for his shortcomings—to promote him, specifically, as a "worker-intellectual." Hal Draper, who provides the essential details, explains why: "The importance to Marx of such a proletarian cadre . . . could eliminate or reduce the need for bourgeois intellectuals in the movement. Eccarius, like Wilhelm Wolff [to whom Marx dedicated *Capital*], was prized because his successes showed that proletarian elements could eventually do the jobs that tended to be monopolized by the 'eddicated' bourgeois whose corruptive role Marx and Engels so often denounced."[21]

What Lenin found so attractive about Malinovsky in their initial encounter at the Prague conference was that he was an industrial worker and a leader of the most revolutionary of the unions in St. Petersburg, the metal workers—a most valuable acquisition for the Bolsheviks. In his deposition to the investigating commission, Lenin said Malinovsky was known in RSDLP circles as "the Russian Bebel" (it's no coincidence that Engels spent innumerable hours in forging August Bebel into a "worker-intellectual"). And like Marx and Engels, Lenin had long "denounced" the "corruptive role" of petit-bourgeois intellectuals for the workers' movement. In his first letter to Malinovsky after the resignation, who was then in a German prison of war camp, Lenin was solicitous about his intellectual needs: "Can anything be sent to you, and what do you need? Do you read Russian newspapers and books?" A couple of months later, Lenin wrote, "We [Krupskaya and I] were very glad to hear that you have a library there and the opportunity to study and give lectures."[22] Like Marx, Lenin, I suspect, bent over backward to give Malinovsky the benefit of the doubt in the absence of concrete evidence exactly because he was a worker who had the potential for being a "worker-intellectual." That combination of facts, I think, explains what has been a conundrum only for Lenin's enemies.

CHAPTER 3: THE "GREAT WAR," 1917, AND BEYOND

The issue about whether the five Duma fraction members agreed with Lenin's theses on the war, particularly the one that called for "revolution-ary defeatism," has been the subject of much discussion. Though Badayev admitted that "certain formal amendments were suggested" to them at the meeting—brought prematurely to an end by the police invasion—he wrote that "no objections were raised to the principles outlined." McKean disagrees on the basis of credible evidence that many Bolsheviks, lead-ers and rank and file inside Russia, opposed Lenin's stance. He may be right, but he provides—as he is wont to do—no concrete evidence about the fraction members to support his claim. The best that he can mount is the fact that in his trial statement Petrovsky didn't explicitly embrace Lenin's theses. But that raises the question of why Lenin praised what he said while denouncing Kamenev, who explicitly did distance himself from the theses.[23] And then there is Figes, who also has an aversion for evidence when it's inconvenient for his agenda: "The Bolsheviks were the only socialist party to remain broadly united in their opposition to the war, although they too had their own defensists during the early days before Lenin had imposed his views."[24] He doesn't explain to the reader how Lenin could manage such a feat, since he didn't attend the meeting where the fraction adopted his stance. He clearly could not have relied on Kamenev doing it for him.

McKean's real aim, in keeping with the thesis of his book about the disconnect between the émigrés and the internal movements, is to go after Lenin for his "extremist stance," which put him, "once again," at "loggerheads" with the Bolsheviks inside Russia. His reformist-minded brain, however, is incapable of understanding that a communist like Lenin was obligated to begin not with "the dangers and difficulties of propagating the concept of their country's defeat at a time of heightened patriotic feelings" but rather with the objective needs of the proletariat internationally.[25] When the Guns of August exploded, the most impor-tant task was to prevent the working class from becoming cannon fod-der for their bourgeois governments. An extreme situation required an extreme policy. Nothing was more convincing to other working classes in the other belligerent countries of the sincere commitment of one's own working class to an antiwar policy and proletarian internationalism than the hope for the defeat of the government of one's own bourgeoisie. Lenin argued that to carry out such a line within Russia, "though undoubtedly difficult, is the only task worthy of a proletarian, the only socialist task." And the Russian proletariat had a special obligation to take the lead: "It is the proletariat in the most backward of the belligerent Great Powers which, through the medium of their party, have had to adopt—especially in view of the shameful treachery of the German and French Social-Democrats—revolutionary tactics that are quite unfeasible unless they 'contribute to the defeat' of their own government, but which alone lead to a European revolution, to the permanent peace of socialism, to the liberation of humanity from the horrors, misery, savagery and brutality now prevailing."[26] Because of his animus toward Lenin, little in McKean's otherwise very rich account helps the reader to understand why the Bolsheviks successfully led the proletariat to power in 1917 and were able to defend that power.

Probably no moment in the Russian Revolution has attracted as much attention from its foes as the dissolution of the Constituent Assembly in January 1918. In the tradition of Kautsky, Service attempts to skew Lenin as the chief culprit. About Lenin's election to it in November, he fumes,

> Seldom has a parliament acquired a member so disdainful of his achievement in being elected. Only in the pre-October months of 1917 had he ever spoken warmly about the Constituent Assembly; and even then it was mainly with the purpose of undermining public confidence in the Provisional Government's will to convoke the Assembly. He had no abiding fondness for institutions elected by universal suffrage. His manipulativeness and lack of public candor was so extreme that, while the Second Congress of Soviets of Workers' and Soldiers' Deputies was in session, he implored his Bolshevik Central Committee colleagues to announce a postponement of the Constituent Assembly elections . . . [H]is central colleagues overruled his proposed tergiversation on 26 October, arguing that it would damage the party politically.[27]

The key charge is that Lenin never really wanted a Constituent Assembly, owing to his long-in-place lack of "fondness for institutions elected by universal suffrage." Careful readers of this book will now understand why there's a deafening silence in Service's narrative about Lenin's electoral/parliamentary strategy prior to the October Revolution. His claim, in fact, sounds other-worldly. In many ways this book is a detailed refutation of Service's fantasies.

Beginning with Chapter 2 of *LES1905*, the reader can verify that Lenin by at least 1899 advocated that social democrats should call for a "Zemsky Sobor of representatives of the people for the elaboration of a constitution"—what had been a demand of Russian social democrats since 1885. In his Draft Program of 1902, he added what had not been in Plekhanov's document: "For its part, the Russian Social-Democratic Labor Party is firmly convinced that the complete, consistent, and lasting implementation of the indicated political and social changes can be achieved only by overthrowing the autocracy and convoking a Constituent Assembly, freely elected by the whole people."[28] Once the revolutionary movement began in 1905, Lenin made clear that the soviets were a superior form of representative democracy and should be prioritized. But he never abandoned the possibility of a Constituent Assembly, as was clear in his April Theses of 1917, which Service gives only superficial attention to and understandably. The last thesis stated, "I argued that *without* the Soviets of Workers' and Soldiers' Deputies the convocation of the Constituent Assembly is not guaranteed and its success is impossible." Drawing on, as always, the lessons of the Paris Commune, Lenin prioritized, which he never hid from the public, soviet governance as preferable to parliamentary governance. If it was one or the other, the soviets were preferable, because they were much more democratic. And it is exactly that argument about which Service et al. never engage Lenin. It's easier to resort to slander and innuendo. No one who knew Lenin's politics since at least 1899 should have been surprised that he called for pulling the plug on the Constituent Assembly in January 1918. Figes, in his slanderous spin on the Constituent Assembly event, at least acknowledges Lenin's argument: "Lenin had always been contemptuous of the ballot box and had made it clear as early as the April Theses that he viewed Soviet power as a higher form of democracy than the Constituent Assembly."[29] What critics like Figes and Service have always had trouble in explaining is why wasn't there a real constituency in the new Soviet Russia ready to defend with its feet parliamentary democracy via the Constituent Assembly as there was for soviet democracy. The proletarian and peasant masses by then, I argue, saw the latter as their organ of representative democracy and not the former. Lenin knew this to be true exactly because, contra Service and Figes, he took universal suffrage so seriously—the elections to the municipal dumas and the soviets in the months preceding the October Revolution.

CONCLUSION

As I was concluding the manuscript for this book, I wrote to Alexander Rabinowitch to get his opinion of my claim to have connected the dots between the strategy of Marx and Engels and the Bolshevik triumph in

1917 via the electoral/parliamentary arenas. He responded immediately on December 20, 2012, as follows: "I appreciated your writing to me with regard to your work on Lenin's electoral strategy in 1917. However, based on my lifetime of painstaking research on the Petrograd Bolsheviks between 1917 and 1919 I regret to say that your hypotheses regarding the importance of elections to Lenin seems completely implausible to me. A rereading of my *The Bolsheviks Come to Power* and *The Bolsheviks in Power* should certainly clarify my reasoning in this regard, as will the book I am now writing on *The Petrograd Bolsheviks in 1919–1920*." For the record, here is the part of my letter to which Rabinowitch responded and another opportunity for readers to reacquaint themselves with the key evidence I mount:

> Lenin's electoral/parliamentary strategy is the project's focus and as far as I can tell it's never been given serious attention, at least in book form. One of my four claims is that it was squarely rooted in the politics of Marx and Engels and another is that his strategy goes a long way in explaining Bolshevik success in October. Only now, after a year of writing, do I feel confident in connecting the dots between both claims and a key piece of evidence was signaled in your *Bolsheviks Come to Power* book. I think— and this is where your opinion would be valuable—this is the first book, certainly, to make the links.
>
> First, a brief overview of the Marx-Engels evidence. In their *Address of March, 1850*—which Lenin, according to Riazanov, committed to memory—Marx and Engels argued that the working class party had to run its own candidates in elections, not with the expectation they would win but an opportunity to "count their forces." The document also raised the possibility of armed struggle. Fast forward to 1884 Engels's *Origins of the Family, Private Property, and State* where he states: "On the day the thermometer of universal suffrage registers boiling point among workers, both they and the capitalists will know where they stand." And then later in 1892 his letter—without the fear of Bismarck's censors—to Paul Lafargue about the value of universal suffrage: "it indicates with the most perfect accuracy the day when a call to armed revolution has to be made." The evidence is quite clear that Lenin knew well the first two texts, if not the third; but his reading of the sub-text in *Origins* is exactly, I argue, what Engels told Lafargue. The bulk of my text is about how Lenin was guided by Marx and Engels's perspective in the work he did around the four state dumas.
>
> In 1917 Lenin gave detailed attention to elections to not only the soviets but the local dumas. My reading of the details you provide on pp. 91–93 is that they bear Lenin's finger prints. The fours state duma experiences, I claim, served him well; he said, as you know, the same in *Left-Wing Communism*—"indispensable," according to him, in the triumph in October. From the July Days onward the "thermometer" metaphor came

increasingly into play. William Rosenberg's article on the municipal duma
elections, which your book pointed me to, is especially valuable. Post-
October Bolshevik memoirs, he notes, said the elections were a "means of
'taking the revolutionary temperature of the masses'"—the "thermometer
metaphor," I argue, in Engels's *Origins*. Furthermore, there's Lenin's constant usage of the election returns to the soviets and municipal dumas as
"objective facts," as he called it, in his efforts to win the rest of the Central Committee to his position about the need to strike in October. And
then later, his 1919 article on the Constituent Assembly elections—which
seems to be ignored in the standard accounts—offers, I think, convincing
evidence that he was right to employ election returns to calculate when to
stage the insurrection. He argued that the data would predict the outcome
of the civil war and it seems—your opinion would also be useful here—
that he was correct.

Is it accurate to say that this is the first study to make at least a credible case, if not a conclusive one, that Marx and Engels's electoral strategy
informed Lenin's? And second, if true, was that advice consequential for
Bolshevik success in not only taking power but keeping it?

I'm told on good authority that Rabinowitch believes that my claim
is "completely implausible" because Lenin "simply didn't trust elections."
This suggests that he subscribes to the standard Leninological fare a la
Service and Figes: respectively, "He had no abiding fondness for institutions elected by universal suffrage" and "Lenin had always been contemptuous of the ballot box" (since the latter's account is synthetic, I
suspect Service is the real author of the calumny). The reader of this book
knows by now how utterly false this claim is and why, therefore, there is a
deafening silence in both accounts about Lenin's electoral/parliamentary
strategy. If Service and Figes's charges are true, why would Lenin—to
begin with the earliest evidence—have devoted so much space in his *One
Step Forward, Two Steps Back* book to a roll-call analysis of voting blocs
at the Second Congress of the RSDLP of 1903, the first instance of his
penchant for crunching election results? And then afterward, why would
he spend innumerable hours poring over, analyzing, and writing about
election returns—and recommend that his comrades do the same—for
all four State Duma elections, for the municipal dumas of 1917, and then
later the Constituent Assembly elections? Why did he take Bolshevik participation in the latter elections so seriously? What about all the election
campaign literature he wrote, the resolutions he composed on how the
Bolsheviks should conduct themselves in the election arena, his incessant
urging of his comrades to take part in elections? Why did he constantly
harp on the educational value of elections for the working class? Maybe
he was obsessive—as some of his opponents charge—and had nothing

better to do with his time. More likely, he was dead serious about elections, of every kind.

If the real charge is that Lenin didn't see elections in the bourgeois electoral arena as an end in themselves, then the accusers are correct. As a Marxist, Lenin was thoroughly convinced (correctly, in my view) that fundamental social change has never been achieved through elections. What takes place outside the parliamentary arena, especially in the streets and on the barricades, is decisive in politics—as history has repeatedly shown. To believe otherwise is to be afflicted with "parliamentary cretinism" and what I call "voting fetishism." These were the premises with which he, like his mentors Marx and Engels, addressed the electoral process. Even in the best settings that bourgeois democracy had to offer, elections—owing to their rules, structures, and socioeconomic context—register at best an approximation of working-class opinion; his Swiss exile, again, was most informative. What he said about elections in the United States regarding the role of money in them is as current as ever if not more so. And yet he defended them against apologists for Czarist rule. That was because elections under bourgeois conditions could for the working class be an important means toward an end—a way to "count their forces," as Marx and Engels put it in 1850—and thus they should be taken seriously. The most democratic elections in the public arena that bourgeois society could offer are what the Paris Commune and the revolutions of 1905 and February 1917 ushered in—elections to the Commune and to the soviets. Yes, it's true that Lenin in July–August 1917 began to have doubts about the soviets. But that in no way suggested he gave up on elections as a means; he was prepared to prioritize the local duma elections. What was decisive for Lenin is when the masses went into the streets to defend the soviets—the best of all kinds of elections, voting with one's feet. Certainly, after October 1917 there can be no doubt about his commitment to elections to the soviets. And can there be any question about his commitment to elections for the revolutionary party? Even the most animated Lenin-bashers have never claimed otherwise. Last, there is that most inconvenient document for Lenin skeptics: *Left-Wing Communism*, written in 1920, whose central message was that aspiring Bolsheviks elsewhere needed to emulate what Lenin and his comrades did—that is, take bourgeois elections seriously.

I reread, as Rabinowitch suggested, the relevant sections of his two books. Basically, there is nothing in either that is inconsistent with my argument. In fact, he provides in *The Bolsheviks Come to Power*, as I pointed out to him, useful material to help me make my case, such as the details around the local duma elections at the end of August 1917. But I realize (admittedly in hindsight) that there is a glaring omission in his otherwise persuasive explanation for why the Bolsheviks succeeded in 1917. He correctly recognizes Lenin's crucial role in what unfolded. Referring to Lenin's success in winning over—registered by a vote!—the overwhelming number of members of the Bolshevik Central Committee to his view for the need for an armed uprising, Rabinowitch concludes, "Few modern historical episodes better illustrate the sometimes decisive role of an individual in historical events."[30] But is it exactly for that reason it is all so important to know what informed Lenin's steely confidence to be able to win others to his point of view, specifically his calculus for success—what other members of the Central Committee would have been familiar with. Unfortunately, that's missing in Rabinowitch's account. He reproduces, for example, key passages from Lenin's letters to the Central Committee about the urgent need to carry out an armed uprising, which make repeated claims that "the majority is with us now" or some variant, and points to "Bolshevik victories in local elections in Moscow and increases in Bolshevik support among soldiers" or "that the Bolsheviks had majorities in many soviets."[31] But this was precisely Lenin's electoral strategy in action, what more than a decade of training since 1905 had made possible—"to count their forces."

Another example of why it's so important to know Lenin's electoral strategy has to do with his call for a boycott of the Democratic State Conference and Preparliament in the weeks leading up to the armed uprising. Rabinowitch gives due attention to both calls but hardly offers an explanation. Lenin's position was informed by years of debate beginning in 1905 that he was at the center of—knowing when and how to use the tactic of the boycott as part of a revolutionary electoral strategy. That's just what Lenin is referring to in one of the letters Rabinowitch quotes where he denounced Bolsheviks who didn't boycott the Conference: "an erroneous attitude toward parliamentarism in moments of revolutionary (and not constitutional) crisis"—here I suspect most readers of *The Bolsheviks Come to Power* have no idea what he's talking about; I certainly didn't in my initial read many years ago. The logic of Lenin's strategy also explains his stance toward the Constituent Assembly leading up to and after October. I argue that coupled with what this book has unearthed, Rabinowitch's most informative narrative about 1917 would be even more persuasive were he to take into account Lenin's electoral/parliamentary strategy.

Rabinowitch admits in his response to my inquiry that his "lifetime of painstaking research" focuses on "the Petrograd Bolsheviks between 1917 and 1919," for which we're all truly indebted. But to fully understand Lenin's actions in 1917—since the paper trail for much of the year, as Rabinowitch points out, is thin owing to his being on the run or in hiding—requires knowing his politics long before then, at least back to 1905. Lenin repeatedly stated that the Revolution of 1905–7 was "the dress rehearsal for 1917," and to not take that seriously requires an explanation. For the last three decades, my research, which this book is the major product of, has been about understanding and detailing Lenin's continuity with Marx and Engels. Rabinowitch, of course, can't necessarily be faulted for not knowing about Lenin's electoral/parliamentary strategy and its roots in Marx and Engels, since until now neither friend nor foe has ever unearthed that rich history (I leave aside the problem of temporal balkanization in much of mainstream historical scholarship).

It's important to recognize that I'm not proposing an original explanation of Lenin's calculus, nor do I claim that it was always accurate. I rely mainly on what he reports he did leading up to and after the October Revolution and show that he had long experience in making such calculations that trace their origin to the historic program of Marx and Engels— what gave him the political authority to win skeptical Central Committee members to his position. My work is mainly an excavation, and all I pretend to do is to make the connections. Again, the burden of proof is on skeptics like Rabinowitch to show why Lenin was wrong to think that his electoral strategy was "indispensable" in the Bolshevik triumph. Scholars like him have never been reluctant to point out when they disagree with Lenin. And Rabinowitch, who has played a most valuable role in challenging orthodoxy, has the credentials to make a credible case.

Last, there is my claim about the "indispensability" of Lenin and the "subjective factor"—leadership and program. Theda Skocpol's *States and Social Revolutions* (1979) continues to influence how political scientists and sociologists understand the Russian Revolution. For Skocpol, social revolutions are the product solely of social structures, economic crises, and geopolitical realities. Any contention, she argues, that a "purposive revolutionary movement" is also necessary is bogus. The "fact is that historically no successful social revolution has ever been 'made' by a mass-mobilizing, avowedly revolutionary movement."[32] While admitting that the Bolsheviks had out-organized their rivals to take power—without even once mentioning Lenin—she insists on her nonpurposive thesis for the Russian case. The reader of this book knows how utterly unsustainable is that claim. Skocpol correctly recognizes that "no modern social revolution has been as thorough-going as the Russian."[33] What she fails to grasp is how central to those transformations was the worker-peasant alliance that no one did more to forge than Lenin. And his electoral strategy, this book demonstrates, figured significantly in that success.

NOTES

CHAPTER 5

1. Geoffrey A. Hosking, *The Russian Constitutional Experiment: Government and Duma, 1907–1914* (Cambridge, UK: Cambridge University Press, 1973), p. 44.
2. V. I. Lenin, *Collected Works*, vol. 15 (Moscow: Progress Publishers, 1978), pp. 457–58. Hereafter, citations from his *Collected Works* will be designated as in this case: *15*, pp. 457–58.
3. *13*, p. 21.
4. Ibid., pp. 25–26.
5. Ibid., p. 35.
6. Ibid., pp. 42–43.
7. Ibid., pp. 44–48. Victoria E. Bonnell, *Roots of Rebellion: Workers' Politics and Organizations in St. Petersburg and Moscow, 1900–1914* (Berkeley: University of California Press, 1983), pp. 338–44, provides evidence that Lenin was essentially right about the "upswing" in Moscow—that it was indeed "partial" and that the Bolsheviks who thought it signaled a new upsurge were wrong.
8. *13*, p. 59.
9. For a few details, see Alfred Levin, *The Third Duma, Election and Profile* (Hamden, CT: Archon Books, 1973), pp. 46–47.
10. Richard Pipes, ed., *The Unknown Lenin: From the Secret Archive* (New Haven, CT: Yale University Press, 1996), p. 36.
11. Karl Marx and Frederick Engels, *Collected Works*, vol. 46 (New York: International Publishers, 1975–2004), pp. 197–98.
12. *13*, p. 81.
13. Ibid., pp. 85–86.
14. See August H. Nimtz, *Lenin's Electoral Strategy from Marx and Engels through the Revolution of 1905: The Ballot, the Streets—or Both* (New York: Palgrave Macmillan, 2014), pp. 30–31. Hereafter, the first volume is referred to as *LES1905*.
15. *13*, pp. 90–91.
16. See *LES1905*, p. 11.

17. Though critical of Bebel's actions, these were "the mistakes of a person with whom we are going the same way" (*34*, p. 371; see also *13*, pp. 164–65). Regarding "agitation among the youth," see Lenin's article on the experience of Social Democratic parties in doing such work: *41*, pp. 204–7.

18. *13*, pp. 91–93.

19. Nadezhda Krupskaya, *Memories of Lenin* (London: Panther Books, 1970), p. 145.

20. Hosking, p. 42.

21. Alfred Levin, *The Second Duma: A Study of the Social-Democratic Party and the Russian Constitutional Experiment* (New Haven, CT: Yale University Press, 1940), p. 341.

22. *15*, p. 502n119.

23. Hosking, p. 43.

24. *13*, p. 518.

25. This, and the following, draws on Levin's account in *The Third Duma*, which provides some details on the RSDLP campaign, the difficulties they faced, and the election itself (pp. 85–111)—despite his tendentious spin on Lenin. It reveals that the Russian-language edition of the *Lenin Collected Works* is more informative than the English edition.

26. Levin, *The Third Duma*, p. 71.

27. Ibid., p. 98.

28. Ibid., pp. 100 and 104.

29. Ibid., p. 107. This is a telling admission from someone who didn't agree with Lenin's revolutionary working-class approach to the electoral process.

30. *13*, pp. 123–33.

31. Ibid., p. 518n75.

32. Ibid., pp. 146 and 519n77.

33. Ibid., p. 140. For background, see pp. 133–34.

34. Ibid., pp. 153–60.

35. For the larger context and useful details, see Hosking, ch. 8, "Towards the First World War."

36. *13*, pp. 479–84.

37. *15*, pp. 220–29.

38. Ibid., pp. 22–27.

39. Ibid., pp. 17–21.

40. Ibid., pp. 155–57.

41. *13*, pp. 52–53.

42. *15*, pp. 291–300.

43. Ibid., pp. 36–37.

44. Ibid., p. 353.

45. Ibid., pp. 325 and 328.

46. Ibid., pp. 352–53.

47. Krupskaya, p. 161.

48. *15*, pp. 422–23.

NOTES 469

49. Ibid., p. 413. There is a not-too-subtle difference in the tone of the two articles. While praising the fraction, the one in *Proletary* points to a few weaknesses, though constructively so. I suspect Lenin wrote it with an eye toward those Bolsheviks who were skeptical about Duma work.

50. Ibid., pp. 431–32 and 451. Regarding Leninological spin on what happened, see "A Critical Review of the Relevant Literature: Chapter 1."

51. *41*, p. 228.

52. Ibid., p. 227. In a letter at the end of August, Lenin mentions his indispensable "work on the Promotion Commission for the Duma Social-Democratic group, which has its headquarters in Paris" (*15*, p. 476).

53. *16*, pp. 24–28.

54. Ibid., p. 64.

55. Ibid., p. 69.

56. Ibid., p. 151.

57. Was this "subcommittee" the "Promotion Commission" that Lenin earlier referred to (*15*, pp. 352–53)?

58. *16*, pp. 110–16.

59. See, for example, Lenin's 1917 "Postscript" to his *The Agrarian Program of Social-Democracy in the First Russian Revolution, 1905–1907* (*13*, pp. 430–31).

60. See Hosking, ch. 4, for details.

61. *16*, pp. 176–78.

62. For details, see Hosking, pp. 106–16.

63. *16*, p. 81.

64. Ibid., pp. 173–75. In addition to his article, Lenin evidently gave a lecture, probably in Paris to the large exile Russian community, in which he included "*Support of the revolutionary* movement in *Persia*—protest against the *Finnish* campaign" (*41*, p. 231).

65. *16*, pp. 198–205.

66. Ibid., p. 33.

67. Ibid., p. 390. Kautsky, *Neue Zeit*'s editor, refused to print Lenin's response—not for the first time.

68. In a letter to Maxim Gorky about six months later, Lenin confirmed that the "Mensheviks predominate in the Duma group" (*34*, p. 446). He also revealed that working with the Menshevik deputies was one thing; working with the Menshevik leaders like Plekhanov was another. The only distinction Lenin thought worth making about the fraction concerned the attitude toward the liquidationists: "The liquidationist *Zhivoye Dyelo* counts among its permanent contributors *two* members of the group in the Duma—Astrakhantsev and Kuznetsov.* In the anti-liquidationist *Zvezda* there are eight members of the group—Voronin, Voiloshnikov, Yegorov, Zakharov, Pokrovsky, Predkaln, Pole-tayev, and Surkov. Two members of the Duma, Chkheidze and Gegechkori, contribute to neither of these organs. One (Shurkanov) contributes to both (*Until recently there was also Belousov. Now this extreme liquidator . . . has resigned from the group in the Duma. The latter has publicly warned all the voters of this; and has demanded his resignation from the Duma. A minor

example showing to what lengths consistent liquidationism goes at times!)" (*17*, p. 545).

69. *16*, pp. 34–35.
70. Ibid., pp. 305–12.
71. Ibid., pp. 347–51.
72. *17*, pp. 173–78.
73. Ibid., pp. 253–56.
74. Ibid., p. 172.
75. Ibid., p. 256.
76. Ibid., pp. 338–41.
77. Ibid., p. 524.
78. Ibid., pp. 471–72. The only Leninologist who at least pays attention to Lenin's State Duma work has a different opinion. See "A Critical Review of the Relevant Literature: Chapter 1."

CHAPTER 6

1. V. I. Lenin, *Collected Works*, vol. 17 (Moscow: Progress Publishers, 1978), p. 278. Hereafter, citations from his *Collected Works* will be designated as in this case: *17*, p. 278.
2. Ibid., p. 397.
3. Ibid., pp. 278–83.
4. Karl Marx and Frederick Engels, *Collected Works*, vol. 27 (New York: International Publishers, 1975–2004), pp. 226–27. Hereafter, citations from the *MECW* are designated as follows: *MECW* 27, pp. 226–27. See *LES1905*, p. 28.
5. Ibid., p. 219.
6. *17*, pp. 421–23.
7. Ibid., p. 436.
8. Ibid., p. 569.
9. Ibid., pp. 378–84.
10. Nadezhda Krupskaya, *Memories of Lenin* (London: Panther Books, 1970), p. 199.
11. On the inevitable debate about who was or was not invited, see Lenin's informative letter in *35*, pp. 25–26.
12. *17*, pp. 468–71.
13. Ibid., p. 473.
14. There was a two-line resolution about *Pravda* but not the later and more well-known one. It referred to the newspaper Trotsky published in Vienna; the Conference annulled an agreement the Central Committee had concluded with him in January 1910. Trotsky, it should be noted, called a "unity" meeting in Vienna in August for those grouped around *Pravda* as an alternative to the Prague Conference. The so-called August Bloc, as it became known, proved, however, to be a feckless challenge to what Lenin had organized. As Lenin accurately predicted, "Let someone try to set up a different R.S.D.L.P. *with* the liquidators! It would be laughable" (*35*, p. 26). On Trotsky's later admission

that Lenin was right and his conciliationist position was wrong—"its profound erroneousness had been long ago demonstrated in both theory and practice"—see his *Stalin: An Appraisal of the Man and His Influence* (New York: Universal Library, 1941), p. 112.

15. *17*, p. 481. For the Leninological view of the conference on this and other points, see "A Critical Review of the Relevant Literature: Chapter 2."

16. *35*, pp. 34–35.

17. *17*, p. 616.

18. *18*, pp. 17 and 102.

19. For useful details about the origins and course of *Pravda*, despite neither understanding nor agreeing with Lenin's politics, see Ralph Carter Elwood, "Lenin and *Pravda*, 1912–1914," *Slavic Review* 31, no. 2 (June 1972): 355–80.

20. *35*, p. 23.

21. Ibid., p. 26. See also Lenin's letter to Gorky, May 27, 1911 (*34*, p. 446), regarding the reality of *Zvezda*.

22. *18*, p. 207.

23. *43*, p. 769; Elwood, "Lenin and *Pravda*, 1912–1914," p. 358n11.

24. *18*, pp. 111–14.

25. Ibid., p. 120.

26. *35*, p. 40.

27. Ibid., p. 20.

28. In addition to *Pravda*, a new version of *Zvezda* appeared with a new name, *Nevskaya Zvezda* [*The Neva Star*], a weekly that lasted until October 1912.

29. *35*, pp. 40–41.

30. Ibid., p. 48.

31. Ibid., pp. 42–43.

32. Elwood, "Lenin and *Pravda*, 1912–1914," p. 364. For more details, see Trotsky, *Stalin*, pp. 138–42, who contends Stalin did so for opportunistic reasons.

33. *18*, pp. 136–42.

34. Ibid., p. 239.

35. Ibid., p. 199.

36. Ibid., pp. 196–97.

37. Ibid., pp. 237–38.

38. *17*, p. 482.

39. *18*, p. 310.

40. Ibid. p. 335.

41. Ibid., pp. 339–40.

42. Ibid., p. 352.

43. Ibid., p. 353.

44. Krupskaya, p. 208.

45. "For at least a couple of days on end Ilyich pumped us full of instructions"—cited in Trotsky, *Stalin*, p. 142.

46. For some useful details, see R. C. Elwood, *Inessa Armand: Revolutionary and Feminist* (New York: Cambridge University Press, 1992), pp. 92–95. September 14 is inconsistent with other details Elwood supplies; see below, fn. 49. See also

Robert B. McKean, *St. Petersburg between the Revolutions: Workers and Revolutionaries, June 1907–February 1917* (New Haven, CT: Yale University Press, 1990), p. 92, who claims that Armand and Safarov were not successful in one of their tasks: reviving the St. Petersburg branch.

47. *35*, p. 58.

48. *18*, p. 348.

49. McKean, p. 138. For very useful data on the election of the factory delegates, see pp. 134–38. His interpretation of the entire process, less a victory for the Bolsheviks (pp. 131–40), differs from that of Badayev's account.

50. Lenin labeled one of the three Mensheviks, P. Sudakov, a "turncoat," charging that he had been duplicitous in the lead-up to the elections. He initially "'sided with *Pravda*,' [but on] the next day," after the elections, he flirted with the liquidationists; *41*, pp. 266–67.

51. Elwood, *Inessa Armand*, pp. 94–95, says that she was involved in these negotiations when arrested. While the details he supplies makes that a credible claim—making her role even more significant—it is inconsistent with the dates that Badayev gives, even taking into account the Old and New Calendar differences.

52. A. Badayev, *The Bolsheviks in the Tsarist Duma* (New York: International Publishers, 1932), pp. 3–24. Trotsky suggests that the second edition of Badayev's recollections bear the hand of Stalin, who wanted the book to put him in the best possible light given his conciliationist stances while working with the editorial board of *Pravda* (*Stalin*, pp. 143, 149)—thus the reason I say the "instructions to the delegates" were "apparently" drafted by Stalin. The original Russian edition was published about 1929; therefore the 1932 International Publishers edition is probably a translation of the second edition.

53. Although Badayev didn't elaborate on the campaign, Lenin provides some details and suggestions on how the Bolsheviks should respond to defend his election; see *18*, pp. 428–29.

54. *18*, p. 505.

55. *35*, pp. 61–62.

56. *41*, p. 269.

57. *18*, p. 460.

58. Ibid., pp. 493–518.

59. Ibid., p. 438.

60. *35*, p. 103.

61. Ibid., pp. 424–26. Lenin suggested that the Bolshevik deputies along with the St. Petersburg branch of the party issue a statement, which he drafted, to correct the "mistake" (ibid., p. 428).

62. Ibid., pp. 413–23.

63. Badayev, pp. 43–44.

64. Ibid., p. 52.

65. *18*, pp. 460–61. Another legal venue that Lenin insisted that the Bolsheviks participate in—that can only be noted here—were the elections for the boards of the "workers' sick benefit funds," a palliative the regime threw at the workers in a futile attempt to quell disquiet; see the resolution, "The Insurance

Campaign" (pp. 461–62). According to Krupskaya, Lenin "attached great importance to the election and believed that the election campaign would strengthen our contacts with the masses" (p. 226).

66. The three provisions were later lost. Related here is what the editors of the *Lenin Collected Works* provide—*18*, p. 636n178, which is consistent with other documentation. Badayev remembers, "after a lapse of fifteen years" (p. 63), somewhat differently. But the two accounts are not, as I suggest next, necessarily incompatible.

67. Badayev, pp. 58–64.

68. *35*, p. 70.

69. Ibid., p. 84.

70. On Badayev's activities, much of which consisted of defending workers in St. Petersburg from the assaults of both bosses and the state, see Badayev, pp. 71–99. For instructive details on how the two deputies from the Ukraine carried out this work in their constituencies, see R. C. Elwood, *Russian Social Democracy in the Underground: A Study of the RSDLP in the Ukraine, 1907–1914* (Assen: Van Gorcum, 1974), pp. 188–89.

71. *35*, p. 65. This challenges Badayev's claim, "From the moment that the fraction was formed it made newspaper work one of its chief tasks" (pp. 179–80).

72. It's interesting to note that the resolution was first published in 1956, three years after Stalin's death.

73. *41*, pp. 272–73.

74. Badayev, p. 64.

75. *35*, pp. 78–79.

76. Ibid., pp. 82 and 86.

77. Ibid., p. 93.

78. *19*, p. 64.

79. *35*, pp. 93–96.

80. Ibid., pp. 88–89, 99–100.

81. Krupskaya, pp. 200 and 225; Lenin's later article about Chernomazov, *23*, pp. 362–64; Elwood, "Lenin and *Pravda*," p. 374, and *Russian Social Democracy in the Underground*, pp. 182–83.

82. *35*, p. 111.

83. Elwood, "Lenin and *Pravda*," p. 376.

84. For details, see the resolution that Lenin and the Bolshevik deputies composed: *19*, p. 425. Regarding McKean's claim that Lenin's charges were "mostly demonstrably false" (p. 141), see "A Critical Review of the Relevant Literature: Chapter 2."

85. *18*, pp. 530–31.

86. *35*, p. 95.

87. *19*, pp. 44–46.

88. *41*, p. 275.

89. *19*, p. 492.

90. Ibid., p. 424.

91. Ibid., pp. 425–26.

92. Ibid., pp. 458–74.
93. Ibid., p. 472. As for McKean's claim that these facts were "the flimsiest of pretexts [for the split] . . . which were mostly demonstrably false" (p. 141), see "A Critical Review of the Relevant Literature: Chapter 2."
94. _20_, pp. 538–39.
95. For informative details on how the fraction and *Pravda* assisted the Baku oil workers' strike in 1914, for example, see Badayev, pp. 168–69.
96. Badayev, p. 126.
97. Ibid., p. 132.
98. _18_, p. 365.
99. _19_, p. 56.
100. Ibid., p. 274.
101. _41_, p. 276.
102. _19_, p. 547; _20_, p. 64.
103. _20_, pp. 254–58.
104. Lenin's opinion was warranted. It was later learned that Bernstein—and evidently with some complicity by Bebel—carried out the "greatest bowdlerization" in the history of the Marxist movement; Roger Morgan, *The German Social Democrats and the First International, 1864–1872* (London: Cambridge University Press, 1965), p. 248.
105. _19_, pp. 553–54.
106. Ibid., pp. 298–99. See Chapter 1.
107. _36_, p. 243.
108. Ibid., p. 235.
109. _43_, pp. 406–7.
110. Badayev, p. 174.
111. Ibid., p. 135.
112. Ibid., pp. 149–50.
113. _31_, p. 45.
114. Badayev, p. 163. Much has been made of Lenin having been duped by Malinovsky. See "A Critical Review of the Relevant Literature: Chapter 2," for a discussion.
115. Richard Pipes, ed., *The Unknown Lenin: From the Secret Archive* (New Haven, CT: Yale University Press, 1996), p. 39.
116. Badayev, p. 177.

CHAPTER 7

1. New scholarship reveals that Nicholas was the real instigator and that the "Guns of August" actually began in July. See Sean McMeekin, *The Russian Origins of the First World War* (Cambridge, MA: Harvard University Press, 2011). McMeekin's research sustains Lenin's long-held charge about the Czar's imperial ambitions.
2. Orlando Figes, *A People's Tragedy: A History of the Russian Revolution* (New York: Viking, 1996), p. 293.

3. V. I. Lenin, *Collected Works*, vol. 21 (Moscow: Progress Publishers, 1978), p. 29. Hereafter, citations from his *Collected Works* will be designated as in this case: *21*, p. 29.

4. *35*, pp. 177–78.

5. A. Badayev, *The Bolsheviks in the Tsarist Duma* (New York: International Publishers, 1932), p. 198.

6. For an informative historiography of the declaration, see D. A. Longley, "The Russian Social Democratic Statement to the Duma on 26 July (8 August) 1914: A New Look at the Evidence," *English Historical Review* 102, no. 187 (July 1987): 599–621. Longley (pp. 607–8) questions Badayev's claim about the censorship of the declaration.

7. The St. Petersburg branch of the party did issue a statement that made no concessions to the patriotic fervor. See "Petersburg Bolshevik Appeal against the War," in *Lenin's Struggle for a Revolutionary International: Documents: 1907–1916, The Preparatory Years*, ed. John Riddell (New York: Pathfinder, 1986), pp. 131–32.

8. Badayev, pp. 200–202 (including note).

9. Ibid., pp. 206–7. See Robert B. McKean, *St. Petersburg between the Revolutions: Workers and Revolutionaries, June 1907–February 1917* (New Haven, CT: Yale University Press, 1990), pp. 362–64, for details on the differences among the Mensheviks.

10. Longley, p. 617.

11. *35*, p. 165.

12. Ibid. See Badayev, pp. 207–8, for the response. McKean says that Lenin "in as yet unpublished correspondence, criticized the Bolsheviks' reply to Vandervelde" (p. 366). That wouldn't be inconsistent with Lenin's comment in his letter of October 17 if McKean is referring to a draft response. Unfortunately, McKean doesn't let his readers know what he has apparently seen that might suggest otherwise. See "A Critical Review of the Relevant Literature: Chapter 3," for a discussion of McKean.

13. *21*, pp. 16–17.

14. Ibid., p. 18.

15. According to Trotsky, "Not one of the Russian organizations or groups of the party took the openly defeatist position which Lenin came out for abroad" (*The History of the Russian Revolution* [New York: Pathfinder Press, 2009], p. 59).

16. *21*, pp. 30–31.

17. Badayev, p. 212. Regarding McKean's suggestion that the "amendments" repudiated Lenin's revolutionary defeatist stance (p. 360), see "A Critical Review of the Relevant Literature: Chapter 3." Figes's claim that "Lenin had imposed his views" on the fraction and the party (p. 294) is addressed there as well.

18. *35*, p. 175.

19. Badayev, p. 220.

20. Ibid., pp. 223–32.

21. *21*, p. 322.

22. Ibid., p. 256.

23. Ibid., p. 323.
24. Ibid., p. 176.
25. Ibid., p. 258.
26. Ibid., pp. 401–2.
27. Ibid., p. 482n164. For more details on the elections and a different interpreta-
    tion, see McKean, pp. 380–84. Another but considerably less significant legal
    arena were the workers' insurance boards. Though Lenin made no mention of
    them, a few supplemental elections to them took place at the beginning of 1916
    and the Bolsheviks scored some successes; see McKean, pp. 401–3, for details.
28. _21_, pp. 401–2.
29. _35_, p. 235.
30. For details, see Farrell Dobbs, *Teamster Bureaucracy* (New York: Pathfinder,
    2002).
31. _21_, pp. 251–56.
32. _22_, pp. 169–78.
33. Lenin lived in Switzerland for seven years (though not consecutively) begin-
    ning in 1895. It was during his last stay, August 1914 to April 1917, that he
    participated in Swiss working-class politics as a member of the Swiss Social
    Democratic Party.
34. _23_, pp. 141–42.
35. Ibid., p. 253.
36. Ibid., pp. 289–90.
37. Ibid., pp. 292–93.
38. Ibid., pp. 324–31 and 352.
39. _24_, p. 86.
40. Ibid., pp. 22–25.
41. See "Paris Commune (1871)," MIA: Encyclopedia of Marxism: Glossary of
    Organisations, http://marxistsfr.org/glossary/orgs/p/a.htm#paris-commune.
42. _24_, pp. 38–39.
43. Ibid., p. 69.
44. Ibid., pp. 44–53.
45. Ibid., pp. 210–11.
46. Ibid., p. 181.
47. This is Trotsky in his own words from his rare book *Lenin* (1925) in the Trotsky
    Archives (http://www.marxists.org/archive/trotsky/1925/lenin) and at variance
    with the account in Isaac Deutscher, *The Prophet Armed: Trotsky 1879–1921*
    (New York: Vintage Books, 1965), pp. 255–56.
48. _24_, p. 543.
49. Deutscher, pp. 84–97; Trotsky, "Report of the Siberian Delegation," Trotsky
    Archives, http://www.marxists.org/archive/trotsky/1903.
50. _35_, p. 285.
51. See Krupskaya's point about Lenin's ability to "approach the opponent of yes-
    terday as a comrade" (Nadezhda Krupskaya, *Memories of Lenin* [London: Law-
    rence and Wishart, 1970], p. 217). The record of the 14-year estrangement
    reveals that Lenin made more overtures for reconciliation than Trotsky.

52. _24_, pp. 241–42.
53. Ibid., pp. 295–96.
54. Ibid., pp. 311–12.
55. Ibid., p. 334.
56. Ibid., pp. 373–74.
57. _25_, pp. 18–26.
58. Figes, pp. 397–98.
59. _25_, p. 155.
60. For the best eyewitness/participant account, see Trotsky's _History of the Russian Revolution_, pp. 501–82.
61. _25_, pp. 179–80.
62. See _LES1905_, ch. 3.
63. _25_, pp. 310–12.
64. Trotsky, _History of the Russian Revolution_, p. 795.
65. There are, it seems, two party resolutions possibly composed by Lenin—which I haven't seen—and apparently never translated into English that would no doubt be of significance. At the Sixth Congress of the RSDLP (Bolshevik) at the end of July, there were two agenda items, "Elections to the Constituent Assembly" and "Elections," and, probably, resolutions that codified the decisions taken. Regarding the meeting, see _25_, pp. 526–30. As for the official record of the congress, see Alexander Rabinowitch, _The Bolsheviks Come to Power: The Revolution of 1917 in Petrograd_ (New York: W. W. Norton, 1976), p. 329n1.
66. _24_, pp. 97–101.
67. Ibid., pp. 471–73.
68. Ibid., p. 512.
69. Ibid., p. 511.
70. William G. Rosenberg, "The Russian Municipal Duma Elections of 1917: A Preliminary Computation of Returns," _Soviet Studies_ 21, no. 2 (October 1969), pp. 131–63.
71. Ibid., p. 162.
72. Quoted in Rabinowitch, _The Bolsheviks Come to Power_, p. 92.
73. Krupskaya, pp. 303–6.
74. _24_, pp. 211–12.
75. Trotsky, _History of the Russian Revolution_, pp. 523–24.
76. _25_, p. 308.
77. Trotsky, _History of the Russian Revolution_, p. 795.
78. _24_, p. 245.
79. _25_, pp. 427–29.
80. Krupskaya, p. 163.
81. _25_, p. 497.
82. _25_, p. 374. On August 25 the Czarist commander of the army, General Kornilov, launched, with a wink and nod from Kerensky, a counterrevolutionary putsch that was soon put down owing to mass mobilizations led by the Bolsheviks—a decisive turning point in the Russian Revolution.

83. *26*, p. 19.

84. *27*, p. 25.

85. *26*, p. 25. It is no accident that Lenin reemploys "parliamentary cretinism" at this moment. He had been reading, as his letter to the Central Committee "Marxism and Insurrection" shows, Marx and Engels on the German Revolution of 1848. That was the context in which they coined the term. See *LES1905*, ch. 1.

86. Ibid., p. 33.

87. Ibid., pp. 54–55.

88. *41*, pp. 446–48.

89. Ibid., pp. 597–98n554; *25*, p. 530n97.

90. *12*, pp. 109–12.

91. For useful details on the election campaign, see Alexander Rabinowitch, *The Bolsheviks in Power: The First Year of Soviet Rule in Petrograd* (Bloomington: Indiana University Press, 2007), pp. 62–69.

92. Ibid., p. 416n50, on data on peasant meetings that demonstrated more support for soviet governance than the Constituent Assembly.

93. *26*, pp. 437–39. Regarding Robert Service's allegations about Lenin's supposed attitude toward the Constituent Assembly, see "A Critical Review of the Relevant Literature: Chapter 3."

94. *29*, p. 311.

95. *29*, pp. 485–86. Exit polls for the 2012 US presidential election indicated that 59 percent of voters said the economic system favors the rich.

96. *28*, p. 272.

97. Ibid., p. 256. It is to be noted that the Czar and his family were denied the right to vote by the new government that came to rule in March 1917.

98. *29*, p. 125. In the United States, four states permanently disenfranchise ex-felons. In Florida it is estimated that nearly a quarter of its voting-age black population is not eligible to vote because of a felony record.

99. Ibid., p. 184.

100. Ibid., p. 125.

101. Ibid., pp. 371–72.

102. Ibid., pp. 107–8.

103. About the data, "[H]is point of view was by no means as biased as one might expect, for he consciously sought in the figures the lessons they contained for his party, whether flattering or otherwise, and his deductions constitute a thoroughgoing and penetrating analysis of the results." Oliver Radkey, *Russia Goes to the Polls: The Elections to the All-Russian Constituent Assembly, 1917* (Ithaca, NY: Cornell University Press, 1990), p. 6.

104. *30*, pp. 265–66.

105. *21*, p. 253.

106. *27*, p. 146.

107. Regarding the debate at the Second Congress on this issue, see John Riddell, ed., *Workers of the World and Oppressed Peoples, Unite! Proceedings and Documents of the Second Congress, 1920* (New York: Pathfinder, 1991), pp. 420–82.

108. *31*, p. 21.
109. Ibid., p. 27.
110. Ibid., p. 36.
111. Ibid., p. 61.
112. Ibid., p. 64.
113. Ibid., p. 98.
114. Riddell, *Workers of the World and Oppressed Peoples, Unite!*, p. 459.
115. *31*, p. 65.
116. Riddell, *Workers of the World and Oppressed Peoples, Unite!*, p. 769.
117. Georg Lukács, *History and Class Consciousness: Studies in Marxist Dialectics*, trans. Rodney Livingstone (Cambridge, MA: MIT Press, 1971), pp. xiii–xiv. I thank Howard Kling for bringing this to my attention.
118. *32*, p. 48. For details, see George Fyson, ed., *Lenin's Final Fight: Speeches and Writings, 1922–23* (New York: Pathfinder, 1995).
119. Rabinowitch, *The Bolsheviks in Power*, ch. 2, also subscribes—looking at other factors—to a contingential argument.
120. Robert Daniels, ed., *A Documentary History of Communism*, vol. 2 (New York: Vintage Books, 1962), p. 116.
121. Trotsky, *History of the Russian Revolution*, p. 1193.
122. Just as in the 1930s, the current global capitalist crisis has shaken the confidence of defenders of liberal democracy. Symptomatic is the May 2013 report of the Transatlantic Academy, "The Democratic Disconnect," as well as the cover story for that month of the British monthly *Prospect*, "Has Democracy Had Its Day? Electoral Politics Has Had a Bad Decade."

CONCLUSION

1. Karl Marx and Frederick Engels, *Collected Works*, vol. 10 (New York: International Publishers, 1975–2004), p. 284. Hereafter, citations from the *MECW* are designated as follows: *MECW* 10, p. 284.
2. David Riazanov, *Karl Marx and Friedrich Engels: An Introduction to Their Lives and Works* (New York: Monthly Review, 1973), p. 100.
3. Robert Service, *Lenin: A Political Life*, vol. 2 (Bloomington: Indiana University Press, 1991), p. 353n32. On the retrieval of the materials in 1920, see Helen Rappaport, *Conspirator: Lenin in Exile* (New York: Basic Books, 2010), p. 253.
4. Israel Getzler, *Martov: A Political Biography of a Russian Social Democrat* (Melbourne: Melbourne University Press, 1967), ch. 6, pp. 113–37, provides inter alia a few details on Martov's Duma work.
5. *MECW* 6, p. 519.
6. Hal Draper, *The Adventures of the Communist Manifesto* (Berkeley: Center for Socialist History, 1994), p. 321, argues convincingly that Engels substituted "whenever" for "as soon as" in the aforementioned sentence for the 1888 translation of the Manifesto that he supervised. He did so to acknowledge that the expectation in the original 1848 document about the bourgeoisie was not fulfilled.

7. *MECW* 10, p. 284.
8. *MECW* 27, p. 271.
9. Leon Trotsky, *The Young Lenin* (New York: Doubleday, 1972), p. 187.
10. V. I. Lenin, *Collected Works*, vol. 21 (Moscow: Progress Publishers, 1978), p. 16. Hereafter, citations from his *Collected Works* will be designated as in this case: *21*, p. 16.
11. My article, "A Return to Lenin—But without Marx and Engels?" *Science & Society* 73, no. 4 (October 2009): 452–73, details how Lenin began to have second thoughts about the German party before August 1914.
12. V. I. Lenin, *Collected Works*, vol. 13 (Moscow: Progress Publishers, 1978), p. 81. Hereafter, citations from his *Collected Works* will be designated as in this case: *13* p. 81.
13. I elaborate on this point in "A Critical Review of the Relevant Literature: Conclusion."
14. Leon Trotsky, "The Class, the Party, and the Leadership," Marxists.org (1940), http://www.marxists.org/archive/trotsky/1940/xx/party.htm.
15. For the best-known example of the claim that the subjective factor was inconsequential in the Russian Revolution, Theda Skocpol's *States and Social Revolutions: A Comparative Analysis of France, Russia and China* (Cambridge, UK: Cambridge University Press, 1979), see "A Critical Review of the Relevant Literature: Conclusion."
16. I'll always remember the student in my Cuban Revolution class at the University of Minnesota in 2008 who, after reading the Second Declaration and being persuaded by it, seemed skeptical about the presentation of the vice-presidential candidate for the Socialist Workers Party that year whom I invited to speak to the class. The essence of his question was, Didn't her candidacy legitimize the capitalist electoral process? Alyson Kennedy, the candidate, drew on the legacy that her party inherited in response. That moment was motivation in part for writing this book.
17. Joe Hansen's "The Seven Errors Made by Che Guevara," in *Dynamics of the Cuban Revolution: The Trotskyist View* (New York: Pathfinder, 1978), is most instructive on the consequences of this turn.
18. The focus here is on books that claim to be overviews of Lenin's life. Therefore, works such as Paul LeBlanc's *Lenin and the Revolutionary Party* (Atlantic Highlands, NJ: Humanities Press International, 1990) or Lars Lih's *Lenin Rediscovered: What Is to Be Done? in Context* (Leiden: Brill, 2006), which respectively look at Lenin's organizational ideas and his famous book, are not discussed here.
19. Neil Harding, *Lenin's Political Thought: Theory and Practice in the Democratic and Socialist Revolutions* (Chicago: Haymarket Books, 2009), p. 25. While it's possible to treat his book as sympathetic to Lenin, his *Leninism* (Durham, NC: Duke University Press, 1996) is a different story. There he repeats the standard anti-Lenin formulas—for example, the "elitist and anti-democratic disposition of Leninism" (p. 174). These failings, he asserts, can be traced to Marx and Engels; the central claim of the book is that "Leninism was authentic Marxism"

(p. 6). As for what he thinks of "authentic Marxism," his tendentious and dishonest review of my Marx-Engels book (*Democratization* 8, no. 2 [Summer 2001]) leaves no doubt.

20. Alan Woods, *Bolshevism: The Road to Power: A History of the Bolshevik Party from the Early Beginnings to the October Revolution* (London: Wellred Publications, 1999). That he hardly acknowledges Lenin's *Two Tactics of Social Democracy in the Democratic Revolution*, in what poses as a thorough reading of Bolshevism, is telling—an egregious attempt to turn Lenin into a supporter of Trotsky's theory of permanent revolution.

21. Christopher Read, *Lenin: A Revolutionary Life* (London: Routledge, 2005).

22. Lars T. Lih, *Lenin* (London: Reaktion Books, 2011).

23. At the panel that the two of us participated in at the Historical Materialism Conference in London, November 2012 (which is somewhere in cyberspace), I asked Lih if he had an explanation for the silence. He didn't reply. I posed the same question shortly afterward in an email, and he wrote that he would get back to me with an answer. I've yet, as of August 2013, to receive his response.

24. I am thankful to my colleagues at the University of Minnesota, of different generations, who responded to my informal inquiry about which texts introduced them to Lenin.

25. Bertram D. Wolfe, *Three Who Made a Revolution: A Biographical History* (New York: Stein and Day, 1984).

26. See "A Critical Review of the Relevant Literature: Chapter 2" regarding a most egregious fabrication performed by Wolfe on one of Lenin's texts.

27. Alfred G. Meyer, *Leninism* (New York: Fredrick A. Praeger, 1957).

28. "A Critical Review of the Relevant Literature: Chapter 2" also critiques some of Meyer's misrepresentations.

29. Louis Fischer, *The Life of Lenin* (New York: Harper and Row, 1965), p. 523.

30. Robert Service, *Lenin: A Political Life*, vols. 1–3 (Bloomington: Indiana University Press, 1985–1995).

31. See "A Critical Review of the Relevant Literature: Chapter 2" for details. In Service's *Lenin: A Biography* (Cambridge, MA: Harvard University Press, 2000), the pickings are even slimmer. It's worth noting that Service's *Trotsky: A Biography* (Cambridge, MA: Belknap Press of Harvard University, 2009) has rightly reaped scathing criticism for its shoddy scholarship driven by a political agenda.

32. Richard Pipes, ed., *The Unknown Lenin: From the Secret Archive* (New Haven, CT: Yale University Press, 1996). For the most informed critical review, see Lars T. Lih's review of Pipes's collection, which he compares with the more complete, 420-document, and more accurately translated and less tendentious Russian edition, in *Canadian-American Slavic Studies* 35, nos. 2–3 (Summer/Fall 2001): 301–6.

33. Leo Panitch, Greg Albo, and Vivek Chibber, eds., *Socialist Register 2013: The Question of Strategy* (Pontypool, Wales: Merlin, 2013).

34. Ibid., p. xi.

35. Charles Post, "What Is Left of Leninism? New European Left Parties in Historical Perspective," in *Socialist Register*, pp. 175–97.

36. *33*, pp. 430–31.

37. Leon Trotsky, *The Revolution Betrayed: What Is the Soviet Union and Where Is It Going?* (New York: Pathfinder Press, 1972), p. 186.

38. Ibid.

39. Post, p. 179.

40. Michael Hardt and Antonio Negri, *Empire* (Cambridge, MA: Harvard University Press, 2000). I predicted as much in my "Class Struggle under 'Empire': In Defence of Marx and Engels," *International Socialism* no. 96 (Autumn 2002): 47–70.

41. In September 1973, the Social Democratic government of Salvador Allende in Chile was overthrown in a coup d'état headed by General Augusto Pinochet and supported by the US government. Though the working-class masses asked to be armed to defend his government and the conquests they had made, Allende declined, saying the military in Chile, unlike elsewhere in Latin America, had always respected civilian rule.

42. See my "Class Struggle under 'Empire': In Defence of Marx and Engels."

43. Atilio Borom, "Strategy and Tactics in Popular Struggles in Latin America," in *Socialist Register*, p. 249.

44. Ibid., p. 253.

45. Michalis Spourdalakis, "Left Strategy in the Greek Cauldron: Explaining Syriza's Success," in *Socialist Register*, pp. 108; Aristides Baltas, "The Rise of Syriza: An Interview," in *Socialist Register*, pp. 131–32.

46. Hillary Wainwright, "Transformative Power: Political Organization in Transition," in *Socialist Register*, pp. 138 and 143.

47. Forever etched on my brain when I first read them more than thirty years ago are the all-so-instructive lines in Leon Trotsky's *The History of the Russian Revolution* (New York: Pathfinder Press, 2009) about the decisive moments in the drama of 1917: "The Bolsheviks did not summon the masses for the April demonstration. The Bolsheviks will not call the armed masses into the streets at the beginning of July. Only in October will the party finally fall in step and march out at the head of the masses, not for a demonstration, but for a revolution" (p. 369).

48. Baltas, p. 124.

49. At the end of 2012, Syriza held a national conference to begin the process of transforming itself into a political party, and the differences between those who want to moderate its message in order to become the governing party and those who want to stay with the radical vision quickly manifested itself. Engels's comment made in 1887 about a workers' party "getting bourgeois" is apropos: "It is a misfortune that overtakes all extreme parties as soon as the day for them to become 'possible' draws near." Karl Marx and Frederick Engels, *Collected Works*, vol. 48 (New York: International Publishers, 1975–2004), p. 115. Hereafter, citations from the *MECW* are designated as follows: *MECW* 48, p. 115. In his speech to the party convention in July 2013, Alexis Tsipras made a number of proposals about the electoral process and party

discipline but didn't make clear if Syriza's parliamentary group would be subordinate to the will of its rank and file.

50. Post, p. 191.

51. Susan Spronk, "Twenty-First Century Socialism in Bolivia: The Gender Agenda," in *Socialist Register*, p. 259.

52. In the draft I mistakenly wrote "1912"; I probably had in mind the Lena goldfields strike in Siberia, when miners there—like the gold and platinum miners in South Africa—went out on strike and helped revive the revolutionary process in Russia leading eventually to 1917.

53. Mandela, evidently, according to new revelations prompted by his death on December 5, 2013, had in fact been a member of the SACP. See Bill Keller, "Nelson Mandela, Communist," *New York Times*, December 8, 2013, p. 8.

54. Longtime SACP leader Joe Slovo's 1989 document "Has Socialism Failed?," written as the USSR and its sycophant regimes in Eastern Europe were about to implode, appeared to be the analysis that many thought provided an explanation for what went wrong with the Stalinist option. In hindsight, admittedly, it could never have been an honest discussion, because there were too many skeletons in the SACP's closet and too many people were still alive who were responsible for them being there. Former SACP leader Raymond Suttner's recent denunciation of the ANC/SACP/COSATU alliance for its venality, "South Africa: The Tripartite Alliance Has Sold Its Soul," *Mail & Guardian*, September 27, 2013, is telling. Like Slovo's document, it fails to get to the root of the problem—the counterrevolutionary character of Stalinism.

55. The latest news from South Africa suggests this may now be underway. The largest trade union—Numsa, the miners—announced that it would break with the Triple Alliance and "would seek to start a socialist party aimed at protecting the interests of the working class." See Lydia Polgreen, "South Africa's Biggest Trade Union Pulls Its Support for A.N.C.," *New York Times*, December 20, 2013.

56. *MECW* 50, p. 236.

57. August H. Nimtz, *Marx, Tocqueville, and Race in America: The "Absolute Democracy" or "Defiled Republic"* (Lanham, MD: Lexington Books, 2003), p. 213. I didn't employ a crystal ball for my prediction about the crisis but the analysis that the US Socialist Workers' Party began making with the 1987 Wall Street stock-market crash.

58. Thomas Sugrue's op-ed piece in the *New York Times* (December 14, 2012) about the Michigan defeat is accurate about the failed course of the once-powerful United Auto Workers union: "[T]hey have used their dwindling resources to influence elections . . . rather than confronting employers directly. At a moment when the voting machine has replaced the picket line as the last bastion of union strength, right-to-work advocates hope to weaken what remains of the movement's clout. Without a strong voice representing them, Michigan workers will remain outmatched in what was already a tough defensive battle for economic security."

59. Joan Sangster and Meg Luxton, "Feminism, Co-optation and the Problems of Amnesia: A Response to Nancy Fraser," in *Socialist Register*, p. 303.
60. Barbara Epstein, "Occupy Oakland: The Question of Violence," in *Socialist Register*, pp. 72–74.
61. *33*, p. 431.
62. "If from the outset the democrats come out resolutely and terroristically against the reactionaries, the influence of the latter in the elections will be destroyed in advance." *MECW* 10, p. 284.
63. Alex Callinicos, "Alain Badiou and the Idea of Communism," in *Socialist Register*, p. 341.
64. "Inevitable" (or, in its original German, *unvermeidlich*) appears only once in the *Manifesto*, at the very end of Part One, immediately followed by Part Two, "Proletarians and Communists," about the latter's tasks.

APPENDIX A

1. Original text available at http://www.marxists.org/archive/lenin/works/1908/ 5thconfr/3.htm.

APPENDIX B

1. Original text available at http://www.marxists.org/archive/lenin/works/1909/ confreeb/part3.htm.
2. [Footnote from source] *Vlasov*—A. I. Rykov.
3. [Footnote from source] *The private meeting*—a meeting of Leninist Bolsheviks called by Lenin on the eve of the conference of the extended editorial board of *Proletary*. Lenin gave the meeting full information concerning the state of affairs in the Bolshevik section and the struggle against the otzovists, the ultimatumists and the god-builders. The theses contained in Lenin's report formed the basis for the resolutions adopted by the conference of the extended editorial board.

APPENDIX C

1. Original text available at http://www.marxists.org/archive/lenin/works/1909/ oct/00b.htm.
2. [Footnote from source] The first part of the first chapter of the explanatory note should include a popular account, written in as propagandist a manner as possible, of the reasons in favour of the eight-hour working day, from the point of view of the productivity of labour, the health and cultural interests of the proletariat, and the interests in general of its struggle for emancipation.—*Lenin*
3. [Footnote from source] *Zubatov, S. V.*—colonel of gendarmerie and chief of the Moscow Secret Police, who carried out a policy known as "police socialism." In 1901–03, on his initiative legal workers' organisations were set up in order to divert the workers from the political struggle against the autocracy.

Zubatov's activity in setting up legal workers' organisations was supported by V. K. Plehve, Minister of the Interior. Zubatov tried to direct the working-class movement towards the achievement of purely economic demands and, to make the workers think that the government was ready to meet their demands. The first Zubatov organisation was set up in Moscow in May 1901 under the name "Society for the Mutual Assistance of Workers in Mechanical Industry." Zubatov organisations were set up also in Minsk, Odessa, Vilna, Kiev and other cities.

4. [Footnote from source] Jules Guesde, *Le Problème et la solution; les huit heures à la chambre*, Lille. (*The Problem and Its Solution; the Eight-Hour Day in Parliament—Ed.*)

5. [Footnote from source] M. Schippel, *Sozial-Demokratisches Reichstagshandbuch* (*Social Democratic Handbook to the Reichstag—Ed.*) Berlin, 1902, pp. 882 and 886.

6. [Footnote from source] Parvus, *Die Handelskrisis und die Gewerkschaften*. Nebst Anhang, Gesetzentwurf über den achtstundigen Normalarbeitstag. München: 1901 (Parvus, *The Trade Crisis and the Trade Unions*. With appendix: Bill on the Eight-Hour Normal Working Day Munich, 1901.—*Ed.*)

7. [Footnote from source] On the question of the *gradual* introduction of the eight-hour working day Parvus says, in our opinion quite rightly, that this feature of his Bill arises "not from the desire to come to an understanding with the employers but from the desire to come to an understanding with the workers. We should follow the tactics of the trade unions: they carry out the reduction of the working day extremely gradually for they are well aware that this is the easiest way to counteract a *reduction of wages*" (Parvus's italics, ibid., pp. 62–63).—*Lenin*

APPENDIX D

1. Original text available at http://www.marxists.org/archive/lenin/works/1912/6thconf/efd.htm.

APPENDIX E

1. [Footnote from source] Lenin wrote "*The Election Platform of the R.S.D.L.P.*" in Paris, early in March 1912, shortly after the Prague Conference. "The Election Platform" was published in Russia by the Central Committee of the Party as a separate leaflet and distributed in 18 localities including the main working-class centres. Reprinted from the leaflet, it appeared as a supplement to No. 26 of *Sotsial-Demokrat*. It was also reprinted by many local Bolshevik organisations and by the Russian Bureau of the C.C. of the R.S.D.L.P. in Tiflis. The significance of this document is dealt with by V. I. Lenin in his article "The Platform of the Reformists and the Platform of the Revolutionary Social-Democrats." Original text available at http://www.marxists.org/archive/lenin/works/1912/mar/00c.htm.

2. [Footnote from source] *Khodynka Tsar*—at Khodynka Field on the outskirts of Moscow, a carnival was arranged on the occasion of the coronation of Tsar

Nicholas II on May 18, 1896. Criminal negligence on the part of the authorities led to a tremendous crush in which about 2,000 people lost their lives and tens of thousands were injured.

3. [Footnote from source] *The law of March 4, 1906*—temporary regulations providing for a certain freedom of associations, unions and meetings, but which at the same time laid down a number of obstacles, and in fact reduced the law to a scrap of paper. It gave the Minister of the Interior the right not only to suppress associations and unions, but also to refuse official recognition to new unions.

APPENDIX F

1. Original text available at http://www.marxists.org/archive/lenin/works/1914/mar/28.htm.

APPENDIX G

1. Original text available at http://www.marxists.org/archive/lenin/works/1917/petcconf/22b.htm.

APPENDIX H

1. Original text available at http://www.marxists.org/archive/lenin/works/1919/dec/16.htm.

APPENDIX I

1. Original text available at http://www.marxists.org/history/international/comintern/2nd-congress/ch08a.htm.

A CRITICAL REVIEW OF THE RELEVANT LITERATURE

1. For a useful introduction to this literature, see "Review Forum: Documentary History and Political Parties," *Kritika: Explorations in Russian and Eurasian History* 5, no. 1 (Winter 2004): 107–232.
2. Robert Service, *Lenin: A Political Life*, vol. 1 (Bloomington: Indiana University Press, 1991), p. 186.
3. Orlando Figes, *A People's Tragedy: A History of the Russian Revolution* (New York: Viking, 1996), pp. 388–89.
4. Nadezhda Krupskaya, *Memories of Lenin* (London: Panther Books, 1970), p. 172.
5. V. I. Lenin, *Collected Works*, vol. 31 (Moscow: Progress Publishers, 1978), p. 35. Hereafter, citations from his *Collected Works* will be designated as in this case: *31*, p. 35.
6. Robert B. McKean, *St. Petersburg between the Revolutions: Workers and Revolutionaries, June 1907–February 1917* (New Haven, CT: Yale University Press, 1990), p. 131.

7. Service, vol. 2, p. 18.

8. *18*, p. 494.

9. Geoffrey A. Hosking, *The Russian Constitutional Experiment: Government and Duma, 1907–1914* (Cambridge, UK: Cambridge University Press, 1973), p. 183.

10. Service, vol. 2, p. 18.

11. Ibid., p. 19.

12. Ibid., p. 24.

13. McKean, p. 84.

14. Leon Trotsky, *Stalin: An Appraisal of the Man and His Influence* (New York: Universal Library, 1941), p. 112.

15. McKean, p. 141.

16. Ibid., p. 525n37.

17. Service, vol. 2, p. 50.

18. Louis Fischer, *The Life of Lenin* (New York: Harper and Row, 1965), p. 83. But Fischer couldn't resist at least one fabrication. He claims that Lenin, despite Malinovsky's plea that he do so, did not attend his trial (p. 84). In fact, he did, according to R. C. Elwood, *Russian Social Democracy in the Underground: A Study of the RSDLP in the Ukraine, 1907–1914* (Assen: Van Gorcum, 1974), p. 66.

19. Richard Pipes, ed., *The Unknown Lenin: From the Secret Archive* (New Haven, CT: Yale University Press, 1996), pp. 37–38. According to Pipes, "Lenin pretended in 1917 that he had had no contact with Malinovsky after he resigned from the Duma" (p. 24). That claim is contradicted by Lenin's point that the investigating commission, of which he was a member, "arranged personal confrontations with Malinovsky" (p. 37).

20. Trotsky, *Stalin*, p. 151.

21. Hal Draper, *Karl Marx's Theory of Revolution*, vol. 2 (New York: Monthly Review, 1977–90), p. 653.

22. Pipes, pp. 31–32.

23. *21*, p. 172.

24. Figes, p. 294.

25. McKean, p. 361.

26. *21*, p. 280.

27. Service, vol. 2, p. 304.

28. *6*, p. 31.

29. Figes, p. 507.

30. Alexander Rabinowitch, *The Bolsheviks Come to Power: The Revolution of 1917 in Petrograd* (New York: W. W. Norton, 1976), p. 208.

31. Ibid., inter alia, pp. 194–204.

32. Theda Skocpol, *States and Social Revolutions: A Comparative Analysis of France, Russia, and China* (Cambridge, UK: Cambridge University Press, 1979), p. 17.

33. Ibid., p. 206.

BIBLIOGRAPHY

PRIMARY SOURCES

Daniels, Robert, ed. *A Documentary History of Communism*. Vol. 2. New York: Vintage Books, 1962.

Fyson, George, ed. *Lenin's Final Fight: Speeches and Writings, 1922–23*. New York: Pathfinder, 1995.

Institute of Marxism-Leninism. *The General Council of the First International: Minutes, 1866–1872*. Moscow: Progress Publishers, 1974.

Lenin, V. I. *Collected Works*. Vols. 1–45. Moscow: Progress Publishers, 1977. This English edition is a translation of the fourth, enlarged Russian edition prepared by the Institute of Marxism-Leninism, Central Committee of the Communist Party of the Soviet Union.

Marx, Karl, and Frederick Engels. *Collected Works*. Vols. 1–50. New York: International Publishers, 1975–2005.

1903: Second Ordinary Congress of the RSDLP. Complete Text of the Minutes. Translated and annotated by Brian Pearce. London: New Park Publications, 1978.

Riddell, John, ed. *Lenin's Struggle for a Revolutionary International: Documents: 1907–1916, The Preparatory Years*. New York: Pathfinder, 1986.

———, ed. *Workers of the World and Oppressed Peoples Unite! Proceedings and Documents of the Second Congress, 1920*. New York: Pathfinder, 1991.

SECONDARY SOURCES

Badayev, Aleksei. *The Bolsheviks in the Tsarist Duma*. New York: International Publishers, 1932.

Baltas, Aristides. "The Rise of Syriza: An Interview." In *Socialist Register 2013: The Question of Strategy*, edited by Leo Panitch, Greg Albo, and Vivek Chibber. Pontypool, Wales: Merlin, 2013.

Bartolini, Stefano. *The Political Mobilization of the European Left, 1860–1980: The Class Cleavage*. New York: Cambridge University Press, 2000.

Berman, Sheri. *The Primacy of Politics: Social Democracy and the Making of Europe's Twentieth Century*. Cambridge, UK: Cambridge University Press, 2006.

Borom, Atilio. "Strategy and Tactics in Popular Struggles in Latin America." In *Socialist Register 2013: The Question of Strategy*, edited by Leo Panitch, Greg Albo, and Vivek Chibber. Pontypool, Wales: Merlin, 2013.

Brenner, Johanna, and Nancy Holmstrom. "Socialist-Feminist Strategy Today." In *Socialist Register 2013: The Question of Strategy*, edited by Leo Panitch, Greg Albo, and Vivek Chibber. Pontypool, Wales: Merlin, 2013.

Callinicos, Alex. "Alain Badiou and the Idea of Communism." In *Socialist Register 2013: The Question of Strategy*, edited by Leo Panitch, Greg Albo, and Vivek Chibber. Pontypool, Wales: Merlin, 2013.

Cliff, Tony. *Lenin: Building the Party, 1893–1914*. Chicago: Haymarket Books, 2002.

Deutscher, Isaac. *The Prophet Armed: Trotsky 1879–1921*. New York: Vintage Books, 1965.

Dobbs, Farrell. *Teamster Bureaucracy*. New York: Pathfinder, 2002.

Draper, Hal. *The Adventures of the Communist Manifesto*. Berkeley: Center for Socialist History, 1994.

———. *The "Dictatorship of the Proletariat" from Marx to Lenin*. New York: Monthly Review, 1987.

———. *Karl Marx's Theory of Revolution*. Vols. 1–4. New York: Monthly Review, 1977–90.

Elwood, Ralph Carter. *Inessa Armand: Revolutionary and Feminist*. New York: Cambridge University Press, 1992.

———. "Lenin and *Pravda*, 1912–1914," *Slavic Review* 31, no. 2 (June 1972): 355–80.

———. *Roman Malinovsky: A Life without a Cause*. Newtonville, MA: Oriental Research Partners, 1977.

———. *Russian Social Democracy in the Underground: A Study of the RSDLP in the Ukraine, 1907–1914*. Assen: Van Gorcum, 1974.

Figes, Orlando. *A People's Tragedy: A History of the Russian Revolution*. New York: Viking, 1996.

Fischer, Louis. *The Life of Lenin*. New York: Harper and Row, 1965.

Getzler, Israel. *Martov: A Political Biography of a Russian Social Democrat*. Melbourne: Melbourne University Press, 1967.

Gindin, Sam. "Rethinking Unions, Registering Socialism." In *Socialist Register 2013: The Question of Strategy*, edited by Leo Panitch, Greg Albo, and Vivek Chibber. Pontypool, Wales: Merlin, 2013.

Hansen, Joe. *Dynamics of the Cuban Revolution: The Trotskyist View*. New York: Pathfinder, 1978.

Hardt, Michael, and Antonio Negri. *Empire*. Cambridge, MA: Harvard University Press, 2000.

Hellman, Stephen. "Whatever Happened to Italian Communism? Lucio Magri's *The Tailor of Ulm*." In *Socialist Register 2013: The Question of Strategy*, edited by Leo Panitch, Greg Albo, and Vivek Chibber. Pontypool, Wales: Merlin, 2013.

Hosking, Geoffrey A. *The Russian Constitutional Experiment: Government and Duma, 1907–1914*. Cambridge, UK: Cambridge University Press, 1973.

Krupskaya, Nadezhda. *Memories of Lenin*. London: Panther Books, 1970.

Lane, David. *Leninism: A Sociological Interpretation*. Cambridge, UK: Cambridge University Press, 1981.

Le Blanc, Paul. *Lenin and the Revolutionary Party*. Atlantic Highlands, NJ: Humanities Press International, 1990.

Levin, Alfred. *The Second Duma: A Study of the Social-Democratic Party and the Russian Constitutional Experiment*. New Haven, CT: Yale University Press, 1940.

———. *The Third Duma, Election and Profile*. Hamden, CT: Archon Books, 1973.

Lih, Lars. *Lenin*. London: Reaktion Books, 2011.

———. *Lenin Rediscovered: What Is to Be Done? in Context*. Leiden: Brill, 2006.

———. Review of Richard Pipe's *The Unknown Lenin: From the Secret Archive*. *Canadian-American Slavic Studies* 35, nos. 2–3 (Summer/Fall 2001): 301–6.

Longley, D. A. "The Russian Social Democratic Statement to the Duma on 26 July (8 August) 1914: A New Look at the Evidence," *English Historical Review* 102, no. 187 (July 1987): 599–621.

Lukács, Georg. *History and Class Consciousness: Studies in Marxist Dialectics*. Translated by Rodney Livingstone. Cambridge, MA: MIT Press, 1971.

McKean, Robert B. *St. Petersburg between the Revolutions: Workers and Revolutionaries, June 1907–February 1917*. New Haven, CT: Yale University Press, 1990.

McMeekin, Sean. *The Russian Origins of the First World War*. Cambridge, MA: Harvard University Press, 2011.

Meyer, Alfred G. *Leninism*. New York: Fredrick A. Praeger, 1957.

Nimtz, August H. "Class Struggle under 'Empire': In Defence of Marx and Engels," *International Socialism* no. 96 (Autumn 2002): 47–70.

———. "Marx and Engels's Electoral Strategy: The Alleged versus the Real," *New Political Science* 32, no. 3 (September 2010): 367–87.

———. *Marx, Tocqueville, and Race in America: The "Absolute Democracy" or the "Defiled Republic."* Lanham, MD: Lexington Books, 2003.

———. "A Return to Lenin—But without Marx and Engels?" *Science & Society* 73, no. 4 (October 2009): 452–73.

Panitch, Leo, Greg Albo, and Vivek Chibber, eds. *Socialist Register 2013: The Question of Strategy*. Pontypool, Wales: Merlin, 2013.

Pipes, Richard, ed. *The Unknown Lenin: From the Secret Archive*. New Haven, CT: Yale University Press, 1996.

Pocaro, Mimmo. "Occupy Lenin." In *Socialist Register 2013: The Question of Strategy*, edited by Leo Panitch, Greg Albo, and Vivek Chibber. Pontypool, Wales: Merlin, 2013.

Post, Charles. "What Is Left of Leninism? New European Left Parties in Historical Perspective." In *Socialist Register 2013: The Question of Strategy*, edited by Leo Panitch, Greg Albo, and Vivek Chibber. Pontypool, Wales: Merlin, 2013.

Rabinowitch, Alexander. *The Bolsheviks Come to Power: The Revolution of 1917 in Petrograd*. New York: W. W. Norton, 1976.

———. *The Bolsheviks in Power: The First Year of Soviet Rule in Petrograd*. Bloomington: Indiana University Press, 2007.

Radkey, Oliver. *Russian Goes to the Polls: The Elections to the All-Russian Constituent Assembly, 1917*. Ithaca, NY: Cornell University Press, 1990.

Rappoport, Helen. *Conspirator: Lenin in Exile*. New York: Basic Books, 2010.

Read, Christopher. *Lenin: A Revolutionary Life*. London: Routledge, 2005.

"Review Forum: Documentary History and Political Parties," *Kritika: Explorations in Russian and Eurasian History* 5, no. 1 (Winter 2004): 107–232.

Riazanov, David. *Karl Marx and Friedrich Engels: An Introduction to Their Lives and Works*. New York: Monthly Review, 1973.

Rosenberg, William. "The Russian Municipal Duma Elections of 1917: A Preliminary Computation of Returns," *Soviet Studies* 21, no. 2 (October 1969): 131–63.

Saul, John S. "On Taming a Revolution: The South African Case." In *Socialist Register
2013: The Question of Strategy*, edited by Leo Panitch, Greg Albo, and Vivek Chibber. Pontypool, Wales: Merlin, 2013.

Service, Robert. *Lenin: A Biography*. Cambridge, MA: Harvard University Press, 2000.

———. *Lenin: A Political Life*. Vols. 1–3. Bloomington: Indiana University Press,
1991.

———. *Trotsky: A Biography*. Cambridge: Belknap Press of Harvard University Press,
2009.

Skocpol, Theda. *States and Social Revolutions: A Comparative Analysis of France, Russia,
and China*. Cambridge, UK: Cambridge University Press, 1979.

Spekr, Christoph. "Die Linke Today: Fears and Desires." In *Socialist Register 2013:
The Question of Strategy*, edited by Leo Panitch, Greg Albo, and Vivek Chibber.
Pontypool, Wales: Merlin, 2013.

Spourdalakis, Michalis. "Left Strategy in the Greek Cauldron: Explaining Syriza's Success." In *Socialist Register 2013: The Question of Strategy*, edited by Leo Panitch,
Greg Albo, and Vivek Chibber. Pontypool, Wales: Merlin, 2013.

Spronk, Susan. "Twenty-First Century Socialism in Bolivia: The Gender Agenda." In
Socialist Register 2013: The Question of Strategy, edited by Leo Panitch, Greg Albo,
and Vivek Chibber. Pontypool, Wales: Merlin, 2013.

Trotsky, Leon. "The Class, the Party, and the Leadership," Marxists.org (1940),
http://www.marxists.org/archive/trotsky/1940/xx/party.htm.

———. *The History of the Russian Revolution*. New York: Pathfinder Press, 2009.

———. *The Revolution Betrayed: What Is the Soviet Union and Where Is It Going?*
New York: Pathfinder Press, 1972.

———. *Stalin: An Appraisal of the Man and His Influence*. New York: Universal
Library, 1941.

———. *The Young Lenin*. New York: Doubleday, 1972.

Wainwright, Hilary. "Transformative Power: Political Organization in Transition." In
Socialist Register 2013: The Question of Strategy, edited by Leo Panitch, Greg Albo,
and Vivek Chibber. Pontypool, Wales: Merlin, 2013.

Wolfe, Bertram. *Three Who Made a Revolution: A Biographical History*. New York:
Stein and Day, 1984.

Woods, Alan. *Bolshevism: The Road to Power: A History of the Bolshevik Party from the
Early Beginnings to the October Revolution*. London: Wellred Publications, 1999.

Zaretsky, Eli. "Reconsidering the American Left." In *Socialist Register 2013: The Question of Strategy*, edited by Leo Panitch, Greg Albo, and Vivek Chibber. Pontypool,
Wales: Merlin, 2013.

INDEX

Russian Social Democratic Labor Party (RSDLP) Duma fraction or group in First (Witte) Duma; Russian Social Democratic Labor Party (RSDLP) Duma fraction or group in Second Duma; *What Is to Be Done?*

party control of electoral/parliamentary process, 249–50, 302, 362, 391, 403, 413–14, 416–17, 427–28, 449–51. See also Prague Conference

Parvus, 422, 485n7

Pathfinder Press, 381–82

Peasant Question in France and Germany (Engels), 31–32

peasantry, 4, 25, 37, 39, 41, 45–46, 52–53, 123–24, 149–50, 153–59, 163–64, 175–76, 229, 240–43, 286, 291, 334–35, 340, 352, 356, 367, 369, 417, 430, 432, 451, 461. See also agrarian question; Trudoviks; *Two Tactics of Social-Democracy in the Democratic Revolution*; worker-peasant alliance

Persecutors of the Zemstvo and the Hannibals of Liberalism, 84–85

Persia, 239–40, 278, 210

Petrovsky, Grigory, 297, 298, 325, 459

Pipes, Richard, 387, 481n32, 487n19

Plekhanov, Georgi, 40, 44, 47–49, 55, 68, 70, 80, 87, 115, 126, 137, 145, 161, 163, 188, 202n29, 233, 276, 294, 320, 373, 461, 469n68

Pokrovsky, Mikhail, 235–37

Poland and Poles, 276, 435

political rights and revolution: Marx and Engels, 48–49; nationalities, 48–49; peasantry, 52; religion, 62; workers, 48–54, 57–58

Popular Front policy, 363, 373, 382, 390, 407, 409–12

Porcaro, Mimmo, 391–95

Post, Charles, 389–91, 305

Potemkin, 87

Potresov, Alexander, 68, 205n92

Prague Conference (1912), 267, 275–77, 280–81, 286, 288, 293, 312, 372,

425–28, 433, 455–56, 458

Pravda [St. Petersburg], 277, 282–90, 296, 299–301, 305–6, 310, 314–16, 323, 335, 338–39, 342–43, 346–48, 369, 471n19

Pravda [Vienna], 470n14

"Preface," *Letters by Johannes Becker, Joseph Dietzgen, Frederick Engels, Karl Marx, and Others to Friedrich Sorge and Others*, 159–61, 310–11

Pre-Parliament, 447, 448, 465

"professional revolutionary," 71–72, 79

proletarian internationalism, 258–59, 322, 326–27, 404, 459–60

proletariat, 223, 231, 238, 245, 258, 272–73, 284, 350, 353, 355, 398, 441–42. See also dictatorship of the proletariat

Proletary [Finland], 128, 136, 139

Proletary [St. Petersburg], 347

Proletary [Vyborg, Geneva, Paris], 222, 225, 230, 237, 241, 243, 245–46, 251–52, 254, 415–17, 454

proportional representation, 345, 437

protest vote, 28, 97, 108

provisional government, 87, 91, 95, 175–77, 224, 333–38, 342, 349, 354, 437, 457, 460

Przeworski, Adam, 186–87, 197n21

public education, 345

Question of Strategy—Socialist Register 2013, The (eds. Leo Panitch, Greg Albo, Vivek Chibber), 388–412

Rabinowitch, Alexander, 461–66

Rabochaya Gazeta [St. Petersburg], 284

race, 27, 407–10

Read, Christopher, 384–85

recallists or otzovists, 246–49, 252, 260–61, 270

reforms and reformism, 23, 30, 32–33, 47, 55, 85, 121–22, 253, 255, 261, 263–64, 278, 312, 331, 332, 400–401, 413–14, 416, 419, 430, 433, 443–44, 459. See also opportunism;

ABOUT HAYMARKET BOOKS

Haymarket Books is a radical, independent, nonprofit book publisher based in Chicago.

Our mission is to publish books that contribute to struggles for social and economic justice. We strive to make our books a vibrant and organic part of social movements and the education and development of a critical, engaged, international left.

We take inspiration and courage from our namesakes, the Haymarket martyrs, who gave their lives fighting for a better world. Their 1886 struggle for the eight-hour day—which gave us May Day, the international workers' holiday—reminds workers around the world that ordinary people can organize and struggle for their own liberation. These struggles continue today across the globe—struggles against oppression, exploitation, poverty, and war.

Since our founding in 2001, Haymarket Books has published more than five hundred titles. Radically independent, we seek to drive a wedge into the risk-averse world of corporate book publishing. Our authors include Noam Chomsky, Arundhati Roy, Rebecca Solnit, Angela Y. Davis, Howard Zinn, Amy Goodman, Wallace Shawn, Mike Davis, Winona LaDuke, Ilan Pappé, Richard Wolff, Dave Zirin August H. Nimtz is professor of political science and African American and African studies and Distinguished Teaching Professor at the University of Minnesota. He is the author of Marx and Engels: Their Contribution to the Democratic Breakthrough (2000), Marx, Tocqueville, and Race in America: The 'Absolute Democracy' or 'Defiled Republic' (2003), and a number of related articles in edited volumes and journals., Keeanga-Yamahtta Taylor, Nick Turse, Dahr Jamail, David Barsamian, Elizabeth Laird, Amira Hass, Mark Steel, Avi Lewis, Naomi Klein, and Neil Davidson. We are also the trade publishers of the acclaimed Historical Materialism Book Series and of Dispatch Books.

ALSO AVAILABLE FROM HAYMARKET BOOKS

1905
Leon Trotsky

Eyewitnesses to the Russian Revolution
Edited by Todd Chretien

History of the Russian Revolution
Leon Trotsky, Translated by Max Eastman

Leaflets of the Russian Revolution: Socialist Organizing in 1917
Edited and translated by Barbara Allen

Leninism under Lenin
Marcel Liebman

Lenin's Moscow
Alfred Rosmer, Introduction by Ian Birchall

Lessons of October
Leon Trotsky

Red Petrograd: Revolution in the Factories, 1917-1918
S. A. Smith

Returns of Marxism: Marxist Theory in a Time of Crisis
Edited by Sara R Farris

Revolutionary Democracy: Emancipation in Classical Marxism
Soma Marik

Socialism From Below
Hal Draper

Ten Days that Shook the World
John Reed

The Women's Revolution: Russia 1905–1917
Judy Cox

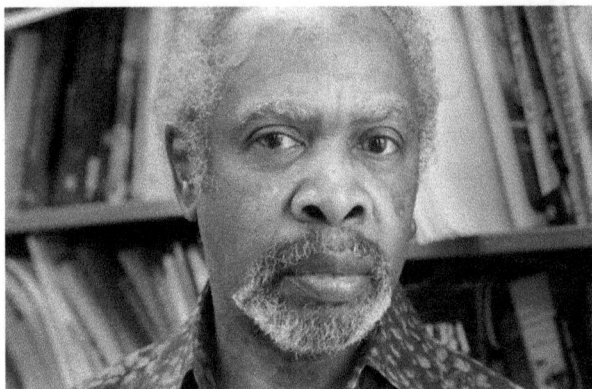
PHOTO BY JACOB VAN BLARCOM

ABOUT THE AUTHOR

August H. Nimtz is professor of political science and African American and African studies and Distinguished Teaching Professor at the University of Minnesota. He is the author of *Marx and Engels: Their Contribution to the Democratic Breakthrough* (2000), *Marx, Tocqueville, and Race in America: The 'Absolute Democracy' or 'Defiled Republic'* (2003), and a number of related articles in edited volumes and journals. His most recent book is *Marxism versus Liberalism: Comparative Real-Time Political Analysis* (2019).

www.ingramcontent.com/pod-product-compliance
Lightning Source LLC
Chambersburg PA
CBHW070857030426
42336CB00014BA/2237